Tanja Leppäaho • Sarah Jack
Editors

The Palgrave Handbook of Family Firm Internationalization

palgrave
macmillan

Editors
Tanja Leppäaho
LUT University
Lappeenranta, Finland

Sarah Jack
House of Innovation, Stockholm School of
Economics, Stockholm, Sweden

Lancaster University Management School,
Lancaster, UK

ISBN 978-3-030-66736-8   ISBN 978-3-030-66737-5   (eBook)
https://doi.org/10.1007/978-3-030-66737-5

© The Editor(s) (if applicable) and The Author(s), under exclusive license to Springer Nature Switzerland AG 2021
This work is subject to copyright. All rights are solely and exclusively licensed by the Publisher, whether the
whole or part of the material is concerned, specifically the rights of translation, reprinting, reuse of illustrations,
recitation, broadcasting, reproduction on microfilms or in any other physical way, and transmission or information storage and retrieval, electronic adaptation, computer software, or by similar or dissimilar methodology
now known or hereafter developed.
The use of general descriptive names, registered names, trademarks, service marks, etc. in this publication does
not imply, even in the absence of a specific statement, that such names are exempt from the relevant protective
laws and regulations and therefore free for general use.
The publisher, the authors and the editors are safe to assume that the advice and information in this book are
believed to be true and accurate at the date of publication. Neither the publisher nor the authors or the editors
give a warranty, expressed or implied, with respect to the material contained herein or for any errors or omissions
that may have been made. The publisher remains neutral with regard to jurisdictional claims in published maps
and institutional affiliations.

Cover illustration: Zoonar GmbH / Alamy Stock Photo

This Palgrave Macmillan imprint is published by the registered company Springer Nature Switzerland AG.
The registered company address is: Gewerbestrasse 11, 6330 Cham, Switzerland

To our family members
To family entrepreneurs all around the world

Foreword 1: Breaking New Ground

I was very excited when Tanja Leppäaho and Sarah Jack invited me to write this Foreword for this first-ever *Handbook on Family Firm Internationalization*. Family firm internationalization attracts growing scholarly interest, including critical reviews (Kontinen and Ojala, 2010; Pukall & Calabrò, 2014), state-of-the-art statements (Metsola et al., 2020), new theoretical developments within and beyond the traditional family business field (Arregle et al., 2019; Reuber, 2016; Verbeke et al., 2019), empirical analysis of internationalization theory (Cesinger et al., 2016), and meta-analyses (Arregle et al., 2017). However, cumulatively, we do not sufficiently understand family firm internationalization, its uniqueness and differences against non-family firms, heterogeneity among family firms themselves, or whether existing internationalization theories must change when considering the family firm (e.g. Arregle et al., 2019; Cesinger et al., 2016). This list is by no means exhaustive, and a plethora of questions remain unanswered. The decision for researchers then is *what* to prioritize for study to generate truly new insights. In many ways, this decision is one that this first-ever *Palgrave Handbook on Family Firm Internationalization* sets out to richly inform—a feat it certainly achieves!

A general conclusion from studies of family firm internationalization to date is that "family matters" for internationalization (Arregle et al., 2017). This is hardly surprising to most family firm scholars. However, further scrutiny reveals a general tendency toward ownership and governance, economic and non-economic goals, socioemotional wealth, family relationships and network ties, and institutions as essential considerations. The compilation of 17 chapters residing in this *Handbook* addresses individually or in combination these essential themes, and each gives rise to new considerations vital to

viii   **Foreword 1: Breaking New Ground**

spearheading novel research. I do not see this *Handbook* as a "how to" guide, but instead a "where to" guide that gives birth to exciting new questions for family firm internationalization research. It addresses these underlying themes, reveals potent theoretical considerations, and inspires new questions. I would like to share with the reader my observations and lessons.

Ownership and Governance

Ownership and governance are two of the most widely studied features of family business (Suess, 2014; Hu & Hughes, 2020; Madison et al., 2016). Family firms differ from non-family firms owing to the unification, not separation, of ownership and control (Carney, 2005). While such an arrangement was expected to ameliorate traditional agency problem, giving rise to stewardship, dysfunction, conflict, nepotism, and asymmetric power can occur among family agents (Carney, 2005; Madison et al., 2016; Schulze et al., 2001) and affect family firm strategy (Scholes et al., 2020). The power of the family can come at the expense of non-family members and minority investors, for example. Internally directed governance mechanisms (such as the family status of the CEO or board chair, composition of the board of directors or management) can also solidify family power. In contrast, the general alignment of interests among family members can encourage stewardly behaviour, interest alignment, and protection of the firm and the family's (good) name (Davis et al., 1997; Miller & Le Breton-Miller, 2006). Ultimately, governance in the family business literature to date is a problem posed by ownership and answered through agency or stewardship theories.

What is interesting about the research at the interface of family business and international business is the emergence of *new* governance considerations in the form of resource use (and disposal) and dysfunctional behaviour. In this *Handbook*, Kano et al. (Chap. 1) build on the work of Verbeke et al. (2020) on a "bifurcation bias" among family firms. Defined as a tendency to separate assets and routines into heritage-based and commodity-based categories depending on family ownership and control, a bifurcation bias suggests that families create affect-based governance practices that may clash with boundedly rational economic consideration in guiding international strategy. Batas et al. (Chap. 12) extend this notion of bifurcation bias to suggest a relationship with family structure and institutional traditions concerning family (e.g. hierarchy) in religion and culture to understand their international networking behaviour. Rienda et al. (Chap. 2), however, adopt the classic perspective of governance to consider how family ownership, CEO, management, and generation affect the degree of internationalization.

I see an opportunity to combine both perspectives to understand the configuration of a family firm's governance and decisions to do with its international strategy (and especially the composition of entry modes, degree of internationalization, location, etc.). My one concern, however, mirrors the thoughts of Scholes et al. (2020): while capable of directing behaviour (Madison et al., 2016), governance is still long-linked to family firm (international) strategy and may be subject to contingencies and intermediate factors in bearing effects (e.g. a bifurcation bias in asset or routine terms may be offset by external corporate governance initiatives such as family councils and family trusts). Developing models in which independent, dependent, and intervening variables are causally adjacent (Scholes et al., 2020) is perhaps necessary to accumulate fine-grained knowledge to explain family firm's internationalization heterogeneity.

Goals: Economic and Non-economic Goals, and Socioemotional Wealth

The socioemotional wealth (SEW) thesis is the only home-grown theory of family business to date. Generally speaking, the theory of socioemotional wealth assumes that family firm strategic behaviour will be governed first and foremost by a desire to protect and grow their non-financial, socioemotional, or affective utilities including preserving the family's control and influence, perpetuating family identity, serving the family's prestige and status, supporting family bonds, preventing access to family firm assets, controlling decision rights, and prolonging their ability to transfer the business to future generations (Berrone et al., 2010, 2012; Gómez-Mejía et al., 2007, 2010). SEW theory is grounded in bounded rationality and behavioural theory (Cesinger et al., 2016). Under this logic, the family firm will be willing to absorb short-term financial losses if it means preserving or protecting SEW. However, while often conceived of as a single body of wealth, studies acknowledge that families have different attitudes to what precise dimension of SEW they prioritize or will seek to protect the most (Miller et al., 2015). When endangered (or perhaps conversely, when opportunities to accumulate its stock are presented), their attitudes towards strategies or specific courses of action may change.

Several chapters in this *Handbook* present interesting insights into the role and functioning of SEW in family firm internationalization. For instance, Metsola et al. (Chap. 3) hypothesize that SEW preservation has a negative association with a family SME's degree of internationalization. SEW dimensions of family-heritage maintenance, family-controlled decision-making, familial relationship-building, and emotional decision-making also moderated the positive effects of networking and family SMEs' degree of internationalization. I find this interesting as it enriches the insights of Cesinger et al. (2016) who found that although family firms appear to internationalize gradually, it is due to SEW considerations and not the gradual accumulation of knowledge predicted under Johanson and Vahlne (1977, 2009). Indeed, Metsola et al. reaffirm the restraining role of SEW and the economizing role of networking in offsetting the dysfunction of SEW. The effects of SEW appear more far-reaching, though. Kampouri and Plakoyiannaki (Chap. 8) find that initial entry node decisions are shaped by family owners' identification with the business. But, instead of changing entry nodes thereafter, family firms tended to maintain relationships with their initial entry nodes rather than searching for new international partners, due to the emotional attachment of the family owners with their entry nodes. This is consistent with studies that report family firms prioritizing trust (Cesinger et al., 2016; Scholes et al., 2015) and relationships with actors with which they share common interests and values (Kontinen & Ojala, 2012). Through familiarity and extended periods of interaction, trust mitigates concerns that non-family members (as outsiders) potentially endanger SEW (Cesinger et al., 2016; Chrisman et al., 2007). Indeed, Metsola (Chap. 10) shows that family firms with higher levels of SEW were more active in building close foreign partner relationships, consistent with this logic. As a note of caution, however, Metsola draws attention to how studies are yet to provide evidence on how family firms balance economic and non-economic (SEW) goals in their internationalization endeavours.

These insights create an opportunity to consider what happens to these relationships when SEW preservation is in jeopardy (e.g. such as in crisis times) and whether family firms modulate their behaviour. The relationship between SEW and networking (essential for the internationalization of family firms, as this *Handbook* makes very clear), and their co-functioning in unleashing or restraining the degree of internationalization, is a complex and nuanced one. First, we still know relatively little about the goal-setting process in family firms (Kotlar & De Massis, 2013). Kuiken et al. (Chap. 5) attempt to unpack the role played by multiple goals from the viewpoint of behavioural theory of the firm in understanding family firm internationalization. This is a helpful starting point for future research. Second, we know little about the priority family firms attach to different dimensions of SEW or what happens when different combinations of SEW dimensions are either at risk or face opportunity for enrichment (Miller et al., 2015). Simply put, SEW is not a single, homogeneous body of non-economic wealth. Third, generally, our current body of assumptions about SEW originates from (relatively) stable times.

However, internationalization may become a requirement for survival, and not a choice, when domestic markets deteriorate or face considerable disruption (Georgiadou et al., 2020).

Family Social Capital Relationships and Network Ties

It is very clear from this *Handbook* that networks and relationships play a fundamental role in the internationalization of family firms. In many ways, networks and relationships are vital for the vast majority of SMEs who internationalize, whether "born global" or late, traditional internationalizing SMEs (Hughes et al., 2019). Networks can be considered from at least three different vantage points: network structure, network content, and network behaviour (Hughes et al., 2014). Effort to develop network relationships results in social capital. Family firms are unique because they possess a separate category of social capital, family social capital (Herrero & Hughes, 2019), that non-family firms can only reproduce imperfectly (Herrero, 2018). Social capital is a potentially powerful asset enabling access to new resources and knowledge. However, it is not without its limitations. Greater embeddedness in strong ties can generate dependence, redundancy, and, for family firms, complex lock-ins that prevent new information, ideas, knowledge, and resources from entering the network and the family firm (Herrero & Hughes, 2019; Hughes & Perrons, 2011; Hughes et al., 2014). As a rule, family firms need a combination of internal family ties (its family social capital) and external organizational ties (its organizational social capital) to perform well or risk dysfunctional effects including ignoring new information and impeding innovation, transfer of dysfunctional family characteristics into the family firm's broader network, and restrict new external ties from causing organizational advantages to vanish (Adler & Kwon, 2002; Arregle et al., 2007; Herrero & Hughes, 2019; Leana & Van Buren, 1999; Nahapiet & Ghoshal, 1998; Portes, 1998; Uzzi, 1996; Zahra, 2010). We still have much to learn about the role of network ties and social capital in family firm outcomes (including internationalization).

Korhonen et al. (Chap. 7) shed interesting new light on phenomena akin to social capital these authors build on the notion of the "social legacy" of founders in family firms in conjunction with their interpersonal networks and its effects on the ties of their successors over an intergenerational period of time. I find this contribution fascinating because it draws attention to the public and private component of social capital. For instance, social capital held by one person in the family firm may support another, but only partly. I ask whether a founder's social capital, or social legacy, can transfer to a next-generation successor and whether in doing so it loses strength, fidelity, or usefulness. Korhonen et al. further observe that historical contingencies work to endorse the founders' "social legacies" in the successor generations' international networking, putting forward the concept of "international networking legacy". Moreover, Batas et al. (Chap. 12) find that different family structures were linked to inherited social capital. Crucially, this legacy may be an advantage or a disadvantage for successors' own approaches to international networking.

A frequently neglected factor compared to network structure is network behaviour (Hughes et al., 2014). I am relieved to see a discussion of network behaviour in this *Handbook*. Fuerst (Chap. 14) reveals from a micro-perspective the networking behaviour of family and non-family member entrepreneurs in a Columbian case study, shedding light on how networking unfolds over time. San Román et al. (Chap. 11) present the case of the Spanish family multinational, Iberostar Group, documenting how its efforts to bed itself as a trustworthy partner for foreign partners led to its domestic and international growth, providing access to foreign markets and activating a learning process that developed its ability to venture internationally. This social capital provided reputation and trust, reliability and long-term vision, and, perhaps curiously, appeared to cross borders, shedding new light on the potential reach of social capital. Relatedly, Caffarena and Discua Cruz (Chap. 14) show the power of social capital and ethnic networks to support migrant families to internationalize their family business. Their work draws attention to whether social capital is a single, homogenous asset or one potentially specific to and different across groups within which it is conceived. Caffarena and Discua Cruz also suggest a continued reliance on specific networks to aide in internationalization. This may suggest that family firms' tendencies to rely on trust and long-standing relationships (as discussed above) risk dependence. Dependence can be destructive to future endeavours (Bouncken et al., 2020; Hughes and Perrons, 2011).

Many new research opportunities arise from the chapters dedicated to family firms' networks and relationships for the study of family firm internationalization. I will comment on a few that strike me as especially interesting. First, a pertinent question after reading the chapter in this *Handbook* dedicated to network relationships and family firm internationalization is whether we can ever study the latter without at least some consideration of the former. It seems, at the minimum, that network ties or some relational components should be considered as control variables to guard against alternative explanations in future studies. Second, I would argue that much more work is needed on network behaviour to understand how family firms build trust and guard against its loss. Concurrently, research is needed to understand how the behaviour of family firms change when distrust emerges in their relationships or in instances of trust violations. Firms can rarely abandon ties, and given the priority family firms attach to long-lasting, trusting relationships, a higher degree of dependence is likely to be a feature of these ties. Even in instances of trust violations then, family firms are unlikely to be able to simply abandon those relationships, creating a series of potential implications. Third, and perhaps relatedly, we cannot exclude the probability that the preference of family firms for long-lasting, enduring relationships is simultaneously connected to SEW and its preservation. That such long-lasting ties are purposefully built indicates a deliberate strategy. Since strategic decisions in family firms are directly connected to SEW, its preservation, and its growth, decisions about network content, structure, and behaviour are likely to revolve around such parameters of SEW that are especially meaningful to a family firm. Fourth, I am intrigued by the question of how might social capital function across borders considering the likely relationship between SEW and network behaviour. SEW preservation extends to the international context. Assuming a bifurcation bias, family firms may keep relationships quite separate creating little pockets of social capital, dyadic, and perhaps idiosyncratic to each relationship, with little spillover (because greater spillover implies a larger network less amenable to control with greater expectations of reciprocity that would require more investment from the family firm). The Iberostar case by San Román et al. (Chap. 11) is then quite intriguing because it departs from this logic.

Institutions

Institutions are an inescapable reality for any internationalizing business. The (family) firm experiences pressure from the socio-cultural, regulatory, and political institutions of its host country that compel obedience in exchange for legitimacy. The concept is rooted in institutional theory and ideas of isomorphism (DiMaggio & Powell, 1983), defined as pressures that could cause an organization to alter its structure and behaviour and conform to an institutional pattern (Mellahi et al., 2013). Isomorphism can be coercive (where patterns are imposed on firms by a powerful authority to obtain legitimacy), mimetic (resulting from standardized responses to uncertainty wherein firms duplicate the patterns of successful rivals or standard bearers), or normative (informed by professionalism, where firms adopt patterns considered appropriate for the host environment). For the family firm, such institutions are potentially problematic as they require some ceding of control (contrary to SEW preservation). However, the family firm may also seek institutional approval as a signal of its good name. Nonetheless, whether the firm converges with or diverges from these host institutions depends on a second source of institutional pressure: the firm itself. Institutional duality (Kostova & Roth, 2002), the notion that a subsidiary is buffeted by the institutional pressure of both its host environment and its parent organization, affects the performance of subsidiaries (Hughes et al., 2017). For example, the parent organization (the headquarters) often seeks to transfer a reservoir of practices based on well-established capabilities (Dunning, 1988; He et al., 2013; Peng, 2001), pressurizing the internal legitimacy of the subsidiary (Hughes et al., 2017; Kostova & Roth, 2002; Mellahi et al., 2013). The inescapable conclusion then is that for the family firm, venturing internationally—be it through exports, joint ventures, or subsidiaries (etc.)—will lead the family business inexorably to encounter strong institutional pressures. It must then decide how it will respond to those pressures.

Several chapters in this *Handbook* (implicitly or explicitly) draw attention to institutions and their potential effects on family firm internationalization. Sestu (Chap. 4) provides a framework for family firms' foreign entry strategies; Laari-Salmela et al. (Chap. 6) draw attention to the MNC as a complex web of interdependent relationships with subsidiaries embedded in their own local networks, implicitly suggesting the presence of institutional duality; and Debellis and Rondi (Chap. 9) consider the global factory model proposing the control that large family multinational enterprises will seek to implant on their global value chains, again implicitly raising questions of institutions. More directly, Kahor and Stranskov (Chap. 16) focus on the effects of home country institutions and institutional processes that shape firms' ability to access resources in their home environment. Interestingly, these authors suggest that these institutional factors may enhance the legitimacy of foreign operations and activities but that informal and poor home country institutional factors may restrain firms' internationalization. In a study of a developing-country family SME in Guatemala (Chap. 17 by Godinez and Sierra), however, a potentially different role is set out for domestic resources in comparison to the position set out by Kalhor and Stranskov, and these authors also acknowledge the role of networks in substituting or filling resource gaps. Finally, Jayakumar (Chap. 15) considers how strong host-country push and specific family factors (i.e. institutional pressures) may reverse their internationalization journey, de-internationalizing in the process.

Institutions represent a green-field opportunity for research on family firm internationalization. First, the chapters in this *Handbook* point to tensions between home and host country institutions that are of interest to understanding the motivation for internationalization. Second, the functioning of host country institutions and their relative pressure against those from the parental organization may affect the ability of family subsidiaries to function effectively when internationalizing. Third, it is not yet known how family firms respond to competing institutional pressures. Finally, we tend to think of internationalization as a continuous process which, once started, escalates in its magnitude and commitment. Studies of de-internationalization are refreshing for the new insights they can create on existing phenomena when (family) firms choose to scale back their international operations.

Concluding Remarks

This is an excellent *Handbook*. It will serve as a superb reference and resource for scholars across the family business and international business domains. It stands out as a powerful anchor point to inform and spearhead future research at the interface of the family and internationalization. It provides an overview and reference point about the status of family firm internationalization and contains interesting and insightful chapters, provoking new questions for family business and international business scholarship. It is compelling reading for those in need of a single source of knowledge and inspiration of family firm internationalization research. As I hope is apparent from my enthusiasm in writing this Foreword, this is an exciting time to be working on family firm internationalization. While I endeavour to report on the things that pique my interest and highlight important opportunities, there are many questions and opportunities to discover within these pages. I encourage readers to deep dive into these chapters and absorb the wealth of insights available! You can be assured that this *Handbook*, the first of its kind, provides you with the latest concepts and ideas, and will expand your knowledge of this important phenomenon.

Loughborough, UK   Mathew Hughes

References

Adler, P. S., & Kwon, S. W. (2002). Social capital: Prospects for a new concept. *The Academy of Management Review, 27*, 17–40.

Arregle, J. L., Duran, P., Hitt, M. A., & Van Essen, M. (2017). Why is family firms' internationalization unique? A meta-analysis. *Entrepreneurship Theory and Practice, 41*(5), 801–831.

Arregle, J.-L., Hitt, M. A., & Mari, I. (2019). A missing link in family firms' internationalization research: Family structures. *Journal of International Business Studies, 50*, 809–825.

Arregle, J., Hitt, M. A., Sirmon, D. G., & Very, P. (2007). The development of organizational social capital: Attributes of family firms. *Journal of Management Studies, 44*(1), 73–95.

Berrone, P., Cruz, C., Gómez-Mejía, L. R., & Larraza-Kintana, M. (2010). Socioemotional wealth and corporate responses to institutional pressures: Do family-controlled firms pollute less? *Administrative Science Quarterly, 55*, 82–113.

Berrone, P., Cruz, C., & Gómez-Mejía, L. R. (2012). Socioemotional wealth in family firms: Theoretical dimensions, assessment approaches, and agenda for future research. *Family Business Review, 25*, 258–279.

Bouncken, R. B., Hughes, M., Ratzmann, M., Cesinger, B., & Pesch, R. (2020). Family firms, alliance governance, and mutual knowledge creation. *British Journal of Management*, in press. https://doi.org/10.1111/1467-8551.12408

Carney, M. (2005). Corporate governance and competitive advantage in family-controlled firms. *Entrepreneurship Theory and Practice, 29*(3), 249–265.

Cesinger, B., Hughes, M., Mensching, H., Bouncken, R., Fredrich, V., & Kraus, S. (2016). A socioemotional wealth perspective on how collaboration intensity, trust, and international market knowledge affect family firms' multinationality. *Journal of World Business, 51*(4), 586–599.

Chrisman, J. J., Chua, J. H., Kellermanns, F. W., & Chang, E. P. (2007). Are family managers agents or stewards? An exploratory study in privately held family firms. *Journal of Business Research, 60*, 1030–1038.

Davis, J., Schoorman, F., & Donaldson, L. (1997). Toward a stewardship theory of management. *Academy of Management Review, 22*(1), 20–47.

DiMaggio, P. J., & Powell, W. W. (1983). The iron cage revisited: Institutionalism and collective rationality in organizational fields. *American Sociological Review, 48*, 147–160.

Dunning, J. H. (1988). The eclectic paradigm of international production: A restatement and some possible extensions. *Journal of International Business Studies, 19*, 1–31.

Georgiadou, E., Hughes, M., & Viala, C. (2020). Commercial diplomacy as a mechanism for passive-reactive SME internationalization: Overcoming liabilities of outsidership. *European Journal of International Management*, in press. https://doi.org/10.1504/ejim.2021.10029764

Gómez-Mejía, L. R., Haynes, K. T., Núñez-Nickel, M., Jacobson, K. J. L., & Moyano-Fuentes, J. (2007). Socioemotional wealth and business risks in family-controlled firms: Evidence from Spanish olive oil mills. *Administrative Science Quarterly, 52*, 106–137.

Gómez-Mejía, L. R., Makri, M., & Larraza Kintana, M. (2010). Diversification decisions in family-controlled firms. *Journal of Management Studies, 47*, 223–252.

He, X., Brouthers, K. D., & Filatotchev, I. (2013). Resource-based and institutional perspectives on export channel selection and export performance. *Journal of Management, 39*, 27–47.

Herrero, I., (2018). How familial is Family Social Capital? Analysing bonding social capital in family and nonfamily firms. *Family Business Review, 31*(4), 441–459.

Herrero, I., & Hughes, M. (2019). When family social capital is too much of a good thing. *Journal of Family Business Strategy, 10*(3), 100271.

Hu, Q., & Hughes, M. (2020). Radical innovation in family firms: A systematic analysis and research agenda. *International Journal of Entrepreneurial Behavior & Research*, in press. https://doi.org/10.1108/IJEBR-11-2019-0658

Hughes, M., & Perrons, R. (2011). Shaping and re-shaping social capital in buyer-supplier relationships. *Journal of Business Research, 64*(2), 164–171.

Hughes, M., Cesinger, B., Cheng, C.-F., Schüßler, F., & Kraus S. (2019). A configurational analysis of network and knowledge variables explaining Born Globals' and late internationalizing SMEs' international performance. *Industrial Marketing Management, 80*, 172–187.

Hughes, M., Morgan, R. E., Ireland, R. D., & Hughes, P. (2014). Social capital and learning from network relationships: A problem of absorptive capacity. *Strategic Entrepreneurship Journal, 8*(3), 214–233.

Hughes, M., Powell, T. H., Chung, L., & Mellahi, K. (2017). Institutional and resource-based explanations for subsidiary performance. *British Journal of Management, 28*(3), 407–424.

Johanson, J., & Vahlne, J.-E. (1977). The internationalization process of the firm—A model of knowledge development and increasing foreign market commitments. *Journal of International Business Studies, 18*, 23–32.

Johanson, J., & Vahlne, J.-E. (2009). The Uppsala internationalization process model revisited: From liability of foreignness to liability of outsidership. *Journal of International Business Studies, 40*, 1411–1431.

Kontinen, T., & Ojala, A. (2010). The internationalisation of family businesses: A review of extant research. *Journal of Family Business Strategy, 1*, 97–107.

Kontinen, T., & Ojala, A. (2012). Social capital in the international operations of family SMEs. *Journal of Small Business and Enterprise Development, 19*, 39–55.

Kostova, T., & Roth, K. (2002). Adoption of an organizational practice by subsidiaries of multinational corporations: Institutional and relational effects. *Academy of Management Journal, 45*, 215–233.

Kotlar, J., and De Massis, A. (2013). Goal setting in family firms: Goal diversity, social interactions, and collective commitment to family-centered goals. *Entrepreneurship Theory and Practice, 37*(6), 1263–1288.

Leana, C. R., & Van Buren, H. J. (1999). Organizational social capital and employment practices. *Academy of Management Review, 24*, 538–555.

Madison, K., Holt, D. T, Kellermanns, F. W., & Ranft, A. L. (2016). Viewing family firm behavior and governance through the lens of agency and stewardship theories. *Family Business Review, 29*(1), 65–93.

Mellahi, K., Demirbag, M., Collings, D., Tatoglu, E., & Hughes, M. (2013). Similarly different: A comparison of HRM practices in MNE subsidiaries and local firms in Turkey. *International Journal of Human Resource Management, 24*(12), 2239–2368.

Metsola, J., Leppäaho, T., Paavilainen-Mäntymäki, E., & Plakoyiannaki, E. (2020). Process in family business internationalisation: The state of the art and ways forward. *International Business Review, 29*(2), 101665.

Miller, D., and Le Breton-Miller, I. (2006). Family governance and firm performance: Agency, stewardship, and capabilities. *Family Business Review, 19*(1), 73–87.

Miller, D., Wright, M., Le Breton-Miller, I., & Scholes, L. (2015). Resources and innovation in family businesses: The Janus-face of socioemotional preferences. *California Management Review, 58*(1), 20–41.

Nahapiet, J., & Ghoshal, S. (1998). Social capital, intellectual capital, and the organizational advantage. *Academy of Management Review, 23*, 242–266.

Peng, M. W. (2001). The resource-based view and international business. *Journal of Management, 27*, 803–829.

Portes, A. (1998). Social capital: Its origins and applications in modern sociology. *Annual Review of Sociology, 24*, 1–24.

Pukall, T. J., & Calabrò, A. (2014). The internationalisation of family firms: A critical review and integrative model. *Family Business Review, 27*(2), 103–125.

Reuber, A. R. (2016). An assemblage-theoretic perspective on the internationalization processes of family firms. *Entrepreneurship Theory and Practice, 40*(6), 1269–1286.

Scholes, L., Hughes, M., Wright, M., De Massis, A., & Kotlar, J. (2020). Family management and family guardianship: Governance effects on family firm innovation strategy. *Journal of Family Business Strategy*, conditionally accepted.

Scholes, L., Mustafa, M., & Chen, S. (2015). Internationalization of small family firms: The influence of family from a socioemotional wealth perspective. *Thunderbird International Business Review, 58*, 131–146.

Schulze, W. S., Lubatkin, M. H., Dino, R. N., & Buchholtz, A. K. (2001). Agency relationships in family firms: Theory and evidence. *Organization Science, 12*(2), 99–116.

Suess, J. (2014). Family governance–Literature review and the development of a conceptual model. *Journal of Family Business Strategy, 5*(2), 138–155.

Uzzi, B. (1996). The sources and consequences of embeddedness for the economic performance of organizations: The network effect. *American Sociological Review, 61*(4), 674–698.

Verbeke, A., Yuan, W., & Kano, L. (2020). A values-based analysis of bifurcation bias and its impact on family firm internationalization. *Asia Pacific Journal of Management, 37*, 449–477.

Zahra, S. A. (2010). Harvesting family firms' organizational social capital: A relational perspective. *Journal of Management Studies, 47*(2), 345–366.

Foreword 2: Reflections on the Family Firm Internationalization Literature

Introduction

Worldwide, family firms are in the majority, some are major international players, and yet they have received less attention in the international business literature than large firms with dispersed ownership. There is still no consensus on the impact of the family mode of governance on a firm's internationalization level and processes. We do not know whether family firms are more or less likely than non-family firms to sell to foreign customers, whether they internationalize differently, or whether and how their internationalization is influenced by home and host country institutions.

Interest in family firms is growing. In the past ten years, there has been a marked increase in the number of scholarly articles devoted to them (Casillas & Moreno-Menendez, 2017). All the same, after meta-analysing 76 empirical studies of the impact of family governance on internationalization, Arregle et al. (2017) concluded that "the association between the family vs. non-family dimension is basically null and characterized by its high variance (heterogeneity)" (Arregle, Hitt & Mari, 2019: 809). In this Foreword, I suggest possible reasons for the lack of definite answers to some of the research questions posed in this book.

What Features of Family firm Governance Are Likely to Impact Its Internationalization?

To study family firm internationalization is to research the relationship between two concepts, family firms on one hand and internationalization on the other. A useful starting point is to look at what is meant by "family firm", and to ascertain whether there is a fit between how family firms have been defined and operationalized in the literature and the theories used to explain their internationalization.

The most restrictive way to define a family firm is a firm fully owned and managed by a family, with a history (or intent) of intergenerational succession (Salvato, Chirico, Melin & Seidl, 2019). A broader definition looks at family ownership, differentiating between when a family has sufficient ownership to exercise control over a firm—even if it does not manage it, that is, a family-owned firm—and when it has neither undisputed control nor participation in management, that is, a family-influenced one.

One would expect to observe differences in the extent of internationalization between family and non-family firms only if they act in fundamentally different ways. In other words, if family firms are defined in such a way as to make them almost indistinguishable from other types of firms, then one would not expect to see marked differences in their degree of internationalization.

What is then truly distinctive about family firms? One possibility is concentrated ownership. In this case, there is no principal-agent problem because full ownership aligns the goals of firm owners with those of managers. Note that this does not ipso facto mean that managers/owners will maximize profits. Being undisputed owners, managers of family-managed firms are able to maximize whatever they wish. The literature on socioemotional wealth (SEW) makes this clear (Berrone, Cruz, & Gomez-Mejia, 2011). Monetary income is only one of many parameters in an individual's utility function, so unless fully constrained by principals to maximize profits, agents can be expected to engage in activities that provide other sources of utility. A start-up entrepreneur with easy access to funds may spend them on peripheral hobbies or on lavish office decor. A CEO of a large company with dispersed shareholders and a compliant board can indulge in personal whims (with sometimes disastrous results as in the case of Jean-Marie Messier and Vivendi). So, ownership concentration per se may not lead to clear differences in behaviour between family firms and other firms. To argue that SEW maximization will lead to different outcomes for family firms, one needs to look at other family firm characteristics than just concentrated ownership. Firms owned by family members, but not managed by them, may behave more like non-family firms than those which are both family-owned and managed because the separation of ownership and management has re-created a principal-agent problem, a conjecture supported by Kim, Hoskisson, and Zyung (2019). Likewise, sharing ownership with non-family owners leads to principal-principal problems, as the goals of the family and those of other shareholders may conflict. Then, depending on the institutional context, for example, the extent of legal protection of minority shareholders (Arregle et al., 2017), family firms may be forced to curb their pursuit of non-financial goals and to behave like non-family firms.

The intent and practice of leaving ownership and management to one's offspring would seem to be an important dimension of family firm governance. It makes it possible to distinguish family-managed firms from entrepreneurial start-ups owned and managed by their founder(s) (alone or in partnership). A start-up founder, intending to sell the firm as soon as possible to other firms or to the general public through an IPO, is bound to have a shorter-term horizon than a family firm owner eager to pass the firm to descendants. As in family firms, the coherence of the management team in start-up partnerships comes from co-ownership in contrast to firms with dispersed ownership where the interests of the managers may not align with those of the owners. But there is one subtle difference: A family has a wider panoply of tools to maintain management team cohesion than a partnership with non-family partners. A family can use the threat of ostracism, for instance, a deviant family manager might no longer be included in family events (Pollak, 1985). It is also easier for family managers to monitor one another since they have deeper knowledge of each other, often built over a long period of time, than is usually the case with start-up partners.

Multi-generation succession also facilitates the build-up of social capital. Owners of family firms will be trusted because they are less likely to engage in opportunism or bounded reliability today as it might damage the prospects for their offspring in the future. In other words, multi-generation succession lengthens the shadow of the future. It raises the pay-off of maintaining a good reputation because it strengthens the identification of the manager with the firm. Misbehaving CEOs of firms with dispersed ownership have less at stake than managers of family firms, whose firms often bear their name, and who are embedded in the social fabric of the community where the firm is located. One would therefore expect family firms with intergeneration intent to care more about protecting firm reputation than family firms without such intent and, of course, more than firms in which family plays no part at all. As I argue below, a stellar reputation allows family firms with intergeneration intent to develop trusting relationships with customers and suppliers, making it possible, for example, to co-develop products with them.

In short, what strongly distinguishes family firms from other types of firms are family management and transgenerational intent. Partial family ownership introduces principal-principal conflicts which may cause family-owned

xxiv   Foreword 2: Reflections on the Family Firm Internationalization...

Table 1 Match between theories and family-firm types

Impact on internationalization scale and scope	Family-influenced	Family-owned	Family-owned and managed	Family-owned and managed with intergenerational intent
Family firms selling mass-market products			−−	−−
Family firms selling niche products		+	+	++
Impact of SEW			−−	−−

firms to behave in ways that do not differ much from other firms. Ownership sans management will result in principal-agent problems, just as it does in other firms. It is also difficult to argue that the time orientation of family-firm owners who do not intend to pass on the firm to offspring differs in any significant way from that of any other types of firms. In short, the sharper contrasts between family firms and non-family firms are likely to be observed between non-family firms where shareholders effectively constrain managers to maximize profits, and family-owned and managed firms with intergenerational succession intent.

Table 1 summarizes these arguments, with two minus or plus signs signifying strong predicted differences between family firms and other firms in the extent of internationalization, one plus or minus indicating a weak effect, and no sign signifying no effect.

How to Measure Internationalization

Internationalization is the extent (scale) and the inter-country distribution (scope) of sales to foreign customers. A firm can serve such customers through exports from the home country or through production in a foreign country. Sometimes firms use a mix of the two modes, so both must be taken into account. Only foreign-based production destined for local or third-country customers should be considered, as production abroad for domestic customers does not constitute foreign sales. Internationalization scale is generally measured by the ratio of foreign sales to total sales (FSTS) (e.g. Fang et al., 2018), although some (e.g. Bhaumik, Driffield & Pal, 2010) have used the ratio of foreign assets to total assets (FATA), a measure which assumes that all foreign sales arise from overseas production and sales subsidiaries (i.e. that excludes exports). FSTS and FATA have limitations. First, because they are ratios, they are affected by changes in both the numerator (foreign sales; foreign assets) and the denominator (total sales; total assets), so changes in the ratios may result from changes in domestic sales or assets only. A second limitation is that they do not reflect the diversity of foreign markets served. Hence, a firm can have an FSTS ratio of 0.9, with either 90% of its sales to a culturally similar country across the border, say a Swiss firm located in the German-speaking part of Switzerland selling to Germany, or 10% of its sales going to nine culturally distant countries (Hennart, 2011; Verbeke & Forootan, 2012).

Some authors (e.g. Singla, Veliyath & George, 2014) have used a firm's total number of foreign subsidiaries, or the ratio of its foreign subsidiaries to its total number of subsidiaries, as reported in annual reports or other administrative documents. Subsidiaries, however, are administrative units, with only an approximate correspondence to actual production units, so the measure can be unreliable.[1]

The inter-country dispersion of sales is called internationalization scope. This has been measured by the number of countries where the firm has at least one subsidiary and by the entropy index of foreign sales. Both of these measures have serious drawbacks. Counting the number of countries where the firm has subsidiaries (as in Zhara, 2003 and Arregle et al., 2017) is problematic because it does not provide information on the geographical distribution of sales: a firm may have subsidiaries in 150 foreign countries, but most of its sales in a single one, with others performing minor operations. Other studies have measured international scope with an entropy index, which is meant to measure the geographic dispersion of a firm's total sales (e.g. Bauweraerts, Sciascia, Naldi & Mazzola, 2019; D'Angelo, Majocchi & Buck, 2016; Sanchez-Bueno & Usero, 2014).[2] The problem with an entropy index is that it only measures dispersion, not scale. Hence, an SME selling half of its production at home and small amounts (say €1000 each) to five different foreign countries has exactly the same entropy index as a firm selling €500 million at home and €100 million to five different foreign countries (Hennart, Majocchi & Forlani, 2019). This is highly problematic if international scope is meant to measure the degree of commitment to international markets and the resources needed to achieve it. Another drawback is that the highest value

---

[1] For example, the list of Enron's foreign subsidiaries in its 2000 10K report to the US Securities and Exchange Commission runs to 64 pages. Many of them appear to be tax-avoiding special purpose entities—692 subsidiaries are incorporated in the Cayman Islands and 151 in the Netherlands, two countries where Enron did not have any physical activities at the time. Many foreign activities are in subsidiaries incorporated in Enron's home country, the United States. Enron's ill-fated Dabhol Indian power plant, for example, was owned by a Mauritius subsidiary, itself owned by a Dutch company, itself owned by a Cayman Island subsidiary, which was then owned by a Delaware subsidiary of Enron, Enron India, LLC. A superficial reading would count Dabhol as a domestic subsidiary of Enron. It is clear in Enron's case that there is little correspondence between administrative units and activities.

[2] D'Angelo, Majocchi, and Buck (2016) calculate this entropy ratio on the FSTS ratio for each major world region.

of the index is when every country has exactly the same share of sales; however, even if a firm were to be successful at developing sales in each of the world's countries or regions, the share of its sales would not be the same in all countries, as some countries have more potential customers than others. In other words, an entropy index does not tell us the extent to which a firm has saturated all the foreign markets available.

To remedy these weaknesses, some authors have used composite measures. Purkayastha, Manolova, and Edelman (2018), for instance, sum up a firm's FSTS, FATA, the absolute number of countries where the firm has subsidiaries, and the ratio of the number of countries where it has subsidiaries over the number of countries where firms in the sample have at least one subsidiary. Such composite indexes suffer from all the criticisms that can be levied against their constituent parts; moreover, the choice of the measures to include and their respective weight is arbitrary.

A much more theoretically satisfying solution is to use a gravity model. Gravity models have been successful at predicting the level of a country's exports to other countries (see the survey by Wang, Wei & Liu, 2010). They are based on Newton's law of gravity that states that the attraction between two objects is proportional to their mass and inversely proportional to the distance between them. By analogy, Tinbergen (1962) posited that the level of economic transactions between two countries depends on their respective economic size—proxied by their respective GDP—and by the distance—geographical, economic, institutional, political, and cultural—between them. A gravity model can be used to predict the sales of a given firm to a given foreign country—or foreign region; we can then test whether family firm governance affects the level of those sales, keeping constant other firm characteristics, such as size and age. This approach makes it possible to simultaneously measure a firm's depth and breadth of internationalization since it compares its actual and potential sales in each country. For instance, firms which sell much less in most countries than predicted by a gravity model, but much more in a few others, have a low level of international scope. As far as I know, with the exception of Hennart et al. (2019), gravity models have not been used in the family firm internationalization literature.

Traditional Theories of Family Firm Internationalization

The Uppsala model, as developed by Johanson and Vahlne (1977, 2009) and their followers, explicitly argues that internationalization is a slow, gradual process, and implicitly argues that it is costly and risky. For those authors, foreign countries differ in culture, language, and economic conditions from the internationalizing firm's home base, and from each other. The internationalizing firm must therefore find out, for each foreign country, how to identify foreign customers and persuade them to buy, and how to adapt the marketing mix to their tastes and use conditions. Uppsala scholars also posit that the most efficient way to serve foreign customers is through foreign manufacturing plants, often an expensive and risky endeavour requiring an in-depth knowledge of each foreign country as it involves hiring and supervising a foreign labour force, finding local suppliers, and dealing with host country governments. Uppsala scholars assume that a firm will commit to developing sales in a foreign country if, and only if, it has accumulated experience of that country. That experience can only be had by being physically present in the country; so, because this takes time, the firm will slowly and progressively expand in one foreign market at a time, slowing down the internationalization process. A more recent version of the Uppsala model (Johanson & Vahlne, 2009) puts greater emphasis on the need to penetrate foreign country networks. Since being accepted in a network takes time and repeated interactions, this does not affect the model's core prediction that internationalization is a slow market-by-market endeavour that requires the internationalizing firm to accumulate local knowledge—in this version, knowledge of which host country networks to enter.

The main theories of family firm internationalization (see the surveys by Kontinen & Ojala, 2010, Fernández & Nieto, 2013 and Pukall & Calabrò, 2014) have all been heavily influenced by this view. The argument is that family firms will internationalize less than other types of firms because they do not have (1) internationally experienced managers and (2) sufficient funds to undertake international expansion. Family firms are said to lack the needed internationally experienced managers in-house because their skill pool is limited to family members and they are reluctant to recruit internationally experienced managers from the outside (Graves & Thomas, 2006). They are also supposed to lack the necessary financial resources because of their unwillingness to tap outside finance, since it may dilute their control of the business (Claver et al., 2009; Gallo et al., 2004; Gomez-Mejia et al., 2010, 2011;

Fernández & Nieto, 2006; Muñoz-Bullon & Sanchez-Bueno, 2012; Sanchez-Bueno & Usero, 2014). A more recent argument as to why family firms may have difficulty internationalizing is that the backgrounds of family members are likely to be more homogeneous than those of outside managers (Tsang, 2018). Consequently, the networks of their management team are more redundant than those of outside managers. Their networks are also likely to be more domestic—and if international, more regional—than those of firms that bring in managers from the outside (Banalieva & Eddleston, 2011; Kontinen & Ojala, 2012).

To sum up, family firm internationalization scholars have assumed that the Uppsala way of foreign expansion, which requires managers with extensive experience of target foreign countries, insidership in their networks, and substantial financial resources, applies across the board to all firms. Since they believe that family-managed firms do not have—and are unwilling to acquire—these resources, they conclude that family-managed firms will have a lower level of internationalization than non-family firms.

Niche Business Models and Family Firm Internationalization

In essence, all of the aforementioned arguments as to why family-managed firms will find it difficult to sell abroad are rooted in the Uppsala assumptions that (1) selling abroad requires a huge investment to introduce a product to consumers and educate them about it, to adapt it to country-specific conditions, and to set up production facilities abroad, and (2) that each foreign market is fundamentally different, and hence successful foreign market penetration requires country-specific experience. Hennart (2014) and Hennart, Majocchi, and Forlani (2019) argue, on the other hand, that such difficulties are only faced by firms with a mass-market business model. Many family-managed firms, however, have adopted a totally different business model, a global niche model. That business model is well suited to a family-managed firm with intergenerational succession intent, and this explains why, despite the arguments widely found in the family firm internationalization literature, many family-managed firms are highly internationalized (e.g. Colli, Garcia-Canal & Guillen, 2013; De Massis, Audretsch, Uhlaner & Kammerlander, 2018; Magnani & Zucchella, 2019).

Niche products are unique and cater to the specialized needs and tastes of a limited number of customers (Toften & Hammervoll, 2013). As a result, they have very few, if any, substitutes, giving their producers some degree of market power (Merrilees & Tiessen, 1999). Their uniqueness may be based on advanced technology, artistic design, high-quality workmanship, or unique provenance.

A niche business model allows for easy and extensive internationalization. In their 2019 article, Hennart et al. use the example of the Ciclotte, an exercise bike designed and built by Lamiflex in Bergamo, Italy. The Ciclotte is artistically designed and exquisitely built of high-quality carbon fibre, and fits beautifully in a luxury mansion or on the deck of an expensive yacht. In contrast to exercise bikes found on Amazon with retail prices starting at around €100, the Ciclotte sells upward from €10,000 (Hedd Magazine, 2018), and it is targeted at affluent customers located all over the world, members of a global, cosmopolitan elite who share a taste for high design and luxury. They may be one in a million and, for that simple reason, most of them are located outside Italy.

How does an SME like Lamiflex reach potential customers? Let's revisit the challenges of selling abroad identified by the Uppsala model. The first is to make foreign consumers aware of the offering and to persuade them to buy. While this is challenging for sellers of garden-variety exercise bikes in foreign markets where there are domestic substitutes, buyers of niche products—luxury products or specialized B2B ones—are few in number and belong to communities of experienced users, who often exchange information about suppliers and their products. Such users often directly approach sellers, saving the latter the cost of customer acquisition. Users of niche products, whether luxury or technical, tend to have homogeneous tastes, so niche products do not have to be adapted to each foreign country, as is the case for mass-market goods. Buyers of mass-market products are unlikely to pay high shipping charges to import them from overseas because they can find local substitutes. This forces manufacturers of mass-market products—even of those with a higher-than-average price tag like a Volvo car—to locate production relatively close to buyers. Niche products, on the other hand, have few or no local substitutes, so their buyers are willing to absorb shipping charges, making it possible for their sellers to export from a home base at very low marginal costs (Hennart, 2014).[3] Note also that niche sellers do not need to become insiders in the networks of each target foreign country, as argued in the literature (e. g. Xu, Hitt & Dai, 2020; Banalieva & Eddleston, 2011), but instead need

---

[3] An additional reason for serving foreign customers through exports from the home base is that part of the attraction of niche products comes from their geographical provenance. The Ciclotte website emphasizes that the bike is manufactured in Italy (Hennart et al., 2019).

only penetrate one network—that of the international users of their product. Entry into that kind of network does not require foreign country experience, only familiarity with the product and its users, which family firms pursuing niche strategies are likely to have, especially if they are multi-generational.

In sum, the internationalization handicaps that family firm international-ization scholars have assumed family-managed firms must face—lack of inter-nationally experienced managers, of target country network insidership, and of finance—do not apply if they sell niche products. Because their customers have homogeneous tastes that can be served by exports, increasing the scale and scope of international activities will not pose managerial challenges for niche sellers.

In fact, one could go further and argue that family-managed firms are uniquely suited to carrying out a global niche strategy. One major risk with that strategy is that larger competitors might attempt to invade the niche. There are two main defences against this. One is to maintain distinctiveness by continuously improving the product. Simon (2014) cites the motto of Flexi, a German family firm with a 70% world market share for retractable dog leashes: "We will do only one thing, but we do it better than anyone else". The second defence is to establish and maintain strong links with customers by responding flexibly to their needs, even anticipating them. Magnani and Zucchella (2019: 149) write that the comparative advantage of the niche firms they observed was "based on the proactive identification of customers wherever they are located, anticipating their needs, solving their problems and ultimately co-creating value and innovating through customer interactions".

Family-managed firms are in a good position to carry out these two strate-gies (Hennart et al., 2019). Continuous improvement of product and pro-cesses requires a long-term outlook, which family-managed firms, free from the short-term demands of external shareholders, are more likely to have. This culture of high quality is often passed generations,[4] as is the importance of maintaining strong bonds with suppliers and customers. Such bonds, the result of a long history of honest dealings, are a sine-qua-non condition for co-innovating with them (Coleman, 1990). Family-managed firms with intergeneration intent maximize in the long run, knowing that the reputation of the firm is tightly linked to that of the owning and managing family mem-bers because the firm bears their name. Reputation is always vulnerable to free-riding and a potential problem in publicly owned firms where managers

---

[4] Hennart et al. (2019) cite Andrea Illy, the CEO of Illycaffé, manufacturer of one of the world's best coffee: "When Grandfather Francesco founded the company he wanted to sell the best coffee in the world, and we are still working on it" (Fontevecchia, 2013).

have a relatively short tenure—indeed, their opportunistic behaviour is often discovered after they have left the firm. By contrast, the managers of family-managed firms are usually co-owners, whose interests are aligned with the firm itself. Employees of family firms tend also to have a longer tenure and a closer relationship with management than in publicly held firms (Miller & Le Breton-Miller, 2005; Simon, 2009). This increases the chance that they will uphold the firm's reputation. In sum, family-managed firms with intergeneration intent possess the resources required to carry out global niche strategies, and those strategies allow them to internationalize with limited financial resources and purely domestic managers who are complete outsiders in foreign country networks (Hennart, 2014).

Hennart et al. (2019) tested this hypothesis on 9214 French, German, Italian, and Spanish SMEs. Correcting for endogeneity, they find that the higher the percentage of family members within the managerial team of family-owned SMEs (their measure of family management), the lower the sales to eight foreign regions (compared to SMEs with lower or zero family management). Family-managed firms that sold niche products, on the other hand, were able to partially close the gap. Their results were robust. They were found in the overall sample, but also for each country, even though they have their own culture and institutions.

Implications for the Study of Family Firm Internationalization

There are many other issues in family firm internationalization, but space constraints prevent me from discussing them here. One of them is endogeneity. Family governance is not randomly assigned to firms, so research that seeks to uncover performance differences between family firms and other firms needs to control for endogeneity. Very few family firm studies do (but see Hennart et al., 2019). There are also other sources of heterogeneity in family firms not discussed here, for instance, family structures (Arregle et al., 2019). Nevertheless, this short survey has a number of implications for future research.

For one, it is important to match theory to family firm type. The Uppsala-derived argument that family firms will be less likely to internationalize because they do not have the required managerial and financial resources to sell abroad only applies to family firms selling mass-market products and which are both family-owned and managed, since family firms with non-family owners and those not managed by family members have already opened themselves to outside capital and to non-family managers. Equally, Uppsala-based arguments do not apply to family-managed firms, especially those with transgenerational intent, which are following a global niche strategy. This strategy, which demands a long-term vision and the maintenance of a good reputation, will be harder to conduct if the family firm has minority shareholders clamouring for immediate profits and/or if it is implemented by non-family managers presumably with less emotional attachment to the firm. Likewise, the argument that SEW preservation will lead family firms to eschew internationalization because it is risky would seem to apply only to those family-managed firms which follow mass-market internationalization strategies.

A second point is that a much better job of measuring internationalization is needed across the board. Specifically, research should make clear what exactly is being measured and how any measure might be affected by family firm attributes.[5]

A third implication is the need to relax the assumption that all family firms need to follow an Uppsala-type mass-market business model. As I have shown, family-managed firms that follow niche strategies are perfectly able to sell substantial amounts in a large number of foreign countries. While it seems plausible to expect that, in the case of family-managed firms following mass-market strategies, expanding into a "broader set of countries places significant demands on the ability of managers to deal with diverse institutional environments, creating substantial managerial challenges" (Arregle et al., 2017: 821), and that this constrains their internationalization breadth, this is not a challenge facing family-managed firms following niche strategies: for them, selling in twenty foreign countries requires the same level of management expertise as selling in one. Since the global niche strategy is suited to family-managed firms, while the Uppsala mass-market one is not, one might question why family-managed firms would ever attempt to pursue mass-market strategies. Perhaps family-managed firms are of two types: some will not engage at all in foreign sales, while others will be significant internationalizers. The overall effect observed when comparing the scale and scope of internationalization of family-managed versus other firms would then depend on the relative share of these two types of family-managed firms in the sample. This may explain why Arregle et al. (2017) and Hennart et al. (2019) find that family-managed firms internationalize less than other types of firms, but that

---

[5] Arregle et al. (2017) note that the results of their meta-analysis of family firm internationalization hinge on the way internationalization is measured.

Hennart et al. find the negative impact of family governance greatly reduced when family-managed firms follow niche strategies. Further research might elucidate this puzzle.

Tilburg, Netherlands   Jean-Francois Hennart

References

Arregle, J., Duran, P. Hitt, M., & van Essen, P. (2017). Why is family firms' internationalization unique? A meta-analysis. *Entrepreneurship Theory and Practice, 41*(5), 801–831.

Arregle, J., Hitt, M., & Mari, I. (2019). A missing link in family firms' internationalization research: Family structures. *Journal of International Business Studies, 50*(5), 809–825.

Arregle, J., Naldi, L., Nordquist, M., & Hitt., M. (2012). Internationalization of family-controlled firms: A study of the effects of external involvement in governance. *Entrepreneurship Theory and Practice, 36*(6), 1115–1143.

Banalieva, E., & Eddleston, K. (2011). Home regional focus and performance of family firms: The role of family vs. non-family leaders. *Journal of International Business Studies, 42*(8), 1060–1072.

Bauweraerts, J., Sciascia, S., Naldi, L., & Mazzola, P. (2019). Family CEO and board service: Turning the tide for export scope in family SMEs. *International Business Review, 28*(5), 101583.

Bhaumik, S., Driffield, N., & Pal, S. (2010). Does ownership structure of emerging market firms affect their outward FDI? The case of the Indian automotive and pharmaceutical sectors. *Journal of International Business Studies, 41*, 437–450.

Berrone, P., Cruz, C., & Gomez-Mejia, L. (2012). Socioemotional wealth in family firms: Theoretical dimensions, assessment approaches, and agenda for future research. *Family Business Review, 25*(3), 258–279.

Casillas, J., & Moreno-Menendez, A. (2017). International business and family business: Potential dialogue between disciplines. *European Journal of Family Business, 7*(1–2), 25–40.

Claver, E., Rienda, L., & Quer, D. (2009). Family firm's international commitment: The influence of family-related factors. *Family Business Review, 22*(2), 125–135.

Coleman, J. (1990). *Foundations of social theory.* Cambridge, MA: Harvard University Press.

Colli, A., Garcia-Canal, E., & Guillen, M. (2013). Family character and international entrepreneurship: A historical comparison of Italian and Spanish "new multinationals". *Business History, 55*(1), 119–138.

De Massis, A., Audretsch, D., Uhlaner, L., & Kammerlander, N. (2018). Innovation with limited resources: Management lessons from the German Mittelstand. *Journal of Production and Innovation Management, 35*(1), 125–146.

Fang, H., Kotlar, J., Memili, E., Chrisman, J., & De Massis, A. (2018). The pursuit of international opportunities in family firms: Generational differences and the role of knowledge-based resources. *Global Strategy Journal, 8*(1), 136–157.

Fernández, Z., & Nieto, M. (2013). Internationalization of family firms. In L. Melin, M. Nordqvist, & P. Sharma (Eds.), *The Sage handbook of family business*. Los Angeles: Sage.

Fontevecchia, A. (2013). Illy's espresso revolution: A luxury business model and the search for the perfect coffee. *Forbes*, December 10. Retrieved November 10, 2015, from http://www.forbes.com/sites/afontevecchia/2013/12/10/illys-espresso-revolution-a-luxury-business-model-and-the-search-for-the-perfect-coffee/

Gallo, M., Tapies, J., & Cappuyns, K. (2004). Comparison of family and non-family business: Financial logic and personal preferences. *Family Business Review, 17*(4), 303–318.

Gomez-Mejia, L., Cruz, C., Berrone, P., & de Castro, J. (2011). The bind that ties: Socioemotional wealth preservation in family firms. *Academy of Management Annals, 5*(1), 653–707.

Gomez-Mejia, L., Makri, M., & Larraza-Kintana, M. (2010). Diversification decisions in family-controlled firms. *Journal of Management Studies, 47*(2), 223–252.

Graves, C., & Thomas, J. (2006). Internationalization of Australian family firms: A managerial capabilities perspective. *Family Business Review, 19*(3), 207–224.

Hedd Magazine. (2018). Ride in style with Ciclotte—World first designer exercise bike. Retrieved September 4, 2020, from www.Heddmagazine.com/2018/11/02/ciclotte-designer-exercise-bike/

Hennart, J. F. (2011). A theoretical assessment of the empirical literature on the impact of multinationality on performance. *Global Strategy Journal, 1*(1–2), 135–151.

Hennart, J. F. (2014). The accidental internationalists: A theory of born globals. *Entrepreneurship Theory and Practice, 38*(1), 117–135.

Hennart, J. F., Majocchi, A., & Forlani, E. (2019). The myth of the stay-at-home family firm: How family-managed SMEs can overcome their internationalization limitations. *Journal of International Business Studies, 50*(5), 758–782.

Johanson, J., & Vahlne, J. E. (1977). Internationalization process of firm—A model of knowledge development and increasing foreign market commitments. *Journal of International Business Studies, 8*(1), 23–32.

Johanson, J., & Vahlne, J. E. (2009). The Uppsala internationalization process model revisited: From liability of foreignness to liability of outsidership. *Journal of International Business Studies, 40*(3), 1411–1431.

Kim, H., Hoskisson, R., & Zyung, J. (2019). Socioemotional favoritism: Evidence from foreign divestitures in family multinationals. *Organization Studies, 40*(6), 917–940.

Kontinen, T., & Ojala, A. (2010). The internationalization of family business: A review of extant research. *Journal of Family Business Strategy, 1*(2), 97–107.

Kontinen, T., & Ojala, A. (2012). Social capital in the international operations of family SMEs. *Journal of Small Business and Enterprise Development, 19*(1), 39–55.

Magnani, G., & Zucchella, A. (2019). Coping with uncertainty in the internationalisation strategy: An exploratory study on entrepreneurial firms. *International Marketing Review, 36*(1), 131–163.

Merrilees, B., & Tiessen, J. H. (1999). Building generalizable SME international marketing models using case studies. *International Marketing Review, 16*(4/5), 326–344.

Miller, D., & Le Breton-Miller, I. (2005). *Managing for the long run: Lessons in competitive advantage from great family businesses.* Boston, MA: Harvard Business School Press.

Muñoz-Bullon, F., & Sanchez-Bueno, M. (2012). So family ties shape the performance consequences of diversification? Evidence from the European Union. *Journal of World Business, 47*(3), 469–277.

Pollak, R. (1985). A transaction cost approach to families and households. *Journal of Economic Literature, 23*(2), 581–608.

Pukall T., & Calabrò, A. (2014). The internationalization of family firms: A critical review and integrative model. *Family Business Review, 27*(2), 103–125.

Purkayastha, S., Manolova, T., & Edelman, L. (2018). Business group effects on the R&D intensity-internationalization relationship: Empirical evidence from India. *Journal of World Business, 53*(2), 104–117.

Salvato, C., Chirico, F., Melin, L., & Seidl, D. (2019). Coupling family business research with organization studies: Interpretations, issues, and insights. *Organization Studies, 40*(6), 775–791.

Sanchez-Bueno, M., & Usero, B. (2014). How may the nature of family firms explain the decisions concerning international diversification? *Journal of Business Research, 67*(7), 1311–1320.

Simon, H. (2009). *Hidden champions of the 21st century.* Berlin: Springer.

Simon, H. (2014). The global success of midsized companies. *The German Times for Europe*, May 30. Retrieved June 30, 2015, from http://www.german-times.com/index.php?option=com_content&task=view&id=43501&Itemid=244

Singla, C., Veliyath, R., & George, R. (2014). Family firms and internationalization-governance relationships: Evidence of secondary agency issues. *Strategic Management Journal, 35*, 606–616.

Tinbergen, J. (1962). *Shaping the world economy.* New York: Twentieth Century Fund.

Toften, K., & Hammervoll, T. (2013). Niche marketing research: Status and challenges. *Marketing Intelligence and Planning, 31*(3), 272–285.

Tsang, E. (2020). Family firm internationalization: An organizational learning perspective. *Asia Pacific Journal of Management, 37*, 205–225.

Verbeke, A., & Forootan, Z. (2012). How good are Multinationality-Performance (M-P) empirical studies? *Global Strategy Journal, 2*, 332–344.

Wang, C., Wei, Y., & Liu, X. (2010). Determinants of bilateral trade flows in OECD countries: Evidence from gravity panel data models. *The World Economy, 33*(7), 894–915.

Xu, K., Hitt, M., & Dai, L. (2020). International diversification of family-dominant firms: Integrating socioemotional wealth and behavioral theory of the firm. *Journal of World Business, 55*(3), 101071.

Zahra, S. (2003). International expansion of US manufacturing family businesses: The effect of ownership and involvement. *Journal of Business Venturing, 18*(4), 495–512.

Foreword 3

The Palgrave *Handbook on Family Firm Internationalization* by Tanja Leppäaho and Sarah Jack is the pleasing result of enthusiastic and tireless research done to advance our knowledge and understanding of family firm internationalization. Meeting Tanja and Sarah at the Centre for Family Business, Lancaster University Management School, allowed me to discover the passion Tanja adds to her work, and to see Sarah's charisma in prompting research as a priority to advance knowledge creation and sharing. Their efforts have melded the work of the contributors into a useful and vital volume.

Family business internationalization has received attention only in the last ten years, with scant earlier contributions. The literature reviews by Kontinen and Ojala (2010) and Pukall and Calabrò (2014) give full credit to this stream of literature, highlighting the importance of looking at this topic from novel perspectives. They consider how internationalization theories and models could be adapted and changed to better explain the behaviours of businesses run by families that look for opportunities abroad—opportunities outside their comfort zone. The family business context offers opportunity to challenge the assumptions of existing internationalization models, providing novel explanations to understand reasons, modes, and processes of international expansion. Over time, we have assisted in an increasing number of articles that look at this phenomenon, especially the special issues advancing our knowledge of family business internationalization (Baù, et al., 2017; De Massis et al., 2018; Eddleston et al., 2020).

The handbook complements and advances the ongoing debates on family business internationalization by offering a rich and diverse set of contributions to crystallize the most up-to-date and challenging perspectives on the topic. The reader of the book will delve into four core areas of research: family

xxxvii

firm-specific view on internationalization; internationalization process, networks in family firm internationalization, and family firm internationalization from emerging markets. The contributions collected in this handbook are arranged in a way that highlights the idiosyncratic characteristics of family businesses and their role in advancing knowledge on internationalization.

The first part of the book leverages on debated concepts and theoretical perspectives that have flourished in family business studies. The authors suggest that a decision such as internationalization is strongly dependent on affect-related dimensions: the prioritization of family assets and routines (bifurcation bias, cf. Kano, Verbeke, and Johnston—Chap. 1); intergenerational differences in the way the business is looked after (family stewards, cf. Ruenda, Claver, and Andreu—Chap. 2); paradoxical tensions in preserving the interests of the family in business, while building networks to expand the family business (socioemotional wealth, cf. Metsola, Torkkeli, Leppäaho, Arenius, and Haapanen—Chap. 3); as well as considerations about costs and resources from the family and the business perspective (integration of family and business, cf. Sestu—Chap. 4).

The second part of the book embraces the view that internationalization is not considered as an event, rather as a process. Through this perspective, the reader has the opportunity to reflect on other three core features of family firms that make them focus differently on their businesses and the strategies employed abroad. Indeed, using a behavioural perspective, Kuiken, Naldi, and Nordqvist (Chap. 5) suggest family firms have to manage a discontinuous process in their international expansion. From a different angle and looking at the evolution of the family business into a multinational company, Laari-Salmela, Mainela, Pernu, and Puhakka (Chap. 6) show how family values can affect the management model of the family business subsidiaries in other countries. Moreover, underlying the salience of the founder's social legacy for a family business, Korhonen, Leppäaho, Amdam, and Jack (Chap. 7) advance how family heritage is intertwined with networking activities, introducing and explaining the concept "international networking legacy".

The first two parts of the handbook on family firm-specific views and process views lead the reader to observe that there is a *fil rouge* across the contributions collected there, as networking emerges as a *leitmotiv* in several chapters. Accordingly, the third part of the book not surprisingly addresses this aspect of family firm internationalization. The authors of these contributions challenge the reader's view on the topic. In Chap. 8, Kampouri and Plakoyiannaki offer insights on entry modes, suggesting that identification to the business and emotional attachment make family firms stick to their nodes in the international network they created in the first move. Embracing the notion of global value chair, in Chap. 9, Debellis and Rondi highlight how relational control, along with vertical integration, characterizes the networking activities of family businesses. Investigating foreign partner relationships, in Chap. 10, Jaakko clarifies how the existence of both economic and non-economic goals influence family firms' behaviour with their partners, who are considered as an "extended international family". In Chap. 11, San Román, Gil-López, Díez-Vial, and Jack advance how a family firm can learn working with international partners and, at the same time, leverage on family reputation and trust, reliability and long-term vision. Finally, concerning international networking behaviour of family firms, in Chap. 12, Batas, Guiderdoni-Jourdain, and Leppäaho discuss how different family structures leverage on inherited social capital, thus affecting their internationalization endeavours.

The last section of the handbook tackles a growing theme, looking at family firm internationalization from emerging markets. The contributions in this section offer inspiring insights and learnings from family firms that move abroad by expanding their activities from developing and transition economies. Fuerst suggests the importance of networking activities of both family and non-family entrepreneurs in the internationalization process of a family business established in Colombia (Chap. 13). With a focus on the social network of migrant families, Centeno Caffarena and Discua Cruz discuss the relevance of social resources used by a German family in business in Nicaragua, leveraging in particular the ethnic group to overcome contextual challenges (Chap. 14). Jayakumar relies on the ability-willingness framework to discuss various internationalization pathways of small Indian family businesses (Chap. 15). Kalhor and Strandskov develop a conceptual model that offers an overview of institutional processes to access resources, focusing on informal and poor institutions, which legitimize operations abroad (Chap. 16). Finally, presenting a family SME in Guatemala, Godinez and Solís Sierra advance that, to develop an effective exporting strategy, a family business initially establishes a trustful relationship with an intermediary to enter the targeted foreign market (Chap. 17). Overall, these contributions broaden a very well-established North American and Western European perspective, embracing evidence from different contexts.

I am confident that researchers, family business owners, and consultants likewise will find this handbook a vital source to understand family firm internationalization, and a trigger to foster new ideas, practices, and policies.

Lancaster, UK

Giovanna Campopiano

References

Baù, M., Block, J. H., Discua Cruz, A., & Naldi, L. (2017). Locality and internationalization of family firms. *Entrepreneurship & Regional Development, 29*(5–6), 570–574.

De Massis, A., Frattini, F., Majocchi, A., & Piscitello, L. (2018). Family firms in the global economy: Toward a deeper understanding of internationalization determinants, processes, and outcomes. *Global Strategy Journal, 8*(1), 3–21.

Eddleston, K. A., Jaskiewicz, P., & Wright, M. (2020). Family firms and internationalization in the Asia-Pacific: The need for multi-level perspectives. *Asia Pacific Journal of Management, 37*, 345–361.

Kontinen, T., & Ojala, A. (2010). The internationalization of family business: A review of extant research. *Journal of Family Business Strategy, 1*(2), 97–107.

Pukall, T. J., & Calabrò, A. (2014). The internationalization of family firms: A critical review and integrative model. *Family Business Review, 27*(2), 103–125.

Foreword 4

In recent years, research on family firm internationalization has attracted increasing attention amongst both academics and practitioners. Recently, by working on an integrative literature review on the topic and examining four evolutionary waves of family firm internationalization research, I realized that although the seeds of this research were planted in the beginning of the 1990s, a clear understanding of the distinctive challenges connected with internationalization of family firms is far from being developed. What is more, we are still quite far from connecting international and family business theories, and this research area suffers from both theoretical limitations and empirical indeterminacy issues. Such issues unquestionably point to the pressing need of directing further attention to the how, the what, and the why of family firm internationalization.

This timely handbook challenges existing knowledge on family firm internationalization and makes an important step forward in advancing our understanding of the distinctive features of internationalization in the family firm setting. Overall, the volume provides a clear and well-reasoned overview of the features making family firm internationalization unique, the processual aspects associated with internationalization in this distinctive organizational setting, original network and social capital perspectives that can enrich our understanding of family firm internationalization dynamics, and a number of timely aspects related to family firm internationalization from emerging markets.

More specifically, the handbook offers a systematization of existing knowledge that is useful to understand the effect of family involvement in a business organization on its internationalization goals, decision-making processes, and behaviours. It goes even further by taking into account the role played by the

xli

family system in shaping international business behaviours through an in-depth examination of family dynamics that goes beyond a mere examination of the effect of family ownership and management. At the same time, the volume challenges the predominant focus on exports in the family firm internationalization literature by proposing a more variegated examination of international business activities. Overall, the different chapters organized in four sections shed light on a number of important topics, involving both established and emerging academics in this area.

The two co-editors, Professor Tanja Leppäaho and Professor Sarah Jack, and the authors of the eighteen chapters discuss in a clear and comprehensive way the importance of taking a family business and social capital view on internationalization issues, and the volume offers important contributions to the existing body of knowledge on international issues of firms with family involvement—the most ubiquitous form of business organization in any world economy. It examines a particularly timely phenomenon from different perspectives by providing a multifaceted and fine-grained understanding of it, drawing on both mainstream theories and new, pioneering research streams that open new avenues for future research.

I strongly recommend this reading to anyone interested in appreciating the role of family involvement in shaping a firm's internationalization strategy and its ensuing management challenges, and to those scholars who are eager to know how considering the idiosyncrasies of family firms can influence their internationalization determinants, processes, and outcomes. The two co-editors have succeeded in the important task of disseminating the latest research insights to the benefit of a large community of stakeholders that extends well beyond the academic network.

Lancaster, UK   Alfredo De Massis

Preface

The specific features of the growth and internationalization of family firms deserve specific attention (see Arregle et al., 2019; Hennart et al., 2019; Kontinen & Ojala, 2010; Metsola et al., 2020; Pukall & Calabro, 2014), not least during adverse economic times, such as the current coronavirus pandemic. The coronavirus crisis has put almost all firms under huge pressure due to governmental restrictions and changing customer behaviour. Nevertheless, it has been shown that family firms can sustain relatively profitable businesses during adverse economic climates (Dyer & Whetten, 2006; Sirmon & Hitt, 2003). Indeed, especially at this time, there may be increased appreciation of the stability and prolonged time horizons, survivability capital, strong social capital, and patient financial capital (Sirmon & Hitt, 2003) possessed by some family firms (Nordqvist & Jack, 2020).

Family firms form the majority (about 80%) of all firms around the world, and some are major international players. They account for an enormous percentage of the employment, revenues, and GDP of national economies at a global level (EFB, 2012; Hennart et al., 2019; Shanker & Astrachan, 1996; Westhead & Cowling, 1998) but also at national and local levels (Gomez-Mejia, Haynes, Nunez-Nickel, Jacobson, & Moyano-Fuentes, 2007). All types of family firm internationalization strategies deserve attention, given that internationalization could well prove a requirement for survival rather than a choice, when domestic markets deteriorate or face considerable disruption (Georgiadou et al., 2020).

For family firms, a quartile typically consists of a whole generation (25 years) rather than three months. Typically, there is a desire to pass the firm on to the next generation and to cherish the heritage of previous generations. The well-being of family members typically takes precedence over the success of the business (Berrone, Cruz, & Gomez-Mejia, 2012; Gomez-Mejia et al., 2007), with non-economic values being prioritized over economic returns (Verbeke et al., 2018). Family firms act as an engine of stability and long-term growth, and also as natural incubators of an entrepreneurial culture, fostering the next generation of entrepreneurs (EFB, 2012).

We are delighted to have with us now the very first *Palgrave Handbook on Family Firm Internationalization*. Family firms have been close to our hearts ever since we started to be interested in entrepreneurship and began our research careers in academia. This book is the outcome of our view that family firm internationalization is different from the internationalization of other types of firm (see e.g. Arregle et al., 2019; DeMassis et al., 2018) to the extent that it deserves a book of its own. The present book is focused around topics that existing reviews (see Arregle et al., 2019; Debellis et al., 2020; Hennart et al., 2019; Kontinen & Ojala, 2010; Metsola et al., 2020; Pukall & Calabro, 2014) have also regarded as deserving more attention, in order to take the field forward. These have touched on (1) family firm-specific views (e.g. Kontinen & Ojala, 2010; Pukall & Calabro, 2014), (2) the process nature of internationalization (see Metsola et al., 2020 in particular), (3) the role of networks in the internationalization of family firms (see Kampouri et al., 2017; Kontinen & Ojala, 2010), and (4) the internationalization of family firms located in emerging economies (see especially Leppäaho et al., 2016; Metsola et al., 2020).

Part I of the book on *family firm-specific views* starts with the insightful study (Chap. 1) of Kano et al., discussing how the prioritization of family assets and routines (i.e. bifurcation bias) creates affect-based governance practices that may clash with rational economic considerations in guiding international strategy. Rienda et al. (Chap. 2) use the stewardship lens to discuss intergenerational differences in the way the business is looked after. They conclude that later generations seem to opt for non-control entry modes. In Chap. 3—which is based on the only "home-grown" theory of family business research field to date, that is, socioemotional wealth (SEW)—Metsola et al. tackle the paradoxical tensions that occur in preserving the interests of the family in business, while building networks to expand the family business. They found that emotional decision-making has a strong negative relationship, and networking has a strong positive relationship with the degree of internationalization. In Chap. 4, Sestu provides an integrative framework on how family firms choose between different entry modes, examining the integration of family and business aspects.

Part II of the book discusses the *internationalization process*. On a general level, recent academic, public, and political discourses have focused strongly on high-growth and rapidly internationalizing firms. Some family firms do indeed fall into this category (see Hennart et al., 2019; Kontinen & Ojala, 20102; Kontinen, 2014), but most do not (see Kontinen & Ojala, 2010; Pukall & Calabro, 2014). The emphasis on high growth is unsurprising, given that the goals (and most often the realities) of national economic wealth have been based on constantly increasing or stable growth rates. However, there has been a tendency to overlook the fundamental economic role played by firms that have grown more slowly over many years—of which family firms form the largest cohort.

Generally speaking, family firms are regarded as slow to internationalize, in the manner portrayed in the Uppsala model (see e.g. Kontinen & Ojala, 2010; Pukall & Calabro, 2014). However, some have been shown to follow a born-global or born-again global approach to internationalization (Kontinen & Ojala, 2012; Kontinen, 2014). These typically represent a global niche strategy (Hennart, 2014; Hennart et al., 2019) rather than provision of a mass-market commodity. The chapters in this book shed new light on the internationalization process, for example, by discussing the discontinuous nature of the internationalization process, the development of a network in a transitional incumbent–successor context, and how family values shape the development of the family firm into a multinational company.

In Chap. 5, applying a behavioural perspective, Kuiken et al. suggest that rather than a continuous process, internationalization is often in reality a discontinuous process in which firms internationalize, de-internationalize, and, potentially, re-internationalize. This is an important aspect, given the longitudinal time horizons and changing context that family firms have to deal with and live through. Chapter 6 by Laari-Salmela et al. discusses the evolution of a family business into a multinational company, showing how family values can affect the management model of the family business subsidiaries in other countries. For their part, Korhonen et al. (Chap. 7) apply two longitudinal case histories to show how, within a transitional incumbent–successor context, the founder-entrepreneurs' domestic and international identity-based and calculative ties emerged and further evolved within and across country borders. They demonstrate how the family heritage is intertwined with networking activities, and they introduce and explain the concept of an "international networking legacy".

Part III of the book focuses on *networks in family firm internationalization*. Family firms rely on a complex web of family and professional relationships in their internationalization and may indeed possess particularly long-lasting network ties. In-depth understandings of such webs are still nascent (Ciravegna et al., 2019; Kampouri et al., 2017; Kontinen & Ojala, 2010, 2012; Pukall & Calàbro, 2014). Nevertheless, this book offers several new approaches to the

xlvi   Preface

understanding of international networking among family firms and does much to expand knowledge and understanding of the topic.

In Chap. 8, Kampouri and Plakoyiannaki suggest that identification with the business and emotional attachment causes family firms to stick to familiar nodes within the international network that they created in their initial move. Chapter 9 by Debellis and Rondi discusses the distinctive characteristics of family firms in the global value chain, suggesting that family firms foster vertical integration—limiting outsourcing to those activities that are difficult or impossible to internalize (e.g. due to lack of raw materials)—and relational control. Metsola (Chap. 10) examines the foreign partner relationships of family firms via the lens of SEW, concluding that firms with higher levels of SEW are more active in building close foreign partner relationships; this suggests that family firms with high levels of SEW build an "extended international family".

Chapter 11 by San Román et al. draws on a historical longitudinal case. It elaborates how the efforts of a family firm to embed itself as a trustworthy partner for foreign partners can lead to domestic and international growth, despite a constrained domestic market. Chapter 12 by Batas et al. explores how family firms with a range of inherited family structures and values networked to internationalize. It appears that the Taiwanese case in the study based its international networking decisions on tradition and security, while the Finnish and French cases based their decisions on conformity, related to the protection of family members.

Part IV of the book includes five studies in the *emerging markets* context, noting how these deserve increased attention in research on family firm internationalization. Fuerst (Chap. 13) presents a case from Colombia, encompassing international networking. It shows us how a family member together with a non-family member built a base for internationalization, thus revealing micro-processes in long-term international networking. Centeno-Caffarena and Discua Cruz (Chap. 14) report on a family firm in agribusiness, owned and managed by a family of German migrants in Nicaragua. They demonstrate the power of social capital and ethnic networks in helping migrant families to internationalize their family business. In so doing, the authors also reveal how contextual challenges can foster an early and continued reliance on ethnic networks in efforts to internationalize.

Jayakumar (Chap. 15) explores eight small Indian family firms. She presents an integrated model of small family-firm internationalization in fast-growing emerging economies, bringing together environmental, state, and change variables, plus family factors, to show how these influence the family firm's ability and willingness to internationalize. Kalhor and Strandskov

(Chap. 16) focus on informal and weak institutions; they develop a conceptual model which encompasses how a family firm, faced with strong host-country push and specific family factors, may reverse its internationalization journey. Last, but not least, through their coffee-exporting family firm case from Guatemala, Godinez and Solís Sierra (Chap. 17) advance understanding of how a family firm may develop an effective exporting strategy. They show how a family firm initially established a trustful relationship within its domestic borders, endeavouring to discover whether it could establish a trust-based working relationship with an intermediary in the foreign market. This was followed by the firm exporting on its own, with the family firm leveraging its family structure to exploit its experiential resources.

We would not have been able to provide such an insightful outcome without the dedicated work by the distinguished authors of our four forewords, and the authors of all the 17 chapters. The material as a whole offers conceptual advancement, archival longitudinal studies, statistical regressions, and multiple and single case studies, drawing on data from Northern and Southern Europe, with cases also from India, and from countries in Asia and South America.

We believe that the forewords and individual chapters provide several fruitful research directions, and we would warmly recommend you to read these thoughtful works in full. However, we would briefly like to offer some further ideas for future investigations. Firstly, we would like to emphasize the need to study *family firm heterogeneity* (see also Arregle et al., 2017; 2019; De Massis et al., 2018; Hennart et al., 2019; Hughes et al., 2018; Metsola et al., 2020; Verbeke et al., 2018) to enhance theorization in the field. The field would benefit from additional perspectives on ownership, management, and continuity (see Gersick et al., 1997) to determine how different combinations of ownership, control, and management, plus the desire to pass the firm from one generation to the next generation, are manifested in internationalization strategies. Family firms do indeed differ from non-family firms in the aspect of unification of ownership and control (Carney, 2005). Nevertheless, the management of family-owned firms varies greatly. Some family firms are owned by family members, but not managed by them; some are owned and managed by family members, but with no desire for continuity to the next generation; others are owned and managed by family members, with the strong pursuit of continuity. In line with the foreword by Hennart, the transgenerational intent is also related to longer time horizons. Firms with family ownership, but with no family management or desire for transgenerational succession, may behave more like non-family firms than do those which are both family-owned and managed.

xlviii   Preface

Secondly, and related to the above, the study of *internationalization processes* could be more directed to explaining the heterogeneity of the internationalization processes among family firms, and with more investigation of the continuity/discontinuity aspects of the internationalization process over time. As discussed by Kuiken et al. in Chap. 5 of this book, a typical longitudinal process will include entries, exits, re-entries, increases/decreases in the range of activities and networks, and so on. Furthermore, we need elaboration on how and why a family firm can be a born-global firm (Kontinen, 2014), a born-again global firm (Graves & Thomas, 2008; Kontinen & Ojala, 2012), a global niche player with a significant international presence (Hennart et al., 2019), or a traditional slow growing enterprise (following the Uppsala model). Studies along these lines will increase our understanding of the heterogeneity of family firms in their internationalization strategies and the reasons behind them.

Thirdly, we see considerable potential in contextualizing family firm internationalization research (see e.g. Delios, 2017; Michailova, 2011; Leppäaho, Chetty, & Dimitratos, 2018). Changing historical contexts and situational sensitivities should be an integral element in the analyses of internationalization, with the activities of both individuals and firms viewed as evolving in parallel with the context (Cantwell et al., 2010). Family firms with long historical backgrounds through different times provide excellent potential for this type of theorization, as indicated by the longitudinal analyses of Korhonen et al. (Chap. 7) and San Roman et al. (Chap. 11). The contexts of developed and developing economies offer family firm cases with a range of background features, including notably the starting point. Taken together, these features have the potential to enrich theory and to provide new openings for conceptual development.

Fourthly, an in-depth understanding of the network view could offer even more insights on the specific features of family firm internationalization, including the ways in which firms tend to nurture their network carefully, and, having done so, pass it on to the next generation. Chapters 6, 7, 11, 12, and 13 in this book offer views on transgenerational networks, collaborative partnering networks, family values in a growing international network, and the micro-processes of international networking. They provide excellent examples of the stepping stones involved with this perspective. Future research could well encompass the role of immigrant networks in aiding internationalization (see Chap. 14), the role of domestic partners in testing and initiating the market (see Chap. 17), and collaboration with non-family partners (see Chap. 13). Neither should one overlook the strength of multi-country data sets, in which the different cultural and institutional origins of family firms can give rise to theorization (see Chap. 12).

Lappeenranta, Finland   Tanja Leppäaho
Stockholm, Sweden   Sarah Jack

References

Arregle, J., Duran, P. Hitt, M., & van Essen, P. (2017). Why is family firms' internationalization unique? A meta-analysis. *Entrepreneurship Theory and Practice, 41*(5), 801–831.

Arregle, J. L., Hitt, M. A., & Mari, I. A. (2019). A missing link in family firms' internationalization research: Family structure. *Journal of International Business Studies, 50*(5), 809–825.

Berrone, P., Cruz, C., & Gomez-Mejia, L. R. (2012). Socioemotional wealth in family firms: Theoretical dimensions, assessment approaches, and agenda for future research. *Family Business Review, 25*(3), 258–279.

Ciravegna, L., Kano, L., Rattalino, F., & Verbeke, A. (2019). Corporate diplomacy and family firm longevity. *Entrepreneurship Theory and Practice, 44.*

Debellis, F., Rondi, E., Plakoyiannaki, E., & De Massis, A. (2020). Riding the waves of family firm internationalization: A systematic literature review, integrative framework, and research agenda. *Journal of World Business.*

Delios, A. (2017). The death and rebirth (?) of international business research. *Journal of Management Studies, 54*(3), 391–397.

De Massis, A., Frattini, F., Majocchi, A., & Piscitello, L. (2018). Family firms in the global economy: Toward a deeper understanding of internationalization determinants, processes, and outcomes. *Global Strategy Journal, 8*(1), 3–21.

Georgiadou, E., Hughes, M., & Viala, C. (2020). Commercial diplomacy as a mechanism for passive-reactive SME internationalization: Overcoming liabilities of outsidership. *European Journal of International Management*, in press. https://doi.org/10.1504/EJIM.2021.10029764

Gersick, K. E., Davis, J. A., Hampton, M. M., & Lansberg, I. (1997). *Generation to generation: Life cycles of the family business.* Harvard Business Press.

Dyer, W. G., Jr., & Whetten, D. A. (2006). Family firms and social responsibility: Preliminary evidence from the S&P 500. *Entrepreneurship Theory and Practice, 30*(6), 785–802.

Gómez-Mejía, L. R., Haynes, K. T., Núñez-Nickel, M., Jacobson, K. J., & Moyano-Fuentes, J. (2007). Socioemotional wealth and business risks in family-controlled firms: Evidence from Spanish olive oil mills. *Administrative Science Quarterly, 52*(1), 106–137.

Graves, C., & Thomas, J. (2008). Determinants of the internationalization pathways of family firms: An examination of family influence. *Family Business Review, 21*(2), 151–167.

Hennart, J. F. (2014). The accidental internationalists: A theory of born globals. *Entrepreneurship Theory and Practice, 38*(1), 117–135.

Hennart, J. F., Majocchi, A., & Forlani, E. (2019). The myth of the stay-at-home family firm: How family-managed SMEs can overcome their internationalization limitations. *Journal of International Business Studies, 50*, 758–782.

Hughes, M., Filser, M., Harms, R., Kraus, S., Chang, M. L., & Cheng, C. F. (2018). Family firm configurations for high performance: The role of entrepreneurship and ambidexterity. *British Journal of Management, 29*, 595–612.

Jack, S., & Nordqvist, M. (2020). The Wallenberg family of Sweden—Sustainable business development since 1856. In P. Sharma & S. Sharma (Eds.), *Pioneering sustainable family firms' patient capital strategies*. Northampton, MA: Edward Elgar Publishing Inc. [Forthcoming].

Kampouri, K., Plakoyiannaki, E., & Leppäaho, T. (2017). Family business internationalization and networks: Emerging pathways. *Journal of Business & Industrial Marketing, 32*, 357–370.

Kano, L., & Verbeke, A. (2018). Family firm internationalization: Heritage assets and the impact of bifurcation bias. *Global Strategy Journal, 8*, 158–183.

Kontinen, T. (2014). Biohit: A global, family–owned company embarking on a new phase. *Entrepreneurship Theory and Practice, 38*(1), 185–207.

Kontinen, T., & Ojala, A. (2012). Social capital in the international operations of family SMEs. *Journal of Small Business and Enterprise Development, 19*.

Kontinen, T., & Ojala, A. (2010). The internationalization of family businesses: A review of extant research. *Journal of Family Business Strategy, 1*, 97–107.

Leppäaho, T., Chetty, S., & Dimitratos, P. (2018). Network embeddedness in the internationalization of biotechnology entrepreneurs. *Entrepreneurship & Regional Development, 30*(5–6), 562–584.

Leppäaho, T., Plakoyiannaki, E., & Dimitratos, P. (2016). The case study in family business: An analysis of current research practices and recommendations. *Family Business Review, 29*(2), 159–173.

Metsola, J., Leppäaho, T., Paavilainen-Mäntymäki, E., & Plakoyiannaki, E. (2020). Process in family business internationalisation: The state of the art and ways forward. *International Business Review, 29*(2), 101665.

Michailova, S. (2011). Contextualizing in international business research: Why do we need more of it and how can we be better at it? *Scandinavian Journal of Management, 27*(1), 129–139.

Pukall, T. J., & Calabrò, A. (2014). The internationalization of family firms: A critical review and integrative model. *Family Business Review, 27*, 103–125.

Shanker, M. C., & Astrachan, J. H. (1996). Myths and realities: Family businesses' contribution to the US economy—A framework for assessing family business statistics. *Family Business Review, 9*(2), 107–123.

Sirmon, D. G., & Hitt, M. A. (2003). Managing resources: Linking unique resources, management, and wealth creation in family firms. *Entrepreneurship Theory and Practice, 27*(4), 339–358.

Verbeke, A., Yuan, W., & Kano, L. (2018). A values-based analysis of bifurcation bias and its impact on family firm internationalization. *Asia Pacific Journal of Management*, 1–29.

Acknowledgements

We want to cordially thank the financial assistance by the Academy of Finland (grant number 308667, 434 485 EUR, 1.1.2017-31.7.2022) and Foundation for Economic Education.

We want to cordially thank all the contributors of this book, including the authors of the forewords. Thank you so much for taking the field forward. Second, we send our warmest thanks to all the anonymous reviewers of the *Handbook*. Without your dedicated and detailed work, we would not have been able to develop the message of the chapters to where they are now.

Contents

Part I	**Family Firm-Specific Views and Internationalization**	1
1	**Internationalization Decisions in Family Firms: The Impact of Bifurcation Bias** *Liena Kano, Alain Verbeke, and Andrew Johnston*	3
2	**Internationalisation and Family Involvement: A Stewardship Approach in the Hotel Industry** *Laura Rienda, Enrique Claver, and Rosario Andreu*	37
3	**Socioemotional Wealth and Networking in the Internationalisation of Family SMEs** *Jaakko Metsola, Lasse Torkkeli, Tanja Leppäaho, Pia Arenius, and Mika Haapanen*	63
4	**An Integrative Framework of Family Firms and Foreign Entry Strategies** *Maria Cristina Sestu*	103
Part II	**Internationalization Process of Family Firms**	133
5	**Internationalization of Family Firms as a Discontinuous Process: The Role of Behavioral Theory** *Andrea Kuiken, Lucia Naldi, and Mattias Nordqvist*	135

lvi   Contents

6   One Family Firm, Four Families: Developing Management
     Models of a Family Values-Based MNC   173
     Sari Laari-Salmela, Tuija Mainela, Elina Pernu, and Vesa Puhakka

7   The "Unwritten Will" in Interpersonal Network Ties: Founder
     Legacy and International Networking of Family Firms in
     History   199
     *Satu Korhonen, Tanja Leppäaho, Rolv Petter Amdam, and
     Sarah Jack*

Part III   Networks in Family Firm Internationalization   235

8   Entry Nodes in Foreign Market Entry and Post-Entry
     Operations of Family-Managed Firms   237
     Katerina Kampouri and Emmanuella Plakoyiannaki

9   How Do Family Firms Orchestrate Their Global Value Chain?   265
     Francesco Debellis and Emanuela Rondi

10   Coexistence of Economic and Noneconomic Goals in Building
     Foreign Partner Relationships: Evidence from Small Finnish
     Family Firms   289
     Jaakko Metsola

11   Networking from Home to Abroad: The Internationalization
     of The Iberostar Group   327
     *Elena San Román, Agueda Gil-López, Isabel Díez-Vial, and
     Sarah Jack*

12   Social Capital and Values in the Internationalization of Family
     Firms: A Multi-Country Study   361
     Spiros Batas, Karine Guiderdoni-Jourdain, and Tanja Leppäaho

Contents   lvii

Part IV   Family Firm Internationalization from Emerging Markets   393

13   The Network Dynamics During Internationalization of a Family Firm: The Case of a New Venture from Colombia   395
Sascha Fuerst

14   Internationalisation of a Migrant Family Firm and Contextual Uncertainty: The Role of Ethnic Social Networks   431
Leonardo Centeno-Caffarena and Allan Discua Cruz

15   Internationalization of Small Indian Family-Firms: An Emergent Theory   461
Tulsi Jayakumar

16   Family Firms' Internationalization: The Importance of Home Country Institutions   519
Elham Kalhor and Jesper Strandskov

17   Internationalization Process of Developing-Country Family SMEs: The Case of Solanos Hermanos S.A. of Guatemala   553
Jose Godinez and José Solís Sierra

Index   571

Notes on Contributors

Rolv Petter Amdam is Professor of Business History at BI Norwegian Business School. His main research interests are internationalization processes of MNEs in general and business schools in particular. He has been the Alfred D. Chandler Jr. Visiting Scholar in International Business History at Harvard Business School and SCANCOR fellow at the Weatherhead Center of International Affairs, Harvard. In addition to several books within business history, his articles have appeared in journals such as *Business History, Business History Review, Management & Organizational History, Academy of Management Executives*, and *Journal of World Business*.

Rosario Andreu is Associate Professor of Management at the University of Alicante. She holds a PhD from the University of Alicante. Her primary research interests are focused on the internationalization of hotels and tourism firms. Her research articles have appeared in journals such as *International Business Review, International Journal of Hospitality Management, Current Issues in Tourism, International Journal of Contemporary Hospitality Management*, and *Journal of Hospitality & Tourism Management*.

Pia Arenius is Professor of Entrepreneurship and Innovation at RMIT University, Australia. Her research interests include nascent entrepreneurs, emotion, self-regulation, and opportunity processes. Arenius has worked in various roles in universities in Finland, Switzerland, USA, and Australia for the past 25 years. Her research has been published in highly ranked journals including *Journal of Business Venturing, Small Business Economics, Research Policy*, and *International Small Business Journal*. She serves on the editorial review board of *Entrepreneurship Theory and Practice*.

lx   **Notes on Contributors**

Spiros Batas is Senior Lecturer in International Business at University of Greenwich, London, UK. He holds his PhD in International Business and Strategy from University of Edinburgh and was examined by Professor Jan Johanson of Uppsala University. He is a member of the AIB-UKI Executive Board. He has worked as a consultant for Edinburgh World Heritage (EWH) where he led a project related to the valuation of Edinburgh's World Heritage Site in economic terms. His research interests include social capital, family firms, international new ventures, and institutional logics.

Leonardo Centeno-Caffarena is a researcher and director of the Centre for the Promotion and Development of the Family Business (CEPRODEF) in Nicaragua. He holds a PhD and his articles have appeared in *Entrepreneurship & Regional Development, Cross Cultural & Strategic Management*, and in *Sociedad y Utopía* and has also published book chapters on family business and entrepreneurship. His research interests focus on families in business, corporate governance, and institutions.

Enrique Claver is Professor of Management and Strategic Management at the University of Alicante, Spain. He holds a PhD in Business and Economics. His doctoral dissertation focused on corporate social responsibility, but his primary areas of research cover tourism management and strategic management also. Likewise, he is member of the Tourism Research Institute at UA. He is the author of several books, book chapters, and international articles related to strategic, tourism, and human resource management.

Francesco Debellis is postdoctoral researcher and the chair of International Business at the University of Vienna, Austria. Prior to joining Vienna, Francesco has been a research associate at the Centre for Family Business Management of the Free University of Bozen-Bolzano, Italy. He has been working as business consultant of several SMEs, and he has also earned research experience as a visiting scholar at the University of Leeds, UK, Witten Institute for Family Businesses, Germany, Henley Business School, UK, Old Dominion University, USA, and Zhejiang University, China. His research focuses on governance and internationalization of family firms. His articles have appeared, among others, in the *Journal of World Business* and *Journal of International Management*.

Isabel Díez-Vial is Associate Professor of Business Administration at Complutense University of Madrid where she co-coordinates the research group "Growth strategies". Her research topics are clusters, science parks, and networks. Her articles have appeared in *Journal of Management Studies*,

Technovation, Journal of Knowledge Management, Journal of Small Business Management, The Journal of Technology Transfer, among others.

Allan Discua Cruz is a senior lecturer at the Entrepreneurship and Strategy Department (ENST) in Lancaster University Management School. He is a founding member of the Centre for Family Business and a member of the Pentland Centre for Sustainability in Business. He holds a PhD and his articles have appeared in journals such as *Organization & Environment, Entrepreneurship Theory and Practice, Journal of Business Ethics, Entrepreneurship & Regional Development, Business History, Cross Cultural & Strategic Management, Journal of Family Business Strategy,* and *International Small Business Journal* and has also published in book compilations. His research focuses on sustainable family enterprises as well as internationalization of family businesses.

Sascha Fuerst is Research Professor of Entrepreneurship and Innovation at EGADE Business School, Tecnologico de Monterrey, Mexico. He also holds an affiliation as researcher in international entrepreneurship with Turku School of Economics at the University of Turku, Finland. He holds a PhD in International Business with distinction from the Turku School of Economics. His research interest is focused on the intersection of entrepreneurship, innovation, and international business, and particularly entrepreneurial internationalization from a process perspective.

Águeda Gil-López is Assistant Professor of Economics at Universidad Francisco de Vitoria, Madrid, Spain. She holds a PhD in Economics from Universidad Complutense de Madrid, with a European mention, and was awarded with the Complutense Extraordinary PhD Prize of Economics in 2018. Her research interests include business history, family business, and entrepreneurship. She belongs to the research team of a competitive project funded by the Spanish Ministry of Education.

Jose Godinez is Assistant Professor of Management at the Robert J. Manning School of Business, University of Massachusetts Lowell. His work lays at the intersection of the strategy, international business, entrepreneurship, and business ethics disciplines, and he focuses on strategies for firms to operate ethically in locations characterized by high corruption levels. He holds a PhD from the University of Edinburgh Business School, and his article has appeared in journals such as *International Business Review, Journal of Business Ethics,* and *Business and Politics.*

lxii   Notes on Contributors

Karine Guiderdoni-Jourdain is Assistant Professor of Management Science in Aix-Marseille University, France. She is affiliated to the Institute of Labor Economics and Industrial Sociology (LEST-CNRS 7317). She is leading research on international support services for SME and on the internationalization of family-managed SME through a network perspective and in a multi-country cross-cultural approach. She has also led projects on pedagogical innovations, especially on the use of serious games in management courses for students.

Mika Haapanen is Associate Professor of Economics at University of Jyväskylä, Finland. His primary research interests include economics of education, regional economics, and labour economics. He has written empirical research papers, for example, about returns to education and labour migration. His article has appeared in *Oxford Economic Papers*, *Labour Economics*, *Regional Studies*, *Journal of Regional Science*, *Journal of Development Studies*, among others. He is an associate editor for the journal *Regional Studies, Regional Science*.

Sarah Jack is the Jacob and Marcus Wallenberg Professor of Innovative and Sustainable Business Development at the House of Innovation, Stockholm School of Economics, and Professor of Entrepreneurship at Lancaster University Management School. Her primary research interests relate to the social dimensions of entrepreneurship, where she draws on social capital and social network theory to extend understanding using qualitative method. Her articles have appeared in *Journal of Management Studies*, *Academy of Management Learning and Education*, *Entrepreneurship Theory and Practice*, and *Journal of Business Venturing*.

Tulsi Jayakumar is Professor of Economics and Chairperson, Family Managed Business, at Bhavans S.P. Jain Institute of Management and Research (SPJIMR), Mumbai. Her research spans across areas of economics and family business. Other than articles in prestigious peer-reviewed journals, her cases have consistently been acclaimed as 'Global Best-Selling' and 'Most Popular' cases on global case repositories, Harvard and Ivey. She writes extensively in the media and is recognized as a thought leader in her chosen areas. She works closely with Indian family businesses and is also a member of Indian industrial bodies, where she acts as a voice for the SMEs.

Andrew Johnston is a PhD student and research assistant at the Haskayne School of Business, University of Calgary. He holds an MBA from the University of Calgary, an MSc in Comparative Politics from the London School of Economics, and a BA(Hons) in Social Sciences from Leeds Beckett

University. In addition to theories of family firm internationalization, Johnston's research interests also focus on transactions between resource extraction firms, government regulators, and Indigenous groups.

Elham Kalhor is a PhD research fellow in international businesses and entrepreneurship in the Department of Marketing and Management at the University of Southern Denmark. Her research area is family businesses and, in particular, the effects of institutional environments on the internationalization process in family firms. Her investigations have been accepted to be presented in international conferences such as the Academy of International Business (AIB) 2020, European Academy of Management (Euram) 2019, and Babson Conference (2018). Her articles have appeared in the *European Journal of International Management (EJIM)* and *Sinergie Italian Journal of Management.*

Katerina Kampouri is a postdoctoral researcher at the University of Macedonia, Greece, and business consultant for Greek small and medium enterprises. She holds a PhD from the Aristotle University of Thessaloniki, Greece. Her research interests focus on family firm internationalization, partner selection, and emotion research. Her research appears in peer-reviewed academic journals, scientific volumes, and various conference proceedings.

Liena Kano is Associate Professor of Strategy and Global Management at the Haskayne School of Business, University of Calgary, Canada. Her research interests lie at the intersection of strategic management, international business, and entrepreneurship, with a particular focus on novel applications of internalization theory, and on microfoundations that underlie complex international governance decisions. Her article has appeared in top academic journals such as the *Journal of International Business Studies, Journal of World Business, Entrepreneurship Theory and Practice,* among others.

Satu Korhonen is a Finnish scholar and holds a PhD in Business and Economics from Lappeenranta-Lahti University of Technology, Finland, where she also works as a researcher. Her primary research interests comprehend the individuals in and social dimensions of entrepreneurship and internationalization of small firms. Her methodological interests reside in qualitative process research and especially in the narrative enquiry. In addition to her involvement in family firm research over the recent years, she has about a decade of experience as a board member of her father's industrial management consulting business.

lxiv   Notes on Contributors

Andrea Kuiken is a lecturer at the Faculty of Economics and Business, University of Groningen, the Netherlands. She holds a PhD in Business Administration from Jönköping International Business School, Sweden. Her research interests are in the areas of internationalization process, de-internationalization, SME internationalization, and family ownership.

Sari Laari-Salmela is an associate professor at the University of Oulu Business School. Her interests are in the areas of strategy and organization studies, information systems, and industrial networks, and her articles have appeared in reputed international journals including *Industrial Marketing Management*, *Journal of Business Ethics*, and *Journal of Strategic Information Systems*. She has over ten years of work experience in an international family firm.

Tanja Leppäaho (previously Kontinen) works as Professor of Growth Entrepreneurship and Academy of Finland Research Fellow at LUT University, Finland. Her research focuses on internationalization of family firms and SMEs, networking, social capital, and qualitative research. Her articles have appeared in E*ntrepreneurship Theory and Practice*, *Family Business Review*, *Entrepreneurship and Regional Development*, and *International Business Review*, among others. She is also closely involved with business practice through her Academy of Finland-funded research project on the internationalization of family firms (see http://ife.fi).

Tuija Mainela is Professor of International Business at the University of Oulu Business School, Finland. Her research interests include international entrepreneurship, internationalization of firms, international opportunity development, and dynamics of business networks. She leads a research project focused on innovation and change in health care sector. Her articles have appeared in reputed journals, such as *Journal of Business Venturing* and *Industrial Marketing Management*, and has contributed to several books as an author of chapters.

Jaakko Metsola works as a postdoctoral researcher at the School of Business and Management at LUT University, Lappeenranta, Finland. His primary research interests include internationalization and international marketing of family SMEs.

Lucia Naldi is Professor of Business Administration at Jönköping International Business School and Vice President for Research at Jönköping University. She holds a PhD from JIBS and an MSc from the University of Florence. Her main research and teaching are in the areas of entrepreneurship, international business, and strategy. Her research focuses on growth and internationalization of small and young firms. She is also interested in entrepreneurship in different contexts, including family firms and firms located in rural areas. Naldi's research has been published in several journals and as book chapters. Naldi is affiliated with the Centre for Family Entrepreneurship and Ownership (CeFEO) and the Centre for Entrepreneurship and Spatial Economics (CEnSE).

Mattias Nordqvist is Professor of Entrepreneurship at the House of Innovation at Stockholm School of Economics, Sweden. He is also Professor of Business Administration and affiliated with the Center for Family Entrepreneurship and Ownership (CeFEO) at Jönköping International Business School, Jönköping University, Sweden.

Elina Pernu holds a PhD in Marketing from the University of Oulu Business School, Finland. Her main research interests include multinational corporations, internal networks, sense-making in organizations, key account management, and global customer relationships. Her research has appeared in academic journals, such as *Industrial Marketing Management* and *Advances in International Management*.

Emmanuella Plakoyiannaki is Chair of International Business at the University of Vienna, Austria, and a visiting professor at Leeds University Business School, UK. She serves as an associate editor in the *British Journal of Management*. Her expertise lies in the areas of SMEs and family firm internationalization and qualitative research. Her articles have appeared in various academic outlets including the *Academy of Management Review*, *Journal of International Business Studies*, *Journal of Management Studies*, and *Journal of World Business*.

Vesa Puhakka is Professor of Management and Organization and Head of Department of Marketing, Management and International Business at the University of Oulu Business School, Finland. His research interests include international entrepreneurship, opportunity creation, and entrepreneurial leadership, and he leads the Center for Entrepreneurship and Sustainable Business. His articles have appeared in reputed journals, such as *Journal of Business Venturing* and *Industrial Marketing Management* and has contributed to several books as an author of chapters.

Laura Rienda is Associate Professor of Management at the University of Alicante, and her research interest is related to family businesses, international strategy, and emerging markets. She holds a PhD from the University of

lxvi   Notes on Contributors

Alicante and her articles have appeared in different journals such as *Family Business Review*, *Asia Pacific Journal of Management*, *Management Decision*, *International Journal of Hospitality Management*, and *Current Issues in Tourism*.

Elena San Román is Associate Professor of Economic History at Complutense University of Madrid, Spain and an associate member of the Spanish Royal Academy of History. Her research interests are focused on business history, family business, entrepreneurship, and international business in the twentieth century. She is the co-principal researcher of a competitive research project funded by the Spanish Ministry of Education, focused on the study of collective entrepreneurship and innovation in the Spanish service industry.

Emanuela Rondi is Assistant Professor at the Department of Management of the Università degli Studi di Bergamo (Italy). She holds a PhD in Management (2016) from Lancaster University (UK) and was research member of the Center for Family Business Management of the Free University of Bozen-Bolzano (Italy). Her research lies at the intersection of family business and social networks, with a specific interest on the role that family relationships exerts on succession, innovation, and internationalization. Her research articles have appeared in leading academic journals as *Entrepreneurship Theory and Practice*, *Journal of Management*, *Journal of Management Studies* and *Journal of World Business*.

Maria Cristina Sestu is an assistant professor at the University of Groningen. She holds a PhD (Doctor Europaeus) in Economics and Management from the University of Padua in 2017. She was a visiting scholar at the Université Jean Moulin Lyon3 and Sussex University. Her research interests are in international business, entry modes, family firms, and SMEs.

José Solís Sierra is Director of Finance and Corporate Compliance master's programme at UVG Masters at Universidad de Valle de Guatemala and Professor of Finance at the same institution. He holds an MSc from EADA Business School, and his research interests include business ethics and behavioural finance in emerging economies. Recently, he participated as the main author for Guatemala in the first Latin-American study *Status of Business Anti-Bribery Practices; First Latin American Study* in collaboration with Principles for Responsible Management Education (PRME), a United Nations-supported initiative founded in 2007.

Jesper Strandskov is Emeritus Professor of International Business at the Department of Marketing and Management, University of Southern Denmark. His research interests include firm internationalization, business development, corporate governance, and business history. His articles have appeared in academic journals such as *International Business Review*, *Business History*, *Scandinavian Journal of Economic History Research*, *Journal of Global Marketing*, and *Academy of Management Review*.

Lasse Torkkeli is an associate professor at the School of Business and Management at LUT University at Lappeenranta, Finland. He is also Adjunct Professor of International Business in the Turku School of Economics at the University of Turku. Torkkeli's research interests are in the international entrepreneurship and international business domains, and include SME internationalization, business networks and capabilities, and sustainable entrepreneurship.

Alain Verbeke is Professor of International Business and the McCaig Chair in Management at the Haskayne School of Business, University of Calgary. He is also the Inaugural Alan M. Rugman Memorial Fellow at the Henley Business School, University of Reading, and editor-in-chief of the *Journal of International Business Studies*. He is an adjunct professor at the Solvay Business School, Vrije Universiteit Brussel, and a Dean's Circle Distinguished Fellow at Florida International University. He was elected a fellow of the AIB (2007) and EIBA (2019). His research agenda focuses on the strategic management of MNEs, and on effective governance design for managing new resource combinations internationally.

List of Figures

Fig. 1.1	International governance decisions and outcomes in family firms	7
Fig. 2.1	Family involvement and internationalisation	46
Fig. 4.1	Entry modes and family firms' characteristics. (Source: Author)	111
Fig. 4.2	Integrative framework. (Source: Author)	118
Fig. 6.1	The emergence of practice-based management models in MNCs. (Source: Authors)	179
Fig. 7.1	Case Ahlström. (Source: Authors)	209
Fig. 7.2	Case Serlachius. (Source: Authors)	209
Fig. 8.1	Entry situations and entry nodes (Source: Sandberg, 2013, p. 109)	243
Fig. 8.2	Example from Atlas (Source: Authors)	250
Fig. 8.3	Entry nodes of the investigated family-managed SMEs (prior to first entrance to foreign markets)	251
Fig. 8.4	Entry nodes of the investigated family-managed SMEs (after the first entrance to international markets)	256
Fig. 10.1	Theoretical framework of the study. (Source: Author)	296
Fig. 10.2	Directed content analysis applied in forming the category 'Close FPR-building for maintaining both economic and noneconomic goals' with Firm B's answers as an example. (Source: Author)	304
Fig. 10.3	SEW levels of case firms, A–H. (Source: Author)	305
Fig. 10.4	Coexistence of noneconomic and economic goals in driving small FFs' active and close relationship-building with foreign partners for promoted internationalisation (Source: Author)	312
Fig. 11.1	Timeline of Iberostar Group history. (Own elaboration from San Román, 2017)	336

lxix

lxx   List of Figures

Fig. 12.1   Social capital, bifurcation bias, family values, and family structures in the internationalization of FFs. (Source: Elaborated by the authors)   368

Fig. 13.1   Networking activities along different development periods. (Source: Author)   403

Fig. 15.1   Three-circle framework of internationalization literature: finding a research gap. (Source: Author)   463

Fig. 15.2   Family-firm internationalization: Institutional-level, family-level and firm-level drivers. (Source: Author)   474

Fig. 15.3   An integrated model of fast-growing emerging economy small family-firm internationalization. (Source: Author)   476

Fig. 15.4   Ability-willingness (A-W) matrix of small family-firm internationalization in fast-growing emerging economies. (Source: Author)   510

Fig. 15.5   Internationalization pathways followed by fast-growing emerging economy small family-firms. (Source: Author)   511

Fig. 16.1   Moderating effects of home country institutional processes on family firm internationalization. A conceptual model. (Source: Author)   532

Fig. 17.1   Solanos Hermanos S.A. value chain. (Source: Author)   562

List of Tables

Table 2.1	Sample description	47
Table 2.2	Descriptive statistics and correlations	51
Table 2.3	Results of linear and logistic regressions	52
Table 3.1	The results of the PCA for the SEW-related factors	76
Table 3.2	Correlations of dependent, independent and control variables within family SMEs (scores within nonfamily SMEs in parentheses)	82
Table 3.3	Results of the linear regression for each independent variable separately with the dependent variable DOI	84
Table 3.4	Results of the multiple linear regression models with the dependent variable DOI	85
Table 4.1	Insights for future research	122
Table 5.1	Main findings in family business internationalization literature in relation to key concepts in the behavioral theory of the firm	146
Table 5.2	Summary of the areas for empirical research	151
Table 6.1	Interview data of the case study	181
Table 6.2	Comparison of subsidiary management and market features	187
Table 6.3	Comparison of the subsidiary management models	191
Table 7.1	Antti's domestic and international identity-based and calculative ties	211
Table 7.2	Walter's domestic and international identity-based and calculative ties	214
Table 7.3	Gustaf's domestic and international identity-based and calculative ties	216
Table 7.4	Gösta's domestic and international identity-based and calculative ties	219
Table 8.1	Information on the investigated family-managed FFs	248

lxxii   List of Tables

Table 8.2	Profile of the interviewees	249
Table 8.3	Entry nodes and post-entry nodes of the investigated firms	255
Table 9.1	GVC orchestration of family and non-family firms	273
Table 10.1	Basic information regarding the case firms and interviews	300
Table 10.2	SEW, FPR-building activity, and importance of FF status in FPRs and internationalisation	308
Table 11.1	Summary of data	338
Table 12.1	Background on FFs	370
Table 12.2	Interviews and informants	371
Table 12.3	Cross-case analysis: Family values, structure, and networks	375
Table 13.1	Observation period and data sources	401
Table 13.2	Networking characteristics of both entrepreneurs	417
Table 14.1	Contextual framework in the Nicaraguan coffee industry context	439
Table 14.2	Important dates for the Kühl family and the Selva Negra Farm. Source: Kühl family	442
Table 14.3	Data coding	444
Table 15.1	Studies on internationalization of small family-firms	465
Table 15.2	Studies on internationalization of Indian family-firms	472
Table 15.3	Definitions of micro, small and medium-sized enterprises	480
Table 15.4	Characteristics of case firms included in the study	482
Table 15.5	Details of the internationalization behaviour of the case firms	486
Table 15.6	Analysis of family factors affecting internationalization in the case firms	496
Table 15.7	Internationalization pathways of small Indian family-firms: An Augmented framework (based on Bell et al., 2003)	506

Part I

Family Firm-Specific Views and Internationalization

1

Internationalization Decisions in Family Firms: The Impact of Bifurcation Bias

Liena Kano, Alain Verbeke, and Andrew Johnston

Introduction

Family firms play a major role in the world economy. As at June 2018, the world's top 750 family firms generated annual revenues of over $9 trillion USD and employed nearly 30 million people (Davis, 2019). Moreover, in 2019, the top 500 global family firms outperformed the Fortune 500, with total annual revenues growing by 9.9% versus 8.6% for the Fortune 500—a testament to the ability of family-owned multinational enterprises (MNEs) to compete effectively in the global arena (EY & University of St. Gallen, 2019).

The ubiquity and apparent success of family firms in the global marketplace have attracted much scholarly attention in the past two decades, and the field continues to grow. In a first comprehensive review of family firm internationalization studies, Kontinen and Ojala (2010) identified a total of 25 articles on family firm internationalization published in academic peer-reviewed

---

L. Kano (✉) • A. Johnston
Haskayne School of Business, University of Calgary, Calgary, AB, Canada
e-mail: liena.kano@haskayne.ucalgary.ca; andrew.johnston1@haskayne.ucalgary.ca

A. Verbeke
Haskayne School of Business, University of Calgary, Calgary, AB, Canada

Vrije Universiteit Brussel (VUB), Brussels, Belgium

Henley Business School, University of Reading, Reading, UK
e-mail: alain.verbeke@haskayne.ucalgary.ca

© The Author(s), under exclusive license to Springer Nature Switzerland AG 2021
T. Leppäaho, S. Jack (eds.), *The Palgrave Handbook of Family Firm Internationalization*,
https://doi.org/10.1007/978-3-030-66737-5_1

journals prior to 2009. In an extension of Kontinen and Ojala's work, Pukall and Calabrò (2014) showed that research on family firm internationalization had grown significantly in the years following the first review: they found that 42 family firm internationalization studies had been published in the short, four-year period between 2008 and 2012 (as compared with Kontinen and Ojala's sample of 25 studies over a 20 year period). Arregle, Duran, Hitt, and van Essen (2017) analysed 76 studies conducted between 2003 and 2013. Most recently, a review of the family firm literature by Metsola, Leppäaho, Paavilainen-Mäntymäki, and Plakoyiannaki (2020) identified 172 empirical studies on the internationalization of family firms conducted between 1998 and 2018. Much of this research is conducted from the family business, rather than international business (IB), perspective and utilizes general management and family business theoretical lenses (most frequently the agency and socio-emotional wealth [SEW] perspectives), with IB theory somewhat underrepresented in this body of work. Recent work has been concerned with the dynamic and strategic elements of family firm internationalization to a greater extent than earlier work: for example, Metsola et al.'s (2020) analysis focuses on developing a process model of family firm internationalization. Still, most extant studies included in the above reviews focus on comparing the levels of internationalization between family firms and those with dispersed ownership (Arregle et al., 2017).

The empirical results of these inquiries have tended to be inconclusive, if not contradictory. Studies by Fernández and Nieto (2006), Gomez-Mejia, Makri, and Larraza-Kintana (2010), and Graves and Thomas (2006), among others, found family firms to be less internationalized than their nonfamily counterparts, whereas other studies, for example, Singh and Gaur (2013) and Zahra (2003), have found them to be more internationalized. Still other studies (Cerrato & Piva, 2012; Pinho, 2007) have found no significant difference in internationalization levels between family and nonfamily firms. This latter conclusion has been confirmed more recently in a meta-analysis by Arregle et al., which found that "the association between a firm's ownership (i.e., family vs. nonfamily) and internationalization is null" (Arregle et al., 2017, p. 823). It has been suggested that the reason for these contradictory results stems from the omission of variables accounting for family firm heterogeneity at macro, firm, family and individual levels, such as, *inter alia*, differences in external operating environments (Carney, Gedajlovic, & Strike, 2014; Cruz, Larraza-Kintana, Garcés-Galdeano, & Berrone, 2014; Wright, Chrisman, Chua, & Steier, 2014), uniqueness of resource bundles and firm-level strategies (De Massis, Di Minin, & Frattini, 2015; Majocchi & Strange, 2012), differences in structures and types of founding families (Arregle, Hitt, &

Mari, 2019), and individual-level characteristics and decision-making biases that ultimately impact family firms' internationalization paths (Eddleston, Sarathy, & Banalieva, 2019; Kano & Verbeke, 2018; Majocchi, D'Angelo, Forlani, & Buck, 2018).

Given the ambiguity of these empirical findings, it seems appropriate to focus on idiosyncratic family firm features that afffect not only the extent of these firms' internationalization, but also more complex, dynamic aspects of international strategic governance. Several studies have made progress in this direction. A study by Graves and Thomas (2008) identifies three key variables of family firm internationalization: commitment levels, availability of financial resources and capacity for the development of capabilities critical for cross-border expansion. Banalieva and Eddleston (2011) find that family firms with nonfamily managers perform better when expanding outside of the home region, while family firms with family managers perform better when internationalization is home region-oriented. More recently, Hennart, Majocchi, and Forlani (2019) argued that success of family firms' internationalization is contingent on a business model adopted by the firm, with high-quality global niche business models being particularly suited for family-controlled firms. Eddleston et al. (2019) refined these findings by suggesting that family firms' ability to pursue successfully a high-quality niche business model is contingent on macro- and firm-level factors, such as a country of origin effect at the macro level, and professionalization practices at the firm level. Arregle et al. (2019) further elaborated that family firms' ability and propensity to deploy a high-quality niche business model depend on the structure of the owning family.

Xu, Hitt, and Dai (2020) conducted a nuanced investigation of the effect of family firms' idiosyncratic features on the scale and scope of their internationalization. They found that financial performance influences the role of non-economic goals in foreign market entry decisions. Metsola et al. (2020) focused on temporal aspects of family firm internationalization, and suggested that unique features of family governance, both facilitative and constraining ones, influence family firms' international strategies differently at various stages of the internationalization process. The above studies have augmented significantly our knowledge on family firm internationalization, but did not aim to develop a general, integrative conceptual approach to describe and explain this phenomenon in a fine-grained fashion.

With that in mind, this chapter adopts an internalization theory perspective in order to explain and predict the ways in which family firms differ from each other, and from their nonfamily counterparts, in organizing and governing cross-border transactions. Internalization theory and its "sister" theory, transaction cost economics (TCE), are somewhat underrepresented in the study of family firm internationalization, with the exception of several studies exploring family firms' choices of international market entry modes (e.g., Kao, Kuo, & Chang, 2013; Sestu & Majocchi, 2018). Recently, internalization theory scholars have suggested that family firms are subject to a unique barrier to efficient international governance in the form of *bifurcation bias* (Kano & Verbeke, 2018). Bifurcation bias is an affect-based decision-making logic that prioritizes *heritage assets* (assets with familial connections) over non-family assets, which are treated as lower-value *commodity*-type assets (Verbeke & Kano, 2012). In the context of internationalization, bifurcation bias affects both the success of cross-border activity and the specific internationalization paths adopted by family firms. In this chapter, we argue that the notion of bifurcation bias can serve as a "common denominator" to help explain internationalization behaviour of family firms. We explore the causes, symptoms, and specific impacts of bifurcation bias on international strategy.

The remainder of the chapter is structured as follows. First, we give a brief overview of core theoretical constructs, namely internalization theory and bifurcation bias. Second, we discuss how bifurcation bias can lead to governance structures that are comparatively sub-optimal in the short- to medium-run. Third, we link bifurcation bias to extant theoretical constructs, namely the Schwartzian theory of values (Schwartz, 1992, 2006) and socioemotional wealth (SEW) (Gomez-Mejia, Haynes, Núñez-Nickel, Jacobson, & Moyano-Fuentes, 2007) to further investigate potential antecedents and consequences of bifurcation bias. Fourth, we discuss strategies to combat the formation of bifurcation bias, and to mitigate its effects. Figure 1.1 visualizes our new conceptual model, linking these various streams of research and summarizing our arguments.

Internalization Theory and the Family Firm

Internalization theory is a branch of comparative institutional analysis that, in its current form, combines elements of Williamson's (1996) version of transaction cost economics (TCE), the resource-based view (RBV), and entrepreneurship theory (Buckley & Casson, 1976; Narula & Verbeke, 2015). Internalization theory predicts that firms will, in the long run, select the modes of governance that are most efficient for conducting transactions across international borders (although inefficient structures and modes of operating may prevail in the short- to medium-term). Internalization theory also predicts that firms will choose the internal and external contracting arrangements

1 Internationalization Decisions in Family Firms: The Impact… 7

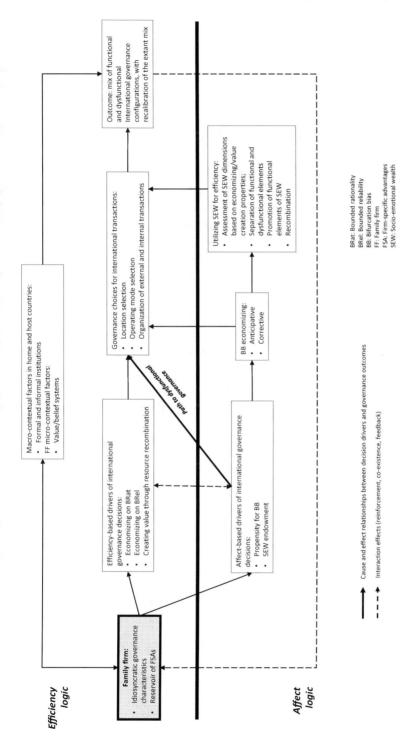

Fig. 1.1 International governance decisions and outcomes in family firms

8   L. Kano et al.

that best facilitate the successful recombination of resources across international borders in order to create value for the firm's owners. The selected governance arrangements may also need to be adapted and/or restructured over time in order to efficiently address changes in the internal and/or external operating environments.

The key governance decisions faced by a multinational enterprise (MNE) are (1) determining the boundaries of the firm: which activities to perform in-house versus externally, that is, the "make or buy" decision; (2) the organization of externalized activities: contract type and duration, types of alliances and/or partnerships and so on; and (3) the organization of internal activities: choices surrounding organizational structure, administrative relationships, human resource practices and so on. In addressing these issues, the most efficient forms of governance will be those that: (1) economize most effectively on bounded rationality;[1] (2) economize most effectively on bounded reliability[2] (Kano & Verbeke, 2015; Verbeke & Greidanus, 2009) and (3) provide the most favourable environment for the creation of value through resource recombination (Grøgaard & Verbeke, 2012; Verbeke & Kenworthy, 2008).

In the absence of bifurcation bias, both family and nonfamily firms will approach the above decisions in an economizing way, based on their unique resource bundles and (internal and external) environmental contexts. Further, with respect to family firms, the most efficient governance structure is the one that uses the optimal mix of family and nonfamily resources both in home and in host countries. However, bifurcation bias can inhibit resource utilization and recombination, as we discuss in the following section.

---

[1] *Bounded rationality* is one of two behavioural assumptions which undergird Williamsonian TCE. Bounded rationality was defined canonically by Herbert Simon as behaviour which is "*intendedly* rational, but only *limitedly* so" (Simon, 1961, p. xxiv). Simon's concept of bounded rationality provides a more useful and realistic cognitive-behavioural framework than strict rationality (as found in neoclassical economics) for describing the actions of economic actors with limited capacities for accessing and processing complex information, evaluating options and making optimal decisions.

[2] *Bounded reliability* explains sources of commitment failure and is an extension of the second behavioural assumption of Williamsonian TCE—opportunism, described by Williamson as "self-interest seeking with guile" (Williamson, 1981, p. 1545), or "calculated efforts to mislead, distort, disguise, obfuscate or otherwise confuse" (Williamson, 1985, p. 47). Bounded reliability still allows for opportunistic behaviour as a cause of commitment failure, but also recognizes cases of commitment failure that materialize despite the *ex ante* good faith intentions of the unreliable actor (Verbeke & Greidanus, 2009), and includes such distinct manifestations as benevolent preference reversal and identity-based discordance (Kano & Verbeke, 2015). Thus, the behavioural assumption of bounded reliability takes into account the propensity of human actors (assumed technically competent) to fail in their commitments, but without the default assumption of malevolence implied by the narrower concept of opportunism.

Bifurcation Bias: An Overview

Bifurcation bias is "a unique, affect-based barrier to short and medium run efficient decision making in family firms, which manifests itself in two simultaneous, diverging patterns of behaviour towards family vs. nonfamily assets, applied systematically and by default" (Kano & Verbeke, 2018, p. 163). In bifurcation-biased firms, assets with a family connection are treated as *heritage* assets and assigned unique value, whereas nonfamily assets engender a negative affect and are typically viewed as generic and fungible. Bifurcation bias is therefore an expression of bounded rationality, as well as a potential source of bounded reliability in a family firm.

When decisions are made using this affect heuristic instead of (boundedly) rational economic logic, the firm's performance may suffer due to sub-optimal choices and prioritization of heritage assets, which in turn can create an environment that promotes severe bounded reliability. Not all family firms are bifurcation-biased; however, unlike firms with dispersed ownership, family firms exhibit an inherent propensity towards this dysfunctional bias (Verbeke & Kano, 2012); the family ownership and management also make it more difficult to correct the bias as compared to a traditional Chandlerian hierarchy, where dysfunctionalities are easier to observe and correct.

Heritage assets can include both human and non-human assets. In the case of human assets, in a bifurcation-biased firm, employees who are family members will be treated as high-potential, high-value, and loyal agents of the firm, irrespective of their actual performance or actual potential for value creation. By contrast, nonfamily members may be viewed as less reliable, less loyal, and less valuable. In these instances, bifurcation bias will manifest itself in practices such as reluctance to monitor or discipline family employees while simultaneously displaying a generalized and unwarranted distrust for nonfamily employees (Dyer, 2006). Bifurcation bias towards human assets can affect routines related to recruitment, promotion, performance evaluation, compensation, and resource allocation. The common practice of appointing highly competent, nonfamily managers to key leadership roles on an interim basis only until these positions can be filled permanently by family members (Lee, Lim, & Lim, 2003) is an example of bifurcation bias.

Physical assets, product lines, locations, and investment projects are all examples of non-human assets that can be subject to bifurcation bias. Non-human heritage assets may also include intangibles such as firm knowledge and ways of doing things: processes, intellectual property, and so on. Attachment to such heritage assets can manifest itself in either functional or dysfunctional ways. In many situations, assets and governance mechanisms connected to the family owners will serve economizing purposes and support the continued health of the firm (see discussion below on SEW pursuits). However, in instances where bifurcation bias is present, there will be an inappropriate prioritization of these heritage assets versus perceived commodity assets. Such "inflexible attachment to existing assets and strategies characteristic of family firms" (Holt & Daspit, 2015, p. 83) and simultaneous neglect of potentially valuable resources and opportunities treated as commodity can lead to sub-optimal outcomes. For example, firms showing dysfunctional favouritism toward family-connected groups such as workers, investors, and community members (Bennedsen & Foss, 2015) may limit their social capital to the home community and thus fail to develop social ties with outside stakeholders that may aid international expansion (Ciravegna, Kano, Rattalino, & Verbeke, 2020).

In many instances, bifurcation bias will arise in situations where changes in the internal and/or external environment mean that family assets that once served an economizing purpose no longer do so, but the family owners are not able or willing to engage in a sober reassessment of the place of these heritage assets in the firm. It is exactly this type of situation that the family firm often faces when pursuing international expansion into a new host market: assets which have served the family well in previous settings may no longer do so in the host country environment (Arregle et al., 2017; Verbeke & Kano, 2012). In such situations, a bifurcation-biased firm will overestimate the value creation potential of heritage assets and make decisions based on these false assessments. These decisions can lead to significant inefficiencies, as discussed in the next section.

Bifurcation Bias and International Governance Decisions

Successful internationalization generally requires an MNE to transfer, recombine, and/or upgrade its firm-specific advantages (FSAs) across national borders, in a way that allows achieving value creation and capture in host markets (Verbeke, 2013). Bifurcation bias can impair successful transfer, deployment and recombination of FSAs in the following ways:

* The transferability and deployability of heritage assets across borders can be overestimated by the family firm. This can exacerbate the *global illusion*

effect (to which family and nonfamily firms alike are susceptible), whereby a firm overestimates the extent to which its resources can be deployed outside the home market. In this scenario, the family firm may try to deploy a heritage FSA in a host market where there is in fact little potential for profitable exploitation.

- The firm may choose to internalize cross-border "heritage-asset rich" transactions that would be more efficiently conducted externally in the host-market, while neglecting to internalize "commodity-asset rich" transactions that may represent core or vulnerable activities that should be performed in-house.
- The selection of host country location may be impaired by the non-economic preferences of a bifurcation-biased family member (e.g., quality of life factors).
- The recombination of heritage assets with host market resources, necessary for successful international expansion (Hennart, 2009), may be impaired by a dysfunctional distrust of outsiders (Banfield, 1958). In this instance, the family owners may be reluctant to recombine the firm's heritage assets with the resources of nonfamily "outsiders", thereby limiting responsiveness and adaptability to the host market environment.

These hazards can further complicate situations where family firm managers may already be grappling with the challenges posed by compounded cultural, administrative, geographic and economic distance (Ghemawat, 2001; Rugman, Verbeke, & Nguyen, 2011). Specific governance decisions affected by bifurcation bias include location and entry mode choices and host country partner selection.

Bifurcation Bias and Host Country Location Selection

When assessing location advantages, some of the variables that need to be considered in host country selection are comparative cost of contracting, the strength of labour markets, the strength of financial markets, the nature of demand, the strength of local institutions, and so on. In selecting a host location, managers must compare the location advantages of different markets and assess the cost of adapting their MNE's FSAs in these new markets. In most cases, successful utilization of FSAs requires recombination of resources with host country assets. The accessibility and complementarity of these host country assets is a critical factor in the location selection decision (Hennart, 2009; Verbeke, 2013).

Here, MNEs with dispersed ownership and unbiased family MNEs are likely to choose the location that has both the lowest costs for FSA adaption and the best access to required third-party complementary assets (Grøgaard & Verbeke, 2012). However, if a firm suffers from bifurcation bias, it may prioritize the non-economic objectives of family members to the detriment of the firm's long-term economic goals. Family members' preferences—personal location preference, presence of family networks, and so on—can lead to a sub-optimal geographic configuration of international activity (Kano & Verbeke, 2018). Writing about the expansion of the Rothschild banking empire during the 1830s, economic historian Niall Ferguson argued that "[w]ith the benefit of hindsight, the historian can see that the greatest omission of the period was the failure to establish a stable and reliable Rothschild base in the United States of America" (Ferguson, 1998, p. 354). While the five Rothschild brothers had enjoyed enormous success in the establishment of banking houses in the large European centres, none of their sons could be persuaded to take up the mantle and establish operations in the booming financial market of the United States. Commenting on this fact, Ferguson writes:

> What James [Rothschild] really wanted was for a Rothschild to go to America. But who? The debate on this question was to bedevil the Rothschilds' America policy for decades to come: no one wanted to go there. (Ferguson, 1998, p. 370)

James' difficulty in establishing a strong base in America due to the unwillingness of his nephews to relocate there was further exacerbated by his reluctance to give the job to an "outsider"—a prime example of bifurcation bias, whereby outside managers are viewed as incompetent, untrustworthy, or both: "to place our trust entirely in the hands of strangers is difficult" (Ferguson, 1998, p. 371). As employing a nonfamily manager to run American operations appeared unfeasible, the lucrative expansion opportunity was essentially abandoned.

A desire to control the deployment of heritage assets abroad can also drive dysfunctionality in host country selection—that is, the family MNE may prioritize locations that will enable them to maintain maximum control over heritage assets, for example, locating production facilities only in those jurisdictions that permit full foreign ownership. In such a setting, host-country regulations regarding foreign direct investment (and the extent to which they may limit or reinforce family ownership) may prove decisive. Finally, biased preferences, such as loyalty to a home community, may prevent family MNEs from achieving efficiency through offshoring—a situation observed in the French family-owned automotive company Peugeot, where the founding family's continued insistence on keeping a large share of production in France almost led the company to bankruptcy (Fainsilber, 2014).

Nevertheless, it is important to reemphasize that the pursuit of non-economic goals (e.g., quality-of life seeking motive for international expansion) is not evidence of bifurcation bias in and of itself. Rather, it is when the pursuit of these non-economic goals is detrimental to the firm's economic goals that it becomes dysfunctional and results in sub-optimal performance of the MNE. In many instances, the presence of network relationships and other family-connected factors can and do align with the best economic interests of the firm in host country selection and may in fact enable transactions that otherwise would not take place (e.g., relying on family networks in environments characterized by opportunistic competitive behaviour and weak legal and contracting institutions; see Ilias, 2006). Mustafa and Chen (2010) have shown that the presence of family networks in target host countries can endow family firms with significant advantages. Such networks provide access to resources that facilitate expansion. In these cases, the pursuit of non-economic goals harmonizes with the economic interests of the firm, provided that the functional elements of these non-economic pursuits outweigh the dysfunctional ones.

Bifurcation Bias and Operating Mode Selection

Internalization theory predicts that, in the long run, an MNE will select the mode of operation that maximizes efficiency of deployment for its FSAs and economizes on the costs of recombining firm resource bundles with required complementary resources in the host country (Hennart, 2009). Based on these considerations, the MNE will choose whether to pursue a market exchange, a wholly owned subsidiary (either through a greenfield entry or an acquisition) or a cooperative entry with a local or international partner. If the MNE's FSAs are vulnerable to appropriation by third parties and the required complementary assets are easily accessible in the host market, an equity-based full-ownership operating mode will likely be the most appropriate. If the FSAs in question are less vulnerable to appropriation (or less critical to value creation), then a cooperative or externally contracted operating mode is more efficient (Grøgaard & Verbeke, 2012; Rugman et al., 2011).

However, in the presence of bifurcation bias, a family firm will overvalue heritage FSAs and undervalue perceived commodity FSAs. This will lead to the internalization of potentially low-value heritage FSAs that could be more efficiently exploited through external contracting, while deploying in contracts with external parties the potentially high-value commodity-type FSAs that are at risk of third-party appropriation or otherwise unsuitable for external transacting.

The former scenario—that is, family firms' tendency to gravitate towards operating modes that facilitate greater control (Boellis, Mariotti, Minichilli, & Piscitello, 2016; Memili, Chrisman, & Chua, 2011)—is fairly well explored in family firm literature. Protecting valuable heritage assets through internalization can be justified. Yet, dysfunctionality arises when emotional attachment to heritage routines, processes, or product lines prevents a biased family firm from outsourcing non-essential/low-value-added activities that involve standardized knowledge. The family may perceive a need to control fully the knowledge associated with these activities, even if that knowledge is not in fact subject to appropriation. This decision is connected to the location choice discussed above, as conducting heritage activities in the home country, or seeking host markets that allow for full ownership, may present the best way to exercise control over these activities. Italian confectionery company Ferrero, for example, internationalized sales and production under the leadership of legendary Michele Ferrero. However, the firm entered foreign markets using exclusively wholly owned subsidiaries that produced goods developed by Ferrero itself, and bearing Ferrero brands. Ferrero's insistence on entering new markets only where it could launch its own brands and avoid acquisitions and diversification might have limited the extent and scope of its internationalization, which, perhaps not coincidentally, focused mainly on markets characterized by a relatively low distance, such as France and Germany (Ferrero Italia, 2017). Interestingly, Ferrero's international strategy contrasts with that of its competitor Mars (also family owned), which acquired several related businesses in different markets (Mars, 2017), and that of Nestle, which owns a large and diversified portfolio of products and brands. After Michele's death in 2015, Ferrero's strategy seems to have changed. In 2015, the firm acquired Thorntons, a confectionery producer based in the UK, stating that it will keep Thorntons' production facilities and brands. In 2016, Ferrero purchased Delacre, a Belgium-based biscuit manufacturer (Bricco, 2017). This suggests that under its new generation of management, the firm has become more willing to experiment with different entry modes, and to cede control over the development and branding of some of its products. In 2017, for the first time, Ferrero appointed a nonfamily CEO, signalling further change from the era of the family's personal control of most of the firm's activities (Murray Brown, 2017).

The other scenario—that is, misguided externalization, following the least cost logic—is largely unexplored in family firm research, as family firms are argued to be prone to excessive internalization rather than excessive outsourcing (Memili, Chrisman, & Chua, 2011). Yet, dysfunctional externalization of activities wrongly perceived as using commodity-like resources is highly possible in bifurcation-biased family MNEs. It is exemplified in the history of the Fiat Group, an iconic Italian carmaker, presided over for decades by the late Giovanni ("Gianni") Agnelli Jr. While Gianni Agnelli has arguably led Fiat to many international successes, he is also famous for prioritizing his personal aspirations, preferences and connections (Tagliabue, 2003). Agnelli's personal fixation on the Fiat brand entailed under-investment in Alfa Romeo and Lancia, two other brands of Fiat automotive division, specialized in higher niche vehicles. As a consequence, both Alfa Romeo and Lancia exited from the racing competitions that made them famous, eroding the brand value they developed by being at the forefront of international motor racing—as examples, Enzo Ferrari worked at Alfa Romeo before founding Ferrari, and Ferrari was initially a spin out of Alfa Romeo. Lancia to this day remains a winner of the highest number of titles in the World Rally Championship, in spite of having exited that competition in the early 1990s. After years of the company's under-investment in product development of other brands in order to boost Fiat, Alfa Romeo and Lancia sales declined, and both brands lost their significance in international markets (Berta, 2006).

Another example of potentially bifurcation-biased approaches to operating mode selection is the propensity of family firms to pursue cooperative entry modes only when other family firms are available as potential alliance partners, and to disproportionately select kin-controlled partners (Memili, Chrisman, & Chua, 2011) over partners with dispersed ownership. Generally speaking, firms tend to favour other firms of similar status when engaging in transactions (Podolny, 1994), but this tendency is even more pronounced in family firms, which attach a socially constructed meaning of reliability to family governance (Reuber, 2016). Similar backgrounds and perceived shared values foster a "common bond" (Gomez-Mejia et al., 2010, p. 82) between the two families, which is seen by the focal MNE's founding family as a safeguard against bounded reliability of partners. A recent empirical study by Sestu and Majocchi (2018) found that family firms are more likely to choose a joint venture mode of entry (versus a wholly owned subsidiary) if the partner organization in the host country is also a family firm.

This may seem to be a reasonable economizing mechanism against bounded reliability, yet, evaluating potential alliance partners based, first and foremost, on ownership, could be an expression of bifurcation bias when this evaluation supersedes assessment of partners' capabilities to perform adequately the outsourced task. Dysfunctionality will arise if the partner lacks requisite capabilities to perform the desired function in the host market, or if other, nonfamily-owned partners could perform those functions more efficiently. In unbiased family firms, entering into an agreement with a family-owned partner must be supplemented by careful due diligence, whereby potential partners are assessed based on the nature, level and complementarity of their FSAs, as well as the expected costs and benefits of collaboration (Rugman & Verbeke, 2003; Yamin, 2011). Further, de facto excluding nonfamily firms from the consideration set may lead to adverse selection. Family ownership, as discussed in much family firm literature, has a dark side (Lubatkin, Schulze, Ling, & Dino, 2005) and thus, on its own, cannot serve as a safeguard against bounded reliability.

The Magnitude and Impact of Bifurcation Bias: Cultural Factors

As mentioned above, not all family firms are bifurcation biased, and those firms that indeed exhibit bifurcation bias may do so to varying degrees. The firm's propensity towards bifurcation bias, as well as the magnitude of this bias's dysfunctional impact, depend on a number of factors, including, *inter alia*, individual-level characteristics of the firm members, and the cultural, institutional, economic and technological contexts within which the firm operates.

The role of formal macro-level institutions in family firm internationalization is fairly well researched, with a general consensus that country-level institutions (e.g., minority stakeholder protection, inheritance laws, regulatory practices separating ownership and control, export orientation of the economy) are critical to explaining family firm internationalization (Arregle et al., 2017; Lehrer & Celo, 2017; Wright et al., 2014). In terms of bifurcation bias, it has been argued that strong formal institutions can serve as macro-level safeguards against firm-level biased behaviour (Verbeke & Kano, 2012).

In this section, we focus on the interplay between bifurcation bias and *informal* institutions, namely individual and societal cultural values. Schwartz and Rubel define values as "transituational goals, varying in importance, that serve as guiding principles in the life of a person or a group" (Schwartz & Rubel, 2005, p. 1008). In the family firm setting, these values often form an integral part of the firm's DNA and inform decision-making related to both economic and non-economic goal pursuit (Arregle et al., 2017; Zellweger, Kellermanns, Chrisman, & Chua, 2012).

Schwartz[3] (Schwartz, 2010) identifies two levels of values: those held at the personal level and those held at the cultural/societal level. In the setting of the family MNE, firm-level values may be affected both by the personally held values of influential individual family members and by the dominant cultural values of the firm's home country (Verbeke, Yuan, & Kano, 2019).

Personal Values and Bifurcation Bias

As a manifestation of affect-based decision-making, the roots of bifurcation bias can be traced back to the values held by influential members of the owning family. Schwartz (1992) specifies ten basic human values which are grouped within four "higher-order" values. The higher-order values operate on a two-dimensional spectrum. Along one dimension are the values of openness to change versus conservation. Along the second dimension are the values of self-transcendence versus self-enhancement. Verbeke et al. (2019) argue that within the context of family firm internationalization, the values most relevant to the formation and resultant effects of bifurcation bias are those related to openness versus conservation, and self-transcendence. Here, openness values encompass stimulation and self-direction; conservation values refer to conformity, tradition and security. The self-transcendence dimension includes universalism versus benevolence values, whereby universalism emphasizes tolerance and appreciation for the welfare of others, and benevolence emphasizes the welfare of in-group members (e.g., the family) (Schwartz, 1992).

Verbeke et al. (2019) suggest that families with strong conservation and benevolence values are more prone to bifurcation bias, and more likely to select lower levels of internationalization and make lower-quality international governance decisions. Such firms will naturally prioritize family-connected assets and resources over nonfamily ones in order to provide security, conformity, and adherence to tradition within the firm, and therefore may be reluctant to deploy nonfamily employees to manage foreign

---

[3] While extant international business research has tended to use Hofstede's (1980) framework of values as a default measurement instrument of cross-cultural differences, Schwartz's dual theory of values has been somewhat underutilized, with some notable exceptions—see, for example, Duran et al. (2017). Although Schwartz's dual theory is somewhat more complicated—Schwartz himself has acknowledged this difficulty (Schwartz, 2011)—the allowance which it makes for within-country variation of individual values provides for a subtlety of analysis which is useful when examining the critical role played by the individually held values of influential family firm owners and managers. Other conceptualizations of values commonly used in IB, such as Hofstede or GLOBE, appear to confuse the level of the individual with the level of the society (Schwartz, 2011), which makes Schwartz's model superior for the purpose of our analysis.

18 L. Kano et al.

operations, and/or pursue expansion into such geographic and product areas where full control by the family is not an option. This pattern has been confirmed by studies such as that of Kets de Vries (1996), which highlights the tendency within family firms to provide secure employment and other privileges for family members.

Conversely, family firms where key family members exhibit openness to change and universalism values are less prone to bifurcation bias; the direct effect of these values on internationalization, as well as the indirect effect through bifurcation bias, is likely to be positive. That is, such firms are likely to exhibit higher internationalization levels and make higher-quality international governance decisions. Here, international governance choices are expected to be made according to comparative institutional logic, involving the most competent individuals, whether family or nonfamily.

Societal Values and Bifurcation Bias

While individual firm owners within the same country can and do vary in the personal values which they espouse, the dominant societal values of the firm's home country nevertheless play a significant normative role in setting the expectations and context in which the firm operates. Both internal firm functions (such as the socializing of staff and the managing of interactions between teams) and external firm functions (such as the formation of network relationships with clients and suppliers) are influenced by the dominant cultural values in the firm's home country. These values also form the expectations and norms to which the family firm owners must conform in order to achieve legitimacy within their host communities. Thus, although individual firm owners' personal values may vary, they will nevertheless be shaped and constrained by the macro-values of the environment in which the firm operates.

Schwartz (2006) outlines seven dominant cultural values: (1) embeddedness versus (2) intellectual autonomy, and/or (3) affective autonomy; (4) egalitarianism versus (5) hierarchy; and (6) mastery versus (7) harmony. Various combinations of the above values prevailing in a given society shape the cultural background and context in which the firm must operate. While individual firms and firm owners may vary in their degree of conformity to the values of their culture, significant deviation from societal expectations will cause problems for the firm, leading to ostracism and possibly even political and/or legal censure. Schwartz identifies seven historical cultural groups that correspond to the seven societal/cultural values: Confucian; South Asian;

African/Middle-Eastern; Western European; Eastern European; English-speaking; and Latin American.

Verbeke et al. (2019) argue that of the seven societal values outlined by Schwartz, the ones that are most relevant to the development of bifurcation bias are (1) those that address the nature of the relationship between the individual and the group (embeddedness versus intellectual autonomy, and/or affective autonomy): and (2) those that ensure the preservation of societal fabric (egalitarianism versus hierarchy). The dimension of embeddedness versus autonomy defines the relationship between the individual and the group and, thus, plays a significant role in determining how family members view family and nonfamily employees, as well as determining how family and nonfamily employees view themselves within the firm. Embeddedness values prioritize group solidarity, family security, social order and deference to the collective interests of the group. Individuals that are part of an embeddedness society are more likely to view the preferential treatment of family members within the firm as both normal and acceptable, in keeping with the values of the wider society in which the firm operates. By supporting such attitudes and behaviours, nonfamily employees within embeddedness cultures are both more likely to encourage the manifestation of bifurcation bias within the firm, and more likely to mitigate its negative impact by avoiding agency-type reactions.

The dimension of hierarchy versus egalitarianism addresses the way individuals view and interact with each other. In egalitarian cultures, individuals view each other as moral equals and are socialized to promote and expect a cooperative form of interaction in their relationships. Hierarchical cultures, on the other hand, ascribe well-defined roles to different individuals within a clear and well-understood structure of authority. Individuals operating within a hierarchical culture are more likely to accept obligations attached to their specified roles as a given and treat authority relationships with the deference prescribed by their position within the hierarchy. In societies characterized by strong hierarchical values, family firm owners are more likely to demonstrate preferential treatment of family employees as the natural consequence of their role-based authority positions within the firm, while nonfamily employees are more likely to view this preferential treatment as the normal and acceptable privilege that is due based on that position. Nonfamily employees are therefore more likely to respond to manifestations of bifurcation bias with stewardship-type behaviour and continue to remain loyal and committed to the family owners and the firm.

Verbeke et al. (2019) further suggest that societal values impact the role of bifurcation bias in cross-border transfer and recombination of FSAs in family firms. As mentioned above, bifurcation-biased family firms are generally likely to overestimate the transferability, deployment and profitable exploitation potential of heritage FSAs, while underestimating the potential of commodity FSAs (Kano & Verbeke, 2018). Somewhat paradoxically, value similarities between home and host countries can exacerbate the dysfunctional impact of bifurcation bias on international governance. Cultural proximity may encourage foreign entry (Duran, Kostova, & van Essen, 2017), but discourage careful assessment of FSA transferability, with firm owners viewing the similarity of societal values as a guarantee of a seamless transfer of heritage FSAs. Here, the family may underestimate the need for FSA adaptation and novel resource combinations, which will impede value creation in the host market.

SEW Pursuit and Family Firm Internationalization

Socioemotional wealth (SEW) refers to "the nonfinancial aspects of the firm that meet the family's affective needs, such as identity, the ability to exercise family influence, and the perpetuation of the family dynasty" (Gomez-Mejia et al., 2007, p. 106). SEW represents a dominant conceptual lens in family firm research and has been invoked extensively in the study of family firm internationalization. SEW-related objectives are argued to impact family firm diversification strategies (Gomez-Mejia et al., 2007), innovation (Patel & Chrisman, 2014), and internationalization paths (Gomez-Mejia et al., 2010), in that family firms are likely to select strategies that carry the least likelihood of SEW dissipation. Unchecked emphasis on various SEW dimensions may clash with comparative efficiency-based evaluation of international governance alternatives. For example "make or buy" decisions, decisions regarding the interface with the external environment (e.g., partner selection), and internal organization decisions for each cross-border transaction or a class of transactions will not be made at the service of economizing/value creation objectives, but will aim to first and foremost preserve SEW.

SEW Versus Bifurcation Bias

SEW is related to, but not synonymous with, bifurcation bias. Bifurcation bias represents a systemic *dysfunctional* pursuit of socioemotional preferences and usage of heritage assets. It can impair the economic health of the firm. SEW pursuit, on the other hand, can dovetail harmoniously with economizing behaviour. Miller et al. (2015, p. 21) refer to the functional and complementary pursuit of SEW as "creating an evergreen organization". Functional elements of SEW include the emphasis on positive reputation, preservation of a family network, long-term horizons of strategic decision-making, and other priorities and activities which help the firm create value in host markets. For example, concentrated control allows family firms significant latitude in decision-making in the realm of international strategy (De Massis, Kotlar, Chua, & Chrisman, 2014). Identification with and emotional attachment to the firm foster commitment to quality (Hennart et al., 2019) and help family firms establish positive reputations in host countries. Focusing on social ties leads to advanced relational capabilities (Ward, 2004), which can be critical for overcoming the liability of outsidership (Johanson & Vahlne, 2009). Dynastic aspirations contribute patient capital (Chrisman, Chua, De Massis, Frattini, & Wright, 2015) to international operations. SEW dimensions can thus foster unique FSAs that family firms can leverage to support their international activity.

However, the above potential benefits of SEW are likely to accrue only to those family firms that actively monitor for and economize against bifurcation bias. Bifurcation bias economizing constrains SEW pursuit: In unbiased family firms, SEW objectives are assessed based on their compatibility with efficient governance choices, and are promoted only if they have economizing and value-creating properties in host countries (Kano, Verbeke, & Ciravegna, 2020). For example, a family MNE may pursue internalization in a host country if sustained family control afforded by internalization reduces transaction costs through simplified decision-making, better intellectual property protection, or greater strategic flexibility; conversely, if family control does not serve efficiency purposes (i.e., if the cost of market transactions is lower than the cost of organizing interdependencies inside the MNE, Hennart & Park, 1993), alternative operating modes (e.g., a joint venture or market transactions) will be selected.

Conversely, in bifurcation-biased family firms driven by unconstrained SEW goals, SEW is *de facto* prioritized and guides international strategy decisions, which can lead to dysfunctional governance. Decisions related to the boundaries of the firm, the organization of the external interface, and internal organization will likely veer towards arrangements that enable greater control and monitoring of dispersed operations by the family (Banalieva & Eddleston, 2011). For example, pursuit of sustained family control may lead to a rejection of external investors, over-reliance on wholly owned operating modes (Boellis et al., 2016; Memili, Chrisman, & Chua, 2011; Memili, Chrisman, Chua, Chang, & Kellermanns, 2011; Sestu & Majocchi, 2018), and a preference for top-down internal management systems that facilitate hands-on involvement but may not match the complexity of international operations (Alessandri, Cerrato, & Eddleston, 2018). Unconstrained SEW pursuit means that these governance arrangements will be selected even if they are inferior in terms of their actual efficiency properties.

Facilitative Role of SEW in Unbiased Firms: The Imperative of Recombination

We have argued above that constrained SEW pursuit can equip family firms with unique advantages vis-à-vis their nonfamily counterparts. However, family firms also suffer from a number of resource weaknesses in international markets, which are essentially "the flip side" of their advantages (Hennart et al., 2019, p. 763), and fall into three general and interrelated categories. First, SEW-based desire for control leads to particularistic human resources practices (Carney, 2005) and a consequent shortage of sophisticated managerial capabilities, which are important in complex international environments (Banalieva & Eddleston, 2011; Graves & Thomas, 2006). Second, family MNEs' preference for internally generated equity over debt and outside financing, stemming from unwillingness to dilute control, restricts financial resources necessary for internationalization (Hennart et al., 2019). Third, emphasis on control and binding social ties may lead to isolation from other firms and from external actors, which negatively affects family firms' knowledge related to internationalization; this knowledge includes, inter alia, information about host country institutions, business intermediaries, competition, and consumer preferences.

In addition, family firms' FSAs that stem from their SEW preferences are frequently location-bound: specifically, social ties and reputation are often focused on the home community and cannot always be efficiently relied upon in international transactions (Arregle, Hitt, & Sirmon, 2007; Kano, Ciravegna, & Rattalino, 2021). Even when theoretically transferable, FSAs such as superior relational capabilities and long-term orientation are not guaranteed to be profitable in host markets (Verbeke, 2013), as they need to be supplemented by host country–specific knowledge and access to local networks in order to be exploited efficiently.

Internalization theory posits that weaknesses in firms' host country FSA portfolios can be compensated through recombination, which means leveraging the firm's own FSAs in alternative configurations and/or integrating complementary resources of external actors in host markets. Recombination capability is a higher-order FSA in its own right, and a critical prerequisite for international competitive success (Collinson & Narula, 2014; Narula, 2014; Verbeke, 2013). In the context of family firms, SEW-driven idiosyncratic resources and capabilities add value in foreign markets only if productively linked with complementary resources, so as to compensate for extant FSA weaknesses and to address differences between home and host markets. Frescobaldi, a 700-year old Italian wine producer currently in the 31st generation of family management, achieved such linkage by forming a joint venture with family-owned Mondavi, one of the leading US wine producers. At the time of its entry into the US market, Frescobaldi was an established wine producer, with a stellar domestic reputation, sophisticated modern production technologies, and wine-making techniques and recipes that have been honed over centuries. Yet, the company lacked advanced management practices, knowledge about foreign market dynamics, host country marketing tactics, and efficient use of media. These resources and capabilities were supplied by the joint venture partner, and a new wine developed through the partnership went on to become one of Frescobaldi's most successful products in international markets (interview with Lamberto Frescobaldi, President and 30th-generation family leader, 2017[4]).

It should be noted that recombination may require family firms to surrender a certain degree of control (particularly when required capabilities are owned by outside actors), to shed resources, and to depart from traditional routines. This may be difficult in the presence of bifurcation bias, and, as such, successful recombination is conditional on the presence of strategies to economize on bifurcation bias, which we discuss next.

Economizing on Bifurcation Bias

Internalization theory predicts that the inefficiencies brought by bifurcation bias will cause sub-optimal governance decision in the short- to medium-run. In the long run, the systemic inefficiencies bifurcation bias causes will be eliminated—either through a change in specific practices and routines, a major change in governance (i.e., by converting to a Chandlerian hierarchy), or by the firm simply ceasing to exist. It is therefore imperative that family firms learn to implement economizing strategies to combat bifurcation bias in order to survive as profitable family-owned MNEs. This means aligning the

---

[4] The interview was conducted in 2017 as part of data collection for a large-scale family firm governance research project.

24   L. Kano et al.

firm's non-economic goals with efficient international strategy in a way that limits bifurcation bias in the firm's decision-making.

General Economizing Strategies

Kano and Verbeke (2018) outline six strategies that can help family firms combat the formation of bifurcation bias and mitigate its potential impacts: (1) cross-border operational meritocracy; (2) targeted international education of family managers; (3) structured processes for making international expansion decisions; (4) rigorous measurement of international performance (e.g., benchmarking); (5) purposeful exposure to unbiased scrutiny; and (6) intentional implementation of *reverse* bifurcation bias in decision-making. These strategies are briefly discussed below.

1. *Cross-border operational meritocracy.* Research has demonstrated that the quality of international operations and decision-making can be improved significantly by the implementation of explicitly merit-based, professionalized HR practices including hiring, promotion and role allocation (Chrisman, Memili, & Misra, 2014; Eddleston et al., 2019; Holt & Daspit, 2015; Verbeke & Kano, 2012). Implementing a rigorous merit-based HR policy ensures that competent and unbiased employees oversee complex international business decisions. The term "operational meritocracy" was first coined by the Merck family—the family in charge of the German pharmaceutical and chemical firm Merck. Merck exemplifies this practice, intentionally protecting the firm's international governance and operations by entrusting managerial responsibility to those who are deemed to be most competent, irrespective of their family affiliation or lack thereof (Glemser & Leleux, 2011). Importantly, nonfamily managers must have full authority over their domains, rather than playing a ceremonial role, with the family routinely overriding strategic decisions made by nonfamily executives (Ciravegna et al., 2020).
2. *Targeted international education of family managers.* Research has shown that if family firms neglect to properly invest in the training and education of family members, they can suffer negative ramifications in technically and managerially complex settings in which MNEs operate (Miller et al., 2015; Verbeke & Kano, 2012). Successful family MNEs, such as Merck and Mars, ensure that prospective family managers are trained and educated appropriately. In the case of Merck, this involves sending future family employees abroad for an international education in order to expose

them to aspects of international culture and business (Neumann & Tapies, 2007). Mars stipulates that in order for family members to be considered for a high-level position within the firm, they must first have successfully launched and managed an independent international business venture on their own (Clark, 2008; Kaplan, 2013).

3. *Structured processes for international decision-making.* Family firms are generally observed to have low levels of formalization due to their relational style of management and direct ownership control (König, Kammerlander, & Enders, 2013). However, this informal/relational approach to firm management can create an environment in which bifurcation bias goes unchecked. In the complex operating environment of the MNE, it is necessary to put in place formalized and objective decision-making processes in order to economize on bounded rationality and reliability and manage potential instances of bifurcation bias.

4. *Measurement of international performance.* Recent research has shown that family firms can reduce dysfunctional management decision-making by introducing performance benchmarking against other international firms (De Massis, Kotlar, Mazzola, Minola, & Sciascia, 2018). This type of objective self-assessment is practiced by successful international family firms, such as the aforementioned Merck pharmaceutical group, as well as Carlson Group (a US-based hotel and travel MNE).

5. *Purposeful exposure to unbiased scrutiny.* Opening up the firm to unbiased third-party scrutiny is a very effective way to uncover and address bifurcation bias. This can be accomplished in a number of ways, including the use of external consulting firms, the presence of a strong board of directors and/or taking the firm public. A recent empirical study by Bauweraerts, Sciascia, Naldi, and Mazzola (2019) found that, among the 248 Belgian SMEs in the dataset, the presence of a strong and active board that included external directors was a significant predictor of superior internationalization performance for family firms versus their nonfamily competitors.

6. *Reverse bifurcation bias.* The final way in which a family firm can combat bifurcation bias is by engaging in deliberate reverse bifurcation bias. This entails flipping the bias around so that heritage assets are held to a higher standard of scrutiny and performance evaluation than nonfamily ones (Jennings, Dempsey, & James, 2018). By adding an extra layer of scrutiny and scepticism to the assessment of family assets, family firms can exercise a self-conscious awareness of their propensity to bifurcation bias and take measures to compensate for it.

Timing and Scale of Bifurcation Bias Economizing

The question arises as to when corrections for bifurcation bias are likely to occur. Verbeke and Fariborzi (2019) outline two dimensions along which MNEs differ in their implementation of governance changes in response to observed inefficiencies: (1) the timing of adaptation (anticipative versus corrective) and (2) the scale of adaptation (large-scale versus small-scale).

Anticipative adaptation seeks to implement economizing solutions at the level of the firm's overarching governance features before problems arise. Because anticipative adaption interacts with the firm's strategy formation, it tends to be large-scale and targets all relevant operations. Within the family-owned MNE, anticipative economizing on bifurcation bias may include strategies such as targeted international education of family members or an intentionally fostered culture of operational meritocracy that sees nonfamily employees occupying senior roles within the firm (see above). Crucially, and as its name implies, anticipative economizing strategies are put in place *before* bifurcation bias creates a crisis for the firm.

When anticipative strategies are not put in place to combat bifurcation bias, or when extant anticipative practices prove ineffective, crises may arise which require the firm to pursue *corrective* adaptations to meet the challenges caused by sub-optimal (i.e., bifurcation-biased) decisions. Corrective economizing measures can be taken at the localized or firm-wide level. Localized corrective measures attempt to address the pain-point directly, for example, by the replacement of an underperforming family manager in a foreign subsidiary with a competent, local, nonfamily manager. While this type of localized corrective economizing may address the immediate crisis at hand, it often risks addressing isolated "symptoms" rather than the systemic issues that are causing them. Large-scale corrective adaptations, on the other hand, while also triggered as a response to a specific problem or crisis-point, seek to address issues of bifurcation bias at the firm's overall governance level.

In some cases, however, the options available for corrective economizing may not suffice to reverse the damage caused by previous bifurcation-biased decisions (i.e., too-little and/or too-late). As mentioned above, in these instances internalization theory predicts that the firm will fail in a given market or, in extreme cases, cease to exist as a family firm or cease to exist at all (Verbeke & Kano, 2012). This may have been the case with the Dutch apparel and clothing retailer C&A, founded in the nineteenth century. C&A entered the US market in 1948, mainly because of the controlling family's life-long aspirations to have a US market presence. During the 1950s, the firm had to close several of its US branches because of heavy losses. The family later concluded that management had underestimated the differences of the US market, primarily the higher wages, higher pressure on prices, greater competition, and difficulties in establishing long-term relationships with suppliers. This assessment of performance, however, did not immediately spur corrective action. The firm remained in the US market until 2000, sustaining losses for a prolonged period of time. C&A eventually exited the market, in spite of the dramatic expansion of the business concept it helped pioneer—affordable, mass-produced, fast fashion clothing and apparel (Spoerer, 2016).

Conclusion

In this chapter, we have focused on the concept of bifurcation bias as a way to explain unique internationalization features of family firms, and these firms' potential deviation from efficient international governance. Using internalization theory as our conceptual lens, we have argued that family and nonfamily firms are subject to the same economic logic: in the long run, they will select the most efficient international governance structures. However, in the short run, the presence of bifurcation bias can lead to sub-optimal international governance decisions. The firm's propensity towards such dysfunctionality, as well as the magnitude of the negative impact of sub-optimal decisions on the firm's long-term viability, depends on a number of factors discussed above, including personal values and aspirations of the owners, the cultural characteristics of home and host countries, the firm's recombination capabilities, and, importantly, the firm's ability and willingness to implement systematically a set of strategies to identify and safeguard against affective decision biases, as summarized in Fig. 1.1.

It should be noted that nonfamily firms can also display biases that result in sub-optimal international governance. MNEs with dispersed ownership are susceptible to numerous impediments to sound decision-making in the short- and medium-term, resulting from bounded rationality and bounded reliability challenges. These types of barriers to efficient international decision-making can affect all firms, but only family firms are subject to bifurcation bias. On the positive side, family firms can benefit from unique features that make them competitive in international markets vis-à-vis their nonfamily counterparts. These benefits represent functional features of SEW and include, *inter alia*, superior reputation, emphasis on quality, managerial and employee dedication to the firm, strong networks, and long-term horizons of strategic decision-making (Carney, Dieleman, & Taussig, 2016; Duran, Kammerlander, van Essen, & Zellweger, 2015; Erdener & Shapiro, 2005; Hennart et al., 2019). The paradox of the family firm is that unconstrained promotion of SEW, in the absence of bifurcation bias economizing, will fail future family generations in terms of both economic wealth and SEW preservations. The pursuit of intergenerational, economic and socioemotional family wealth is what differentiates family firms from nonfamily ones, but such pursuit, if it is to be successful, must necessarily go at the expense of managerial practices that indiscriminately reward family heritage and family membership.

Although still relatively new to the family firm internationalization literature, the concept of bifurcation bias is already proving a fruitful avenue for both conceptual and empirical enquiry (Arregle et al., 2019; Bauweraerts et al., 2019; Eddleston et al., 2019; Jennings et al., 2018; Metsola et al., 2020). It is our hope that future research into the phenomenon of bifurcation bias will provide further insights for family firm and IB scholars, as well as additional strategic tools for managers of international family firms.

References

Alessandri, T. M., Cerrato, D., & Eddleston, K. A. (2018). The mixed gamble of internationalization in family and nonfamily firms: The moderating role of organizational slack. *Global Strategy Journal, 8*(1), 46–72.

Arregle, J.-L., Duran, P., Hitt, M. A., & van Essen, M. (2017). Why is family firm's internationalization unique? A meta-analysis. *Entrepreneurship Theory and Practice, 41*(5), 801–831.

Arregle, J.-L., Hitt, M. A., & Mari, I. (2019). A missing link in family firms' internationalization research: Family structures. *Journal of International Business Studies, 50*(5), 809–825.

Arregle, J.-L., Hitt, M. A., & Sirmon, D. G. (2007). The development of organizational social capital: Attributes of family firms. *Journal of Management Studies, 44*(1), 73–95.

Banalieva, E. R., & Eddleston, K. A. (2011). Home-region focus and performance of family firms: The role of family vs non-family leaders. *Journal of International Business Studies, 42*(8), 1060–1072.

Banfield, E. C. (1958). *The moral basis of a backward society.*. Glencol.

Bauweraerts, J., Sciascia, S., Naldi, L., & Mazzola, P. (2019). Family CEO and board service: Turning the tide for export scope in family SMEs. *International Business Review, 28*(5), 101583.

Bennedsen, M., & Foss, N. (2015). Family assets and liabilities in the innovation process. *California Management Review, 58*(1), 65–81.

Berta, G. (2006). *La Fiat dopo la Fiat.* Mondadori.

Boellis, A., Mariotti, S., Minichilli, A., & Piscitello, L. (2016). Family involvement and firms' establishment mode choice in foreign markets. *Journal of International Business Studies, 47*(8), 929–950.

Bricco, P. (2017). Quarta acquisizione in due anni: Se il "made in Italy" non e solo una preda. *Il Sole 24 Ore-Digital Replica Edition*. March 2017.

Buckley, P. J., & Casson, M. (1976). *The future of the multinational enterprise*. London: Palgrave Macmillan.

Carney, M. (2005). Corporate governance and competitive advantage in family-controlled firms. *Entrepreneurship Theory and Practice, 29*(3), 249–265.

Carney, M., Dieleman, M., & Taussig, M. (2016). How are institutional capabilities transferred across borders? *Journal of World Business, 51*(6), 882–894.

Carney, M., Gedajlovic, E., & Strike, V. M. (2014). Dead money: Inheritance law and the longevity of family firms. *Entrepreneurship Theory and Practice, 38*(6), 1261–1283.

Cerrato, D., & Piva, M. (2012). The internationalization of small and medium-sized enterprises: the effect of family management, human capital and foreign ownership. *Journal of Management & Governance, 16*(4), 617–644.

Chrisman, J. J., Chua, J. H., De Massis, A., Frattini, F., & Wright, M. (2015). The ability and willingness paradox in family firm innovation. *Journal of Product Innovation Management, 32*(3), 310–318.

Chrisman, J. J., Memili, E., & Misra, K. (2014). Nonfamily managers, family firms, and the winner's curse: The influence of noneconomic goals and bounded rationality. *Entrepreneurship Theory and Practice, 38*(5), 1103–1127.

Ciravegna, L., Kano, L., Rattalino, F., & Verbeke, A. (2020). Corporate diplomacy and family firm longevity. *Entrepreneurship theory and practice, 44*(1), 109–133.

Clark, A. (2008, May 2). Life in Mars: reclusive dynasty behind one of world's most famous brands. *The Guardian*. Retrieved November 18, 2019, from https://www.theguardian.com/business/2008/may/02/mars.wrigley.secretive

Collinson, S., & Narula, R. (2014). Asset recombination in international partnerships as a source of improved innovation capabilities in China. *Multinational Business Review, 22*(4), 394–417.

Cruz, C., Larraza-Kintana, M., Garcés-Galdeano, L., & Berrone, P. (2014). Are family firms really more socially responsible? *Entrepreneurship Theory and Practice, 38*(6), 1295–1316.

Davis, J. (2019, January 3). Why family businesses matter so much to the world economy. *Family Capital*. Retrieved October 20, 2019, from https://www.famcap.com/2019/01/why-family-businesses-matter-so-much-to-the-world-economy/

De Massis, A., Di Minin, A., & Frattini, F. (2015). Family-driven innovation: Resolving the paradox in family firms. *California Management Review, 58*(1), 5–19.

De Massis, A., Kotlar, J., Chua, J. H., & Chrisman, J. J. (2014). Ability and willingness as sufficiency conditions for family-oriented particularistic behavior: Implications for theory and empirical studies. *Journal of Small Business Management, 52*(2), 344–364.

De Massis, A., Kotlar, J., Mazzola, P., Minola, T., & Sciascia, S. (2018). Conflicting selves: Family owners' multiple goals and self-control agency problems in private firms. *Entrepreneurship Theory and Practice, 42*(3), 362–389.

Duran, P., Kammerlander, N., van Essen, M., & Zellweger, T. (2015). Doing more with less: Innovation input and output in family firms. *Academy of Management Journal, 59*(4), 1224–1264.

Duran, P., Kostova, T., & van Essen, M. (2017). Political ideologies and the internationalization of family-controlled firms. *Journal of World Business, 52*(4), 474–488.

Dyer, W. G. (2006). Examining the "family effect" on firm performance. *Family Business Review, 19*(4), 253–273.

Eddleston, K. A., Sarathy, R., & Banalieva, E. R. (2019). When a high-quality niche strategy is not enough to spur family-firm internationalization: The role of external and internal contexts. *Journal of International Business Studies, 50*(5), 783–808.

Erdener, C., & Shapiro, D. M. (2005). The internationalization of Chinese family enterprises and Dunning's eclectic MNE paradigm. *Management and Organization Review, 1*(3), 411–436.

EY & University of St. Gallen. (2019, February 18). EY and University of St. Gallen global family business index. *How the world's largest family businesses are responding to the Transformative Age.* Retrieved October 20, 2019, from http://familybusinessindex.com/

Fainsilber, D. (2014, February 19). Les difficiles relations des patrons du groupe avec la famille Peugeot. *Les Echos.* Retrieved November 18, 2019, from https://www.lesechos.fr/2014/02/les-difficiles-relations-des-patrons-du-groupe-avec-la-famille-peugeot-273495.

Ferguson, N. (1998). *The House of Rothschild: Money's Prophets, 1798-1848.* London: Penguin.

Fernández, Z., & Nieto, M. J. (2006). Impact of ownership on the international involvement of SMEs. *Journal of International Business Studies, 37*(3), 340–351.

Ferrero Italia. (2017). Storia. Retrieved March 25, 2017, from https://www.ferrero.it/azienda/il-gruppo/una-storia-di-famiglia/una-grande-azienda.

Ghemawat, P. (2001). Distance still matters. *Harvard Business Review, 79*(8), 137–147.

Glemser, A.-C., & Leleux, B. (2011). *The Mercks of Darmstadt: What a family can do (A).* Lausanne, Switzerland: IMD International.

Gomez-Mejia, L. R., Haynes, K. T., Núñez-Nickel, M., Jacobson, K. J. L., & Moyano-Fuentes, J. (2007). Socioemotional wealth and business risks in family-controlled firms: Evidence from Spanish olive oil mills. *Administrative Science Quarterly, 52*(1), 106–137.

Gomez-Mejia, L. R., Makri, M., & Larraza-Kintana, M. L. (2010). Diversification decisions in family-controlled firms. *Journal of Management Studies, 47*(2), 223–252.

Graves, C., & Thomas, J. (2006). Internationalization of Australian family businesses: A managerial capabilities perspective. *Family Business Review, 19*(3), 207–224.

Graves, C., & Thomas, J. (2008). Determinants of internationalization pathways of family firms: An examination of family influence. *Family Business Review, 21*(2), 151–167.

Grøgaard, B., & Verbeke, A. (2012). Twenty key hypotheses that make internalization theory the general theory of international strategic management. In *Handbook of research in international strategic management* (pp. 7–30). Cheltenham: Edward Elgar.

Hennart, J.-F. (2009). Down with MNE-centric theories! Market entry and expansion as the bundling of MNE and local assets. *Journal of International Business Studies, 40*(9), 1432–1454.

Hennart, J.-F., Majocchi, A., & Forlani, E. (2019). The myth of the stay-at-home family firm: How family-managed SMEs can overcome their internationalization limitations. *Journal of International Business Studies, 50*(5), 758–782.

Hennart, J.-F., & Park, Y. R. (1993). Greenfield vs. acquisition: The strategy of Japanese investors in the United States. *Management Science, 39*(9), 1054–1070.

Hofstede, G. (1980). *Culture's consequences: International differences in work-related values*. London: Sage.

Holt, D. T., & Daspit, J. J. (2015). Diagnosing innovation readiness in family firms. *California Management Review, 58*(1), 82–96.

Ilias, N. (2006). Families and firms: Agency costs and labor market imperfections in Sialkot's surgical industry. *Journal of Development Economics, 80*(2), 329–349.

Jennings, J. E., Dempsey, D., & James, A. E. (2018). Bifurcated HR practices in family firms: Insights from the normative-adaptive approach to stepfamilies. *Human Resource Management Review, 28*(1), 68–82.

Johanson, J., & Vahlne, J. E. (2009). The Uppsala internationalization process model revisited: From liability of foreignness to liability of outsidership. *Journal of International Business Studies, 40*(3), 1411–1431.

Kano, L., Ciravegna, L., & Rattalino, F. (2021). The family as a platform for FSA development: Enriching new internalization theory with insights from family firm research. *Journal of international Business Studies, 52*(1), 148–160.

Kano, L., & Verbeke, A. (2015). The three faces of bounded reliability: Alfred Chandler and the micro-foundations of management theory. *California Management Review, 58*(1), 97–122.

Kano, L., & Verbeke, A. (2018). Family firm internationalization: Heritage assets and the impact of bifurcation bias. *Global Strategy Journal, 8*(1), 158–183.

Kano, L., Verbeke, A., & Ciravegna, L. (2020). Internationalization of family firms: When is a managerial focus on socio-emotional wealth effective? In K. Mellahi, K. Meyer, R. Narula, I. Surdu, & A. Verbeke (Eds.), *The Oxford handbook of international business strategy*. Oxford: Oxford University Press, forthcoming.

Kao, M. S., Kuo, A., & Chang, Y. C. (2013). How family control influences FDI entry mode choice. *Journal of Management & Organization, 19*(4), 367–385.

Kaplan, D. (2013, January 17). Mars Incorporated: A pretty sweet place to work. *Fortune*. Retrieved November 18, 2019, from https://fortune.com/2013/01/17/mars-incorporated-a-pretty-sweet-place-to-work/.

Kets de Vries, M. F. (1996). *Family business: Human dilemmas in the family firm*. London: International Thomson Business Press.

König, A., Kammerlander, N., & Enders, A. (2013). The family innovator's dilemma: How family influence affects the adoption of discontinuous technologies by incumbent firms. *Academy of Management Review, 38*(3), 418–441.

Kontinen, T., & Ojala, A. (2010). The internationalization of family businesses: A review of extant research. *Journal of Family Business Strategy, 1*(2), 97–107.

Lee, K. S., Lim, G. H., & Lim, W. S. (2003). Family business succession: Appropriation risk and choice of successor. *Academy of Management Review, 28*(4), 657–666.

Lehrer, M., & Celo, S. (2017). Boundary-spanning and boundary-buffering in global markets: A German perspective on the internationalization of family firms. *Review of International Business and Strategy, 27*(2), 161–179.

Lubatkin, M. H., Schulze, W. S., Ling, Y., & Dino, R. N. (2005). The effects of parental altruism on the governance of family-managed firms. *Journal of Organizational Behavior, 26*(3), 313–330.

Majocchi, A., D'Angelo, A., Forlani, E., & Buck, T. (2018). Bifurcation bias and exporting: Can foreign work experience be an answer? Insight from European family SMEs. *Journal of World Business, 53*(2), 237–247.

Majocchi, A., & Strange, R. (2012). International diversification: The impact of ownership structure, the market for corporate control and board independence. *Management International Review, 52*(6), 879–900.

Mars. (2017). About Mars: History timeline. Retrieved March 28, 2017, from http://www.mars.com/uk/en/about-mars/history.aspx

Memili, E., Chrisman, J. J., & Chua, J. H. (2011). Transaction costs and outsourcing decisions in small- and medium-sized family firms. *Family Business Review, 24*(1), 47–61.

Memili, E., Chrisman, J. J., Chua, J. H., Chang, E. P., & Kellermanns, F. W. (2011). The determinants of family firms' subcontracting: A transaction cost perspective. *Journal of Family Business Strategy, 2*(1), 26–33.

Metsola, J., Leppäaho, T., Paavilainen-Mäntymäki, E., & Plakoyiannaki, E. (2020). Process in family business internationalisation: The state of the art and ways forward. *International Business Review*. https://doi.org/10.1016/j.ibusrev.2020.101665

Miller, D., Wright, M., Le Breton-Miller, I. L., & Scholes, L. (2015). Resources and innovation in family businesses: The Janus-face of socioemotional preferences. *California Management Review, 58*(1), 20–40.

Murray Brown, J. (2017). Ferrero appoints first non-family CEO. *The Financial Times-Online*. Retrieved May 31, 2017, from https://www.ft.com/content/b0583c87-40b5-3fb3-979c-b3878009f56d

Mustafa, M., & Chen, S. (2010). The strength of family networks in transnational immigrant entrepreneurship. *Thunderbird International Business Review, 52*(2), 97–106.

Narula, R. (2014). Exploring the paradox of competence-creating subsidiaries: Balancing bandwidth and dispersion in MNEs. *Long Range Planning, 47*(1-2), 4–15.

Narula, R., & Verbeke, A. (2015). Making internalization theory good for practice: The essence of Alan Rugman's contributions to international business. *Journal of World Business, 50*(4), 612–622.

Neumann, A., & Tapies, J. (2007). *Balancing family and business needs at Merck KGaA*. IESE.

Patel, P. C., & Chrisman, J. J. (2014). Risk abatement as a strategy for R&D investments in family firms. *Strategic Management Journal, 35*(4), 617–627.

Pinho, J. C. (2007). The impact of ownership: Location-specific advantages and managerial characteristics on SME foreign entry mode choices. *International Marketing Review, 24*(6), 715–734.

Podolny, J. M. (1994). Market uncertainty and the social character of economic exchange. *Administrative Science Quarterly, 39*(3), 458–483.

Pukall, T. J., & Calabrò, A. (2014). The internationalization of family firms: A critical review and integrative model. *Family Business Review, 27*(2), 103–125.

Reuber, A. R. (2016). An assemblage-theoretic perspective on the internationalization processes of family firms. *Entrepreneurship Theory and Practice, 40*(6), 1269–1286.

Rugman, A. M., & Verbeke, A. (2003). Extending the theory of the multinational enterprise: Internalization and strategic management perspectives. *Journal of International Business Studies, 34*(2), 125–137.

Rugman, A. M., Verbeke, A., & Nguyen, Q. T. K. (2011). Fifty years of international business theory and beyond. *Management International Review, 51*(6), 755–786.

Schwartz, S. H. (1992). Universals in the content and structure of values: Theoretical advances and empirical tests in 20 countries. In *Advances in experimental social psychology* (pp. 1–65). London: Academic Press.

Schwartz, S. H. (2006). A theory of cultural value orientations: Explication and applications. *Comparative sociology, 5*(2–3), 137–182.

Schwartz, S. H. (2010). Values: Individual and cultural. In S. M. Breugelmans, A. Chasiotis, & F. J. R. van de Vijver (Eds.), *Fundamental questions in cross-cultural psychology* (pp. 463–493). Cambridge: Cambridge University Press.

Schwartz, S. H. (2011). Studying values: Personal adventure. future directions. *Journal of Cross-Cultural Psychology, 42*(2), 307–319.

Schwartz, S. H., & Rubel, T. (2005). Sex differences in value priorities: Cross-cultural and multimethod studies. *Journal of Personality and Social Psychology, 89*(6), 1010–1028.

Sestu, M. C., & Majocchi, A. (2018). Family Firms and the Choice Between Wholly Owned Subsidiaries and Joint Ventures: A Transaction Costs Perspective. *Entrepreneurship Theory and Practice*, 1042258718797925.

Simon, H. (1961). *Administrative behavior* (2nd ed.). New York: Palgrave Macmillan.

Singh, D. A., & Gaur, A. S. (2013). Governance structure, innovation and internationalization: Evidence from India. *Journal of International Management, 19*(3), 300–309.

Spoerer, M. (2016). *C&A: Ein Familienunternehmen in Deutschland, den Niederlanden und Großbritannien*. CH Beck.

Tagliabue, J. (2003). Giovanni Agnelli, Fiat patriarch and a force in Italy dies at 81. *The New York Times-Online*. Retrieved March 25, 2017, from http://www.nytimes.com/2003/01/25/business/giovanni-agnelli-fiat-patriarch-and-a-force-in-italy-dies-at-81.html

Verbeke, A. (2013). *International business strategy*. Cambridge: Cambridge University Press.

Verbeke, A., & Fariborzi, H. (2019). Managerial governance adaptation in the multinational enterprise: In honour of Mira Wilkins. *Journal of International Business Studies, 50*(8), 1213–1230.

Verbeke, A., & Greidanus, N. S. (2009). The end of the opportunism vs trust debate: Bounded reliability as a new envelope concept in research on MNE governance. *Journal of International Business Studies, 40*(9), 1471–1495.

Verbeke, A., & Kano, L. (2012). The transaction cost economics theory of the family firm: Family-based human asset specificity and the bifurcation bias. *Entrepreneurship Theory and Practice, 36*(6), 1183–1205.

Verbeke, A., & Kenworthy, T. P. (2008). Multidivisional vs metanational governance of the multinational enterprise. *Journal of International Business Studies, 39*(6), 940–956.

Verbeke, A., Yuan, W., & Kano, L. (2019). A values-based analysis of bifurcation bias and its impact on family firm internationalization. *Asia Pacific Journal of Management*. Retrieved October 20, 2019, from http://link.springer.com/10.1007/s10490-018-9598-4

Ward, J. L. (2004). *Perpetuating the family business: 50 lessons learned from long-lasting, successful families in business*. London: Palgrave Macmillan.

Williamson, O. E. (1981). The modern corporation: Origins, evolution. *attributes. Journal of Economic Literature, 19*, 1537–1568.

Williamson, O. E. (1985). *The economic institutions of capitalism: Firms, markets, relational contracting*. New York: Free Press.

Williamson, O. E. (1996). *The mechanisms of governance*. Oxford: Oxford University Press.

Wright, M., Chrisman, J. J., Chua, J. H., & Steier, L. P. (2014). *Family enterprise and context*. London: SAGE Publications Sage CA.

Xu, K., Hitt, M. A., & Dai, L. (2020). International diversification of family-dominant firms: Integrating socioemotional wealth and behavioral theory of the firm. *Journal of World Business, 55*(3). https://doi.org/10.1016/j.jwb.2019.101071

Yamin, M. (2011). A commentary on Peter Buckley's writings on the global factory. *Management International Review, 51*(2), 285–293.

Zahra, S. A. (2003). International expansion of US manufacturing family businesses: The effect of ownership and involvement. *Journal of Business Venturing, 18*(4), 495–512.

Zellweger, T. M., Kellermanns, F. W., Chrisman, J. J., & Chua, J. H. (2012). Family Control and Family Firm Valuation by Family CEOs: The Importance of Intentions for Transgenerational Control. *Organization Science, 23*(3), 851–868.

2

Internationalisation and Family Involvement: A Stewardship Approach in the Hotel Industry

Laura Rienda, Enrique Claver, and Rosario Andreu

Introduction

Research on the internationalisation process of family firms (FFs) continues investigating the influence of family on different aspects of the process. Different theories are employed to explain the behaviour of FFs and to balance the two most important issues in these companies: the family and the business. Emotional reactions can be in opposition to, or in line with, managerial and organisational considerations.

The stewardship theory proposes that firms take decisions based on a steward prioritising pro-organisational and collectivistic behaviours over individualistic and self-serving behaviours. Through this theory, the steward (manager) believes that by working towards business aims, personal needs are met (Davis, Schoorman, & Donaldson, 1997). Stewardship behaviour should be related with trust, involvement, collectivism, commitment and long-term orientation. According to the stewardship theory, internationalisation is viewed as an opportunity to make the business more competitive and increase the chances of successful growth (Segaro, 2012). This perspective also tries to align the interests of the family and the company and helps us to understand some specific behaviours of family managers (Chrisman, Chua, Kellermanns, & Chang, 2007; Corbetta & Salvato, 2004; Le Breton-Miller & Miller, 2009;

L. Rienda (✉) • E. Claver • R. Andreu
Department of Management, University of Alicante, Alicante, Spain
e-mail: laura.rienda@ua.es

© The Author(s), under exclusive license to Springer Nature Switzerland AG 2021
T. Leppäaho, S. Jack (eds.), *The Palgrave Handbook of Family Firm Internationalization*,
https://doi.org/10.1007/978-3-030-66737-5_2

37

Miller & Le Breton-Miller, 2006). Family managers are strongly committed to the enterprise and act for its good, even if that implies personal sacrifice (Davis, Schoorman, Mayer, & Tan, 2000). FFs thus adopt a longer-term vision and are able to take riskier strategic decisions with the aim of preserving the continuity of the firm for future generations. Amongst these strategic decisions, internationalisation arises as one of the main challenges for FFs (Spanish Family Firm Institute, 2018). Despite the potential risk involved in this strategy, internationalisation can be an attractive long-term strategy because it can bring competitive advantages (Claver, Rienda, & Quer, 2009). In this case the risk is considered necessary for the business to prosper.

In this study we will focus on the Spanish hotel industry, a sector with a large percentage of FFs (Andreu, Claver, Quer, & Rienda, 2019). A great number of firms in this sector are highly internationalised (Assaf, Josiassen, & Oh, 2016). Following the premises of the stewardship theory, we analyse the influence of family on two important decisions for international FFs: the degree of internationalisation and the entry mode used in each market. This analysis allows us to evaluate the impact of different characteristics associated with FF involvement in internationalisation. More precisely, the influence of family ownership and management, a family CEO and the current generation on the internationalisation process of family hotels, underlining the importance of considering the heterogeneity of FFs in this sector.

The contribution of this study is twofold. First, it considers the heterogeneity of FFs, and how this heterogeneity potentially influences key strategy decisions such as internationalisation. Although it is a topic that has received attention previously, the results are not conclusive, so new empirical evidence is necessary. Second, it is focused on an important sector in Spain, the hotel sector. This sector is made up of a high percentage of family businesses. However, the relationship between the characteristics of family hotel companies and their internationalisation has received little attention. This study provides new empirical evidence about one of the main growth options for these specific family businesses.

The rest of the study is divided as follows. First, the literature review section includes a revision of different studies on FFs and internationalisation, focusing on the hotel industry. Second, the methodology section describes the sample and the variables included in our study. Third, the results section shows the main results and the confirmation of the previously developed hypotheses. The study continues with a discussion section, which explains the relationships we found linked with the premises of the stewardship theory. Contributions, limitations and future research are also included. And, finally, the conclusion section concludes the chapter.

Literature Review

Definition and Heterogeneity of FFs

Different definitions of FFs have been considered, according to the presence of family in ownership or management (Abdellatif, Amann, & Jaussaud, 2010; Kraus, Mensching, Calabrò, Cheng, & Filser, 2016), or different kinds of firms in which family involvement plays a crucial role (Andreu et al., 2019; Arregle, Duran, Hitt, & van Essen, 2017; Casillas & Acedo, 2005). The consensus is to identify a firm as an FF when family members own a majority of shares, are involved in management, are present on the board of directors and wish to pass on the firm to subsequent generations (Mazzi, 2011). Family involvement brings a new point of view to the definition of FFs. Multiples studies focus on determining whether a firm is an FF or not, but it is more interesting to analyse the degree of *familiness* to reveal heterogeneity in FFs. *Familiness* is considered to be the identification of "resources and capabilities that are unique to the family's involvement and interactions in the business" (Pearson, Carr, & Shaw, 2008, p. 949). Considering different aspects related to the family in business may contribute to a better understanding of FF characteristics (Alayo, Maseda, Iturralde, & Arzubiaga, 2019; Chua, Chrisman, Steier, & Rau, 2012).

The role of the family could change the direction of a business. As Fang, Kellermanns and Eddleston (2019, p. 70) point out, "the degree to which the family is involved in the day-to-day operations and the strategic direction of the firm are likely to serve as distinguishing features that influence family business behaviour and goals". Family involvement is related with their level of control and it is defined as the level of power held by family members (Gersick, Davis, Hampton, & Lansberg, 1997). Attending to ownership and management, high levels of concentrated control in the family indicates that the power in the organisation is limited to family members or to an individual founder, showing a high family involvement, whereas lower levels suggest that many individuals share power in the FF (Eddleston & Kellermanns, 2007). In terms of generations, founder(s) and generation(s) close to the founder usually have a high level of control and this is related to greater family involvement (Miller, Le Breton-Miller, Lester, & Cannella, 2007).

Some authors consider family involvement in a single variable when studying the internationalisation process of FFs, grouping different family aspects together (Andreu et al., 2019; Arregle et al., 2017). However, in line with other studies, our research considers these aspects individually, that is, the effect of ownership and management (Chen, Hsu, & Chang, 2014); the role of a family CEO (Westhead & Howorth, 2006) and the influence of a later generation on corporate strategy decisions (Claver et al., 2009; Fernández & Nieto, 2005). This approach will allow us to better identify the incidence of family involvement in internationalisation, taking into account the heterogeneity that FFs present.

Agency Theory, Socioemotional Wealth Theory and Stewardship Theory

Traditionally, different theories have justified the strategic decision-making process of the firm by considering the role of each power group and who has control (Segaro, 2012). A greater or lesser organisational outcome, according to the coincidence or not of the ownership and the management in the same person, was a key study in management (Donaldson & Davis, 1991; Muth & Donaldson, 1998). For example, the agency theory argues that managers could display opportunistic behaviour at the expense of shareholder interests (Williamson, 1995). This theory proposes that managers try to maximise their individual utility (Jensen & Meckling, 1976). Also, when the CEO holds the dual role of chair, then the interests of management prevail over the interests of owners. Agency loss appears in this case, emphasising the search of self-interest by managers. For FFs, ownership and management interests are aligned and agency costs are low (Jensen & Meckling, 1976). Nevertheless, as Chua, Chrisman, and Sharma (2003) point out, the validity of the assumption of low- or no-agency costs in family firms depends on the presence of reciprocal altruism or stewardship on the part of managers.

In recent years, the socioeconomic wealth (SEW) perspective has gained widespread attention in FF studies (Hauck & Prügl, 2015). This theory explores the decision process of FFs and advocates for more conservative long-term behaviour in these firms (Calabrò, Minola, Campopiano, & Pukall, 2016). From an agency perspective the focus is on misalignments of interest among organisational actors, emphasising a short-term orientation. The SEW premises offer an alternative viewpoint. It points out that wealth is the priority for FFs and the family owners and managers work to protect this wealth (Gómez-Mejía, Haynes, Núñez-Nickel, Jacobson, & Moyano-Fuentes, 2007). The preservation of the family's wealth leads managers to take less risky decisions, forgoing opportunities such as international activities (Zahra, 2005).

A different view is provided by the stewardship theory. From this perspective, managers should be good stewards of corporate assets (Donaldson &

Davis, 1991). A dual role of CEO and chair could align the interests of the firm with those of the shareholders when there is long-term compensation. Managerial behaviour leans towards a range of non-financial motives acting in the benefit of shareholders (Muth & Donaldson, 1998). Therefore, "stewardship theory defines situations in which managers are not motivated by individual goals, but rather are stewards whose motives are aligned with the objectives of their principals" (Davis et al., 1997, p. 21). This perspective proposes that managers take decisions in favour of the organisation and with collectivistic over individualistic behaviours. Pro-organisational objectives, as opposed to self-interested objectives, are promoted.

Despite its potential, the stewardship theory has not been extensively adopted in family-business studies. Nevertheless, some authors admit that stewardship relationships may exist, or even prevail, at least in some FFs (Chrisman et al., 2007; Vallejo, 2009). In this study we consider that the stewardship theory could provide a useful framework to explain the dynamics and relationships observed in family hotels (Corbetta & Salvato, 2004).

FF Internationalisation

FF literature includes studies on international strategy with different and mixed findings (Arregle et al., 2017). On the one hand, we found studies that emphasise the aversion to risk of FFs and how this aversion could hamper international activity (Graves & Thomas, 2006). Nevertheless, other authors stress the positive attributes of FFs and how they can positively affect the internationalisation process (Zahra, 2003). Attending to these inconclusive results, the difference in degrees of internationalisation could be due to the variance emanating from the differences in the level of family involvement.

Some studies highlight the idea that FFs link emotional and managerial aspects, and this link leads the firm to take less risky decisions. More precisely, decisions related to the internationalisation process are considered riskier because they could entail uncertainty to the managers (Gómez-Mejía, Makri, & Larraza, 2010; Kraus et al., 2016; Pukall & Calabrò, 2014). Internationalisation implies entering a new market, usually with different rules, which in many cases is unknown, and which requires significant investment. The SEW theory has studied this area of research and it points out that FFs could be less internationalised. The goal is to reduce all the risks that could lead to losing the family business (Chen, Huang, & Chen, 2009; Ray, Mondal, & Ramachandran, 2018). The possible loss of legacy makes the FFs more conservative and limits international expansion.

Nevertheless, from the stewardship theory, strategic decisions by FFs are taken with an organisational and collectivistic purpose, prioritising managerial objectives—such as business growth and long-term orientation—over emotional ones—such as risk aversion (Segaro, 2012). The business works to preserve and secure the family, not taking risk-averse decisions but strategic decisions that allow future continuity.

In the case of the hotel industry, the more recent literature found that family involvement can facilitate internationalisation, considering the ideas of the stewardship theory (Andreu et al., 2019; Andreu, Claver, Quer, & Rienda, 2018; Rienda, Claver, & Andreu, 2020), emphasising the benefits of aligning family and business goals (Le Breton-Miller & Miller, 2009; Schulze, Lubatkin, & Dino, 2003). The need to continue the business in the future leads the firm to take riskier decisions.

One important decision for family hotels is their international commitment. Although a more restrictive approach usually argues that FFs are less internationalised, Spanish family hotels have a high level of international activity (Andreu et al., 2018). In accordance with the stewardship theory, business activity is seen as a way to support the family in the future, to provide continuity and security for future generations (Chu, 2009; Miller, Breton-Miller, & Scholnick, 2008; Miller & Le Breton-Miller, 2006). That is why these enterprises invest in creating the conditions required to ensure long-term benefits for all family members (Gómez-Mejía et al., 2007). Seeking to guarantee long-term continuity and survival, FFs will tend to undertake strategies aimed at rapid growth. This may lead them to achieve a larger market share in the current markets or even to expand towards new markets, as is the case with an internationalisation strategy.

Zahra (2003) observed how greater family involvement is likely to have a positive influence on the decision to compete internationally. According to the stewardship theory, the objectives of managers join those of owners and seek to attain organisational objectives such as business growth (Davis et al., 1997). The majority of ownership and management in the hands of a family has been studied from the same definition as FF. The most common way to define an FF was through a combination of ownership and management criteria (Kontinen & Ojala, 2010) and the authors found a negative impact (Sciascia, Mazzola, Astrachan, & Pieper, 2012), a positive impact (Andreu et al., 2019; Zahra, 2003) or even an insignificant impact on internationalisation (Arregle et al., 2017). Considering the stewardship theory, positive family interactions can enhance an FF because relationship conflict diminishes and a participative strategy process arises (Eddleston & Kellermanns, 2007). In this line, a greater level of control is an important family-based resource that may contribute to FF success. We propose that the hotel industry is highly internationalised due to, among others, the family involvement of each firm. When family ownership and management are high, the level of family involvement is also high, and this has a positive impact on the degree of internationalisation. Therefore we propose that:

H1a: Greater family involvement, through family ownership and management of an FF, is positively related with the degree of internationalisation of family hotels.

The presence of a family CEO is another important factor in international decisions. A family CEO can facilitate the alignment of interests between ownership and management. A family CEO may also provide better internal control mechanisms and better access to resources (Peng & Jiang, 2010). In some studies, the presence of family CEO increases family involvement (Al-Dubai, Ismail, & Amran, 2014; Baronchelli, Bettinelli, Del Bosco, & Loane, 2016). From the stewardship theory, if the CEO is a member of the family, the CEO should show a long-term orientation towards the firm's survival, and the level of internationalisation would be positively influenced (Zahra, 2005) since growing across borders helps to strengthen the business in the long run (Pukall & Calabrò, 2014). CEOs in FFs are committed to international expansion decisions to improve the long-term prospects of their businesses (Chen, Liu, Ni, & Wu, 2015; Miller et al., 2008). This leads us to propose the following:

H1b: Greater family involvement, due to the presence of a family CEO, is positively related with the degree of internationalisation of family hotels.

Generation has also been analysed in previous studies, although many of them consider it as a control variable (Arregle et al., 2017). Some authors found that generation has no impact on internationalisation (Mitter, Duller, Feldbauer-Durstmüller, & Kraus, 2014), following the same argument as the stewardship theory, a younger generation could also affect internationalisation in a positive way (Arregle et al., 2017; Claver, Rienda, & Quer, 2007; Okoroafo, 1999). The family increases in complexity with successive generations, and firm managers will perceive more risk from the search for market information, customer needs or the firm's internal relations, increasing market threats and reducing the exploitation of market opportunities (Bobillo, Rodríguez-Sanz, & Tejerina-Gaite, 2013). Over the years, FFs become more conservative and less inclined to take the risks involved in business activities that might undermine the economic value creation process (Zahra, 2005). Later generations managing the company make it difficult to integrate the family's interests and, according to the stewardship theory, this impedes long-term growth decisions such as internationalisation. This is why we propose Hypothesis H1c as follows:

H1c: Greater family involvement, due to the presence of the first or a younger generation, is positively related with the degree of internationalisation of family hotels.

Foreign Entry Modes of FFs

The internationalisation of FFs has also been studied from different points of view, such as foreign location choices (Filatochev, Lien, & Piesse, 2005; Hernández, Nieto, & Boellis, 2018) or entry modes used by the firm (Andreu et al., 2019; Claver et al., 2007; Pongelli, Carolli, & Cucculelli, 2016). Foreign-market entry mode choice represents an important research topic because this may be an irreversible decision and because there are multiple variables that influence this choice (Agarwal & Ramaswami, 1992). One of the most critical strategic decisions for the internationalisation process is the choice of foreign market entry mode (Brouthers & Hennart, 2007). Traditionally, international business research considered entry mode choices from the perspective of control and risk (Anderson & Gatignon, 1986). And due to the characteristics of FFs, the choice between control and risk foreign entry modes is an important decision (Kao & Kuo, 2017), which could determine the potential risks and rewards for firms entering new international markets. A high-control mode can increase profitability and risk, and a low-control mode diminishes the commitment of resources but frequently at the expense of profitability.

In the hotel industry there are different classifications of foreign entry modes. If a firm wants to maximise control, it assumes a greater commitment in terms of resources and risk (Brouthers & Hennart, 2007). Conversely, if a firm opts to relinquish control, it can use contractual methods, which are very common in the hotel industry (Dimou, Chen, & Archer, 2003; Kruesi, Kim, & Hemmington, 2017). In this context, FFs traditionally tend to keep control, although, in an international context, it implies a higher risk (Andreu, Quer, & Rienda, 2020).

The stewardship theory proposes that managers, acting as stewards, take riskier decisions with the aim of gaining long-term objectives such as business growth. High-control entry modes, although riskier, allow the firm better control of units in other markets. The need for control is a characteristic of FFs and previous studies point out that these firms are very closed and want to keep control in the hands of the family (Claver et al., 2009). In FFs, family owners tend to have distinctive family-related priorities and risk preferences,

2 Internationalisation and Family Involvement: A Stewardship... 45

and this may influence decisions on entry mode choices. Therefore, if FFs want to keep control of their subsidiaries, it is assumed that, despite the risk, they opt for high-control foreign entry modes. In the same way, high-control entry modes exclude external partners that may dilute family shares and decision-making power (Gómez-Mejía et al., 2010).

In addition, we found some differences in the influence of each family involvement component. In relation to family ownership and management, FFs traditionally opt for high-control entry modes (Claver et al., 2007). As previously mentioned, the need to control is higher when the presence of family is also higher. In line with the stewardship theory, a higher level of family control facilitates the achievement of organisational objectives (Davis et al., 1997) even if they entail greater risk. Therefore, internationalisation decisions such as high-control entry modes, while oriented towards riskier options, are preferred for FFs (Kao & Kuo, 2017). This leads us to propose the next hypothesis related to the entry mode choice by FFs in the hotel industry:

H2a: Greater family involvement, due to family ownership and management, is positively associated with high-control entry mode choices in family hotels.

A similar argument could be applied when there is a family member in the firm's CEO position. A family CEO means greater family involvement in the business and may favour the use of entry modes that keep control in family hands (Andreu et al., 2019). The stewardship theory advocates growth-oriented decisions and an alignment of the objectives of managers and owners. With high-control entry modes—an important goal for FFs—the firm could develop effective ways to achieve internationalisation, preserving the business, increasing legitimacy and improving the profitability of future generations (Andreu et al., 2020). Therefore, we can propose the next relationship:

H2b: Greater family involvement, due to the presence of a family CEO, is positively associated with high-control foreign entry mode choice in family hotels.

Finally, if we focus on later generations, they bring a new perspective because new ideas are incorporated with each new generation and a gap appears regarding the more conservative ideas of the founder generation (Zahra, 2005). Some studies found that later generations didn't increase the likelihood of using entry modes that involve a high level of resource commitment (Claver et al., 2009). Following the stewardship theory, a lower achievement of long-term commitment goals and a decrease of the managerial identification with the firm appear with the passing of generations (Miller et al., 2007). The passing of generations may cause a greater misalignment of interests as ownership becomes scattered among different family members.

Accordingly, Claver et al. (2007) found that first generations perceive less risk when doing business abroad. To the extent that risk aversion increases with successive generations, the use of non-control modes could be positively related to later generations. For the hotel industry this was recently found in the study of Andreu et al. (2019). The authors identified a lower risk aversion of the founders, with a tendency to use high-control entry modes, compared to the second and subsequent generations. With all these arguments we can propose the last hypothesis:

H2c: Greater family involvement, due to the presence of the first or a younger generation, is positively associated with non-control foreign entry mode choice in family hotels.

Figure 2.1 shows the model proposed with all the hypotheses.

Methodology

The sample was collected from the *Alimarket Hotel and Catering Yearbook* for the year 2016. The database contains financial and commercial data of the most important hotel chains with Spanish-based headquarters (including both national chains and international groups). From a total of 697 hotel chains, we only analysed internationalised chains. That is, hotel chains with at least one hotel abroad. We identified 76 internationalised Spanish hotel chains with 981 hotels abroad, and these chains make up our final sample. Table 2.1 provides a description of the sample.

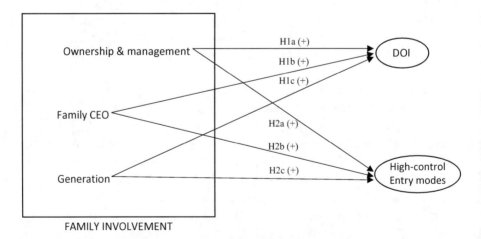

Fig. 2.1 Family involvement and internationalisation

Table 2.1 Sample description

Variables	
Family involvement	
1. Without	52.6%
2. Low	10.5%
3. Medium	21.1%
4. Higher	15.8%
Family CEO	
Yes	7.9%
No	92.1%
Generation	
First	25.7%
Second	60.0%
Third and subsequent	14.3%
DOI (mean)	
	36.67%
Entry modes	
High-control	256 (26.1%)
Non-control	725 (73.9%)

Dependent Variables

Degree of internationalisation (DOI). The ratio of sales abroad over total sales is often used to measure DOI (Grant, Jammine, & Thomas, 1988; Miller et al., 2008). Due to the seasonality of the hotel industry, the most frequently used ratio is the number of rooms abroad over the total number of rooms (Lee, Upneja, Özdemir, & Sun, 2014). This measure has been used in previous studies on internationalisation in the hotel industry (Brida, Ramón-Rodriguez, Such-Devesa, & Driha, 2016; Lu & Beamish, 2004; Ramón, 2002; Tallman & Li, 1996). The higher the ratio, the higher the DOI. In this study we used this measure to find the intensity of internationalisation.

Entry mode. We considered entry mode as a dummy variable as follows: (0) non-control entry modes (such as franchising agreements), and (1) high-control entry modes (such as management contracts, lease agreements and equity-based entry modes). In the hotel industry there are different classifications of foreign entry modes. Both franchising and management agreements are contractual methods, but management agreements offer more operational and strategic control, thus being closer to a quasi-internalised transaction (Contractor & Kundu, 1998; Plá-Barber, Sánchez-Peinado, & Madhok, 2010). However, despite not entailing large investments, management contracts involve a certain level of resource commitment. This is due to the need to transfer assets—such as knowledge for local management training or the expatriation of staff from one country to another—as well as the need to acquire local information and the pre-opening costs (Dimou et al., 2003). In turn, a franchising agreement not only means lesser resource commitment but also a lower level of control, thus making it a quasi-market transaction (Kruesi et al., 2017). Therefore, management agreements, lease contracts (which can almost be considered an equity-based entry mode) and the ownership of hotels abroad are entry modes which, in addition to involving greater resource commitment, allow the firm to exercise more control (Dimou et al., 2003; Kruesi et al., 2017).

Independent Variables

Family ownership and management. One definition of family business considers that the majority of ownership and management of the firm should be in family hands (Claver et al., 2009; Graves & Thomas, 2004). Nevertheless, the FF and non-FF classification could be more detailed when we include different situations that show the heterogeneity of FFs. Following Andreu et al. (2019) and Arregle et al. (2017), we established four categories that combine different degrees of ownership and management: (1) Firms with less than 10% of the corporate capital in the hands of the family and fewer than two family managers. These are classified as "firms without family involvement" (Gómez-Mejía et al., 2010). (2) Firms with more than 10% of the firm's capital in the hands of the family and more than two managers in management positions but whose percentage is still a minority in both ownership and management (firms with low family involvement). (3) Firms with a majority presence of family members in management positions but not in ownership (family-managed firms) or firms with a majority percentage of family presence in ownership but not in management positions (family-owned firms). (4) Firms with a majority family presence in both ownership and management positions (family-owned and family-managed firms). In this last situation the firm has a "greater family involvement".

Family CEO. The presence of the family in management, more precisely in the CEO position, has been widely studied (García-Castro & Aguilera, 2014). Family involvement increases when a managerial position is occupied by a family member. The influence exerted by owners who hold top management positions, such as CEO, allows them to enjoy the discretion of acting with the possibility to influence corporate decisions (Miller & Le Breton-Miller, 2006). Hence, we included a dummy variable that takes the value of 1, when one of the family members is the firm's CEO, and 0, otherwise.

2 Internationalisation and Family Involvement: A Stewardship... 49

Generation. Some previous studies analysed the influence of generation on FF internationalisation. Some studied its impact on international commitment (Claver et al., 2009; Fernández & Nieto, 2005) and others its impact on certain decisions such as foreign entry mode (Andreu et al., 2019; Claver, Rienda, & Quer, 2008). In our case, the current generation was collected through different databases and consulting the corporate websites of each hotel chain. We checked the information obtained in secondary databases by contacting each hotel chain. Finally, in order to collect and differentiate between higher and lower family involvement, with respect to the generation that is currently in charge of the company, we created a dummy variable. As Sharma (2004) points out, founders could exert considerable influence on the culture and values of the company. Therefore, we created a variable which adopts the value 1 when the founder (first generation) manages the firm, and 0 when it is the second or subsequent generations that have joined the company. This variable is also used in the paper of Ramón-Llorens, García-Meca, and Duréndez (2017).

Control Variables

Firm size. Firms may adopt different patterns of internationalisation based on their financial and managerial resource limitations (Brida, Driha, Ramón-Rodríguez, & Scuderi, 2015). Hence, we controlled for firm size using the average income of each hotel chain in the last three years, with a logarithmic transformation to normalise the variable distribution (Brida et al., 2016; García de Soto & Vargas, 2015).

International experience. International experience is also a determinant factor for international firms (Gatignon & Anderson, 1988). International experience allows the company to better adapt to the characteristics of the host market (Niñerola, Campa, Hernández, & Sánchez, 2016). Companies with no international experience are likely to have more difficulties in managing foreign operations, thus preferring entry modes demanding lower resource commitment (Agarwal & Ramaswami, 1992). We measured international experience with the total number of years the company has operated abroad (Brida et al., 2016; León-Darder, Villar-García, & Plá-Barber, 2011).

Cultural distance. Cultural distance is a very important factor that influences decisions on entry modes in international markets (Demirbag, Tatoglu, & Glaister, 2008). In different cultures, executives perceive high uncertainty, and transaction costs could be reduced when home and host countries share cultural values. We measured the cultural distance between Spain and each

50   L. Rienda et al.

host country following the Kogut and Singh (1988) index, based on the extended Hofstede's model with six dimensions: power distance, uncertainty avoidance, individualism vs collectivism, masculinity vs femininity, long-term vs short-term orientation, and indulgence vs restraint. Countries with values close to 0 for cultural distance are culturally similar to Spain. This index has been widely used in previous international business research (Barkema & Vermeulen, 1998; Demirbag et al., 2008) and FF studies (Strike, Berrone, Sapp, & Congiu, 2015).

Hotel category. The category of hotels abroad was determined by means of a categorical variable according to the number of stars that each hotel has (between 1 and 5). This variable has been used in several studies to assess the importance of a hotel's intangible assets, understanding that the higher the level of importance, the more control the firm will want to exert over it, which in turn can influence foreign entry mode (León-Darder et al., 2011; Plá-Barber, León-Darder, & Villar, 2011).

Results

A correlation analysis is presented in Table 2.2, together with the mean and standard deviation of each variable of our model. We also calculated the variance inflation factor (VIF) in order to detect multicollinearity problems. The VIF values are from 1.05 to 3.39. The highest value is below 10, the cut-off point recommended by Kutner, Nachtsheim, Neter, and Li (2005). Therefore, we have ruled out the presence of multicollinearity in our data. Finally, Table 2.3 presents the regressions used to test the hypotheses: a linear regression with Models 1 and 2 (Hypotheses 1a, 1b and 1c) and a binomial regression with Models 3 and 4 (Hypotheses 2a, 2b and 2c). Moreover, in order to have a better interpretation of our results, in Table 2.3-Model 4 we included the odd ratios to calculate the effect sizes of each variable in terms of entry mode decisions.

In Model 2, with respect to Hypothesis 1a, the results show a positive and significant relationship between family ownership/management and internationalisation (9.49, p<0.001), in line with the positive approach of the stewardship theory. Hypothesis 1b is also confirmed in Model 2; we can conclude that the presence of a family CEO is a determinant factor in FF internationalisation (5.56, p<0.05). Finally, in relation to the generation that runs the firm, later generations increase the DOI of the FF (-22.36, p<0.001). That is, contrary to expectations, the founder or early generations are less likely to engage in internationalisation. Hypothesis 1c is not confirmed and we found

Table 2.2 Descriptive statistics and correlations

	Mean	SD	VIF	(1)	(2)	(3)	(4)	(5)	(6)	(7)	(8)
(1) DOI	58.62	18.86									
(2) Entry mode	.74	.43		.13**							
(3) Family ownership & management	2.47	1.26	1.05	-.10**	-.07*						
(4) Family CEO	.98	.12	1.13	.15**	.03	-.00					
(5) Generation	.12	.33	1.58	-.51**	.08	.12**	.05				
(6) Firm size	4.33	.62	2.74	.41**	-.00	.11**	.22**	-.25**			
(7) International experience	20.83	9.02	3.39	.38**	-.01	.44**	.13**	-.51**	.63**		
(8) Cultural distance	7.12	3.83	1.17	.14**	-.13**	.17**	-.00	-.18**	.03	.18**	
(9) Hotel category	4.24	.74	1.15	.22**	-.11**	.21**	-.03	-.14**	.08**	.21**	.33**

** p<0.05

52 L. Rienda et al.

Table 2.3 Results of linear and logistic regressions

Variables	DOI (N=76)		Entry modes[a] (N=981)	
	Model 1	Model 2	Model 3	Model 4
Control variables				
Firm size	7.92***	7.87***	0.42***	-0.62*
		(0.24)		(0.53)
International experience	0.45***	0.23*	-0.01	0.03*
		(0.13)		(1.04)
Cultural distance			-0.06**	-0.06**
				(0.94)
Hotel category			-0.03	0.05
				(1.00)
Independent variables				
Family ownership and management		9.49***		0.43**
		(0.33)		(1.54)
Family CEO		8.56*		1.62*
		(0.07)		(5.07)
Generation		-22.36***		0.70*
		(-0.43)		(2.03)
Adjusted R^2	0.187	0.508		
F	113.462***	123.270***		
Chi-square			244.407***	125.225***
Pseudo R^2			0.224	0.193

[a](1) High-control entry modes: management and lease agreements, and equity-based entry modes;
(0) Non-control entry modes: franchising.
Standardised coefficients (Model 2) and odds ratio (Model 4) in parentheses.
*** $p<0.001$, ** $p<0.01$, * $p<0.05$.

a significant relationship in the opposite direction. Therefore, a higher family concentration in ownership and management, the presence of family in CEO positions and later generations, positively impacts on the international commitment of family hotels.

If we observe Model 4, the three independent variables are also significant. Family ownership and management are positively related with high-control entry modes. Thus, Hypothesis 2a is confirmed (0.43, $p<0.01$). We calculated the effect size of family ownership and management as the standard deviation of this variable (1.26) multiplied by the odds ratio (1.54). This leads us to conclude that a standard deviation increase in family ownership and management would make the decision of a high-control entry mode 1.94 times more attractive. In the same way Hypothesis 2b is also confirmed (1.62, $p<0.05$). The presence of a family CEO in the firm is positively associated with entry modes in which family could exert more control. We calculated the effect size of family CEO as the standard deviation of this variable (0.12) multiplied by the odds ratio (5.07). Thus, we can state that a standard deviation increase in the family CEO variable would make the decision of a high-control entry mode 0.6 times more attractive. Finally, we proposed that later generations could opt for non-control entry modes because the passing of generations increases the divergence of interests in FFs. This relationship is also confirmed in our model (0.70, p<0.05). We also calculated the effect size for this variable as the standard deviation (0.33) multiplied by the odds ratio (2.03). Thus, we can state that a standard deviation increase in the generation variable would make the decision of a high-control entry mode 0.66 times more attractive.

Finally, we performed several robustness checks to assess the sensitivity of our findings (Lu & White, 2014). First, we excluded the firm with the greatest number of investments. We then repeated the regression analyses and the results were consistent with those reported in Table 2.3. Second, we also excluded investments made in Europe, since this area received the largest number of investments. As in the previous case, omitting this data did not change the results of our initial analysis. Finally, we re-ran the models considering that companies that have less than 50% of capital in the hands of a family are not FFs. The results in this case are similar to those described in Table 2.3.

Discussion

From a family heterogeneity approach, different aspects of family involvement have been studied to find the influence of each one on the internationalisation process of Spanish hotels. More precisely, the degree of family ownership and management, the presence of a family member as CEO and the current generation have been analysed. Following the ideas of the stewardship theory, a higher family involvement is associated with risk-taking strategies facilitating entry to international markets (Chen et al., 2014). The concentration of power in the family, in business ownership and management, is a factor that positively conditions the hotels' DOI. This is also true when a family member is the CEO. Therefore, the stewardship theory is postulated as a good reference to study FFs and their internationalisation process. Nevertheless, a different result is found for the generation of the FFs. Although we proposed that first generations have a higher degree of family involvement and could be related with a higher DOI, our results showed that the later generations are related to a greater DOI (Fernández & Nieto, 2005; Menéndez-Requejo, 2005), considering the foreign market as an alternative way of growth (Graves & Thomas, 2004). The new generations could be more qualified, with a greater knowledge of languages and more cross-cultural training, which facilitate internationalisation (Fernández & Nieto, 2005; Kontinen & Ojala, 2012; Menéndez-Requejo, 2005). These attributes may contribute to greater internationalisation in later generations.

Foreign market entry mode decisions have also been analysed. A higher family ownership and management, and a family CEO, are associated with high-control entry modes in Spanish family hotels. As the stewardship theory sets out, the alignment of interests between family and business promotes future business continuity. Therefore, a higher presence of family in the business leads to greater control (Claver et al., 2009). This is why family hotels prefer high-control entry modes attending to these dimensions of family involvement. Moreover, the effect sizes provided enhance the great effect of family involvement, attending to family ownership and management, in decisions about entry modes for Spanish family hotels. In terms of generation, although new generations have been associated with a higher DOI, new ideas coming from these generations could be linked with non-control entry modes (Pongelli et al., 2016). A great divergence of interest, due to the greater number of family members incorporated in the firm over time, could attenuate the need to control and could affect some international decisions. With these results, we can conclude that Spanish family hotels, with a greater family involvement, tend to internationalise by choosing entry options that allow greater control of activities abroad. Although authors such as Kruesi et al. (2017) show that in recent years hotel firms make more use of non-control foreign entry modes such as franchising, when these firms are FFs this relationship changes. It could be interesting in the future to continue with this research line.

This study addresses a scarcely covered topic: internationalisation of family hotels. It fills a research gap in the tourism management literature by examining the strategy of internationalisation. The contributions of the chapter are twofold. First, from a stewardship theory approach, our results help reinforce the positive perspective of the role of family involvement in firm's strategic decisions. We can conclude that for Spanish family hotels, family involvement matters for international decisions, but with nuances. It is interesting to analyse the different aspects that are included in family involvement to reach a better understanding of the FF-internationalisation relationship (Rienda et al., 2020). In this sense, we have enlarged the studies that consider the stewardship theory as a good approach to FF research.

Second, the study of Spanish family hotels helps to explain how family involvement affects internationalisation and hence contributes to the FF and internationalisation literature, particularly in the hotel industry. The vast majority of internationalisation studies have focused on the manufacturing sector (Kruesi, Hemmington, & Kim, 2018; Pla & Ghauri, 2012). New outcomes and knowledge in the service sector are needed. And combining these new insights with FF research make the study more interesting.

Moreover, this research provides practical implications for managers in the hotel industry. The findings of this study help managers to know how the role of the family affects some strategic decisions. This information should be integrated in the decision-making framework of hotel FFs when they attempt to internationalise their business. In other words, managers need to make strategic decisions, acknowledging that their decisions can be affected by various family factors, such as family ownership and management, the presence of a family CEO and the current generation, in a positive or negative way.

Limitations and Future Research

One limitation of our study is related with the sample. We have focused on Spanish family hotels and a single-country study should not be generalised to FFs in other countries (Arregle et al., 2017). The relationship between FFs and internationalisation may be considered as a multilevel question. Future research could analyse the country effect on international strategy and shed more light on this relationship. In addition, a second limitation arises from the measures of some variables. Secondary data provide us with valid information but primary data, for example with an interview or questionnaire, could provide another way of measuring the variables used as well as alternative explanations to our results. The next step in our study goes in this line in order to continue exploring the heterogeneity of the FFs and their influence on the internationalisation process.

Conclusions

International activities are very important to the Spanish hotel industry, which includes an important number of FFs. We have analysed the effects of different dimensions of family involvement on DOI for family hotels, and the influence of these dimensions on foreign market entry mode decisions. Our results show that family involvement matters in FFs. Greater family ownership and management, the presence of family in CEO positions and later generations are associated with a greater DOI in family hotels. In the same way, greater family ownership and management, and a family CEO are related with high-control entry modes, while later generations are linked with entry modes that require less control.

References

Abdellatif, M., Amann, B., & Jaussaud, J. (2010). Family versus nonfamily business: A comparison of international strategies. *Journal of Family Business Strategy, 1*, 108–116.

Agarwal, S., & Ramaswami, S. N. (1992). Choice of foreign market entry mode: Impact of ownership, location and internalisation factors. *Journal of International Business Studies, 23*(1), 1–27.

Alayo, M., Maseda, A., Iturralde, T., & Arzubiaga, U. (2019). Internationalization and entrepreneurial orientation of family SMEs: The influence of the family character. *International Business Review, 28*, 48–59.

Al-Dubai, S. A. A., Ismail, K. N. I. K., & Amran, N. A. (2014). Family involvement in ownership, management, and firm performance: Moderating and direct-effect models. *Asian Social Science, 10*(14), 193–205.

Anderson, E., & Gatignon, H. (1986). Modes of foreign entry: A transaction cost analysis and propositions. *Journal of International Business Studies, 17*(3), 1–26.

Andreu, R., Claver, E., Quer, D., & Rienda, L. (2018). Family ownership and Spanish hotel chains: an analysis of their expansion through internationalization. *Universia Business Review, 59*, 40–75.

Andreu, R., Claver, E., Quer, D., & Rienda, L. (2019). Family involvement and Spanish hotel chains' entry modes abroad. *Current Issues in Tourism, 23*(11), 1375–1393.

Andreu, R., Quer, D., & Rienda, L. (2020). The influence of family character on the choice of foreign market entry mode: An analysis of Spanish hotel chains. *European Research on Management and Business Economics, 26*, 40–44.

Arregle, J. L., Duran, P., Hitt, M. A., & van Essen, M. (2017). Why is family firms' internationalization unique? A meta-analysis. *Entrepreneurship Theory and Practice, 41*(5), 801–831.

Assaf, A. G., Josiassen, A., & Oh, H. (2016). Internationalization and hotel performance: The missing pieces. *Tourism Economics, 22*(3), 572–592.

Barkema, H. G., & Vermeulen, F. (1998). International expansion through start-up or acquisitions: a learning perspective. *Academy of Management Journal, 41*(1), 7–26.

Baronchelli, G., Bettinelli, C., Del Bosco, B., & Loane, S. (2016). The impact of family involvement on the investments of Italian small-medium enterprises in psychically distant countries. *International Business Review, 25*(4), 960–970.

Bobillo, A. M., Rodríguez-Sanz, J. A., & Tejerina-Gaite, F. (2013). Shareholder activism and internationalization in the family firm. *Journal of Business Economics and Management, 14*(5), 867–885.

Brida, J. G., Driha, O., Ramón-Rodríguez, A. B., & Scuderi, F. (2015). Dynamics of internationalisation of the hotel industry: The case of Spain. *International Journal of Contemporary Hospitality Management, 27*(5), 1024–1047.

Brida, J. G., Ramón-Rodriguez, A. B., Such-Devesa, M. J., & Driha, O. (2016). The inverted-U relationship between the degree of internationalization and the performance: The case of Spanish hotel chains. *Tourism Management Perspectives, 17*, 72–81.

Brouthers, K. D., & Hennart, J.-F. (2007). Boundaries of the firm: Insights from international entry mode research. *Journal of Management, 33*(3), 395–425.

Calabrò, A., Minola, T., Campopiano, G., & Pukall, T. (2016). Turning innovativeness into domestic and international corporate venturing: The moderating effect of high family ownership and influence. *European Journal of International Management, 10*(5), 505–533.

Casillas, J. C., & Acedo, F. J. (2005). Internationalisation of Spanish family SMEs: An analysis of family involvement. *International Journal of Globalisation and Small Business, 1*(2), 134–151.

Chen, H. L., Hsu, W. T., & Chang, C. Y. (2014). Family ownership, institutional ownership, and internationalization of SMEs. *Journal of Small Business Management, 52*(4), 771–789.

Chen, Y.-M., Liu, H.-H., Ni, Y.-T., & Wu, M.-F. (2015). A rational normative model of international expansion: Strategic intent perspective, market positions, and founder CEOs/family-successor CEOs. *Journal of Business Research, 68*(7), 1539–1543.

Chen, Y.-R., Huang, Y.-L., & Chen, C.-N. (2009). Financing constraints, ownership control, and crossborder M&As: Evidence from nine East Asian economies. *Corporate Governance: An International Review, 17*(6), 665–680.

Chrisman, J., Chua, J., Kellermanns, F. W., & Chang, E. P. C. (2007). Are family managers agents or stewards? An exploratory study in privately held family firms. *Journal of Business Research, 60*, 1030–1038.

Chu, W. (2009). The influence of family ownership on SME performance: Evidence from public firms in Taiwan. *Small Business Economics, 33*(3), 353–373.

Chua, J. H., Chrisman, J. J., & Sharma, P. (2003). Succession and nonsuccession concerns of family firms and agency relationship with nonfamily managers. *Family Business Review, 16*(2), 89–108.

Chua, J. H., Chrisman, J. J., Steier, L. P., & Rau, S. B. (2012). Sources of heterogeneity in family firms: An introduction. *Entrepreneurship Theory and Practice, 36*(6), 1103–1113.

Claver, E., Rienda, L., & Quer, D. (2007). The internationalisation process in family firms: Choice of market entry strategies. *Journal of General Management, 33*(1), 1–16.

Claver, E., Rienda, L., & Quer, D. (2008). Factores familiares y compromiso internacional: Evidencia empírica en las empresas españolas. *Cuadernos de Economía y Dirección de la Empresa, 11*, 7–25.

Claver, E., Rienda, L., & Quer, D. (2009). Family firms' international commitment: The influence of family-related factors. *Family Business Review, 22*(2), 125–135.

Contractor, F. J., & Kundu, S. K. (1998). Modal choice in a world of alliances: Analyzing organizational forms in the international hotel sector. *Journal of International Business Studies, 29*(2), 325–356.

Corbetta, G., & Salvato, C. (2004). Self-serving or self-actualizing? Models of man and agency costs in different types of family firms: A commentary on 'comparing the agency costs of family and non-family firms: Conceptual issues and exploratory evidences'. *Entrepreneurship. Theory and Practice, 28*(4), 355–362.

Davis, J. H., Schoorman, F. D., & Donaldson, L. (1997). Toward a stewardship theory of management. *The Academy of Management Review, 22*(1), 20–47.

Davis, J. H., Schoorman, F. D., Mayer, R. C., & Tan, H. H. (2000). The trusted general manager and business unit performance: empirical evidence of a competitive advantage. *Strategic Management Journal, 21*(5), 563–576.

Demirbag, M., Tatoglu, E., & Glaister, K. W. (2008). Factors affecting perceptions of the choice between acquisition and greenfield entry: The case of western FDI in an emerging market. *Management International Review, 48*(1), 5–38.

Dimou, I., Chen, J., & Archer, S. (2003). The choice between management contracts and franchise agreements in the corporate development of international hotel firms. *Journal of Marketing Channels, 10*(3–4), 33–52.

Donaldson, L., & Davis, J. H. (1991). Stewardship theory or agency theory: CEO governance and shareholder returns. *Australian Journal of Management, 16*(1), 49–64.

Eddleston, K. A., & Kellermanns, F. W. (2007). Destructive and productive family relationships: A stewardship theory perspective. *Journal of Business Venturing, 22*(4), 545–565.

Fang, H., Kellermanns, F. W., & Eddleston, K. A. (2019). Empirical modeling in testing for family firm heterogeneity. In E. Memili & C. Dibrell (Eds.), *The palgrave handbook of heterogeneity among family firms* (pp. 69–85). London: Palgrave Macmillan.

Fernández, Z., & Nieto, M. J. (2005). Internationalization strategy of small and medium-sized family businesses: Some influential factors. *Family Business Review, 18*(1), 77–89.

Filatochev, I., Lien, Y. C., & Piesse, J. (2005). Internationalization strategy of small and medium-sized family business: Some influential factors. *Asia Pacific Journal of Management, 22*(3), 257–283.

García de Soto, E., & Vargas, A. (2015). Choice of entry mode, strategic flexibility and performance of international strategy in hotel chains: An approach based on real options. *European Journal of Tourism Research, 9*, 92–114.

García-Castro, R., & Aguilera, R. V. (2014). Family involvement in business and financial performance: A set-theoretic cross-national inquiry. *Journal of Family Business Strategy, 5,* 85–96.

Gatignon, H. A., & Anderson, E. (1988). The multinational corporation's degree of control over foreign subsidiaries: An empirical test of a transaction cost explanation. *Journal of Law, Economics and Organization, 4*(2), 305–336.

Gersick, K. E., Davis, J. A., Hampton, M. M., & Lansberg, I. (1997). *Generation to generation: Life cycles of the family business.* Harvard Business School press.

Gómez-Mejía, L., Haynes, K. T., Núñez-Nickel, M., Jacobson, K. J. L., & Moyano-Fuentes, J. (2007). Socioemotional wealth and business risks in family-controlled firms: Evidence from Spanish olive oil mills. *Administrative Science Quarterly, 52*(1), 106–137.

Gómez-Mejía, L. R., Makri, M., & Larraza, M. (2010). Diversification decisions in family-controlled firms. *Journal of Management Studies, 47*(2), 223–252.

Grant, R. M., Jammine, A. P., & Thomas, H. (1988). Diversity, diversification, and profitability among British manufacturing companies. *Academy of Management Journal, 31,* 771–801.

Graves, C., & Thomas, J. (2004). Internationalisation of the family business: A longitudinal perspective. *International Journal of Globalisation and Small Business, 1*(1), 7–27.

Graves, C., & Thomas, J. (2006). Internationalization of Australian Family Businesses: A Managerial Capabilities Perspective. *Family Business Review, 19*(3), 207–224.

Hauck, J., & Prügl, R. (2015). Innovation activities during intra-family leadership succession in family firms: An empirical study from a socioemotional wealth perspective. *Journal of Family Business Strategy, 6*(2), 104–118.

Hernández, V., Nieto, M. J., & Boellis, A. (2018). The asymmetric effect of institutional distance on international location: Family versus nonfamily firms. *Global Strategy Journal, 8*(1), 22–45.

Jensen, J., & Meckling, W. (1976). Theory of the firm: Managerial behavior, agency costs and capital structure. *Journal of Financial Economics, 3*(4), 305–360.

Kao, M.-S., & Kuo, A. (2017). The effect of uncertainty on FDI entry mode decisions: The influence of family ownership and involvement in the board of directors. *Journal of Family Business Strategy, 8,* 224–236.

Kogut, B., & Singh, H. (1988). The effect of national culture on the choice of entry mode. *Journal of International Business Studies, 19*(3), 411–432.

Kontinen, T., & Ojala, A. (2010). The internationalization of family businesses: A review of extant research. *Journal of Family Business Strategy, 1,* 97–107.

Kontinen, T., & Ojala, A. (2012). Internationalization pathways among family-owned SMEs. *International Marketing Review, 29*(5), 496–518.

Kraus, S., Mensching, H., Calabrò, A., Cheng, C.-F., & Filser, M. (2016). Family firm internationalization: A configurational approach. *Journal of Business Research, 69*(11), 5473–5478.

Kruesi, M., Kim, P. B., & Hemmington, N. (2017). Evaluating foreign market entry mode theories from a hotel industry perspective. *International Journal of Hospitality Management, 62,* 88–100.

Kruesi, M. A., Hemmington, N. R., & Kim, P. B. (2018). What matters for hotel executives? An examination of major theories in non-equity entry mode research. *International Journal of Hospitality Management, 70,* 25–36.

Kutner, M. H., Nachtsheim, C. J., Neter, J., & Li, W. (2005). *Applied linear statistical models.* London: McGraw-Hill/ Irwin.

Le Breton-Miller, I., & Miller, D. (2009). Agency vs. stewardship in public firms: A social embeddedness reconciliation. *Entrepreneurship Theory and Practice, 33*(6), 1169–1191.

Lee, S., Upneja, A., Özdemir, Ö., & Sun, K.-A. (2014). A synergy effect of internationalization and firm size on performance. US hotel industry. *International Journal of Contemporary Hospitality Management, 26*(1), 35–49.

León-Darder, F., Villar-García, C., & Plá-Barber, J. (2011). Entry mode choice in the internationalisation of the hotel industry: A holistic approach. *The Service Industries Journal, 31*(1), 107–122.

Lu, J. W., & Beamish, P. W. (2004). International Diversification and Firm Performance: The S-curve Hypothesis. *Academy of Management Journal, 47*(4), 598–609.

Lu, Z., & White, H. (2014). Robustness checks and robustness tests in applied economics. *Journal of Econometrics, 178*(1), 194–206.

Mazzi, C. (2011). Family business and financial performance: Current state of knowledge and future research challenges. *Journal of Family Business Strategy, 2*(3), 166–181.

Menéndez-Requejo, R. (2005). Growth and internationalisation of family businesses. *International Journal of Globalisation and Small Business, 1*(2), 122–133.

Miller, D., Le Breton-Miller, I., & Scholnick, B. (2008). Stewardship vs. stagnation: An empirical comparison of small family and nonfamily businesses. *Journal of Management Studies, 45,* 51–78.

Miller, D., & Le Breton-Miller, I. (2006). Family governance and firm performance: Agency, stewardship and capabilities. *Family Business Review, 19*(1), 73–87.

Miller, D., Le Breton-Miller, I., Lester, R. H., & Cannella, A. A. (2007). Are family firms really superior performers? *Journal of Corporate Finance, 13*(5), 829–858.

Mitter, C., Duller, C., Feldbauer-Durstmüller, B., & Kraus, S. (2014). Internationalization of family firms: The effect of ownership and governance. *Review of Managerial Science, 8*(1), 1–28.

Muth, M., & Donaldson, L. (1998). Stewardship theory and board structure: A contingency approach. *Corporate Governance: An International Review, 6*(1), 5–28.

Niñerola, A., Campa, F., Hernández, A. B., & Sánchez, M. V. (2016). The experience of Meliá Hotels International in China: A case of internationalisation of a Spanish hotel group. *European Journal of Tourism Research, 12,* 191–196.

Okoroafo, S. C. (1999). Internationalization of family businesses: Evidence from Northwest Ohio, USA. *Family Business Review, 12*(2), 147–158.

Pearson, A. W., Carr, J. C., & Shaw, J. C. (2008). Toward a theory of familiness: A social capital perspective. *Entrepreneurship Theory and Practice, 32*(6), 949–969.

Peng, M. W., & Jiang, Y. (2010). Institutions behind family ownership and control in large firms. *Journal of Management Studies, 47*(2), 253–273.

Pla, J., & Ghauri, P. N. (2012). Internationalization of service industry firms: Understanding distinctive characteristics. *Service Industries Journal, 32*(7), 1007–1010.

Plá-Barber, J., León-Darder, F., & Villar, C. (2011). The internationalization of soft-services: Entry modes and main determinants in the Spanish hotel industry. *Service Business, 5*(2), 139–154.

Plá-Barber, J., Sánchez-Peinado, E., & Madhok, A. (2010). Investment and control decisions in foreign markets: Evidence from service industries. *British Journal of Management, 21*(3), 736–753.

Pongelli, C., Carolli, M. G., & Cucculelli, M. (2016). Family business going abroad: the effect of family ownership on foreign market entry mode decisions. *Small Business Economics, 47*(3), 787–801.

Pukall, T. J., & Calabrò, A. (2014). The internationalization of family firms: A critical review and integrative model. *Family Business Review, 27*(2), 103–125.

Ramón, A. (2002). Determining factors in entry choice for international expansion. The case of the Spanish hotel industry. *Tourism Management, 23*(6), 597–607.

Ramón-Llorens, M. C., García-Meca, E., & Duréndez, A. (2017). Influence of CEO characteristics in family firms internationalization. *International Business Review, 26*(4), 786–799.

Ray, S., Mondal, A., & Ramachandran, K. (2018). How does family involvement affect a firm's internationalization? An investigation of Indian family firms. *Global Strategy Journal, 8*(1), 73–105.

Rienda, L., Claver, E., & Andreu, R. (2020). Family involvement, internationalisation and performance: An empirical study of the Spanish hotel industry. *Journal of Hospitality and Tourism Management, 42*, 173–180.

Schulze, W. S., Lubatkin, M. H., & Dino, R. N. (2003). Exploring the agency consequences of ownership dispersion among the directors of private family firms. *Academy of Management Journal, 46*(2), 179–194.

Sciascia, S., Mazzola, P., Astrachan, J. H., & Pieper, T. M. (2012). The role of family ownership in international entrepreneurship: Exploring nonlinear effects. *Small Business Economics, 38*(1), 15–31.

Segaro, E. (2012). Internationalization of family SMEs: the impact of ownership, governance, and top management team. *Journal of Management & Governance, 16*, 147–169.

Sharma, P. (2004). An overview of the field of family business studies: Current status and directions for the future. *Family Business Review, 17*(1), 1–36.

Spanish Family Firm Institute. (2018). *Factores de Competitividad y Análisis Financiero en la Empresa Familiar*. Barcelona, Spain: Family Firm Institute.

Strike, V. M., Berrone, P., Sapp, S. G., & Congiu, L. (2015). A socioemotional wealth approach to CEO career horizons in family firms. *Journal of Management Studies, 52*(4), 555–583.

Tallman, S., & Li, J. (1996). Effects of international diversity and product diversity on the performance of multinational firms. *Academy of Management Journal, 39*(1), 179–196.

Vallejo, M. C. (2009). The effects of commitment of non-family employees of family firms from the perspective of stewardship theory. *Journal of Business Ethics, 87*, 379–390.

Westhead, P., & Howorth, C. (2006). Ownership and management issues associated with family firm performance and company objectives. *Family Business Review, 19*, 301–319.

Williamson, O. E. (1995). *The mechanisms of governance*. Oxford: Oxford University Press.

Zahra, S. A. (2003). International expansion of U.S. manufacturing family businesses: The effect of ownership and involvement. *Journal of Business Venturing, 18*, 495–512.

Zahra, S. A. (2005). Entrepreneurial risk taking in family firms. *Family Business Review, 18*(1), 23–40.

3

Socioemotional Wealth and Networking in the Internationalisation of Family SMEs

Jaakko Metsola, Lasse Torkkeli, Tanja Leppäaho, Pia Arenius, and Mika Haapanen

Introduction

Family firms constitute the most dominant firm type in the world (European Commission, 2019a; Schulze, Lubatkin, & Dino, 2002; Shanker & Astrachan, 1996). These firms, in which family members control ownership and managerial positions (e.g. Arregle, Naldi, Nordqvist, & Hitt, 2012), differ from non-family firms in their tendency to preserve socioemotional wealth (SEW). SEW refers to 'non-financial aspects of the firm that meet the family's affective needs, such as identity, the ability to exercise family influence, and the perpetuation of the family dynasty' (Gómez-Mejía, Haynes, Núñez-Nickel, Jacobson, & Moyano-Fuentes, 2007, p. 106). In family firms, decision-making aimed at increasing and preserving affective endowments may even take priority over rational economic decision-making (e.g. Gomez-Mejia, Cruz, Berrone, & De Castro, 2011). SEW preservation might make family

---

J. Metsola (✉) • L. Torkkeli • T. Leppäaho
LUT University, Lappeenranta, Finland
e-mail: jaakko.metsola@lut.fi

P. Arenius
RMIT University, Melbourne, VIC, Australia

M. Haapanen
University of Jyväskylä, Jyväskylä, Finland

© The Author(s), under exclusive license to Springer Nature Switzerland AG 2021
T. Leppäaho, S. Jack (eds.), *The Palgrave Handbook of Family Firm Internationalization*,
https://doi.org/10.1007/978-3-030-66737-5_3

firms bifurcation-biased, that is, preferring affect-based and dysfunctional family assets over economising and functional nonfamily assets, leading to inefficient decision-making, at least in the short or the medium term (Kano & Verbeke, 2018).

However, we know very little about the role of SEW in family firms' decision-making and strategies, due to the lack of SEW measurement in family-firm research (Miller & Le Breton-Miller, 2014), despite the availability of alternative SEW measurement scales (e.g. Berrone, Cruz, & Gomez-Mejia, 2012; Debicki, Kellermanns, Chrisman, Pearson, & Spencer, 2016; Hauck, Suess-Reyes, Beck, Prügl, & Frank, 2016). The lack of measurement also concerns the internationalisation of family firms, which, as a research theme per se, has attracted an increasing number of studies over the past two decades (Arregle, Duran, Hitt, & van Essen, 2017). Although SEW is increasingly included in some empirical analyses, primarily yielding findings on its restraining effect on internationalisation propensity and intensity (e.g. Alessandri, Cerrato, & Eddleston, 2018), it mostly appears as a higher-order theoretical perspective or becomes operationalised through proxies of family control, without any deeper measurement capturing its various dimensions.

In this study, we provide new empirical insights into the relationship of SEW and family-firm internationalisation, considering two key issues concerning SEW. First, in terms of measurement, this study applies the FIBER scale by Berrone et al. (2012) to analysing the association of SEW with the successful international expansion of family firms. Both of the FIBER-related scales that Debicki et al. (2016) and Hauck et al. (2016) developed consist of three SEW dimensions, although they differ in emphasis. Debicki et al.'s SEWi scale focuses on the affective importance of SEW, and Hauck et al.'s REI-scale focuses on the core affective endowments of SEW. Given also that these scales are based on family firms operating from large economies, namely the United States (Debicki et al., 2016) and Germany (Hauck et al., 2016), conducting our own factor analysis seemed useful. Based on the FIBER scale and derived from data from the smaller and more internationalisation-dependent economy of Finland, our factor analysis aimed to not only clarify or extend existing scales but also to apply SEW more directly to the context of internationalisation.

Second, we emphasise the relational role of SEW in family firms and in internationalisation. SEW relates to maintaining social relationships and family benefit among the family members inside family firms (Berrone et al., 2012; Zellweger, Chrisman, Chua, & Steier, 2019). The prominent role of SEW *inside* family firms suggests that it is important, yet challenging, to engage in *external* and *international* networking to promote internationalisation. The essentiality of networking particularly concerns family-owned small- and medium-sized enterprises (family SMEs), since SMEs tend to heavily depend on networks that compensate for limited resources and, thus, enable successful internationalisation (e.g. Eberhard & Craig, 2013; Torkkeli, Saarenketo, & Nummela, 2015; Zain & Ng, 2006). Smaller family firms are also more likely than larger family firms to use SEW as a primary reference point in decision-making (Gomez-Mejia et al., 2011). Therefore, studying whether family SMEs can 'cut loose', at least partially, from internal intrafamily social bonding stemming from SEW preservation, and engage in external interfirm networking needed for internationalisation, is relevant.

Thus, we conducted a multiple regression analysis to study whether SEW and family SMEs networking are related to the degree of internationalisation (DOI). The analysis utilises observations from 47 Finnish family SMEs (used in SEW-related factor analysis), together with a reference group of 42 Finnish nonfamily SMEs. The results partially confirmed our hypotheses. Of the four new SEW constructs derived from the factor analysis, emotional decision-making has a statistically significant strong negative relationship with the DOI of family SMEs. On the other hand, the results for the effects of the other three SEW constructs (family-heritage maintenance, family-controlled decision-making, familial relationship-building) were not statistically significant. Networking has a statistically significant strong positive relationship with the DOI of family SMEs. Moderation effects were not statistically significant.

In sum, the results of this study indicate that if family SMEs focus on networking and avoid the tendency to make decisions emotionally, they can reach higher degrees of internationalisation. The study and these results contribute both methodologically and conceptually to the research on family-firm internationalisation. First, the four reconstructed SEW dimensions provide elaborate validation of Gómez-Mejía et al.'s (2007), Debicki et al.'s (2016), and Kano, Ciravegna, and Rattalino's (2020) conceptualisations of SEW, as well as an extension of Hauck et al.'s (2016) FIBER-based scale, by underscoring SEW's role in the ways that family firms make decisions in the long run, using affective and relational needs and preferences. Second, we pinpoint emotional decision-making as a key restrictive SEW factor in the internationalisation of family SMEs. Third, we emphasise the role of networking as a key economic and functional 'counterforce' to noneconomically perceived and often dysfunctional emotional decision-making inherent in family SMEs. Thus, we contribute to understanding the role of bifurcation bias in family firms and their internationalisation (Kano et al., 2020; Kano & Verbeke, 2018).

Socioemotional Wealth and Networking in Family Firm Internationalisation

Socioemotional wealth (SEW) that builds on the triad of family, business and ownership (see Gersick, Davis, Hampton, & Lansberg, 1997) has emerged to explain the uniqueness of family firms in the years since the appearance of the first article to explicitly discuss it, by Gómez-Mejía et al. (2007). The concept of SEW consists of understanding such noneconomic rewards or affective endowments as emotional attachment and family-member involvement, which family members in the organisation seek to preserve and draw from the family business (Gomez-Mejia et al., 2011; Gómez-Mejía et al., 2007). Based on the behavioural agency model (BAM) (Wiseman & Gomez-Mejia, 1998), SEW is an important 'affective wealth-at-risk' (Gomez-Mejia et al., 2014, p. 1354), the loss of which is avoided even at the risk and expense of financial decisions and wealth (Debicki et al., 2016; Gómez-Mejía et al., 2007). Berrone et al. (2012) suggest five central SEW dimensions that encapsulate the important SEW assemblage that family firms may want to preserve: family control and influence, family members' identification with the firm, binding social ties, emotional attachment and renewal of family bonds with the firm through dynastic succession. Thus, SEW broadly covers the family dynamics in the management, ownership and decision-making of family firms.

Gomez-Mejia et al. (2011) argue that 'socioemotional wealth is the defining feature of a family business [...] central, enduring, and unique to the dominant family owner, influencing everything the firm does' (p. 692). The fear of losing SEW might lead to decision-making guided by noneconomic and affect-based factors, rather than more rational economic factors, for instance, manifesting as contractual arrangements benefitting family, reluctance to join cooperatives or avoidance of diversification (Cruz, Gómez-Mejia, & Becerra, 2010; Gómez-Mejía et al., 2007; Gomez-Mejia, Makri, & Kintana, 2010). The family firm is regarded as an extension of family (including non-family employees), and the members of the organisation feel a strong identification with the business, care for the reputation of the firm and commit to and benefit extended-family members through reciprocal relationships (Berrone, Cruz, Gomez-Mejia, & Larraza-Kintana, 2010; Miller & Le Breton-Miller, 2005; Miller, Lee, Chang, & Le Breton-Miller, 2009).

SEW preservation, bringing members of a family firm closer in order to pursue collective efforts to maintain noneconomic aspects of the business, has a largely negative image, though in some contexts its image is a positive one in relation to internationalisation. The 'mixed gamble', that is, the trade-offs between potential SEW gains and losses that figure in making strategic (economic) decisions (Gomez-Mejia et al., 2014; Martin, Gomez-Mejia, & Wiseman, 2013), may result in family firms staying in domestic or nearby markets and not expanding to distant markets that are riskier for the preservation of SEW (Alessandri et al., 2018). The notion of the mixed gamble means that family firms might take the 'gamble' if they deem some strategic and entrepreneurial decisions helpful in accumulating assets for the SEW endowment (Gomez-Mejia, Patel, & Zellweger, 2018); however, the risks of internationalisation might be too great a trade-off to discover. As De Massis, Frattini, Majocchi, and Piscitello (2018) point out, the many aspects of heterogeneity among family firms, such as behavioural propensities and strategic drivers, include weighing family benefits against internationalisation benefits and ultimately preventing family from committing to economically driven internationalisation if it will not benefit family and noneconomic aspects of the business. This could be a generational question; younger generations are less oriented towards preserving SEW and more oriented towards capitalising on internationalisation than older generations (Fang, Kotlar, Memili, Chrisman, & De Massis, 2018).

One possible reason that SEW preservation may act as a significant deterrent to the internationalisation of family firms is the required formation of external business relationships. With increased access to information and enhanced logistics (Coviello, Kano, & Liesch, 2017; Van Alstyne & Brynjolfsson, 2005), the modern, digitalised global business environment has pushed firms to be proactive, entrepreneurial and networked, to capitalise on opportunities and competitive advantages in business exchanges (Vahlne & Johanson, 2017). SEW dimensions strongly relate to intrafamily social relationships (Zellweger et al., 2019), manifesting in maintenance of family control, emotional attachment, binding social ties, identification and generational continuity (Berrone et al., 2012). 'Exposure' to external relationships might appear to threaten family legacy, goals, decision-making and harmony.

The role of SEW in managerial decision-making decreases as the family-firm size increases (Gomez-Mejia et al., 2011). Thus, the threat of losing SEW might pose a big concern, particularly for SME-sized family firms. Their relatively small size might reinforce the effects of various SEW dimensions, for example, identification with the firm and emotional attachment, in a close community of family-member owners and managers, possibly making them risk-averse to entering the outside world and seeking growth opportunities in international markets. Yet, SMEs engaging in networking to complement their limited resources and internationalise profitably seems particularly important (Buciuni & Mola, 2014). In family SMEs, SEW preservation within the close family and distrust of outsiders negatively influence the formation of international network relationships and the development of resources for shifting from an exporting and domestic focus to joint ventures and more distant markets (Scholes, Mustafa, & Chen, 2016). Family SMEs engage in less interorganisational networking for internationalisation (Eberhard & Craig, 2013). Once they form international network relationships, they may stick with just a few and miss out on profitable opportunities outside that immediate network (Kontinen & Ojala, 2012). Thus, SEW preservation might restrain not only internationalisation propensity but also internationalisation intensity, stagnating the internationalisation process through limited networks.

However, SEW preservation can also encourage family SMEs to go international. Family-firm members might see internationalisation as a survival strategy that is then persistently executed with strong inherent stewardship and a long-term orientation (Kraus, Mensching, Calabro, Cheng, & Filser, 2016; Muñoz-Bullón & Sánchez-Bueno, 2012; Zahra, 2003). From this perspective, family SMEs are not necessarily inward-looking and distrustful of outsiders but, rather, able to extend their strong internal social capital externally to international customers and partner relationships (Cesinger et al., 2016; Graves & Shan, 2014; Tasavori, Zaefarian, & Eng, 2018). Banalieva and Eddleston (2011) argue that family management is beneficial regionally and nonfamily management is beneficial globally. Family-managed firms can more easily leverage and maintain their inherent social capital, long-term orientation and reputation interorganisationally, in nearby locations. Hennart, Majocchi, and Forlani (2019) specifically point to family members' strong identification and emotional attachment to the family SME, showing powerful determination and desire to develop their products and services in the long run for external stakeholders also. They find that family SMEs may have competitive advantages in producing and marketing high-quality products in global niches, where foreign customers and partners require reliable and close relationships and communication with suppliers. If these foreign customers and partners are themselves family firms that possess similar values, mutual trust and long-term orientation, relationships may have even more potential to thrive (Fernández & Nieto, 2005; Gallo & Pont, 1996; Mitter & Emprechtinger, 2016; Swinth & Vinton, 1993). Leppäaho and Metsola (2020) found two types of international networking among family SMEs, which align with the notions above: (i) narrow network maximisers that mostly rely on network relationships that are few, but strong, and relational embeddedness to drive long-term and sustainable internationalisation regionally or globally; and (ii) broad network enablers that have a more extensive network of relationships of varying strengths globally, enabling widespread growth, mostly in global niches, while maintaining community-level social capital among the network partners. In both networking strategies, family-firm-specific attributes and choices, such as social capital, long-term orientation and choosing similar family firms as foreign partners, are conducive to promoting successful internationalisation with either a narrow or broad scope.

Thus, research indicates that the distinctive organisational culture, SEW preservation and distrust of outsiders, discourages family firms from engaging in relationships with external and nonfamily organisations (Dyer, 1988; Eberhard & Craig, 2013; Roessl, 2005). Nonetheless, family-SME idiosyncrasies and SEW preservation are not automatically negative noneconomic hindrances to internationalisation but can indicate a passion for running an economically sound business and developing superior products and relationships with foreign customers and partners. SEW preservation poses both a challenge and an opportunity for family-SME internationalisation. Specifically, each SEW dimension might encompass two sides of the same coin. For instance, identification, emotional attachment and binding social ties might restrain the formation of external networks and broadening of those networks without too strong a shackle on existing ones. However, these dimensions might also create social capital, both within the family firm and externally, which then creates trustworthy and long-term partner and customer relationships in foreign markets. High levels of family control and renewal of family bonds might restrain acquiring competent nonfamily managers with internationalisation knowledge and contacts, but these dimensions might also enable agility for internationalisation decision-making and effective transfer of accumulated knowledge through generations, for a persistent, long-term and sustainable internationalisation process.

Indeed, Kano et al. (2020) suggest that SEW-related family assets can be transformed into firm-specific advantages (FSAs), namely social capital, long-term orientation and reputation. However, that essentially requires openness to nonfamily and external involvement in management, ownership and network relationships. Building the optimal structure for the organisation to implement a successful internationalisation process, with a view to leveraging internal family-specific factors on the one hand and 'external exposure' on the other, challenges family firms. Several studies point to the benefits of diversity and heterogeneity in the management and board of family firms (e.g. D'Angelo, Majocchi, & Buck, 2016; Kraus et al., 2016), but such firms have a tendency to operate under family control over generations (e.g. Pongelli, Caroli, & Cucculelli, 2016; Ray, Mondal, & Ramachandran, 2018).

This tendency of family-firm owners and managers to treat family assets and nonfamily assets differently, regardless of their actual contribution to value creation within particular bounds of rationality and reliability, is 'bifurcation bias' (Verbeke & Kano, 2012). Kano and Verbeke (2018) argue that bifurcation bias can inhibit the decision-making and goal orientations of family firms during their internationalisation processes and international operations in the short or medium run, but more efficient economising practices and routines can replace them in the long run. In practice, this can happen by appointing managers for their cross-border operational merits, providing international education to family members, and making internationalisation-related decision-making and performance-measurement processes more structured, rigorous and transparent. However, given that bifurcation bias is 'the de facto preferential treatment of assets that hold a special emotional meaning for the family' (Kano et al., 2020, p. 2), family firms might have difficulty altering decision-making by resorting less to family-priorities and including less emotional, nonfamily considerations.

Overall, the family-firm-internationalisation research has mostly considered factors specific to family firms as negative factors for internationalisation (e.g. Fernandez & Nieto, 2006; Monreal-Pérez & Sánchez-Marín, 2017), although other studies perceive some benefits for internationalisation resulting from factors specific to family firms (e.g. Muñoz-Bullón & Sánchez-Bueno, 2012; Zahra, 2003). One possible reason for not reaching a widespread consensus in this regard might be that the models describing family-firm internationalisation often do not include SEW or its dimensions as independent variables. SEW captures the distinctive essence of family firms and their strategic decision-making, especially in family SMEs. By balancing the positive and negative sides of SEW based on the existing literature discussed above, we hypothesise that its effect is inversely related to the degree of internationalisation.

H1
The higher the priority on SEW in family SMEs is, the less is their degree of internationalisation.

As the international expansion of SMEs depends heavily on their networks (Eberhard & Craig, 2013; Musteen, Datta, & Butts, 2014; Zain & Ng, 2006) and capabilities for developing networks with other individuals and firms (Mort & Weerawardena, 2006; Torkkeli et al., 2015; Zhou, Wu, & Luo,

2007), we would expect a similar tendency in family SMEs. Internationalisation depends largely on the ability to avoid 'liability of outsidership', through involvement in and learning from network relationships (Johanson & Vahlne, 2009) that provide new and complementary resources, capabilities and knowledge that facilitate and speed up foreign-market entries and expansions (Agndal, Chetty, & Wilson, 2008; Arenius, 2005; Chetty & Holm, 2000; Yli-Renko, Autio, & Tontti, 2002). Chetty and Holm (2000) define a network as 'a set of two or more connected business relationships, in which each exchange relation is between business firms that are conceptualized as collective actors' (p. 79). Thus, networks or network relationships, ranging from buyer to supplier relationships, are strategic environments in which SMEs can cooperate, gain benefits and even develop competitive advantages for internationalisation (Coviello & Munro, 1995). The existence of networks per se may not yield benefits and profitable internationalisation, but the activity and extent to which SMEs use these networks, receive support from them and collaborate through them (i.e. engage in *networking* activities) are important for internationalisation (Dimitratos, Amorós, Etchebarne, & Felzensztein, 2014; Johanson & Mattsson, 1988).

Obviously, family SMEs are no exception, and networking benefits can apply to them as they do to nonfamily SMEs. For instance, family SMEs can obtain crucial knowledge for internationalisation by intense collaboration with and trust in network partners (Cesinger et al., 2016). Making intense networking activity even more important for family SMEs is the simultaneous preservation of SEW, as the closer and longer relationship-building process with these partners supports family SMEs' accumulating international market knowledge and trust in the improbability that these partners will jeopardise SEW (Cesinger et al., 2016). Kraus et al. (2016) suggest that the higher the level of SEW endowment, the greater the need for external involvement in management and ownership, as well as the family firm's involvement in international networks, to achieve successful internationalisation. These economising and functional activities can then mitigate bifurcation bias and equip family SMEs with the necessary resources and capabilities that serve internationalisation operations in the long run (Kano et al., 2020).

However, as discussed earlier, SEW can also negatively affect the development of international network relationships in family SMEs (Scholes et al., 2016). Strong desire to maintain intrafamily social relationships, family harmony and decision-making under family control could result in a desire to preserve SEW (Berrone et al., 2012; Zellweger et al., 2019), to which engagements in external relationships pose a considerable threat. Thus, following the network view of internationalisation that Johanson and Vahlne (2009) present could raise the question of whether family firms nurture 'insidership' excessively within the close circle around the family, rather than promote it for opportunities outside the close family. The tendency to preserve SEW might be one of the reasons behind family SMEs' reluctance to engage in interorganisational networking in the first place (Eberhard & Craig, 2013) and expand networks as the internationalisation process progresses (Kontinen & Ojala, 2012). However, besides the studies by Cesinger et al. (2016) and Scholes et al. (2016), no studies explicitly consider SEW as an antecedent, moderator or outcome of international networking within family SMEs.

Thus, we posit that to the extent a family SME does engage in networking, those networks can help offset the negative impact of SEW on international expansion hypothesised in H1 above. However, based on the prominent role of SEW as a relational construct, we also expect it to negatively moderate the effect of networking on the internationalisation of family SMEs. Therefore, we hypothesise:

H2
The more that family SMEs engage in networking, the higher is their DOI.

H3
In family SMEs, SEW negatively moderates the relationship between networking and DOI.

Data and Methods

Data Collection and Sample Selection

The data used to test the hypotheses were collected from Finnish family and nonfamily SMEs that had been identified in 2012 in a similar internationalisation-related data collection but without SEW-related questions. At that time, we identified 4343 exporting SMEs (using a Finnish credit-information organisation, Asiakastieto Ltd, and Finnish Customs), of whom 734 (17%) responded to our survey. Respondents were deliberately chosen senior managers (in most cases, CEOs), the most informed about the firm strategy and, thus, in the best position to respond knowledgeably. Following the European Commission (2019b), we defined SMEs as firms that employ less than 250 employees and whose turnover is under 50 million euro. In 2017, we contacted all these respondents and additional firms again for a survey that included similar internationalisation-related questions but also SEW-related questions. Requests were sent to 908 SMEs by email. An additional 830 respondents were contacted by phone, of whom 384 promised to answer the survey. Eventually, after sending reminders to those who had promised to take part but did not respond in time, we received 187 survey responses. As a result, the response rate in relation to the e-mail requests sent was 20%. Most of the respondents answered the questionnaire in full and included both family and nonfamily SMEs.

The survey questions focused on family ownership, networking, SEW and the internationalisation and international activities of the firms. In addition to more general family-specific questions (e.g. the presence of family members in management and different generations), we aimed to obtain information about SEW dimensions by using the questionnaire that Berrone et al. (2012) suggested. When studying SEW, one should distinguish between family-controlled and family-influenced firms. Family-controlled firms—in which family members own at least 50% of the shares and constitute a presence in management and governance (e.g. Arregle et al., 2012)—may have stronger SEW-preservation tendencies than firms that are merely family-influenced, with less control and decision-making power in family-member hands (Arregle et al., 2012; Berrone et al., 2012; Gómez-Mejía et al., 2007; Zellweger, Kellermanns, Chrisman, & Chua, 2012). The degree of family control per se has been used as a proxy for SEW (Kotlar, Signori, De Massis, & Vismara, 2018; Zellweger et al., 2012). Therefore, we selected from the sample only family-controlled SMEs meeting the definition above. We also selected non-family SMEs (0% family ownership) to act as a reference group for selected family SMEs.

Furthermore, we noticed that despite the initial identification of exporters, some firms in the sample had importing or wholesale business as a main source of revenue. Since we examined external and international networking, we wanted exporters that had personally manufactured products for sale abroad and would require a search for partners and customers 'from scratch'. Eventually, after selecting family-controlled and nonfamily SMEs by product manufactured and removing those with missing values for key variables and clear outliers, the final sample comprised 89 firms, of which 47 were family SMEs and 42 were nonfamily SMEs.

Dependent Variables

To capture the degree of internationalisation (hereafter DOI), we used the ratio of foreign sales to total sales (cf. Arregle et al., 2012; Fernhaber & McDougall-Covin, 2009; Gomez-Mejia et al., 2010; Zahra, Ireland, & Hitt, 2000). The SME-internationalisation literature broadly uses this ratio as an indicator of DOI (e.g. Graves & Shan, 2014; Lu & Beamish, 2001). The DOI data is based on the 2017 survey.

Independent Variables

We adopted measures for the central constructs from the literature. We included in the questionnaire the list of survey items (27 questions/claims) that Berrone et al. (2012) suggest to capture each five SEW dimensions in the FIBER scale (i.e. *Family control and influence, family members' Identification with the firm, Binding social ties, Emotional attachment and Renewal of family bonds to the firm through dynastic succession*). For each item, we used a seven-point Likert scale ranging from 'strongly disagree' to 'strongly agree'. In the context of internationalisation, the FIBER scale (Berrone et al., 2012) has seldom been used (e.g. Kraus et al., 2016). Furthermore, the five SEW dimensions overlap to some extent (e.g. family control and renewal of family bonds through dynastic succession, identification and emotional attachment), which encourages reassessing and identifying potential new constructs that contain items from different SEW dimensions.

One such option could have been relating the REI scale by Hauck et al. (2016) to the FIBER scale. It encompasses three dimensions of the FIBER scale (i.e. renewal of family bonds through dynastic succession, emotional attachment of family members and identification of family members with the firm) with a focus on nine key affective items of these dimensions. Thus, the REI scale encapsulates the affective endowments of SEW very narrowly, and we deemed it a possible alternative reconstruction of the FIBER scale. Another option for measuring SEW through different dimensions would have been using the SEWi scale that Debicki et al. (2016) suggest. They developed their scale with a focus on *importance* rather than on the *level* of SEW in family firms (cf. Berrone et al., 2012). We wanted to use the scale by Berrone et al. (2012), the most often referenced conceptualisation of SEW through different dimensions, despite the fact that it lacks empirical evidence as a measured variable in the extant research. Moreover, two of the three dimensions by Debicki et al. (2016), *family continuity* and *family prominence* (the third is

3 Socioemotional Wealth and Networking in the Internationalisation... 75

family enrichment), overlap with some dimensions of the FIBER scale. Contextually, a new assessment of the FIBER scale using family SMEs from Finland, a smaller economy than Germany's (used for the REI scale by Hauck et al., 2016) and that of the United States (used for the SEWi scale by Debicki et al., 2016), could provide interesting comparative SEW dimensions. Firms from a small and open economy like Finland's also must internationalise more, as the domestic markets may not provide enough demand for the firm to compete and survive (Bell, 1995; Torkkeli, Kuivalainen, Saarenketo, & Puumalainen, 2016). Obtaining views on SEW from family owners and managers of Finnish family SMEs could facilitate identifying associations of SEW with internationalisation.

We conducted a principal component analysis (PCA) to further explore and extract the latent constituents of SEW. As a result of the analysis, four SEW-related factors (average summated scales) emerged, with the latent root criterion and eigenvalue more than 1 (advised for use with 20–50 measures) specified in Table 3.1. The first, called 'family-heritage maintenance', consists of six measures that primarily indicate the tendency of family firms to preserve and maintain family business and related heritage. Accordingly, most measures loaded to it came from the SEW dimension of renewal of family bonds through dynastic succession, but it also involved items from family control and identification (Berrone et al., 2012). Despite different original associations, they could be linked together, for example, in terms of long-term orientation and pride and value in having family in the business. Hence, we decided to include all of them under the label of 'family-heritage maintenance' as one construct. Using Debicki et al.'s (2016) categorisation, family-heritage maintenance reflected both family prominence and family continuity.

The second factor was named 'family-controlled decision-making' because it consisted of five measures indicating the role of family in management and governance as well as family-member influence in strategic and investment decisions. The third factor was named 'emotional decision-making' and comprised four measures revolving around decision-making, as in the second factor, but emphasising the role of emotions. While these four measures belonged to the SEW dimension labelled 'emotional attachment' by Berrone et al. (2012), the two more general items about warmth between family members and self-concept were excluded (cf. Hauck et al.'s, 2016 E-dimension with these excluded items, labelled the same as the original dimension in Berrone et al.'s, 2012 scale). Thus, labelling the factor as 'emotional attachment', as in the original dimension, would not have clarified it to the extent that refining it to encompass 'emotional decision-making' did, based on the new assemblage of items. The warmth and self-concept items, together with items on

76   J. Metsola et al.

Table 3.1 The results of the PCA for the SEW-related factors

Measure[a]	Family-heritage maintenance	Family-controlled decision-making	Familial relationship-building	Emotional decision-making	Communality
Preservation of family control and independence are important goals for my family business (family control).	0.72				0.68
Being a member of the family business helps define who we are (identification).	0.63				0.63
Family members are proud to tell others that we are part of the family business (identification).	0.52				0.66
Continuing the family legacy and tradition is an important goal for my family business (renewal of family bonds through dynastic succession).	0.82				0.79
Family members would be unlikely to consider selling the family business (renewal of family bonds through dynastic succession).	0.91				0.74

(*continued*)

3 Socioemotional Wealth and Networking in the Internationalisation... 77

Table 3.1 (continued)

Measure[a]	Family-heritage maintenance	Family-controlled decision-making	Familial relationship-building	Emotional decision-making	Communality
Successful business transfer to the next generation is an important goal for family members (renewal of family bonds through dynastic succession).	0.80				0.77
In my family business, family members exert control over the company's strategic decisions (family control).		0.76			0.58
In my family business, most executive positions are occupied by family members (family control).		0.54			0.69
In my family business, nonfamily managers and directors are named by family members (family control).		0.85			0.71
The board of directors is mainly composed of family members (family control).		0.69			0.70

(*continued*)

Table 3.1 (continued)

Measure[a]	Family-heritage maintenance	Family-controlled decision-making	Familial relationship-building	Emotional decision-making	Communality
Family owners are less likely to evaluate their investment on a short-term basis (renewal of family bonds through dynastic succession)	0.66				0.69
In my family business, nonfamily employees are treated as part of the family (binding social ties).			0.53		0.88
Building strong relationships with other institutions (i.e. other companies, professional associations, government agents, etc.) is important for my family business (binding social ties).			0.67		0.84
Strong emotional ties among family members help us maintain a positive self-concept (emotional attachment).			0.71		0.80

(*continued*)

3 Socioemotional Wealth and Networking in the Internationalisation... 79

Table 3.1 (continued)

Measure[a]	Family-heritage maintenance	Family-controlled decision-making	Familial relationship-building	Emotional decision-making	Communality
In my family business, family members feel warmth for each other (emotional attachment).			0.77		0.69
Emotions and sentiments often affect decision-making processes in my family business (emotional attachment).				0.79	0.85
Protecting the welfare of family members is critical to us (emotional attachment).				0.68	0.80
In my family business, the emotional bonds among family members are very strong (emotional attachment).				0.62	0.68
In my family business, affective considerations are often as important as economic considerations (emotional attachment).				0.78	0.63
Cronbach's alpha	0.91	0.83	0.83	0.78	

Notes: The text in parentheses after each SEW measure indicates the measure's original inclusion of some of the five SEW dimensions of Berrone et al. (2012). The values under each factor indicate the factor loadings of certain SEW measures. The MSA overall (Kaiser's measure of sampling adequacy) is 0.82.

[a]Question format in the survey: Assess on a scale from 1 to 7 from 'strongly disagree' to 'strongly agree' how well the following statements apply to you...

regarding nonfamily employees as part of the family and the importance of strong relationships with other stakeholders, were loaded into the fourth factor, named 'familial relationship-building', due to the combination of emotional and relational measures.

In addition to the link to Debicki et al.'s (2016) categorisation, the reconstructed four SEW factors (especially family-heritage maintenance) can be linked to the suggestion by Kano et al. (2020) that SEW can materialise in three major resource inputs for family firms: social capital, long-term orientation and reputation. The item contents in all the factors also tapped mostly into the call by Debicki et al. (2016) for measuring the importance of SEW (e.g. 'are important'; 'is critical'; 'helps define'), despite the usage of Berrone et al.'s (2012) level-oriented items, as well as the behavioural role of SEW called for by such researchers as Miller and Le Breton-Miller (2014) (e.g. 'would be unlikely to consider'; 'exert control over'; 'often affect decision-making'; see Table 3.1 for detailed information). Thus, we were confident that these four factors were valid and reliable for encapsulating and measuring SEW for Hypotheses 1 and 3. In summary, the factors referred to the affective preferences or needs in family firms' decision-making and relationships, thus reflecting both the pioneering conceptualisation of SEW by Gómez-Mejía et al. (2007), emphasising the affective side of SEW, and the recent elaborations that focus on the relational side of SEW (e.g. Zellweger et al., 2019).

We conducted the necessary diagnostics to ensure the quality of the developed SEW factors. The communalities of the measures were all over 0.50, implying good internal consistency. The four factors explained 56% of the total variance. The Kaiser's measure of sampling adequacy (MSA) value was 0.82, and the Cronbach's alphas ranged from 0.78 to 0.91, exceeding the threshold of 0.70 suggested for adapted scales (Hair, Black, Babin, & Anderson, 2009). Thus, we considered this four-factor solution adequate for hypotheses testing.

Since network ties and networking in the SME context have been studied relatively more than family-firm-specific SEW, with largely consensual findings on the resources, capabilities and knowledge gained from networks, we decided not to employ exploratory PCA for identifying key constructs. The networking measures were derived from the literature on SMEs, especially manufacturing SMEs, and their managers' use of interpersonal and interorganisational network ties, including industry authorities and trade fairs, for identifying international opportunities, increasing DOI and enhancing exporting and firm performance (e.g. Al-Hyari, Al-Weshah, & Alnsour, 2012; Fernhaber, McDougall-Covin, & Shepherd, 2009; Kontinen & Ojala, 2011; Musteen, Francis, & Datta, 2010; Nordman & Melén, 2008; Peng & Luo, 2000; Senik, Scott-Ladd, Entrekin, & Adham, 2011). We created a summated scale that included measures of the importance of prior international experience, trade-fair participation and existing business partners in international opportunity identification, and of the extent to which firms have utilised personal ties, networks and connections with foreign buyers, foreign suppliers and industry authorities for internationalisation during the previous three years. Thus, the scale was a combination of use and importance considerations. We followed Dimitratos et al. (2014) by naming this factor 'networking' since the measures capture the extent to which collaboration with and support from external stakeholders are used for SME internationalisation. Despite looking like a conceptual outlier, we included prior international experience that may indirectly encompass the involvement of such foreign stakeholders as customers and partners in accumulating knowledge gained from experiential learning. Engaging in networking as such encompasses learning opportunities and increased knowledge for SME internationalisation (e.g. Prashantham & Dhanaraj, 2010; Zahra & Hayton, 2008).

Control Variables

We controlled the variables that earlier literature found to affect the international networking and internationalisation of family SMEs, namely, firm age and family ownership (e.g. Eberhard & Craig, 2013). Firm age in years was the difference between the year of the firm's establishment and the year 2017, when survey responses were produced. Family ownership was calculated as the share of family-member ownership in the firm (*a priori* controlling was already considered by selecting only family-controlled firms with more than 50% family ownership; the average family ownership in the family-SME sample was a high 92%).

Correlations

Table 3.2 presents the descriptive statistics and between-item correlations of the variables used in the analysis. Since all the correlations, except for the correlation between emotional decision-making and familial relationship-building with a slightly exceeding 0.60, are below 0.56, the maximum value for testing multicollinearity (e.g. Leiblein, Reuer, & Dalsace, 2002), the data did not exhibit correlations between the items that would have caused clear multicollinearity concern. The statistically significant correlations existed between the independent and dependent variables, thus providing preliminary and reasonable evidence that networking and emotional decision-making, the second SEW factor constructed, can affect DOI.

Table 3.2 Correlations of dependent, independent and control variables within family SMEs (scores within nonfamily SMEs in parentheses)

	Mean	Std. Dev.	1	2	3	4	5	6	7	8
1. Degree of internationalisation (DOI)	44.34 (50.62)	30.53 (31.07)	1							
2. Family-heritage maintenance	4.49	1.57	-0.11	1						
3. Family-controlled decision-making	5.18	1.64	-0.16	0.42**	1					
4. Familial relationship-building	4.76	1.21	-0.11	0.52**	0.55**	1				
5. Emotional decision-making	4.22	1.21	-0.34*	0.44**	0.47**	0.60**	1			
6. Networking	4.74 (4.68)	0.80 (0.97)	0.43**	-0.22	-0.15	-0.01	-0.08	1		
7. Family ownership	92	16.64	0.04	0.11	0.24	0.27†	0.20	0.13	1	
8. Firm age	37.04 (38.67)	17.09 (25.75)	0.05	0.23	0.06	0.06	-0.03	-0.04	0.22	1

Notes: **p<0.01, *p<0.05, †p<0.1

Common Method Bias

In cross-sectional survey settings with single respondents and similarly constructed (usually Likert-scale) measures, common method bias can be an issue, and mitigating it requires ex ante procedures in data collection (Podsakoff, MacKenzie, Lee, & Podsakoff, 2003; Podsakoff, MacKenzie, & Podsakoff, 2012), as well as preferable ex post statistical tests, such as Harman's single-factor test (Podsakoff & Organ, 1986). As Chang, van Witteloostuijn, and Eden (2010) point out, the international-business research domain is no stranger to such issues. Therefore, we took a few precautions in collecting the data to counter any potential common method bias issues.

First, the focal items were placed in different parts of the questionnaire, and negatively worded items were included to minimise any halo effects. Second, the focal measures were made to seem like part of a larger survey covering a range of issues for SMEs, beyond internationalisation. As Chang et al. (2010) note, 'respondents are unlikely to be guided by a cognitive map that includes difficult-to-visualise interaction and non-visual effects' (p. 179). Besides, we conducted two ex post tests to check for any common method bias issues. First, we conducted Harman's single-factor test, and the results indicated that total variance was less than 50% for all the single factors. Thus, we concluded that no single factors that could have caused a concern in the empirical analysis underlie the data. Second, as Harman's test can be criticised (e.g. Podsakoff et al., 2003), it was complemented by applying the marker variable technique (cf. Lindell & Whitney, 2001). We chose the measure of the number of people listed in upper management as the marker variable, since the literature on family-firm internationalisation does not indicate that variable is directly and highly dependent on SEW or networking. We observed that the marker variable had nonsignificant correlations with the theoretically relevant predictors and criterion variables, and there were no major changes in the magnitude or significance of the correlations between the independent and dependent variables when controlling for the marker variable in partial correlation analysis. Since both the ex ante and ex post precautions taken to mitigate common method bias indicated no issues in this regard, the data were considered suitable for proceeding to hypotheses testing.

84   J. Metsola et al.

Results

We first ran linear regressions for each independent variable separately (see Table 3.3), which suggested that networking has a strong positive relationship with DOI in family SMEs (β=0.43, p<0.01). A statistically weaker indication of positive relationship was also found in nonfamily SMEs (β=0.26, p<0.1). Emotional decision-making in family SMEs has a strong negative relationship with DOI (β=-0.34, p<0.05). To further check multicollinearity and having multiple variables in a model, we verified the variance inflation factor (VIF). The VIF scores range from 1.11 to 2.06, considerably lower than 10, and as a result, we can employ models involving multiple variables. We also ran the Breusch-Pagan/Cook-Weisberg test, which yielded a p-value above 0.05, suggesting that there is no heteroskedasticity issue.

We then ran four models to examine the hypotheses, first focusing on networking and then adding SEW-related factors, complemented by control variables. Table 3.4 presents each model's results. Model 1 involves only nonfamily SMEs (n=42) and the association of networking with DOI among them. The following models involve only family SMEs (n=47), the first with only networking as the independent variable, the second also with all the SEW factors and the third also with interaction effect between emotional decision-making and networking, since it was the only SEW factor with statistically significant results in relation to DOI and, thus, could also initially indicate significance in interaction with networking. Networking is positively associated with DOI in Models 2 and 3 (β=0.44 in Model 2 and β=0.42 in Model 3, p<0.01). Model 1 and the effect of networking for nonfamily

Table 3.3 Results of the linear regression for each independent variable separately with the dependent variable DOI

Independent variable	Parameter estimate
Sample: Non-family SMEs	
Firm age	0.05 (0.19)
Networking	0.26[†] (4.88)
Sample: Family SMEs	
Firm age	0.05 (0.26)
Family ownership	0.04 (0.27)
Networking	0.43** (5.12)
Family-heritage maintenance	-0.11 (2.88)
Emotional decision-making	-0.34* (3.53)
Family-controlled decision-making	-0.16 (2.74)
Familial relationship-building	-0.11 (3.74)

Notes: Each line reports an estimate from separate linear regression on DOI (a constant term is not reported). **p<0.01, *p<0.05, [†]p<0.1; standard errors in parentheses

3 Socioemotional Wealth and Networking in the Internationalisation...

Table 3.4 Results of the multiple linear regression models with the dependent variable DOI

Variables	Model 1 β	Std. err.	Model 2 β	Std. err.	Model 3 β	Std. err.	Model 4 β	Std. err.
Firm age	0.07	0.19	0.08	0.25	0.02	0.26	0.01	0.25
Family ownership			-0.04	0.26	0.03	0.27	0.04	0.27
Networking	0.26	4.94	0.44**	5.28	0.42**	5.38	-0.36	21.61
Family-heritage maintenance					0.12	3.33	0.10	3.29
Family-controlled decision-making					-0.01	3.14	0.05	3.18
Familial relationship-building					0.07	4.86	0.04	4.83
Emotional decision-making					-0.40*	4.43	-1.76	24.50
Emotional decision-making x Networking							1.53	5.06
Diagnostics								
Adj. R^2		0.02		0.14		0.17		0.20
F-value		1.48		3.43*		2.38*		2.39*

Notes: **$p<0.01$, *$p<0.05$

SMEs are not statistically significant. Regarding SEW-related factors, only emotional decision-making has a statistically significant and strong negative association with DOI (Model 3, $\beta=-0.40$, $p<0.01$). However, the moderating effect of emotional decision-making on the effect of networking was not statistically significant. We also ran post hoc analyses on the moderation effect of the other three SEW factors but did not obtain statistically significant results.

Consequently, H1 is partially supported, H2 is supported and H3 is not supported. Regarding H1, the results suggest that the higher the level of emotional decision-making is, the lower is the DOI in family SMEs. A one-standard-deviation increase in emotional decision-making leads to a 0.42-standard-deviation decrease in predicted DOI, with the other variables held constant. Regarding H2, the results suggest that networking indeed has a positive association with DOI. A one-standard-deviation increase in networking leads to a 0.40-standard-deviation increase in predicted DOI, with the other variables held constant.

The results in Model 1 further support these conclusions and indicate a weaker positive association of networking with DOI, without statistical significance, in the context of nonfamily SMEs. Networking seems particularly important for the internationalisation of family SMEs that must deal with the inherent inclination towards emotional decision-making inside the firm and avoid its potential negative hindrance to initiating and intensifying internationalisation. The components of emotional decision-making capture the role of emotions among family members, decision-making, protection of family welfare and their coordinate status with financial aspects and goals of the business. The networking construct components stress the role of prior international experience, trade-fair participation, existing business partners and using personal ties, networks and connections to foreign buyers, suppliers and industry authorities. These represent the opposite of emotional decision-making, namely, the willingness and actions of family SMEs to engage in external relationships for the benefit of internationalisation and not merely to settle for internal family relationships. Our findings show that those family SMEs that concentrate more on networking and, hence, achieve a higher DOI may have more focus on economic, growth-related orientations than family SMEs with lower levels of networking and, thus, lower DOI, as well as a greater tendency to value noneconomic and emotional aspects of the family firm and stability.

The average DOI of the 42 nonfamily SMEs in our sample was 50.6% (44.3% in family SMEs) and the average networking score was 4.68 (4.74 in family SMEs). These figures suggest that emotional decision-making in family SMEs, stemming from high levels of family ownership and involvement and not directly comparable to the potential emotional decision-making in nonfamily SMEs, plays a significant role in restraining family SMEs' internationalisation. As the descriptive statistics show, both family and nonfamily SMEs may engage in networking per se. In fact, family SMEs are slightly more engaged in networking than non-family SMEs. Accordingly, emotional-decision-making is a key distinguishing socioemotional factor that can challenge family SMEs in the context of internationalisation.

The insignificant result regarding the interaction between emotional decision-making and networking in relation to DOI suggests that each independent variable has either a positive or negative influence on DOI—that is, neither one increases or decreases the other's effect in the internationalisation process. This further emphasises the Model 3 results, indicating that just increasing networking activity *or* decreasing emotional decision-making may not be enough to influence the effect of the other. Rather, *both* increasing networking *and* decreasing emotional decision-making are needed to have best possible overall effect on DOI.

Discussion

Our results largely align with existing literature on the association of SEW with internationalisation. Scholes et al. (2016) found that SEW preservation reinforces the maintenance of family harmony and distrust of outsiders, restraining external network formation and the necessary resources and capabilities to advance the internationalisation process. SEW preservation and related risk aversion negatively affect both export propensity and intensity, but especially propensity (Monreal-Pérez & Sánchez-Marín, 2017; Yang, Li, Stanley, Kellermanns, & Li, 2018).

However, our results also partly diverge and provide a more specific explanation of the association. The concept of family harmony that Scholes et al. (2016) describe can be partially associated with our emotional decision-making construct, but otherwise, existing research has not explicitly specified certain SEW dimensions related to the internationalisation of family SMEs. The role of emotional decision-making stood out in our analysis, suggesting that at least emotional decision-making is a significant SEW-related factor in family SMEs' internationalisation. According to our construct, emotional decision-making relates to the strategic role of emotions and family benefit in family SMEs' decision-making. Internationalisation itself is a strategic decision, influenced by such internal family business characteristics as the desire to maintain control and influence (Gallo, Tàpies, & Cappuyns, 2004). Thus, our results suggest that emotional decision-making plays a key role as a restraint (noneconomic decision) on family SMEs intensifying internationalisation, rather than a driver (economic decision) to do so.

Emotions form an inseparable part of every organisation (Ashforth & Humphrey, 1995), but especially of family firms (Eddleston & Kellermanns, 2007), where shared history and knowledge shape and intertwine social relationships (Berrone et al., 2012; Kets de Vries, 1996; Zellweger et al., 2019), blurring the boundaries among family, business and ownership (Baron, 2008; Berrone et al., 2010; Gersick et al., 1997). The relatively small sizes of family SMEs make more difficult the 'artificial' avoidance and decrease of emotional decision-making because the intermingling of relationships becomes stronger in a tight community with close interactions and knowledge sharing. Not surprisingly, explicitly emotional aspects arise from all the SEW items, showing their importance in family-SME decision-making and internationalisation. Gomez-Mejia et al. (2011) emphasise a strong 'emotional overtone' as one of the three key factors that distinguish family firms (p. 964). Family members at high levels of family control tend to bring emotions into business activities (Baron, 2008), which might cause them to neglect market forces and rational, economically sound business (Ward, 2004). This strong emotional overtone and blindness to sound, globally competitive business might exist in some of family SMEs with strong inclinations towards emotional decision-making. Networking embodies readiness to pursue international market opportunities and seize them, even at the expense of emotional attachment to the family business.

We note that the mean of emotional decision-making among family SMEs in our data was 4.22 (with individual values ranging from 1.25 to 7.00). Accordingly, emotional decision-making is present to some extent in all family SMEs and, in most, above the scale median of 4.00. As the networking construct implicitly indicates the intensity and importance of close foreign network relationships for internationalisation, those family SMEs with high levels of networking may use their emotional decision-making to convince foreign partners and customers to trust active relationship-building as well as their manufactured products. Given the slightly higher mean for networking than in nonfamily SMEs, this suggestion would align with Cesinger et al.'s (2016) finding that family SMEs can obtain crucial knowledge for internationalisation and preserve SEW at the same time, through collaboration intensity and network trust of network partners. Similarly, Hennart et al. (2019) mention emotional attachment as an affective attribute of family SMEs for building long-term, trustworthy business relationships with foreign partners and customers and gaining competitive advantage. The association of emotions with positive feelings towards an object can manifest in family SMEs as 'rational pride' in the products and firm history, rather than 'irrational sensitivity' towards maintaining family benefit and status in the firm at any cost.

Indeed, a SEW dimension can lead to both positive and negative performance outcomes. Gomez-Mejia et al. (2011) suggest the possibility that 'positives neutralize the negatives and vice versa'—for instance, regarding 'affective commitment versus more time spent handling emotions or long-term orientation versus entrenchment' (p. 691). However, our study more clearly indicates that family SMEs should prioritise economically driven networking and avoid noneconomically driven emotional decision-making if they want to increase DOI. Family SMEs cannot ignore the widespread conclusions from the general SME literature that their limited resources often force them to use foreign and other partners to provide necessary resources and knowledge, with a view to expanding abroad (Agndal et al., 2008; Arenius, 2005; Chetty & Holm, 2000; Yli-Renko et al., 2002). Our results partially diverge from those of Eberhard and Craig (2013), who found that high levels of family

3 Socioemotional Wealth and Networking in the Internationalisation...

ownership negatively moderate the effect of interorganisational networking on internationalisation, leading to less export intensity for family SMEs than for nonfamily SMEs. According to our study, family SMEs' networking activity and importance resemble or even exceed those of nonfamily SMEs, and networking is a key factor for the successful internationalisation of family SMEs. However, emotional decision-making, derived from high levels of family ownership, acts as a negative antecedent, rather than as a moderator that restrains internationalisation and, thus, associated networking in the first place. Moreover, all the family SMEs in our sample had over 50% family ownership (mean = 92%), with an average age of 37 years. In addition, 39 firms had a family CEO and only 8 had a nonfamily CEO. Thus, many of these family SMEs seem less than eager to shake up their family ownership and involvement in management to include a greater nonfamily presence and 'internally external readiness' to intensify internationalisation.

One reason for lack of support for the role of family-heritage maintenance in affecting the DOI of family SMEs might reside in its looser connection to decision-making than that of emotional decision-making. Family-heritage maintenance encompasses maintaining family business and related heritage with a more explicit orientation towards long-term preservation over generations, while the affective items of emotional decision-making more explicitly relate to operational and shorter-term decision-making. Thus, SEW preservation channelled through family-heritage maintenance can provide both positive long-term orientation/stability in the execution of internationalisation strategies (e.g. Kraus, Mitter, Eggers, & Stieg, 2017; Mitter & Emprechtinger, 2016) and negative risk aversion and conservativeness in restraining internationalisation efforts (e.g. Monreal-Pérez & Sánchez-Marín, 2017; Olivares-Mesa & Cabrera-Suarez, 2006). However, it might not be closely present in shorter-term decision-making dealing with upcoming foreign market entries, expansions and overall internationalisation management at a grass-roots level. For instance, the items of emotional decision-making reflect emotional bonds and protection of family welfare among family members on one hand and, on the other hand, the role of emotional/affective considerations in decision-making on an equal footing with economic considerations. Thus, strong emotional decision-making could manifest in family SMEs' tendency to have incompetent family members in charge of key managerial positions, which could inhibit internationalisation if its opportunities are not recognised or assessed objectively.

Family-controlled decision-making could have been expected to be significant for the internationalisation of family SMEs, as earlier research finds that the controlling role of family members in their firms' decision-making, through ownership and managerial roles, influences internationalisation. On the positive side, intertwined family ownership and management enable family members to be both agile and long-term-oriented in decision-making (Gallo & Pont, 1996). For instance, such efficient decision-making can facilitate joint product and international diversification and, thereby, both the firm's and the family's success and survival in the long run (Muñoz-Bullón & Sánchez-Bueno, 2012). On the other hand, as discussed earlier, the strong role of family members in managerial decision-making and ownership can restrain internationalisation, due to dysfunctional SEW preservation and risk aversion (e.g. Alessandri et al., 2018). Despite the more explicit reflection of decision-making, family-controlled decision-making resembles family-heritage maintenance as a construct in its orientation towards long-term, rather than shorter-term, decision-making. As such, it can be relevant for internationalisation, providing consistency and 'main lines' for internationalisation strategy and execution. However, one reason for the insignificance of the factor in our study could reside in its remoteness from internationalisation decisions at the operational level and in the short term. Moreover, family SMEs generally may have shorter decision-making horizons than larger firms, as their limited resources force them to follow effectual reasoning (i.e. the means, resources and stakeholders available at hand) to seize international opportunities, rather than careful causation logic with predetermined goals and decision-making processes (Sarasvathy, Kumar, York, & Bhagavatula, 2014). In such a situation, emotions, rather than sanity, can easily—and insidiously—guide firm decision-making.

Familial relationship-building was also of promising significance for internationalisation, comprising interorganisational and social relationship-building and potentially reflecting their relational importance in the internationalisation of family SMEs operating with limited resources and capabilities. Like emotional decision-making, but without decision-making, this factor (including aspects of warmth between family members and familial inclusion of nonfamily employees in the firm) is probably too loosely connected to the internationalisation of family SMEs, lacking enough substance for relevance to strategic and challenging internationalisation.

Overall, our findings align with the bifurcation-bias theory of Kano and Verbeke (2018), who suggest that family firms tend to make dysfunctional SEW-related internationalisation decisions in the short and medium run, ignoring functional economising practices (e.g. cross-border operational meritocracy in human resources and rigorous data-driven decision-making) for assessing and planning internationalisation performance. The insignificant results for all the other three SEW factors, except emotional decision-making, suggest the difficulty that family owners and family-SME managers have in transforming family and SEW-related resources to firm-level and international firm-specific advantages (FSAs)—that is, social capital, long-term orientation and reputation (Kano et al., 2020)—which can clearly manifest themselves in high DOI or their lack in low DOI. The three insignificant factors, reflecting the importance of strong relationships and long-term-oriented decision-making, could be conducive to the SEW-related FSAs per se but remain inconclusive. One condition for productive deployment is the access of nonfamily/external managers and owners to these resources (Kano et al., 2020). In that light, our data regarding family control in both management and ownership indicate that family SMEs in this study are not ready for this interaction from the outset. Yet, at the same time, the visibly dysfunctional emotional decision-making and visibly functional networking 'fill the void' emphatically in family SMEs' internationalisation, steered either by bifurcation-biased decision-making with emotional overtones or by economising decision-making with adoption of active networking.

Accordingly, bifurcation-bias theorising also supports the strong positive impact of networking on the internationalisation of family SMEs. Networking with existing business partners, industry authorities, foreign suppliers and buyers, with trade-fair participation and accumulated international experience gained in networking activities, can bring functional economising practices, resources and capabilities to family SMEs. These relational and periodic activities, conducted with shorter- and longer-term horizons, may equip owning and managing family members with not only new knowledge and skills but also a new mindset and attitude towards regarding internationalisation as a strategy for ensuring long-term growth of the business and, thereby, the survival and stability of the family firm. Thus, networking may actually help to preserve SEW dimensions perceived as important in the long term, provided that at least in the short and medium term, dysfunctional and family-centred liabilities, such as emotional decision-making, do not overpower the crucial importance of networking for international opportunity recognition and establishing an efficient value chain and contact base. In the long run, aspects of emotional decision-making might become attributes through pride and 'softer' values in decision-making, which yield trust and reciprocity in international network relationships. Contacts and profitable business relationships gained through active networking are strengthened and long-term competitive advantages achieved (Hennart et al., 2019).

Earlier research provides evidence that the main concern regarding the internationalisation of family firms is indeed internationalisation propensity and promotion in the early phases of the process. Moreover, indications for success in the later phases are similar to or even better than those for nonfamily firms (Evert, Sears, Martin, & Payne, 2018; Graves & Shan, 2014; Monreal-Pérez & Sánchez-Marín, 2017; Yang et al., 2018). Based on the large-scale literature review, Metsola, Leppäaho, Paavilainen-Mäntymäki, and Plakoyiannaki (2020) encapsulate the dominance of 'liabilities', including SEW-related factors, in the early phases of internationalisation and the increasing potential for 'capabilities', including networking-related factors, which can offset the initial restraints of liabilities in the long run, in line with bifurcation-bias theory. Not finding support for the moderating effect of emotional decision-making or other SEW factors of this study on the effect of networking in relation to DOI, which reflects internationalisation intensity rather than propensity, further suggests that noneconomically driven SEW, through emotional decision-making, may not have enough 'power' to mitigate the positive economic effect of networking on increasing international growth of family SMEs. However, in turn, networking might not have enough power to mitigate the negative effect of emotional decision-making if it is deeply rooted in family-SME practices, with no signs of change under strong family control. Accordingly, the results of this study elaborate such studies as Metsola et al. (2020) that capabilities (networking) and liabilities (emotional decision-making), both with high impacts, may not be able to co-exist in family-SME internationalisation processes. Nonetheless, there must be enough 'room' for mitigating possible emotional decision-making and increasing networking in the long run. Given the high number of family CEOs (and not nonfamily CEOs) and the high average of family ownership in the family-SMEs sample, the circumstances have most likely been conducive in all family SMEs for emotional decision-making and bifurcation bias from the beginning. However, some family SMEs have been more able or willing to adopt economising such practices and capabilities as networking, resulting in higher DOI, while others have been more inclined towards emotional decision-making and other family-related liabilities, resulting in lower DOI. Noting that bifurcation bias essentially revolves around emotional aspects of family firms (Kano et al., 2020), emotional decision-making—and *only* that, among all the SEW-related factors—can be expected to affect internationalisation negatively and is difficult for some family SMEs to avoid. These conclusions will obviously require further longitudinal data and future analysis for more validation.

Conclusions

Using cross-sectional survey data on 89 Finnish SMEs from 2017 and conducting multiple linear regression analyses, we found that those family SMEs that actively network and consider it important have a higher degree of internationalisation than those with strong inclinations towards emotional decision-making. Family SMEs engaged in high levels of networking might have greater economic motivation to seek growth through exports and international networks, while family SMEs characterised by strong emotional decision-making might have a more noneconomic and risk-averse motivation to a maintain domestic and family-centred business focus.

The contributions of this study relate to illustrating how SEW, specifically through affective preferences and needs in decision-making, and family-SME networking connect to firm internationalisation. Thus, the study extends the literature on both family-firm internationalisation (e.g. Fernandez & Nieto, 2006; Kontinen & Ojala, 2012; Torkkeli, Uzhegova, Kuivalainen, Saarenketo, & Puumalainen, forthcoming) and the role of SEW in family firms (e.g. Berrone et al., 2012; Gomez-Mejia et al., 2011; Miller & Le Breton-Miller, 2014) and their internationalisation (e.g. Kraus et al., 2016; Scholes et al., 2016), as well as the role of networking in SME internationalisation (e.g. Eberhard & Craig, 2013; Torkkeli et al., 2015; Zain & Ng, 2006). Specifically, we contribute to demonstrating the lack and ambiguity of validating the role of SEW in family-firm internationalisation, for which varying SEW-measurement scales have been offered (Berrone et al., 2012; Debicki et al., 2016; Hauck et al., 2016), most without applying those scales to analysis (e.g. Alessandri et al., 2018; Stieg, Cesinger, Apfelthaler, Kraus, & Cheng, 2018). We aimed at elaborating the role of SEW in the internationalisation of family SMEs through rigorous PCA, using items from the seminal FIBER scale (Berrone et al., 2012). Then, for use in further internationalisation-related analyses, we reconstructed four SEW constructs significant to family SMEs: family-heritage maintenance, family-controlled decision-making, familial relationship-building and emotional decision-making. The further significance of emotional decision-making for the internationalisation of family SMEs suggests that affective preferences and needs, manifesting in shorter-term and more operational decision-making than those more general and long-term aspects of family-heritage maintenance and family-controlled decision-making, are SEW-related factors that can closely influence the family firm's strategic behaviour. Thus, in the context of internationalisation, this study and its results contribute to the strong need in family-firm research to identify specific SEW dimensions that manifest in firm behaviour (Chrisman & Patel, 2012; Debicki et al., 2016; Miller & Le Breton-Miller, 2014). High levels of family control per se or SEW as a whole might not be enough to clarify the role of SEW in family firms' behaviour. Most family SMEs in this study were highly family-controlled, yet showed varying levels of emotional decision-making and corresponding levels of internationalisation.

In addition, our research contributes to studies discussing bifurcation bias (Kano et al., 2020; Kano & Verbeke, 2018; Verbeke & Kano, 2012) in the family-business context, suggesting that too-strong emotional decision-making deeply rooted in family SMEs may fuel bifurcation bias and restrain family SMEs from gaining economically sound external involvement for internationalisation, inside and outside of the firm. However, that early, strong focus on networking can mitigate bifurcation bias and increase the degree of internationalisation in the long run. Family SMEs provide a specific context for highlighting bifurcation bias, as they have truly been under the strong influence of family members through ownership and management positions, thereby growing the breeding ground for emotional decision-making over years and generations. Our results contribute to the literature on family-firm internationalisation, indicating that some family SMEs have avoided the potential restraining effect on internationalisation of strong family involvement by capitalising on networking. But, for some family SMEs, strong family involvement has presumably kept the firm in the realm of strong emotional decision-making and at a lower level of internationalisation.

Although we contribute to SEW measurement in family-firm research (Miller & Le Breton-Miller, 2014) by conducting PCA and suggesting emotional decision-making as a key SEW-related construct in the internationalisation of family SMEs, we acknowledge the limited sample size and specific single-country context for our SEW analysis. Thus, we encourage future studies to continue validating and elaborating Berrone et al.'s (2012) underutilised FIBER scale and use our four-dimension SEW structure in different country contexts, hoping that we can approach a more consensual agreement on the much-debated SEW as such and its connection to internationalisation.

The cross-sectional nature of the study also calls for future research applying longitudinal panel data and for cross-cultural studies with lagged and control variables to test causalities. Qualitative approaches to describing the development and impact of SEW on international expansion and strategy of family firms longitudinally may also yield richer descriptions of the specific nature of the dynamics between SEW and networking, unravelling how non-economic/affective and economic/rational decision-making and goals manifest in practice.

References

Agndal, H., Chetty, S., & Wilson, H. (2008). Social capital dynamics and foreign market entry. *International Business Review, 17*(6), 663–675.

Alessandri, T. M., Cerrato, D., & Eddleston, K. A. (2018). The mixed gamble of internationalization in family and nonfamily firms: The moderating role of organizational slack. *Global Strategy Journal, 8*(1), 46–72.

Al-Hyari, K., Al-Weshah, G., & Alnsour, M. (2012). Barriers to internationalization in SMEs: Evidence from Jordan. *Marketing Intelligence & Planning, 30*(2), 188–211.

Arenius, P. (2005). The psychic distance postulate revised: From market selection to speed of market penetration. *Journal of International Entrepreneurship, 3*(2), 115–131.

Arregle, J. L., Duran, P., Hitt, M. A., & Van Essen, M. (2017). Why is family firms' internationalization unique? A meta-analysis. *Entrepreneurship Theory and Practice, 41*(5), 801–831.

Arregle, J. L., Naldi, L., Nordqvist, M., & Hitt, M. A. (2012). Internationalization of family–controlled firms: A study of the effects of external involvement in governance. *Entrepreneurship Theory and Practice, 36*(6), 1115–1143.

Ashforth, B. E., & Humphrey, R. H. (1995). Emotion in the workplace: A reappraisal. *Human Relations, 48*(2), 97–125.

Banalieva, E. R., & Eddleston, K. A. (2011). Home-region focus and performance of family firms: The role of family vs non-family leaders. *Journal of International Business Studies, 42*(8), 1060–1072.

Baron, R. A. (2008). The role of affect in the entrepreneurial process. *Academy of Management Review, 33*(2), 328–340.

Bell, J. (1995). The internationalization of small computer software firms: A further challenge to "stage" theories. *European Journal of Marketing, 29*(8), 60–75.

Berrone, P., Cruz, C., & Gomez-Mejia, L. R. (2012). Socioemotional wealth in family firms: Theoretical dimensions, assessment approaches, and agenda for future research. *Family Business Review, 25*(3), 258–279.

Berrone, P., Cruz, C., Gomez-Mejia, L. R., & Larraza-Kintana, M. (2010). Socioemotional wealth and corporate responses to institutional pressures: Do family-controlled firms pollute less? *Administrative Science Quarterly, 55*(1), 82–113.

Buciuni, G., & Mola, L. (2014). How do entrepreneurial firms establish cross-border relationships? A global value chain perspective. *Journal of International Entrepreneurship, 12*(1), 67–84.

Cesinger, B., Hughes, M., Mensching, H., Bouncken, R., Fredrich, V., & Kraus, S. (2016). A socioemotional wealth perspective on how collaboration intensity, trust, and international market knowledge affect family firms' multinationality. *Journal of World Business, 51*(4), 586–599.

Chang, S. J., van Witteloostuijn, A., & Eden, L. (2010). From the editors: Common method variance in international business research. *Journal of International Business Studies, 41*(2), 178–184.

Chetty, S., & Holm, D. B. (2000). Internationalisation of small to medium-sized manufacturing firms: A network approach. *International Business Review, 9*(1), 77–93.

Chrisman, J. J., & Patel, P. C. (2012). Variations in R&D investments of family and nonfamily firms: Behavioral agency and myopic loss aversion perspectives. *Academy of Management Journal, 55*(4), 976–997.

Coviello, N., Kano, L., & Liesch, P. W. (2017). Adapting the Uppsala model to a modern world: Macro-context and microfoundations. *Journal of International Business Studies, 48*(9), 1151–1164.

Coviello, N. E., & Munro, H. J. (1995). Growing the entrepreneurial firm: Networking for international market development. *European Journal of Marketing, 29*(7), 49–61.

Cruz, C. C., Gómez-Mejia, L. R., & Becerra, M. (2010). Perceptions of benevolence and the design of agency contracts: CEO-TMT relationships in family firms. *Academy of Management Journal, 53*(1), 69–89.

D'Angelo, A., Majocchi, A., & Buck, T. (2016). External managers, family ownership and the scope of SME internationalization. *Journal of World Business, 51*(4), 534–547.

De Massis, A., Frattini, F., Majocchi, A., & Piscitello, L. (2018). Family firms in the global economy: Toward a deeper understanding of internationalization determinants, processes, and outcomes. *Global Strategy Journal, 8*(1), 3–21.

Debicki, B. J., Kellermanns, F. W., Chrisman, J. J., Pearson, A. W., & Spencer, B. A. (2016). Development of a socioemotional wealth importance (SEWi) scale for family firm research. *Journal of Family Business Strategy, 7*(1), 47–57.

Dimitratos, P., Amorós, J. E., Etchebarne, M. S., & Felzensztein, C. (2014). Micro-multinational or not? International entrepreneurship, networking and learning effects. *Journal of Business Research, 67*(5), 908–915.

Dyer, W. G. (1988). Culture and continuity in family firms. *Family Business Review, 1*, 37–50.

Eberhard, M., & Craig, J. (2013). The evolving role of organisational and personal networks in international market venturing. *Journal of World Business, 48*(3), 385–397.

Eddleston, K. A., & Kellermanns, F. W. (2007). Destructive and productive family relationships: A stewardship theory perspective. *Journal of Business Venturing, 22*(4), 545–565.

European Commission. (2019a). Family business. Retrieved November 20, 2019, from https://ec.europa.eu/growth/smes/promoting-entrepreneurship/we-work-for/family-business_en

European Commission. (2019b). What is an SME? Retrieved November 25, 2019, from https://ec.europa.eu/growth/smes/business-friendly-environment/sme-definition_en

Evert, R. E., Sears, J. B., Martin, J. A., & Payne, G. T. (2018). Family ownership and family involvement as antecedents of strategic action: A longitudinal study of initial international entry. *Journal of Business Research, 84*, 301–311.

Fang, H., Kotlar, J., Memili, E., Chrisman, J. J., & De Massis, A. (2018). The pursuit of international opportunities in family firms: Generational differences and the role of knowledge-based resources. *Global Strategy Journal, 8*(1), 136–157.

Fernández, Z., & Nieto, M. J. (2005). Internationalization strategy of small and medium-sized family businesses: Some influential factors. *Family Business Review, 18*(1), 77–89.

Fernandez, Z., & Nieto, M. J. (2006). Impact of ownership on the international involvement of SMEs. *Journal of International Business Studies, 37*(3), 340–351.

Fernhaber, S. A., & McDougall-Covin, P. P. (2009). Venture capitalists as catalysts to new venture internationalization: The impact of their knowledge and reputation resources. *Entrepreneurship Theory and Practice, 33*(1), 277–295.

Fernhaber, S. A., Mcdougall-Covin, P. P., & Shepherd, D. A. (2009). International entrepreneurship: Leveraging internal and external knowledge sources. *Strategic Entrepreneurship Journal, 3*(4), 297–320.

Gallo, M. A., & Pont, C. G. (1996). Important factors in family business internationalization. *Family Business Review, 9*(1), 45–59.

Gallo, M. Á., Tàpies, J., & Cappuyns, K. (2004). Comparison of family and nonfamily business: Financial logic and personal preferences. *Family Business Review, 17*(4), 303–318.

Gersick, K. E., Davis, J. A., Hampton, M. M., & Lansberg, I. (1997). *Generation to generation: Life cycles of the family business.* Boston, MA: Harvard Business Press.

Gomez-Mejia, L. R., Campbell, J. T., Martin, G., Hoskisson, R. E., Makri, M., & Sirmon, D. G. (2014). Socioemotional wealth as a mixed gamble: Revisiting family firm R&D investments with the behavioral agency model. *Entrepreneurship Theory and Practice, 38*(6), 1351–1374.

Gomez-Mejia, L. R., Cruz, C., Berrone, P., & De Castro, J. (2011). The bind that ties: Socioemotional wealth preservation in family firms. *Academy of Management Annals, 5*(1), 653–707.

Gómez-Mejía, L. R., Haynes, K. T., Núñez-Nickel, M., Jacobson, K. J., & Moyano-Fuentes, J. (2007). Socioemotional wealth and business risks in family-controlled firms: Evidence from Spanish olive oil mills. *Administrative Science Quarterly, 52*(1), 106–137.

Gomez-Mejia, L. R., Makri, M., & Kintana, M. L. (2010). Diversification decisions in family-controlled firms. *Journal of Management Studies, 47*(2), 223–252.

Gomez-Mejia, L. R., Patel, P. C., & Zellweger, T. M. (2018). In the horns of the dilemma: Socioemotional wealth, financial wealth, and acquisitions in family firms. *Journal of Management, 44*(4), 1369–1397.

Graves, C., & Shan, Y. G. (2014). An empirical analysis of the effect of internationalization on the performance of unlisted family and nonfamily firms in Australia. *Family Business Review, 27*(2), 142–160.

Hair, J. F., Black, W. C., Babin, B. J., & Anderson, R. E. (2009). *Multivariate data analysis* (7th ed.). Upper Saddle River, NJ: Prentice Hall.

Hauck, J., Suess-Reyes, J., Beck, S., Prügl, R., & Frank, H. (2016). Measuring socio-emotional wealth in family-owned and-managed firms: A validation and short form of the FIBER Scale. *Journal of Family Business Strategy, 7*(3), 133–148.

Hennart, J. F., Majocchi, A., & Forlani, E. (2019). The myth of the stay-at-home family firm: How family-managed SMEs can overcome their internationalization limitations. *Journal of International Business Studies, 50*(5), 758–782.

Johanson, J., & Mattsson, L. G. (1988). Internationalisation in industrial systems – a network approach. In Hood, N. & Vahlne, J. E. (Eds.), *Strategies in Global Competition*. London: Croom Helm, 287–314.

Johanson, J., & Vahlne, J.-E. (2009). The Uppsala internationalization process model revisited: From liability of foreignness to liability of outsidership. *Journal of International Business Studies, 40*, 1411–1431.

Kano, L., Ciravegna, L., & Rattalino, F. (2020). The family as a platform for FSA development: Enriching new internalization theory with insights from family firm research. *Journal of International Business Studies, 1*, 1–13.

Kano, L., & Verbeke, A. (2018). Family firm internationalization: Heritage assets and the impact of bifurcation bias. *Global Strategy Journal, 8*(1), 158–183.

Kets de Vries, M. (1996). *Human dilemmas in family business*. London: Routledge.

Kontinen, T., & Ojala, A. (2011). Network ties in the international opportunity recognition of family SMEs. *International Business Review, 20*, 440–453.

Kontinen, T., & Ojala, A. (2012). Internationalization pathways among family-owned SMEs. *International Marketing Review, 29*(5), 496–518.

Kotlar, J., Signori, A., De Massis, A., & Vismara, S. (2018). Financial wealth, socio-emotional wealth, and IPO underpricing in family firms: A two-stage gamble model. *Academy of Management Journal, 61*(3), 1073–1099.

Kraus, S., Mensching, H., Calabro, A., Cheng, C. F., & Filser, M. (2016). Family firm internationalization: A configurational approach. *Journal of Business Research, 69*(11), 5473–5478.

Kraus, S., Mitter, C., Eggers, F., & Stieg, P. (2017). Drivers of internationalization success: A conjoint choice experiment on German SME managers. *Review of Managerial Science, 11*(3), 691–716.

Leiblein, M. J., Reuer, J. J., & Dalsace, F. (2002). Do make or buy decisions matter? The influence of organizational governance on technological performance. *Strategic Management Journal, 23*(9), 817–833.

Leppäaho, T., & Metsola, J. (2020). *Family firm internationalisation: A network perspective*. Cham: Palgrave Pivot.

Lindell, M. K., & Whitney, D. J. (2001). Accounting for common method variance in cross-sectional research designs. *Journal of Applied Psychology, 86*(1), 114.

Lu, J. W., & Beamish, P. W. (2001). The internationalization and performance of SMEs. *Strategic Management Journal, 22*(6-7), 565–586.

Martin, G. P., Gomez-Mejia, L. R., & Wiseman, R. M. (2013). Executive stock options as mixed gambles: Revisiting the behavioral agency model. *Academy of Management Journal, 56*(2), 451–472.

Metsola, J., Leppäaho, T., Paavilainen-Mäntymäki, E., & Plakoyiannaki, E. (2020). Process in family business internationalisation: The state of the art and ways forward. *International Business Review, 1*, 101665.

Miller, D., & Le Breton-Miller, I. (2005). Management insights from great and struggling family businesses. *Long Range Planning, 38*(6), 517–530.

Miller, D., & Le Breton-Miller, I. (2014). Deconstructing socioemotional wealth. *Entrepreneurship Theory and Practice, 38*(4), 713–720.

Miller, D., Lee, J., Chang, S., & Le Breton-Miller, I. (2009). Filling the institutional void: The social behavior and performance of family vs non-family technology firms in emerging markets. *Journal of International Business Studies, 40*(5), 802–817.

Mitter, C., & Emprechtinger, S. (2016). The role of stewardship in the internationalisation of family firms. *International Journal of Entrepreneurial Venturing, 8*(4), 400–421.

Monreal-Pérez, J., & Sánchez-Marín, G. (2017). Does transitioning from family to non-family controlled firm influence internationalization? *Journal of Small Business and Enterprise Development, 24*(4), 775–792.

Mort, G. S., & Weerawardena, J. (2006). Networking capability and international entrepreneurship: How networks function in Australian born global firms. *International Marketing Review, 23*(5), 549–572.

Muñoz-Bullón, F., & Sánchez-Bueno, M. J. (2012). Do family ties shape the performance consequences of diversification? Evidence from the European Union. *Journal of World Business, 47*(3), 469–477.

Musteen, M., Datta, D. K., & Butts, M. M. (2014). Do international networks and foreign market knowledge facilitate SME internationalization? Evidence from the Czech Republic. *Entrepreneurship Theory and Practice, 38*(4), 749–774.

Musteen, M., Francis, J., & Datta, D. K. (2010). The influence of international networks on internationalization speed and performance: A study of Czech SMEs. *Journal of World Business, 45*(3), 197–205.

Nordman, E. R., & Melén, S. (2008). The impact of different kinds of knowledge for the internationalization process of born globals in the biotech business. *Journal of World Business, 43*(2), 171–185.

Olivares-Mesa, A., & Cabrera-Suarez, K. (2006). Factors affecting the timing of the export development process: Does the family influence on the business make a difference? *International Journal of Globalisation and Small Business, 1*(4), 326–339.

Peng, M. W., & Luo, Y. (2000). Managerial ties and firm performance in a transition economy: The nature of a micro-macro link. *Academy of Management Journal, 43*(3), 486–501.

Podsakoff, P. M., MacKenzie, S. B., Lee, J. Y., & Podsakoff, N. P. (2003). Common method biases in behavioral research: A critical review of the literature and recommended remedies. *Journal of Applied Psychology, 88*(5), 879.

Podsakoff, P. M., MacKenzie, S. B., & Podsakoff, N. P. (2012). Sources of method bias in social science research and recommendations on how to control it. *Annual Review of Psychology, 63*, 539–569.

Podsakoff, P. M., & Organ, D. W. (1986). Self-reports in organizational research: Problems and prospects. *Journal of Management, 12*(4), 531–544.

Pongelli, C., Caroli, M. G., & Cucculelli, M. (2016). Family business going abroad: The effect of family ownership on foreign market entry mode decisions. *Small Business Economics, 47*(3), 787–801.

Prashantham, S., & Dhanaraj, C. (2010). The dynamic influence of social capital on the international growth of new ventures. *Journal of Management Studies, 47*(6), 967–994.

Ray, S., Mondal, A., & Ramachandran, K. (2018). How does family involvement affect a firm's internationalization? An investigation of Indian family firms. *Global Strategy Journal, 8*(1), 73–105.

Roessl, D. (2005). Family businesses and interfirm cooperation. *Family Business Review, 18*(3), 203–214.

Sarasvathy, S., Kumar, K., York, J. G., & Bhagavatula, S. (2014). An effectual approach to international entrepreneurship: Overlaps, challenges, and provocative possibilities. *Entrepreneurship Theory and Practice, 38*(1), 71–93.

Scholes, L., Mustafa, M., & Chen, S. (2016). Internationalization of small family firms: The influence of family from a socioemotional wealth perspective. *Thunderbird International Business Review, 58*(2), 131–146.

Schulze, W. S., Lubatkin, M. H., & Dino, R. N. (2002). Altruism, agency, and the competitiveness of family firms. *Managerial and Decision Economics, 23*(4-5), 247–259.

Senik, Z. C., Scott-Ladd, B., Entrekin, L., & Adham, K. A. (2011). Networking and internationalization of SMEs in emerging economies. *Journal of International Entrepreneurship, 9*(4), 259–281.

Shanker, M. C., & Astrachan, J. H. (1996). Myths and realities: Family businesses' contribution to the US economy—A framework for assessing family business statistics. *Family Business Review, 9*(2), 107–123.

Stieg, P., Cesinger, B., Apfelthaler, G., Kraus, S., & Cheng, C. F. (2018). Antecedents of successful internationalization in family and non-family firms: How knowledge resources and collaboration intensity shape international performance. *Journal of Small Business Strategy, 28*(1), 14–27.

Swinth, R. L., & Vinton, K. L. (1993). Do family-owned businesses have a strategic advantage in international joint ventures? *Family Business Review, 6*(1), 19–30.

Tasavori, M., Zaefarian, R., & Eng, T. Y. (2018). Internal social capital and international firm performance in emerging market family firms: The mediating role of participative governance. *International Small Business Journal, 36*(8), 887–910.

Torkkeli, L., Kuivalainen, O., Saarenketo, S., & Puumalainen, K. (2016). Network competence in Finnish SMEs: Implications for growth. *Baltic Journal of Management, 11*(2), 207–230.

Torkkeli, L., Saarenketo, S., & Nummela, N. (2015). The development of network competence in an internationalized SME. In *Handbook on international alliance and network research*. Cheltenham: Edward Elgar Publishing.

Torkkeli, L., Uzhegova, M., Kuivalainen, O., Saarenketo, S., & Puumalainen, K. (forthcoming). Internationalisation of Family Enterprises: The Role of Entrepreneurial Orientation and International Growth Orientation. *International Journal of Business and Globalisation*.

Vahlne, J. E., & Johanson, J. (2017). From internationalization to evolution: The Uppsala model at 40 years. *Journal of International Business Studies, 48*(9), 1087–1102.

Van Alstyne, M., & Brynjolfsson, E. (2005). Global village or cyber-balkans? Modeling and measuring the integration of electronic communities. *Management Science, 51*(6), 851–868.

Verbeke, A., & Kano, L. (2012). The transaction cost economics theory of the family firm: Family–based human asset specificity and the bifurcation bias. *Entrepreneurship Theory and Practice, 36*(6), 1183–1205.

Ward, J. L. (2004). *Perpetuating the family business: 50 lessons learned from long-lasting successful families in business*. New York: Palgrave Macmillan.

Wiseman, R. M., & Gomez-Mejia, L. R. (1998). A behavioral agency model of managerial risk taking. *Academy of Management Review, 23*(1), 133–153.

Yang, X., Li, J., Stanley, L. J., Kellermanns, F. W., & Li, X. (2018). How family firm characteristics affect internationalization of Chinese family SMEs. *Asia Pacific Journal of Management, 37*(2), 417–448.

Yli-Renko, H., Autio, E., & Tontti, V. (2002). Social capital, knowledge, and the international growth of technology-based new firms. *International Business Review, 11*(3), 279–304.

Zahra, S. A. (2003). International expansion of U.S. manufacturing family businesses: The effect of ownership and involvement. *Journal of Business Venturing, 18*(4), 495–512.

Zahra, S. A., & Hayton, J. C. (2008). The effect of international venturing on firm performance: The moderating influence of absorptive capacity. *Journal of Business Venturing, 23*(2), 195–220.

Zahra, S. A., Ireland, R. D., & Hitt, M. A. (2000). International expansion by new venture firms: International diversity, mode of market entry, technological learning, and performance. *Academy of Management Journal, 43*(5), 925–950.

Zain, M., & Ng, S. I. (2006). The impacts of network relationships on SMEs' internationalization process. *Thunderbird International Business Review, 48*(2), 183–205.

Zellweger, T. M., Chrisman, J. J., Chua, J. H., & Steier, L. P. (2019). Social structures, social relationships, and family firms. *Entrepreneurship Theory and Practice, 43*(2), 207–223.

Zellweger, T. M., Kellermanns, F. W., Chrisman, J. J., & Chua, J. H. (2012). Family control and family firm valuation by family CEOs: The importance of intentions for transgenerational control. *Organization Science, 23*(3), 851–868.

Zhou, L., Wu, W. P., & Luo, X. (2007). Internationalization and the performance of born-global SMEs: The mediating role of social networks. *Journal of International Business Studies, 38*(4), 673–690.

4

An Integrative Framework of Family Firms and Foreign Entry Strategies

Maria Cristina Sestu

Introduction

Family firms are the most common form of business entity around the world (Faccio & Lang, 2002).

From a historical point of view, it is impossible to locate precisely in place or time the origin of the organisational form of the family firm (Colli, 2003). "They were in the absolute majority during the first industrial revolution, as well as in the pre-industrial period, going from the urban artisan workshop to the famous Medici Bank … to the sophisticated commercial and trading company of Andrea Barbarigo, 'Merchant of Venice' " (Colli, 2003, p. 8).

Nowadays family business still plays a key role in the worldwide economy. They account for two-thirds of all businesses around the world and are responsible for 70–90 per cent of global GDP (Family Firm Institute, 2017). Common wisdom associates the idea of family businesses to small and domestic firms, but even some of the largest companies in the world, that is, Ford, Samsung, Wal-Mart, and with popular brands, that is, Benetton, Lego, Mars, are family firms. The peculiar presence of family members both in ownership and in the management, and the combination of family values and

M. C. Sestu (✉)
Department of Global Economics and Management, University of Groningen, Groningen, Netherlands
e-mail: m.c.sestu@rug.nl

© The Author(s), under exclusive license to Springer Nature Switzerland AG 2021
T. Leppäaho, S. Jack (eds.), *The Palgrave Handbook of Family Firm Internationalization*,
https://doi.org/10.1007/978-3-030-66737-5_4

non-economic goals with business goals affecting firms' strategies, require specific knowledge to understand their mechanisms and choices. Indeed, prior literature has largely demonstrated that corporate governance characteristics (e.g. ownership structure) affect the firm's strategic decisions (see Aguilera, Marano, & Haxhi, 2019 for an excellent review), for example, internationalisation. Academic research showed that also the shareholder type affects the firm's strategies (Calabrò, Torchia, Pukall, & Mussolino, 2013; Sanders & Carpenter, 2015; Sciascia, Mazzola, Astrachan, & Pieper, 2012; Zahra, 2003). Thus, different kinds of ownership affect international strategies (Filatotchev, Strange, Piesse, & Lien, 2007; Oesterle, Richta, & Fisch, 2013), because they have different values, incentives, temporal preferences and risk attitude (Lin, 2012). International business literature concerning family firms largely investigated the degree of internationalisation (Pukall & Calabrò, 2014). Indeed, it has been showed that family-related variables, as the involvement of family members in management, affect the degree (international sales) and the geographic scope (number of countries) of internationalisation (Arregle, Naldi, Nordqvist, & Hitt, 2012; Zahra, 2003). Moreover, they may also influence the timing of internationalisation. However, while there is extensive research on the internationalisation process of family firms (Metsola, Leppäaho, Paavilainen-Mäntymäki, & Plakoyiannaki, 2020), for a long time it has been largely ignoring the family firms' choice between different entry modes (Lin, 2012), and only recently studies in this area are emerging. Indeed, the extensive empirical research on entry modes mostly focused on country, industry and firm-specific determinants (Zhao, Luo, & Suh, 2004), overlooking the role of corporate governance and ownership type, family ownership in particular. Scholars that over the past decades have extensively studied foreign entry strategies clearly demonstrate that these strategies are crucial for firms moving their first steps in a foreign country. Indeed, choosing the right entry mode affects the success, performance and future development in the host country. Given the crucial relevance of these strategies and the key role in the economy played by family firms, recently, a growing body of studies started to investigate family firms' entry modes (Boellis, Mariotti, Minichilli, & Piscitello, 2016; Pongelli, Caroli, & Cucculelli, 2016; Sestu & Majocchi, 2020).

On the one hand, we have an extensive literature both on family firms' peculiarities and on their internationalisation (De Massis, Frattini, Majocchi, & Piscitello, 2018; Pukall & Calabrò, 2014), on the other hand, international business scholars have largely explored foreign entry strategies (Zhao et al., 2004). Decades of entry mode research left scholars with the question, "Do we really need more entry mode studies?" (Shaver, 2013). The significant and interesting results of the recent studies exploring family firms' foreign entry strategies show that the research in this field needs to be developed further (Xu, Hitt, & Miller, 2020). Indeed, our knowledge on how family firms choose their entry mode and why they prefer one mode to another is still limited and deserves more attention. Thus, we surely need more entry mode research to understand clearly how family firms choose between different entry modes. Indeed, we know that family firms are different, that their international expansion is different as well as the process that they follow to internationalize, but how do they choose between equity and non-equity mode of entry, or between joint venture and wholly owned subsidiary? How can we reconcile this belief that we do not need more entry mode research with the family business literature that clearly demonstrated that the overlapping of economic and non-economic goals in these firms significantly influences their strategies at all levels? This chapter aims to answer these questions. What is missed in the literature is a bridge between these two streams of research, in order to organize their points of conjunction and to identify fruitful insights for future research. The aim of this chapter is to provide an integrative framework of entry mode and family firms' literature in order to guide future research on family firms' foreign entry strategies. Indeed, an integration between entry modes theories and family business theories is necessary to investigate fruitfully family firms' foreign entry strategies. Different scholars have indeed called for an integration of family theories and internationalisations theories (De Massis et al., 2018). As highlighted by De Massis et al. (2018), first attempts in this direction have been made by scholars integrating internationalisation, corporate governance and family firm theories, and agency and stewardship theories into transaction cost theory. However, further integration is needed regarding transaction cost and resource-based view. On the one hand, entry mode research has been extensively investigated through the lens of transaction cost theory and resource-based view. On the other hand, the complex and broad area of family businesses have been described and analysed using multiple theories from agency theory to stewardship and stagnation perspectives, from resource-based view and socioemotional wealth perspectives, to transaction cost theory. While all of these theories can offer valuable insights to the research on family firms' entry strategies, the integration of the transaction cost theory and resource-based view developed in parallel from both the entry mode and family firm research should be combined. Using an integrative framework of these two theories will help scholars investigate more in-depth family firms' entry strategies. Indeed, despite some studies have examined family firms' entry mode choices, our knowledge on this topic is still limited and many aspects need to be explored further. The purpose of this chapter is to highlight the existing gap in the literature regarding the relationship between family businesses and entry strategies, providing insights for future research integrating family firms' theories with entry mode research.

This chapter aims to contribute to both the entry mode research and family business literature. First, it identifies common points between these stream of research. Second, it provides a discussion of several aspects that still need to be investigated for a continuous and fruitful interaction between entry mode research and family business literature.

The chapter is organised into three main sections. The first section starts by briefly introducing the main family firms' peculiarities. This introduction is useful to explain why these firms might choose different entry modes in comparison to non-family firms. Then, it reviews the entry mode determinants, focusing on the transaction cost and resource-based view in order to develop an integrative framework. The second section aims to reconcile the literature on family businesses and entry modes, underlining how firm ownership is another important determinant of entry modes. Finally, the last section presents concluding remarks and insights for future research.

Theoretical Framework

Does corporate governance affect entry mode? Corporate governance mechanisms (e.g. ownership concentration and board of directors) affect the firm's strategies, as entry mode choices. A single shareholder having enough voting rights, directly or through pyramids, is able to control the firm and shape its strategies. Shareholders with a high percentage of equity stakes, indeed, are more motivated to influence managers' decisions (Shleifer & Vishny, 2007). Therefore, the goals and the risk attitude of the main shareholder affect the entry strategies. Because entry modes affect the firm's performance and consequently shareholders' wealth, more wealth the shareholder has invested in the company, the more he or she will be affected. Thus, it is of primary importance to identify the type of the shareholder, such as individual or family, financial company or state authority, because they have different goals and risk attitudes. Moreover, a family controlling a company through ownership might magnify its control having other family members in the management team, reducing agency costs of the first type (principal-agent). The owning family might influence the firm's strategy also through the board of directors. Indeed, because the board has two primary functions, monitoring and advisory, directors influence the strategies of the firm through their experience and

4 An Integrative Framework of Family Firms and Foreign Entry... 107

demographic characteristics as managers do. Thus, the presence of family directors might influence their advisory role.

Despite the common acceptance that corporate governance affects firms' strategic decisions, only recently scholars started to investigate its role played on affecting foreign entry strategies (Sestu & Majocchi, 2020; Xu et al., 2020). In international business some scholars studied the effect of corporate governance on the scope and intensity of firms' internationalisation. However, with few exceptions (Filatotchev et al., 2007; Musteen, Datta, & Herrmann, 2009) they failed to study how the same governance characteristics affect entry mode choice.

The few empirical studies on the choice between joint venture and wholly owned subsidiary (the most studied choice in entry mode research) obtain inconsistent results, and more research is needed. Although they agree into arguing that ownership structure affects the choice (Filatotchev et al., 2007), the direction of the effect is still not clear. To exemplify, on the one hand, Musteen et al. (2009) found that institutional owners are more likely to choose a wholly owned subsidiary rather than a joint venture. Indeed, institutional shareholders, due to their large equity ownership in the firm and difficulties to disinvest rapidly, have a long-term orientation. On the other hand, Filatotchev et al. (2007), distinguishing between foreign and domestic institutional shareholders, found that foreign shareholders are more likely to prefer a full ownership investment, while domestic institutional investors prefer a low ownership commitment mode.

Scholars also showed a relation between managers' payment scheme and the probability to choose a wholly owned subsidiary rather than a joint venture. Indeed, managers with a high percentage of stakes in the firm are more likely to choose a full ownership mode rather than shared ownership (Datta, Musteen, & Herrmann, 2009; Musteen et al., 2009). Moreover, some scholars found that managers with compensations linked to long-term performance are more likely to choose a wholly owned subsidiary (Datta et al., 2009; Musteen et al., 2009). In the extant research, there are only a few attempts to investigate corporate governance effects on the establishment mode. Interesting in this sense are the results of Matta and Beamish (2008). They found that CEOs with a longer career prospect are more likely to make an acquisition. However, their study is limited to the effect on the probability to make an acquisition or not. It would be interesting to study if the CEO career horizon also affects the choice between acquisition and greenfield. Moreover, Datta et al. (2009) found that firms with a high percentage of outside directors prefer a full acquisition over a joint venture. The crucial role of directors is not limited to the monitoring function. They influence managers' choice, and they provide valuable experience and knowledge. Accordingly, Lai, Chen and Chang (2012) found that directors with a previous acquisition or joint venture experience encourage managers to make an acquisition.

Family Firms

One of the key aspects of firms' corporate governance is related to concentration and type of shareholder. Family is the most common type of ownership. Despite the relevance of family businesses in the worldwide economy, only in the 1990s, the field became a separate academic discipline (Bird, Welsch, Astrachan, & Pistrui, 2002). The development of the new field proceeded slowly, at least until 1995. Indeed, before that year, the number of the articles published in the field was limited, even if the first journal entirely dedicated to family firms, the *Family Business Review*, had been released by 1988. Accordingly, academic research began to study family firms' internationalisation only in the last three decades (Kontinen & Ojala, 2010).

Despite a huge number of articles published in the field from different perspectives (Corporate Governance, Accounting, Business History, Organisational Studies and International Business), research still lacks a unique definition (Chua, Chrisman, & Sharma, 1999). Variations in the definitions might produce considerably different results (Colli, 2003). Indeed, reviewing studies on the effect of family control on firm's performance (see Dyer (2006) for a review) and internationalisation (Arregle, Duran, Hitt, & van Essen, 2017), the obtained evidence is so far inconclusive. What emerges from the review of this vast variety of requirements is that researchers applying different definitions fail to motivate theoretically the importance of the components used to define a family firm (Chrisman, Chua, & Sharma, 2005). Furthermore, the lack of consensus on a unique definition might make difficult to compare the findings of previous researchers. However, differences between countries, regarding culture and institutional environments, may affect the concept of the family firm, making difficult the use of a unique definition (Carney, 2005).

Also, with reference to the theories, there is a wide variety. Indeed, researchers approaching family firms' internationalisation ground on different theories: agency theory, stewardship perspective, resource-based view, stagnation and socioemotional wealth perspectives, and transaction cost theory. These theories highlighted the key characteristics of family firms that in turn might affect their entry modes.

Authors highlight the following family firms' characteristics: the conservatism, the importance to maintain control of the business, and consequently their tendency to do not raise debt, preferring an almost permanent lack of financial resources (Molly, Laveren, & Deloof, 2010). However, this reluctance to increase debt limits the financial resources and consequently the possibility to make investments in order to grow and/or internationalise. Because the increase of debt financing can be easily translated in a loss of control, family firms might be reluctant raising debt and change the capital structure of the company.

Moreover, scholars using the expression "socioemotional wealth" highlighted the idiosyncratic family businesses' characteristics regarding the affective sphere (Berrone, Cruz, & Gomez-Mejia, 2012). Gomez-Meija et al. defined the socioemotional wealth as the "non-financial aspects of the firm that meet the family's needs, such as identity, the ability to exercise family influence, and the perpetuation of the family dynasty" (Gomez-Mejia, Haynes, Nunez-Nickel, Jacobson, & Moyano-Fuentes, 2007, p. 106). Thus, the risk propensity of family businesses varies with regard to their socioemotional wealth. To preserve it they are willing to take high-risk investment decisions, and at the same time, they are strongly risk-averse if the risk concerns the loss of the socioemotional wealth. Thus, the willingness to take risk is high if this is necessary to retain the direct control of the firm and to increase the business with entrepreneurial activities. On the contrary, if the encompassed risk is to lose the family wealth, family businesses are more risk-averse than non-family firms (Naldi, Nordqvist, Sjöberg, & Wiklund, 2007).

Entry Modes: An Overview

Entry mode research concerns the decision about how to enter a foreign market, and specifically on the choice between at least two different entry modes. These are usually long-term strategies difficult to change, particularly when they imply long-term contracts or require a significant resource commitment. Moreover, entry mode choices affect firms' international success and their performance (Hill, Hwang, & Kim, 1990). For this reason, foreign entry strategies have been a crucial theme in international business research for the past three decades. Referring to family firms, we can immediately link these aspects to their peculiar features. Indeed, while the entry mode literature defines entry modes as long-term strategies, previous studies have also established that family firms are more long-term oriented in comparison to non-family firms. This long-term orientation will, therefore, influence differently their entry mode choices.

Entering a new market means to make two important and long-term decisions. Firstly, the choice between contracts and equity and in the latter case the level of ownership. Second, the establishment mode: greenfield or acquisition. Anderson and Gatignon (1986) ground their seminal paper, one of the first papers on entry modes, in the transaction cost analysis as formulated by Williamson (1979). They stress the importance of trade-off between control and resource commitment and they provide a series of testable propositions to study entry modes. They delineate a framework in which the entry mode choice is affected by the MNE's desired degree of control. Choosing the level of control over the investment, the firm is choosing simultaneously the resource commitment and the position in the trade-off risk and adjusted return associated with the investment. They state that the entry mode choice is a continuum of increasing resource commitment, control and risk (E. Anderson & Gatignon, 1986). The seventeen entry modes identified in their article are classified in a continuum of increasing control, looking at the control as the determiner of risk and return, and therefore efficiency. The optimal choice between complete integration and complete non-integration of an activity depends on the four constructs of transaction cost theory: asset specificity, uncertainty, information asymmetries, high frequency. In their framework, the available options of entry mode range from contracts to wholly owned subsidiaries, with the joint venture seen as an intermediate point, between hierarchy and contracts (E. Anderson & Gatignon, 1986). These three concepts (i.e. resources, control, and risk) that have been the milestones for entry mode research, for different reasons, are also crucial for family business literature. First, scholars have identified a lack of resources (financial and managerial resources) as one of the key characteristics of these firms. Thus, while entry mode research states that all firms entering a foreign market have to make choices on their desired resource commitment, this choice is even more significant for family firms, and it is again determined by the mix of their peculiarities that affect also the resource availability that might be employed to enter a new market. Second, control is a recurring concept in family business literature (Gomez-Mejia, Cruz, Berrone, & De Castro, 2011). Indeed, family firms aiming to maintain control over the business to pass to the next generations, when they have to choose the level of control in an entry mode, must take into consideration also other non-economic aspects. Finally, regarding the third concept, risk, an intense debate on the risk attitude of family firms is ongoing. Indeed, some scholars consider family firms more risk-averse, because family wealth is completely invested in the business.

4 An Integrative Framework of Family Firms and Foreign Entry...

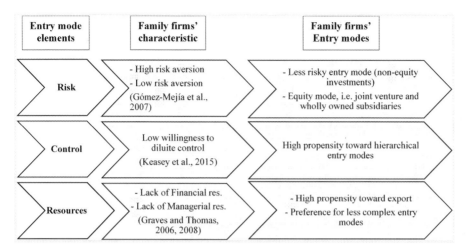

Fig. 4.1 Entry modes and family firms' characteristics. (Source: Author)

While other studies consider family firms with a high-risk attitude because of their need to maximize the investment for future generations. More likely, in family firms, the risk attitude is a trade-off between different aspects, both economic and not. As reported in Fig. 4.1, it is possible to combine the key aspects of entry mode research to some family firms' features in order to identify their more likely entry mode choices. Thus, while the general theory on entry mode sees these choices as a continuum of increasing of risk, for family firms we should consider their risk attitude generated by the overlapping of family and non-family economic goals. Therefore, ceteris paribus, family firms might be less likely to opt for equity investments than non-family firms. Moreover, because more risky investments are also those with more control, family firms will be more likely to opt for equity investments in order to maintain full control over the business also abroad. Equity modes require a high level of financial and managerial resource commitment. However, family firms with less managerial resources will be less able to manage the increasing complexity derived by international expansion. Therefore, ceteris paribus, they will be more likely to choose export over other entry modes in comparison to non-family firms. Similar reasoning applies to financial resources. Small family firms with lack of financial resource (Sestu, D'Angelo, & Majocchi, 2020) are more likely to choose export strategies rather than equity investments in comparison to non-family firms.

Entry Mode and Family Firms: The Theoretical Approaches

Authors investigating entry mode determinants ground their arguments in different theories: transaction cost theory, resource-based view, institutional theory, evolutionary process (Uppsala model) and the real option perspective. Although the vast literature, entry modes cannot be entirely explained through the use of a unique theory (Hill et al., 1990; Zhao et al., 2004). While the transaction cost and the resource-based view are the most applied frameworks in entry mode research, these theories, being used also to investigate family firms' characteristics, are ideal to investigate family firms' entry strategies. This section is dedicated to offering integration of these two theories in order to identify the most relevant aspects for family firms' entry modes.

Since the seminal paper of Coase in 1937 and the revised version by Williamson (1979), the transaction cost theory has been applied in a wide range of studies. In international business this theory has been the most used to explain foreign entry strategies (E. Anderson & Gatignon, 1986; Hennart, 1982; Rugman & Verbeke, 1992). Indeed, the trade-off between integration and non-integration of Williamson's (1979) framework has an extensive range of application, from the analysis of market versus hierarchy in daily activities, from the decision making or buy in defining the boundaries of the firms, to the choice of the right mode to enter a foreign market (Hennart, 1982).

The key determinants of the transaction cost theory in entry modes and at the same time most relevant for family firms' entry strategies are the asset specificity and the uncertainty of the transaction. The specificity of an asset is related to the degree of which an asset is dedicated to specific use in a specific transaction with another firm and it is not differently utilisable. Williamson (1985) describes six kinds of assets specificity related to investment: site specificity, physical asset, dedicated assets, human asset, brand name capital and temporal specificity (Zhao et al., 2004). However, empirical entry mode research often fails to find a proxy for all these kinds of specificity (Zhao et al., 2004). The variable most used to measure asset specificity is the research and development intensity. Scholars argue that firms with high R&D intensity, having more technological capabilities and thus more specific knowledge needed to be protected from a partner's opportunism, prefer a wholly owned subsidiary over a joint venture (Gatignon & Anderson, 1988; Makino & Neupert, 2000). However, other important kinds of assets (knowledge and capabilities) might justify the joint venture choice. Chen and Hennart (2002), for instance, found that marketing resources are more important in determining the joint venture choice. An important aspect of asset specificity pointed out by Hennart is the difficulty to transact an asset and who owns that. Hennart (2009) state that the entry mode choice depends on whether the asset is easy or difficult to transact. Moreover, the choice depends on whether the asset difficult to transact is owned by the foreign firm aiming to enter a host country, or by a local firm that owns a difficult to transact complementary asset needed by the foreign firm. In Hennart's model, the MNE entering a foreign country needs access to complementary assets owned by a local firm. These assets might be difficult or easy to transact. At the same time also the MNE owns some assets that can be difficult or easy to transact. It is the combination of the assets of both the MNE and the local firm that determines the entry mode choice. Thus, for instance, if both firms own assets difficult to transact, neither of them will be able to acquire the other company. In this case, the MNE will enter the foreign country with a JV to share ownership of the assets with the local firm. When the MNE owns an asset difficult to transact, while the local firm owns assets that are easy to transact, the MNE will fully acquire the local company and it will enter the foreign country through a wholly owned subsidiary (Hennart, Sheng, & Pimenta, 2015). Hennart provides a practical example of this model using the example of knowledge, which is typically an asset difficult to transact, especially if it is tacit and not codifiable.

Recently the transaction cost theory has been also applied family firms (Memili, Misra, Chrisman, & Welsh, 2017; Verbeke, Yuan, & Kano, 2019), providing interesting explanations on family-specific assets, that can be in turn used to explain entry modes. While the general theory on entry mode has sometimes failed to find an adequate proxy for asset specificity according to transaction cost theory, transaction cost theorists in family business literature agree that family firms are able to develop specific assets, completely different from those of non-family firms. Indeed, some authors (Gedajlovic & Carney, 2010; Verbeke & Kano, 2010, 2012) apply the concept of specific assets of the transaction cost theory to the idiosyncratic characteristics of family firms (Verbeke & Kano, 2012). Williamson distinguished between specific and generic assets, arguing that the latter is easy to transact and therefore are generally traded through markets. Gedajlovic and Carney (2010), grounding on Williamson's work, added that even generic assets might be difficult to transact. Thus, there are generic non-tradable assets, which have a wide variety of application inside the company but are sticky to the firm (Gedajlovic & Carney, 2010). They identified the family businesses' resources analysed by the above-presented theories, such as social capital, reputation and tacit knowledge, are generic non-tradable assets. In addition, family firms' governance structure fosters the capabilities to developing, sustaining and appropriating value from these assets (Gedajlovic & Carney, 2010; Verbeke & Kano, 2010). The transaction cost model of Hennart (2009) can thus be extended to family firms' assets. Indeed, while Hennart describes his model using the example of knowledge difficult to transact, we can extend it to family firms' reasoning on the tacit knowledge developed inside these firms (Gedajlovic & Carney, 2010). Furthermore, we can extend the model more generally to family-specific assets that being sticky to the company, non-tradable, perfectly fit the Hennart's model. Thus, these assets, depending on whether they are owned by a family MNE or a local family firm, will affect differently the entry mode choice (Sestu & Majocchi, 2020). Moreover, family firms, because of the social bonding and bridging capital that they developed, might build stronger networks in the local context. This capability may influence the choice of a MNE investing in a foreign country because it may prefer to have as a partner a local family firm rather than a non-family firm to exploit its local knowledge and related networks, which are another form of important assets difficult to transact.

Moreover, family firms' have different behaviours depending on whether the assets involved in the decision are strictly linked to the family or not. Thus, their decisions suffer from a "bifurcation bias" towards family-assets (Verbeke & Kano, 2012). Family firms' behaviours are thus affected by these specific family assets and might be explained through the transaction cost lens. Recent studies applying transaction cost theory to family businesses in general (Kano & Verbeke, 2018; Memili et al., 2017; Verbeke et al., 2019) and family firms' entry modes (Sestu & Majocchi, 2020) more specifically show that this stream of literature deserves more attention and further research.

Another determinant of the transaction costs in entry mode research is the uncertainty related to the transaction. This might be internal or external to the company, concerning the environment in which the corporation invest. Uncertainty, in the case of either internal or external, has been denoted in a wide variety of ways. For instance, internal uncertainty has been denoted as international experience and cultural distance. External uncertainty has been connoted as governance quality (Kaufmann, Kraay, & Mastruzzi, 2004); political stability (perceived or from secondary data); government effectiveness; regulatory quality; rule of law; corruption (Slangen & van Tulder, 2009); country risk; industry growth; industry concentration ratio; the size of the market; the perceived measure of target market volatility and diversity; perceived economic stability; perceived market potential and cultural distance.

Thus, we can consider uncertainty as a source of risk. Previous literature has established that family ownership varies in terms of risk taking, which in turn may influence the choice to expand internationally (Zahra, 2003). With reference to the risk attitude of family firms, there are opposite views. Often the family business literature qualified family firms as risk-averse because their entire wealth is invested in the family business (Gomez-Mejia et al., 2007). Other authors argue that family firms show higher entrepreneurial risky behaviour in comparison to non-family businesses (Naldi et al., 2007; Zahra, 2005; Zahra, Neubaum, & Larraneta, 2007). Grounding on the "socioemotional wealth", scholars state that family firms are risk-willing and risk-averse at the same time, depending on how the decision affects the preservation of the "socioemotional wealth" (Gomez-Mejia et al., 2007). Risk aversion in family business research assumed mostly the connotation of financial risk aversion and it is measured as the proportion of debt (González, Guzmán, Pombo, & Trujillo, 2013). However, given the relevance that non-financial aspects assume in family firms, other measures of risk attitudes coming from entrepreneurial research are relevant as the risk attitude towards the involvement in risky activities, for example, international alliances and new foreign markets entries (Zahra, 2005).

Finally, some empirical studies focused on the effect of another transaction cost determinant, not expressively included in Coase's and Williamson's works: the free-riding risk. This is defined as the reputation damages that a firm may incur allowing another company to use its brand abroad. Indeed, the opportunistic behaviours of the overseas firm using the brand have consequences directly to the image of the brand owner. The literature has emphasised the relevance of a large variety of non-economic goals for family firms. Most of them require a long-term orientation, that is, special attention to maintain and nurture a corporate reputation, the desire to maintain direct control over the business and pass it to the next generations. Reputational assets are crucial for family firms especially because often the name of the firm coincides with the name of the family. Thus, given the prominence of reputation for family firms, they might be even more cautious in avoiding free-riding risk. This might influence partner selection in joint venture decisions. Indeed, ceteris paribus, a firm that does not want to damage its reputation and, if possible, increase its quality would be a better partner. Together with the long-term orientation of family firms, this increases the likelihood of joint ventures for family firms. Indeed, their long-term orientation will decrease the chances of failure in the joint venture.

The basic concepts of the resource-based view (Barney, 1991, 2001) (resources that are valuable, rare, inimitable and non-substitutable are a source of competitive advantage), extended to include the knowledge base perspective (focused on knowledge as a resource) and the organisational capability view (focused on the capabilities owned by a firm), have been the theoretical frame for different empirical studies on foreign entry strategies. Scholars using this perspective explain the entry mode choice on the basis of the resources owned by the firm. According to this broad perspective, firms choosing a hierarchical governance mode are able to protect their resources and to maintain the full control of them, while developing routines in the foreign subsidiaries they increase the value of their resources (Brouthers, Brouthers, & Werner, 2008). The mixed results obtained by the general studies on entry mode might be eventually overcome by investigating more in detail the source of the resources. For instance, looking at the owner of these resources. Is the owner of these resources a family firm? Do family firms develop different resources in comparison to non-family firms? Scholars point out that family firms control unique inimitable resources, deriving from the family relationships, which allow them to build and sustain a competitive advantage over the other type of companies (Habbershon, 2006; Habbershon & Williams, 1999; Zahra, Hayton, & Salvato, 2004). Habbershon and Williams (1999) developed the concept of familiness to identify "the unique bundle of resources a particular firm has because of the systems interaction between the family, its individual members, and the business". Furthermore, the familiness is a concept that helps us to see the business, the family ownership and management, and family culture as a continuum of interactions and not just as a static system where ownership and management overlap (Habbershon, Williams, & MacMillan, 2003). This system of interconnected relationships and the shared culture makes inimitable the family firms' assets (Zahra et al., 2004). Indeed informal interactions among family owners and family managers simplify the communication inside the company and speed the decision-making process (Carr & Bateman, 2009). Reputation is another key resource in the family business. Often the name of the controlling family is closely associated with the name of the firm, or even it is included in the company name. Controlling families consider the business as a continuum of the family; hence, they carefully consider the firm's reputation. Thus, family and firm reputation coincide. Families build over generations a good image and strong reputation of the firm, which facilitates relationships with customers, partners and suppliers. Moreover, previous studies have debated the lack of financial or managerial resources. Thus, the application of the resource-based view to entry mode research should be deepened to include also these family firms' peculiarities from the familiness as an additional resource, to the lack of resources (i.e. financial and managerial). They might affect entry mode choices differently in comparison to non-family firms. For instance, the lack of resources might positively influence the choice of non-equity modes. At the same time, the familiness might be positively influenced by equity investments in order to exploit this competitive advantage also in foreign countries. However, according to the entry mode scholars, the advantages derived from the resources are highly context-specific (Brouthers et al., 2008). Indeed, the institutional environment moderates the effect of resources-specific advantage. Different normative and regulatory environments have different effects on firms' decisions. Firms adopt the most implemented strategy in each institutional context, mimicking the other incumbent firms (Ang, Benischke, & Doh, 2015). In accordance with the institutional theory, entering a foreign country with strong institutions moderates the costs of alternative organisational forms (Meyer, Estrin, Bhaumik, & Peng, 2009; Williamson, 1985). Thus, to understand entry mode choices is important to investigate the role of different institutional settings (Brouthers, 2013). This will shed light on the firms' ability to exploit and enhance their competitive advantage that varies in accordance with the institutional framework. This argument assumes particular relevance for family firms as family firms' characteristics, as well as institutions, are highly context-specific. Thus, studying family firms, and more specifically family firms' entry mode, require particular attention to the interaction and relationship between family firms' characteristics and institutional context.

Scholars interested in investigating family firms' entry strategies will find it beneficial to ground their arguments on both transaction cost and resource-based view, integrating aspects highlighted by entry mode research and finding the corresponding aspects in the same theory using the family business literature. First, entry mode research found that according to transaction cost theory the higher is the assets specificity the higher is the probability of equity modes in comparison to non-equity and wholly owned subsidiary in comparison to a joint venture. Scholars applying the transaction cost theory to family firms have identified some generic non-tradeable assets (Gedajlovic & Carney, 2010). These family-specific assets are therefore sticky to the company and difficult to transact. Therefore, family firms are more likely to choose equity investments rather than a non-equity mode of entry in comparison to non-family firms. The uncertainty (internal and external to the firm) in entry mode research has been identified as an important determinant negatively related to the choice of risky investments. This might mean either equity investments or entry in high-risk countries. The higher is the uncertainty, the lower is the probability of high commitment entry mode (wholly owned subsidiary, or joint ventures) (Delios & Henisz, 2003). At the same time, when the uncertainty is related to the scarce knowledge of the host country, firms may opt for a joint venture with a local partner. These findings should be integrated with the mixed arguments on the risk attitude of family firms.

Grounding on the resource-based view, entry mode research state that lack of resources negatively relates to the probability to enter a foreign country with an equity mode. Moreover, resources are more important the more the host country is unfamiliar (Mutinelli & Piscitello, 1998). These findings should be integrated with the resource-based view applied to family firms. Indeed, while the debate on lack of financial resources of family firms is still open, authors agree that family firms develop an important system of resources, that is, the familiness. Thus, in investigating family firms' entry modes it is important to understand how the familiness affects the choice.

Finally, to complete an integrative framework of family firms' entry mode the uncertainty identified through the lens of transaction cost is assimilable to the result of resource-based view that resources are more relevant in unfamiliar countries and therefore when the international experience or the ability to handle a specific institutional context is low. Moreover, the transaction cost theory established that family firms develop specific assets, while the resource-based view argues that family firms develop a complex system of resources named familiness (Chrisman, Chua, & Steier, 2005). These concepts can be integrated to understand how family-specific assets/resources affect entry mode choice. Thus, an integrative framework is possible both for the same theory from the two different lenses of entry mode research and family

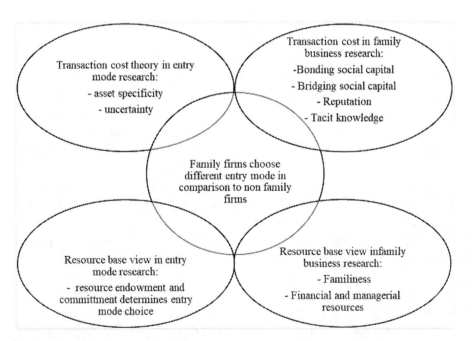

Fig. 4.2 Integrative framework. (Source: Author)

4 An Integrative Framework of Family Firms and Foreign Entry... 119

literature and at the same time between the two different theoretical frameworks, that is, transaction cost and resource-based view. Figure 4.2 summarizes the integrative framework of the different aspects that scholars interested in this field might take into consideration.

Family firms and foreign entry strategies. While a recent literature review (Metsola et al., 2020) on family firms' internationalisation process identified 172 empirical papers on this topic, the number of papers on the specific area of entry mode choice is still narrow. As mentioned above with this concept we refer to papers that investigate the choice between at least two entry modes, excluding the extensive literature on the family firms' export strategies (Majocchi, D'Angelo, Forlani, & Buck, 2018). Currently, the body of research on family firms' foreign entry strategies is growing consistently, showing that it is an interesting topic and it deserves more empirical investigation to shed light on practical implications for practitioners other than to contribute to the academic literature. Previous studies showed that this process is incremental and follows the evolutionary process model. Claver, Rienda and Quer (2007) show that family companies started to internationalise through export because the resource commitment and the risk related to this entry mode are low. As companies gain experience, they choose other strategies with higher requirements than export. Family firms increase their international commitment gradually, with the growth of their international experience and starting in countries that are closed from a geographic and cultural point of view (Chang, Kao, & Kuo, 2014; Claver et al., 2007; Claver, Rienda, & Quer, 2009). Moreover, they found a positive relationship between international experience and commitment and found that large firms are able to reach a higher degree of international commitment. Despite the interesting propositions developed by the authors, they base their study only on six companies from exclusively a small geographic area. Thus, more empirical research is needed to investigate whether these results hold in different empirical settings. Indeed, in a completely different context (Taiwanese listed firms) Lin (2012) found that family ownership positively affects the speed of internationalisation, while negatively influences the scope and the regularity of the foreign expansion. These findings might suggest that family firms, rather than follow an evolutionary process, choose an irregular rhythm of internationalisation and a narrow scope as a way to preserve the family's long-term wealth. In addition, contrary to what we would expect from an evolutionary process, Lin (2012) states that family firms are more likely to build greenfield or implement acquisitions than their counterparts.

Focusing on equity entry mode choice, Abdellatif, Amann and Jaussaud (2010) found that family businesses, due to their strong desire to keep control of the firm, establish lesser joint ventures than non-family firms do. Similarly, Pongelli et al. (2016), using a sample of Italian SMEs, found that firms owned by the founder family are more likely to choose an equity mode of entry rather than a cooperative solution. Differently, Filatotchev et al. (2007) demonstrated that a high level of family ownership is associated with entry mode with low levels of equity commitment, measured by the percentage of the equity stake in the foreign subsidiary.

Kuo, Kao, Chang and Chiu (2012) state that what really affects the choice between different equity modes is the firms' international experience. Indeed, they found that family firms with low international experience, compared to inexperienced non-family businesses, are more likely to choose joint ventures over wholly owned subsidiaries because they have a greater need for local partner' knowledge. Experienced family firms, compared with experienced non-family firms, are more likely to choose wholly owned subsidiaries over joint ventures. The study of Chang et al. (2014) adds on this specific entry mode choice (i.e. joint venture versus wholly owned subsidiary) showing that businesses tend to choose wholly owned subsidiaries when they enter a host country with high-quality governance, and this tendency is stronger for family firms. They highlighted the importance of political risk and legal and institutional environments as a determinant of the entry mode. Moreover, they state that the impact of governance quality of the host country is not the same for all firms. Low governance quality may discourage some firms from investing in that country, while other companies may exploit market opportunities (Chang et al., 2014). High level of risk in the host country may affect the entry mode choice. How family firms deal with institutional challenges and how these differences influence their foreign market entry strategies need further investigation. Moreover, the existence of support programs in the home and host country (Laufs & Schwens, 2014) might be another determinant of entry choices. Sestu and Majocchi (2020) add to the transaction cost theory and the literature on the choice between a joint venture and wholly owned subsidiaries studying it as a bilateral choice and not as the previous studies as a unilateral decision made by the MNE. Thus, they base their analysis on family firms' characteristics of both the MNE and the local firms. They found that a joint venture is more likely when both companies are family-owned and -managed. On the contrary, when the local firm is not family controlled, a wholly owned subsidiary is more likely. In line with these results, Xu et al. (2020) showed that family-dominant firms prefer equity modes that preserve the socioemotional wealth and partial equity mode (i.e. joint venture), rather than wholly owned subsidiary as institutional investors.

Regarding the establishment mode, only the study of Boellis et al. (2016) investigated the choice between greenfield and acquisition. Using a sample of Italian firms, they found that the family involvement in ownership and management fosters the propensity towards a greenfield investment.

What emerges even from the literature in this small area of research is the presence of many different definitions which make difficult the comparison of empirical results. However, the mixed results of previous studies confirm that more research is needed to shed light on the entry mode choices of family businesses and the related effects on firms' post-performance.

Future Research and Conclusions

Previous research has shown that corporate governance characteristics, and in particular family's ownership and its involvement in managerial positions and the board of directors, affect firms' strategies in different ways. Irrespective of the different definitions used family firms adopt peculiar strategies to internationalise. These studies focus on the scope and intensity of family firms' internationalisation, but as shown in the last section there is still limited, but growing, research on family firms' foreign entry modes. Entry modes have been analysed through different theoretical frameworks, and scholars have described clearly some key determinants affecting them (e.g. assets specificity, resource endowment, uncertainty and risk). However, among the various determinants, the type of the controlling shareholder has been largely overlooked. This chapter presented an integrative framework of the two most used theories in entry mode research and largely applied also to study family firms. Integrating the parallel analyses of these theories developed by entry mode and family business literature, a clear framework that can guides future research on family firms' entry modes emerges. Moreover, an integration between transaction cost and resource-based view is also possible in order to have a more coherent analysis and explore different entry mode determinants at the same time. Indeed, the complexity of these strategies makes it impossible to explore it in-depth using only one theory. The integrative framework is helpful in order to identify research questions and future research might investigate that. Table 4.1 reports some of them.

Given the peculiar characteristics of family firms, future research might investigate whether family firms differ from non-family firms regarding foreign market entry strategies. As stated above, for family firms to maintain control of the business is crucial. At the same time, some researchers have underlined the fact that fewer resources characterise family firms than

122   M. C. Sestu

Table 4.1 Insights for future research

Theoretical background	Entry mode determinant	Family firms' characteristic	Research question
Transaction cost Resource-based view (insights from socioemotional wealth arguments)	Trade-off control (resource commitment) and risk	Lack of resources Family firms desire to maintain control Risk attitude	"How does the trade-off between control and risk is affected by family firms resource endowment-desire to maintain control and risk attitude?"
Transaction cost Resource-based view	Asset specificity	Family-specific assets Familiness	"How do family firms' assets affect establishment mode choice?"
Transaction cost Resource-based view	Asset specificity	Family-specific assets Familiness	"How being a family firm affects entry mode strategies both in the case of the investing company and of the local firm?"
Transaction cost (insights from real option)	Risk	Risk attitude	"Do family firms prefer gradual investments because of their risk aversion?"
Transaction cost	Risk	Risk attitude	"Are family firms less likely to choose equity rather non-equity modes of entry?"
Transaction cost Resource-based view	Risk Resource commitment Control	Risk attitude Non-economic goals	"Does the fear of failure differently affect family and non-family firms' entry modes?"
Transaction cost	Free-riding risk, partner selection, resource commitment, control	Long-term orientation	"Are family firms more likely to choose equity mode rather that non-equity mode of entry?"
Resource-based view	Resources	Family managers	"How family managers characteristics (demographic and professional) influence a firm's entry mode choices?"
Resource-based view	Resource commitment	Lack of financial and managerial resources	"Does family firms' resource lack affect their entry strategies?"

(continued)

Table 4.1 (continued)

Theoretical background	Entry mode determinant	Family firms' characteristic	Research question
Transaction cost	General theory	General characteristics	"Do family firms have lower/higher post-entry performance compared to non-family firms?"

Source: Author

non-family firms. The high propensity to preserve the control of the company on the one hand, and on the other hand the lack of resources that characterise family firms, and therefore a lower possibility to commit resources to enter new markets, might affect their entry mode decisions. Thus, the socioemotional wealth perspective could be integrated with the transaction cost theory as interpreted by Anderson and Gatignon (E. Anderson & Gatignon, 1986) focusing on the trade-off between control (resource commitment) and risk.

Family ownership governance promotes the desire to maintain the direct control of the firm, this because of family strong personal attachment, commitment and identification with the company (Lin, 2012). The concept of family control, defined as the family's power to influence the business through ownership and managers, is strongly related to the long-term orientation of family firms. Indeed, the owning family considers the control of the firm as a way through which they preserve and maximise the family wealth for the next generations. Having control of the firm is indispensable for the family to achieve its non-economic goals (Zellweger, Kellermanns, Chrisman, & Chua, 2012). Thus, future research might integrate this desire to keep control over the firm with the entry mode literature. Indeed, the desire of family firms to maintain the control could translate in the choice of wholly owned subsidiary rather than a joint hierarchy (i.e. joint venture).

Building on the concepts of familiness from the resource-based view and asset specificity from the transaction cost, future studies might explore further how family firms' entry strategies are affected by these assets, for instance, in the establishment mode choice. The recent and still limited stream of research that applied the transaction cost theory to family firms (Verbeke & Kano, 2010) might offer important insights into the study of entry mode choices of family firms. Indeed, the peculiar characteristics of family businesses or their "familiness" might be analysed as the specific asset that is difficult to transact when a company needs to decide how to enter a foreign market. This asset might be owned by the investing firm, by the local firm, or both, complicating the transactions and affecting the decision. Further research is required to extend our knowledge regarding the role of local firms' assets in entry mode choices. Indeed, it is important to draw attention even on the assets owned by the local firm. Previous research has mostly ignored the local firm characteristics. However, the entry mode choice is not a univocal decision (Hennart, 2009). Thus, it is important to fill this gap in the literature and investigate how being a family firm affects entry mode strategies in the case of both the investing company and of the local firm. A first step in this direction has been made by Sestu and Majocchi (2020) which focused on the choice between joint venture and wholly owned subsidiary, but many other different entry mode choices need to be explored.

Two important aspects of family firms are related to their managerial and financial resource endowments. Indeed, empirical research demonstrated that family firms in comparison to non-family firms have less managerial resources (Graves & Thomas, 2006). Family ownership prefers a manager from the kinship rather than to hire an external professional manager (Bhaumik, Dimova, Burkart, Panunzi, & Shleifer, 2014). However, the second generation of family members might have access to a qualified education more oriented to the involvement in the family business (Casillas & Acedo, 2005). Moreover, the business-specific knowledge that family members acquire since their childhood in some aspects overcome the disadvantages arising from the lack of professional managers (Miller, Minichilli, & Corbetta, 2013). In addition to managerial capabilities, financial resources assume a crucial role in family business literature. Researchers have pointed out that family businesses usually have lower financial resources than non-family firms, mainly because of their reluctance to increase debt proportion (R. C. Anderson & Reeb, 2003). Grounding on this literature future research might integrate these results with the resource-based view applied to entry mode choice, to investigate whether and to what extent family firms' lack of resources affect their entry strategies. Thus, for instance, if it is true that they have fewer resources we could expect them choosing entry modes that require less resource commitment and thus less control (E. Anderson & Gatignon, 1986).

Family firms are often characterised by the involvement of a member of the owning family in management operations. They may serve as CEO and/or Chairman or occupy other positions inside the top management team or in the board of directors. Previous literature has showed how demographic characteristics affect the firm's decision-making process. Surprisingly, what is still missing in the literature is how these characteristics affect the entry mode choices. Thus, we could expect that certain demographic characteristics and certain experience are more linked to specific entry modes. For instance,

CEO/Chairman/Directors with international experience are more likely to choose risky equity investments, or perhaps long-tenure managers, who are also likely to have international experience, prefer equity mode. Less experienced managers, on the other hand, may prefer cooperative entry modes, as a joint venture with a local partner. Moreover, it would be interesting to compare the effect of these managers' characteristics and their effect on entry mode choice distinguishing between family and non-family managers.

Moreover, because family firms have generally a longer time horizon than non-family ones this could affect their entry mode choices which are long-term strategies. The literature has emphasised the relevance of a large variety of non-economic goals for family firms. Most of them require a long-term orientation, that is, special attention to maintain and nurture a corporate reputation, the desire to maintain direct control over the business and pass it to the next generations. Thus, in order to pass the business to the next generation, it might be more likely that family firms prefer equity modes (wholly owned subsidiary, joint venture) rather non-equity (licensing, franchising and strategic alliances). Also, their long-term orientation might affect their establishment mode choice between greenfield and acquisition.

Family ownership varies also in terms of risk taking, which in turn may influence the choice to expand internationally (Zahra, 2003). Because with reference to the risk attitude of family firms, there are opposite views, future studies should also explore how family firms choose the level of risk involved when they enter a foreign country. Future research on family firms' entry mode could integrate both the socioemotional wealth perspective and the transaction cost theory to explore how whether family firms are more likely to choose risky entry modes (hierarchy) or low level of risk and thus also a low level of control of the investment. This should be related to family desire to maintain control of the business.

Previous literature has established the relevance of non-financial aspects in family firms. For this reason, as stated above, other measures of risk attitudes coming from entrepreneurial research are relevant (Zahra, 2005). We need more research in this direction, and introducing the concept of fear of failure to family business might shed some light on the risk attitude of these firms (Cacciotti & Hayton, 2015). Indeed, especially in family firms, the fear to obtain negative results that might affect other family members or the fear to be judged negatively by the family might have significant effects on the business.

Furthermore, the research might be extended to study other types of entry mode choice other than equity solutions (e.g. licensing, franchising, export, strategic alliances). Family business literature has investigated the performance of family firms in comparison to non-family businesses, while scant research is made on the post-entry performance of entry modes. Future studies might explore this topic of post-entry performance of family firms. Recently IB literature is investigating the post-entry decision, for instance, the disinvestment or the re-entry after disinvestment (Surdu, Mellahi, & Glaister, 2019). Given the preference for long-term orientation of family firms, future studies might explore if the same results applied also to them. Moreover, on the one hand, family business literature call for more studies exploring the heterogeneity of family firms; on the other hand, international business literature has explored different aspects of corporate governance, other than at the firm level, affecting internationalisation (Aguilera et al., 2019). More research is needed to investigate family firms' heterogeneity, considering the different corporate governance context in which they operate in both home and host countries, to understand how this affects the entry mode choice. To this aim, it might be fruitful to integrate the family business literature with the institutional theory used in entry mode research.

The use of the real option theory might also offer useful insights into the family business field. Indeed, if it is true that family firms are risk-averse, they might prefer a real option investment. Indeed, according to this theory, the best option for a firm entering a new foreign market is to make a gradual investment. Given that our knowledge on family firms' establishment mode decision is limited to the study of Boellis et al. (2016), future studies could integrate the real option theory with the stagnation and socioemotional wealth perspective to shed more light on this area.

Last, future studies could explore the foreign entry strategies (both ownership mode and establishment mode) of family firms compared to other constituencies (state-owned firms, financial firms, widely held). Grounding on the literature that claims that different shareholders have different risk attitudes and different goals, it could be interesting to investigate how these results are related to different entry strategies. Also, nothing is known regarding the preference of family firms with reference to licensing, franchising and strategic alliances. Future studies could investigate also family firms' preference for non-equity investments.

In conclusion, entry modes are crucial strategies affecting firms' international success. Although extant literature has established that family firms implement different strategies in comparison to non-family firms, more research is needed to understand how they choose between different entry modes in order to succeed abroad. Further research on foreign entry strategies can make significant contributions to both entry mode research and family business literature.

References

Abdellatif, M., Amann, B., & Jaussaud, J. (2010). Family versus nonfamily business: A comparison of international strategies. *Journal of Family Business Strategy, 1*(2), 108–116.

Aguilera, R. V., Marano, V., & Haxhi, I. (2019). International corporate governance: A review and opportunities for future research. *Journal of International Business Studies, 50*(4), 457–498.

Anderson, E., & Gatignon, H. (1986). Modes of foreign entry: A transaction cost analysis and propositions. *Journal of International Business Studies, 17*(3), 1–26.

Anderson, R. C., & Reeb, D. M. (2003). Founding-family ownership, corporate diversification, and firm leverage. *Journal of Law and Economics, 46*(2), 653–684.

Ang, S. H., Benischke, M. H., & Doh, J. P. (2015). The interactions of institutions on foreign market entry mode. *Strategic Management Journal, 36*(10), 1536–1553.

Arregle, J.-L., Duran, P., Hitt, M. A., & van Essen, M. (2017). Why is family firms' internationalization unique? A meta-analysis. *Entrepreneurship: Theory and Practice, 41*(5), 801–831.

Arregle, J.-L., Naldi, L., Nordqvist, M., & Hitt, M. A. (2012). Internationalization of family-controlled firms: A study of the effects of external involvement in governance. *Entrepreneurship: Theory and Practice, 36*(6), 1115–1143.

Barney, J. B. (1991). Firm resources and sustained competitive advantage. *Journal of Management, 17*(1), 99–120.

Barney, J. B. (2001). Is the resource-based "view" a useful perspective for strategic management research? Yes. *Academy of Management Review, 26*(1), 41–56.

Berrone, P., Cruz, C., & Gomez-Mejia, L. R. (2012). Socioemotional wealth in family firms: Theoretical dimensions, assessment approaches, and agenda for future research. *Family Business Review, 25*(3), 258–279.

Bhaumik, S., Dimova, R., Burkart, M., Panunzi, F. S., & Shleifer, A. (2014). Family firms. *How Family Firms Differ, 58*(5), 2167–2201.

Bird, B., Welsch, H., Astrachan, J. H., & Pistrui, D. (2002). Family business research: The evolution of an academic field. *Family Business Review, 15*(4), 337–350.

Boellis, A., Mariotti, S., Minichilli, A., & Piscitello, L. (2016). Family involvement and firms' establishment mode choice in foreign markets. *Journal of International Business Studies, 47*(8), 929–950.

Brouthers, K. D. (2013). Institutional, cultural and transaction cost influences on entry mode choice and performance. *Journal of International Business Studies, 44*(1), 14–22.

Brouthers, K. D., Brouthers, L. E., & Werner, S. (2008). Resource-based advantages in an international context. *Journal of Management, 34*(2), 189–217.

Cacciotti, G., & Hayton, J. C. (2015). Fear and entrepreneurship: A review and research agenda. *International Journal of Management Reviews, 17*(2), 165–190.

Calabrò, A., Torchia, M., Pukall, T. J., & Mussolino, D. (2013). The influence of ownership structure and board strategic involvement on international sales: The moderating effect of family involvement. *International Business Review, 22*(3), 509–523.

Carney, M. (2005). Corporate governance and competitive advantage in family-controlled firms. *Entrepreneurship Theory and Practice, 29*(3), 249–265.

Carr, C., & Bateman, S. (2009). International strategy configurations of the world's top family firms. *Management International Review, 49*(6), 733–758.

Casillas, J. C., & Acedo, F. J. (2005). Internationalisation of Spanish family SMEs: An analysis of family involvement. *International Journal of Globalisation and Small Business, 1*(2), 134–151.

Chang, Y.-C., Kao, M.-S., & Kuo, A. (2014). The influences of governance quality on equity-based entry mode choice: The strengthening role of family control. *International Business Review, 23*(5), 1008–1020.

Chen, S.-F., & Hennart, J.-F. (2002). Japanese investors' choice of joint ventures versus wholly-owned subsidiaries in the US: The role of market barriers and firm capabilities. *Journal of International Business Studies, 33*(1), 1–18.

Chrisman, J. J., Chua, J. H., & Sharma, P. (2005). Trends and directions in the development of a strategic management theory of the family firm. *Entrepreneurship Theory and Practice, 29*(5), 555–575.

Chrisman, J. J., Chua, J. H., & Steier, L. (2005). Sources and consequences of distinctive familiness: An introduction. *Entrepreneurship Theory and Practice, 29*(3), 237–247.

Chua, J. H., Chrisman, J. J., & Sharma, P. (1999). Defining the family business by behavior. *Entrepreneurship: Theory & Practice Summer99, 23*(4), 19.

Claver, E., Rienda, L., & Quer, D. (2007). The internationalisation process in family firms: Choice of market entry strategies. *Journal of General Management, 33*(1), 1–14.

Claver, E., Rienda, L., & Quer, D. (2009). Family firms' international commitment. *Family Business Review, 2009*(2), 125–135.

Colli, A. (2003). *The History of Family Business, 1850–2000.* Cambridge: Cambridge University Press.

Datta, D. K., Musteen, M., & Herrmann, P. (2009). Board characteristics, managerial incentives, and the choice between foreign acquisitions and international joint ventures. *Journal of Management, 35*(4), 928–953.

De Massis, A., Frattini, F., Majocchi, A., & Piscitello, L. (2018). Family firms in the global economy: Toward a deeper understanding of internationalization determinants, processes, and outcomes. *Global Strategy Journal, 8*(1), 3–21.

Delios, A., & Henisz, W. J. (2003). Policy uncertainty and the sequence of entry by Japanese firms. *Journal of International Business Studies, 34*(3), 227–241.

Dyer, W. G. (2006). Examining the "family effect" on firm performance. *Family Business Review, 19*(4), 253–273.

Faccio, M., & Lang, L. H. P. (2002). The ultimate ownership of Western European corporations. *Journal of Financial Economics, 65*(3), 365–395.

Family Firm Institute. (2017). *Global data points.*

Filatotchev, I., Strange, R., Piesse, J., & Lien, Y.-C. (2007). FDI by firms from newly industrialised economies in emerging markets: Corporate governance, entry mode and location. *Journal of International Business Studies, 38*(4), 556–572.

Gatignon, H., & Anderson, E. (1988). The multinational corporation's degree of control over foreign subsidiaries: An empirical test of a transaction cost explanation. *Journal of Law, Economics, & Organization, 4*(2), 305–336.

Gedajlovic, E. R., & Carney, M. (2010). Markets, hierarchies, and families: Toward a transaction cost theory of the family firm. *Entrepreneurship: Theory and Practice, 34*(6), 1145–1172.

Gomez-Mejia, L. R., Cruz, C., Berrone, P., & De Castro, J. (2011). The bind that ties: Socioemotional wealth preservation in family firms. *The Academy of Management Annals, 5*(1), 37–41.

Gomez-Mejia, L. R., Haynes, K. T., Nunez-Nickel, M., Jacobson, K. J. L., & Moyano-Fuentes, J. (2007). Socioemotional wealth and business risks in family-controlled firms: Evidence from Spanish olive oil mills. *Administrative Science Quarterly, 52*(1), 106–137.

González, M., Guzmán, A., Pombo, C., & Trujillo, M.-A. (2013). Family firms and debt: Risk aversion versus risk of losing control. *Journal of Business Research, 66*(11), 2308–2320.

Graves, C., & Thomas, J. (2006). Internationalization of Australian family businesses: A managerial capabilities perspective. *Family Business Review, 19*(3), 207–224.

Habbershon, T. G. (2006). Commentary: A framework for managing the familiness and agency advantages in family firms. *Entrepreneurship Theory and Practice, 30*(6), 879–886.

Habbershon, T. G., Williams, M., & MacMillan, I. C. (2003). A unified systems perspective of family firm performance. *Journal of Business Venturing, 18*(4), 451–465.

Habbershon, T. G., & Williams, M. L. (1999). A resource-based framework for assessing the strategic advantages of family firms. *Family Business Review, 12*(1), 1–25.

Hennart, J.-F. (1982). *A theory of multinational enterprise.* University of Michigan Press.

Hennart, J.-F. (2009). Down with MNE-centric theories! market entry and expansion as the bundling of MNE and local assets. *Journal of International Business Studies, 40*(9), 1432–1454.

Hennart, J.-F., Sheng, H. H., & Pimenta, G. (2015). Local complementary inputs as drivers of entry mode choices: The case of US investments in Brazil. *International Business Review, 24*(3), 466–475.

Hill, C. W. L., Hwang, P., & Kim, W. C. (1990). An eclectic theory of the choice of international entry mode. *Strategic Management Journal, 11*(2), 117–128.

Kano, L., & Verbeke, A. (2018). Family firm internationalization: Heritage assets and the impact of bifurcation bias. *Global Strategy Journal, 8*(1), 158–183.

Kaufmann, D., Kraay, A., & Mastruzzi, M. (2004). Governance matters III: Governance indicators for 1996, 1998, 2000, and 2002. *World Bank Economic Review, 18*(2), 253–287.

Kontinen, T., & Ojala, A. (2010). The internationalization of family businesses: A review of extant research. *Journal of Family Business Strategy, 1*(2), 97–107.

Kuo, A., Kao, M.-S., Chang, Y.-C., & Chiu, C.-F. (2012). The influence of international experience on entry mode choice: Difference between family and non-family firms. *European Management Journal, 30*(3), 248–263.

Lai, J.-H., Chen, L.-Y., & Chang, S.-C. (2012). The board mechanism and entry mode choice. *Journal of International Management, 18*(4), 379–392.

Laufs, K., & Schwens, C. (2014). Foreign market entry mode choice of small and medium-sized enterprises: A systematic review and future research agenda. *International Business Review, 23*(6), 1109–1126.

Lin, W.-T. (2012). Family ownership and internationalization processes: Internationalization pace, internationalization scope, and internationalization rhythm. *European Management Journal, 30*(1), 47–56.

Majocchi, A., D'Angelo, A., Forlani, E., & Buck, T. (2018). Bifurcation bias and exporting: Can foreign work experience be an answer? Insight from European family SMEs. *Journal of World Business, 53*(2), 237–247.

Makino, S., & Neupert, K. E. E. (2000). National Culture, transaction costs, and the choice between joint venture and wholly owned subsidiary. *Journal of International Business Studies, 31*(4), 705–713.

Matta, E., & Beamish, P. W. (2008). The accentuated CEO career horizon problem: Evidence from international acquisitions. *Strategic Management Journal, 29*(7), 683–700.

Memili, E., Misra, K., Chrisman, J. J., & Welsh, D. H. B. (2017). Internationalisation of publicly traded family firms: A transaction cost theory perspective and longitudinal analysis. *International Journal of Management and Enterprise Development, 16*(1–2), 80–108.

Metsola, J., Leppäaho, T., Paavilainen-Mäntymäki, E., & Plakoyiannaki, E. (2020). Process in family business internationalisation: The state of the art and ways forward. *International Business Review, 29*(2), 101665.

Meyer, K. E., Estrin, S., Bhaumik, S. K., & Peng, M. W. (2009). Institutions, resources, and entry strategies in emerging economies. *Strategic Management Journal, 30*(1), 61–80.

Miller, D., Minichilli, A., & Corbetta, G. (2013). Is family leadership always beneficial? *Strategic Management Journal, 34*(5), 553–571.

Molly, V., Laveren, E., & Deloof, M. (2010). Family Business Succession and Its Impact on Financial Structure and Performance. *Family Business Review, 23*(2): 131–147.

Musteen, M., Datta, D. K., & Herrmann, P. (2009). Ownership structure and CEO compensation: Implications for the choice of foreign market entry modes. *Journal of International Business Studies, 40*(2), 321–338.

Mutinelli, M., & Piscitello, L. (1998). The entry mode choice of MNEs: An evolutionary approach. *Research Policy, 27*(5), 491–506.

Naldi, L., Nordqvist, M., Sjöberg, K., & Wiklund, J. (2007). Entrepreneurial orientation, risk taking, and performance in family firms. *Family Business Review, 20*(1), 33–47.

Oesterle, M.-J., Richta, H. N., & Fisch, J. H. (2013). The influence of ownership structure on internationalization. *International Business Review, 22*(1), 187–201.

Pongelli, C., Caroli, M. G., & Cucculelli, M. (2016). Family business going abroad: The effect of family ownership on foreign market entry mode decisions. *Small Business Economics, 47*(3), 787–801.

Pukall, T. J., & Calabrò, A. (2014). The internationalization of family firms: A critical review and integrative model. *Family Business Review, 27*(2), 103–125.

Rugman, A. M., & Verbeke, A. (1992). A note on the transnational solution and the transaction cost theory of multinational strategic management. *Journal of International Business Studies, 23*(4), 761–771.

Sanders, W. M. G., & Carpenter, M. A. (2015). Internationalization and firm governance: The roles of CEO compensation, top team composition. *and board structure. Academy of Management Journal, 41*(2), 158–178.

Sciascia, S., Mazzola, P., Astrachan, J. H., & Pieper, T. M. (2012). The role of family ownership in international entrepreneurship: Exploring nonlinear effects. *Small Business Economics, 38*(1), 15–31.

Sestu, M. C., D'Angelo, A., & Majocchi, A. (2020). No Title. *European Journal of International Management.*

Sestu, M. C., & Majocchi, A. (2020). Family firms and the choice between wholly owned subsidiaries and joint ventures: A transaction costs perspective. *Entrepreneurship Theory and Practice, 44*(2), 211–232.

Shaver, J. M. (2013). Do we really need more entry mode studies? *Journal of International Business Studies, 44*(1), 23–27.

Shleifer, A., & Vishny, R. W. (2007). A survey of corporate governance. *Corporate Governance and Corporate Finance: A European Perspective, LII*(2), 52–90.

Slangen, A. H. L., & van Tulder, R. J. M. (2009). Cultural distance, political risk, or governance quality? Towards a more accurate conceptualization and measurement of external uncertainty in foreign entry mode research. *International Business Review, 18*(3), 276–291.

Surdu, I., Mellahi, K., & Glaister, K. W. (2019). Once bitten, not necessarily shy? Determinants of foreign market re-entry commitment strategies. *Journal of International Business Studies, 50*(3), 393–422.

Verbeke, A., & Kano, L. (2010). Transaction cost economics (TCE) and the family firm. *Entrepreneurship Theory and Practice, 34*(6), 1173–1182.

Verbeke, A., & Kano, L. (2012). The transaction cost economics theory of the family firm: Family-based human asset specificity and the bifurcation Bias. *Entrepreneurship: Theory and Practice, 36*(6), 1183–1205.

Verbeke, A., Yuan, W., & Kano, L. (2019). A values-based analysis of bifurcation bias and its impact on family firm internationalization. *Asia Pacific Journal of Management, 37*, 449–477.

Williamson, O. E. (1979). Transaction-cost economics: The governance of contractual relations. *Journal of Law and Economics, 22*(2), 233–261.

Williamson, O. E. (1985). *The economic institutions of capitalism: Firms, markets, relational contracting*. Free Press.

Xu, K., Hitt, M. A., & Miller, S. R. (2020). The ownership structure contingency in the sequential international entry mode decision process: Family owners and institutional investors in family-dominant versus family-influenced firms. *Journal of International Business Studies, 51*(2), 151–171.

Zahra, S. A. (2003). International expansion of U.S. manufacturing family businesses: The effect of ownership and involvement. *Journal of Business Venturing, 18*(4), 495–512.

Zahra, S. A. (2005). Entrepreneurial risk taking in family firms. *Family Business Review, 18*(1), 23–40.

Zahra, S. A., Hayton, J. C., & Salvato, C. (2004). Entrepreneurship in family vs. non-family firms: A resource-based analysis of the effect of organizational culture. *Entrepreneurship Theory and Practice, 28*(4), 363–381.

Zahra, S. A., Neubaum, D. O., & Larraneta, B. (2007). Knowledge sharing and technological capabilities: The moderating role of family involvement. *Journal of Business Research, 60*(10), 1070–1079.

Zellweger, T. M., Kellermanns, F. W., Chrisman, J. J., & Chua, J. H. (2012). Family control and family firm valuation by family CEOs: The importance of intentions for transgenerational control. *Organization Science, 23*(3), 851–868.

Zhao, H., Luo, Y., & Suh, T. (2004). Transaction cost determinants and ownership-based entry mode choice: A meta-analytical review. *Journal of International Business Studies, 35*(6), 524–544.

Part II

Internationalization Process of Family Firms

5

Internationalization of Family Firms as a Discontinuous Process: The Role of Behavioral Theory

Andrea Kuiken, Lucia Naldi, and Mattias Nordqvist

Introduction

Following the first article on internationalization of family firms by Gallo and Sveen (1991) research in this area has steadily increased (Casillas & Moreno-Menéndez, 2017; Kontinen & Ojala, 2010; Pukall & Calabrò, 2014). Family firms are firms where the majority shareholding is owned by family members and the family controls the firm through involvement in management and/or the board of directors (e.g., Gallo & Sveen, 1991; Sharma, 2004). Family firm owners have a large part of their wealth invested in the firm and because family members are often involved in managing the firm, family firms' internationalization decisions are influenced by financial and non-financial goals (Gómez-Mejía, Haynes, Núñez-Nickel, Jacobson, & Moyano-Fuentes, 2007). Prior research has mainly studied whether family firms internationalize more or less than non-family firms (e.g., Fernández & Nieto, 2005; George, Wiklund, & Zahra, 2005; Sciascia, Mazzola, Astrachan, & Pieper, 2012; Zahra, 2003) or which family firm characteristics influence its

---

A. Kuiken (✉)
University of Groningen, Groningen, Netherlands
e-mail: a.kuiken@rug.nl

L. Naldi
Jönköping International Business School, Jönköping, Sweden

M. Nordqvist
Stockholm School of Economics, Stockholm, Sweden

© The Author(s), under exclusive license to Springer Nature Switzerland AG 2021
T. Leppäaho, S. Jack (eds.), *The Palgrave Handbook of Family Firm Internationalization*,
https://doi.org/10.1007/978-3-030-66737-5_5

internationalization (e.g., Arregle, Naldi, Nordqvist, & Hitt, 2012; Calabro, Brogi, & Torchia, 2016; D'Angelo, Majocchi, & Buck, 2016).

While internationalization—commonly defined as the involvement in activities across national borders (Jones, 1999, 2001; Welch & Luostarinen, 1988)—is a process in nature (Metsola et al., 2020), only a few existing studies (Graves & Thomas, 2008; Kontinen & Ojala, 2012) have adopted a processual and longitudinal perspective on family firms' internationalization and studied their internationalization paths. In addition, reviews of these process-based studies conclude that family firms tend to gradually internationalize as is predicted by the Uppsala model (Metsola et al., 2020; Pukall & Calabrò, 2014). Thus, these studies conceptualize internationalization as a continuous process in which it is assumed that once a family firm has entered a foreign market it stays there and over time it continues to increase its commitment in terms of investments, sales, and geographical presence in this market.

However, internationalization is associated with a variety of challenges, as a result of which a family firm's internationalization is often better characterized as a discontinuous process. Internationalization as a discontinuous process entails that firms do not necessarily continue to grow internationally over time, but that firms can go through periods of de-internationalization and potential re-internationalization. De-internationalization can take different forms like a complete stop to all international activities, a reduction in international scope by withdrawing from one foreign market but not from others, or a reduction in commitment to a market through a change in its operational mode (Benito & Welch, 1997; Turcan, 2011). After a time-out period, firms may renew their international operations by re-entering foreign markets that they previously de-internationalized from, enter new foreign markets, or use a higher-commitment operation mode, which is referred to as re-internationalization (Vissak, 2010; Welch & Welch, 2009). Re-internationalization is different from the initial foreign market because the willingness to and process of re-internationalization are influenced by past international experience (Crick, 2004; Javalgi, Deligonul, Dixit, & Cavusgil, 2011; Welch & Welch, 2009).

Despite increasing interest among scholars in international business (Benito & Welch, 1997; Bernini, Du, & Love, 2016; Dominguez & Mayrhofer, 2017; Surdu, Mellahi, & Glaister, 2018; Vissak, Francioni, & Musso, 2012), internationalization as a discontinuous process is poorly understood in the context of family firms, both conceptually and empirically. In this conceptual chapter, we argue that refocusing attention on the theoretical framework of the behavioral theory of the firm provides a theoretical background for conceptualizing internationalization of family firms as a discontinuous process and identifying important areas for empirical research to understand this phenomenon and its complexity.

The behavioral theory of the firm aims at understanding how micro-processes in a firm explain its decisions relating to aspects like price and output (Cyert & March, 1963). The behavioral theory of the firm has been highly influential in business research in general (Gavetti, Greve, Levinthal, & Ocasio, 2012), and in international business and family business research in particular. The Uppsala model (Johanson & Vahlne, 1977), as the main internationalization process model, is directly related to the behavioral theory of the firm through the incorporation of problemistic search, uncertainty avoidance, and learning. Not only internationalization process literature has built on the behavioral theory of the firm, family business research is also directly and indirectly influenced by the behavioral theory of the firm. For example, in line with the behavioral theory of the firm, family business scholars have recognized that a variety of goals can exist within a family firm which can conflict with each other (Kotlar & De Massis, 2013; Tagiuri & Davis, 1992). Moreover, literature on family firm risk taking and the related concept of socioemotional wealth (SEW)—defined as non-financial aspects of the firm that meet the family's affective needs (Gómez-Mejía et al., 2007)—relies on the idea of the behavioral theory of the firm in that decisions are influenced by a potential failure to meet non-financial goals. Hence, literature on internationalization processes and family firms is rich, but it only borrows part of the concepts and ideas of the behavioral theory of the firm and disregards others.

In this chapter, we first analyze existing literature on family business internationalization and present how the behavioral theory of the firm has contributed to this field. To structure this analysis, we rely on Cyert and March's (1963) four key concepts to understand decision-making: (1) quasi resolution of conflict, (2) uncertainty avoidance, (3) problemistic search, and (4) learning. We then discuss how the existing use of the behavioral theory of the firm can contribute to an understanding of family firm internationalization as a discontinuous process and identify areas in the behavioral theory of the firm which have not been used but could potentially contribute to an understanding of internationalization as a discontinuous process. Although the behavioral theory of the firm can also provide avenues for future research on the internationalization process of family firms in general, we focus on de-internationalization and re-internationalization as key elements of *internationalization as a discontinuous process*. Specifically, we seek to provide a conceptual background for understanding the internationalization of family firms as a discontinuous process and identifying central concepts. We also suggest specific areas and questions for future research.

Theoretical Background

Family Firms and Internationalization

In their pioneering article Gallo and Sveen (1991) listed a number of factors that can stimulate and restrain the internationalization of family firms which have formed the basis of a growing body of research on family firms' internationalization. The dominant question in existing research is: how does family ownership influence the likelihood of a family firm's internationalization and the degree of internationalization? To answer this question, researchers have adopted two opposing approaches: the restrictive approach and the facilitating approach (Arregle, Duran, Hitt, & Van Essen, 2017). Although Gallo and Sveen (1991) put forward that family firms have characteristics that can facilitate internationalization as well as characteristics that can restrain internationalization, these approaches emphasize one or the other. According to the restrictive approach, family firms internationalize less than non-family firms due to factors like limited resources (Arregle et al., 2012; Fernández & Nieto, 2005; Graves & Thomas, 2008; Liu, Lin, & Cheng, 2011), lack of necessary managerial capabilities (Graves & Thomas, 2006), risk aversion (Claver, Rienda, & Quer, 2007), strong reliance on local networks (Kontinen & Ojala, 2011b), and a fear of losing SEW (Gomez-Mejia, Makri, & Kintana, 2010). The facilitating approach emphasizes that aspects like patient capital (Zahra, 2003), greater alignment of interests within the firm (Chen, Hsu, & Chang, 2014), and altruism (Calabro et al., 2016) increase the likelihood of family firms' internationalization. In response to these mixed findings, family firms' internationalization literature examines several forms of heterogeneity.

Heterogeneity in research on family firms' internationalization most often refers to differences in ownership and control. For example, Sciascia et al. (2012) reconcile the mixed findings by examining an inverted U-shaped relationship between family ownership and internationalization and showing that the internationalization of family firms is maximized at moderate levels of family ownership. Others (Alessandri, Cerrato, & Eddleston, 2018; Arregle et al., 2012; D'Angelo et al., 2016) examine the influence of external involvement—defined as involvement of non-family members—in a firm's management and its board of directors. External involvement can provide access to resources, knowledge, and capabilities which can reduce concerns about SEW, reduce bifurcation bias, and, as a result, increase the degree and pace of internationalization (Arregle et al., 2012; Calabro, Campopiano, Basco, & Pukall, 2017; Calabrò, Mussolino, & Huse, 2009; D'Angelo et al., 2016). Similarly, having multiple owners can provide access to resources for internationalization and stimulate family firms' international growth (Fernandez & Nieto, 2006). Whereas having another family firm as owner might have little impact on internationalization, financial institutions might positively influence international diversification (Sanchez-Bueno & Usero, 2014). Another source of heterogeneity within family firms can be the generational involvement in a firm. Gallo and Sveen (1991) put forward that a new generation entering the business can be a reason for family firms to internationalize. Incoming generations can have different perceptions and knowledge about internationalization and risk-taking, and as such a new generation taking over a firm can spur internationalization (Calabro et al., 2016). However, if family firms have not internationalized in the first and second generations, they are unlikely to internationalize after this (Okoroafo & Koh, 2009).

Heterogeneity can also relate to different internationalization strategies that family firms pursue. A rich stream of literature has emerged on the influence that family firm heterogeneity has on internationalization, though only a few studies consider heterogeneity in the internationalization strategies that are pursued by family firms (Hennart, Majocchi, & Forlani, 2017). Generally, it is argued that if family firms internationalize, they will internationalize into markets that are relatively close so as to reduce risks of losing SEW (Gomez-Mejia et al., 2010). However, a more nuanced understanding can be achieved by combining heterogeneity of family firms with different internationalization strategies. In line with this, Banalieva and Eddleston (2011) distinguish between a home-region strategy and a global strategy and find that family firms with family leaders tend to have a stronger home-region focus, whereas non-family leaders are beneficial for pursuing a global strategy. Moreover, family firms that sell niche market products are less affected by the factors that restrain the internationalization of family firms and hence they are more likely to adopt a global strategy (Hennart et al., 2017).

Export is the dominant mode of internationalization documented in studies on small,- and medium-sized family firms' internationalization (e.g., D'Angelo et al., 2016; Fernández & Nieto, 2005; Sciascia et al., 2012). Interestingly, Arregle et al. (2017) did not find any difference between family and non-family firms measuring internationalization as exports. But differences were observed when the focus was on foreign direct investment (FDI). The adoption of international operation modes that require higher international commitment like FDI is associated with a long-term vision and the presence of non-family managers (Claver, Rienda, & Quer, 2009). When adopting a foreign operation mode which requires higher commitment, family firms are more likely to follow a greenfield strategy rather than acquiring a

140   A. Kuiken et al.

foreign subsidiary because greenfield investments are more flexible, can be gradually built, can be better controlled, and tend to be less complex than international acquisitions (Boellis, Mariotti, Minichilli, & Piscitello, 2016).

The few existing studies that examine the internationalization process of family firms (Claver et al., 2007; Graves & Thomas, 2008; Kontinen & Ojala, 2012) follow the Uppsala model and are based on case research. In the Uppsala model, firms first enter markets that are relatively close and over time increase their international commitment (Johanson & Vahlne, 1977). More generally, studies on the internationalization of family firms tend to focus more on describing the process, than explaining why it occurs in the first place. These studies tend also to rely on the implicit assumption that internationalization is a continuous process. As mentioned, recent literature on internationalization challenge this assumption and acknowledge that firms might follow a discontinuous process in which they can internationalize, de-internationalize, and re-internationalize (Bernini et al., 2016; Dominguez & Mayrhofer, 2017; Vissak, 2010).

Internationalization as a Discontinuous Process

Internationalization is often described as a process of continuous growth—increasing involvement in international activities—though in reality it is more likely to be a discontinuous process which entails periods of internationalization, de-internationalization, and re-internationalization (Vissak, 2010; Welch & Paavilainen-Mäntymäki, 2014). An abundant amount of research exists on internationalization which examines issues like internationalization decisions, processes, timing, entry modes, and market choices (Buckley & Casson, 1998; Ellis, 2011; Johanson & Vahlne, 1977; Oviatt & McDougall, 1994). Even though there is a rich understanding of internationalization, episodes in which firms de-internationalize and re-internationalize and the connections between these different episodes are less understood. Relatedly, some scholars have even questioned the extent to which internationalization literature has truly conceptualized internationalization as a process (Welch, Nummela, & Liesch, 2016).

From a discontinuous process perspective, de-internationalization is defined as reduced involvement in foreign operations. As such it includes complete withdrawal from foreign markets, changes in operation modes, or a reduction in the breadth and depth of foreign operations (Benito & Welch, 1997; Turcan, 2011). Financial reasons, like poor performance abroad and a firm's inability to sustain foreign operations, are put forward as major reasons for de-internationalization (Boddewyn, 1979; Sousa & Tan, 2015). However, also other antecedents have been identified. Internal factors that potentially influence de-internationalization include changes in leadership (Cairns, Quinn, Alexander, & Doherty, 2010), international experience (Choquette, 2018; Delios & Beamish, 2001), strategic fit (Sousa & Tan, 2015), and speed of internationalization (Mohr, Batsakis, & Stone, 2018). Examples of external factors are changes in exchange rates and tariffs (Fitzgerald & Haller, 2018) and a decline in demand in the host country (Benito, 1997). In addition, scholars (Boddewyn, 1983; Jackson, Mellahi, & Sparks, 2005; Matthyssens & Pauwels, 2000) have investigated the de-internationalization process rather than the motivation for de-internationalization. Boddewyn (1983) suggests a process that starts with detecting a discrepancy in the foreign environment which results in a performance that is below aspirations, followed by a period in which limited action is taken due to exit barriers. For de-internationalization to take place, a firm often needs a new manager who can persuade the management team and organize support for de-internationalization. Matthyssens and Pauwels (2000) describe the de-internationalization process as one where firms simultaneously go through a process of escalating commitment and creating strategic flexibility.

After a time-out period from a foreign market, firms can decide to re-internationalize by re-entering markets that they previously de-internationalized from, re-entering other foreign markets, or increasing their commitment to foreign markets by changing their operation modes (Welch & Welch, 2009). The de-internationalization experience is likely to influence re-internationalization, a negative experience can result in lack of confidence in a foreign market, and a residual mindshare might make re-entry into an international market difficult (Javalgi et al., 2011). However, since managers tend to learn more from their failures than from their successes (Shepherd, 2003), de-internationalization can also result in learning and a redefinition of the internationalization strategy. Surprisingly, recent studies suggest that prior experience does not increase the speed of re-entry (Surdu, Mellahi, Glaister, & Nardella, 2018); it also does not result in changes in the degree of commitment when the firms re-enter (Surdu, Mellahi, & Glaister, 2018).

Instead of studying one of the episodes, some studies have examined internationalization as a discontinuous process by considering de-internationalization and re-internationalization together. Early studies focus on establishing that the internationalization process can be discontinuous (Vissak et al., 2012; Vissak & Francioni, 2013), whereas later studies have started to explain the reasons and mechanisms underlying such a discontinuous process. Intermittent exporting, as an example of a discontinuous internationalization process, is found to be strongly influenced by changes in the external environment (Bernini et al., 2016). Dominguez and Mayrhofer (2017) relate a variety of internal and external factors to different stages in a discontinuous internationalization process. They find that foreign divestment is mainly associated with lack of preparation, knowledge, and access to networks as well as loss of competitiveness in the market, whereas re-internationalization is triggered by changes in ownership in combination with growing foreign demand.

Thus, international business scholars have started recognizing that internationalization can be discontinuous but research on family firms' internationalization sees internationalization as a static presence, or a continuous process at best. As Reuber (2016) concluded, it would be valuable to complement existing approaches with one that considers the temporality and dynamics of the internationalization of family firms and the family as a major actor in this. In addition, Welch et al. (2016: 794) reclaim the importance of the behavioral paradigm, where process is embedded, and managerial decisions are 'history dependent'. Relatedly, Coviello, Kano, and Liesch (2017) make a plea for considering the role of individuals—that is, the decision makers either individually or as part of a group, including families—as a core micro-foundation of the internationalization process, while Håkanson and Kappen (2017) propose an alternative model of the internationalization process of the firm, where firms enter foreign markets in wave-like patterns rather than incrementally. What is needed for this is a theory which provides a process perspective including insights into the micro-processes underlying family firms' internationalization (Reuber, 2016). In the next section, we argue that the behavioral theory of the firm, which has influenced research on family firms as well as research on the internationalization process, can provide an appropriate theoretical lens for studying family firms' internationalization as a discontinuous process.

Internationalization of Family Firms and the Behavioral Theory of the Firm

Theories Used in Research on Family Firms' Internationalization

A large number of studies on family firms' internationalization rely on agency theory or stewardship theory (e.g., Banalieva & Eddleston, 2011; George et al., 2005; Graves & Shan, 2014; Sciascia et al., 2012). Since the introduction of the SEW (Gómez-Mejía et al., 2007), many studies refer to the notion of SEW in their arguments (e.g., Alessandri et al., 2018; Boellis et al., 2016; Sanchez-Bueno & Usero, 2014) but only a few measure SEW or one of its dimensions and its impact on family firms' internationalization (Cesinger et al., 2016; Kraus, Mensching, Calabrò, Cheng, & Filser, 2016). Alternatively, scholars adopt a resource-based view or a resource dependence perspective to argue that family firms have a different set of resources which influence their internationalization (Arregle et al., 2012; Calabro et al., 2017; Fernandez & Nieto, 2006; Graves & Thomas, 2006). These theories can provide insights into the characteristics of family firms, which influence the likelihood of their internationalization and internationalization strategies, but they provide only limited insights into how the internationalization process evolves over time.

To understand the processes scholars have mainly drawn upon the Uppsala model and the alternative paths of born-globals and born-again globals (Calabrò et al., 2016; Graves & Thomas, 2008; Kontinen & Ojala, 2012). These studies establish that the process predicted by the Uppsala model is the most common but pay less attention to the underlying mechanisms of experiential learning and networking in family firms. While Johanson and Vahlne (1977) recognize that firms can also reduce their international involvement, they do not directly integrate this option in the Uppsala model. For the Uppsala model to contribute to an understanding of internationalization as a discontinuous process, Santangelo and Meyer (2017) suggest that the evolutionary theory has to be incorporated to a larger degree in the model. Instead of adding a theory, we suggest that a closer integration of the key concepts of the behavioral theory of the firm can provide a better understanding of internationalization of family firms as a discontinuous process.

The Behavioral Theory of the Firm and Family Firms' Internationalization

The main question that Cyert and March (1963) address in the behavioral theory of the firm is how economic decisions like price and output decisions are made within the complex setting of a firm. They developed a set of sub-theories and key concepts to understand the micro-processes that underlie managerial decisions.

Underlying assumptions. Cyert and March (1963) define an organization as a coalition of individuals. They assume that these individuals are likely to have different goals and these goals can conflict with each other. Second, individual goals result in organizational objectives through a continuous bargaining process among the individuals in a firm. The outcome of this bargaining process is not a maximizing solution but a satisfying solution because not all goals can be prioritized. Third, they assume that individuals are boundedly rational, meaning that individuals only know about a small fraction of all possible alternatives (Simon, 1972). To become aware of different alternative solutions to a problem, individuals search for information and stop doing so only when they find an alternative that provides a satisfactory solution to the problem. This search starts in the areas that a firm is most familiar with and the extent of the search is influenced by organizational slack. Finally, they assume that firms operate within an uncertain environment. An uncertain environment complicates the gathering of necessary information for taking strategic decisions. To deal with this, individuals use rules and standard operating procedures. The rules are influenced by the environment and the behavioral theory of the firm assumes that there is imperfect environmental matching. so if the environment changes, the decision rules do not always change with the environment.

Sub-theories and key concepts. The behavioral theory of the firm includes a set of variable categories and a set of relational concepts. The variable categories are a set of three sub-theories: organizational goals, organizational expectations, and organizational choice (Cyert & March, 1963). The theory of organizational goals includes two sets of variables that affect organizational goals—the dimensions of goals and the aspiration level. The dimensions of goals focus on what is important within the coalition whereas the aspiration level is the performance target with regard to a certain goal. The theory of organizational expectations argues that organizational expectations are shaped by search activities. The success of search activities is influenced by the extent to which the goals are achieved and the amount of organizational slack. Where organizational slack is defined as the resources that are currently owned by a firm but are not necessary for its demand (Cyert & March, 1992, p. 42). The theory of organizational choice holds that the variables that affect the choice are the variables that influence the definition of a problem, the standard decision rules, and the order in which alternatives are considered. Standard decision rules are in turn influenced by past experience and past organizational slack. In addition, Cyert and March (1963) developed four basic concepts which link the three theories and are key to an understanding of the decision-making process: quasi resolution of conflict, uncertainty avoidance, problemistic search, and organizational learning. These concepts are fundamental for understanding firms' decision-making processes (Cyert & March, 1992). Most of the literature on family firms' internationalization provides an indirect link to the behavioral theory of the firm due to its focus on multiple goals and the emphasis on avoiding uncertainty in relation to SEW outcomes. A relatively small number of studies on family firms' internationalization can be directly linked to the behavioral theory of the firm through their focus on the role of organizational slack (Alessandri et al., 2018; Liu et al., 2011) and learning (Cesinger et al., 2016; Fernández-Olmos, Gargallo-Castel, & Giner-Bagües, 2016). Table 5.1 provides an overview of the arguments in family firms' internationalization research in relation to the four basic concepts of the behavioral theory of the firm.

Quasi resolution of conflict addresses the assumption that a firm is a coalition of individuals with different goals and therefore internal consensus is unlikely. The dimensions of goals address what is perceived as important. Cyert and March (1992) suggest taking into account the goals of different sub-units in the firm, compared to non-family firms, the boundaries of the family firm are extended and consider the coalition of individuals in the firm on the one hand and the owning-family on the other. This results in an overlap between the family unit and the non-family unit which, in turn, results in a larger variety of goals (Berrone, Cruz, & Gomez-Mejia, 2012; Gómez-Mejía et al., 2007; Kotlar & De Massis, 2013). It is argued that internationalization is either facilitated because owner-managers perceive it as a strategy that facilitates the long-term growth of a firm and with that jobs for the next generation (Zahra, 2003) or family firms are unlikely to internationalize because they might not meet their non-financial goals if they do so (Cesinger et al., 2016; Gomez-Mejia et al., 2010). Moreover, if family firms internationalize they might be more likely to take suboptimal internationalization decisions if family members involved in the firm pursue goals associated with enhancing the quality of their personal lives (Kano & Verbeke, 2018). This bifurcation bias—that is, the prioritization of dysfunctional family assets over functional assets—has been observed in several studies on family firms' internationalization, even if these studies might not have made explicit use of this concept. For example, Bauweraerts, Sciascia, Naldi and Mazzola (2019) find that family CEOs might be more likely to prioritize family considerations and goals when taking exporting decision, unless they are supported—in strategic decision-making—by their board of directors.

According to the behavioral theory of the firm, goal conflict is resolved by prioritizing different goals at different points in time. Which goals are prioritized depends on the power that different coalitions have in the bargaining process. A high degree of family ownership and control tends to put more emphasis on non-financial goals and with that reducing the likelihood of internationalization (Liu et al., 2011; Sanchez-Bueno & Usero, 2014; Sciascia

Table 5.1 Main findings in family business internationalization literature in relation to key concepts in the behavioral theory of the firm

Key concept	Focus	Examples	Main findings
Quasi resolution of goal conflict	Different goals	Zahra (2003), Westhead (2003), Gomez-Mejia et al. (2010), Kano and Verbeke (2018)	The potential to create wealth for owner-managers and future generations can result in a prioritization of internationalization. However, a strong emphasis on non-financial goals like a focus on maintaining reputation and status in the local community and protecting SEW can result in less emphasis on internationalization. Moreover, a focus on enhancing the personal quality of life and bias towards prioritizing heritage assets can result in suboptimal internationalization decisions.
	Influence of different coalitions	Chen et al. (2014), Sanchez-Bueno and Usero (2014), George et al. (2005), Fernández and Nieto (2005), Banalieva and Eddleston (2011), Holt (2012), Sciascia, Mazzola, Astrachan, and Pieper (2013), D'Angelo et al. (2016)	A high degree of family ownership and control tends to reduce family firms' internationalization. External shareholders like venture capitalists may shift attention to internationalization, because they can provide access to external resources and they might align the owner-manager's interests with those of the top management team. Besides external shareholders, external managers can have a positive influence on internationalization because they bring a different set of skills and experience and can hence change the firm's priorities.

Uncertainty avoidance	Decision-rules	Claver et al. (2009), Gomez-Mejia et al. (2010), Banalieva & Eddleston, 2011, Lin (2012), Boellis et al. (2016)	Potential downside effects on SEW are weighted heavier than potential financial gains, as a result of which family firms are less likely to internationalize. When going international, family firms avoid uncertainty by entering markets that are relatively close and use operation modes that allow for flexibility and control. Family firms prefer a narrow international scope or an irregular internationalization rhythm to maintain long-term family wealth.
Problemistic search	Initiation of internationalization	Okoroafo (1999), Kontinen and Ojala (2011a), Fernández-Olmos et al. (2016)	Family firms do not regularly scan the international market place. Internationalization tends to be initiated by unsolicited orders or through opportunities arising in the network.
	Organizational slack	Liu et al. (2011), Alessandri et al. (2018)	Presence of organizational slack does not necessarily facilitate internationalization of family firms; on the contrary, a high degree of available slack might result in even stronger self-serving behavior and protection of SEW. However, recoverable slack can stimulate a search for international opportunities.
Organizational learning		Basly (2007), Fernández-Olmos et al. (2016), Cesinger et al. (2016)	Family business conservatism may limit organizational learning from international experiences. However, family firms' long-term orientation can allow them to accumulate international experience and build the capabilities that are necessary for long-term growth.

148   **A. Kuiken et al.**

et al., 2012). Changes in the prioritization of goals are influenced by experience and the extent to which aspiration levels are met. This is a key aspect in the behavioral agency model and the relating SEW perspective. Internationalization can result in potential losses in SEW, that is, a failure to meet non-economic goals, which reduces the likelihood of family firms internationalizing (Gomez-Mejia et al., 2010). Literature on family firms' goals addresses goals as relatively static and, hence, few scholars consider changes in the prioritization of goals or changes in aspirations over time. However, it is recognized that changes in succession, external involvement in a firm's management, and external ownership are associated with changes in family firms' internationalization strategies (Arregle et al., 2012; Kontinen & Ojala, 2012; Sanchez-Bueno & Usero, 2014) which could be an indication of changes in the prioritization of goals and the differences in aspirations.

Second, firms must deal with uncertainty in the decision-making process. Firms avoid uncertainty by using decision rules, focusing on short-term problems rather than the long-run, and by creating a negotiated environment through industry-wide good business practices, budgeting, and strategic planning (Cyert & March, 1963). The firms' aim is avoiding uncertainty while reaching a solution that satisfies the coalition and other demands of a firm rather than finding a maximizing solution. Potential gains or losses in SEW are weighted heavier than financial gains or losses by family firms (Gómez-Mejía et al., 2007). As such, a satisfying solution in family firms is likely to be one where losses in SEW are minimized which can be at the cost of financial gains (Martin & Gomez-Mejia, 2016). Therefore, family firms can be more risk averse than non-family firms and are thus more likely to diversify within the home market than internationally (Gomez-Mejia et al., 2010). If family firms internationalize, they tend to enter markets that are relatively close (Eddleston & Kellermanns, 2007; Gomez-Mejia et al., 2010) and use operation modes which allow them to be flexible and maintain control (Boellis et al., 2016).

Third, problemistic search addresses the idea that a search for solutions starts only in response to a problem (Cyert & March, 1963). A problem is recognized when a firm fails to satisfy one or more of its goals or when this is anticipated in the future. Whereas problemistic search is a key concept in the behavioral theory of the firm and in the Uppsala model (Johanson & Vahlne, 1977) and addressed by Gómez-Mejía et al. (2007) in their discussion on SEW in family firms, few studies consider why family firms internationalize. Gallo and Sveen (1991) suggest that internationalization can be initiated by family firms for creating jobs for the next generation. Other studies (Jansson & Söderman, 2012; Kontinen & Ojala, 2011a) suggest that like many SMEs, family firms mainly respond to unsolicited orders and opportunities that arise in their formal networks. According to the behavioral theory of the firm, problemistic search continues until a satisfying alternative is found (Cyert & March, 1963). The search for solutions is generally simple minded, that is, the search is conducted in an area that causes the problem and an area where previous solutions to similar problems have been found. Traditionally, literature on family firms' internationalization suggested that family firms have limited knowledge about international markets and limited access to international networks (Gallo & Sveen, 1991; Kontinen & Ojala, 2011b) which may impact their search strategies by focusing on solutions that are present in the domestic market. For example, Okoroafo (1999) found that family firms did not regularly scan international markets for opportunities. The search process was highly influenced by past experience which addresses the last key concept in the behavioral theory of the firm.

Within a firm, knowledge is translated into routines and decision-rules and these shape future decisions and learning (Levitt & March, 1988). Based on learning from current experience, firms change their goals, shift attention to certain parts of the environment, and/or revise their procedures for the search (Cyert & March, 1963). Literature on family firms' internationalization suggests that due to limited knowledge about internationalization and foreign markets, family firms experience barriers to internationalization (Gallo & Sveen, 1991). However, there is also fear of losing control which can result in a conservative approach to internationalization and can limit the development of internationalization and market knowledge (Basly, 2007). External owners and non-family board members (Arregle et al., 2012; D'Angelo et al., 2016; Sciascia et al., 2013) and strong network relations (Kontinen & Ojala, 2011b) can help family firms overcome such barriers and stimulate their internationalization. However, these studies do not consider how family firms learn from their international experience and how this impacts internationalization decisions after the initial market entry.

Future Research Directions on Family Firms' De-internationalization and Re-internationalization

The above comparison of the behavioral theory of the firm with literature on family firms' internationalization suggests that scholars have built on and borrowed different elements of the behavioral theory of the firm. However, whereas the behavioral theory of the firm provides a process perspective, literature on family firms' internationalization tends to incorporate mainly static elements of the behavioral theory of the firm. Next, we discuss areas for empirical research and future research questions that arise when taking the behavioral theory of the firm as a lens for studying internationalization of family firms as a discontinuous process. As a starting point, we use the four key concepts that Cyert and March (1963) introduced as being essential for understanding decision-making. Incorporating all four concepts provides a more comprehensive view, but also the opportunity to highlight avenues of research that so far have received less attention. Table 5.2 provides an overview of future research areas and relevant research questions that can be asked to deepen our current understanding of the internationalization process of family firms, with a specific focus on de-internationalization and re-internationalization.

Goals and Quasi Resolution of Goal Conflict

Besides heterogeneity in terms of family ownership, family firms can also be heterogeneous from the perspective of which goals they prioritize (Kammerlander & Ganter, 2015) and, according to the behavioral theory of the firm, this can vary over time. Literature on family firms' internationalization mainly relies on the assumption that there are two types of goals—financial and non-financial—which are relatively static over time. But the behavioral theory of the firm suggests that a larger variety of goals can be prioritized at different points of time (Cyert & March, 1963). Following this idea, family business scholars (Berrone et al., 2012; Kotlar & De Massis, 2013) have suggested a number of goals that family firms can pursue, which can be divided into financial family goals, non-financial family goals, financial non-family goals, and non-financial non-family goals. Financial family goals relate to family control and family wealth, while non-financial family goals relate to family harmony, social status, and identity. Further, financial non-family goals relate to growth, survival, and economic performance of the firm, and non-financial non-family goals are associated with internal serenity and external relations. While the distinction between different goals is made in the family business literature in general, family business internationalization literature mainly distinguishes between financial and non-financial goals and rarely studies the impact of different goals empirically. Although it is true that poor performance, so a difficulty in meeting financial non-family goals, is identified as a major reason for de-internationalization (Dominguez & Mayrhofer,

5 Internationalization of Family Firms as a Discontinuous Process... 151

Table 5.2 Summary of the areas for empirical research

	De-internationalization	Re-internationalization
Quasi resolution of conflict	*Prioritization of goals* • Which goals are prioritized when family firms take a decision to de-internationalize? • How do non-financial goals influence family firms' de-internationalization processes? • Do family firms prioritize goals in the de-internationalization process that are different from those of non-family firms? *Bargaining power* • Which coalitions in a family firm play a role in the de-internationalization decision? • How do external managers and owners influence the prioritization of goals and subsequent de-internationalization?	*Prioritization of goals* • Which goals are prioritized when family firms take a decision to re-internationalize? • How do different goals influence the likelihood of re-internationalization? • Are the goals that are prioritized in times of re-internationalization different from those prioritized during the initial internationalization decision? *Bargaining power* • How do changes in ownership influence the likelihood of re-internationalization? To what extent and how do external managers influence re-internationalization?
Uncertainty avoidance	*Response to short-term problems* • How do family firms balance between long-term orientation and de-internationalization as a potential response to short-term problems? *Planning and routines* • How does the extent of planning for internationalization influence the likelihood of de-internationalization? • To what extent do family firms plan for de-internationalization? • What kind of routines do family firms that go through multiple de-internationalization experiences develop?	*Planning and routines* • To what extent do family firms plan for re-internationalization? • How do international strategies and routines change when family firms re-internationalize? • What kind of routines do family firms develop when they go through multiple re-internationalization experiences? • To what extent are routines for re-internationalization in the same market different from routines for a new market entry?

(continued)

152   A. Kuiken et al.

Table 5.2 (continued)

	De-internationalization	Re-internationalization
Problemistic search	*Failure to meet aspirations* • To what extent is de-internationalization triggered by a failure to meet financial aspirations and to what extent is it triggered by a failure to meet non-financial aspirations? *Search process* • Which alternatives do family firms consider when aspirations are not met? Do family firms consider other alternatives before de-internationalization as compared to non-family firms? • How does family firms' patient capital influence the search process before de-internationalization? • How does family firms' patient capital influence the degree of their de-internationalization?	*Failure to meet aspirations* • Which aspirations influence the search process that leads to re-internationalization of family firms? Are these different from those considered by non-family firms? • Under what circumstances is re-internationalization a viable strategy for family firms that do not meet their performance aspirations? *Search process* • To what extent are the alternatives considered for re-internationalization similar to the alternatives considered at the initial foreign market entry?
Learning	• How does international experience influence a family firm's decision to de-internationalize? Do family firms respond differently to international experience as compared to non-family firms? • How does family ownership and control influence learning from de-internationalization? • How does the de-internationalization experience influence family firms' aspirations? • How does the de-internationalization experience influence the family and its goals?	• How do family firms utilize their past international experience in the re-internationalization decision? • How does the de-internationalization experience influence family firms' likelihood of re-internationalization? • How does a family firm's heterogeneity influence the extent to which it uses past experience in the re-internationalization decision?

2017; McDermott, 2010), due to the variety of goals present within the family firm the final decision might be driven by different goals. Which goals are prioritized depends on the framing of the situation, meaning that an expected current loss in SEW can result in a decision that is different from the one taken for expected future gains in financial wealth (Gomez-Mejia et al., 2010; Gomez-Mejia, Patel, & Zellweger, 2018; Martin & Gomez-Mejia, 2016). Different non-financial goals can also result in diverse behavioral outcomes. For example, a focus on emotions can result in organizational inertia (Kammerlander & Ganter, 2015). This could be a potential reason for family firms to continue international activities, despite financial losses. On the other hand, a desire for control and power can result in timely recognition of changes in the environment, thereby generating a response that is beneficial for meeting economic goals (Kammerlander & Ganter, 2015), which can take the form of timely de-internationalization or later re-internationalization. Like the notion that prioritization of non-financial goals can result in forgoing financial goals, non-financial goals can conflict with each other resulting in shifting priorities between different non-financial goals over time (Chua, Chrisman, & De Massis, 2015).

Time might come into play as well. Balancing financial and non-financial goals might require a 'mixed gamble' logic (e.g., Gomez-Mejia et al., 2014, Gomez-Mejia et al., 2018, Kotlar, Signori, De Massis, & Vismara, 2018), entailing complex trade-offs among current (now) and perspective (future) financial and non-financial goals (Chirico et al., 2020). While a few studies have used the mix-gamble logic in study of family firms' internationalization (e.g., Alessandri et al., 2018), additional insights on (de)internationalization decisions over time can be gained by considering the priority that family firms may attribute to current financial goals versus prospective non-financial goals or vice versa. This also relates the potential of bifurcation bias, which is an expression of bounded rationality reflected in the de facto prioritization of dysfunctional family assets over functional non-family assets (especially human assets) in the short- and medium-term internationalization (Verbeke & Kano, 2012, Kano & Verbeke, 2018). Mixed gamble logic and bifurcation bias might influence the (dis)continuous internationalization of family firms where financial and non-financial (family) considerations are intertwined in an evolutionary way.

While the distinction between financial and non-financial goals is prominent in literature on family firms' internationalization, the distinction between family and non-family goals is less common. However, non-family goals potentially play an important role in changes in the international activities of the firm. Recruitment of new managers, for instance, influences de-internationalization as well as re-internationalization (Boddewyn, 1983; Dominguez & Mayrhofer, 2017). Following the behavioral theory of the firm, this can result in changes in the coalition and power of different coalitions within the firm, potential for goal conflict, and possibly a stronger focus on non-family goals within the decision-making process of the family firm. Family business internationalization literature has, so far, rarely addressed these underlying mechanisms, but doing so can provide new insights in the dynamics of the internationalization process of family firms. Following the discussion so far, some questions that can be addressed in future research are: Which goals are prioritized when family firms take a decision to de-internationalize or re-internationalize? How do external managers and owners influence the prioritization of goals and the subsequent de-internationalization? Which goals are pursued during the de-internationalization and re-internationalization processes?

Changes in the prioritization of goals can occur as a result of changing bargaining power. Whereas succession might be a driver of internationalization, questions arise as to how changes in family ownership and generational changes influence discontinuity in the internationalization process. Changes in the percentage of family ownership and succession can result in changes in the bargaining powers of different individuals in a family firm and the owning-family (Arregle et al., 2012; Fernandez & Nieto, 2006; Okoroafo 1999). It has been established that different degrees of family ownership, involvement in the management, and changes in family ownership through succession might also influence internationalization (Mitter, Duller, Feldbauer-Durstmüller, & Kraus, 2014; Pukall & Calabrò, 2014). This can result in changes in the bargaining powers of different coalitions and prioritization of different goals (Cyert & March, 1963). Since changes in management might be a necessary prerequisite for de-internationalization (Boddewyn, 1983; Dominguez & Mayrhofer, 2017), not only the recruitment of external managers can influence de-internationalization and re-internationalization, but also changes in family ownership and involvement can potentially result in a change in the prioritization of goals and the internationalization strategy. Hence, to extend our understanding of family firms' internationalization as a discontinuous process, future research can consider how changes in the bargaining powers of a family firm's owners and managers change the prioritization of goals and how this is related to decisions on de-internationalization and re-internationalization. Recognizing the different coalitions in a firm and the possible changes in their bargaining powers over time raises research questions like: How do changes in ownership influence de-internationalization and re-internationalization?

Uncertainty Avoidance

Family firms' internationalization can potentially benefit from a long-term orientation within the firm because family firms do not expect direct returns on investments and therefore have more time to learn from their experiences (Zahra, 2003). This is at odds with the behavioral theory of the firm which argues that firms avoid uncertainty by acknowledging that they cannot anticipate future events correctly and instead solve pressing problems rather than having a long-term focus (Cyert & March, 1963). The SEW perspective is more in line with this notion in the behavioral theory of the firm because it argues that family firms tend to respond to short-term problems that put SEW at risk (Gomez-Mejia et al., 2010). To reconcile these two different notions, Kammerlander and Ganter (2015) suggest that different goals can be associated with different time horizons. Trade-offs and inter-relations between short-term responses to problems and the family firms' long-term orientation can vary across different types of strategic decisions and this is often highly complex (Lumpkin & Brigham, 2011). The extent to which de-internationalization and re-internationalization might be influenced by long-term orientation versus short-term responses to problems can potentially explain the degree of de-internationalization and the approach to re-internationalization by family firms. For example, intermittent exporting is often associated with an ad hoc response to short-term external opportunities (Samiee & Walters, 1991), while more committed exporters might first continue to commit for some more time trying to address the problems in the market before taking a decision to de-internationalize (Matthyssens & Pauwels, 2000). Hence, questions can be raised about how family firms balance between a long-term orientation and responses to short-term problems in their internationalization processes in general and about the timing of the de-internationalization and re-internationalization in particular to extend the current understanding of family firm internationalization beyond the initial stages.

In addition to responding to short-term problems, firms avoid uncertainty by developing a negotiated environment through aspects like industry traditions and strategic plans and routines (Cyert & March, 1963). While some internationalization strategies are identified that help family firms avoid uncertainty, the behavioral theory of the firm can provide a richer understanding of this by focusing on strategic planning and routines. Strategic planning is important not only for international growth, since most firms will go through some form of de-internationalization at some point in time, firms might also consider strategies for de-internationalization (Welch & Luostarinen, 1988). Family firms' strategic planning and business routines are expected to differ from those of non-family firms because of the overlap between the family and the firm which influences strategic planning (Gersick, Lansberg, Desjardins, & Dunn, 1999). Several reasons have been provided for why family firms are less likely to develop strategic plans including lack of knowledge about foreign markets, lack of necessary tools to scan the environment, challenges in incorporating the family's goals, and owner-manager's reluctance to plan because it reduces decision-making flexibility (Ward, 1988). In particular, de-internationalization can be related to poor planning of the initial international entry (Reiljan, 2006) pointing toward the relevance of understanding how and to what extent family firms plan their internationalization and the subsequent likelihood of de-internationalization. In addition, the extent to which family businesses adjust their plans for international growth when they decide to re-internationalize can be questioned. In family firms, strongly held family values and routines might provide a distinct frame of reference for decision-making and strategic planning which influences strategic planning, actions, and outcomes (Hall, Melin, & Nordqvist, 2008); these are also likely to influence the extent to which adjustments are made when family firms re-internationalize. While recent findings indicate that firms in general do not adjust their operation modes when they re-internationalize (Surdu, Mellahi, & Glaister, 2018), these characteristics might influence the likelihood of family firms' re-internationalizing and the extent to which plans and routines change in comparison to the initial internationalization. Although general insights exist on strategic planning in family firms and family firm routines, our current understanding on how these play a role in the internationalization process of family firms in order to deal with uncertainty is limited. Hence, future research can address questions about the extent to which family firms plan for de-internationalization and re-internationalization and to what extent family firms develop routines to deal with discontinuities in the internationalization process.

Problemistic Search

According to Cyert and March (1963), financial performance that is below aspirations triggers a search process. As stated before, de-internationalization is often associated with poor financial performance (Dominguez & Mayrhofer, 2017; Reiljan, 2006), suggesting that performance is below aspirations before firms de-internationalize. Since family firms tend to prioritize non-financial goals in their decision-making processes, it can be questioned whether the search process that results in de-internationalization in family firms is always triggered by a failure to meet financial goals. Similarly, initial market entry is associated with performance below aspiration levels which results in a search for new ways of doing business, resulting in more risk taking and increased commitment to internationalization (Cyert & March, 1963; Wennberg & Holmquist, 2008). Whereas it can be argued that the same holds true for re-internationalization, several scholars have suggested that re-internationalization is not the same as the initial internationalization because of the de-internationalization experience (Javalgi et al., 2011; Welch & Welch, 2009).

Several factors can influence re-internationalization, of which a change in management is an important one because new managers are less influenced by negative emotions associated with de-internationalization (Dominguez & Mayrhofer, 2017; Javalgi et al., 2011). However, family firms often have a lower turnover in their management teams as compared to non-family firms due to the involvement of the family (Stewart & Hitt, 2012). Hence, for family firms the solutions that they search for are also likely to be relatively stable. For example, if internationalization has led to positive results in the past, they might pursue the same strategy again. However, it can also be argued that re-internationalization is less likely to be considered because of potential negative experiences associated with de-internationalization (Javalgi et al., 2011).

Hence, for family firms the type of solutions searched for is also likely to be relatively stable. This raises questions about the motivations for re-internationalization of family firms like which kind of problems or opportunities do family firms respond to when they re-internationalize, are these problems different from those of non-family firms, and do family firms respond to different problems when they re-internationalize than they do during their initial internationalization efforts?

A firm starts its search in areas that it is familiar with (Cyert & March, 1963). Hence, when search is initiated, questions arise about the alternatives considered and how this is influenced by a family firm's characteristics. Because family firms are characterized by patient capital (Sirmon & Hitt, 2003), de-internationalization might not be the first option considered when performance is below financial aspirations. When considering different types of goals that family firms can prioritize, there can be different responses to a failure to meet financial goals. For example, due to patient capital, family firms might want to be more willing to continue to invest even though the performance is below aspirations as compared to non-family firms and they search for different alternatives to increase profitability in the market.

However, following the SEW logic, current threats to family firms' SEW can have the opposite effect and increase chances of de-internationalization among these firms. Little is known about the process that leads to de-internationalization (Jackson et al., 2005) and even less about re-internationalization (Welch & Welch, 2009). Questions about the problems that family firms respond to when they de-internationalize and re-internationalize, the processes that these problems trigger, and the variety of alternatives considered before de-internationalizing or re-internationalizing can provide new insights into the internationalization of family firms as a discontinuous process.

Finally, family firms' characteristics can result in different perceptions of what is a satisfying solution. Due to concerns about SEW and due to limited resources, family firms prefer certain international operation modes over others (Boellis et al., 2016; Gallo & Sveen, 1991) and these factors might influence de-internationalization and re-internationalization as well. De-internationalization can take different forms like reduced commitment to a foreign market by changing to an operation mode that requires less resources, complete withdrawal from one foreign market but continued operations in others, or complete de-internationalization from all foreign markets (Turcan, 2011).

Moreover, family firms tend to be strongly embedded in the local environment of the home market with strong local relationships (Berrone et al., 2012; Kontinen & Ojala, 2011b) and by supporting and subsidizing institutions (Campopiano, De Massis, & Chirico, 2014). This local embeddedness can result in a preference for complete de-internationalization since family firms have more knowledge about the home market and the local environment. However, recently it is found that international family firms can pursue niche strategies which increase their international presence (Hennart et al., 2017). For these firms, complete de-internationalization might not be a satisfying solution because it threatens their SEW so they might consider other solutions instead. Hence, incorporating such family firms' characteristics is needed to fully understand the responses to the problems that arise. Similarly, re-internationalization can be concerned about entry into the same markets as the firm previously de-internationalized from or different foreign markets and the use of the same or different operation modes (Surdu, Mellahi, & Glaister, 2018; Welch & Welch, 2009).

Family firms are less likely to search for solutions that are new and increase chances of unexpected outcomes as compared to non-family firms (Gómez-Mejía et al., 2007). This might increase the likelihood of these firms entering the same or similar markets following the same operation modes. Hence, future research can provide new insights into family firms' internationalization as a discontinuous process by considering which family firms' characteristics and goals are associated with which type of satisfying solutions for de-internationalization and re-internationalization.

Learning

Existing research suggests that family firms are limited in their internationalization due to limitations in their knowledge about internationalization. However, existing literature on internationalization of family firms rarely considers experiential learning from internationalization. Family firms' characteristics can have different effects on their learning from international experience (Basly, 2007; Zahra, 2012). In line with a facilitative approach, family firms can be a setting where learning is stimulated more than in non-family firms because success and the long-term survival of a firm and a family's wealth depend on learning and using new skills for addressing challenges and opportunities (Zahra, 2012). Moreover, family cohesion, alignment of goals among individuals, and a higher frequency of meetings at which information is shared can facilitate learning within the owning-family and the firm (Basly, 2007). A restrictive approach suggests that family firms' core assumptions, beliefs, and routines can result in resistance or ignoring information that is not in line with these characteristics (Davis, 1983). Moreover, the presence of a dominant decision-maker can reduce the variety in knowledge flows into the company, thus limiting learning experiences (Zahra, 2012).

An interpretation of new information is influenced by the family's routines and decision-rules and following literature on SEW, family firms might be reluctant to de-internationalize if they expect a potential loss to their SEW, even if this means that they have to accept some financial losses. Hence, the characteristics of family firms and decision-rules can result in different interpretations of the knowledge gained from international experience and hence different responses to challenges in a foreign market. Relevant questions can help address family firms' learning from international experience, the likelihood and form of de-internationalization, and how family firms' routines and decision-rules influence de-internationalization decisions.

Given their de-internationalization experience, the likelihood and strategies for re-internationalization might be different for family firms as compared to non-family firms. Usually individuals need time to reflect on experiences and incorporate this knowledge in their current strategies. When de-internationalization is associated with failure, more time might be needed to forget the negative experience (Javalgi et al., 2011; Welch & Welch, 2009). For the owning-family, besides being a source of income, the firm is also a source of pride as it reflects the family's identity. As a result, de-internationalization can trigger a stronger negative emotional response in the owning-family and family members involved in the firm than in managers of non-family firms (Shepherd, 2003). This negative emotional response can result in focusing on activities associated with the actual de-internationalization, rather than reflecting on what led to the de-internationalization. This means that subsequent learning from experiences might be limited.

Hence, if re-internationalization is considered a viable strategy at all, the question arises: to what extent do family firms adjust their internationalization strategies based on their learning from previous experiences? In line with the notion of learning in the behavioral theory of the firm, future research could examine how experiences associated with de-internationalization and re-internationalization influence future strategic decisions and whether differences exist between family and non-family firms. As there are different perspectives on how family ownership can influence learning, it will be valuable to recognize that family firms are a heterogeneous group of firms with different knowledge bases and opportunities for knowledge sharing. Hence, different family firms can have different ways of incorporating internationalization and de-internationalization experiences in their decisions.

Learning not only influences behavior but it can also influence the prioritization of goals. The behavioral theory of the firm suggests that learning from experience can influence goals in two ways. First, aspiration levels can be adjusted depending on past personal achievements as well as the achievements of a reference group (Cyert & March, 1963). Although goals are central in understanding family firms' behavior, learning from experience and the subsequent effect of this learning on a firm and family's goals are not often acknowledged in literature on family firms (Williams Jr, Pieper, Kellermanns, & Astrachan, 2018). One possible reason for this could be that in recent years the SEW perspective has strongly influenced research on family firms. However, this perspective is based on the prospect theory which mainly focuses on adjusting behavior in response to a risk of not meeting aspirations (Wiseman & Gomez-Mejia, 1998) rather than how these responses affect aspirations.

Besides potential adjustments in behavior as a result of a search process, the behavioral theory of the firm also suggests that aspiration levels associated with different goals can be adjusted. Changes in aspiration levels can change the degree of commitment to a foreign market. In existing literature on family firms' internationalization, family firms' goals are implicitly assumed as static.

However, a more dynamic view can be provided by building on key concepts of the behavioral theory of the firm's goal adjustments. This leads to research questions on how family firms adjust their aspiration levels in response to learning from the initial internationalization and de-internationalization experience and whether family firms respond differently to a de-internationalization experience as compared to non-family firms.

Second, experience can shift attention to different goals (Cyert & March, 1963). Family firms and family members cannot respond to a large variety of goals at once. Most of the literature on family firms' internationalization examines how family owners influence international development and only a few studies have examined internationalization's influence on family firms' financial performance (Fernández-Olmos et al., 2016). Little attention is also paid to how experiences associated with internationalization influence a family and its goals.

The impact of internationalization experiences is likely to relate to the characteristics and the stage of internationalization. For example, de-internationalization from one export market which only captured a small percentage of a firm's sales might have a different impact on the family, its learning, and its ability to achieve goals than divestment of a foreign subsidiary. In case there is the divestment of a foreign subsidiary, commitment to foreign operations and therefore the time and money invested are higher. These have a more serious impact on the firm's financial wealth (Benito & Welch, 1997). Since financial wealth is a pre-requisite for a family firm to survive and achieve non-financial goals (Holt, Pearson, Carr, & Barnett, 2017), divestment of foreign subsidiaries can have a stronger influence on family cohesion and the family's ability to achieve non-financial goals than exiting from an export market. Moreover, the family's attachment to the firm's international operations that are stopped can trigger shifts in attention.

De-internationalization might be more difficult for family members who worked to create international activities (Feldman, Amit, & Villalonga, 2013). In these situations, conflicts might arise when family members prioritize different goals which can destabilize the family (Williams Jr et al., 2018). This suggests that besides considering the potential impact of international experience on a family and the attention it pays to its goals, questions can be raised about contingency conditions like the degree of initial international commitment or emotional involvement in the international activities that the family firm de-internationalizes which influence a shift in attention between different goals.

Conclusions

The conceptual study in this chapter contributes to our scholarly understanding of family firms' internationalization in two ways. First, we outline how the behavioral theory of the firm, as one of the main theories underlying studies on family firms as well as internationalization process studies, has so far contributed to our knowledge of family firms' internationalization processes. This includes an overview of which elements of the behavioral theory of the firm that have been less influential in previous research. We conclude that literature on family firms' internationalization has borrowed some of the concepts of the behavioral theory of the firm, but disregarded others. The notion that firms are composed by a coalition of individuals with a variety of goals is incorporated by distinguishing between financial and non-financial goals in family firms' internationalization. However, in general, research on family firms has established a larger variety of goals and as such distinguishing between financial and non-financial goals might be too narrow a focus for understanding internationalization as a discontinuous process.

Moreover, family firms avoid uncertainty in their internationalization processes by entering similar markets and by preferring certain operation modes over others. The behavioral theory of the firm provides a process perspective which is less prominent in literature on family firms' internationalization because it treats goals as relatively static. The notions of learning and problemistic search, which are prominent in internationalization process studies, have also received little attention.

Second, we contribute by building on the four key concepts that Cyert and March (1963) introduced as essential for an understanding of decision-making processes to provide ideas for new research. The future research agenda is focused on areas that scholars might address to more fully understand the internationalization of family firms as a discontinuous process. We rely on the notion that family firms are a coalition of individuals with different goals leading to that family firms may prioritize different goals at different points in time. In doing so, our study opens up for seeing a family's and firm's goals and their impact on internationalization as a discontinuous process.

In addition, incorporating the notion of problemistic search can provide new insights into which problems family firms respond to when they de-internationalize or re-internationalize. It can also help to understand whether a variety of alternative strategies are considered before de-internationalization to prevent it or whether de-internationalization is the only option for ensuring that aspirations are met. Similarly, incorporating the idea of problemistic search can provide insights into why family firms re-internationalize. Finally, we suggest that to what extent family firms learn from their past international experience and incorporate this learning in future strategic planning and organizational routines can influence the internationalization process. As such, learning is essential for understanding how and why firms de-internationalize or re-internationalize and how different phases in the internationalization process are linked to each other.

References

Alessandri, T. M., Cerrato, D., & Eddleston, K. A. (2018). The mixed gamble of internationalization in family and nonfamily firms: The moderating role of organizational slack. *Global Strategy Journal, 8*(1), 46–72. https://doi.org/10.1002/gsj.1201

Arregle, J. L., Duran, P., Hitt, M. A., & Van Essen, M. (2017). Why is family firms' internationalization unique? A meta–analysis. *Entrepreneurship Theory and Practice, 41*(5), 801–831.

Arregle, J. L., Naldi, L., Nordqvist, M., & Hitt, M. A. (2012). Internationalization of family-controlled firms: A study of the effects of external involvement in governance. *Entrepreneurship Theory and Practice, 36*(6), 1115–1143. https://doi.org/10.1111/j.1540-6520.2012.00541.x

Banalieva, E. R., & Eddleston, K. A. (2011). Home-region focus and performance of family firms: The role of family vs non-family leaders. *Journal of International Business Studies, 42*(8), 1060–1072.

Basly, S. (2007). The internationalization of family SME: An organizational learning and knowledge development perspective. *Baltic Journal of Management, 2*(2), 154–180.

Bauweraerts, J., Sciascia, S., Naldi, L., & Mazzola, P. (2019). Family CEO and board service: Turning the tide for export scope in family SMEs. *International Business Review, 28*(5), 101583.

Benito, G. R. (1997). Divestment of foreign production operations. *Applied Economics, 29*(10), 1365–1378.

Benito, G. R., & Welch, L. S. (1997). De-internationalization. *MIR: Management International Review, 37*, 7–25.

Bernini, M., Du, J., & Love, J. H. (2016). Explaining intermittent exporting: Exit and conditional re-entry in export markets. *Journal of International Business Studies*, 1–19. https://doi.org/10.1057/s41267-016-0015-2

Berrone, P., Cruz, C., & Gomez-Mejia, L. R. (2012). Socioemotional wealth in family firms theoretical dimensions, assessment approaches, and agenda for future research. *Family Business Review, 25*(3), 258–279.

Boddewyn, J. J. (1979). Foreign divestment: Magnitude and factors. *Journal of International Business Studies, 10*, 21–27.

Boddewyn, J. J. (1983). Foreign and domestic divestment and investment decisions: Like or unlike? *Journal of International Business Studies, 14*(3), 23–35.

Boellis, A., Mariotti, S., Minichilli, A., & Piscitello, L. (2016). Family involvement and firms' establishment mode choice in foreign markets. *Journal of International Business Studies, 47*(8), 929–950.

Buckley, P. J., & Casson, M. C. (1998). Analyzing foreign market entry strategies: Extending the internalization approach. *Journal of International Business Studies, 29*(3), 539–561.

Cairns, P., Quinn, B., Alexander, N., & Doherty, A. M. (2010). The role of leadership in international retail divestment. *European Business Review, 22*(1), 25–42.

Calabro, A., Brogi, M., & Torchia, M. (2016). What does really matter in the internationalization of small and medium-sized family businesses? *Journal of Small Business Management, 54*(2), 679–696. https://doi.org/10.1111/jsbm.12165

Calabro, A., Campopiano, G., Basco, R., & Pukall, T. (2017). Governance structure and internationalization of family-controlled firms: The mediating role of international entrepreneurial orientation. *European Management Journal, 35*(2), 238–248. https://doi.org/10.1016/j.emj.2016.04.007

Calabrò, A., Mussolino, D., & Huse, M. (2009). The role of board of directors in the internationalisation process of small and medium sized family businesses. *International Journal of Globalisation and Small Business, 3*(4), 393–411. https://doi.org/10.1504/IJGSB.2009.032259

Campopiano, G., De Massis, A., & Chirico, F. (2014). Firm philanthropy in small- and medium-sized family firms: The effects of family involvement in ownership and management. *Family Business Review, 27*(3), 244–258.

Casillas, J. C., & Moreno-Menéndez, A. M. (2017). International business & family business: Potential dialogue between disciplines. *European Journal of Family Business, 7*(1–2), 25–40.

Cesinger, B., Hughes, M., Mensching, H., Bouncken, R., Fredrich, V., & Kraus, S. (2016). A socioemotional wealth perspective on how collaboration intensity, trust, and international market knowledge affect family firms' multinationality. *Journal of World Business, 51*(4), 586–599. https://doi.org/10.1016/j.jwb.2016.02.004

Chen, H. L., Hsu, W. T., & Chang, C. Y. (2014). Family ownership, institutional ownership, and internationalization of SMEs. *Journal of Small Business Management, 52*(4), 771–789.

Chirico, F., Criaco, G., Baù, M., Naldi, L., Gomez-Mejia, L. R., & Kotlar, J. (2020). To patent or not to patent: That is the question. Intellectual property protection in family firms. *Entrepreneurship Theory and Practice, 44*(2), 339–367.

Choquette, E. (2018). Import-based market experience and firms' exit from export markets. *Journal of International Business Studies, 50*, 1–27.

Chua, J. H., Chrisman, J. J., & De Massis, A. (2015). A closer look at socioemotional wealth: Its flows, stocks, and prospects for moving forward. *Entrepreneurship Theory and Practice, 39*(2), 173–182.

Claver, E., Rienda, L., & Quer, D. (2007). The internationalisation process in family firms: Choice of market entry strategies. *Journal of General Management, 33*(1), 1–14.

Claver, E., Rienda, L., & Quer, D. (2009). Family firms' international commitment: The influence of family-related factors. *Family Business Review, 22*(2), 125–135.

Coviello, N., Kano, L., & Liesch, P. (2017). Adapting the Uppsala model to a modern world: Macro-context and microfoundations. *Journal of International Business Studies, 48*(9), 1151–1164.

Crick, D. (2004). UK SMEs' decision to discontinue exporting: An exploratory investigation into practices within the clothing industry. *Journal of Business Venturing, 19*(4), 561–587.

Cyert, R. M., & March, J. G. (1963). *A behavioral theory of the firm* (Vol. 2). Englewood Cliffs, NJ: Prentice-Hall.

Cyert, R. M., & March, J. G. (1992). *A behavioral theory of the firm* (2nd ed.). Oxford, UK: Blackwell Publishers.

D'Angelo, A., Majocchi, A., & Buck, T. (2016). External managers, family ownership and the scope of SME internationalization. *Journal of World Business, 51*, 534–547.

Davis, P. (1983). Realizing the potential of the family business. *Organizational Dynamics, 12*(1), 47–56.

Delios, A., & Beamish, P. W. (2001). Survival and profitability: The roles of experience and intangible assets in foreign subsidiary performance. *Academy of Management Journal, 44*(5), 1028–1038.

Dominguez, N., & Mayrhofer, U. (2017). Internationalization stages of traditional SMEs: Increasing, decreasing and re-increasing commitment to foreign markets. *International Business Review, 26*(6), 1051–1063.

Eddleston, K. A., & Kellermanns, F. W. (2007). Destructive and productive family relationships: A stewardship theory perspective. *Journal of Business Venturing, 22*(4), 545–565.

Ellis, P. D. (2011). Social ties and international entrepreneurship: Opportunities and constraints affecting firm internationalization. *Journal of International Business Studies, 42*(1), 99–127.

Feldman, E. R., Amit, R. R., & Villalonga, B. (2013). *Corporate divestitures and family control.* Paper presented at the Academy of Management Proceedings.

Fernández, Z., & Nieto, M. J. (2005). Internationalization strategy of small and medium-sized family businesses: Some influential factors. *Family Business Review, 18*(1), 77–89.

Fernandez, Z., & Nieto, M. J. (2006). Impact of ownership on the international involvement of SMEs. *Journal of International Business Studies, 37*(3), 340–351. https://doi.org/10.1057/palgrave.jibs.8400196

Fernández-Olmos, M., Gargallo-Castel, A., & Giner-Bagües, E. (2016). Internationalisation and performance in Spanish family SMES: The W-curve. *BRQ Business Research Quarterly, 19*(2), 122–136.

Fitzgerald, D., & Haller, S. (2018). Exporters and shocks. *Journal of International Economics, 113*, 154–171. https://doi.org/10.1016/j.jinteco.2018.04.005

Gallo, M. A., & Sveen, J. (1991). Internationalizing the family business: Facilitating and restraining factors. *Family Business Review, 4*(2), 181–190. https://doi.org/10.1111/j.1741-6248.1991.00181.x

Gavetti, G., Greve, H. R., Levinthal, D. A., & Ocasio, W. (2012). The behavioral theory of the firm: Assessment and prospects. *The Academy of Management Annals, 6*(1), 1–40.

George, G., Wiklund, J., & Zahra, S. A. (2005). Ownership and the internationalization of small firms. *Journal of Management, 31*(2), 210–233. https://doi.org/10.1177/0149206304271760

Gersick, K. E., Lansberg, I., Desjardins, M., & Dunn, B. (1999). Stages and transitions: Managing change in the family business. *Family Business Review, 12*(4), 287–297.

Gomez–Mejia, L. R., Campbell, J. T., Martin, G., Hoskisson, R. E., Makri, M., & Sirmon, D. G. (2014). Socioemotional wealth as a mixed gamble: Revisiting family firm R&D investments with the behavioral agency model. *Entrepreneurship Theory and Practice, 38*(6), 1351–1374.

Gómez-Mejía, L. R., Haynes, K. T., Núñez-Nickel, M., Jacobson, K. J., & Moyano-Fuentes, J. (2007). Socioemotional wealth and business risks in family-controlled firms: Evidence from Spanish olive oil mills. *Administrative Science Quarterly, 52*(1), 106–137.

Gomez-Mejia, L. R., Makri, M., & Kintana, M. L. (2010). Diversification decisions in family-controlled firms. *Journal of Management Studies, 47*(2), 223–252. https://doi.org/10.1111/j.1467-6486.2009.00889.x

Gomez-Mejia, L. R., Patel, P. C., & Zellweger, T. M. (2018). In the horns of the dilemma: Socioemotional wealth, financial wealth, and acquisitions in family firms. *Journal of Management, 44*(4), 1369–1397.

Graves, C., & Shan, Y. G. (2014). An empirical analysis of the effect of internationalization on the performance of unlisted family and nonfamily firms in Australia. *Family Business Review, 27*(2), 142–160.

Graves, C., & Thomas, J. (2006). Internationalization of Australian family businesses: A managerial capabilities perspective. *Family Business Review, 19*(3), 207–224.

Graves, C., & Thomas, J. (2008). Determinants of the internationalization pathways of family firms: An examination of family influence. *Family Business Review, 21*(2), 151–167. https://doi.org/10.1111/j.1741-6248.2008.00119.x

Håkanson, L., & Kappen, P. (2017). The 'casino model' of internationalization: An alternative Uppsala paradigm. *Journal of International Business Studies, 48*(9), 1103–1113.

Hall, A., Melin, L., & Nordqvist, M. (2008). 14 Understanding strategizing in the family business context. In *Handbook of Research on Family Business* (Vol. 253). Cheltenham: Edward Elgar.

Hennart, J.-F., Majocchi, A., & Forlani, E. (2017). The myth of the stay-at-home family firm: How family-managed SMEs can overcome their internationalization limitations. *Journal of International Business Studies, 50*(5), 1–25.

Holt, D. T. (2012). Article Commentary: Strategic Decisions within Family Firms: Understanding the Controlling Family's Receptivity to Internationalization. *Entrepreneurship Theory and Practice, 36*(6), 1145–1151.

Holt, D. T., Pearson, A. W., Carr, J. C., & Barnett, T. (2017). Family firm (s) outcomes model: Structuring financial and nonfinancial outcomes across the family and firm. *Family Business Review, 30*(2), 182–202.

Jackson, P., Mellahi, K., & Sparks, L. (2005). Shutting up shop: Understanding the international exit process in retailing. *The Service Industries Journal, 25*(3), 355–371.

Jansson, H., & Söderman, S. (2012). Initial internationalization of Chinese privately owned enterprises – The take-off process. *Thunderbird International Business Review, 54*(2), 183–194.

Javalgi, R. R. G., Deligonul, S., Dixit, A., & Cavusgil, S. T. (2011). International market reentry: A review and research framework. *International Business Review, 20*(4), 377–393.

Johanson, J., & Vahlne, J.-E. (1977). The internationalization process of the firm – A model of knowledge development and increasing foreign market commitments. *Journal of International Business Studies, 8*, 23–32.

Jones, M. V. (1999). The internationalization of small high-technology firms. *Journal of International marketing, 7*(4), 15–41.

Jones, M. V. (2001). First steps in internationalisation: Concepts and evidence from a sample of small high-technology firms. *Journal of International Management, 7*(3), 191–210.

Kammerlander, N., & Ganter, M. (2015). An attention-based view of family firm adaptation to discontinuous technological change: Exploring the role of family CEOs' noneconomic goals. *Journal of Product Innovation Management, 32*(3), 361–383.

Kano, L., & Verbeke, A. (2018). Family firm internationalization: Heritage assets and the impact of bifurcation bias. *Global Strategy Journal, 8*(1), 158–183. https://doi.org/10.1002/gsj.1186

Kontinen, T., & Ojala, A. (2010). The internationalization of family businesses: A review of extant research. *Journal of Family Business Strategy, 1*(2), 97–107.

Kontinen, T., & Ojala, A. (2011a). International opportunity recognition among small and medium-sized family firms. *Journal of Small Business Management, 49*(3), 490–514.

Kontinen, T., & Ojala, A. (2011b). Social capital in relation to the foreign market entry and post-entry operations of family SMEs. *Journal of international entrepreneurship, 9*(2), 133–151.

Kontinen, T., & Ojala, A. (2012). Internationalization pathways among family-owned SMEs. *International Marketing Review, 29*(5), 496–518. https://doi.org/10.1108/02651331211260359

Kotlar, J., & De Massis, A. (2013). Goal setting in family firms: Goal diversity, social interactions, and collective commitment to family–centered goals. *Entrepreneurship Theory and Practice, 37*(6), 1263–1288.

Kotlar, J., Signori, A., De Massis, A., & Vismara, S. (2018). Financial wealth, socioemotional wealth, and IPO underpricing in family firms: A two-stage gamble model. *Academy of Management Journal, 61*(3), 1073–1099.

Kraus, S., Mensching, H., Calabrò, A., Cheng, C.-F., & Filser, M. (2016). Family firm internationalization: A configurational approach. *Journal of Business Research, 69*(11), 5473–5478.

Levitt, B., & March, J. G. (1988). Organizational learning. *Annual Review of Sociology, 14*(1), 319–338.

Lin, W. T. (2012). Family ownership and internationalization processes: Internationalization pace, internationalization scope, and internationalization rhythm. *European Management Journal, 30*(1), 47–56.

Liu, Y., Lin, W.-T., & Cheng, K.-Y. (2011). Family ownership and the international involvement of Taiwan's high-technology firms: The moderating effect of high-discretion organizational slack. *Management and Organization Review, 7*(2), 201–222. https://doi.org/10.1111/j.1740-8784.2011.00220.x

Lumpkin, G. T., & Brigham, K. H. (2011). Long-term orientation and intertemporal choice in family firms. *Entrepreneurship Theory and Practice, 35*(6), 1149–1169.

Martin, G., & Gomez-Mejia, L. (2016). The relationship between socioemotional and financial wealth: Re-visiting family firm decision making. *Management Research: Journal of the Iberoamerican Academy of Management, 14*(3), 215–233.

Matthyssens, P., & Pauwels, P. (2000). Uncovering international market-exit processes: A comparative case study. *Psychology & Marketing, 17*(8), 697–719.

McDermott, M. C. (2010). Foreign divestment: The neglected area of international business? *International Studies of Management & Organization, 40*(4), 37–53.

Metsola, J., et al. (2020). Process in family business internationalisation: The state of the art and ways forward. *International Business Review*, 101665.

Mitter, C., Duller, C., Feldbauer-Durstmüller, B., & Kraus, S. (2014). Internationalization of family firms: The effect of ownership and governance. *Review of Managerial Science, 8*(1), 1–28. https://doi.org/10.1007/s11846-012-0093-x

Mohr, A., Batsakis, G., & Stone, Z. (2018). Explaining the effect of rapid internationalization on horizontal foreign divestment in the retail sector: An extended Penrosean perspective. *Journal of International Business Studies, 49*(7), 779–808. https://doi.org/10.1057/s41267-017-0138-0

Okoroafo, S. C. (1999). Internationalization of family businesses: Evidence from Northwest Ohio, U.S.A. *Family Business Review, 12*(2), 147–158. https://doi.org/10.1111/j.1741-6248.1999.00147.x

Okoroafo, S. C., & Koh, A. C. (2009). Family businesses' views on internationalization: do they differ by generations? *International Business Research, 3*(1), P22.

Oviatt, B. M., & McDougall, P. P. (1994). Toward a theory of international new ventures. *Journal of International Business Studies, 25*, 45–64.

Pukall, T. J., & Calabrò, A. (2014). The internationalization of family firms: A critical review and integrative model. *Family Business Review, 27*(2), 103–125.

Reiljan, E. (2006). De-internationalization motives: A theoretical framework. *Tartu University*, 144–154.

Reuber, A. R. (2016). An assemblage–theoretic perspective on the internationalization processes of family firms. *Entrepreneurship Theory and Practice, 40*(6), 1269–1286.

Samiee, S., & Walters, P. G. (1991). Segmenting corporate exporting activities: Sporadic versus regular exporters. *Journal of the Academy of Marketing Science, 19*(2), 93–104.

Sanchez-Bueno, M. J., & Usero, B. (2014). How may the nature of family firms explain the decisions concerning international diversification? *Journal of Business Research, 67*(7), 1311–1320. https://doi.org/10.1016/j.jbusres.2013.09.003

Santangelo, G. D., & Meyer, K. E. (2017). Internationalization as an evolutionary process. *Journal of International Business Studies, 48*(9), 1114–1130. https://doi.org/10.1057/s41267-017-0119-3

Sciascia, S., Mazzola, P., Astrachan, J. H., & Pieper, T. M. (2012). The role of family ownership in international entrepreneurship: Exploring nonlinear effects. *Small Business Economics, 38*(1), 15–31.

Sciascia, S., Mazzola, P., Astrachan, J. H., & Pieper, T. M. (2013). Family involvement in the board of directors: Effects on sales internationalization. *Journal of Small Business Management, 51*(1), 83–99. https://doi.org/10.1111/j.1540-627X.2012.00373.x

Sharma, P. (2004). An overview of the field of family business studies: Current status and directions for the future. *Family business review, 17*(1), 1–36.

Shepherd, D. A. (2003). Learning from business failure: Propositions of grief recovery for the self-employed. *Academy of Management Review, 28*(2), 318–328.

Simon, H. A. (1972). Theories of bounded rationality. *Decision and Organization, 1*(1), 161–176.

Sirmon, D. G., & Hitt, M. A. (2003). Managing resources: Linking unique resources, management, and wealth creation in family firms. *Entrepreneurship Theory and Practice, 27*(4), 339–358.

Sousa, C. M., & Tan, Q. (2015). Exit from a foreign market: Do poor performance, strategic fit, cultural distance, and international experience matter? *Journal of International Marketing, 23*(4), 84–104.

Stewart, A., & Hitt, M. A. (2012). Why can't a family business be more like a nonfamily business? Modes of professionalization in family firms. *Family Business Review, 25*(1), 58–86.

Surdu, I., Mellahi, K., & Glaister, K. W. (2018). Once bitten, not necessarily shy? Determinants of foreign market re-entry commitment strategies. *Journal of International Business Studies, 50*(3), 1–30.

Surdu, I., Mellahi, K., Glaister, K. W., & Nardella, G. (2018). Why wait? Organizational learning, institutional quality and the speed of foreign market re-entry after initial entry and exit. *Journal of World Business, 53*(6), 911–929. https://doi.org/10.1016/j.jwb.2018.07.008

Tagiuri, R., & Davis, J. A. (1992). On the goals of successful family companies. *Family Business Review, 5*(1), 43–62.

Turcan, R. V. (2011). *De-internationalization: A conceptualization.* Paper presented at the AIB-UK & Ireland Chapter Conference 'International Business: New Challenges, New Forms, New Practices,' April.

Verbeke, A., & Kano, L. (2012). The transaction cost economics theory of the family firm: Family–based human asset specificity and the bifurcation bias. *Entrepreneurship Theory and Practice, 36*(6), 1183–1205.

Vissak, T. (2010). Nonlinear internationalization: A neglected topic in international business research. *Advances in International Management, 23*, 559–580.

Vissak, T., & Francioni, B. (2013). Serial nonlinear internationalization in practice: A case study. *International Business Review, 22*(6), 951–962. https://doi.org/10.1016/j.ibusrev.2013.01.010

Vissak, T., Francioni, B., & Musso, F. (2012). MVM's nonlinear internationalization: A case study. *Journal of East-West Business, 18*(4), 275–300. https://doi.org/10.1080/10669868.2012.736081

Ward, J. L. (1988). The special role of strategic planning for family businesses. *Family Business Review, 1*(2), 105–117.

Welch, C., Nummela, N., & Liesch, P. (2016). The internationalization process model revisited: An agenda for future research. *Management International Review, 56*, 783–804.

Welch, C., & Paavilainen-Mäntymäki, E. (2014). Putting process (back) In: Research on the internationalization process of the firm. *International Journal of Management Reviews, 16*(1), 2–23.

Welch, C. L., & Welch, L. S. (2009). Re-internationalisation: Exploration and conceptualisation. *International Business Review, 18*(6), 567–577.

Welch, L. S., & Luostarinen, R. (1988). Internationalization: Evolution of a concept. *The Internationalization of the Firm, 14*, 83–98.

Wennberg, K., & Holmquist, C. (2008). Problemistic search and international entrepreneurship. *European Management Journal, 26*(6), 441–454.

Westhead, P. (2003). Company performance and objectives reported by first and multi-generation family companies: a research note. *Journal of Small Business and Enterprise Development, 10*(1), 93–105.

Williams Jr., R. I., Pieper, T. M., Kellermanns, F. W., & Astrachan, J. H. (2018). Family firm goals and their effects on strategy, family and organization behavior: A review and research agenda. *International Journal of Management Reviews, 20*, S63–S82.

Wiseman, R. M., & Gomez-Mejia, L. R. (1998). A behavioral agency model of managerial risk taking. *Academy of Management Review, 23*(1), 133–153.

Zahra, S. A. (2003). International expansion of U.S. manufacturing family businesses: The effect of ownership and involvement. *Journal of Business Venturing, 18*(4), 495–512. https://doi.org/10.1016/S0883-9026(03)00057-0

Zahra, S. A. (2012). Organizational learning and entrepreneurship in family firms: Exploring the moderating effect of ownership and cohesion. *Small Business Economics, 38*(1), 51–65. https://doi.org/10.1007/s11187-010-9266-7

6

One Family Firm, Four Families: Developing Management Models of a Family Values-Based MNC

Sari Laari-Salmela, Tuija Mainela, Elina Pernu, and Vesa Puhakka

Introduction

Multinational companies (MNCs) are network organisations consisting of a headquarters and often many and various kinds of subsidiaries operating in cross-border business networks (Hedlund, 1986). In such types of international organisations, their management involves complexity that researchers and managers have approached through, for example, questions of organisational design (Bartlett & Ghoshal, 1989; Pedersen, Devinney, Venzin, & Tihanyi, 2014). Organisational design influences the ways in which a firm operates both in local customer networks and within broader industry networks. An additional dimension affecting its ways of operating is whether the MNC is a family firm. In such cases, familiness shapes the behaviours and decisions of the firm, influencing the design of its international operations (Chrisman, Chua, & Sharma, 2005; Kontinen & Ojala, 2012) but there is scant research with primary attention to familiness of MNCs. It has been suggested that family firms maximise socioemotional wealth (Berrone, Cruz, & Gomez-Mejia, 2012), and a values-driven approach is an important feature of family firms (Chrisman et al., 2005), but the approach becomes complicated

---

S. Laari-Salmela • T. Mainela (✉) • E. Pernu • V. Puhakka
Department of Marketing, Management and International Business & Center for Entrepreneurship and Sustainable Business, University of Oulu Business School, Oulu, Finland
e-mail: tuija.mainela@oulu.fi

© The Author(s), under exclusive license to Springer Nature Switzerland AG 2021

T. Leppäaho, S. Jack (eds.), *The Palgrave Handbook of Family Firm Internationalization*, https://doi.org/10.1007/978-3-030-66737-5_6

in MNCs with units in different and distant locations (see Lubatkin, Schulze, Ling, & Dino, 2005). In the present study, we examine the management model emerging through the enactment of family values in different MNC units.

The concept of a management model draws attention to the choices a firm internally makes about how work is accomplished when attending to micro-level strategic and operative processes (Birkinshaw & Ansari, 2015). We will use the concept to characterise the managerial principles vocalised and demonstrated by the headquarters and emerging in practice at the organisational unit level in a family MNC. This allows us to uncover the ways practice and, in particular, enactment of values, produce management models instead of focusing on how managers develop management praxis (cf. Vaara & Whittington, 2012; Whittington, 2006). Furthermore, the management models grow out of practice by individuals representing the firm, and thus, multitudes of management models co-exist within firms (Birkinshaw & Ansari, 2015). Overall, little attention has been given to family influence in the operations of MNCs, that is, the later phases of internationalisation, and the challenges in managing a multinational network organisation through family values. To uncover the complexities of managing a family MNC, the research question of the study is as follows: *How is a values-based management model of a family MNC enacted in the practice of its units?*

Theoretically, we rely on the network view of MNCs and use the practice-oriented management model as a lens through which to analyse how family values are vocalised and enacted. In this way, we can elaborate on the values-defined interface between the internal and external structures of a family MNC as a practice-based design issue. In the empirical part of the study, we examine a family MNC and three of its subsidiaries in Sweden, Russia and the USA. Family MNCs are particularly interesting settings for analysing management models because the headquarters of the various firms tend to emphasise a specific management model as the global way of doing business (see Kontinen & Ojala, 2012). At the same time, local subsidiaries need to develop their management models to fit into particular local communities (Marquis & Battilana, 2009). We rely on interview data to track how the management model develops and is enacted in different ways within an MNC. As a result, we illustrate family values as the nexus that guides operations and sets the direction of the firm, but they take different manifestations in the management models of the subsidiaries.

The contribution of the study is that it elaborates on the informal and underlying processes of internal organising in simultaneously controlled and independent ways within the units of globally operating family MNCs (see

Birkinshaw & Ansari, 2015). Furthermore, through attention to the different manifestations of values-based management principles in the practices of the subsidiaries, we develop a standardisation versus local adaptation view of MNC design (see Bartlett & Ghoshal, 1989; Meyer, Mudambi, & Narula, 2011) further through defining its micro-level determinants. The managerial contribution of the study is bound up in the discussion of how such dynamics can be utilised for coordinated differentiation when organising a network of international sales subsidiaries.

Values-Based Management of a Family MNC

We approach the family MNC as a network organisation to better capture the challenges of managing a group of individual organisations embedded in various local networks in which the firm's headquarters is an outsider (Forsgren, 2008) and the subsidiaries' local environments are emphasised in their operations (Nell, Ambos, & Schlegelmilch, 2011). We then connect this approach to views of familiness in the internationalisation of firms. Towards the end of the section, we propose a values-based management model of a family MNC using the lens of a management model with a practice approach to organisations.

Family MNCs as Internationally Operating Network Organisations

MNCs have evolved from bureaucratic and formal headquarters-led organisations towards increasingly acknowledging the informal and networked relationships at their core (Kostova, Marano, & Tallman, 2016). According to network perspective on MNCs, an MNC is a complex web of interdependent relationships within which individuals operate (Forsgren, 2008). Each subsidiary is acknowledged as firmly embedded in its own local network of relationships, which differ from the networks of other subsidiaries and may develop rather independently from headquarters due to differing business conditions and social and cultural environments (Forsgren, 2008; Ghoshal, Korine, & Szulanski, 1994). The network form of a company in itself is a strategic and competitive device intimately connected to the development of the firm's operations (Cenamor, Parida, Oghazi, Pesämaa, & Wincent, 2019).

Managing MNCs is a question of managing the often conflicting forces initially captured in the integration-responsiveness (IR) framework (Prahalad

& Doz, 1987). According to it, MNCs need to coordinate and integrate activities across borders, and subsidiaries simultaneously need to respond to demands arising from the complex nature of economic, competitive and market forces in the local environment. The need for headquarters to control the development of the MNC stems from the occurrence of strategically inconsistent directions in which subsidiaries might develop (Holm, Johanson, & Thilenius, 1995). Simultaneously, sufficient independence motivates subsidiary managers to establish local relationships for competitive opportunities and contextual risk reduction (Andersson, Forsgren, & Holm, 2002; Luo, 2001). The extent to which subsidiaries become embedded in their local environments influences the possibilities for making local innovations, while on the other hand, the internal embeddedness of subsidiaries within the MNC is crucial for turning local innovations into global innovations (Isaac, Borini, Raziq, & Benito, 2019). Coordinating relationships and organisational designs has been a challenge for global companies throughout their existence (Westney, 2014; Wolf & Egelhoff, 2013).

Successfully managing MNCs requires knowledge located inside and outside the whole network organisation (Cenamor et al., 2019). Quite often, a firm's headquarters lacks sufficient knowledge about the actions of its subsidiaries (Vahlne, Schweizer, & Johanson, 2012). Subsidiaries do not always welcome involvement by headquarters or its interference with local activities (Decreton, Nell, & Stea, 2019) and in an attempt to manage the global organisation, a firm's headquarters may end up demotivating subsidiary managers and employees (Foss, Foss, & Nell, 2012). The network MNC structure creates more occasions for potentially harmful intervention through a low degree of formalisation and the high level of decision-making autonomy granted to subsidiaries (Foss et al., 2012). Negative reactions are more likely to occur when intra-organisational boundaries are strong and individuals within subsidiaries do not feel that they belong to the group, but the boundaries are lowered when a shared understanding and mission exist (Decreton et al., 2019). The question of how to effectively manage a network MNC's operations thus emerges as an intriguing one.

In family firms, previous studies have discovered both factors that facilitate international operations, such as strong social capital, stewardship behaviour and patient capital, and factors that hinder them, such as free riding and shirking (Fernández & Nieto, 2006; Kontinen & Ojala, 2010). Having external parties as owners and on the board of directors can serve as a catalyst for the internationalisation of a family firm (Arregle, Naldi, Nordqvist, & Hitt, 2012) because international experience and the professionalisation of management are helpful in overcoming possible family hesitance about engaging in operations involving more risk (Boellis, Mariotti, Minichilli, & Piscitello, 2016). Still, there is much heterogeneity among family firms: although they have similarities in governance, each firm is unique and demonstrates different strategic behaviour (Kontinen & Ojala, 2012; Melin & Nordqvist, 2007; Sciascia, Mazzola, Astrachan, & Pieper, 2012).

In addition to the composition of governance and 'heterogeneity bias', the role of *values* in internationalisation has been highlighted (Verbeke, Yuan, & Kano, 2020). Family firms are often noted for being traditional, as being more committed to home market-based ways of doing business, keeping control and making mostly incremental changes (Kontinen & Ojala, 2012). The tendency towards risk-aversion is connected to the values underlying the decision-making processes of family-controlled firms. For instance, Koiranen (2002) concluded in his study of Finnish family firms that they valued more desirable modes of conduct than desirable end states, such as good economic return. The personal values of the families are also typically reflected in the values of the firm and its decision-making (Arregle et al., 2017; Zellweger, Kellermanns, Chrisman, & Chua, 2012) and often support a more long-term view (Aronoff & Ward, 2000). Verbeke et al. (2020) noted that values act as guiding principles in how a family firm makes sense of its environment and related resource allocation and strategic decision-making, including internationalisation decisions. In the next section, we elaborate on the influence of family values at the subsidiary practice level with attention to the concept of management model.

Values-Based Management Model of a Family MNC: A Practice Approach

The competing demand to either integrate globally or adapt locally (Marquis & Battilana, 2009) is one of the multifaceted strategic requirements faced by the management of MNCs. The way different firms decide to manage the competing demands depends on the way in which they prioritise different courses of action, and therefore, what they deem *desirable*. The research on family values and their role in internationalisation has focused on these underlying conceptions and ideas of what is desirable in terms of means or end states of action (e.g., Connor & Becker, 1975, p. 551; Guth & Tagiuri, 1965, p. 125). Koiranen (2002, p. 177) defines family business values as those 'explicit or implicit conceptions of the desirable in both family and business life' and continues that such desired end states as shared beliefs underlie the attitudinal and behavioural processes of family members and those involved in business. He emphasises the importance of defining and sharing family business values to form a common ground for the operations.

The values, whether explicitly expressed and shared or not, define the way the firm arranges its management. Birkinshaw and Ansari (2015) coined the term 'management model' to describe those underlying principles that hold beliefs about how the different dimensions of management, such as coordinating activities, making decision, defining objectives and motivating employees, should work. To highlight the differences in beliefs, they formulated archetypes of a 'traditional principle' and 'alternative principle', describing a dichotomy between a more hierarchical, planning-oriented approach and a more modern bottom-up, collective approach to management. In reality, these are not either-or situations, but represent the competing demands faced by an MNC. While a growing MNC typically realises that a more structured approach is needed, it also recognises the need to allow subsidiaries space to develop in terms of the needs of the local environment (see, Regnér, 2003).

To examine the values-based management model of the MNC in question and to better understand the enactment of values in the everyday actions of the individuals managing different units, we adopt a practice approach. Here, we understand values to occur within the field of practices, where practices refer to 'embodied, materially mediated arrays of human activity centrally organized around shared practical understanding' (Schatzki, 2002, p. 11). We draw on Schatzki's conceptualisation of practice in which action consists of three elements: understanding *how to* do things; explicit *rules* of what can be said or done; and a *teleo-affective structure*, which refers to both those aspects that relate to the intended end states of the action and the related emotions, moods and mental states that are acceptable for the participants (the *ought-to-do*). In order to understand how values are enacted through the different practices of both the subsidiaries and the headquarters, we focus on how such 'ought-to-do' practices are manifested in actions: how the desired ends (explicitly expressed as 'values' by the HQ) are reflected in the actions and what forms they take in each context.

In our study, we model the way a family MNC aims to reconcile the competing demands in its organising and form its management model as the 'modus operandi'. This involves looking at how the logic of a firm's operations are vocalised via family values and how family values are enacted in the subsidiary management models, in which the values take form as certain stable tendencies in the operations of the different units (see Fig. 6.1).

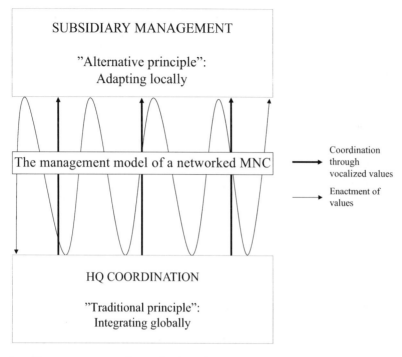

Fig. 6.1 The emergence of practice-based management models in MNCs. (Source: Authors)

Research Methodology

Research Strategy

We adopt an instrumental case study strategy with interest in an in-depth understanding of this particular case as such (Creswell, 2012; Silverman, 2005). Complicated cross-cultural settings can be approached well through the case study method (Marschan-Piekkari & Welch, 2004, pp. 7–8), as case studies provide a unique means for developing theory by utilising the in-depth insights acquired about the phenomenon and its context (Dubois & Gadde, 2002). Qualitative research is well suited to cross-cultural settings because it creates an understanding of the meanings and beliefs behind actions (Marschan-Piekkari & Welch, 2004, pp. 7–8) and case study allows a description of the productive dynamics in real-life events (Piekkari, Welch, & Paavilainen, 2009). We rely on interpretive sensemaking, where the case study consists of detailed, contextual descriptions and is used to understand the subjective experiences of various actors (Welch, Piekkari, Plakoyiannaki, & Paavilainen-Mäntymäki, 2011).

180 S. Laari-Salmela et al.

The MNC under study is a family MNC that publicly and frequently emphasises the importance of family values in its business operations and has provided us access to three of its subsidiaries in different parts of the world. We selected the case purposively and based on theoretical sampling (Silverman, 2005). We saw the firm as well-illustrating the features of our research interest (family ownership, long history, global operations, values-led), and thus it allows us opportunity to develop the conceptual framework further through an in-depth examination of this particular case. The excellence of the case firm has also been recognised through several awards in relation to its internationalisation and growth and its profile as a family firm, a technology firm and a medium-sized firm as well as in terms of entrepreneurship at both individual and company levels.

Examination of this firm allows us to uncover the ways in which the historically developed values of a family MNC are reflected in the management models of its subsidiaries. Through utilising theoretical lenses in the process of casing (Ragin, 1992; see also Stake, 2005), we defined the management model as the case. Our study uses an embedded single-case design (Halinen & Törnroos, 2005) because we explore both the MNC-level values and management principles and their manifestations in the management models of the three subsidiaries. The network MNC viewpoint also leads us to pay attention separately to the headquarters and the subsidiaries and see the multiple management models.

Data Collection and Analysis

Data collection started with the acquisition of publicly available data on the firm. It includes material such as annual reports, histories and press releases as well as news on the firm. We also followed its communications on various internet platforms. This was done to understand the overall characteristics of the firm, its industry and its ways of doing business. To understand the micro level in terms of the values, management principles and the practice of the subsidiaries, we conducted two rounds of interviews.

The first round of interviews began with us meeting the chairman of the board, who is also the son of the founder of the firm. We received an in-depth presentation on the story of the firm that depicted the decades of its development. In selecting the interviewees, we employed a chain sampling strategy (Fletcher & Plakoyiannaki, 2011). The second interview was with the CEO of the firm whom the chairman suggested to be an important interviewee without family background but many years leading the firm. The chairman and the CEO suggested that we concentrate on three subsidiaries based on their different features and operational environments. We then continued by participating in an annual meeting of the subsidiaries, in which the chairman of the board and the managing directors of the three subsidiaries were interviewed. In the interviews, the managing directors were asked to tell about their own experiences with the subsidiary and describe that way its story.

We analysed this data for the purposes of understanding the managing of the MNC and characterising the subsidiaries. After the interviews, the stories of the subsidiaries were written down (see Ghauri, 2004, pp. 117–118). Summaries of the interviews were also reviewed by the interviewees to ensure confirmability of the research (Flint, Woodruff, & Gardial, 2002; Lincoln & Guba, 1985, p. 300), wherein the participants themselves interpreted the phenomenon, as opposed to researchers. This analysis was the starting point for the second round of interviews two years after the first round. We first met with the chairman of the board and the CEO of the firm to discuss further the operations of the three subsidiaries and their relationships with headquarters. We then continued with interviews of the three managing directors of the subsidiaries both to get their reflections on our earlier interpretations and to discuss the latest developments in the subsidiaries. The interviews (see Table 6.1) were otherwise organised in the facilities of the MNC, but the last

Table 6.1 Interview data of the case study

Interviewee	Duration	Focus
Chairman of the board (HQ)	105 min	History of the organisation, internationalisation
CEO of the firm (HQ)	72 min	Present challenges of the firm
Chairman of the board (HQ)	29 min	Internal organising, key individuals
Managing director, Sweden (sub)	61 min	Development of the Swedish subsidiary
Managing director, Russia (sub)	71 min	Development of the Russian subsidiary
Managing director, USA (sub)	57 min	Development of the US subsidiary
Chairman of the board and CEO (HQ)	122 min	Discussion of the subsidiaries on the basis of the analysis from previous interviews
Managing director, Sweden (sub)	68 min	Reflections and latest issues in the Swedish subsidiary
Managing director, Russia (sub)	72 min	Reflections and latest issues in the Russian subsidiary
Managing director, USA (sub)	76 min	Reflections and latest issues in the US subsidiary

Source: Authors

three interviews with the managing directors took place via Skype video. All the interviews were recorded and transcribed by a professional.

As mentioned above, analysis of the data took place in turns with respect to data collection, as is typical in research involving rich, longitudinal, qualitative data (Dubois & Gadde, 2002; Zalan & Lewis, 2004). The first results were captured with a focus on the subsidiary's positioning and the tensions in the subsidiary's interactive spheres. We then continued with attention to the internal operations of the MNC, emphasising the values and managerial principles seen in the management models. The interview data was analysed via a content analytical procedure (Denzin & Lincoln, 2000; Ghauri, 2004). As is typical with embedded case studies, we, first, analysed the headquarters and the subsidiaries separately, with attention given to vocalisations on the values as well as practices in the unit in question. The firm's headquarters has strong guiding values, which were used as a starting point for the data analysis. We then utilised the value concept discussed in the theory section, where values are seen as socially shared views and an inherent part of practices (see Schatzki, 2002). We then proceeded to compare the units with each other, with focus on the ways they act in relationships and compared the values espoused by the firm's headquarters with the subsidiaries' actions. Finally, we depicted the practice-based management models in the values-led family MNC.

Management Models in a Family MNC in the Forest Machine Industry

The MNC under study has been operating for several decades and is currently one of the leading firms in the forest machine industry. Despite being a listed firm, it is still mainly owned by the founding family, now represented by the sons of the founder entrepreneur. The firm operates in approximately 40 countries and exports almost 80% of its products. The early years were rocky, and the firm remained a domestic firm without sales abroad for almost two decades. To intensify internationalisation, the firm was owned by a larger firm for five years, but the entrepreneur acquired full ownership back at the beginning of the 1990s. The company grew at a rather steady pace until 2008, when the financial crisis almost entirely stopped orders. The firm invested heavily in product development and service model renewal and achieved high growth throughout the 2010s; nowadays, the firm is a very profitable company. It has been selected as the best family business, the best international

6 One Family Firm, Four Families: Developing Management Models... 183

company and the most reputable company in its home country. It continues to be a family firm led by inherited values.

> We have never been a family-Sunday-lunch type of business firm, but from the [founder] came very clear directions, and so we have operated.

Historically Developing Values-Base of the Family Firm's Operations

The thinking behind the company's way of working has its roots at the beginning of the twentieth century, in farming and forestry. The founding entrepreneur's family were farmers, very used to hard work. When the husband was away at war, his wife took care of the farm and the family. In addition to a farming background, the founder of the company had been working in timber forests from a young age. The work was heavy, done by hand and horsepower, and the value of one tree trunk was optimised at the site. The effort taken to produce good-quality timber paid off: if forestry representatives had measured the results and found the quality of the timber unsuitable, the reward would have then been lower. Even today, the essence of the MNC's business is conveyed through a picture of a man, a saw and a horse. This is the basis of the first stated family value, 'appreciation of hard work', which goes together with an appreciation of entrepreneurship and an entrepreneurial spirit. The son of the founder described him as a person with a strong belief in the future, a willingness to try and an unwillingness to give up.

> However badly things were today, tomorrow can be a better day. Looking in the rear-view mirror has never been part of it. [...] "Let's try!" was [the founder's] thought.

This value translates into a management principle involving respect for and an understanding of the sense of entrepreneurship. High-quality products and confidential customer relationships are essential; any problems with the machines mean that the forest machine entrepreneurs lose money and may even put at risk the whole business of a small customer owning a single machine. The entrepreneurial spirit is also about innovation. The initial idea of the founder was to make the best forest machine in the world, even though he did not have a high level of education, and that is still the aim of the firm.

The firm also wants to be known for keeping its promises. 'Honesty' is a value inherited from the earlier generations, and trustworthiness is also part of the management principle. The people in this firm are expected to be honest in all their daily interactions and actions. Despite being nowadays a middle-sized, globally operating MNC, there is hope that the decision-making will continue to rely on this value and the related ways of working.

> Grandma said that you have to be honest. Because without honesty, there is no trust, the same thing in personal relationships and business relationships.

The firm was established in a small village in the rural part of the country, in a location that many would see as disadvantageous in terms of distance and availability of resources. For the entrepreneur, the location meant the possibility to rely on communality that forms one of its management principles. Although some people always question your chances for success, many others offered assistance when it was needed. Just as the hard-working children of farmers are used to taking care of the younger siblings, the village provided funding, loans and a reliable workforce for the firm in its early stages. This is the core of the value 'looking after each other'.

> In a big family, responsibility was taken when you took care of the siblings. In normal work, you should be able to look beyond your tasks, asking if a workmate needs help: "How is it with your tasks today? I'm finished with mine".

This value translates into the concept of the extended family of the firm. It means that the firm invests in its employees. The employees are trained and provided with possibilities for learning new skills and for career progress, and their overall working and life conditions are supported with appropriate means. Simultaneously, the people in the firm are given responsibility and space for development.

The space for development by the individuals and the independence of the subsidiaries could be seen in contrast to the founder's idea of family firm management with one face, which could mean centralised decision-making and top management power. However, we can see this 'faced' management principle turn towards the value of 'humbleness'. Hierarchy is intentionally kept to a minimum within the firm; the bosses and the staff sit at the same tables for coffee and lunch, and no one wears a suit or tie to look more important than the others. Humbleness is inherent internally in the idea of the availability of the top management.

> As you see, nobody wears a tie; I cannot even remember the last time that I would have worn a tie in this company's business. One just doesn't have to; it's

6 One Family Firm, Four Families: Developing Management Models...   185

not part of this, this house. [...] If there are issues in a supervisor-supervisee relationship, I believe the people will come to tell if it does not work.

In its customer relationships, the sense of humbleness translates into the availability of the owners of the firm for customer service and their participation in any more or less important smaller and larger customer events. They maintain a grassroots-level touch and emphasise the importance of being at the same level with the customers. As the majority of customers are individual foresters and small businesses, the company wishes to see itself similarly: as a family business without additional hierarchies or bureaucracy. At the same time, the company is a listed company with distributed ownership, but it maintains personified ownership. The family owns the majority of the firm and the other top management is present and visible in much of the daily operations and activities.

> And then one [principle] concerns the ownership: there can be only one master in the house, the owner has a face.

The other side of the principle that the top management be present and visible is the general approachability of the firm and its people. With respect to approachability, the firm relies especially on humour. It cherishes a joy of work and the fact that joking around is an essential part of serious business meetings, too. This translates into the value of 'sincerity'. It also comes with common sense and respect for others as part of the management principle, and it takes form in the unique and relaxed interaction and communication practices of the firm both internally and in relation to various stakeholders. People should not think too highly of themselves, no matter who they are, and they should treat others as their equal and with respect.

> But as a culture and a company, this is easy to approach ... this gang. In the directors' meetings, there is always teasing and joking involved; it is part of the job, this kind of brisk humour.

Over the last ten years, the shift from the founder's era to a new era of expanded operations has been visible. Just as the firm was built on the founder's work and innovation, with him acting as a charismatic leader who was seen as the highest authority in decision-making, the company has of late faced a phase of expansion after the founder's gradual exit from the stage. The company has been searching for a new management and leadership style, and the question of a proper 'management model' has now in new ways arisen. The rational elements of the management model are described as the combination of searching for the new, maintaining strategic direction, managing stakeholder relationships and maintaining a sense of purpose and relatedness with people.

A few years back, the company gave up its vice president-based organisational structure, where the headquarters governed the market areas. Subsidiary managers and regional directors became the persons responsible for the local subsidiaries, having direct contact with local customers. Thus, the aim has been to decentralise responsibility and decision-making, but at the same time management is considering ways to measure the effectiveness of the local management models, which have merged. What the headquarters expects from the subsidiaries is that they function as independent units, reflecting the same core values in their operations but 'thinking for themselves' and making decisions on the spot. The company aims at maintaining contact with the subsidiaries through regular meetings and board activities, but it does not wish to meddle with the everyday operations. Much responsibility is then placed on the shoulders of the subsidiary management. However, there are many questions about how the subsidiaries in various parts of the world represent the MNC. The company is torn between its independent subsidiary approach and the need to build structures and processes to guide the development of the entire MNC.

> how well does the guy in China understand this philosophy of ours, our employee, or in the States or somewhere else, that is something to work upon.

In the following, we will look at the three subsidiaries in terms of their management models as reflections of the historically developed values and management principles of the firm.

Localised Management Models from the Values of Headquarters to the Subsidiaries

On a general level, the subsidiary managers share many common features in their management style based on the core values vocalised by the headquarters. What they have in common is the desire to be close to customers and be easily approachable. Being at the level of the customer is perceived as a competitive advantage and one that differentiates the firm from its competitors. Despite similarities of the subsidiaries, differences also exist. The history of the subsidiary, as well as the type of the market, has a strong effect on the practice of each subsidiary, and each managing director leads the way with

6 One Family Firm, Four Families: Developing Management Models... 187

Table 6.2 Comparison of subsidiary management and market features

Unit	Local management features	Local market features
Swedish subsidiary	Participatory culture Characterised by uncertainty Focus on creating practices	Methods of forestry fully fitting with the company's machines with an emphasis on environmental aspects Innovation emphasis with customers of all sizes Close within-industry relationships
US subsidiary	Management-driven decision-making Customer-driven operations Unique approach to interacting with customers	Dominating methods of forestry clearly divided between northern and southern parts of the country Closeness and commitment to small family firms Training and branding in the local network
Russian subsidiary	Clearly divided responsibilities Customer-driven contacts Focus on dealership coordination	Two alternative ways of forestry methods having about equal shares in the national market Heterogeneous customer base in distant locations Multiple dealers in sales and service

Source: Authors

his/her own style. Table 6.2 collects the main features of the three subsidiaries in terms of the local management and local markets.

We defined above five primary values in the operations of the MNC. The explicitly addressed values and the management principles based on them are the means by which the firm's headquarters achieves integration when dealing with its subsidiaries. The principles and the underlying values form the logic, or 'modus operandi', of the firm's activities, which the subsidiaries also follow in their local operations. However, differences exist between the subsidiaries in the way the values and the management principles are manifested at the level of everyday practices. These differences are defined by the local market type and the relationships in the local networks as well as by the leadership style. All the subsidiaries reflect the values of the company in their activities, but for each subsidiary one of the values especially seems to build the dominating management principle. When the other values and management principles became intertwined with this core value, each subsidiary could be described by the alternative management model that it had adopted.

Sweden is a developed market, and it has long been among the first to adopt new practices and trends in the forestry industry. Also initiatives for innovations often come from the demands of the Swedish market. The launch of a new model that is clearly at the forefront of development can improve the image of the entire company and increase the sales of all machine types in the market. The Swedish subsidiary handles its sales without utilising dealers, but it does use an external maintenance network for service-related matters. The smaller customers are important along with the larger forest industry companies or sawmills, who give projects to the company's customers, meaning that including the customer's customers in the sales processes is essential. Hierarchy in the Swedish organisation is kept to a minimum and employees are encouraged to act together and share information regarding their activities and efforts. Still, the struggle to achieve a larger market share and changes in leadership have led to feelings of uncertainty.

> At first when I came, the situation was really turbulent. Everybody asked, am I the last guy to come in and turn off the lights?—I needed to go meet the customers and every time listen to how our operations have been totally non-Swedish—and then assure [them] that we are not leaving, and we are continuing but in a different way.

An 'appreciation of hard work' is evident in all three of the subsidiaries in terms of respect for entrepreneurship and the entrepreneurial spirit and an appreciation for experimentation. However, in Sweden the pressure to be at the very forefront in innovation, in particular with respect to societal responsibility, has made it appear as a 'demanding family' that always asks somewhat more than one can readily provide.

Most probably because of the forerunner status of the market, there have been some issues with respect to the 'humbleness' value when some salespeople have hesitated to adopt certain practices and with 'honesty' when the customers have been promised some additional service. These issues strengthen the demanding family characterisation, as the managing director has needed to pay continuous attention to the agreed upon sales practices as well as carefully consider the sufficiency of the service network. In the spirit of the 'looking after each other' value, the demands placed on the employees have been supported by investing in human resource management and the personnel. The 'sincerity' has been realised in the form of relaxed, humorous communications with the customers.

In the US market, the company is the market leader in northern parts, but the local forestry traditions make the southern US a difficult market to break into; the mindset and machinery are challenging to change. The customers are mainly small firms, most preferring large engines. A typical customer is a family business with two machines: a harvester and a forwarder. Closeness to customers and active customer contacts are central, and the customers are

6 One Family Firm, Four Families: Developing Management Models... 189

seen as part of the family of the firm. Also, decisions on the location of offices have been made based on customer preferences. The managing director of the American subsidiary has a central role in the organisation and has a clear vision of how the subsidiary should act, but otherwise the organisational structure is low, and the company is described more like a family, where the wellbeing of employees, and customers is central.

> I try to make at least ten calls per day to different people. Just to say hi. Always, when I am in the car, there is nothing to do except make calls—For example, one person wanted a calendar from Finland—so I gave him a calendar.—We do these things differently, and customers are very close. We don't have any layers ... between customers and us, but anybody can walk in from that door and come to talk anytime.

The US subsidiary is unique in its down-to-earth, customer-centric focus. We termed the subsidiary the 'conversational family', by which we are referring to the importance of being available all the time and easily approachable for extended family, customers and partners in the local market. Asking 'how are you?' and showing appreciation for the little things are stressed. The doors are always open for the customers to stop by and chat. These practices carry the value of 'humbleness', working together with the value of 'sincerity', which is characterised in their relaxed, self-made marketing communications. They have sponsorships with, for example, an off-road team, snowboarders and boxers, which have come through the customers' or personnel's affiliations. Their customer events are designed for having fun, with managers, owners, employees and customers all relaxing together. They have not used professional advertising agencies, but all communication materials with a similar attitude have been done by themselves. The 'appreciation of hard work' rests on an understanding of the family business model that the customers represent. The conversational family is also 'looking after each other' when adopting social security practices in relation to the employees.

The Russian subsidiary has three offices, but the main site is in St. Petersburg. Machines and spare parts are imported to Russia through St. Petersburg and from there delivered further to dealers and customers. The Russian market is divided roughly in half between the two machine-based forestry methods. Customers are a heterogeneous group varying from small contractors to multinational companies. The Russian market is not yet technologically advanced, and it is vital that there are no technical problems with the product when sales commence. Hierarchies have traditionally been emphasised in Russia, and the managing director is commonly in charge of everything. The subsidiary has, however, succeeded in sharing the responsibilities among five to six key individuals and delegating the tasks. Also, employee training and education and communicating the core elements of the organisational culture are crucial. The entrepreneurial spirit is emphasised due to the complicated institutional environment. The Russian subsidiary has eight dealers, through whom the customers often approach the firm, and a few partners focusing on service.

> In Russia, the distances are long and logistics less developed than in other parts of Europe; it maybe stresses the need for extra effort so that we can serve the customers, that they have the spare parts and maintenance and workers.—It starts with people's attitudes and expertise—It requires work to get them [employees] to do things in our way and to know our machines and other [practices]—one important job is the training and we have invested a lot in that.

In Russia, a 'supportive family' has emerged that puts much effort into training and providing other types of assistance to both the employees and the dealers. The 'appreciation of hard work' has a solid basis in the large entrepreneurial population, in which there can be found motivated people seeking to develop better practices. The subsidiary management stresses attitude and expertise as well as commitment to cooperation with the MNC in the selection of both employees and dealers. This allows for a type of managing based on 'looking after each other' via an extended family principle by first training and then giving responsibility and space for development to hard-working people. The characterisation is strengthened by the ways in which the value of 'humbleness' takes form in the participation of the owners and top management of the MNC in customer and dealer meetings and the invitations for them to visit the factory in the home country. These practices are much appreciated. 'Honesty' is important in terms of the trustworthiness of the machines and their maintenance because the customer often operates them in remote locations under tough climatic conditions.

The different management models are presented in Table 6.3. Each of the core values has been translated into guiding local management principles in the subsidiaries' operations but we see there a leading management principle that forms the common thread in the story of the subsidiary. For Sweden, it is 'constant development', for the US 'being available' and for Russia 'investing in people' that forms the teleo-affective structure related with the intended end states and the expected and acceptable action of the participants (the *ought-to-do*).

6 One Family Firm, Four Families: Developing Management Models... 191

Table 6.3 Comparison of the subsidiary management models

Unit	Main core value vocalised by HQ and enacted by the subsidiary	Leading management principle (manifestation of the 'ought-to-do')	Demonstrated at the level of action
Swedish subsidiary—A demanding family	Appreciation of hard work	Constant development 'The core feature of the Swedish market is, from the perspective of HQ, that all the new things come from Sweden.'	Reacting to customer feedback Initiating solutions
US subsidiary—A conversational family	Humbleness	Being available 'We gave up of all unnecessary uptightness. … We have been marketing with brisk humour and send them [videos] to clients. They like that kind of stuff.'	Being in contact regularly Building close relationships Small gestures of appreciation
Russian subsidiary—A supporting family	Looking after each other	Investing in people 'It [the dealer network] is very important since we have a large country, and local experience is really important with us here. There are very different kinds of people in different parts of Russia. Without it [the dealer network], we could not get good results.'	Providing support and training for dealers and employees Giving responsibility and delegating

The principles balance the basic contradiction between traditional and alternative principles, or control and emergence (Birkinshaw & Ansari, 2015), which lies at the core of management activities not only in the headquarter model, but also in the models of the subsidiaries. Presently, the MNC leans towards the 'alternative' principle with its bottom-up approach, as it aims to live physically and figuratively close to its customers, partners, suppliers and employees. By deferring to expertise, by leaving decision-making to those people that best know the situation at hand, the MNC also aims, on the one hand, to provide a quick response time, and on the other hand, to learn from those on the front line. The values of the family business provide a solid foundation and a common platform, a nexus, for practices in a variety of international markets that require local sensitivity.

Discussion

The primary contribution of the present study has to do with our use of a micro-level approach to analyse the design choices in the management of family MNCs. We have, first, illustrated the ways that values can become the backbone for dealing with the paradox of a simultaneous need for controlled and independent decision-making and processes in globally operating MNCs (Marquis & Battilana, 2009; Prahalad & Doz, 1987). We searched for the drivers of the contradictory pressures on organising at the subsidiary level of operations and ended up by presenting the practices at various units and how they relate to local circumstances. We concluded that the management models are inevitably numerous within a globally operating, family MNC, but they can come together in an informal nexus of values, even when taking into account different manifestations of them within the different units.

Our micro-level practice approach makes a contribution also to the research on values as determinants of family firm internationalisation (e.g., Verbeke et al., 2020). In general, the family values we noted, as vocalised by the MNC headquarters and enacted by the subsidiaries, included honesty, credibility, quality and working hard, all of which Koiranen (2002) and others have found to form the core of family business values. However, our practice approach highlights the need for the management to focus more on activities and how such activities may reflect the same shared values and understanding in very different ways—ways that fit the local context and people involved. This relates to the complexity of transferring the 'best practice' between units, as the practices are always embedded in local context, and hence, the values need to take different manifestations. The analysis also suggests that each subsidiary might build its practice primarily around one core value and related leading management principle and then circumscribe the other principle around this core. This can, on its part, explain the different spirit and atmosphere that is felt in different units of a single MNC.

Third, we have elaborated on the concept of management model and captured it in more dynamic terms than first presented by Birkinshaw and Ansari (2015). The management model of a family MNC can be defined, on the one hand, as a collection of management principles that guide operations and produce the consistency that can be seen behind managerial decisions and actions. On the other hand, adopting a practice lens in our analysis of company operations helped us reveal the 'modus operandi' of the firm's activities: the logic behind organising. Instead of focusing on those issues that 'can more readily be altered by those in positions of seniority' and are 'more tangible and readily manipulated' (Birkinshaw & Ansari, 2015, p. 91), we featured the MNC management models as the result of both headquarters and subsidiary level managerial practice. The practice approach allowed us to understand the dynamics inherent in the model and focus on the dimensions that, even when not 'managed' by a mere decision, are the ones through which the logics come to be and can be influenced through people's actions. This is especially evident in a family MNC whose activities are driven by family values.

As a result, we also demonstrated how the seemingly contradictory 'traditional' and 'alternative' principles underlying the management model are not so much an either-or choice but rather a question of how much and when the firm decides that a more structured or bureaucratic approach is needed to coordinate activities in different parts of the entire organisation. The design of the management model also depends on the viewpoint taken: while the headquarters of a globally operating MNC is in a continuous process of finding its own way of organising that negotiates between standardisation versus local adaptation (Bartlett & Ghoshal, 1989; Nohria & Ghoshal, 1997) and the need to control and allow for independence, a subsidiary's model perceives the problem as striking a balance between following the guidelines and processes versus maintaining the freedom to appreciate their partners and innovate on the basis of the local needs. Here the management principles developed from the nexus of the shared values are weighted in their power of leading the activity.

The managerial contribution of the study is based on the understanding of the ways these dynamics and contradictions can be utilised for coordinated differentiation when organising a network MNC. The dynamic practice-based approach provides managers with a more realistic picture of the challenges of management by relying not on either-or choices of the planning and strategic management school but building on both-and conflicting demands that need to be balanced. In a family firm, values provide a foundation for leading the international operations, if a sense of familiness can be flexibly applied in different markets. As noted above also the values-based best practice needs to be locally interpreted.

References

Andersson, U., Forsgren, M., & Holm, U. (2002). The strategic impact of external networks: Subsidiary performance and competence development in the multinational corporation. *Strategic Management Journal, 23*(11), 979–996.

Aronoff, C. E., & Ward, J. L. (2000). *More than family: Non-family executives in the family business.* Family Business Leadership Series, No. 13. Marietta, GA: Family Enterprise Publishers.

Arregle, J. L., Naldi, L., Nordqvist, M., & Hitt, M. A. (2012). Internationalization of family–controlled firms: A study of the effects of external involvement in governance. *Entrepreneurship Theory and Practice, 36*(6), 1115–1143.

Arregle, J. L., Duran, P., Hitt, M. A., & Van Essen, M. (2017). Why is family firms' internationalization unique? A meta–analysis. *Entrepreneurship Theory and Practice, 41*(5), 801–831.

Bartlett, C. A., & Ghoshal, S. (1989). *Managing across borders: The transnational solution.* Boston, MA: Harvard Business School Press.

Berrone, P., Cruz, C., & Gomez-Mejia, L. R. (2012). Socioemotional wealth in family firms: Theoretical dimensions, assessment approaches, and agenda for future research. *Family Business Review, 25*(3), 258–279.

Birkinshaw, J., & Ansari, S. (2015). Understanding management models going beyond "what" and "why" to "how" work gets done in organizations. In N. J. Foss & T. Saebi (Eds.), *Business model innovation: The organizational dimension* (pp. 85–103). Oxford: Oxford University Press.

Boellis, A., Mariotti, S., Minichilli, A., & Piscitello, L. (2016). Family involvement and firms' establishment mode choice in foreign markets. *Journal of International Business Studies, 47*(8), 929–950.

Cenamor, J., Parida, V., Oghazi, P., Pesämaa, O., & Wincent, J. (2019). Addressing dual embeddedness: The roles of absorptive capacity and appropriability mechanisms in subsidiary performance. *Industrial Marketing Management, 78*, 239–249.

Chrisman, J. J., Chua, J. H., & Sharma, P. (2005). Trends and directions in the development of a strategic management theory of the family firm. *Entrepreneurship Theory and Practice, 29*(5), 555–575.

Connor, P. E., & Becker, B. W. (1975). Values and the organization: Suggestions for research. *Academy of Management Journal, 18*(3), 550–561.

Creswell, J. W. (2012). *Qualitative inquiry and research design: Choosing among five approaches.* Los Angeles: Sage.

Decreton, B., Nell, P. C., & Stea, D. (2019). Headquarters involvement, socialization, and entrepreneurial behaviors in MNC subsidiaries. *Long Range Planning, 52*(4), 1–12.

Denzin, N. K., & Lincoln, Y. S. (2000). *Handbook of qualitative research.* Thousand Oaks: Sage.

Dubois, A., & Gadde, L. (2002). Systematic combining: An abductive approach to case research. *Journal of Business Research, 55*(7), 553–560.

Fernández, Z., & Nieto, M. J. (2006). Impact of ownership on the international involvement of SMEs. *Journal of International Business Studies, 37*(3), 340–351.

Fletcher, M., & Plakoyiannaki, E. (2011). Case selection in international business: Key issues and common misconceptions. In R. Piekkari & C. Welch (Eds.), *Rethinking the case study in international business and management research* (pp. 171–191). Cheltenham: Edward Elgar.

Flint, D. J., Woodruff, R. B., & Gardial, S. F. (2002). Exploring the phenomenon of customers' desired value change in a business-to-business context. *Journal of Marketing, 66*(4), 102–117.

Forsgren, M. (2008). *Theories of the multinational firm: A multidimensional creature in the global economy*. Cheltenham: Edward Elgar.

Foss, K., Foss, N. J., & Nell, P. C. (2012). MNC organizational form and subsidiary motivation problems: Controlling intervention hazards in the network MNC. *Journal of International Management, 18*(3), 247–259.

Ghauri, P. (2004). Designing and conducting case studies in international business research. In R. Marschan-Piekkari & C. Welch (Eds.), *Handbook of qualitative research methods for international business* (pp. 109–124). Cheltenham: Edward Elgar.

Ghoshal, S., Korine, H., & Szulanski, G. (1994). Interunit communication in multinational corporations. *Management Science, 40*(1), 96–110.

Guth, W. D., & Tagiuri, R. (1965). Personal values and corporate-strategy. *Harvard Business Review, 43*(5), 123–132.

Halinen, A., & Törnroos, J. Å. (2005). Using case methods in the study of contemporary business networks. *Journal of Business Research, 58*(9), 1285–1297.

Hedlund, G. (1986). The hypermodern MNC – A heterarchy? *Human Resource Management, 25*(1), 9–35.

Holm, U., Johanson, J., & Thilenius, P. (1995). Headquarters' knowledge of subsidiary network contexts in the multinational corporation. *International Studies of Management & Organization, 25*(1, 2), 97–119.

Isaac, V. R., Borini, F. M., Raziq, M. M., & Benito, G. R. (2019). From local to global innovation: The role of subsidiaries' external relational embeddedness in an emerging market. *International Business Review, 28*(4), 638–646.

Koiranen, M. (2002). Over 100 years of age but still entrepreneurially active in business: Exploring the values and family characteristics of old Finnish family firms. *Family Business Review, 15*(3), 175–187.

Kontinen, T., & Ojala, A. (2010). The internationalization of family businesses: A review of extant research. *Journal of Family Business Strategy, 1*(2), 97–107.

Kontinen, T., & Ojala, A. (2012). Internationalization pathways among family-owned SMEs. *International Marketing Review, 29*(5), 496–518.

Kostova, T., Marano, V., & Tallman, S. (2016). Headquarters-subsidiary relationships in MNCs: Fifty years of evolving research. *Journal of World Business, 51*(1), 176–184.

Lincoln, Y., & Guba, E. (1985). *Naturalistic inquiry*. Newbury Park: Sage.

Lubatkin, M. H., Schulze, W. S., Ling, Y., & Dino, R. N. (2005). The effects of parental altruism on the governance of family-managed firms. *Journal of Organizational Behavior, 26*(3), 313–330.

Luo, Y. (2001). Determinants of local responsiveness: Perspectives from foreign subsidiaries in an emerging market. *Journal of Management, 27*(4), 451–477.

Marquis, C., & Battilana, J. (2009). Acting globally but thinking locally? The enduring influence of local communities on organizations. *Research in Organizational Behavior, 29*, 283–302.

Marschan-Piekkari, R., & Welch, C. (2004). Qualitative research methods in international business: the state of the art. In R. Marschan-Piekkari & C. Welch (Eds.), *Handbook of qualitative research methods for international business* (pp. 5–24). Cheltenham: Edward Elgar.

Melin, L., & Nordqvist, M. (2007). The reflexive dynamics of institutionalization: The case of the family business. *Strategic Organization, 5*(3), 321–333.

Meyer, K. E., Mudambi, R., & Narula, R. (2011). Multinational enterprises and local contexts: The opportunities and challenges of multiple embeddedness. *Journal of Management Studies, 48*(2), 235–252.

Nell, P. C., Ambos, B., & Schlegelmilch, B. B. (2011). The MNC as an externally embedded organization: An investigation of embeddedness overlap in local subsidiary networks. *Journal of World Business, 46*(4), 497–505.

Nohria, N., & Ghoshal, S. (1997). *The differentiated network: Organizing multinational corporations for value creation.* San Francisco: Jossey-Bass.

Pedersen, T., Devinney, T. M., Venzin, M., & Tihanyi, L. (2014). *Orchestration of the global network organization* (Vol. 27). Bingley: Emerald.

Piekkari, R., Welch, C., & Paavilainen, E. (2009). The case study as disciplinary convention: Evidence from international business journals. *Organizational Research Methods, 12*(3), 567–589.

Prahalad, C. K., & Doz, Y. L. (1987). *The multinational mission: Balancing local demands and global vision.* New York: The Free Press.

Ragin, C. (1992). "Casing" and the process of social inquiry. In C. Ragin & H. Becker (Eds.), *What is a case? Exploring the foundations of social inquiry* (pp. 217–226). Cambridge: Cambridge University Press.

Regnér, P. (2003). Strategy creation in the periphery: Inductive versus deductive strategy making. *Journal of Management Studies, 40*(1), 57–82.

Schatzki, T. R. (2002). *The Site of the social: A philosophical account of the constitution of social life and change.* University Park: Penn State Press.

Sciascia, S., Mazzola, P., Astrachan, J. H., & Pieper, T. M. (2012). The role of family ownership in international entrepreneurship: Exploring nonlinear effects. *Small Business Economics, 38*(1), 15–31.

Silverman, D. (2005). *Doing qualitative research: A practical handbook.* London: Sage.

Stake, R. E. (2005). Qualitative case studies. In N. K. Denzin & Y. S. Lincoln (Eds.), *The Sage handbook of qualitative research* (pp. 443–466). Thousand Oaks: Sage.

Vaara, E., & Whittington, R. (2012). Strategy-as-practice: Taking social practices seriously. *Academy of Management Annals, 6*(1), 285–336.

Vahlne, J., Schweizer, R., & Johanson, J. (2012). Overcoming the liability of outsidership – The challenge of HQ of the global firm. *Journal of International Management, 18*(3), 224–232.

Verbeke, A., Yuan, W., and Kano, L. (2020). A values-based analysis of bifurcation bias and its impact on family firm internationalization. *Asia Pacific Journal of Management, 37*: 449–47.

Welch, C., Piekkari, R., Plakoyiannaki, E., & Paavilainen-Mäntymäki, E. (2011). Theorising from case studies: Towards a pluralist future for international business research. *Journal of International Business Studies, 42*(5), 740–762.

Westney, D. E. (2014). The organizational architecture of the multinational corporation. In T. Pedersen, M. Venzin, T. Devinney, & L. Tihanyi (Eds.), *Orchestration of the global network organization* (pp. 5–22). Advances in International Management, Vol. 27. Bingley: Emerald.

Whittington, R. (2006). Learning more from failure: Practice and process. *Organization Studies, 27*(12), 1903–1906.

Wolf, J., & Egelhoff, W. G. (2013). An empirical evaluation of conflict in MNC matrix structure firms. *International Business Review, 22*(3), 591–601.

Zalan, T., & Lewis, G. (2004). Writing about methods in qualitative research: Towards a more transparent approach. In R. Marschan-Piekkari & C. Welch (Eds.), *Handbook of qualitative research methods for international business* (pp. 507–528). Cheltenham: Edward Elgar.

Zellweger, T. M., Kellermanns, F. W., Chrisman, J. J., & Chua, J. H. (2012). Family control and family firm valuation by family CEOs: The importance of intentions for transgenerational control. *Organization Science, 23*(3), 851–868.

7

The "Unwritten Will" in Interpersonal Network Ties: Founder Legacy and International Networking of Family Firms in History

Satu Korhonen, Tanja Leppäaho, Rolv Petter Amdam, and Sarah Jack

Introduction

Interpersonal network ties, both domestic and international (Arregle, Hitt, Sirmon, & Very, 2007; Harris & Wheeler, 2005; Salvato & Melin, 2008; Zellweger, Chrisman, Chua, & Steier, 2019), are important for providing guidance and support for family firms' internationalization processes (Arregle, Naldi, Nordqvist, & Hitt, 2012; Graves & Thomas, 2008; Kontinen & Ojala, 2012). Illustrative of this, the international networking activities of family

---

S. Korhonen (✉)
School of Business and Management, LUT University,
Lappeenranta, Finland

T. Leppäaho
LUT University, Lappeenranta, Finland
e-mail: satu.korhonen@lut.fi

R. P. Amdam
Department of Strategy and Entrepreneurship, BI Norwegian Business School,
Oslo, Norway

S. Jack
House of Innovation, Stockholm School of Economics, Stockholm, Sweden

Lancaster University Management School, Lancaster, UK

© The Author(s), under exclusive license to Springer Nature Switzerland AG 2021
T. Leppäaho, S. Jack (eds.), *The Palgrave Handbook of Family Firm Internationalization*,
https://doi.org/10.1007/978-3-030-66737-5_7

firms (Kampouri, Plakoyiannaki, & Leppäaho, 2017; Kontinen & Ojala, 2010, 2012; Pukall & Calabrò, 2014) are typically characterized by their embeddedness in an extended family context and network ties with high levels of trust, closeness and long-term commitment (Arregle et al., 2007; Roessl, 2005; Salvato & Melin, 2008; Zellweger et al., 2019). Such interpersonal ties take time and effort to develop into inter-organizational ones (Greve & Salaff, 2003; Larson & Starr, 1993) and can be seen as either assets for or constraints on the firm's development (Kampouri et al., 2017)—when embedded in both domestic and international networks during the internationalization process (Leppäaho, Chetty, & Dimitratos, 2018). There is, however, an emergent yet limited understanding about how these interpersonal ties emerge (Kontinen & Ojala, 2010) at the founder-level, how they take shape (Kampouri et al., 2017) and how they transition to the next generation (Shi, Graves, & Barbera, 2019).

As a further matter, recent literature addresses an underexplored connection between intergenerational succession patterns, including incumbent-successor dynamics, and internationalization of family firms in terms of the next-generation's utilization of the prior interpersonal networks in internationalization and their attitudinal commitment to it (Shi et al., 2019). Paying attention to the embeddedness of different network ties (Arregle et al., 2015) in conjunction with the continuity (Konopaski, Jack, & Hamilton, 2015) and the "founder effect" in family firm evolution (Hammond, Pearson, & Holt, 2016; Kelly, Athanassiou, & Crittenden, 2000) when taking the business "from local to global" (Baù, Block, Discua Cruz, & Naldi, 2017) highlights some underexplored aspects to consider.

Regarding the centrality of the individual actor, that is, the founder-entrepreneur, in a venture's emerging and evolving networks (Coviello, 2006; Hite & Hesterly, 2001), this study embarks from prior notions that the founder-generation's "legacy" is an important grounding dimension in furthering the understanding of a firm's long-term behaviour and strategy (e.g., Ahn, 2018; Baù et al., 2017; Ogbonna & Harris, 2001). "Founder legacy" can be considered as what the founder-entrepreneur leaves behind and how he or she is remembered when no longer working in the family business (Baker & Wiseman, 1998; Harris & Ogbonna, 1999; Hunter & Rowles, 2005), whereas cultivating a "social legacy" of the founder often reflects the maintenance of strong social ties to the community (Hammond et al., 2016) and interest in certain noneconomic goals (McKenny, Short, Zachary, & Payne, 2011; Miller, Steier, & Le Breton-Miller, 2003). To our knowledge, founders' "social legacy" has not been previously discussed in the context of family firm internationalization and networks, though embeddedness of ties between individuals developing in emotional intensity and intimacy, and through reciprocal services (Granovetter, 1973) often mark family firm international

7 The "Unwritten Will" in Interpersonal Network Ties: Founder... 201

networks (Arregle et al., 2007). A "legacy" perspective aligns with our longitudinal research context in which the family firms we study have been managed and developed into international ones over the course of multiple generations and can be seen as cultivating certain social identities within the family firm and their evolving networks (e.g., Jones & Volpe, 2011).

In this study, we examined the social network ties for the internationalization of family firms by focusing on how interpersonal ties (e.g., Hite & Hesterly, 2001) emerged and evolved in the transitional incumbent–successor context of international networking prior to our modern world international business context (Coviello, Kano, & Liesch, 2017) in a time when communication was limited to slow postal systems, travelling, face-to-face visits and interactions and, later, the telegraph. The research questions we pose are (1) "Looking back in history, how did founders' interpersonal ties for internationalization emerge, evolve (and transition) to the next generation?" and (2) "How did the social legacy of the founder become manifested in the succeeding generation's networking?" We draw from the two historical cases—of two founders and their successors—of Ahlström and Serlachius, currently known as the two successful global firms Ahlstrom-Munksjö and the Metsä Group, respectively. Both firms have over time grown into large multinationals. The longitudinal qualitative data we draw on has been generated from public and private archives as well as secondary literary sources.

The contribution of this study lies at the intersection of the literature on family firm internationalization (see, e.g., Arregle, Hitt, & Mari, 2019; De Massis, Frattini, Majocchi, & Piscitello, 2018; Zellweger et al., 2019), international networking (see, e.g.,Kampouri et al., 2017 ; Kontinen & Ojala, 2010, 2012 ; Pukall & Calabrò, 2014), "founder legacy" (see, e.g., Harris & Ogbonna, 1999; Hammond et al., 2016; Baù et al., 2017) and the historical contextualization of internationalization and its micro-foundations including interpersonal network ties (Coviello et al., 2017; Welch & Paavilainen-Mäntymäki, 2014). By exploring the emergence of international networking in family firms (Kampouri et al., 2017; Kontinen & Ojala, 2010, 2012; Pukall & Calabrò, 2014) and the founder-entrepreneurs' interpersonal network ties within and beyond family and national borders (Baù, Chirico, Pittino, Backman, & Klaesson, 2019; Leppäaho et al., 2018), we explicate their emergence and evolvement as both interpersonal identity-based versus calculative (Hite & Hesterly, 2001; Larson & Starr, 1993) and domestic versus international network ties (Kontinen & Ojala, 2010) and their influential role (Coviello, 2006; Elfring & Hulsink, 2007) for the family firms' early internationalization. Our findings highlight how these interpersonal network ties of the founders, embedded in the context of historical contingencies, serve as means to attract like-minded people, that is, ties across industries, societal "elite" and ideological social circles, in addition to business opportunities, that is, new technology and finance. Furthermore, the multi-industry relationships they tied through acquisitions of new estates and factories domestically, established their positions nationally as well as internationally, through which they could draw new technology and machinery providers. Hence, these acquisitions and investments across industry borders through the individual's amalgam of interpersonal ties laid new groundwork for internationalizing the venture.

Then, we add to the understanding of how these interpersonal network ties evolve over time (Kampouri et al., 2017; Kontinen & Ojala, 2010, 2012; Pukall & Calabrò, 2014), and contribute to the embedded continuity and evolution of family firms (Hammond et al., 2016; Kelly et al., 2000; Konopaski et al., 2015). With our longitudinal qualitative historical approach, we could pay attention to the intergenerational embeddedness of the family firms, which as a context has barely been discussed in the literature thus far (Arregle et al., 2015; De Massis et al., 2018). This allows us to see how the nature of both domestic and international interpersonal ties of the central actors over time evolved in the internationalization process of the family firms (Shi et al., 2019). With the acknowledgement of human relations as subject to historical contingencies, our historical approach adds to the longitudinal contextualization internationalization phenomena (Welch & Paavilainen-Mäntymäki, 2014). Related to our "comparison" of the founders' and successors' ties and prevalent networking efforts, we highlight the manifestation and meaning of the founder's "social legacy" (Hammond et al., 2016; Harris & Ogbonna, 1999) in the incumbent–successor context of the Ahlström and Serlachius cases. As an advantage or disadvantage for the successor's international networking (Ellis, 2011; Kellermanns, Eddleston, & Zellweger, 2012; Shi, Shepherd, & Schmidts, 2015) and the family firms' internationalization (Hennart, Majocchi, & Forlani, 2019; Pukall & Calabrò, 2014), we suggest that the cases manifest founders' *international networking legacy*—a mechanism for developing a social legacy of internationalizing family firms.

Theoretical Framework

Interpersonal Networks in Family Firm Internationalization

The international business and international entrepreneurship research on networks (e.g., Coviello & Munro, 1997; Harris & Wheeler, 2005; Mustafa & Chen, 2010; Wright & Nasierowski, 1994) has recognized and conceptualized the important role of relationships—or ties—in the firm internationalization phenomenon (Ellis, 2000; Harris & Wheeler, 2005), as it is essentially a social process, not least in its early stages (e.g., Brydon & Dana, 2011; Byrom & Lehman, 2009; Crick, Bradshaw, & Chaudhry, 2006). A network, defined as "a set of actors and some set of relationships that link them" (Hoang & Antoncic, 2003, p. 167), develops according to the interactions taking place between an individual and others to whom he or she is connected. Whereas inter-organizational networks indicate the firm as the actor, in interpersonal networks the individual is the actor (Chetty & Agndal, 2008). From prior research we can see that interpersonal network ties emerge and develop both as formal and informal relationships in various contexts (Chetty & Agndal, 2008), and involve individuals embedding, that is, increasing trust and commitment with each other, within a given network.

Internationalization literature finds that with regard to networks, interpersonal ties often "offer access to their own network of relationships in other countries, from simple contacts to deeply trusted relationships" (Harris & Wheeler, 2005, p. 189). In addition, such interpersonal relationships can be transformed into inter-organizational relationships, and vice versa (Hite & Hesterly, 2001; Chetty & Agndal, 2008). Prior literature has also pointed out that family firms in particular are able to compensate for most of their weaknesses—for example, lacking financial resources and competence—with respect to internationalization through networks and derived social capital as family-specific resources, which can be categorized as both inter-organizational and interpersonal (e.g., Arregle et al., 2007, 2019; Calabrò & Mussolino, 2013; Zahra, 2003). In addition, formation of non-kin relationships serves as an important dimension in the internationalization processes of family firms (Arregle et al., 2012; Graves & Thomas, 2008; Kontinen & Ojala, 2012). Overall, when discussing their international networking activities (Kampouri et al., 2017; Kontinen & Ojala, 2010, 2012; Pukall & Calabrò, 2014), family firms are typically seen to obtain strong network ties with high levels of trust, closeness and long-term commitment (Arregle et al., 2007; Roessl, 2005; Salvato & Melin, 2008; Zellweger et al., 2019). The stronger ties are perceived to develop over time with respect to their emotional intensity and intimacy, and reciprocal services (Granovetter, 1973). On the contrary, weak ties would be those remaining as superficial, where "the parties do not know each other well and are not emotionally close to each other" (Söderqvist & Chetty, 2013, p. 539).

Founders and Their Interpersonal Ties in Identity-Based and Calculative Networks

Generally, in the initial formation of a new venture's network relationships, the role of the founder-entrepreneur is regarded as central (e.g., Hite & Hesterly, 2001). The networks of the founder-entrepreneur at the interpersonal level are often seen as "virtually synonymous with the firm's network" (Hite & Hesterly, 2001), where "the history of network ties shapes [the firm's] future" (Sharma & Blomstermo, 2003, p. 749; Coviello, 2006), and consequently, its embedding in the networks between individuals (Granovetter, 1973). In general, embeddedness would describe the extent, nature and depth of the entrepreneur's ties to the venturing environment (Anderson & Jack, 2002).

The nature of the founder-entrepreneur's initial relationships (or ties) may be generally broad, spanning informal and more formal situations (Anderson & Jack, 2002; Ellis, 2011; Harris & Wheeler, 2005). As they rarely have all the resources, experience or full capabilities to create and facilitate their entrepreneurial activities, or develop their ventures, entrepreneurs must often rely on their interpersonal, usually social, networks (e.g., Anderson & Jack, 2002; Granovetter, 1985; Greve & Salaff, 2003). Therefore, embedding themselves in networks through various actions such as fundraising for community projects, membership in social clubs or attendance at social functions provides individual entrepreneurial actors with access to previously unattainable resources and assists them in building new networks (Anderson & Jack, 2002; Chetty & Agndal, 2008). Furthermore, the embedded ties (i.e., strong ties) developed over time are those with whom the entrepreneur more regularly discusses his or her business and where the relationships are tightly coupled amalgams of the personal and the professional (Jack, 2005; Uzzi, 1996).

As an assumption, founder-entrepreneurs choose their collaborators and develop interpersonal ties with them to gain access to external knowledge and learning, among other things, in assembling the resources to form and develop their firms (Hervas-Oliver, Lleo, & Cervello, 2017). When looked at from an "egocentric network" perspective (Hite & Hesterly, 2001; Jones & Volpe, 2011), the founder-entrepreneurs' ties are motivated by different things, and—as we will see in family firms—not always only by the expected (economic) benefits. In this vein of the literature, "identity-based" networks are "networks that have a high proportion of ties where some type of personal or social identification with the other actor motivates or influences economic actions" (Hite & Hesterly, 2001, p. 278; see also Uzzi, 1996). These interpersonally unfolding networks are seen to be composed of stronger social ties high in closure and cohesion and stemming from pre-existing relationships with social, family or historically long-held sources (Larson & Starr, 1993; Walker, Kogut, & Shan, 1997). These suggest that the identity of the ties—*who* are the ties?—matters more to the individual entrepreneur than the specific economic functions or resources that certain interpersonal relationships can provide to his or her firm. By contrast, calculative networks and ties suggest that the potential purpose and function of a network tie (*for what* is the tie?) is more important than the "identity" of the tie, and these are said to have the "advantage of providing greater resource availability and mitigating more environmental uncertainty" (Hite & Hesterly, 2001, p. 278; see Williamson, 1993). Unlike identity-based networks, calculative networks are said to be characterized by the dominance of weaker ties (i.e., more market-like than socially embedded), involving a larger and more diverse set of "work-based" ties (Hite & Hesterly, 2001, p. 279).

In contrast to the founder-entrepreneur's role in a family firm and its early stages, taking on a family business as a successor could be seen as a less uncertain task, one reason being the established network relations of the family in the focal industry and local community (Pearson, Carr, & Shaw, 2008) together with a sounder resource base (Sirmon & Hitt, 2003; Zellweger, Sieger, & Halter, 2011). However, despite prior acknowledgements of the importance of (interpersonal) networks in the international growth of family firms from one generation to the next (Shi et al., 2019) in conjunction with the centrality of founders' network ties in the internationalization process of ventures in general, more nuanced understanding of the role and formation of interpersonal ties and networks over time especially in family firms' internationalization appears limited (Kontinen & Ojala, 2011, 2012; Pukall & Calabrò, 2014). Therefore, we now turn to the literature on "founder legacy" as a basic element for a family firm's "social legacy" (Hammond et al., 2016) in order to explore the meaning of founder-entrepreneurs and their evolving interpersonal network ties in the context of family firms' international networking over time.

Legacy: From Founders to Family Firms

Legacy, in terms suggested by Baker and Wiseman (1998), is what the founder-entrepreneurs leave behind and how they are remembered when no longer working in the business. When viewed as an individual-level construct, *founder legacy* can be traced back through psychology and literature on psychosocial development of the individual to a "generativity stage" (i.e., how to "make life count" through one's work career) during one's adult life (Erikson, 1963; see an integrative discussion in Hammond et al., 2016). Such a life stage is featured by one's desire to make a positive contribution to others in the future, whereas stagnation at this stage would lead to a lack of interest in leaving anything to subsequent generations (Hammond et al., 2016).

Furthermore, legacy is what an individual, family or firm stands for (Hunter & Rowles, 2005), and in family-firm context, may influence the long-term survival of a firm (Ahn, 2018). As a theoretical concept, legacy has frequently been proposed (if not tested) to be linked to important family-firm behaviours and described both as an antecedent and outcome of practices in such firms (Hammond et al., 2016). Moreover, in studies of family firms, there is evidence of the "founder effect" that succeeding generations mirror out of respect to the founders' visions and principles as they lead the firm and make key strategic decisions even long after the original founder is gone (Hammond et al., 2016; Kelly et al., 2000). At a strategy level, studies suggest that founder legacy exhibits an "enduring influence of the initial strategic practice or ideology of the founder of an organisation over the actions of successive strategic decision makers following" (Ahn, 2018, p. 2; see also Ogbonna & Harris, 2001) and is key to cultivating socio-emotional wealth—the family-oriented nonfinancial goals and value of the firm (Miller et al., 2003)—which often distinguishes family firms from other types of businesses (Cennamo, Berrone, Cruz, & Gomez-Mejia, 2012).

Furthermore, a family legacy "represents an emergent state whereby important features, values, and perceptions regarding the family, likely introduced originally by the founder or imposed by external conditions, have become 'imprinted' on family members" (Hammond et al., 2016, p. 1214; see also Jaskiewicz, Combs, & Rau, 2015). The sum of certain "valued accomplishments, traditions, assets, histories, experiences, lives, places, and memories that flow from the past through the present into the future" (Taraday, 2013, p. 200) becomes transmitted across generations, for example, by storytelling and family narratives, and conditioned by shared patterns of understanding and collective behavioural norms (see, e.g., Kellas, 2005). In their recent and more nuanced discussion of the elusive family legacy concept, Hammond et al. (2016) indicate different legacy orientations, through which we may first identify "the unique characteristics of a shared legacy" within a family and further the "conditions that arise when the family is involved with the management and operation of a firm" (Hammond et al., 2016, p. 1214). Furthermore, related to how social networks may generate meaning and identities that underpin identification processes (Jones & Volpe, 2011), the formation of a family firm's *social legacy* orientation reflects "the network of meanings associated with the family transferred through the use of stories or broader social tactics (e.g., community involvement)" (Hammond et al., 2016, p. 1215). In preference for deep and long-lasting social ties within the broader community and identification with shared histories and certain beliefs (Hammond et al., 2016), such a social legacy may also become a motivating form of socio-emotional wealth (Chrisman, Chua, & Sharma, 2005; Miller et al., 2003), which operates at "a deep psychological level among family members whose identity is integrally connected to their membership in the family firm" (Debicki, Kellermanns, Chrisman, Pearson, & Spencer, 2016, p. 47). Furthermore, founders should be seen for their influence on future generations as the ones making the "initial endorsement" of the social legacy orientation of the family firm (Hammond et al., 2016, p. 1220), as well as building the social identity of the family firm and its networks (e.g., Jones & Volpe, 2011).

Research Design

In its treatment of the internationalization of family firms, this study appreciates the evolutionary nature of the phenomenon (Coviello & McAuley, 1999). As it seeks the ability to see patterns and changes in a processual phenomenon within an underexplored research context, our research design aligns with longitudinal qualitative approaches (Coviello & Jones, 2004; Jones & Khanna, 2006; Welch & Paavilainen-Mäntymäki, 2014), in which we see historically oriented analysis playing an important role in order to operate between the historian's particular generalizations and the reductionist's general particularizations (Burgelman, 2011).

To explore the interpersonal network ties for internationalization of family firms and focus on how those ties emerge and evolve in a transitional incumbent–successor context, we studied historical cases (Welch, Piekkari, Plakoyiannaki, & Paavilainen, 2011). Our narrative qualitative approach (Welch et al., 2011) enabled us to contextualize the internationalization of family firms in two generations and account for actions being situated in "social time" and "social place" (Abbott, 1998). Family firms tend to endure over time (Konopaski et al., 2015) and two successfully internationalized ones offered us information-rich historical data to investigate. Initially, criterion sampling, which is a strategy of purposeful sampling, was applied (Patton, 2002) through which we selected the cases: (1) the firm was at least 100 years old; (2) the firm has grown successfully into one of the leading forest companies in Finland, allowing us to study the early phases of long-enduring, successful firms; (3) the firm originally operated in the forest industry and was established prior to 1900; (4) the firm exported more than 25% of its production abroad within three years of its actual inception, fulfilling the criteria of an early internationalizing venture (see, e.g., Kuivalainen, Sundqvist, & Servais, 2007); (5) the firm was at least 90% family owned until at least the first decades of the twentieth century; (6) there is good archival data available on the firm and that time period, allowing us access to detailed stories of the cases.

According to our initial sampling, we investigated the two Finnish family firms originating from the ventures launched by Antti Ahlström and Gustaf Serlachius that have since evolved into global multinationals (currently known as Alhstrom-Munksjö and Metsä Group, respectively). The selected cases—Ahlström and Serlachius—were embedded in the forest business of the Nordic countries, the key industry of Finland at the time (Sajasalo, 2002). Consequently, the international venturing of the individuals is investigated with the backdrop of a historical time period of intensified economic activity of a remote and still developing country benefitting from the international expansion of its forest industry at the end of the 1800s and early 1900s (Lamberg, Ojala, Peltoniemi, & Särkkä, 2012). With access to the authentic company documents, archival data were collected from the Central Archives for Finnish Business Records (ELKA) and the Ahlström archives in Noormarkku. In the archives, we prioritized the collection of information from files in the form of international letter correspondence, diaries and meeting minutes, after having consulted existing literature for critical events and years in their international venturing. In addition, we drew on existing history books, research publications and biographies written on the histories of these firms and their entrepreneurs to contextualize our analysis further. The time-lines in Figs. 7.1 and 7.2 provide an overview of the firms' internationalizing business in conjunction with the macro-context between the mid-1800s and the First World War.

In order to explore the emergence and evolvement of interpersonal networks in these cases over time, both our data and analysis cover the timeline from the founders' births to the first decades of the next generation leadership of the family firms. Our analysis makes use of a historical "biographical approach" (Jones, 1998; Fillis, 2015), which, as a type of qualitative narrative approach, constructs analytical narratives describing human action in social and other contexts (Roberts, 2002). Followed by comprehensive and holistic interpretation of events, we initially focused on the biographical data of the founder-entrepreneurs and their domestic and international ties during the ventures' pre-launch phases and their overall early internationalizing orientation (from 1850s to the turn of 1900s). Constitutive of both business and life

7 The "Unwritten Will" in Interpersonal Network Ties: Founder…   209

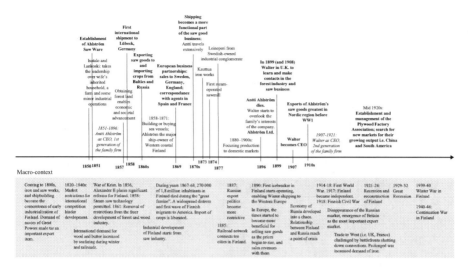

Fig. 7.1 Case Ahlström. (Source: Authors)

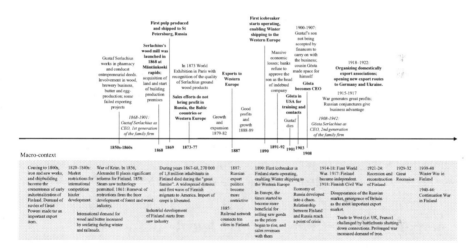

Fig. 7.2 Case Serlachius. (Source: Authors)

documents, such as business correspondence, personal letters and notes, and other material, we explored the biographical data in order to understand the individuals'—both founders' and their successors'—life events and interpersonal ties both "holistically" and "categorically" (Polkinghorne, 1988; Lieblich, Tuval-Mashiach, & Zilber, 1998) as their human relations were subject to historical contingencies. In addition, we traced the "formal" and "informal" relationships and influences (Fernhaber & Li, 2013) on their internationally oriented action at play during the extended intergenerational period of time in its historical setting.

First, to get a picture of their early orientation for internationalization "within" the cases, we explored the role of the founder-entrepreneurs' and the next-generation leaders' interpersonal network ties (e.g., their type, location and strength) in the domestic to international context as categorical-content of the literary data. Then, we sought a holistic-content understanding of the international networking (hi)stories and social legacy of these family firms— the "whole story" in hindsight—by interpreting the meaning of more particular ties and the change in them in light of the overall internationalization process (still very much on the shoulders of the new leader appointed by the family) and the succession. Furthermore, as a "cross-case" type of analysis, comparing these two case narratives pointed us towards the different application of the "founder legacy" as emergent in the next generations' networking. Such notions guided us to interpret manifestations of the founders' *social* legacy in connection to the individuals' embedding to identity-based and/or calculative networks abroad and domestically over time.

Findings

The first part of our findings elaborates on the international networking of the founder and their successors through their interpersonal identity-based and calculative ties within and across country borders. As such, we illustrate the amalgam of the groundwork for the family firms' internationalization in their network ties. Then, by comparing the two historical cases, the latter part of our findings explicates how the founder-entrepreneurs' "social legacy" becomes manifested in the transitional incumbent–successor context.

Emergence of the Interpersonal Identity-Based and Calculative Ties in the Founder and Successor Generations

Case Ahlström

Ahlström as an effort seems largely related to the family background and social identity of *Antti Ahlström*, stemming from his immediate family and marriage context, embedding his persona and interpersonal network ties accordingly. Antti was born and raised in a Western coastal town of Finland as the sixth child of Erkki, a former seaman, and Anna Ahlström. Before his twenties, Antti quit grammar school highly motivated to start his own business career. Helped by his early exposure to wood trading from his father, Antti was quickly immersed in the forestry field, developing a career as a businessman and developing network relationships through exporting saw goods from the coast's harbours (Aho, 1927a, 1927b).

Antti's emerging business venture and the resulting interpersonal network ties could be characterized largely as identity-based ties, emerging initially from his own father's "legacy" of trading internationally, and later from his first wife's legal estate situation and from Antti's strong sense of regional identity (see Table 7.1). From his experience casually networking and selling his own goods (e.g., cigarettes and potatoes) in the harbours since his early teens,

Table 7.1 Antti's domestic and international identity-based and calculative ties

	Domestic network ties	International network ties
Identity-based ties	*Family and extended family* • *Antti's father and brothers played a role in the early phases of his venture becoming internationally oriented.* • *Antti's first wife was influential as her properties were invested into the business. His second wife was a trustee, advisor and partner in his social-welfare efforts.* *Friends and friends of friends* • *Supported Antti's personal and business causes.* *Politics* • *Beneficial from his mid-career. Was himself a member of the Finnish parliament and an active spokesperson for the Finnish language and the needs of women and children. During the famine in the 1860s, Antti donated to the neediest people in Finland.* *Financiers* • *Support for the business developments was initially enabled by the finances of his first wife; strong ties from the beginning.*	*Key employees (e.g., captains) abroad* • *Long-term masters of his sea vessels who later on enabled extended access to international networks.* *Long-term agents and other international shareholders* • *Formed ties from the beginning of his exports; Antti was committed to the ones in whom he invested time, money and heart; learned about the needs and nature of domestic and international customers at Finnish west coast harbours; some of his agents schooled him in the business culture of foreign buyers,* for example, *the Norwegian agent Hamre in Paris and Johnsson & Caston in London.*
Calculative ties	*Multi-industry domestic relationships* • *New knowledge and equity through acquisitions.*	*Providers of technology and machinery* • *International and natural since the early phases of his business phase. Actively renewed technology within his factories, buying technology from abroad.*

Source: Authors

212 S. Korhonen et al.

in addition to his exposure to the wood trading context of his father's business and his own process of becoming strongly embedded into the regional networks, he established personally meaningful networks among his family and friends, from whom would also come the initial financiers. Hence, prior to his first marriage with an affluent widow, Greta, and the official fluent start of his saw business, Antti had a good overview of the forestry business and export situation of the Western coastal cities. Having roots rather tightly knit in a bilingual region, Antti's informal social ties and more formal business ties were embedded in the countryside and Finnish-speaking population in Finland (Aho, 1927a). In 1871, after his first wife died, Antti remarried the daughter of a tradesman. Through this second marriage to Eva and Antti's resultant exposure to her extant social circle of family and friends, Antti's active participation in the politics of his home region as well as the whole country developed into identity-based ties (e.g., with Edvin Avellan, a municipal councillor), which also served as a launchpad for more calculative ties in advocating the development of equal education for the poorer population and the development of the community around the growing business (Schybergson, 1992). With his prolonged presence in parliament and maintenance of a strong position in Western Finland, Ahlström became very well connected domestically (Schybergson, 1992).

In the later stages of his life, he tied multi-industry relationships through acquisitions of new estates and factories and became established nationally as well as internationally, drawing from his networks of technology and machinery providers. As he increased his exports while keeping his relations honest, Antti kept in constant correspondence by post with his European business partners (Aho, 1927b). As an example, one letter from a long-term trusted agent in London reads:

> *Brother Ahlström!*
> *In my yesterday's letter, I forgot to answer your question regarding H. Clarkson Co., but will do it here. You can securely draw bills on them, the sum in question, as the firm is solid and wealthy. Without further remarks from today,*
> *Your true friend,*
> *Henry Caston*[1]

Across national borders, Antti eventually cultivated long-term relationships with his key employees (e.g., trusted captains sailing abroad) and long-term agents, especially in the UK. Along with his expanding forestry venture, his

---

[1] Correspondence between Antti Ahlström and Johnsson & Caston (London); 23rd July 1873. Brev 1872–1874. Box 5. Ahlström Noormarkku Central Office Archives.

reputation as a just and generous man grew, as propelled by his relations both domestically and within the context of international trading. In the 1860s, Antti's ship-building business made him the biggest ship-owner of his Western coastal region, through which his growing exporting efforts to faraway locations (e.g., the Mediterranean and Caribbean), using both his own and others' vessels, soon expanded and turned him into a central player at the intersection of the nation's shipbuilding and export industries.

During the last years of his life, Antti Ahlström travelled extensively, as he wanted to be personally involved in the decision-making of his growing firm. Overall, his domestic ties seem to have become an excellent ground from which to build a sound reputation and fair way of doing business in his national and international networks. While very much involved in his family and regional context, he gradually became more enmeshed in the interpersonal level networks of the coastal wood-processing business, having initially been exposed to these people during and even before grammar school. He soon knew the business from "the roots of the tree," from unloading goods and selling to the export harbours to shipping the goods to the rest of the world.

Walter Ahlström was about 30 years old when he finalized his control over the Ahlström family business. After Antti's sudden death, Walter began practical training in the central office of Ahlström in Noormarkku iron works (Grahn, 2014). Already as a child, Walter had a reputation for being very keen on technical things and was said to be extremely systematic in his deeds (Grahn, 2014; Norrmén, 1927). At the time of the transition from the founder to the successor generation, Eva, Antti's second wife and Walter's mother, controlled the most shares and decision-making power of the company, though in many situations, Walter's opinions were already supported by his mother before becoming CEO, and he was put in charge of critical decisions, as the authorized signatories recognized Walter's knowledge and judgement in technical matters (Schybergson, 1997). Throughout his leadership, his family members, especially his sisters, maintained a clear commitment to ensuring that ownership stayed in the family (Aho, 1927b, p. 36; Grahn, 2014).

With our analysis of Walter's interpersonal network ties, both domestic and international (see Table 7.2), his ties relative to the family firm's internationalization appear more calculative than his father's. When Walter took over the family firm, the business was already well-embedded in the national (both identity-based and calculative) networks established by his father, predominantly consisting of saw operations across Finland: for example, regions covering Southern Western and Central Finland, Southern Eastern Finland and Carelia (Schybergson, 1997), but also from his father's involvement in national

Table 7.2 Walter's domestic and international identity-based and calculative ties

	Domestic ties	International ties
Identity-based ties	*Family and extended family* • *Siblings and mother wanted to maintain transparency, but disagreed with family members.* • *Wife and her family had Norwegian heritage and Swedish-speaking network.*	*Ties from educational trips* • *Especially UK.*
Calculative ties	*Extended family* • *Wife's father and his "elite" connections.* *Key industry people* • *Forest elite: formed a cartel with, for example, Jacob von Julin and others, to strengthen international trade endeavours.* *Multi-industry relationships* • *For example, factory acquisitions; glass industry, water power plant.*	*Ties from business travels* • *Especially UK.* *Multi-industry relationships: for example, providers of technology and machinery* • *Imports of new technology and knowledge from abroad; extensive investments to modernize, for example, old iron works and saw production and build better infrastructure for the domestic industrial development.*

Source: Authors

politics. In 1899 and again in 1908, Walter travelled to the UK in order to study and learn the business. During his time abroad, Walter presumably developed both social (more informal and identity-based) and business ties (more formal and calculative). In 1900, Walter married Hildur "Lilli" Newander, the daughter of Johan Ferdinand Newander, a pharmacist and director of a bank office (Kansallis-Osake-Pankki) in his home region, the Western coast of Finland. This connection provided Walter with useful access to the Swedish-speaking trader elite (Grahn, 2014). The Newander family also had roots in Norway (Grahn, 2014). This marriage, as an identity-based domestic tie with an international dimension, also became beneficial for Walter in terms of a "calculative tie" to his father-in-law, as it would enable both Walter's personal recognition in the region as well as better access to knowledge of international trade. This could be interpreted as sublimating his identity-based ties into calculative network ties in the country as much as broadening his reputation internationally.

7 The "Unwritten Will" in Interpersonal Network Ties: Founder... 215

What is significant about his networking and his contribution to the international business operations of the firm was that during the 1920s, Walter developed friendly ties with the vice chancellor and CEO of a wood-processing factory, Jacob von Julin (1881–1942), and other members of the country's forest elite. Together, the three were key in developing the forestry business environment in Finland and the country's export environment by participating in different networks and organizing various cooperatives supporting the industry's development and competitiveness. Von Julin has been called Walter's close friend, as they interacted and worked intimately to set up and control the plywood cartel in the later 1920s. Walter's desire for the members of the cartel to remain transparent and communicative about their actions, expeditions and travels in order to decrease misinterpretations within the cartel (Helanne, 2019) speaks to the dual meaning of these ties to him as both identity-based and calculative. Both the extent and effect of Walter and von Julin's international ties are evidenced by the number of contracts they were able to make around Europe over the short period of a couple of months in 1926 (Helanne, 2019).

While Walter's domestic interpersonal ties were a resource for sourcing international knowledge and expertise, he also had extensive personal experience in international sales and in forming trade relationships in the British market. Together with von Julin, Gösta Serlachius and other elite members of the country's forest industry, Walter had an influential voice and power in the establishment and management of the Plywood Factory Association, an effort to support the nation's exports to the West during the mid-1820s.[2] The Association's role was to oversee the member companies' sales of plywood both domestically and abroad, and, for example, search for new markets for their growing output through expeditions, including to China and South America, with varying success.

Walter's time in charge of the company deepened the importance of the family firm's place in the industry's and nation's development, but with a seemingly different mindset and orientation than that of his father. Various sources make it evident that his intention was to build "a strong, financially sound and diverse corporation", which also reflected the legacy of his father as an ideological and entrepreneurial man during a favourable time (Grahn, 2014, p. 96).

---

[2] Suomen paperi- ja puutavaralehti, 15.1.1919. The National Library of Finland: Digital Collection. Retrieved November 27, 2019 from https://digi.kansalliskirjasto.fi/sanomalehti/search

Case Serlachius

Gustaf Serlachius, born in 1830, was the second child of Gustaf and Sophia Serlachius. The standard of living of the family was good until the father, in 1843, died of pneumonia, leaving the family with little economic status. Gustaf had started school in Eastern Central Finland but soon needed to quit

Table 7.3 Gustaf's domestic and international identity-based and calculative ties

	Domestic ties	International ties
Identity-based ties	*Family members* • *Close and important for Gustaf.* *Artists* • *Personal interest and taking him on international exhibitions. After some years, these ties were also broken, but after some time he again ordered paintings from Gallén.*	*International business people in Finland* • *Especially Stockmann and his extensive international business network. Had long worked in the pharmacy industry before launching the firm and was able to use them both for domestic and international purposes at different turning points of the firm.*
Calculative ties	*Domestic businesspeople* • *Wide range of businesspeople; shareholders in pharmacy, retail and other fields.* *Financiers* • *Mainly domestic, from pre-launch period onwards.* *Providers of technology and machinery* • *Attracted the very best technicians in the country, but usually lost them very quickly because of his mistreatment of them.* *Politicians and media; the "noble class"* • *Domestically active strong ties; able to write in newspapers about issues of interest to readers and for the business: for example, building a railway to Mänttä groundwood mill, building the first Finnish ice-breaker and improving the status of the Finnish language.*	*Investors* *Expertise and providers of technology and machinery* • *Was able to attract the very best technicians from abroad, one after another, but usually lost them very quickly because of his mistreatment of them.* *Agents* • *Fluctuating between strong and weak since establishment of the firm (80% international). Knew some prospective international intermediaries from his earlier jointly held business, where they had made paper from lump; Serlachius shipped mainly to St Petersburg, Tartu and Riga, but also to the UK and Belgium, depending on the political situation in the market and war.*

Source: Authors

to support the family financially. With the help of his mother, Gustaf found a position as an assistant in a pharmacy (Keskisarja, 2010).

At age 20, Gustaf travelled to St Petersburg to look for opportunities and learn about business life in a global city, after which he bought his pharmacy in Tampere, Southern Central Finland. This sparked Gustaf's international outlook, also affecting his future businesses. Through his early engagement in Finnish pharmacies, Gustaf had extensive access to domestic businesspeople (for details on his ties, see Table 7.3). After buying the pharmacy, Gustaf interacted with a wide range of different stakeholders in his pharmacy, as well as within the retail and other fields. Gustaf acted as an intermediary, buying and selling anything, like a one-man chamber of commerce, which extended his network to all the apothecaries of Finland.

Gustaf's key mentor in international business life was *Georg Franz Stockmann,* a German businessman, who imported liqueurs and chemicals, among other things, for Gustaf. Eventually, via Stockmann, Gustaf formed contacts in Lübeck and Hamburg and began to learn that mutual trust was the most important payment in exports and imports (Keskisarja, 2010). Via Stockmann's beneficial contacts, Gustaf was able to export various goods to Lübeck, Manchester and St Petersburg. Then, in mid-1860s, a notable Finnish businessman Fredrik Idestam appointed Serlachius as the representative of his ground wood mill in Tampere (Keskisarja, 2010), and through Idestam's network, Gustaf became familiar with the manufacturing process at the mill. On the basis of his earlier experience and knowledge networks, and recognizing the rural area of Mänttä in Central Finland for its quality work force, Gustaf began to build a ground wood mill there. Since establishing the firm, exports had come to represent the vast majority of its output. Serlachius had prospective international intermediaries from his earlier jointly held business (paper production from lump). Serlachius shipped mainly to St Petersburg, Tartu and Riga, but also to the UK and Belgium, depending on the political situation, market prices and war.

Gustaf had an innovative, risk-taking personality (Ahvanainen, 1997). Based on our analysis, his approach to networking seemed in general to be rather impulsive and calculating, as seen through his interaction with individual domestic and international businesspeople, financiers, providers of technology and machinery, agents, politicians and media. Gustaf persuaded the best people from his earlier internationally oriented networks in Tampere to work for him. For example, a technical manager of the machine factory with German roots and an engineering background, along with another international technician, advised Gustaf on the process of setting up the ground wood mill. Still, their first successful collaboration ended quickly due to disagreements and Gustaf's violent behaviour (Keskisarja, 2010). Whereas

Gustaf persuaded the very best experts, as well as financer after financer (e.g., Sanmark and C. W. I. Sundman) to invest in his endeavours, his actions and mistreatment soon cost him these ties. It seems that Gustaf's financial problems were not related to debt itself but to his tendency to destroy his networks and have short-term bills of exchange (Keskisarja, 2010). Nevertheless, Stockmann, one of his first international contacts, introduced him to Wilhelm Burjam, a Lübeck-born manager of another bank, Pohjoispankki. He soon recognized that Gustaf conducted business they did not want to finance, but it was too late. When another investor, Sneckenström, withdrew in 1877, the banks concluded that Serlachius' business was worthless, leading Serlachius to tell his financers melodramatically that he was telling his children about the very poor treatment he had received. Interestingly, both Sneckenström and Sanmark cancelled the determination of bankruptcy, and Gustaf Serlachius carried on with his business (Keskisarja, 2010).

Though Gustaf was rather manipulative in his ways of forming new network relations, which also contributed to his disruptive approach to those outside his family, he treated his family ties with unfailing respect. His correspondence with his family seems caring, also in difficult times, which indicates their identity-based quality throughout his life. Still, at the end of his life, being very ill and paralysed, he was unable to manage them well. Gustaf's sickness, together with his short temper, led to worsening relations with some in the family, especially with his son Axel. In relation to this, the account of Gustaf's will and the future of the firm remained unclear for a while after his death in 1901. Some of his other identity-based ties stemmed from his personal interests, such as his political endeavours, and with respect to his writing to newspapers and interacting with the "noble class" and ideological influencers, who had an effect on the societal and business environment in Finland of that time. Moreover, Gustaf had a great personal interest in fine arts and made close friendships with several artists (e.g., Gallén and Wikström), whom he would also support financially, sometimes on a monthly basis. These identity-based ties also took him abroad, for example, to Paris, where he made acquaintances within the international social circles of arts. After some years, his ties to domestic artists were also broken, though eventually, he would start ordering paintings from them again.

Gösta Serlachius represented the successor generation of the business his uncle Gustaf Serlachius had established. Gösta grew up speaking Swedish in Northern Western Finland and learned the Finnish language through visits to his uncle's estate in Mänttä in Central Finland. Gösta joined Gustaf's firm in the late 1890s, when he interrupted his law studies to pursue a more practically oriented career and become a trainee for Gustaf at the age of 21. In the beginning of his work at Serlachius, Gösta was sent to an agent of the firm in the UK. Upon his return, Gustaf assigned him to improve lagging UK exports: Gösta's return to Manchester resulted in a better agreement through a demanding process of negotiations (Silvennoinen, 2012).

With great enthusiasm for his traineeship and successful completion of educational and business trips abroad, Gösta rather quickly mastered the international paper industry and shipping business and oriented his mindset towards the company's international business dealings (for details on Gösta's interpersonal network ties, see Table 7.4). Early in the 1900s, while studying

Table 7.4 Gösta's domestic and international identity-based and calculative ties

	Domestic ties	International ties
Identity-based ties	*Family and extended family* • For example, *first wife is the daughter of Gustaf Sissi, extending his reach in domestic networks but also causing challenges with her mental and alcohol problems.* • *Brother Birger and mother.* *Industry ties* • For example, *Rudolf Walden, Per Schauman, the latter also being part of the government.* • *Finnish-American corporation, trying to expand shipping lines to South America.* • *Development of the human resource aspects of the business.* *War acquaintances and friends* • For example, *Marshal Mannerheim.* • *Development of the country after war.* *People in cultural life and fine arts* • For example, *Architect Valter Thomé.*	*Educational networks* • *Becoming an "expert"; studies in Austria and trips to the UK and US.* • *Enthusiasm for being part of the international paper industry.* *Agents* • *British agents Felber and Jucker: Gösta worked with in the very beginning of his career.* • *Reeve Angel; important for developing his early professional identity?*
Calculative ties	*Domestic Swedish-speaking elite relations and industry* • *Managers of other companies in the cartel.* • *Reputation for his network and ability to lead problematic businesses.*	*Industry people* • *Swedish engineer Sölve Thunström: Got to know in Vienna, helped with production technology.* • *Austrian machinery company he represented in Finland after his study trip.* • *US machinery companies he represented in Finland after his study trip.*

Source: Authors

in Austria, Gösta travelled to the US to visit its large paper factories. He funded his trips by serving as a representative for foreign machinery, evidence not only of Gösta's personal eagerness to invest in developing his international connections but also his professional competence as an international businessman. During his trips, Gösta acquired personal industrial excellence (e.g., steam and paper technology) by visiting factories and reselling their equipment to other Finnish industrial firms (Silvennoinen, 2012). Upon his arrival in Finland he had new foreign companies between which to mediate. Furthermore, his positions representing foreign technology and his other trips abroad provided him with personal connections, especially in the UK, where Gösta met his future business agent for the UK market, H. Reeve Angel. Over the years, Reeve Angel became a close business partner when the temporarily closed route to Western Europe reopened.

Before Gustaf's death, Gösta married Gustaf's daughter Sigrid "Sissi" Serlachius. It was this marriage, an identity-based tie, that can be said to have sealed him the position not only as the potential and probable successor to the family firm but also as an important potential "change-maker" in his father-in-law's and uncle's networks of both identity-based and calculative ties. Moreover, Gösta was personally well-networked with the domestic paper industry elite on his own, which would later set the direction for the long-term development of the country's international business. Prior to taking the mantle from his uncle, Gösta gained leadership experience in Central Finland at the Kangas mill and on the Southern coast at the Kymi mill, the only paper mill shipping large quantities of newspaper to the UK at the time, and he was already domestically recognized as having the skill to lead firms in challenging situations.

By navigating the firms' challenging situations (e.g., financial crises and problems with the Russian market), Gösta had gained experience, learned about rationalization, good paper production, renewed technology and power outlets, as well as become familiar with the peculiarities of the industry's international business in both the Eastern and Western paper markets (Silvennoinen, 2012). Later, along with other influential industry managers, especially Rudolf Walden, Gösta sought new opportunities in Germany—a market that had been closed since the beginning of First World War. In alignment with a long discussion within the industry network, Gösta was there to suggest the establishment of a price cartel (Silvennoinen, 2012).

Like his peers and other patrons prior to him, Gösta began to improve the social well-being around the factory communities of his firm: for example, by building housing for his employees, giving them land and improving the safety of their work conditions (Vesikansa, 1997). During the war, Gösta held a central leadership title; one result of the successful completion of his duty was the good relationship he formed with Marshal Carl G. E. Mannerheim, the future sixth president of Finland, who had a cosmopolitan background (Vesikansa, 1997). In 1918, Gösta served as the consul of Finland in Odessa, Ukraine. Though he did not care for politics, he had good relations with the influential people of the country. Moreover, during his career, Gösta served as a member of several committees (e.g., Red Cross Finland, in which he served along with Marshal Mannerheim) in order to take part in the country's development (both pre- and post-war), which also proved beneficial in solidifying his business ties (Vesikansa, 1997). During the last year of his life, the Ministry of Defence sent Gösta to the UK to use his network to solicit financial help for Finland.

During his own active years in domestic and international identity-based and more calculative network ties, Gösta had also become well-known as a "patron of the arts" and eventually founded the Gösta Serlachius Fine Arts Foundation in 1933 in order to maintain the art collection curated by himself and his uncle (Vesikansa, 1997).

Manifestation of the Founders' "International Networking Legacy" in the Successors' Approach

By comparing the founders' and successors' network ties and taking into consideration the transitional incumbent–successor context, here we provide an account of how the two relevant dimensions—identity-based versus calculative ties and national versus international ties—work as the mechanism endorsing the founders' "social legacy" in the successor generations' own international networking approaches. Their approaches indicate both maintenance of family and regional identity-based ties, as well as an application of the founders' social and industrial legacy (i.e., "elite" position, personal characteristics) in the border-crossing interpersonal networks and more calculative ties with "insider" groups (i.e., agent relations, investors and industry people). According to our findings, we introduce and suggest the founders' interpersonal network ties manifest an *international networking legacy*, which is either considered by successors as more of an advantage or a disadvantage for the successor's own approach to international networking. Our findings suggest that Antti Ahlström's legacy of identity-based domestic ties transformed into a more calculative approach in Walter's domestic and international ties and that Gustaf's legacy of rather scattered networks and disruptive approach to them as calculative ties transformed into the more sound approach of Gösta, who began to "nurture" both the ties he inherited from his uncle (e.g., in the UK) and his own ties, leading them to become more coherent over time.

In comparing *Antti and Walter Ahlström,* we can see that the founder generation's domestic and international ties left behind not only monetary wealth from its steady internal and then expanding international growth but also a strong sense of embedding in the identity-based national and regional ties and strategic international industry networks. Both were determined, independent and strong-willed individuals taking up new opportunities as leaders of the firm, but Antti and Walter participated differently in their networks in different areas of both the domestic and exporting business (e.g., farming, saw/forest industry, politics) (Schybergson, 1992).

Antti's identity-based domestic ties would become cultivated as his first "legacy" as Eva took over the ideological leadership of the family, which was also made visible through Walter's personal interests and deeds within the country. For example, Walter's investments and schemes went beyond his factories, production and expansion exports. In keeping with the "social legacy" of his father, Walter continued, perhaps more calculatedly and strategically, to develop the surrounding communities, for example, in Varkaus in Eastern Finland (Schybergson, 1997); its architectural influence on the particular cities centred on wood exports remains visible to this day. Having been entrusted with a variety of positions of responsibility like his father (or perhaps partially because of him), Walter was well-networked in a rather small but tight internal circle of the international industry.

Antti seems to have been more family oriented in his endeavours than Walter and placed more emphasis than Walter did on the cultivation of friend and family ties and embedding in his "root" networks that also connected him with international networks. He was committed to ongoing actions, in the form of both business and social activities (both formal and informal), which led him to befriend the (often Swedish-speaking) elite in the harbour cities. By comparison, Walter's approach to his family ties appears reserved, as his position as a CEO of the family firm may have demanded that he maintained the emotional distance from his siblings. By further looking into the dimensions of their ties, we can see that from the security Antti had ensured through his domestic ties, Walter Ahlström as his successor would have the advantage of a more strategic approach to and extension of his own networks abroad. Hence, we see that Antti's identity-based national and international interpersonal networking enabled Walter to incorporate such ties into his more calculative national and international networks that would begin to shape his more strategic internationalization of the firm (e.g., later in the "price cartel").

Moreover, as a kind of social entrepreneur, Antti was highly appreciated by people of different statuses and backgrounds despite his own high-level status in the community and country (Aho, 1927a, 1927b), whereas Walter was more socialized into the "elite" and therefore also more oriented towards a luxurious life from the start (Grahn, 2014). Furthermore, based on Walter's character and orientation to developing the firm's operations, we may assume that what Antti had become, Walter had to or wanted to be. In a way, we may detect in Walter's networking behaviour the manifestation of a more calculative way of conducting international business, yet one that was becoming more entangled with his social identity as a leader of his growing "empire" than of a family firm.

What was transferred from Antti to Walter was the respectful and open approach to intra- and inter-organizational relationships, as well as among family and friends. They both valued trust and transparency in their strategic and calculative relationships. Whereas Antti had been loyal to his executive-level employees and long-term friends with whom he shared his business endeavours while home and abroad, Walter maintained open and close relations with those individuals with whom he aimed to cooperate over the long term. While both of them were active in regional development and politics, associations and cooperatives, and advocated an ideology of "Finnishness," for Antti these actions reflected his identity, whereas for Walter they appeared as a strategic choice and task for cultivating his own and his parents' legacy. Walter developed his father's business into a family firm with a sound domestic and international status as a diverse wood-processing business. What then became his own visible legacy was the Walter Ahlström Foundation, which was developed to educate engineers for the Finnish industry and develop exporting industries nationally.

In looking into the case of *Gustaf and Gösta Serlachius*, we detect that Gustaf's legacy of a calculative approach to his domestic and international ties became transformed by Gösta, who from early on developed more sound identity-based ties. Initially, both had a proactive orientation to developing the business both domestically and internationally, where financial returns were not the only motivation (e.g., interest in investing into fine arts). This orientation resulted in their strong local and domestic influence on their political and social environment. Both the founder and successor had on their own behalf gained international exposure, in terms of regular long business trips and receiving education as well as taking personal holidays abroad. In the case of Serlachius, Gösta exploited the "disrupted" and "weakening ties," as he appeared able to use his personal international networking skills to nurture his networks: for example, the vestiges of Gustaf's international network legacy in the form of his UK agency or financers. This appears to have been made possible partly because Gösta had been sent abroad early on but especially because of his personal identity-based network ties.

Whereas Gustaf had a disruptive approach to his networks, both identity-based and calculative ties, Gösta took a more long-term approach to his. Both were advocates for the development of exports in the country but participated in the process differently. Gustaf was known for his radical involvement in political discussions and provision of propaganda to newspapers to advance his own business endeavours, while Gösta generally did not want to go into politics, but would help advance Finnish exports and the status of the country's global competitiveness. Hence, the case reveals perhaps more clearly the critical importance of personality in the initial stage of forming ties and the unconscious way these ties can be handled. The reputation (or legacy) of the earlier entrepreneur—as with Gustaf being rather reckless in his international networking—in the later stages of the family firm becomes managed by the successor within his or her own approach to forming ties. Altogether, our findings on Gustaf and Gösta show how the drivers of and approaches to interpersonal networks were based on their personal characteristics and manifested the "problems" attached to the social legacy of the founder-entrepreneur. For example, perhaps Gustaf's provocative real-time involvement in politics took the form under Gösta's leadership of his more discrete "lobbying" within tighter circles in the industry, grounded in his identity-based ties.

Concluding Discussion

This study has looked into the interpersonal network ties and international networking of two historical family firms in order to better understand how the founder-entrepreneurs' network ties—both identity-based and calculative—for internationalization emerge and further evolve in the transitional incumbent–successor context. From this point of departure, our study elaborates on how the interpersonal ties of the founder-generations seem to work as the mechanism for forming a "social legacy" in the firm's border-crossing networks and, more specifically, manifest in the succeeding generation as the founder-entrepreneur's "international networking legacy."

Firstly, our study adds to the extant literature on the international networking of family firms (Kampouri et al., 2017; Kontinen & Ojala, 2010, 2012; Pukall & Calabrò, 2014) by explicating the emergence of both domestic and international interpersonal network ties (Kontinen & Ojala, 2010) and their role (Elfring & Hulsink, 2007) for the family firms' internationalizing venturing by highlighting the importance of domestic ties for the internationalization process, which is barely discussed in the literature to date. We discovered that the interpersonal *domestic* ties via earlier jobs, personal and family interests, societal commitments, and in border-crossing networks (to the family-like captains of ships, international agents and technology providers, extended family) were necessary not only to identify opportunities, but also to attract like-minded people to advance their internationalizing business. While we see how the founder-entrepreneurs' interpersonal network ties were "as their most valuable asset to provide resources" (Hite & Hesterly, 2001, p. 278; Larson & Starr, 1993), we could recognize the importance of domestic investments and acquisitions across industry borders through interpersonal networks as they laid an important new groundwork for the family firm's internationalization.

Secondly, we add to the literature on family firm internationalization and networking by revealing insights about the continuum of the intergenerational internationalization process (e.g., Shi et al., 2019). We found that the founder-entrepreneurs' interpersonal network ties were meaningful and in different ways influential in regard to the successors' networking. The Ahlström case indicates that both domestic and international ties evolved from identity-based ties of Antti, where calculative ties seemed to have become more emphasized in later stages in the firm (Hite & Hesterly, 2001), especially after the transition to the next generation and Walter's networking. This shows us the business ties with a personal dimension (i.e., Antti's agents in London) becoming more formalized (Chetty & Agndal, 2008) in the next generation and over the course of the firm's internationalization. On the contrary, the Serlachius case represents calculative economic ties as more apparent in the early phase, but either manipulated or managed, as both personal and economic/business ties in the evolvement of the network (Larson & Starr, 1993). Serlachius' approach to his domestic and international ties may have been more "manipulative" than "managerial," but this was over time manoeuvred by his successor, adopting an approach that allowed both identity-based (i.e., Reeve Angelin, UK) and new calculative ties to emerge, increasing the scope of his own international networks while nurturing existing ones. This supplements our notions of how the identity-based network ties, that is, through political interests and societal involvement of the founder-entrepreneurs, did not become less "strong" or influential in the successor's hands (e.g., Greve & Salaff, 2003) but actually served as something like an internationalizing "network identity" of the firm (Coviello, 2006), elevating its ideological reputation both in the region and abroad, and becoming more intentionally managed by the successor (i.e., Gustaf's work for the Finnish political reform and

Gösta's ties with Marshal Mannerheim and development of the country's competitive state after war).

Third, we add to the understanding of both the continuity (Konopaski et al., 2015) and the "founder effect" in family firm evolution beyond national borders (Hammond et al., 2016; Kelly et al., 2000). Our findings illustrate how the "social legacy" (Hammond et al., 2016; McKenny et al., 2011) of the founder through his interpersonal network ties seems to manifest and transfer to the next generation (Shi et al., 2019). In a sense, the cases illustrate how a founder's more or less socially embedded ties (Anderson & Jack, 2002) become the "initial endorsement" (Hammond et al., 2016, p. 1220) of the family firm's internationalizing network behaviour (Arregle et al., 2015). We see how the founder's "unwritten will" manifests in the international networking of the next generation. We may interpret the social legacy of the founder becoming considered by the next generation either as an advantage or a disadvantage—the "dark side" of the embedded ties (Gulati, Nohria, & Zaheer, 2000)—for their own approaches to international networking. As such, we could suggest the *international networking legacy* to be the successors' treatment of interpersonal ties in the networks (Jack, 2005) and further elaborate and contextualize a mechanism that either promotes or inhibits subsequent internationalization (Ellis, 2011; Kellermanns et al., 2012; Shi et al., 2015). As identity-based "outcomes" of the founders' interpersonal ties and international networking, including beneficial marriages into "elite" spheres of money and new ideologies, their evolving social legacy could either enable or hinder positive wealth and status of the family firm (i.e., socioemotional and economic) (Hammond et al., 2016; Hunter & Rowles, 2005), even the cultural legacy of a whole region (Grahn, 2014).

Fourthly, with our methodological approach to the history of interpersonal network ties of internationalizing firms, we contribute to international business and international entrepreneurship literature by embracing both macro-context and micro-foundations of internationalization (Coviello et al., 2017). For example, the establishment of the Finnish Paper Mills' Association with the mutually calculative but strong interpersonal network ties in an inter- and after-war period (beginning of 1900s) ramped up the border-crossing negotiations and agreements of these two family firms, when experiencing a time of more restricted international business. With an acknowledgement of human relations—be it personal or business ties—as subject to historical contingencies, we suggest that these ties as "microfoundations" (Foss & Pedersen, 2016) of our two historical family firms' as well as their modern counterparts' strategic trajectories enact the historical chronology of their industrial and societal surroundings and opportunities (Zahra, Newey, & Li, 2014).

We have shown two cases of international networking against a different backdrop of historical contingencies than the modern world. Whereas contemporary firms may represent more knowledge-intense and service-oriented business with perhaps less limitations in terms of network(ing) and resources for internationalization (Ojala, Evers, & Rialp, 2018), generating meaningful interpersonal ties are still imperative in international venturing and strategies (Coviello, 2006; Ellis, 2011). Moreover, today family businesses still form the core of most national economies and are passed from generation to generation (Jaskiewicz et al., 2015). Therefore, old and new generations ought to find ways to cultivate constructive approaches to their networking strategies, which can further endorse and promote a desired social legacy of the family firm when taking the business "from local to global" (Baù et al., 2017).

Internationalization and networking of family firms are not straightforward processes, but historically contingent, for example, due to societal crisis, economic fluctuation, political objectives, wars, and industries and foreign markets sometimes disappearing and reappearing. This study highlights the need for better understanding of and more research based on the historical contextualization of family firm internationalization (Welch & Paavilainen-Mäntymäki, 2014), especially analysis of international networks, networking and their evolvement in earlier waves of globalization. With both qualitative and quantitative approaches, we may begin to build a broader and deeper understanding of the historical time context of (international) networking and other micro-foundational mechanisms steering firms' internationalization trajectories.

References

Abbott, A. (1998). The causal devolution. *Sociological Methods Research, 27*(2), 148–181.

Ahn, S.-Y. (2018). Founder succession, the imprint of founders' legacies, and long-term corporate survival. *Sustainability, 10*(5), 1–15.

Aho, J. (1927a). *Antti Ahlström 1827–1896. Hänen elämänsä ja työnsä I. Muistokirjoitus*. Noormarkku: A. Ahlström Osakeyhtiö.

Aho, J. (1927b). *Antti Ahlström 1827–1896. Hänen elämänsä ja työnsä II. Muistokirjoitus*. Noormarkku: A. Ahlström Osakeyhtiö.

Ahvanainen, J. (1997). *Serlachius, Gustaf Adolf*. Helsinki: Suomalaisen Kirjallisuuden Seura.

Anderson, A. R., & Jack, S. L. (2002). The articulation of social capital in entrepreneurial networks: A glue or a lubricant? *Entrepreneurship & Regional Development, 14*(3), 193–210.

Arregle, J. L., Hitt, M. A., Sirmon, D. G., & Very, P. (2007). The development of organizational social capital: Attributes of family firms. *Journal of Management Studies, 44*(1), 73–95.

Arregle, J. L., Naldi, L., Nordqvist, M., & Hitt, M. A. (2012). Internationalization of family-controlled firms: A study of the effects of external involvement in governance. *Entrepreneurship: Theory and Practice, 36*(6), 1115–1143.

Arregle, J. L., Batjargal, B., Hitt, M. A., Webb, J. W., Miller, T., & Tsui, A. S. (2015). Family ties in entrepreneurs' social networks and new venture growth. *Entrepreneurship Theory and Practice, 39*(2), 313–344.

Arregle, J. L., Hitt, M. A., & Mari, I. (2019). A missing link in family firms' internationalization research: Family structures. *Journal of International Business Studies, 50*(5), 809–825.

Baker, K. G., & Wiseman, K. K. (1998). Leadership, legacy, and emotional process in family business. *Family Business Review, 11*(3), 207–213.

Baù, M., Block, J. H., Discua Cruz, A., & Naldi, L. (2017). Locality and internationalization of family firms. *Entrepreneurship & Regional Development, 29*(5–6), 570–574.

Baù, M., Chirico, F., Pittino, D., Backman, M., & Klaesson, J. (2019). Roots to grow: Family firms and local embeddedness in rural and urban contexts. *Entrepreneurship: Theory and Practice, 43*(2), 360–385.

Brydon, K., & Dana, L. P. (2011). Globalisation and firm structure: Comparing a family-business and a corporate block holder in the New Zealand seafood industry. *International Journal of Globalisation and Small Business, 4*(2), 206.

Burgelman, R. (2011). Bridging history and reductionism: A key for longitudinal qualitative research. *Journal of International Business Studies, 42*(5), 591–601.

Byrom, J., & Lehman, K. (2009). Coopers Brewery: Heritage and innovation within a family firm. *Marketing Intelligence & Planning, 27*(4), 516–523.

Calabrò, A., & Mussolino, D. (2013). How do boards of directors contribute to family SME export intensity? The role of formal and informal governance mechanisms. *Journal of Management & Governance, 17*(2), 363–403.

Cennamo, C., Berrone, P., Cruz, C., & Gomez-Mejia, L. (2012). Socioemotional wealth and proactive stakeholder engagement: Why family-controlled firms care more about their stakeholders. *Entrepreneurship Theory and Practice, 36*(6), 1153–1173.

Chetty, S., & Agndal, H. (2008). Role of inter-organizational networks and interpersonal networks in an industrial district. *Regional Studies, 42*(2), 175–187.

Chrisman, J. J., Chua, J. H., & Sharma, P. (2005). Trends and directions in the development of a strategic management theory of the family firm. *Entrepreneurship Theory and Practice, 29*(5), 555–576.

Coviello, N. E. (2006). The network dynamics of international new ventures. *Journal of International Business Studies, 37*, 713–731.

Coviello, N. E., & Jones, M. V. (2004). Methodological issues in international entrepreneurship research. *Journal of Business Venturing, 19*(4), 485–508.

Coviello, N. E., & McAuley, A. (1999). Internationalisation and the smaller firm: A review of contemporary empirical research. *Management International Review, 39*(2), 223–257.

Coviello, N. E., & Munro, H. (1997). Network relationships and the internationalisation process of small software firms. *International Business Review, 6*(4), 361–386.

Coviello, N. E., Kano, L., & Liesch, P. W. (2017). Adapting the Uppsala model to a modern world: Macro-context and microfoundations. *Journal of International Business Studies, 48*(9), 1151–1164.

Crick, D., Bradshaw, R., & Chaudhry, S. (2006). 'Successful' internationalising UK family and non-family-owned firms: A comparative study. *Journal of Small Business and Enterprise Development, 13*(4), 498–512.

De Massis, A., Frattini, F., Majocchi, A., & Piscitello, L. (2018). Family firms in the global economy: Toward a deeper understanding of internationalization determinants, processes, and outcomes. *Global Strategy Journal, 8*(1), 3–21.

Debicki, B. J., Kellermanns, F. W., Chrisman, J. J., Pearson, A. W., & Spencer, B. A. (2016). Development of a socioemotional wealth importance (SEWi) scale for family firm research. *Journal of Family Business Strategy, 7*(1), 47–57.

Elfring, T., & Hulsink, W. (2007). Networking by entrepreneurs: Patterns of tie-formation in emerging organizations. *Organization Studies, 28*(12), 1849–1872.

Ellis, P. D. (2000). Social ties and foreign market entry. *Journal of International Business Studies, 31*(3), 443–469.

Ellis, P. D. (2011). Social ties and international entrepreneurship: Opportunities and constraints affecting firm internationalization. *Journal of International Business Studies, 42*(1), 99–127.

Erikson, E. H. (1963). *Childhood and society* (2nd ed.). New York: Norton.

Fernhaber, S., & Li, D. (2013). International exposure through network relationships: Implications for new venture internationalization. *Journal of Business Venturing, 28*(2), 316–334.

Fillis, I. (2015). Biographical research as a methodology for understanding entrepreneurial marketing. *International Journal of Entrepreneurial Behavior & Research, 21*(3), 429–447.

Foss, N. J., & Pedersen, T. (2016). Microfoundations in strategy research. *Strategic Management Journal, 37*(13), E22–E34.

Grahn, M. (2014). *Perheyhtiö ja paikallisuus: A. Ahlström Osakeyhtiön historian perintö Noormarkussa.* Turun yliopisto.

Granovetter, M. S. (1973). The strength of weak ties. *American Journal of Sociology, 78*(6), 1360–1380.

Granovetter, M. (1985). Economic action and social structure: The problem of embeddedness. *American Journal of Sociology, 91*(3), 481–510.

Graves, C., & Thomas, J. (2008). Determinants of the internationalization pathways of family firms: An examination of family influence. *Family Business Review, 21*(2), 151–167.

Greve, A., & Salaff, J. W. (2003). Social networks and entrepreneurship. *Entrepreneurship Theory and Practice, 28*(1), 1–22.

Gulati, R., Nohria, N., & Zaheer, A. (2000). Strategic networks. *Strategic Management Journal, 21*(3), 203–215.

Hammond, N. L., Pearson, A. W., & Holt, D. T. (2016). The quagmire of legacy in family firms: Definition and implications of family and family firm legacy orientations. *Entrepreneurship: Theory and Practice, 40*(6), 1209–1231.

Harris, L. C., & Ogbonna, E. (1999). The strategic legacy of company founders. *Long Range Planning, 32*(3), 333–343.

Harris, S., & Wheeler, C. (2005). Entrepreneurs' relationships for internationalization: Functions, origins and strategies. *International Business Review, 14*(2), 187–207.

Helanne, H. (2019). *Yhdessä vai yksittäin? Suomalainen vanerikartelli 1926–1927.* University of Helsinki.

Hennart, J. F., Majocchi, A., & Forlani, E. (2019). The myth of the stay-at-home family firm: How family-managed SMEs can overcome their internationalization limitations. *Journal of International Business Studies, 50*(5), 758–782.

Hervas-Oliver, J.-L., Lleo, M., & Cervello, R. (2017). The dynamics of cluster entrepreneurship: Knowledge legacy from parents or agglomeration effects? The case of the Castellon ceramic tile district. *Research Policy, 46*(1), 73–92.

Hite, J. M., & Hesterly, W. S. (2001). The evolution of firm networks: From emergence to early growth of the firm. *Strategic Management Journal, 22*(3), 275–286.

Hoang, H., & Antoncic, B. (2003). Network-based research in entrepreneurship. *Journal of Business Venturing, 18*(2), 165–187.

Hunter, E. G., & Rowles, G. D. (2005). Leaving a legacy: Toward a typology. *Journal of Aging Studies, 19*(3), 327–347.

Jack, S. L. (2005). The role, use and activation of strong and weak network ties: A qualitative analysis. *Journal of Management Studies, 42*(6), 1233–1250.

Jaskiewicz, P., Combs, J. G., & Rau, S. B. (2015). Entrepreneurial legacy: Toward a theory of how some family firms nurture transgenerational entrepreneurship. *Journal of Business Venturing, 30*(1), 29–49.

Jones, D. G. B. (1998). Biography as a methodology for studying the history of marketing ideas. *Psychology and Marketing, 15*(2), 161–173.

Jones, G., & Khanna, T. (2006). Bringing history (back) into international business. *Journal of International Business Studies, 37*(4), 453–468.

Jones, C., & Volpe, E. H. (2011). Organizational identification: Extending our understanding of social identities through social networks. *Journal of Organizational Behavior, 32*(3), 413–434.

Kampouri, K., Plakoyiannaki, E., & Leppäaho, T. (2017). Family business internationalisation and networks: Emerging pathways. *Journal of Business & Industrial Marketing, 32*(3), 357–370.

Kellas, J. K. (2005). Family ties: Communicating identity through jointly told family stories. Family Communication Division at the National Communication Association Convention. *Communication Monographs, 72*(4), 365–389.

Kellermanns, F. W., Eddleston, K. A., & Zellweger, T. M. (2012). Extending the socioemotional wealth perspective: A look at the dark side. *Entrepreneurship Theory and Practice, 36*(6), 1175–1182.

Kelly, L. M., Athanassiou, N., & Crittenden, W. F. (2000). Founder centrality and strategic behavior in the family-owned firm. *Entrepreneurship Theory and Practice, 25*(2), 27–42.

Keskisarja, T. (2010). Vihreän kullan kirous. G.A. In *Serlachiuksen elämä ja afäärit*. Helsinki: Siltala.

Konopaski, M., Jack, S., & Hamilton, E. (2015). How family business members learn about continuity. *Academy of Management Learning & Education, 14*(3), 347–364.

Kontinen, T., & Ojala, A. (2010). The internationalization of family businesses: A review of extant research. *Journal of Family Business Strategy, 1*(2), 97–107.

Kontinen, T., & Ojala, A. (2011). Network ties in the international opportunity recognition of family SMEs. *International Business Review, 20*(4), 440–453.

Kontinen, T., & Ojala, A. (2012). Social capital in the international operations of family SMEs. *Journal of Small Business and Enterprise Development, 19*(1), 39–55.

Kuivalainen, O., Sundqvist, S., & Servais, P. (2007). Firms' degree of born-globalness, international entrepreneurial orientation and export performance. *Journal of World Business, 42*(3), 253–267.

Lamberg, J. A., Ojala, J., Peltoniemi, M., & Särkkä, T. (2012). *The Evolution of Global Paper Industry 1800–2050: A Comparative Analysis* (Vol. 17). Springer Science & Business Media.

Larson, A., & Starr, J. A. (1993). A network model of organization formation. *Entrepreneurship Theory and Practice, 17*(2), 5–15.

Leppäaho, T., Chetty, S., & Dimitratos, P. (2018). Network embeddedness in the internationalization of biotechnology entrepreneurs. *Entrepreneurship & Regional Development, 30*(5–6), 562–584.

Lieblich, A., Tuval-Mashiach, R., & Zilber, T. (1998). *Narrative Research: Reading, Analysis, and Interpretation*, Vol. 47. Sage.

McKenny, A. F., Short, J. C., Zachary, M. A., & Payne, G. T. (2011). Assessing espoused goals in private family firms using content analysis. *Family Business Review, 24*(4), 298–317.

Miller, D., Steier, L., & Le Breton-Miller, I. (2003). Lost in time: Intergenerational succession, change, and failure in family business. *Journal of Business Venturing, 18*(4), 513–531.

Mustafa, M., & Chen, S. (2010). The strength of family networks in transnational immigrant entrepreneurship. *Thunderbird International Business Review, 52*(2), 97–106.

Norrmén, P. H. (1927). *Toiminimi Ahlström 1896–1927. Muistokirjoitus.* Noormarkku: A. Ahlström Osakeyhtiö.

Ogbonna, E., & Harris, L. C. (2001). The founder's legacy: Hangover or inheritance? *British Journal of Management, 12*(1), 13–31.

Ojala, A., Evers, N., & Rialp, A. (2018). Extending the international new venture phenomenon to digital platform providers: A longitudinal case study. *Journal of World Business, 53*(5), 725–739.

Patton, M. Q. (2002). *Qualitative research & evaluation methods* (3rd ed.). Thousand Oaks, CA: Sage.

Pearson, A. W., Carr, J. C., & Shaw, J. C. (2008). Toward a theory of familiness: A social capital perspective. *Entrepreneurship Theory and Practice, 32*(6), 949–969.

Polkinghorne, D. E. (1988). *Narrative knowing and the human sciences.* Suny Press.

Pukall, T. J., & Calabrò, A. (2014). The internationalization of family firms. *Family Business Review, 27*(2), 103–125.

Roberts, B. (2002). *Biographical research.* Buckingham: Open University Press.

Roessl, D. (2005). Family businesses and interfirm cooperation. *Family Business Review, 18*(3), 203–214.

Sajasalo, P. (2002). Internationalization of a key industry: Implications for a business and society relationship's development—Case Finland. *Journal of International Business Research, 8*(1), 45–62.

Salvato, C., & Melin, L. (2008). Creating value across generations in family-controlled businesses: The role of family social capital. *Family Business Review, XXI*(3), 259–276.

Schybergson, P. (1992). *Työt ja päivät. Ahlströmin historia 1851–1981.* Helsinki: A. Ahlström.

Schybergson, P. (1997). *Ahlström, Antti.* Helsinki: Suomalaisen Kirjallisuuden Seura.

Sharma, D. D., & Blomstermo, A. (2003). The internationalization process of Born Globals: A network view. *International Business Review, 12*(6), 739–753.

Shi, H. X., Shepherd, D. M., & Schmidts, T. (2015). Social capital in entrepreneurial family businesses: The role of trust. *International Journal of Entrepreneurial Behavior & Research, 21*(6), 814–841.

Shi, H. X., Graves, C., & Barbera, F. (2019). Intergenerational succession and internationalisation strategy of family SMEs: Evidence from China. *Long Range Planning, 52*(4), 101838.

Silvennoinen, O. (2012). *Paperisydän: Gösta Serlachiuksen elämä.* Helsinki: Siltala.

Sirmon, D., & Hitt, M. (2003). Managing resources: Linking unique resources, management, and wealth creation in family firms. *Entrepreneurship Theory and Practice, 27*(4), 339–358.

Söderqvist, A., & Chetty, S. (2013). Strength of ties involved in international new ventures. *European Business Review, 25*(6), 536–552.

Taraday, H. (2013). Book review: Family legacy and leadership: Preserving true family wealth in chal-lenging times. *Family Business Review, 26*(2), 200–202.

Uzzi, B. (1996). The sources and consequences of embeddedness for the economic performance of organizations: The network effect. *American Sociological Review, 61,* 674–698.

Vesikansa, J. (1997). *Serlachius, Gösta.* Helsinki: Suomalaisen Kirjallisuuden Seura.

Walker, G., Kogut, B., & Shan, W. (1997). Social capital, structural holes and the formation of an industry network. In *Organization science* (Vol. 8, pp. 109–125). Elsevier.

Welch, C., & Paavilainen-Mäntymäki, E. (2014). Putting process (back) in: Research on the internationalization process of the firm. *International Journal of Management Reviews, 16*(1), 2–23.

Welch, C., Piekkari, R., Plakoyiannaki, E., & Paavilainen, E. (2011). Theorising from case studies: Towards a pluralist future for international business research. *Journal of International Business Studies, 42*(5), 740–762.

Williamson, O. (1993). Calculativeness, trust, and economic organization. *Journal of Law and Economics, 36*(1 part 2), 453–486.

Wright, P. C., & Nasierowski, W. (1994). The expatriate family firm and cross-cultural management training: A conceptual framework. *Human Resource Development Quarterly, 5*(2), 153–167.

Zahra, S. A. (2003). International expansion of U.S. manufacturing family businesses: The effect of ownership and involvement. *Journal of Business Venturing, 18*(4), 495–512.

Zahra, S. A., Newey, L. R., & Li, Y. (2014). On the frontiers: The implications of social entrepreneurship for international entrepreneurship. *Entrepreneurship: Theory and Practice, 38*(1), 137–158.

Zellweger, T. M., Sieger, P., & Halter, F. (2011). Should I stay or should I go? Career choice intentions of students with family business background. *Journal of Business Venturing, 26*(5), 521–536.

Zellweger, T. M., Chrisman, J. J., Chua, J. H., & Steier, L. P. (2019). Social structures, social relationships, and family firms. *Entrepreneurship Theory and Practice, 43*(2), 207–223.

Part III

Networks in Family Firm Internationalization

8

Entry Nodes in Foreign Market Entry and Post-Entry Operations of Family-Managed Firms

Katerina Kampouri and Emmanuella Plakoyiannaki

Introduction

Research on the internationalisation of family firms (FFs) has flourished since researchers have acknowledged FFs' presence in the international arena (De Massis, Frattini, Majocchi, & Piscitello, 2018; Kraus, Mensching, Calabrò, Cheng, & Filser, 2016) and have differentiated between the international strategic behaviour of different types of firms (e.g. family-managed, family-owned and non-family enterprises) in terms of the family owners versus external managers' different decision-making (Arregle, Naldi, Nordqvist, & Hitt, 2012; Boellis, Mariotti, Minichilli, & Piscitello, 2016). Indeed, in the extant literature many international business (IB) phenomena, such as FFs' international pathways and their entry modes, have been discussed (for example Kontinen & Ojala, 2012; Pongelli, Caroli, & Cucculelli, 2016), while recent FF scholars emphasise the importance of partner relationships in the internationalisation of FFs (Leppäaho & Metsola, 2020a; Pukall & Calabrò, 2014).

K. Kampouri (✉)
School of Business Administration, University of Macedonia, Thessaloniki, Greece
e-mail: kampourikat@uom.edu.gr

E. Plakoyiannaki
Faculty of Business, Economics and Statistics, University of Vienna, Vienna, Austria
e-mail: emmanuella.plakoyiannaki@univie.ac.at

© The Author(s), under exclusive license to Springer Nature Switzerland AG 2021   **237**
T. Leppäaho, S. Jack (eds.), *The Palgrave Handbook of Family Firm Internationalization*,
https://doi.org/10.1007/978-3-030-66737-5_8

238   K. Kampouri and E. Plakoyiannaki

FFs enter foreign markets by establishing international partner relationships with nodes that connect domestic firms to the customers' relationships (Graves & Thomas, 2008; Kontinen & Ojala, 2011a). The nodes that initially connect FFs with other nodes and the relationships to customers initiated and developed through the firms are defined as *entry nodes* in the IB literature (Hilmersson & Jansson, 2012, p. 686). Entry nodes are extremely important and beneficial to all types of firms including FFs, as they offer to firms connections facilitating internationalisation of operations (Elango & Pattnaik, 2007; Graves & Thomas, 2008; Kontinen & Ojala, 2011a). Moreover, entry nodes are important for acquiring experiential knowledge, that is, learning by doing (Sandberg, 2013); without such knowledge, FFs are likely to commit mistakes that incur significant costs and losses due to liabilities of foreignness. Also, they can facilitate partner firms in international opportunity identification (Johanson & Vahlne, 2006; Kontinen & Ojala, 2011a) and provide access to scarce resources (e.g. financial capital, reputation) (Elango & Pattnaik, 2007). The access to scarce resources seems to be extremely important for the FFs that constitute family-managed small- and medium-sized enterprises (SMEs), namely businesses having up to 250 employees (European Commission, 2003), in which family members have substantial ownership and take an active role in management (Hennart, Majocchi, & Forlani, 2017). In particular, family-managed SMEs have limited resources (e.g. financial and managerial) to enter international arena (Graves & Thomas, 2008), appear to lag in the identification of international opportunities (Kontinen & Ojala, 2011a) and seem to have different primary reference points when taking decisions (Berrone, Cruz, & Gómez-Mejía, 2012; Debicki, Kellermanns, Chrisman, Pearson, & Spencer, 2016). The identification and selection of appropriate entry nodes is important for family-managed SMEs since entry nodes help family-managed SMEs either to enter foreign markets (e.g. by providing the necessary resources) or endanger family-managed SMEs' entrance to foreign markets (if the potential international business partner does not have the necessary experiential knowledge).

Due to the importance of entry nodes in international operations of FFs, recent scholarship in the FF internationalisation has emphasised the need to shift the focus from the foreign establishment (entry modes) to the relationship between the internationalising supplier and the foreign partner (entry nodes) (Leppäaho & Metsola, 2020a; Stieg, Cesinger, Apfelthaler, Kraus, & Cheng, 2018). Nevertheless, there is limited research on how family-managed SMEs select entry nodes prior or post first entry (e.g. Cesinger et al., 2016; Kontinen & Ojala, 2011b; Pukall & Calabrò, 2014). We suggest that family-managed SMEs are different from other types of SMEs as the preservation of non-financial or affective utilities, commonly known as socioemotional wealth (SEW), drive family-managed SMEs' intentions or actions and hence entry nodes selection (Cesinger et al., 2016; Debicki et al., 2016; Evert, Sears, Martin, & Payne, 2017; Pongelli et al., 2016). Taking the aforementioned discussion into account, this study addresses a twofold purpose. First *it investigates the types of entry nodes that family-managed SMEs select to enter foreign markets*; and second *it identifies whether family-managed SMEs change their entry nodes after the first entrance to existing foreign markets*. A firm generally enters a foreign market by building either indirect relationships (triads or tetrads) or direct relationships (dyads) with the customers (cf.Holmen & Pedersen, 2000 ; Sandberg, 2013). In a dyad, there is a direct connection of the firm from the home market to the foreign customer, whereas in triads and tetrads, there are more actors involved in the home and host market (Holmen & Pedersen, 2000; Sandberg, 2013). Due to uncertainty when entering foreign markets, indirect relationships seem to be preferable for family-managed SMEs since such relationships may reduce perceived risks (Kontinen & Ojala, 2011b; Pukall & Calabrò, 2014). Triads or tetrads may be useful in the first steps of a family-managed SME incremental internationalisation process, when the firm might lack knowledge of foreign markets and experience of internationalisation. The responsibility then lies with the intermediary, who takes the burden off the exporter (Sandberg, 2013). Nevertheless, triads or tetrads could isolate the family-managed SME from the foreign market, preventing the family-managed SME from gaining any international knowledge and thus to commit further in the international market. On the other hand, dyads may offer the firm the advantages of control and access to information, but dyads are considered as more risky options (Kao & Kuo, 2017; Kao, Kuo, & Chang, 2013). Hence, different types of entry nodes may differently affect family-managed SMEs in their internationalisation.

To address the twofold purpose, this study adopts a network perspective to internationalisation. We draw on Sandberg's theoretical framework on business' entry nodes as well as the SEW perspective on family ownership. It should be noted that such an integration is important since a SEW perspective can enhance understanding of *how* the unique interaction between the business and its family managers influences networking activities and choices and thus the internationalisation process.

In doing so, this study employs a multiple case study design of eight family-managed SMEs operating in the Greek apiculture sector. The findings illustrate that the investigated firms embarked on different entry nodes by building indirect relationships (triads or tetrads) with international partners (foreign or domestic intermediaries) to enter foreign markets. This was mainly due to *family owners' identification* with the business that enabled family owners to maintain balance between family and business needs.

Moreover, the case study evidence suggests that post first entry into existing foreign markets, the investigated family-managed SMEs aimed at maintaining relationships with their entry nodes instead of searching to find new international partners. This was mainly due to an *emotional attachment* of the family owners with their international partners. Emotional attachment enabled the development of strong international business relationships with family-managed SMEs' entry nodes. These strong relationships provided to case study firms a stable international growth to the foreign markets they have already entered. Still, the investigated family-managed SMEs changed the type of the international business relationships with their entry nodes by engaging in higher committed relationships (e.g. exclusive partnerships) in existing and/or new foreign markets. It should be also noted that after the first entrance to international arena, the investigated family-managed SMEs of medium and small size adopted a more active behaviour to internationalisation and embarked on different entry nodes by building either indirect or direct relationships (dyads) with international partners in new international markets.

The results of this study contribute to the FF internationalisation literature. First, this study responds to deficits reported by Pukall and Calabrò (2014) and Leppäaho and Metsola (2020b) on the behaviour of family-managed SMEs in entry nodes selection and extends earlier findings in terms of prior and post-entry operations of family-managed SMEs (Graves & Thomas, 2008; Kontinen & Ojala, 2011b). In particular, this study extends the network perspective by enriching Sandberg's theoretical framework on business' entry nodes with SEW dimensions (family owners identification and family owners' emotional attachment with foreign partners) that explain the entry node selection of family-managed SMEs. Research on SEW dimensions in the context of international networking activities of FFs has only recently started to expand (Cesinger et al., 2016; Pukall & Calabrò, 2014).

This chapter is organised as follows. We firstly discuss the internationalisation of FFs through a network lens, and differentiate between entry modes and entry nodes as well as SEW preservation tendencies of FFs. We then discuss the methodology of the study followed by the findings and conclusions.

Theoretical Background

FF Internationalisation Through a Network Lens

Through a network lens, internationalisation is related to the development of relationships with other firms (or nodes) belonging to a network in a foreign market (Johanson & Mattsson, 1988; Johanson & Vahlne, 2009). The network theory proposes that a firm can compensate for its limited resources by developing its position in an existing network or by establishing new relationships (Johanson & Mattsson, 1988). According to Granovetter (1973) these relationships can be *weak* or *strong*. Kontinen and Ojala (2011a) define a weak tie as "a superficial tie not based on strong trust, and where the parties do not know each other well and are not emotionally close to each other" (Kontinen & Ojala, 2011a, p. 4). A *strong* tie appears when "the partners are close to each other and the relationships are based on mutual respect, trust and commitment" (Kontinen & Ojala, 2011a, p. 4). Independently of the strength of the relationship, common interests motivate firms to develop and maintain international relationships with foreign partners because such partner relationships are of mutual benefit (Kauser & Shaw, 2004; Mohr & Spekman, 1994).

In foreign markets a firm can choose between different types of international partner relationships with different types of actors. To illustrate, firms expand overseas by engaging in four different types of international partner relationships, namely (1) partner relationships with intermediaries (distributors and/or agents), (2) partner relationships with foreign licensees, (3) partner relationships with international franchisees and (4) foreign joint venture partner relationships (Cavusgil, 1998; Kontinen & Ojala, 2011a). When selecting a potential international business partner, firms' behaviour may be active or passive. An active behaviour may be shown when the initiative is taken by the firm, whereas a passive behaviour appears when the initiation comes from the foreign partner's direction (Johanson & Mattsson, 1988).

Until recently research in the FF internationalisation literature that adopts a network perspective has primarily concentrated on the initial networking activities and international partnership building prior FFs' internationalisation (e.g. how FFs find partners when entering a foreign market) (e.g. Eberhard & Craig, 2013; Kontinen & Ojala, 2011a). Extant research has revealed that most family-managed SMEs adopt a passive behaviour by reactively responding to demands from distributors or agents in order to enter a foreign market (Graves & Thomas, 2008; Kontinen & Ojala, 2011a). Family-managed SMEs are mostly seen to internationalising gradually, by building inter-personal or

Entry Nodes Versus Entry Modes

As it is highlighted in the introduction section, *entry nodes* constitute "nodes used initially to connect to domestic firms and the relationships to customers initiated and developed through them" (Hilmersson & Jansson, 2012, p. 686). When the entry node is the final customer, relationships are conceptualised as *direct*, whereas when an entry node constitutes an intermediary, relationships are conceptualised as *indirect* (Hilmersson & Jansson, 2012). This is labelled as the network node configuration, that is, how the relationship with the foreign market is set up (either direct or indirect relationship) (Sandberg, 2013, 2014, p. 21).

In general, *entry modes*, that is, "structural agreements that allow a firm to implement its product market strategy in a host country either by carrying out only the marketing operations (i.e. via export modes), or both production and marketing operations there by itself or in partnership with others (contractual modes, joint ventures, wholly owned operations)" (Sharma & Erramilli, 2004, p. 2), as well as entry nodes represent two different but complementary aspects of foreign market entry (Sandberg, 2013). Entry mode is "subordinated to the entry node by being supportive to the firms' business relationships and adapted to support them" (Hilmersson & Jansson, 2012, p. 691). If FFs are reluctant to build relationships with foreign partners (other firms) their internationalisation and the entry mode selection may suffer (Pukall & Calabrò, 2014). On the other hand, a firm's willingness to build relationships with foreign partners favours its internationalisation pathways. Therefore, entry nodes constitute bridges with foreign market networks (Fernández & Nieto, 2006; Graves & Thomas, 2006) and may be precursors to entry mode decisions (Hilmersson & Jansson, 2012).

In the entry situation (when a firm enters a foreign market network), the internationalising firm sets up different initial network configurations or entry nodes. Sandberg (2013) suggests that network node configurations constitute a dyad (a direct relationship with the customer) or a triad (an indirect

8 Entry Nodes in Foreign Market Entry and Post-Entry Operations...

relationship with the customer) in the form of four entry situations: (1) dyad from the home market, (2) dyad at the foreign market, (3) triad via the home market and (4) triad via the foreign market, each using different types of entry nodes (Fig. 8.1).

To illustrate, there are two types of dyads, dyad from the home market and dyad at the foreign market (Sandberg, 2013). A dyad from the home market refers to a direct connection of the firm from the home market to the foreign customer and the entry node is the foreign customer. A dyad at the foreign market includes a firms' foreign subsidiary in the foreign market which is directly linked to the foreign customer. A triad via the home market refers to an indirect connection to the customer, using an intermediary located in the domestic market as the entry node. A triad via the foreign market entails an indirect relationship with the foreign customer but holds a direct relationship to the market through a foreign intermediary.

Although Sandberg (2013) examined the entry node pattern of SMEs (i.e. the initial entry node and changes in it), we could not be sure if the results of this study could be applied to family-managed SMEs. First of all, Sandberg (2013) does not clarify whether the examined SMEs are family-managed

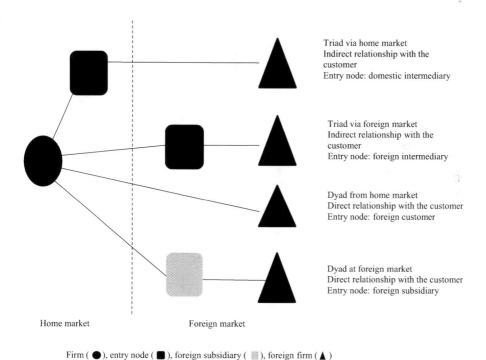

Fig. 8.1 Entry situations and entry nodes (Source: Sandberg, 2013, p. 109)

SMEs or not, hence it may be not clear to the reader whether the results relate to family-managed SMEs or not. Nevertheless, given that family-managed SMEs' behaviour is different compared to other types of firms when family owners take international decisions (Debicki et al., 2016; Gómez-Mejía, Cruz, Berrone, & De Castro, 2011), such a research is important in order to avoid contradictory results in the IB literature.

Second, existing FF literature emphasise family-managed SMEs' preferences on non-equity modes of internationalisation and low committed relationships with foreign partners in the international arena (e.g. Kontinen & Ojala, 2011b; Kontinen & Ojala, 2012; Pukall & Calabrò, 2014). Limited research discusses FFs' preferences on high commitment relationships, yet researchers vastly consider large- and medium-sized companies that select equity modes to internationalisation (e.g. Boers, 2016; Chang, Kao, & Kuo, 2014; Kao et al., 2013; Kao & Kuo, 2017; Sestu, Majocchi, & D'Angelo, 2018). Typically, smaller family-managed firms form triadic relationships by reactively responding to demands from distributors or wholesalers (Kontinen & Ojala, 2011a). Smaller family-managed firms may even choose to develop tetrads to enter foreign markets, that is, an indirect connection to the customer, using four nodes, namely the family-managed SME, the domestic intermediary, the foreign intermediary and the final customer and three relationships created in network (cf. Holmen & Pedersen, 2000) due to the lack of resources. Moreover, a dyad from the foreign market rarely concerns family-managed SMEs as they do not typically own subsidiaries due to lack of resources.

Although the extant literature has highlighted the preferences on family-managed SMEs in their types of international relationships (De Farias, Nataraajan, & Kovacs, 2009; Swinth & Vinton, 1993), research is still limited with regard to family-managed SMEs' entry nodes in the process of internationalisation (Kontinen & Ojala, 2011a; Pukall & Calabrò, 2014). This is important since family-managed SMEs may change (or not) their entry nodes, after they have entered international arena. Such an understanding may enrich our understanding on family-managed SMEs' internationalisation. Moreover, knowledge of family-managed SMEs' entry nodes could provide a roadmap to FF owners in terms of developing relationships with network partners in the international arena.

The SEW Perspective

Within the FF internationalisation literature important strategic decisions on international activities are influenced by SEW preservation tendencies (Cesinger et al., 2016; Pisano, 2018). SEW stems from the behavioural agency theory (Wiseman & Gomez-Mejia, 1998) and explains FFs' strategic decisions and choices (Gómez-Mejía, Haynes, Núñez-Nickel, Jacobson, & Moyano- Fuentes, 2007). SEW is the "single most important feature of a family firm's essence that separates it from other organisational firms" (Berrone et al., 2012, p. 3). It refers to non-economic rewards that owners may derive from their FFs, including their emotional connections to the firm, the family values and their altruistic behaviour (Debicki et al., 2016; Gómez-Mejía et al., 2011).

According to Berrone et al. (2012) the SEW dimensions that influence FFs' managerial attitudes are (1) the ability and desire of family members (usually the owner) to exert control and influence over the FF's strategic decisions, (2) the strong identification of the FF with the family name (e.g. family members seek to perpetuate a positive family image and reputation), (3) the FF's social relationships, that is, the sense of belongingness which is shared not only among family members but also among non-family employees and which promotes a sense of stability and commitment to the firm, (4) the intention of handing the business down to future generations and (5) the family members' emotions that permeate the organisation, influencing the FF's decision-making process (Berrone et al., 2012, p. 279).

Gómez-Mejía et al. (2007) argued that preserving socioemotional endowment is critical for the family and shapes the framing of problems, becoming the primary reference point for guiding strategic decisions and choices. In particular, family managers often face a mixed gamble—considering the possible socioemotional gains and losses (Alessandri, Cerrato, & Eddleston, 2018; Gómez-Mejía et al., 2014). When there is a threat to that endowment (a potential SEW loss), or an opportunity to enhance it (a potential SEW gain), the firm is willing to make decisions that may be not driven by an economic logic, and in fact the family members are willing even to put the firm at risk if this is what it would take to preserve that endowment (Gómez-Mejía et al., 2007). It should be noted, though, that preserving SEW seems to be more critical for family-managed SMEs than in other types of FFs (e.g. family owned but externally managed enterprises) since the intense of SEW preservation tendencies differ (Evert et al., 2017; Pongelli et al., 2016). For example, Pongelli et al. (2016) have mentioned that a manager who does not belong to the family places less priority on the preservation of SEW in entry mode selection. Nevertheless, the preservation of SEW is likely to affect international networking decisions of family-managed SMEs given that the complexity and uncertainty associated with international partner selection generates a range of internationalisation outcomes (Alessandri et al., 2018; Gómez-Mejía et al., 2014).

The aforementioned dimensions may influence family-managed SMEs' strategic behaviour, yet there is a paucity in research that adopts the SEW perspective and examines the behaviour of family-managed SMEs in entry nodes selection (Pukall & Calabrò, 2014; Scholes, Mustafa, & Chen, 2016). Nevertheless, such a perspective is particularly useful in understanding why certain relationships are chosen to others (Pukall & Calabrò, 2014). Moreover it can enhance our understanding of how the unique interaction between the business and the family influences networking activities and choices and thus the internationalisation process.

Methodology

The Qualitative Case Study Approach

In order to address the twofold purpose of our study, namely to (1) investigate the types of entry nodes that family-managed SMEs select to enter foreign markets and (2) identify whether family-managed SMEs change their entry nodes after the first entrance to existing foreign markets, we employed a qualitative multiple case study research. Qualitative case study research was selected for this study as it allowed capturing "how" family-managed SMEs' establish relationships with their entry nodes in order to enter a foreign market and "why" certain relationships are chosen to others (Eisenhardt & Graebner, 2007; Jack, 2010; Reay, 2014). It also served to illuminate the complex and under-investigated phenomenon of family-managed SMEs internationalisation by facilitating the collection of rich data from multiple sources of evidence (cf. Leppäaho, Plakoyiannaki, & Dimitratos, 2016; Yin, 2009). Moreover, case studies also constitute a methodology of choice for the study of IB phenomena (Welch, Piekkari, Plakoyiannaki, & Paavilainen-Mäntymäki, 2011).

The methodological strategy behind this research is mainly abductive. Abduction is especially suitable for case studies in business network research (Järvensivu & Törnroos, 2010) aiming at extending theory (Dubois & Gadde,

2014). We enrich Sandberg's theoretical framework on business' entry nodes by considering the SEW dimensions that influence the entry node selection (Berrone et al., 2012). By constantly iterating between empirical observations and the theoretical insights of the aforementioned authors, we were able to expand our understanding on both network perspective and empirical phenomena (Dubois & Gadde, 2002, p. 555).

Case Study Selection

Multiple case study design was chosen to address the twofold purpose of the study (Dubois & Gadde, 2014). We followed the selection strategy of criterion sampling (Fletcher & Plakoyiannaki, 2011; Patton, 1990) and selected family-managed SMEs that met the following criteria: (1) had at least one year of international experience in foreign market, (2) operated in the Greek apiculture sector and (3) met the general definition of a family-managed SME: "firm owned and run by one family with the intention to shape and pursue the vision of the business held by the family in a manner that it is potentially sustainable across generations" (Arregle et al., 2012; Chua, Chrisman, & Sharma, 1999, p. 28).

First of all, we included case study firms that had at least one year of international experience in order to collect retrospective accounts (Craig-Lees, 2001) on "how" and "why" family-managed SMEs developed international partner relationships that led to internationalisation. Even though a relationship with a partner does not immediately translate to international expansion, it positively influences internationalisation after a short period of time (e.g. a year) (Eberhard & Craig, 2013). Second, the Greek apiculture sector was selected given its growth potential in foreign markets. To illustrate Greece has a unique physical environment for the production of beekeeping products; Greece's flora provide apiculture products with unique organoleptic characteristics with healing properties which enable apiculture firms to gain a competitive advantage compared to other bee products produced in other countries (Thrasyvoulou & Manikis, 1995). This competitive advantage of Greek high-quality beekeeping products has generated an increased demand of Greek apiculture products from foreign markets. Having identified this international growth potential many apiculture family-managed SMEs have proactively and reactively engaged in international operation (International Trade Map, 2017).

Our criterion sampling strategy generated a pool of 20 family-managed SMEs with 100% of family ownership. All case study firms were contacted

248 K. Kampouri and E. Plakoyiannaki

through telephone or e-mail and eight of them agreed to participate in this study. Table 8.1 summarises information on the case study firms. The investigated case study firms market bee products (particularly honey) with firm C and firm D specialising also on organic food products. They are all strong players in the domestic market but they also operate international markets through direct and indirect exports of branded (or bulk) honey for more than ten years. Moreover, the number of personnel varies from 5 to 110 employees.

Data Collection

Following Yin's (2009) suggestions data were collected from multiple sources. We conducted 25 in-depth, open-ended personal interviews with Greek individuals (see also Table 8.2). The interviews were all tape-recorded, transcribed and translated verbatim from Greek to English following the recommendations by Chidlow, Plakoyiannaki, and Welch (2014). They ranged from 60 to 90 minutes and interviewees were invited to elaborate freely on questions such as *"How does your company develop relationships with partners in order to enter foreign markets? Why?"*

In each firm, the owner (usually the founder of the firm) was contacted and served as the primary respondent of the study. It should be also noted that the family owners constituted also the managers of the family-managed SMEs. The primary respondent (CEO & owner) was requested to identify other key respondents who were included in our research through a snowballing technique (Fletcher, Zhao, Plakoyiannaki, & Buck, 2018; Miles & Huberman, 1994). These respondents were chosen due to their direct experience with the family-managed SME's international networking activities (cf. Polkinghorne,

Table 8.1 Information on the investigated family-managed FFs

Family-managed SMEs	Size	Type of firm	Generation on board	Years of international operation	Export branded honey (or not)
Firm A	Medium	Commercial	2	80	Branded
Firm B	Medium	Commercial	1	10	Not branded
Firm C	Small	Commercial	1	27	Branded
Firm D	Small	Productive	1	26	Not branded
Firm E	Small	Commercial	2	20	Branded
Firm F	Micro	Productive	2	35	Not branded
Firm G	Micro	Productive	1	10	Branded
Firm H	Micro	Productive	1	10	Branded

8 Entry Nodes in Foreign Market Entry and Post-Entry Operations... 249

Table 8.2 Profile of the interviewees

Family-managed SMEs	Position of interviewee
Firm A	CEO & owner
	Export manager & owner
	Export supervisor
	Quality assurance manager
	Production manager
	Marketing manager
	Employee in the marketing department
	Employee in the marketing department
Firm B	CEO & owner
	Sales manager
Firm C	CEO & owner
	Export manager
	Sales manager
	Marketing manager
Firm D	CEO & owner
	Export supervisor
Firm E	CEO & owner
	Marketing & sales manager
	Quality assurance manager
Firm F	CEO & owner
	Export supervisor
Firm G	CEO & owner
	Export supervisor
Firm H	CEO & owner
	Export supervisor

2005). Such a selection enhanced the collection of nuanced accounts associated with the purposes of the study.

Secondary materials, such as web pages and documents (e.g. trade press publications and internal presentations), were utilised as well. The secondary material was used to understand the history of each firm as well as to triangulate with the insights gleaned from the interviews (Yin, 2009).

Data Analysis

Data analysis was conducted in two phases: (1) within-case analysis that included write-ups for each family-managed SME and (2) cross-case analysis that involved the identification of cross-case patterns (Eisenhardt, 1989; Miles & Huberman, 1994) across our dataset. Specifically, we followed an abductive approach to analyse rich case study data (Dubois & Gadde, 2002, 2014). This process involved iterating between the data and the existing body of knowledge (Miles & Huberman, 1994). To organise the data collected from multiple contexts and enhance rigour, our analysis was aided by the use of computer-assisted qualitative data analysis software (Atlas) (Sinkovics & Ghauri, 2008). The use of Atlas allowed the categorisation, abstraction and integration of qualitative data (Spiggle, 1994).

In the categorisation phase, we coded and analysed data emerging from interviews and secondary data using Atlas. In vivo coding was used in order to organise the data and to facilitate the identification of themes across the different sources (Saldaña, 2013). For example, the concept of "information sharing" incorporated dimensions such as "institutional knowledge" and the concept of "emotions" incorporated specific emotions of family owners towards international partners such as "pride."

We then employed thematic analysis in order to unveil similar thematic aspects across data sources. In the following stage of data analysis, namely the abstraction stage, we linked the themes into conceptual categories (Spiggle, 1994; cf. Dimitratos, Plakoyiannaki, Pitsoulaki, & Tüselmann, 2010) (see also Fig. 8.2).

In this stage, we reviewed and refined the emerging themes related to our theoretical framework, so as to ensure the quality of the findings, by investigating the relationships between "the everyday language" of our empirical data and the concepts in the existing literature (Dubois-Gadde, 2002, p. 555).

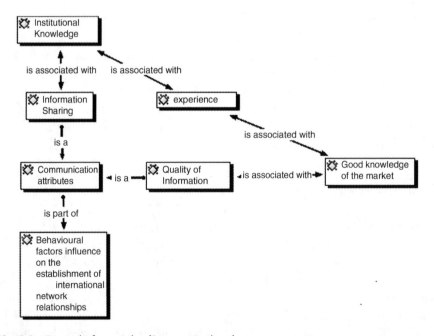

Fig. 8.2 Example from Atlas (Source: Authors)

In the final stage of data analysis, that is, integration, we connected the empirical findings with existing theory. Particularly, in this phase it was crucial to examine the emergent themes and concepts in light of the relevant literature so as to illuminate aspects of FF internationalisation through a network lens.

Findings

The Entry Nodes of Family-Managed SMEs (First Entry to International Markets)

Building upon Sandberg's (2013) four entry situations, our case study evidence illustrates that all the investigated firms chose to build *indirect* relationships to first enter international markets. This was mostly due to risk avoidance. Indeed most of the investigated family-managed SMEs were shown to adopt a passive behaviour to internationalisation and reactively respond to demands from distributors or wholesalers in order to enter a foreign market (Kontinen & Ojala, 2011a).

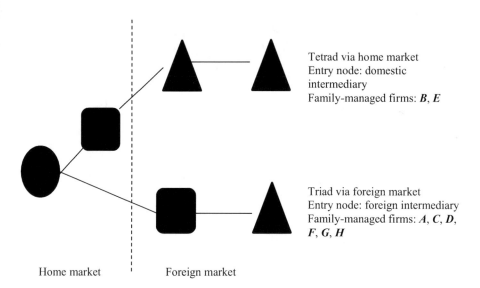

Fig. 8.3 Entry nodes of the investigated family-managed SMEs (prior to first entrance to foreign markets)

In line with the relevant literature, a few investigated firms (firms A, B, E, G and H) firstly met their potential international partners in trade exhibitions (Arregle et al., 2012; Fernandez Moya, 2010). Social networking relationships (e.g. family members and people met at social events) of firms C and D facilitated the connection with their potential partners (Kontinen & Ojala, 2011a), whereas firm F identified its entry node partner online. In addition, the majority of investigated firms (firms A, C, D, F, G and H) developed *triadic* relationships (see also Fig. 8.3).

Triadic entry nodes included intermediaries that constituted a wholesaler or a distributor in the foreign market (firms A, C, D, F, G and H):

> We developed relationships with foreign wholesalers to enter key markets… We prefer to export our products through foreign wholesalers because we do not know the foreign market so well as the foreign wholesalers do. (CEO and owner, firm A)

The quotation above highlights the role of the entry nodes' knowledge of the foreign market as an important factor in FFs' relationship building activities with their entry nodes (Kauser & Shaw, 2004; Mohr & Spekman, 1994; Sandberg, 2013).

Nevertheless, two of the investigated family-managed SMEs (firm B and firm E) started exporting activities via *tetrads*, bringing on board an additional IB relationship, that is, the relationship of the domestic intermediary with the foreign intermediary. A *tetrad via home market* is a system of four nodes that contains three relationships (Holmen & Pedersen, 2000). Particularly, this network node configuration of those case study firms included four nodes, namely the family-managed firm, the domestic intermediary, the foreign intermediary and the final customer, establishing three sets of relationships. These are (1) the relationship of the family-managed SMEs with a domestic intermediary; (2) the relationship of the domestic intermediary with the foreign intermediary and (3) the relationship of the foreign intermediary with the final customer. As quoted below:

> First of all, we are a small family firm and we have not developed our own export department, yet. We prefer to export our products through an intermediary because we do not know the foreign market. So we cannot take the risk of losing time or money. The intermediary cooperates with another company in the foreign market and this foreign intermediary sends our products to supermarkets. (CEO and owner, firm E)

8 Entry Nodes in Foreign Market Entry and Post-Entry Operations... 253

Our case study evidence illustrates that this entry node, that is, the *domestic intermediary*, was extremely significant for the family-managed SMEs' international operations in international markets. Specifically, the domestic intermediary (1) compensated for the lack of knowledge (i.e. language barriers) of the investigated firms and facilitated the development of direct relationships with foreign customers or intermediaries and (2) managed the communication with customers or intermediaries belonging to other business cultures (Kauser & Shaw, 2004; Mohr & Spekman, 1994; Sandberg, 2013). Indeed, all our investigated FFs illustrated that *informational* and *institutional knowledge sharing*, that is, "knowledge that concerns the macro-environment institutions in the foreign country, such as culture and local government" (Sandberg, 2014, p. 22), played a significant role in entering and maintaining themselves to foreign markets.

With regard to SEW preservation tendencies the case study evidence highlights the *family owners' identification with the business*, which influenced the family owners' decisions on entry nodes. As the family owner of the firm H highlighted:

> We are a very small firm and we can produce a certain quantity of honey… When a potential international partner firm asks for a specific quantity of honey, we send the price and ask to deposit the money prior the exportation… we do not take the risk of losing money because our family's survival depends on the company's survival… We select partners that appreciate our brand. (CEO and owner, firm H)

All family owners reported that the production of high-quality Greek honey is limited. Therefore, exporting in large volumes compromised the supply of the domestic market. In light of domestic demand, family owners chose to export only if they were paid in advance to balance the financial risk and preserve the SEW. Moreover, family owners needed to feel appreciated for their production with regard to the quality of the Greek honey. Family members identified themselves with the products and their businesses, and led the family-managed SMEs to evaluate their potential international partners by placing a priority to the family owners' needs. They excluded partners that insisted on price negotiations and bargaining as they perceived that these partners did not appreciate the product quality. They considered these collaborators as threat for SEW preservation and the international future of the FF. This finding is important given that it may be the case that feelings of family owners may affect the family-managed SMEs behaviour and their entry node development.

Moreover, it should be noted that when family owners realised that the potential partner was a Greek expatriate, they generated positive emotions. As quoted below:

> When you realize that the potential partner is Greek you feel happy. A Greek person can better realize the difficulties in the production of the honey and better understands why Greek honey is so expensive compared to others… Most of our initial partners were Greek expatriates. (CEO and owner, firm C)

The positive emotions that family owners felt led to an enhancement of the family owners' tranquillity (SEW gain), and hence it influenced family-managed SMEs' relationship building activities with that potential partner. These insights provide evidence on the SEW perspective and suggest that family owners' identification with the firm may affect family-managed SMEs' entry node development.

The Entry Nodes of Family-Managed SMEs (Post-Entry to International Markets)

After the first entrance to foreign markets, firms A, B, C and D adopted an *active* behaviour to internationalisation. They developed successful and long-term relationships with their entry nodes both in the first entry countries, and in key international markets. Key foreign markets (at the time of investigation) were conceptualised by the interviewees as those markets with a growing demand for the investigated firms' products. As quoted below:

> we had relationships with wholesalers at first… after the first entry to key foreign markets we decided to build partnerships with exclusive representatives and we searched for them within our existing relationship network with wholesalers so as to find the most ideal exclusive representative … Key markets are those markets with a growing demand for honey such as the UK… We selected these partners that seemed promising… We were not fully aware of each one's capabilities, so we selected those that seemed to have good knowledge of the foreign market since they could provide information about customers' preferences… Recently, we have decided to select exclusive representatives in new international markets because our experience has shown that exclusive representatives promote better our brand. (Export manager, firm A)

Post first entry, firm A, firm C and firm D searched for exclusive representatives within their established network of international partners. While they

8 Entry Nodes in Foreign Market Entry and Post-Entry Operations... 255

Table 8.3 Entry nodes and post-entry nodes of the investigated firms

Family-managed SMEs	Entry nodes (first foreign market entry)	Post first entry nodes (new international markets)
Firm A	Foreign wholesaler (UK)	Foreign exclusive sales representative (USA) Foreign customer (UK)
Firm B	Domestic wholesaler (UK)	Foreign wholesaler (USA)
Firm C	Foreign wholesaler (Germany)	Foreign exclusive sales representative (Belgium)
Firm D	Foreign distributor (UK)	Foreign exclusive representative (UK)
Firm E	Domestic distributor (Germany)	Domestic distributor (Germany)
Firm F	Foreign wholesaler (Germany)	Foreign wholesaler (Saudi Arabia)
Firm G	Foreign distributor (Norway)	Foreign distributor (USA)
Firm H	Foreign wholesaler (Germany)	Foreign wholesaler (Switzerland)

did not change the partner, these firms changed the type of relationship with each partner and developed stronger, engaged relationships with them (Kontinen & Ojala, 2012). It should be also noted that firm A, firm C and firm D changed their behaviour, after they have gained international experience, and started international activities in other markets as well by shifting their entry node type selection from wholesalers to exclusive representatives. Moreover, firm B built triadic relationships with foreign intermediaries when entering new international markets (see also Table 8.3).

Nevertheless, firms E, F, G and H remained *passive* in their international relationship building activities and did not change the types of relationships developed in the first foreign market entry. This was mostly due to the limited resources of those small and micro firms and the limited years of experience in international markets (see also Fig. 8.4).

Nevertheless, all investigated firms acknowledged their willingness to develop stable and long-term relationships with their entry nodes post-entry. All investigated family-managed SMEs acknowledged that they had no intention of changing their entry nodes even if relationships were not economically beneficial to them. As quoted below:

Since we are a small firm, we are dependent on our partners in order to survive in the international arena. Therefore, we aim at maintaining those partnerships with partners who understand what we do. (CEO and owner, firm G)

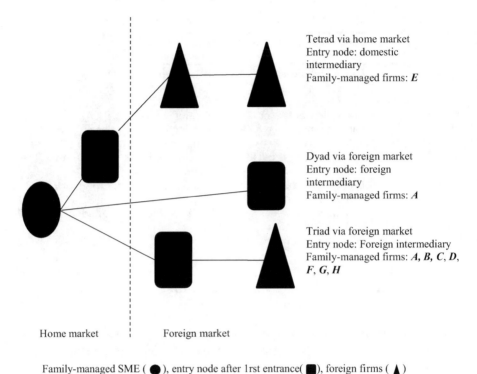

Fig. 8.4 Entry nodes of the investigated family-managed SMEs (after the first entrance to international markets)

Indeed, our interviewees mentioned that institutional pressures rather than partner dissatisfaction determined international partnership termination:

> Currently, we have no intention of changing our relationships with our partners. We feel happy with our partners, we have the same values and we made the right choice to collaborate with them… Some partnerships though were terminated due to legal and institutional problems in the exporting country. For example in Venezuela we found difficulties in introducing our product because the government wanted to protect domestic production. (CEO and owner, firm A)

Investigated owners acknowledged that some partnerships were not as economically beneficial as they expected, still their personal pride—"*we think that we did the right choices*"—and the satisfaction coming from similar personal values among partners—"*we feel happy with our partners*"—were "emotional values" (Zellweger & Astrachan, 2008) that contributed to an *emotional attachment* to their entry nodes. Emotional benefits refer to the value that firm owners derive from power, prestige and satisfaction, whereas emotional costs refer to personal sacrifices, a lack of opportunity to interact, responsibility for the employees and so on (Zellweger & Astrachan, 2008).

This emotional attachment influenced the entry node selection of family-managed SMEs and thus their internationalisation. In particular, this emotional attachment enabled the development of strong international business relationships with family-managed firms' entry nodes. These strong relationships facilitated to case study firms' international growth to the foreign markets they have already entered. Nevertheless, this emotional attachment with entry nodes was not always profitable as they could be; sometimes the emotional attachment of family owners with initial entry nodes compromised opportunities for family-managed SMEs.

These insights provide evidence on the emotional dimension of the SEW perspective and suggest that emotional attachment of family-managed SMEs' owners or founders influences the maintenance of relationships with international partners. This finding is very important since it highlights that emotions influence family-managed SMEs' international strategic decisions (Bee & Neubaum, 2014; Kellermanns, Dibrell, & Cruz, 2014). A better understanding of such emotional attachment with entry nodes may provide a better understanding on how FFs choose their entry nodes.

Discussion and Conclusions

Based on the network perspective to internationalisation and on SEW perspective the purpose of this study was to shed light on family-managed SMEs' entry nodes' pre-entry and post-entry to foreign markets. In doing so, this study examined eight family-managed SMEs form the Greek apiculture sector. Therefore, the study considers the recent calls for future research on FFs' node decisions (Kontinen & Ojala, 2011b; Pukall & Calabrò, 2014) in different country contexts and phases of internationalisation (Leppäaho & Metsola, 2020b). Moreover, it considers calls for the study of networking phenomena of FFs from a SEW perspective (Cesinger et al., 2016; Kampouri, Plakoyiannaki, & Leppäaho, 2017; Pukall & Calabrò, 2014).

The case study evidence coincides with the literature regarding the behaviour of family-managed SMEs that select non-equity modes. Our results indicate that family-managed SMEs adopted a reactive behaviour prior to the first entry to foreign markets by building weak indirect relationships with entry nodes (Graves & Thomas, 2008; Kontinen & Ojala, 2011a). Post-entry, they engaged in active internationalisation by engaging in strong relationships with international partners (Kontinen & Ojala, 2011b). Nevertheless, the case study evidence extends the network perspective on FFs internationalisation by providing two SEW dimensions to Sandberg's earlier work on entry node development, namely *family firms' identification* and *emotional attachment*, which explain the entry node selection of family-managed SMEs. Specifically, this study suggests that family-managed SMEs develop not only triadic relationships but also tetrads to enter foreign markets. These initial triads or tetrads were selected by family-managed SMEs mostly due to a risk-averse behaviour in internationalisation, lack of resources and a protection of SEW. Especially tetrads enabled family-managed SMEs to preserve balance between family and business needs, thereby showing the priority of SEW preservation in entry node development. Moreover, this study indicates that after the first foreign market entry, family owners developed an emotional attachment with their initial international partners (see also De Massis & Foss, 2018; Neubaum, 2018). The emotional attachment of the investigated family-managed SMEs with their initial entry nodes enabled family-managed SMEs' international growth to the initial foreign markets and led the case firms to maintain relationships with their entry nodes instead of searching to find new international partners. Nevertheless, this emotional attachment inhibited the search of new, more profitable opportunities with new business partners.

Finally, this study faces limitations that can potentially offer directions for future research. First of all, this study provides an empirical contribution to the international networking decisions of a particular type of FFs, namely family-managed firms in which family ownership is 100%. Hence, this study does not consider international networking decisions of other types of FFs with lower percentages of family ownership. Future research could investigate other types of FFs and consider the effect of the heterogeneity between international networking decisions of FFs with different ownership structures and different sizes of FFs including large FFs. Viewed in this light, the mixed gamble perspective (Gómez-Mejía et al., 2014; Martin, Gomez-Mejia, & Wiseman, 2013) could explain why FFs' international networking decision may vary among various types of FFs. Second, this study examined international networking decisions of family-managed SMEs that selected non-equity modes to enter international markets, so the results may differ in family-managed large firms that select equity modes (e.g. Kao et al., 2013; Kao & Kuo, 2017). Hence, there is a need for comparative studies between family-managed SMEs and family-managed large firms. Third, this study examined family-managed SMEs from one particular country and one particular sector. Although a single country and a single industry was chosen in our research design to control for the contextual variance of decision-making in family-managed SMEs (Poulis, Poulis, & Plakoyiannaki, 2013), we suggest that future studies could draw from different national and industry contexts to increase our understanding on FF internationalisation and international networking.

References

Alessandri, T. M., Cerrato, D., & Eddleston, K. A. (2018). The mixed gamble of internationalization in family and nonfamily firms: The moderating role of organizational slack. *Global Strategy Journal, 8*(1), 46–72.

Arregle, J. L., Naldi, L., Nordqvist, M., & Hitt, M. A. (2012). Internationalization of family-controlled firms: A study of the effects of external involvement in governance. *Entrepreneurship Theory and Practice, 36*(6), 1115–1143.

Bee, C., & Neubaum, D. O. (2014). The role of cognitive appraisal and emotions of family members in the family business system. *Journal of Family Business Strategy, 5*(3), 323–333.

Berrone, P., Cruz, C., & Gómez-Mejía, L. R. (2012). Socioemotional wealth in family firms theoretical dimensions, assessment approaches, and agenda for future research. *Family Business Review, 25*(3), 258–279.

Boellis, A., Mariotti, S., Minichilli, A., & Piscitello, L. (2016). Family involvement and firms' establishment mode choice in foreign markets. *Journal of International Business Studies, 47*(8), 929–950.

Boers, B. (2016). Go East! How family businesses choose markets and entry modes when internationalising. *International Journal of Globalisation and Small Business, 8*(4), 333–354.

Cavusgil, S. T. (1998). International partnering: A systematic framework for collaborating with foreign business partners. *Journal of International Marketing, 6*(1), 91–107.

Cesinger, B., Hughes, M., Mensching, H., Bouncken, R., Fredrich, V., & Kraus, S. (2016). A socioemotional wealth perspective on how collaboration intensity, trust, and international market knowledge affect family firms' multinationality. *Journal of World Business, 51*(4), 586–599.

Chang, Y. C., Kao, M. S., & Kuo, A. (2014). The influences of governance quality on equity-based entry mode choice: The strengthening role of family control. *International Business Review, 23*(5), 1008–1020.

Chen, T. J. (2003). Network resources for internationalization: The case of Taiwan's electronics firms. *Journal of Management Studies, 40*(5), 1107–1130.

Chidlow, A., Plakoyiannaki, E., & Welch, C. (2014). Translation in cross-language international business research: Beyond equivalence. *Journal of International Business Studies, 45*(5), 562–582.

Chua, J. H., Chrisman, J. J., & Sharma, P. (1999). Defining the family business by behavior. *Entrepreneurship Theory and Practice, 23*(4), 19–39.

Craig-Lees, M. (2001). Sense making: Trojan horse? Pandora's box? *Psychology & Marketing, 18*(5), 513–526.

De Farias, S. A., Nataraajan, R., & Kovacs, E. P. (2009). Global business partnering among family-owned enterprises. *Journal of Business Research, 62*(6), 667–672.

De Massis, A., & Foss, N. J. (2018). Advancing family business research: The promise of microfoundations. *Family Business Review, 31*(4), 386–396.

De Massis, A., Frattini, F., Majocchi, A., & Piscitello, L. (2018). Family firms in the global economy: Toward a deeper understanding of internationalization determinants, processes, and outcomes. *Global Strategy Journal, 8*(1), 3–21.

Debicki, B. J., Kellermanns, F. W., Chrisman, J. J., Pearson, A. W., & Spencer, B. A. (2016). Development of a socioemotional wealth importance (SEWi) scale for family firm research. *Journal of Family Business Strategy, 7*(1), 47–57.

Dimitratos, P., Plakoyiannaki, E., Pitsoulaki, A., & Tüselmann, H. J. (2010). The global smaller firm in international entrepreneurship. *International Business Review, 19*(6), 589–606.

Dubois, A., & Gadde, L. E. (2002). Systematic combining: An abductive approach to case research. *Journal of business research, 55*(7), 553–560.

Dubois, A., & Gadde, L. E. (2014). "Systematic combining"—A decade later. *Journal of Business Research, 67*(6), 1277–1284.

Eberhard, M., & Craig, J. (2013). The evolving role of organisational and personal networks in international market venturing. *Journal of World Business, 48*(3), 385–397.

Eisenhardt, K. M. (1989). Building theories from case study research. *The Academy of Management Review, 14*(4), 532–550.

Eisenhardt, K. M., & Graebner, M. E. (2007). Theory building from cases: Opportunities and challenges. *Academy of Management Journal, 50*(1), 25–32.

Elango, B., & Pattnaik, C. (2007). Building capabilities for international operations through networks: A study of Indian firms. *Journal of International Business Studies, 38*(4), 541–555.

European Commission. (2003). Retrieved December 2017, from https://ec.europa.eu/growth/smes/business-friendly-environment/sme-definition_en

Evert, R. E., Sears, J. B., Martin, J. A., & Payne, G. T. (2017). Family ownership and family involvement as antecedents of strategic action: A longitudinal study of initial international entry. *Journal of Business Research, 84*, 301–311.

Fernandez Moya, M. (2010). A family-owned publishing multinational: The Salvat company (1869–1988). *Business History, 52*(3), 453–470.

Fernández, Z., & Nieto, M. J. (2006). Impact of ownership on the international involvement of SMEs. *Journal of International Business Studies, 37*(3), 340–351.

Fletcher, M., & Plakoyiannaki, E. (2011). Case selection in international business: Key issues and common misconceptions. In R. Piekkari & C. Welch (Eds.),

Rethinking the case study in international business and management research (pp. 171–192). Cheltenham: Edward Elgar.

Fletcher, M., Zhao, Y., Plakoyiannaki, E., & Buck, T. (2018). Three pathways to case selection in international business: A twenty–year review, analysis and synthesis. *International Business Review, 27*(4), 755–766.

Gómez-Mejía, L. R., Campbell, J. T., Martin, G., Hoskisson, R. E., Makri, M., & Sirmon, D. G. (2014). Socioemotional wealth as a mixed gamble: Revisiting family firm R&D investments with the behavioral agency model. *Entrepreneurship Theory and Practice, 38*(6), 1351–1374.

Gómez-Mejía, L. R., Cruz, C., Berrone, P., & De Castro, J. (2011). The bind that ties: Socioemotional wealth preservation in family firms. *Academy of Management Annals, 5*(1), 653–707.

Gómez-Mejía, L. R., Haynes, K. T., Núñez-Nickel, M., Jacobson, K. J., & Moyano-Fuentes, J. (2007). Socioemotional wealth and business risks in family-controlled firms: Evidence from Spanish olive oil mills. *Administrative Science Quarterly, 52*(1), 106–137.

Granovetter, M. (1973). The strength of weak ties. *American Journal of Sociology, 76*(6), 1360–1380.

Graves, C., & Thomas, I. (2006). Internationalization of Australian family businesses: A managerial capabilities perspective. *Family Business Review, 19*(3), 207–224.

Graves, C., & Thomas, J. (2008). Determinants of the internationalization pathways of family firms: An examination of family influence. *Family Business Review, 21*(2), 151–167.

Hennart, J. F., Majocchi, A., & Forlani, E. (2017). The myth of the stay-at-home family firm: How family-managed SMEs can overcome their internationalization limitations. *Journal of International Business Studies, 1*, 1–25.

Hilmersson, M., & Jansson, H. (2012). Reducing uncertainty in the emerging market entry process: On the relationship among international experiential knowledge, institutional distance, and uncertainty. *Journal of International Marketing, 20*(4), 96–110.

Holmen, E., & Pedersen, A. C. (2000). Avoiding triadic reductionism: Serial tetrads–a useful concept for studying connected relationships?. In *Interaction, Relationships and Networks, Proceedings from the 16th IMP Conference*, Bath. Department of Business Studies, Uppsala University.

International Trade Map. (2017). Data derived from. Retrieved December 2017, from https://www.trademap.org/

Jack, S. L. (2010). Approaches to studying networks: Implications and outcomes. *Journal of Business Venturing, 25*(1), 120–137.

Järvensivu, T., & Törnroos, J. Å. (2010). Case study research with moderate constructionism: Conceptualization and practical illustration. *Industrial Marketing Management, 39*(1), 100–108.

Johanson, J., & Mattsson, L.-G. (1988). Internationalization in industrial systems – a network approach. In N. Hood & J.-E. Vahlne (Eds.), *Strategies in global competition* (pp. 303–321). New York: Croom Helm.

Johanson, J., & Vahlne, J. E. (2006). Commitment and opportunity development in the internationalization process: A note on the Uppsala internationalization process model. *Management International Review, 46*(2), 165–178.

Johanson, J., & Vahlne, J. E. (2009). The Uppsala internationalization process model revisited: From liability of foreignness to liability of outsidership. *Journal of International Business Studies, 40*(9), 1411–1431.

Kampouri, K., Plakoyiannaki, E., & Leppäaho, T. (2017). Family business internationalisation and networks: Emerging pathways. *Journal of Business and Industrial Marketing, 32*(3), 1.

Kao, M. S., & Kuo, A. (2017). The effect of uncertainty on FDI entry mode decisions: The influence of family ownership and involvement in the board of directors. *Journal of Family Business Strategy, 8*(4), 224–236.

Kao, M. S., Kuo, A., & Chang, Y. C. (2013). How family control influences FDI entry mode choice. *Journal of Management & Organization, 19*(4), 367–385.

Kauser, S., & Shaw, V. (2004). The influence of behavioural and organizational characteristics on the success of international strategic alliances. *International Marketing Review, 21*(1), 17–52.

Kellermanns, F. W., Dibrell, C., & Cruz, C. (2014). The role and impact of emotions in family business strategy: New approaches and paradigms. *Journal of Family Business Strategy, 5*(3), 277–279.

Kontinen, T., & Ojala, A. (2011a). Network ties in the international opportunity recognition of family SMEs. *International Business Review, 20*(4), 440–453.

Kontinen, T., & Ojala, A. (2011b). Social capital in relation to the foreign market entry and post-entry operations of family SMEs. *Journal of International Entrepreneurship, 9*(2), 133–151.

Kontinen, T., & Ojala, A. (2012). Social capital in the international operations of family SMEs. *Journal of Small Business and Enterprise Development, 19*(1), 39–55.

Kraus, S., Mensching, H., Calabrò, A., Cheng, C. F., & Filser, M. (2016). Family firm internationalization: A configurational approach. *Journal of Business Research, 69*(11), 5473–5478.

Leppäaho, T., & Metsola, J. (2020a). International networking typology, strategies, and paths of family firms. In *Family firm internationalisation* (pp. 73–120). Cham: Palgrave Pivot.

Leppäaho, T., & Metsola, J. (2020b). Conclusions: Implications of family firm internationalisation from a network perspective. In *Family firm internationalisation* (pp. 121–135). Cham: Palgrave Pivot.

Leppäaho, T., Plakoyiannaki, E., & Dimitratos, P. (2016). The case study in family business: An analysis of current research practices and recommendations. *Family Business Review, 29*(2), 159–173.

8 Entry Nodes in Foreign Market Entry and Post-Entry Operations... 263

Martin, G. P., Gomez-Mejia, L. R., & Wiseman, R. M. (2013). Executive stock options as mixed gambles: Revisiting the behavioral agency model. *Academy of Management Journal, 56*(2), 451–472.

Miles, M. B., & Huberman, A. M. (1994). *Qualitative data analysis: An expanded sourcebook*. Thousand Oaks, CA: Sage Publications.

Mohr, J., & Spekman, R. (1994). Characteristics of partnership success: Partnership attributes, communication behavior, and conflict resolution techniques. *Strategic Management Journal, 15*(2), 135–152.

Neubaum, D. O. (2018). Family business research: Roads travelled and the search for unworn paths. *Family Business Review, 31*(3), 259–270.

Patton, M. Q. (1990). *Qualitative evaluation and research methods*. Beverly Hills, CA: Sage Publications.

Pisano, V. (2018). The international entry mode of family-owned enterprises: A socioemotional wealth perspective. *International Journal of Comparative Management, 1*(1), 45–64.

Polkinghorne, D. E. (2005). Language and meaning: Data collection in qualitative research. *Journal of Counseling Psychology, 52*(2), 137.

Pongelli, C., Caroli, M. G., & Cucculelli, M. (2016). Family business going abroad: The effect of family ownership on foreign market entry mode decisions. *Small Business Economics, 47*(3), 787–801.

Poulis, K., Poulis, E., & Plakoyiannaki, E. (2013). The role of context in case study selection: An international business perspective. *International Business Review, 22*(1), 304–314.

Pukall, T. J., & Calabrò, A. (2014). The internationalization of family firms: A critical review and integrative model. *Family Business Review, 27*(2), 103–125.

Reay, T. (2014). Publishing qualitative research. *Family Business Review, 27*, 95–102.

Saldaña, J. (2013). The Coding Manual for Qualitative Researchers. Thousand Oaks,

Sandberg, S. (2013). Emerging market entry node pattern and experiential knowledge of small and medium-sized enterprises. *International Marketing Review, 30*(2), 106–129.

Sandberg, S. (2014). Experiential knowledge antecedents of the SME network node configuration in emerging market business networks. *International Business Review, 23*(1), 20–29.

Scholes, L., Mustafa, M., & Chen, S. (2016). Internationalization of small family firms: The influence of family from a socioemotional wealth perspective. *Thunderbird International Business Review, 58*(2), 131–146.

Sestu, M. C., Majocchi, A., & D'Angelo, A. (2018). Entry mode strategies: Are SMEs any different? In N. Dominguez, & U. Mayrhofer, (Eds.) *Key Success Factors of SME Internationalisation: A Cross-Country Perspective* (chapter 4, 63-68).

Sharma, V. M., & Erramilli, M. K. (2004). Resource-based explanation of entry mode choice. *Journal of Marketing Theory and Practice, 12*(1), 1–18.

Sinkovics, R. R., & Ghauri, P. N. (2008). Enhancing the trustworthiness of qualitative research in international business. *Management International Review, 48*(6), 689–714.

Spiggle, S. (1994). Analysis and interpretation of qualitative data in consumer research. *Journal of Consumer Research, 21*(3), 491–503.

Stieg, P., Cesinger, B., Apfelthaler, G., Kraus, S., & Cheng, C. F. (2018). Antecedents of successful internationalization in family and non-family firms: How knowledge resources and collaboration intensity shape international performance. *Journal of Small Business Strategy, 28*(1), 14–27.

Swinth, R. L., & Vinton, K. L. (1993). Do family-owned businesses have a strategic advantage in international joint ventures? *Family Business Review, 6*(1), 19–30.

Thrasyvoulou, A., & Manikis, J. (1995). Some physicochemical and microscopic characteristics of Greek unifloral honeys. *Apidologie, 26*, 441–452.

Welch, C., Piekkari, R., Plakoyiannaki, E., & Paavilainen-Mäntymäki, E. (2011). Theorising from case studies: Towards a pluralist future for international business research. *Journal of International Business Studies, 42*(5), 740–762.

Wiseman, R. M., & Gomez-Mejia, L. R. (1998). A behavioral agency model of managerial risk taking. *Academy of Management Review, 23*(1), 133–153.

Yin, R. K. (2009). *Case study research: Design and methods.* Thousand Oaks, CA: Sage Publications.

Zellweger, T. M., & Astrachan, J. H. (2008). On the emotional value of owning a firm. *Family Business Review, 21*(4), 347–363.

9

How Do Family Firms Orchestrate Their Global Value Chain?

Francesco Debellis and Emanuela Rondi

Introduction

The current dynamic VUCA (volatility, uncertainty, complexity, ambiguity) context forces firms to re-evaluate their strategies in relation to global operations (Abidi & Joshi, 2018; Buckley, 2019). In this regard, the recent McKinsey Global Institute (Lund et al., 2019) report shows that firms are increasingly compelled to revise the orchestration of their global value chain (GVC). The GVC, that is, "the process by which technology is combined with material and labor inputs, and then processed inputs are assembled, marketed and distributed" (Kogut, 1985, p. 15), is a complex arrangement combining the use of multiple governance types for fine-sliced, disaggregated, and geographically dispersed activities (Coviello, Kano, & Liesch, 2017; Kano,

---

F. Debellis (✉)
Department of Marketing and International Business, University of Vienna, Vienna, Austria

Centre for Family Business Management, Free University of Bozen-Bolzano, Bolzano, Italy
e-mail: francesco.debellis@univie.ac.at

E. Rondi
Centre for Family Business Management, Free University of Bozen-Bolzano, Bolzano, Italy

Department of Management, University of Bergamo, Bergamo, Italy

© The Author(s), under exclusive license to Springer Nature Switzerland AG 2021
T. Leppäaho, S. Jack (eds.), *The Palgrave Handbook of Family Firm Internationalization*,
https://doi.org/10.1007/978-3-030-66737-5_9

2018; Timmer, Erumban, Los, Stehrer, & De Vries, 2014). The Global Factory model that Buckley and Ghauri (2004) developed describes this approach to fine-slicing and managing activities, suggesting that firms should internalize knowledge-intensive activities and outsource operations to minimize the sum of production and contracting costs (Kano, Tsang, & Yeung, 2020; Verbeke & Kano, 2016). This rational cost-driven approach has led many large ownership-dispersed MNEs (e.g. Nike, Apple, Coca Cola) to decouple their intangible and tangible activities by locating the latter in countries with lower manufacturing costs, thereby increasing efficiency and achieving superior financial outcomes.

However, this efficiency logic oriented to profit maximization according to the Global Factory model does not hold for the most diffused business form worldwide: family firms. Indeed, family firms—firms where the owning family substantially influences the decision-making process and strives to transfer the firm across generations (Chua, Chrisman, & Sharma, 1999; De Massis, Kotlar, Chua, & Chrisman, 2014)—have a particularly emotion-dense organizational setting (Kellermanns & Eddleston, 2004; Zellweger & Dehlen, 2012), and are motivated by and committed to their affective endowment (Berrone, Cruz, & Gomez-Mejia, 2012). Hence, family firms pursue a combination of financial and non-financial goals, and their governance is relation-oriented (Gomez-Mejia, Patel, & Zellweger, 2018). Due to these distinctive traits, family firms' international behavior differs from their non-family counterparts (Arregle, Duran, Hitt, & van Essen, 2017; Kontinen & Ojala, 2011).

Despite these critical differences, research has only recently started investigating the idiosyncratic characteristics of family firms' attitude and behavior toward their GVC (Kano et al., 2020), attempting to grasp how they specifically orchestrate their value chain in a global context. In this chapter, we thus aim to respond to the following research question: *How do family firms orchestrate their GVC?* To do so, we revisit the assumptions underlying the Global Factory model in the family business context. Specifically, we adopt a socio-emotional wealth perspective to conceptually unveil the differences between family and non-family firms, building on family firms' intention to preserve their control and influence while taking into account binding social ties. In so doing, we argue that while an efficiency logic oriented toward financial goals alone would suggest internalizing knowledge-intensive activities (Buckley, 2009a, 2009b; Buckley & Ghauri, 2004) and outsourcing all operations to countries with lower manufacturing costs (Mudambi, 2008), family firms are more willing to internalize their activities and externalize only those that cannot be conducted internally. When outsourcing, large ownership-dispersed MNEs usually adopt a captive governance model and exploit their greater power asymmetry, while family firms leverage their internal and external social capital to build a more relational approach based on long-term alliances with their partners. Finally, although seemingly counterproductive in the short term, these choices may lead to highly efficient outcomes beyond mere financial considerations, and greater sustainability in the long term.

Our conceptual investigation offers a threefold contribution to the family firm and international business literature. First, we revisit the Global Factory model, integrating internalization theory (Buckley & Casson, 1976) with socioemotional considerations to determine how family firms design and govern their GVC. In so doing, we contribute to the international business literature by challenging and extending current theory through the specificities of the family firm context (De Massis, Frattini, Majocchi, & Piscitello, 2018; Debellis, Rondi, De Massis & Plakoyiannaki, 2021). Second, we build on the idiosyncratic ability of family firms to develop strong internal social capital (Arregle, Hitt, Sirmon, & Very, 2007; Sharma, 2008), and explore how such relationships and accessible resources can be leveraged to build stronger relationships with international partners, thereby generating inter-organizational social capital. In this endeavor, we corroborate the emerging research stream investigating social capital in internationalization processes (Puthusserry, Child, & Khan, 2019; Zahra, 2018) in terms of breadth—as we frame it in the broader socioemotional wealth perspective—and depth—by disentangling and analyzing its three dimensions. Finally, international business research mostly adopts a transaction cost economics approach based on opportunism, considering recourse to alliances as an alternative to market failure (Reuer, Klijn, van den Bosch, & Volberda, 2011; Williamson, 1975). In adopting a social capital perspective, we challenge the assumption that the success of international strategic partnerships depends only on managing the financial and operational issues, but also relies on their "soft side," that is, developing and managing the relationships in the alliance that in turn facilitate its effective functioning (Debellis, De Massis, Petruzzelli, Frattini, & Del Giudice, 2020). In so doing, we go beyond "what" decisions are made to investigate "why" and "how" family firms engage in internationalization (Reuber, 2016).

GVC and the Global Factory Model

Globalization has led to the increasing disintegration of the GVC through outsourcing non-core manufacturing activities, transforming the global marketplace from the marketing of goods to the marketing of assets (Mudambi, 2013). Gereffi, Humphrey, and Sturgeon (2005) develop a theoretical framework based on three variables to explain GVC governance: the complexity of transactions, the ability to encode transactions, and the capabilities in the supply-base. Kano (2018) enriches this discussion with a transaction cost perspective (Williamson, 1985, 1993), suggesting that an optimal GVC governance system is based on creating an organizational environment that generates new firm-specific advantages and reduces the risks of partners' bounded rationality and bounded reliability. Bounded rationality refers to the limited ability of managers to make optimal decisions due to incomplete information, the limited ability to interpret multiple aspects of information in an international context, and the different assessments of the same information by actors with different backgrounds (Kano, 2018; Verbeke & Yuan, 2005). Bounded reliability instead refers to a scarcity in efforts to make good on open-ended promises, suggesting that economic actors are "intendedly reliable, but only boundedly so" (Kano & Verbeke, 2015, p. 98). A fundamental aspect in this respect is the identity-based discordance between the actors involved, which is likely to emerge between partners in different countries that have limited direct relationships and significant cultural distance (Forsgren, 2016). As a result, several complexities emerge in the design and governance of GVC activities.

Designing the GVC requires choosing what activities to internalize/outsource, where to locate them, and with whom to collaborate. The rational efficiency cost-driven perspective pushes firms to pursue international outsourcing to combine the need to reduce costs and maintain flexibility (Buckley, 2009b). Specifically, decisions regarding GVC governance are explained by the Global Factory model of Buckley and Ghauri (2004). Drawing on internalization theory (Buckley & Casson, 1976), the Global Factory model builds on comparing the relative efficiency of different cross-border governance mechanisms by analyzing the relative costs and benefits of coordinating geographically dispersed activities through vertical integration or recourse to the external market (Buckley & Casson, 1976; Hennart, 1982; Rugman, 1981). According to the Global Factory model, firms should thus focus their main efforts on knowledge-intensive activities, while externalizing operations in different markets (Strange & Humphrey, 2019; Verbeke & Kano, 2016). By externalizing operations, firms can concentrate on their core competences, building their competitive advantage on the complementary resources of strategic partners. In this regard, Mudambi (2008) argues that global value often results in a "smiling curve" of value creation where the activities positioned at the extremes of the curve—that is, knowledge-intensive activities, such as pre-production (e.g. conceptualization, R&D) and post-production (e.g. marketing, after-sales service)—should be largely internalized and located in advanced

9 How Do Family Firms Orchestrate Their Global Value Chain? 269

economies, while those in the middle of the curve should be outsourced to partners in emerging markets. Therefore, the Global Factory model combines internal management and external outsourcing of activities across different locations with the aim of minimizing the production and control costs.

Maintaining control over outsourced activities is crucial for the success or failure of firms (Humprey & Schmitz, 2001; Rondi, Debellis, De Massis, & Garzoni, 2020), a goal that is difficult to achieve through only formal agreements, and even more so when the psychic distance—that is, the distance resulting from the perception of both cultural and business differences (Evans & Mavondo, 2002, p. 517)—between the focal firm and its partners increases (Håkanson, Ambos, Schuster, & Leicht-Deobald, 2016). Buckley and Strange (2011) identify three main complexities related to controlling externalized activities: information costs, that is, the costs of acquiring and transmitting information with strategic partners; coordination costs, that is, the costs of communicating the combined actions of partners; and motivation costs, that is, the costs of supervising and aligning the interests of partners. Therefore, in absence of formal ownership, it becomes difficult to control outsourced activities. For many large ownership-dispersed MNEs, control over externalized activities is exerted through exploiting power asymmetry, making suppliers transactionally dependent and therefore "captive" (Gereffi et al., 2005). In this sense, despite the absence of formal ownership, these MNEs have very high level of monitoring and control over the partner. For instance, Nike is a successful example of how a large ownership-dispersed MNE orchestrates its manufacturing network globally, controlling over 700 factories all over the world and relying on a workforce of roughly 1 million workers (Mudambi & Puck, 2016). In "captive" GVC, suppliers are very dependent on MNEs and kept under control, despite the absence of formal ownership. High power asymmetry combined with the pursuit of financial goals has led many large ownership-dispersed MNEs to literally exploit suppliers and their resources, as shown, for example, in the 1990s' scandals regarding the poor working conditions in contract manufacturing plants and exploiting scarce natural resources at the expense of the local population (Buckley, Doh, & Benischke, 2017). These examples show that GVC governance based on exploitation may engender negative spillovers that undermine the reputation of MNEs worldwide, particularly now that consumers are increasingly sensitive to sustainability issues. To overcome these issues, large ownership-dispersed MNEs, such as Nike, now set their financial goals while paying attention to the health and safety conditions of their suppliers and the environment (Mudambi & Puck, 2016).

From the examination of the current GVC design and governance literature, we identify two assumptions that need to be revised in the family firm context. First, the GVC literature has mainly focused on large MNEs with dispersed ownership, basing the analyses on only financial considerations with regard to GVC orchestration. Second, while large ownership-dispersed MNEs can maintain control over outsourced activities by exploiting their superior legitimacy and power over weaker suppliers, this is not likely to be the case for family firms (De Massis, Frattini, et al., 2018; Eddleston, Jaskiewicz, & Wright, 2019). Indeed, most family firms are motivated by and committed to preserving their socioemotional wealth, thereby also pursuing non-financial goals, and often suffering from financial resource paucity (Carney, 2005), hence not enjoying such power asymmetry. However, the literature remains silent on the mechanisms through which family firms control and make decisions with regard to externalizing operations in developing their GVC (Strange & Humphrey, 2019). Therefore, we seek to understand what drives family firms' decisions in orchestrating their GVC and controlling outsourced activities to foreign partners. By adopting a socioemotional wealth perspective, we consider non-financial goals and family binding social ties as distinctive characteristics that shape family firm GVC design and governance. In so doing, we relax the assumptions underlying the Global Factory model in the context of family firms with important implications for research on international business in general and family firm internationalization in particular.

Family Firm Distinctive Characteristics: Non-financial Goals and Family Social Capital

Family firms are driven by socioemotional considerations, which lead them to frame their decisions differently from their non-family counterparts (Gomez-Mejia et al., 2018; Gomez-Mejia, Haynes, Nuñez-Nickel, Jacobson, & Moyano-Fuentes, 2007). Socioemotional wealth is defined as the firm's non-financial endowment that meets the family's social and affective needs (Gomez-Mejia et al., 2007) and shapes their non-financial goals. The concept of socioemotional wealth can be disentangled into five dimensions (Berrone et al., 2012): (1) family control, that is, the influence the family has on the organization and the goals to preserve (Schulze, Lubatkin, & Dino, 2003; Zellweger, Kellermanns, Chrisman, & Chua, 2012); (2) family identification with the firm, which allows the family to perceive the firm as an extension of its wellbeing (Astrachan, Botero, Astrachan, & Prügl, 2018; Zellweger, Nason,

Nordqvist, & Brush, 2013); (3) binding social ties, that is, kinship ties that generate greater relational trust and commitment to the firm (Arregle et al., 2015; Miller & Le Breton-Miller, 2005); (4) emotional attachment, which refers to the role of values and emotions in the firm (Kellermanns & Eddleston, 2004; Zellweger & Dehlen, 2012); (5) renewal of family bonds, that is, the intention to perpetuate the family values and dynasty through succession (Pongelli, Caroli, & Cucculelli, 2016).

The current literature largely suggests that family owners identify with the firm (Kammerlander, 2016; Kotlar, De Massis, Frattini, & Kammerlander, 2019) and perceive the firm as an extension of the family's wellbeing (Miller & Le Breton-Miller, 2006), especially when the family name is included in the firm's name (De Massis, Kotlar, Mazzola, Minola, & Sciascia, 2018; Deephouse & Jaskiewicz, 2013). This generates psychological appropriation (Kotlar et al., 2019), since over time, the firm becomes part of the owning family's identity (Belk, 1988). Therefore, by pursuing salient non-financial goals, family firms adopt a long-term vision driven by the family's values (Berrone et al., 2012), serving as a reference point in formulating their strategy (Kotlar, De Massis, Fang, & Frattini, 2014; Zahra, 2005). Hence, while non-family firms tend to concentrate on market logic and cost efficiency prescriptions, family firms are driven by their values. In strategic decision-making, family firms face a "mixed gamble" (Alessandri, Cerrato, & Eddleston, 2018; Gomez-Mejia, Neacsu, & Martin, 2019), weighing potential gains and losses from their strategic options in the two non-fungible currencies of financial wealth and socioemotional wealth. Therefore, we contend that the combination of financial and non-financial goals lead family firms to frame their decisions on how to design their GVC (e.g. what activities to internalize/outsource, where to locate them, with whom to develop strategic partnerships) very differently from their non-family counterparts.

Moreover, the presence of the family in the firm engenders binding social ties (Berrone et al., 2012) that are likely to generate a unique bundle of resources with the potential to yield a competitive advantage (Habbershon & Williams, 1999). Given their high emotion-dense organizational setting (Kellermanns & Eddleston, 2004; Zellweger & Dehlen, 2012), stronger social and affective ties are likely to emerge among family firm members (Debellis et al., 2020). Specifically, the intense social interactions at play in family firms, arising from the complex relationships among family members and between family and non-family members, influence the business functioning (Arregle et al., 2017; Gargiulo & Benassi, 2000). The family is simultaneously a source, builder, and user of social capital, "the sum of the actual and potential resources embedded within, available through, and derived from the network of relationships possessed by an individual or social unit" (Nahapiet & Ghoshal, 1998, p. 243), which influences the collective actions in organizations (Bulboz, 2001). Nahapiet and Ghoshal (1998) identify three dimensions of social capital: structural, relational, and cognitive. The structural dimension refers to the configuration of connections among actors, including the presence or absence of network ties and network density. The relational dimension refers to the kind of relationships that actors have developed through past interactions, including trust, norms, sanctions, obligations, and expectations. The cognitive dimension refers to shared representations, interpretations, and systems of meanings among parties, including shared language, codes, values, and beliefs.

Social capital is one of the most distinctive constructs of family firms, since each family firm works as a single entity while involving two forms of social capital: the family's and the firm's (Arregle et al., 2007; Kontinen & Ojala, 2012; Zellweger, Chrisman, Chua, & Steier, 2019). Coherently, scholars have distinguished between family social capital—the relationships and resources among family members (Arregle et al., 2007)—and organizational social capital—the character of social relations and related resources within the firm (Leana & Van Buren, 1999). Family social capital is inimitable or at best imperfectly imitable by non-family firms (Herrero, 2018), and by exerting a significant influence on organizational social capital constitutes a distinctive source of competitive advantage (Arregle et al., 2007). For instance, research has examined the impact of the intertwined relationship between family and organizational social capital on investments in new ventures (Zahra, 2010), innovation (Sanchez-Famoso, Maseda, & Iturralde, 2014), absorptive capacity (Daspit, Long, & Pearson, 2019), information-access and associability (Pearson, Carr, & Shaw, 2008).

Scholars recognize that family social capital leads family firms to behave differently from non-family firms (Hoffman, Hoelscher, & Sorenson, 2006). The strong ties that often bind family members create opportunities to function as a team with informal coordination and information flows that benefit the business (Pearson et al., 2008). Although most research on family firm social capital adopts a family-internal perspective, increasing attention has been dedicated to the influence of family social capital beyond the organizational boundaries (Gedajlovic, Honig, Moore, Payne, & Wright, 2013; Payne, Moore, Griffis, & Autry, 2011). Family firms are found to develop higher social capital in the region where they are located, positively affecting business growth (Baù, Chirico, Pittino, Backman, & Klaesson, 2019) through high local embeddedness, community-level social capital (Lester & Cannella, 2006), and their contribution to the region's social development (Berrone,

Cruz, Gomez-Mejia, & Larraza-Kintana, 2010). Recently, Zahra (2018) highlighted the relevance of social capital beyond local and domestic strategic alliances. Specifically, distinguishing between generalized (relational capital) and restricted (goodwill and reputation) organizational social capital, Zahra (2018) found that family-controlled firms internationalize more than non-family firms when they have technological capabilities and specific (or general) organizational social capital. Therefore, we contend that such distinctive characteristics of family firms differently shape the way they design and govern their GVC compared to their non-family counterparts.

Family Firm Orchestration of the GVC: Design and Governance

Embracing the distinctiveness of socioemotional wealth in family firms, we examine its implications on GVC design and governance. Table 9.1 summarizes the main differences between family and non-family firms in the way they orchestrate GVC in terms of the drivers, design, and governance.

Compared to their non-family counterparts, family firms are more likely to adopt a value-driven approach oriented toward the long-term and based on the family's values. Therefore, we contend that family firms are more likely to internalize their activities than non-family firms, designing vertically integrated GVC mostly located close to the family firm headquarters and relying on local connections in their territory. Under these circumstances, attachment to the local territory and tradition (De Massis, Frattini, Kotlar, Petruzzelli, & Wright, 2016) spurs family firms to opt for less foreign offshoring in order to remain "loyal" to their territory. Due to their close ties with their territory of origin and the identification of the family with the firm, family firms feel more responsible toward their community—within and outside the firm boundaries—and accountable for the quality of their product, hence tending to conduct most production activities internally at the local level, even in

Table 9.1 GVC orchestration of family and non-family firms

	Family firms	Non-family firms
Decision-making drivers	Values	Efficiency
GVC design	High degree of vertical integration	High degree of outsourcing
GVC governance	Relational	Captive

Source: Authors

contrast to the laws of economic efficiency. However, this does not imply underestimating the opportunities of globalization, but interpreting them differently. These firms tend to be oriented toward a global outlet market while preserving production at the local level, so as to maintain the traditions and values handed down from generation to generation as well as control. Moreover, family firms' tendency to develop social capital locally by contributing to social development might also be adopted internationally by contributing to host country development, showing care and long-term interest for the host communities where the non-family employees of partnering family firms live. This approach also pays off financially in the long term (Anderson & Reeb, 2003), whereby the potential tension between preserving the values and international growth gives rise to a paradox that family firms can resolve to the benefit of long-term competitive advantage.

In addition, their value-driven orientation leads family firms to develop partnerships with firms with whom they share similar family values (Sestu & Majocchi, 2018). This implies that the choice of strategic partner, when activities cannot be carried out internally, is based on selection criteria that go beyond mere efficiency assessments. In fact, the objective is to partner with firms with whom they can build strong relationships that are profitable and sustainable for both parties, leading to the development of inter-organizational social capital. In terms of partner selection, the presence of a family in each partner business engenders family as well as internal organizational social capital (Arregle et al., 2007), which becomes a solid platform for the emergence of inter-family firm social capital (Rondi et al., 2020). Therefore, when designing their GVC, family firms are more likely to partner with other family firms with whom they share the motivation and commitment to preserve socioemotional wealth, distinctive elements compared to their non-family counterparts. Hence, we posit:

Proposition 1 *(Non-)family firms are likely to design their GVC by (outsourcing) vertically integrating their operations.*

Regarding the governance of GVC activities, family firms leverage binding social ties to rely less on formal contracting and more on inter-organizational social capital. Family and organizational social capital facilitate information exchange with strategic partners, enhancing cooperation, commitment, and goal alignment (Sundaramurthy, 2008). In particular, when the focal family firm outsources activities to another family firm, the presence of a family in each of the businesses engenders family and organizational social capital, enhancing the intra-partner relationship. Specifically, social capital is a critical

9 How Do Family Firms Orchestrate Their Global Value Chain? 275

source of competitive advantage in the current globalized scenario, with markets consisting of networks of relationships in which firms are embedded and strongly linked (Johanson & Vahlne, 2009). Therefore, relational aspects, such as trust, flexibility, interest alignment, and mutual forbearance, become crucial to guarantee partnership success (Fryxell, Dooley, & Vryza, 2002; Poppo & Zenger, 2002). Following this line of reasoning, social capital is a determinant of the development of relational governance mechanisms that determine the success of GVC control (Enderwick & Buckley, 2017) by limiting information, coordination, and motivation costs.

The longevity and the long-term orientation that often characterize family firms allow families to preserve durable relationships, sometimes across generations, with local stakeholders in the communities where they operate (Arregle et al., 2007). Indeed, moving beyond their local area, their ability to build long-term relationships with external partners has been also identified in franchising strategies (Chirico, Ireland, & Sirmon, 2011). The overlap between the family system and the firm system enables a wider network of relationships that spans the boundaries of the organization, up to the point that binding ties might involve partnering organization. We contend that social capital is crucial for the governance of family firm GVC, more trust-based and long-term oriented control that differs from the more instrumental and formalized control of non-family firms. Although family firms might not always be able to partner with other family firms, we conceptually discuss this as the ideal case for the relational control of GVC. In so doing, we discuss the three dimensions of social capital (structural, relational, and cognitive) by considering partnerships among family firms in the GVC.

Regarding the structural dimension, the network linking partners in the family firm's GVC might include ties between members of different owning families, ties between family members of one firm and non-family members of other firms, and ties among non-family members across organizations. The family's strong identification with and emotional attachment to its business creates an overlap between the two networks of relationships so that inter-organizational connections might also include family members not directly involved in the business (e.g. wife, husband, or offspring who are not active in the firm). The development of ties outside the business allows the family to feel connected beyond instrumental relationships, with implications for the development of trust and inter-organizational closure (Coleman, 1988). Overall, the organizational hierarchy of family firms is likely to influence the development of new connections among non-family members. In particular, when the partnering firm is a family business, the link between the two families at hierarchically higher levels of the business enables developing connections among family members and key non-family firm executives in a cascading reaction that might reach hierarchically lower levels.

On the relational dimension, the development of strong ties, closure, and long-term orientation among family firms leads to the emergence of higher levels of trust critical for GVC control. This relational dimension is pivotal to enhancing cooperation, adaptation, and the development of long-term relations between partners (Debellis et al., 2020). International strategic alliance research shows that relational contracting based on trust is fundamental to alliance success, as it reduces monitoring costs and provides safeguards against opportunistic behavior (Fryxell et al., 2002; Klijn, Reuer, Van den Bosch, & Volberda, 2013). Although psychic distance could undermine the development of trust with foreign partners (Håkanson et al., 2016), owning-families provide the foundations of accepted moral behavior that guides internal cooperation and employee coordination (Bulboz, 2001), thus reducing hazards related to the partner's bounded reliability. When sustained by family members' personal commitment and personalized business relationships (Gedajlovic & Carney, 2010), partnering-owning families might reciprocally identify shared principles that guide their conduct, such as long-term orientation, transgenerational leadership, familial trust, and reciprocity. Such shared principles stimulate the emergence of mutual trust at the inter-family level boosting the development of trust among employees who espouse the internal principles and identify with the family firm. Overall, the set of norms and reciprocal obligations that rule the family firm's internal functioning are reflected in the inter-organizational connections, requiring time to be fine-tuned. However, the low turnover that characterizes family firms also allows trust-based relationships to endure over time.

On the cognitive dimension, while a shared language and vision can be key resources for family firms developed internally from the family roots and instilled in employees through intensive and long-term interactions, its development across family firms collaborating internationally might be problematic. First, before referring to shared narratives, family firms need to build a shared story, in other words, intensive and/or lasting interactions (Chirico & Salvato, 2016). However, in family firms, a shared vision is more likely to emerge from sustainable international collaborations oriented toward the long-term. Mirroring the vision of the owning family, non-family members may also share the vision in terms of their commitment and loyalty toward the family firm, and therefore the strategic alliance. The cognitive dimension of social capital might be more difficult to develop when the psychic distance, shaped by the two countries of origin, is higher. The intervention of cultural brokers (Kwon, Rondi, Levin, De Massis, & Brass, 2020), either members of the organizations or third parties, able to interpret and translate the absorbed information can be crucial to creating shared meanings and representations among the actors (Balachandran & Hernandez, 2018). In this regard, family firms' long-term orientation can benefit their foreign partnerships, allowing them to fine-tune the shared language and norms over time thanks to their lower turnover and stable connections, which in turn become crucial assets for GVC control in the long run.

Even in absence of a family in the foreign partner ownership, family firms' long-term orientation exerts an influence on GVC control, since the lower turnover of the focal family firm allows developing more stable and long-term relationships, with implications on the three social capital dimensions. Moreover, non-family firms supplying a family firm may benefit from its orientation toward non-financial outcomes. Therefore, we propose:

Proposition 2 *(Non-)family firms are likely to adopt a (captive) relational governance of their GVC.*

Discussion

Firms are increasingly called on to compete in the global market, requiring designing and controlling their GVC in terms of which activities to conduct internally or outsource. The Global Factory model suggests establishing relational governance mechanisms to successfully control activities outsourced to foreign partners in the global value chain (Enderwick & Buckley, 2017). However, GVC research has mainly focused on large ownership-dispersed MNEs driven by financial goals with captive control of their value chain. In this study, we relax these assumptions by investigating family firms, organizations committed to preserving their socioemotional wealth, thus driven also by non-financial goals. Therefore, drawing on the socioemotional wealth perspective (Gomez-Mejia et al., 2007), we argue that family firms design and control their GVC in a value-oriented approach. In so doing, we conceptualize that the structural, relational, and cognitive dimensions of family firm social capital developed beyond organizational boundaries lead to relational control over externalized operations, despite the absence of legal ownership, hence requiring lower formal control.

Our study offers three main contributions to the literature on family firm and international strategic alliances. First, by revisiting the assumptions underlying the Global Factory model and contextualizing internalization theory (Buckley & Casson, 1976) to family firms, we pave the way for further investigations of GVC design and control. In this chapter, we adopt a socio-emotional wealth perspective and show that GVC involves various types of social capital embedded in the relationship with family firm stakeholders (Buckley & Strange, 2011). However, international business scholars have mainly taken into account financial considerations, overlooking the importance of the non-financial aspects. Our study aims to advance research in this perspective, acknowledging that the international governance structure of a family firm might not only depend on comparative transaction costs, but requires investigating how the values and relationships with partners affect their ability to control the entire GVC.

Second, prior family firm internationalization research has mainly focused on exports (Debellis et al., 2021; De Massis, Frattini, et al., 2018), which is the most elementary entry mode in foreign markets and exposes the firm to limited risk manageable through contracts. We advance this literature stream by focusing on international partnerships of family firms, which can only be partly governed through contracts and require the combined development of social capital to guarantee long-term success. We thus also contribute to advancing research on social capital in family firms (Arregle et al., 2007; Pearson et al., 2008) by explaining not only how social capital develops within firms, but also how it might be created and developed between different firms for successful international alliances.

Third, the focus of the family firm internationalization literature has tended to be on the input-output relationship, ignoring the processes behind such decisions and the post-decision outcomes (Reuber, 2016). Adopting the socioemotional wealth perspective, we thus advance research going beyond the "what" question by focusing more on "why" and "how" family firms develop their international activities. In this regard, we shed light on the interaction of internal (family and organizational) social capital and external social capital in family firms' strategic alliances relying on the three foundational dimensions thus far not fully explored in the family firm literature. This perspective allows identifying a source of competitive advantage in the involvement of the family in the business, compensating for the potential paucity of resources to formally control partnerships.

Limitations and Future Research Directions

Although our study deepens current understanding of family firm internationalization beyond exports, and complements the financial considerations underlying the Global Factory model, it is not exempt from limitations, which may however open new doors for future research. First, we conceptually theorize family firms' GVC design and control, but do not rely on empirical evidence. We call for future research to explore the development and effects of family firm social capital beyond the boundaries of a single organization, investigating how family firm social capital may help in managing the GVC and how intra-firm social capital is affected by such process. In this regard, embracing a processual perspective could allow to identify the underlying mechanisms through which family firms implement their GVC. In so doing, qualitative methods as multiple case studies or ethnographies are likely to offer the opportunity to directly grasp practices and actions undertaken by family and non-family members in designing and governing their GVC. Furthermore, this line of inquiry might benefit from being temporally contextualized in relation to generational transition, a key process that involves reflections on socioemotional wealth to preserve the legacy of the family in the firm and inter-organizational social capital.

Second, although we have explained the importance of generating social capital with strategic partners and that it is easier to do so with other family firms that share the same family values, a further step would be a more in-depth investigation of supplier selection criteria, how many suppliers family firms rely on, and from where they source (e.g. national or continental vendors). Conceivably, family firms focusing primarily on the quality of relationships aim for a local sourcing strategy, that is, a limited number of suppliers, which allows faster reaction time in case of changes, whereas non-family firms usually opt for a more global sourcing strategy enabling higher bargaining power and cost reduction due to a broader supplier base (Ivanov, Tsipoulanidis, & Schönberger, 2017). We call for further research to shed more light on these neglected aspects by conducting research on large samples, potentially across countries, that considers under which conditions foreign partners operate since contextual aspects as formal and informal institutions are proven crucial in shaping family firms' strategic decisions (Brinkerink & Rondi, 2020).

Third, our conceptualization of social capital focuses on the positive aspects, highlighting only the benefits of this intangible resource for family firm GVC governance. However, social capital may have also a "dark side" and negative implications for social processes, deserving further attention (Gargiulo & Benassi, 1999; Graeff, 2009). For instance, while it is very beneficial for individuals in a firm to develop ties with otherwise disconnected actors to access new resources, an excessively closed network of ties may be inefficient and even detrimental for the organization. We therefore encourage future investigations on whether there is an optimum level of social capital across businesses for GVC control.

Finally, we consider family firms as a homogeneous category that pursues also non-financial goals and can rely on strong internal relationships among their members. However, family firms differ from each other in terms of goals and the relationships might not always be positive (Jaskiewicz & Dyer, 2017). Future research should thus address the issue of the heterogeneity of family firms (Chua, Chrisman, Steier, & Rau, 2012) by taking into account tangible dimensions as ownership and governance but also intangible dimensions. For instance, board composition and ownership dispersion are likely to affect internal social capital and its influence on international partnerships. Furthermore, less tangible aspects as family legacy and tradition might emerge as drivers of their internalization behavior in relation to the orchestration of the GVC. We urge future research to empirically examine the role of social capital and how it affects family firms' internationalization, especially with regard to the development of relational governance mechanisms with foreign strategic partners. This would also contribute to spanning the boundaries of family firm internationalization to other domains, attracting the broader interest of international business scholars and the general management audience.

References

Abidi, S., & Joshi, M. (2018). *The VUCA learner: Future-proof your relevance*. SAGE Publications, Inc.

Alessandri, T. M., Cerrato, D., & Eddleston, K. A. (2018). The mixed gamble of internationalization in family and nonfamily firms: The moderating role of organizational slack. *Global Strategy Journal, 8*, 46–72.

Anderson, R. C., & Reeb, D. M. (2003). Founding-family ownership and firm performance: Evidence from the S&P 500. *The Journal of Finance, 58*, 1301–1328.

Arregle, J. L., Batjargal, B., Hitt, M. A., Webb, J. W., Miller, T., & Tsui, A. S. (2015). Family ties in entrepreneurs' social networks and new venture growth. *Entrepreneurship Theory and Practice, 39*, 313–344.

Arregle, J. L., Duran, P., Hitt, M. A., & van Essen, M. (2017). Why is family firms' internationalization unique? A meta-analysis. *Entrepreneurship Theory and Practice, 41*, 801–831.

Arregle, J. L., Hitt, M. A., Sirmon, D. G., & Very, P. (2007). The development of organizational social capital: Attributes of family firms. *Journal of Management Studies, 44*, 73–95.

Astrachan, C. B., Botero, I., Astrachan, J. H., & Prügl, R. (2018). Branding the family firm: A review, integrative framework proposal, and research agenda. *Journal of Family Business Strategy, 9*, 3–15.

Balachandran, S., & Hernandez, E. (2018). Networks and innovation: Accounting for structural and institutional sources of recombination in brokerage triads. *Organization Science, 29*, 80–99.

Baù, M., Chirico, F., Pittino, D., Backman, M., & Klaesson, J. (2019). Roots to grow: Family firms and local embeddedness in rural and urban contexts. *Entrepreneurship Theory and Practice, 43*, 360–385.

Belk, R. W. (1988). Possessions and the extended self. *Journal of Consumer Research, 15*, 139–168.

Berrone, P., Cruz, C., & Gomez-Mejia, L. R. (2012). Socioemotional wealth in family firms: Theoretical dimensions, assessment approaches, and agenda for future research. *Family Business Review, 25*, 258–279.

Berrone, P., Cruz, C., Gomez-Mejia, L. R., & Larraza-Kintana, M. (2010). Socioemotional wealth and corporate responses to institutional pressures: Do family-controlled firms pollute less? *Administrative Science Quarterly, 55*, 82–113.

Brinkerink, J., & Rondi, E. (2020). When can families fill voids? Firms' reliance on formal and informal institutions in R&D decisions. *Entrepreneurship Theory and Practice*, in press.

Buckley, P. J. (2009a). The impact of the global factory on economic development. *Journal of World Business, 44*, 131–143.

Buckley, P. J. (2009b). Internalisation thinking: From the multinational enterprise to the global factory. *International Business Review, 18*, 224–235.

Buckley, P. J. (2019). The role of international business theory in an uncertain world. In R. V. Tulder, A. Verbeke, & B. Jankowska (Eds.), *International business in a VUCA world: The changing role of states and firms* (Progress in International Business Research, vol. 14) (pp. 23–29). Emerald Publishing Limited.

Buckley, P. J., & Casson, M. (1976). *The future of the multinational enterprise*. Springer.

Buckley, P. J., Doh, J. P., & Benischke, M. H. (2017). Towards a renaissance in international business research? Big questions, grand challenges, and the future of IB scholarship. *Journal of International Business Studies, 48*, 1045–1064.

Buckley, P. J., & Ghauri, P. N. (2004). Globalisation, economic geography and the strategy of multinational enterprises. *Journal of International Business Studies, 35*, 81–98.

Buckley, P. J., & Strange, R. (2011). The governance of the multinational enterprise: Insights from internalization theory. *Journal of Management Studies, 48*, 460–470.

Bulboz, M. (2001). Family as source, user, and builder of social capital. *Journal of Socio-Economics, 30*, 129–131.

Carney, M. (2005). Corporate governance and competitive advantage in family-controlled firms. *Entrepreneurship Theory and Practice, 29*, 249–265.

Chirico, F., Ireland, R. D., & Sirmon, D. G. (2011). Franchising and the family firm: Creating unique sources of advantage through "familiness". *Entrepreneurship Theory and Practice, 35*, 483–501.

Chirico, F., & Salvato, C. (2016). Knowledge internalization and product development in family firms: When relational and affective factors matter. *Entrepreneurship Theory and Practice, 40*, 201–229.

Chua, J. H., Chrisman, J. J., & Sharma, P. (1999). Defining the family business by behavior. *Entrepreneurship Theory and Practice, 23*, 19–39.

Chua, J. H., Chrisman, J. J., Steier, L. P., & Rau, S. B. (2012). Sources of heterogeneity in family firms: An introduction. *Entrepreneurship Theory and Practice, 36*, 1103–1113.

Coleman, J. S. (1988). Social capital in the creation of human capital. *American Journal of Sociology, 94*, S95–S120.

Coviello, N., Kano, L., & Liesch, P. W. (2017). Adapting the Uppsala model to a modern world: Macro-context and microfoundations. *Journal of International Business Studies, 48*, 1151–1164.

Daspit, J. J., Long, R. G., & Pearson, A. W. (2019). How familiness affects innovation outcomes via absorptive capacity: A dynamic capability perspective of the family firm. *Journal of Family Business Strategy, 10*, 133–143.

Debellis, F., De Massis, A., Petruzzelli, A. M., Frattini, F., & Del Giudice, M. (2020). Strategic agility and international joint ventures: The willingness-ability paradox of family firms. *Journal of International Management*, in press.

Deephouse, D. L., & Jaskiewicz, P. (2013). Do family firms have better reputations than non-family firms? An integration of socioemotional wealth and social identity theories. *Journal of Management Studies, 50*, 337–360.

De Massis, A., Frattini, F., Kotlar, J., Petruzzelli, A. M., & Wright, M. (2016). Innovation through tradition: Lessons from innovative family businesses and directions for future research. *Academy of Management Perspectives, 30*, 93–116.

De Massis, A., Frattini, F., Majocchi, A., & Piscitello, L. (2018). Family firms in the global economy: Toward a deeper understanding of internationalization determinants, processes, and outcomes. *Global Strategy Journal, 8*, 3–21.

De Massis, A., Kotlar, J., Chua, J. H., & Chrisman, J. J. (2014). Ability and willingness as sufficiency conditions for family-oriented particularistic behavior: Implications for theory and empirical studies. *Journal of Small Business Management, 52*, 344–364.

De Massis, A., Kotlar, J., Mazzola, P., Minola, T., & Sciascia, S. (2018). Conflicting selves: Family owners' multiple goals and self-control agency problems in private firms. *Entrepreneurship Theory and Practice, 42*, 362–389.

Debellis, F., Rondi, E., Plakoyiannaki, E., & De Massis, A. (2021). Riding the waves of family firm internationalization: A systematic literature review, integrative framework, and research agenda. *Journal of World Business, 56*(1), 101–144.

Eddleston, K. A., Jaskiewicz, P., & Wright, M. (2019). Family firms and internationalization in the Asia-Pacific: The need for multi-level perspectives. *Asia Pacific Journal of Management, 37*, 345–361

Enderwick, P., & Buckley, P. J. (2017). Beyond supply and assembly relations: Collaborative innovation in global factory systems. *Journal of Business Research, 103*, 547–556.

Evans, J., & Mavondo, F. T. (2002). Psychic distance and organizational performance: An empirical examination of international retailing operations. *Journal of International Business Studies, 33*, 515–532.

Forsgren, M. (2016). A note on the revisited Uppsala internationalization process model—The implications of business networks and entrepreneurship. *Journal of International Business Studies, 47*, 1135–1144.

Fryxell, G. E., Dooley, R. S., & Vryza, M. (2002). After the ink dries: The interaction of trust and control in US-based international joint ventures. *Journal of Management Studies, 39*, 865–886.

Gargiulo, M., & Benassi, M. (1999). *The dark side of social capital, corporate social capital and liability* (pp. 298–322). Springer.

Gargiulo, M., & Benassi, M. (2000). Trapped in your own net? Network cohesion, structural holes, and the adaptation of social capital. *Organization Science, 11*, 183–196.

Gedajlovic, E., & Carney, M. (2010). Markets, hierarchies, and families: Toward a transaction cost theory of the family firm. *Entrepreneurship Theory and Practice, 34*, 1145–1172.

Gedajlovic, E., Honig, B., Moore, C. B., Payne, G. T., & Wright, M. (2013). Social capital and entrepreneurship: A schema and research agenda. *Entrepreneurship Theory and Practice, 37*, 455–478.

Gereffi, G., Humphrey, J., & Sturgeon, T. (2005). The governance of global value chains. *Review of International Political Economy, 12*, 78–104.

Gomez-Mejia, L. R., Haynes, K. T., Nuñez-Nickel, M., Jacobson, K. J., & Moyano-Fuentes, J. (2007). Socioemotional wealth and business risks in family-controlled firms: Evidence from Spanish olive oil mills. *Administrative Science Quarterly, 52*, 106–137.

Gomez-Mejia, L. R., Neacsu, I., & Martin, G. (2019). CEO risk-taking and socioemotional wealth: The behavioral agency model, family control, and CEO option wealth. *Journal of Management, 45*, 1713–1738.

Gomez-Mejia, L. R., Patel, P. C., & Zellweger, T. M. (2018). In the horns of the dilemma: Socioemotional wealth, financial wealth, and acquisitions in family firms. *Journal of Management, 44*, 1369–1397.

Graeff, P. (2009). Social capital: The dark side. In G. T. Svendsen & G. L. H. Svendsen (Eds.), *Handbook of social capital* (pp. 143–161). Edward Elgar.

Habbershon, T. G., & Williams, M. L. (1999). A resource-based framework for assessing the strategic advantages of family firms. *Family Business Review, 12*, 1–25.

Håkanson, L., Ambos, B., Schuster, A., & Leicht-Deobald, U. (2016). The psychology of psychic distance: Antecedents of asymmetric perceptions. *Journal of World Business, 51*, 308–318.

Hennart, J.-F. (1982). *A theory of multinational enterprise*. Ann Arbor, MI: University of Michigan Press.

Herrero, I. (2018). How familial is family social capital? Analyzing bonding social capital in family and nonfamily firms. *Family Business Review, 31*, 441–459.

Hoffman, J., Hoelscher, M., & Sorenson, R. (2006). Achieving sustained competitive advantage: A family capital theory. *Family Business Review, 19*, 135–145.

Humprey, J., & Schmitz, H. (2001). Governance in global value chains. *IDS Bulletin, 32*(3), 19–29.

Ivanov, D., Tsipoulanidis, A., & Schönberger, J. (2017). *Global supply chain and operations management: A decision-oriented introduction to the creation of value*. Springer.

Jaskiewicz, P., & Dyer, W. G. (2017). Addressing the elephant in the room: Disentangling family heterogeneity to advance family business research. *Family Business Review, 30*, 111–118.

Johanson, J., & Vahlne, J.-E. (2009). The Uppsala internationalization process model revisited: From liability of foreignness to liability of outsidership. *Journal of International Business Studies, 40*, 1411–1431.

Kammerlander, N. (2016). 'I want this firm to be in good hands': Emotional pricing of resigning entrepreneurs. *International Small Business Journal, 34*, 189–214.

Kano, L. (2018). Global value chain governance: A relational perspective. *Journal of International Business Studies, 49*, 684–705.

Kano, L., Tsang, E. W., & Yeung, H. W. C. (2020). Global value chains: A review of the multi-disciplinary literature. *Journal of International Business Studies, 51*, 577–622.

Kano, L., & Verbeke, A. (2015). The three faces of bounded reliability: Alfred Chandler and the micro-foundations of management theory. *California Management Review, 58*, 97–122.

Kellermanns, F. W., & Eddleston, K. A. (2004). Feuding families: When conflict does a family firm good. *Entrepreneurship Theory and Practice, 28*, 209–228.

Klijn, E., Reuer, J. J., Van den Bosch, F. A. J., & Volberda, H. W. (2013). Performance implications of IJV Boards: A contingency perspective. *Journal of Management Studies, 50*, 1245–1266.

Kogut, B. (1985). Designing global strategies: Comparative and competitive value-added chains. *Sloan Management Review, 26*, 15.

Kontinen, T., & Ojala, A. (2011). Network ties in the international opportunity recognition of family SMEs. *International Business Review, 20*(4), 440–453.

Kontinen, T., & Ojala, A. (2012). Social capital in the international operations of family SMEs. *Journal of Small Business and Enterprise Development, 19*(1), 39–55.

Kotlar, J., De Massis, A., Fang, H., & Frattini, F. (2014). Strategic reference points in family firms. *Small Business Economics, 43*, 597–619.

Kotlar, J., De Massis, A., Frattini, F., & Kammerlander, N. (2019). Motivation gaps and implementation traps: The paradoxical and time-varying effects of family ownership on firm absorptive capacity. *Journal of Product Innovation Management, 37*(1), 2–25.

Kwon, S. W., Rondi, E., Levin, D. Z., De Massis, A., & Brass, D. J. (2020). Network brokerage: An integrative review and future research agenda. *Journal of Management*, in press.

Leana III, C. R., & Van Buren, H. J. (1999). Organizational social capital and employment practices. *Academy of Management Review, 24*, 538–555.

Lester, R. H., & Cannella Jr., A. A. (2006). Interorganizational familiness: How family firms use interlocking directorates to build community–level social capital. *Entrepreneurship Theory and Practice, 30*(6), 755–775.

Lund, S., Manyika, J., Woetzel, J., Bughin, J., Krishnan, M., Seong, J., et al. (2019). *Globalization in transition: The future of trade and value chains*. McKinsey Global Institute.

Miller, D., & Le Breton-Miller, I. (2005). Management insights from great and struggling family businesses. *Long Range Planning, 38*, 517–530.

Miller, D., & Le Breton-Miller, I. (2006). Family governance and firm performance: Agency, stewardship, and capabilities. *Family Business Review, 19*, 73–87.

Mudambi, R. (2008). Location, control and innovation in knowledge-intensive industries. *Journal of Economic Geography, 8*, 699–725.

Mudambi, R. (2013). Flatness: The global disaggregation of value creation. In G. Cook & J. Johns (Eds.), *The changing geography of international business* (pp. 9–16). Palgrave Macmillan.

Mudambi, R., & Puck, J. (2016). A global value chain analysis of the 'regional strategy' perspective. *Journal of Management Studies, 53*, 1076–1093.

Nahapiet, J., & Ghoshal, S. (1998). Social capital, intellectual capital, and the organizational advantage. *Academy of Management Review, 23*, 242–266.

Payne, G. T., Moore, C. B., Griffis, S. E., & Autry, C. W. (2011). Multilevel challenges and opportunities in social capital research. *Journal of Management, 37*, 491–520.

Pearson, A. W., Carr, J. C., & Shaw, J. C. (2008). Toward a theory of familiness: A social capital perspective. *Entrepreneurship Theory and Practice, 32*, 949–969.

Pongelli, C., Caroli, M. G., & Cucculelli, M. (2016). Family business going abroad: The effect of family ownership on foreign market entry mode decisions. *Small Business Economics, 47*, 787–801.

Poppo, L., & Zenger, T. (2002). Do formal contracts and relational governance function as substitutes or complements? *Strategic Management Journal, 23*, 707–725.

Puthusserry, P., Child, J., & Khan, Z. (2019). Social capital development through the stages of internationalization: Relations between British and Indian SMEs. *Global Strategy Journal, 10*(2), 282–308.

Reuber, A. R. (2016). An assemblage-theoretic perspective on the internationalization processes of family firms. *Entrepreneurship Theory and Practice, 40*, 1269–1286.

Reuer, J. J., Klijn, E., van den Bosch, F. A., & Volberda, H. W. (2011). Bringing corporate governance to international joint ventures. *Global Strategy Journal, 1*, 54–66.

Rondi, E., Debellis, F., De Massis, A., & Garzoni, A. (2020). Bonding and bridging social capital in family firm internationalization. *Sinergie Italian Journal of Management*, in press.

Rugman, A. (1981). *Inside the multinationals: The economics of the multinational enterprise.* New York City: Columbia University Press.

Sanchez-Famoso, V., Maseda, A., & Iturralde, T. (2014). The role of internal social capital in organisational innovation. An empirical study of family firms. *European Management Journal, 32*, 950–962.

Schulze, W. S., Lubatkin, M. H., & Dino, R. N. (2003). Toward a theory of agency and altruism in family firms. *Journal of Business Venturing, 18*, 473–490.

Sestu, M. C., & Majocchi, A. (2018). Family firms and the choice between wholly owned subsidiaries and joint ventures: A transaction costs perspective. *Entrepreneurship Theory and Practice, 44*(2), 211–232

Sharma, P. (2008). Commentary: Familiness: Capital stocks and flows between family and business. *Entrepreneurship Theory and Practice, 32*, 971–977.

Strange, R., & Humphrey, J. (2019). What lies between market and hierarchy? Insights from internalization theory and global value chain theory. *Journal of International Business Studies, 50*, 1401–1413.

Sundaramurthy, C. (2008). Sustaining trust within family businesses. *Family Business Review, 21*, 89–102.

Timmer, M. P., Erumban, A. A., Los, B., Stehrer, R., & De Vries, G. J. (2014). Slicing up global value chains. *Journal of Economic Perspectives, 28*(2), 99–118.

Verbeke, A., & Kano, L. (2016). An internalization theory perspective on the global and regional strategies of multinational enterprises. *Journal of World Business, 51*, 83–92.

Verbeke, A., & Yuan, W. (2005). Subsidiary autonomous activities in multinational enterprises: A transaction cost perspective. *Management International Review, 45*, 31–52.

Williamson, O. E. (1975). *Markets and hierarchies: Analysis and antitrust implications.* New York: Free Press.

Williamson, O. E. (1985). *The economic institutions of capitalism: Firms, markets, relational contracting.* New York: Free Press.

Williamson, O. E. (1993). Transaction cost economics and organization theory. *Industrial and Corporate Change, 2*, 107–156.

Zahra, S. A. (2005). Entrepreneurial risk taking in family firms. *Family Business Review, 18*(1), 23–40.

Zahra, S. A. (2010). Harvesting family firms' organizational social capital: A relational perspective. *Journal of Management Studies, 47*, 345–366.

Zahra, S. A. (2018). Technological capabilities and international expansion: The moderating role of family and non-family firms' social capital. *Asia Pacific Journal of Management, 37*(1), 391–415.

Zellweger, T. M., Chrisman, J. J., Chua, J. H., & Steier, L. P. (2019). *Social structures, social relationships, and family firms*. Los Angeles, CA: Sage Publications Sage CA.

Zellweger, T. M., & Dehlen, T. (2012). Value is in the eye of the owner: Affect infusion and socioemotional wealth among family firm owners. *Family Business Review, 25*, 280–297.

Zellweger, T. M., Kellermanns, F. W., Chrisman, J. J., & Chua, J. H. (2012). Family control and family firm valuation by family CEOs: The importance of intentions for transgenerational control. *Organization Science, 23*, 851–868.

Zellweger, T. M., Nason, R. S., Nordqvist, M., & Brush, C. G. (2013). Why do family firms strive for nonfinancial goals? An organizational identity perspective. *Entrepreneurship Theory and Practice, 37*, 229–248.

10

Coexistence of Economic and Noneconomic Goals in Building Foreign Partner Relationships: Evidence from Small Finnish Family Firms

Jaakko Metsola

Introduction

Socioemotional wealth (SEW), the set of noneconomic and affective endowments that *family firms* (FFs) aim at preserving, 'is the defining feature of a family business [...] central, enduring, and unique to the dominant family owner, influencing everything the firm does' (Gomez-Mejia, Cruz, Berrone, & De Castro, 2011, p. 692). Consisting of dimensions such as family control and emotional attachment (Berrone, Cruz, & Gomez-Mejia, 2012), SEW is central to the strategic decision-making of FFs (e.g. Chrisman & Patel, 2012). Since initialising and intensifying *internationalisation* is highly strategic, due to threats and opportunities related to the process, the pursuit of SEW preservation might overshadow economically viable international goals and restrain internationalisation (Fang, Kotlar, Memili, Chrisman, & De Massis, 2018; Gomez-Mejia, Makri, & Kintana, 2010). However, some argue that economic and noneconomic SEW goals can coexist, for example, when FFs form collaborative relationships with foreign network partners (Cesinger et al., 2016; Kraus, Mensching, Calabro, Cheng, & Filser, 2016).

This mixed gamble of economic and noneconomic trade-offs in the internationalisation of FFs has gained increasing attention from research (e.g. Alessandri, Cerrato, & Eddleston, 2018) but with no consensual findings.

J. Metsola (✉)
LUT University, Lappeenranta, Finland
e-mail: jaakko.metsola@lut.fi

© The Author(s), under exclusive license to Springer Nature Switzerland AG 2021
T. Leppäaho, S. Jack (eds.), *The Palgrave Handbook of Family Firm Internationalization*,
https://doi.org/10.1007/978-3-030-66737-5_10

Most studies argue for the negative impact of SEW (e.g. Sánchez-Bueno & Usero, 2014; Yang, Lee, Stanley, Kellermans, & Li, 2020), but some argue for its possible positive impact (e.g. Kraus et al., 2016). Based on the review of 172 empirical FF internationalisation studies, Metsola, Leppäaho, Paavilainen-Mäntymäki, and Plakoyiannaki (2020) found that SEW-related factors tend to be liabilities in the early stages of internationalisation processes, but can be offset by or turned into capabilities in the later stages, provided that mitigation of the so-called bifurcation-biased preference for family assets (Kano & Verbeke, 2018) and adoption of economic-goal orientations occur alongside noneconomic orientations.

Since (i) network relationships are essentially social (Granovetter, 1985) and (ii) SEW manifests itself strongly in internal and external social relationships, for example, via family owners' and managers' use of family resources and decision-making power (Zellweger, Chrisman, Chua, & Steier, 2019), the pathway to understanding the role of SEW in internationalisation might reside in studying foreign partner relationships (FPRs). The concept of FPR, constructed here with reference to relationship marketing literature (e.g. Grönroos, 1990; Johnson & Selnes, 2004), may define the Business-to-business (B2B) relationships of small FFs to foreign agents, distributors and subsidiaries, which conduct selling activities in host countries and which FFs' SEW-preservation activities might influence, due to their strategic and relational importance to the FFs.

Thus, small firms often depend on external relationships (or, more explicitly, partner relationships) to complement their limitations on resources for internationalisation (e.g. Buciuni & Mola, 2014; Chetty & Holm, 2000). Also, due to their size and closer interaction with family owners, managers and nonfamily employees, *small FFs* are more likely than larger FFs to preserve different SEW dimensions in their strategies and operations (Gomez-Mejia et al., 2011; Le Breton-Miller & Miller, 2013). Accordingly, this study focuses on the FPRs of small FFs. Moreover, with the strong influence of family members in the firm via ownership and management positions, *family-controlled* FFs are more likely to embody SEW preservation than *family-influenced* FFs in which family members have weaker decision-making power (e.g. Berrone et al., 2012). However, these considerations have received limited study in the context of internationalisation and international networking (e.g. Scholes, Mustafa, & Chen, 2016). Given that small- and medium-sized enterprises (SME), and especially micro and small firms, are mostly family businesses in Europe (European Commission, 2009) and globally (Hennart, Majocchi, & Forlani, 2019), studying how these FFs can capitalise on international markets amid noneconomic (SEW) and economic goal orientations is also societally important.

Thus, this study aims to answer the following research question via a multiple-case study of eight Finnish FFs: *Considering that small FFs consider SEW in their internationalisation decisions and activities, how do small FFs either confine or utilise SEW in foreign partner relationships (FPRs)?* Based on the literature, the internationalisation of small FFs anticipates SEW's presence. But understanding whether and *how* SEW and its dimensions manifest in FFs and, possibly, in FPR activities requires further in-depth analysis. For that purpose, this paper qualitatively measures and conducts different SEW profiles, based on the dimensions of Berrone et al.'s (2012) FIBER-scale that aims at indicating the real-life importance and manifestations of SEW to the case firms, their relationship dynamics and decision-making (Berrone et al., 2012; Eisenhardt & Graebner, 2007; Yin, 1994).

The analysis reveals that small FFs with at least a moderate level of SEW were more active in building close FPRs than those with SEW below a moderate level. All the case firms with at least a moderate level of SEW aimed at familial FPR relationships, even to the point of including other FFs as foreign partners. Also, they often leveraged the attributes of SEW through the deliberate promotion of FF status and related image factors (e.g. trust, long-term orientation, agile decision-making) in international marketing and relationship-building. However, leveraging SEW attributes from different SEW dimensions in active and close FPR-building also requires concurrent awareness and implementation of economic goals, with pragmatic and financially oriented international sales and marketing activities. Thus, noneconomic SEW and economic goal pursuits coexist and interact; fruitful FPRs can leverage SEW to benefit internationalisation, and economic goals that internationalisation achieves can, in turn, help maintain SEW. Accordingly, SEW acts as both a means and an end for active international networking and internationalisation.

The findings not only elaborate our understanding of how SEW may manifest through binding and trustworthy social ties in internationalisation (Cesinger et al., 2016; Scholes et al., 2016). They also extend that knowledge by describing how FFs behave in those relationships to maintain the pursuit of both noneconomic and economic goals. Rather than a restraint on internationalisation, which earlier FF internationalisation literature largely concluded (e.g. Gomez-Mejia et al., 2010; Sánchez-Bueno & Usero, 2014), SEW can represent an asset that small FFs can derive from various SEW dimensions for successful and sustainable FPRs. Active FPR-building may be a 'must' for small FFs with high SEW-preservation goals. By actively incorporating the

292   J. Metsola

foreign partners within 'the scope of SEW preservation' and building 'an extended international family' with them, small FFs may successfully pursue economic as well as noneconomic SEW goals. The novel way to assess different SEW profiles qualitatively serves as an important reflection point for understanding FFs' FPR activities from a SEW perspective. Thus far, FF internationalisation literature has mainly discussed the effect of SEW on internationalisation through general-level association with family control and its idiosyncrasies, such as risk aversion, without elaborating the role of different FIBER-scale dimensions in the effect (e.g. Alessandri et al., 2018; Cesinger et al., 2016; Stieg, Cesinger, Apfelthaler, Kraus, & Cheng, 2018).

The paper proceeds as follows. First discussed is the theoretical background on networking and SEW, in the context of internationalisation and small FFs, including the theoretical framework of the study. Second is a detailed explanation of the study's methodology. Then, the findings are presented by focusing on the SEW profiles and FPR-building activities of the case firms, including also the theoretical framework updated with key findings. Finally, the relevance and contributions of the findings appear in the discussion section, encapsulated into three propositions, and the final conclusions section summarises the paper, emphasising key managerial and research implications.

Theoretical Background

International Networking of Small FFs

Internationalisation is often a necessary strategy for small firms, especially those from such small and open economies as in the Scandinavian countries (Bell, 1995), so they can compete against larger competitors and seek revenues from abroad. Successful internationalisation involves processes of initiating, developing and maintaining foreign network relationships (Johanson & Mattsson, 1988) in such a way that involvement in and learning from these relationships enable firms to avoid 'liability of outsidership' (Johanson & Vahlne, 2009). Small firms often have limited resources for starting internationalisation that emphasises the significance of cross-border relationships and networks in compensating for resource limitations (Buciuni & Mola, 2014; Eberhard & Craig, 2013). Earlier research found that despite such limitations, active networking (i.e. the firm taking initiative and being entrepreneurial in approaching potential partners and customers, see Johanson &

Mattsson, 1988) has benefitted small-firm internationalisation, for example, in terms of international knowledge acquisition and market entry to new locations (Chetty & Holm, 2000; Gabrielsson, Kirpalani, Dimitratos, Solberg, & Zucchella, 2008; Loane & Bell, 2006).

Research indicates that small FFs pose a special group, in their attitudes towards and behaviour in international networking. Categorising network relationships according to their strength, that is, the extent to which time, emotional intensity, intimacy and reciprocity define the relationships (Granovetter, 1973), small FFs tend to value all of these dimensions and seek strong relationships with their foreign partners and customers (e.g. Kontinen & Ojala, 2012; Mitter & Emprechtinger, 2016). Strong relationships are close and trust-based, with mutual respect and commitment between the parties, whereas weak relationships are more superficial, with less trust and emotional closeness, due to lack of knowledge about each other in the relationship (Söderqvist & Chetty, 2013). Pursuing strong relationships encompasses both positive and negative implications for the internationalisation of small FFs. On one hand, the tendency of small FFs to spend time and resources to find suitable and trustworthy foreign partners and promote strong bonding relationships with a small number of such partners might lead them to miss out on potential international opportunities (Kontinen & Ojala, 2012; Leppäaho & Pajunen, 2018). Distrust of outsiders might make small FFs prefer family members to conduct cross-border operations, in host countries as well, constraining the development of resources and external networks for moving from an export-based and narrowly focused market scope to joint ventures and different markets (Scholes et al., 2016). Orientation towards and confidence in strong relationships and resources found within the family can hinder internationalisation efforts. Weaker relationships that the FF could access relatively quickly, without extensive investments, could provide valuable resources and indirect ties to facilitate internationalisation (Oviatt & McDougall, 2005).

On the other hand, small FFs' pursuit of strong relationships might pay off in certain situations. Small FFs tend to establish relationships, joint ventures and alliances with other FFs in foreign countries. Relationships among FFs with similar values (such as trust, loyalty and a long-term orientation) enhance cross-cultural bridging and facilitate internationalisation (Fernandez & Nieto, 2005; Gallo & Pont, 1996; Swinth & Vinton, 1993). Overall, a network of organisations sharing common interests provides mutual benefits and encourages a long-term relationship (Johanson & Mattsson, 1988; Johanson & Vahlne, 2003). Although risk aversion and resource constraints lead to a cautious and gradual internationalisation process in small FFs, stewardship and long-term orientations behind cautious strategies, careful selection of trustworthy foreign partners and concern for local employees enable sustainable internationalisation with opportunities for long-term competitive advantages (Mitter & Emprechtinger, 2016). Small FFs' international success might reside in mutually beneficial relationships with foreign partners and customers (Mitter & Emprechtinger, 2016). Hennart et al. (2019) argue that small FFs' ability to create strong customer and partner relationships is particularly beneficial in global niches of high-quality products, whose demanding customers require the attributes that small FFs inherently possess: trust, long-term orientation and high levels of social capital, consistently present from internal family relationships to external business relationships.

Indeed, Leppäaho and Metsola (2020) find that both types of international-networking actors that small FFs might become—that is, narrow network maximisers (NNMs) and broad network enablers (BNEs)—can result in successful internationalisation. NNMs rely on regional or global network relationships that are few but strong, with a long-term perspective, enabling sustainable international business (IB). BNEs utilise an extensive network with relationships of varying strength and an agile approach to modifying and expanding the network globally, enabling both fast-growing IB and good risk management. However, both networking strategies must reflect the firm's internal resources and capabilities (e.g. management's IB skills, financial preparedness and risk tolerance) and the compatibility of the firm's product and international market potential (e.g. profitability of internationalisation, extent of international demand for the product). Arguably, one key FF-specific factor in the formation and development of small FFs' network relationships could be socioemotional wealth (SEW).

Socioemotional Wealth as a Liability and a Capability in Strong Network Relationships

According to the SEW perspective, FFs' pursuit of noneconomic rewards may result in economically irrational decision-making, with a reluctance to join cooperatives or avoidance of diversification (Cruz, Gómez-Mejia, & Becerra, 2010; Gomez-Mejia et al., 2010; Gomez-Mejia, Haynes, Núñez-Nickel, Jacobson, & Moyano-Fuentes, 2007). If and when FFs establish foreign network relationships, their tendency to deepen and maintain long-term relationships with existing partners and with other FFs might have an association with the tendency towards SEW preservation (Pukall & Calabrò, 2014). The five dimensions of SEW—the so-called FIBER-scale (*Family control and* *influence, family members' **I**dentification with the firm, **B**inding social ties, **E**motional attachment and **R**enewal of family bonds to the firm through dynastic succession)*—that Berrone et al. (2012) suggest, encompass togetherness and longevity. Accordingly, this paper follows the definitions of strong and weak relationships from Granovetter (1973) and Söderqvist and Chetty (2013), in light of the close relation of elements of SEW to the elements these authors propose for relationships (i.e. time/commitment, emotional intensity/closeness, intimacy, reciprocity, trust). The interrelations of SEW and foreign partner relationships (FPRs) in the context of internationalisation can yield more valid analyses.

The fear of losing SEW may inhibit internationalisation through risk aversion and inward-looking attitudes, but it can also have enhancing effects, including the enhancement of stewardship and, thereby, a long-term orientation towards sustainable internationalisation (Patel, Pieper, & Hair Jr, 2012). After a firm goes international, SEW may remain well preserved, despite the expectation that internationalisation would reduce SEW (Fang et al., 2018; Gomez-Mejia et al., 2010). Kraus et al. (2016) discuss this paradox, considering different internationalisation configurations for FFs with different SEW levels. In one such configuration, high levels of internationalisation resulted from a combination of high SEW endowment and the presence of nonfamily ownership or a nonfamily CEO, plus a wide international network. The FFs' orientation could explain its success, in the sense that they did not regard this 'external involvement' as detrimental to SEW. On the contrary, they viewed it as an opportunity to achieve SEW gains by involving parties from whom they could learn and with whom they could execute strategic internationalisation, achieving both economic and noneconomic goals (Kraus et al., 2016).

Such information on the role and effect of SEW in FFs' international networking (and internationalisation in general) only scratches the surface. In other words, we have little evidence of (i) how family members in FFs feel about SEW and its various dimensions, and (ii) how these conceptions manifest themselves in FF internationalisation at a grassroots level. Arguably, one major reason for this gap could be the lack of using SEW measurement scales or the static use of SEW as a general-level umbrella term for FF behaviour without putting it into practice (see Miller & Le Breton-Miller, 2014). As the five dimensions of SEW (Berrone et al., 2012) show, it is nowhere near being a static concept. It evolves over time and generations, with different conceptions and effects in different kinds of FFs with various types of family members, under different circumstances. Prioritising SEW goals over economic goals is a 'mixed gamble', with various kinds of FFs with different ownership and management structures and diverse views on the balance (Alessandri et al., 2018). Older generations may incline more towards preserving SEW and, thus, resisting internationalisation decisions, while newer generations may have a greater propensity to internationalise (Fang et al., 2018).

As indicated earlier, SEW and its different dimensions manifest themselves in relationships. The effects of SEW might be especially strong in FFs with high levels of family control, that is, strong ownership and involvement in management (Kotlar, Signori, De Massis, & Vismara, 2018; Zellweger, Kellermanns, Chrisman, & Chua, 2012). The controlling family's structural, cognitive and relational embeddedness in the business influence its norms, principles and social relationships (Bird & Zellweger, 2018; Zellweger et al., 2019). Relationships are essentially social, unifying the parties around shared goal setting and achievement (Granovetter, 1985; Johanson & Vahlne, 2009). The controlling family's presence and decision-making power intertwine social relationships within FFs, among its family and nonfamily members and even external stakeholders, affecting the use of firm resources and achievement of economic and noneconomic goals (Zellweger et al., 2019). Arguably, the effect of the controlling family on the realisation of SEW goals via social relationships would have more effect in smaller firms, as the smaller number of employees and external stakeholders enables closer relationship-building. In general, the role of SEW as a primary reference point in managerial decision-making decreases as the FF size increases (Gomez-Mejia et al., 2011). This is apparent in such situations as larger FFs' willingness to join cooperatives (Gomez-Mejia et al., 2007); yet, no clear evidence of dimension-specific manifestations in the context of international networking exists.

Accordingly, this paper aims to take an abductive approach to studying a narrow group of small, highly family-controlled firms and their SEW and FPRs (e.g. foreign agent and distributor relationships) to unravel the dynamics between them. Figure 10.1 depicts the theoretical framework of the present study, which hypothesises the interaction of noneconomic (SEW) and

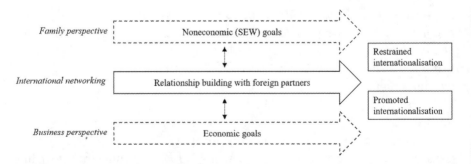

Fig. 10.1 Theoretical framework of the study. (Source: Author)

economic goals with the relationship-building with foreign partners. The nature and activity of FPR-building that noneconomic and economic goal orientations influence are likely to indicate internationalisation that is either restrained (passive FPR-building with narrow and strong relationships, focus on noneconomic goals and strong SEW preservation) or promoted (active FPR-building with broad and weak relationships, focus on economic goals and weaker SEW preservation).

Methodology

Case studies form linkages between phenomena and their context and can identify different relationship patterns (Eisenhardt, 1989; Eisenhardt & Graebner, 2007; Piekkari, Welch, & Paavilainen, 2009; Yin, 1994). Thus, the case-study method is suitable for studying the complex processes that occur when small FFs, with different levels of SEW, build FPRs. Berrone et al. (2012), the developers of the FIBER-scale for measuring SEW, brought up case studies as informative ways to unravel the nature of SEW in certain situations and when the level of family control varies. The ability of case studies to grasp the real-world environment is important for understanding SEW, because the social environment, family and business become closely intertwined in FFs (Berrone, Cruz, Gomez-Mejia, & Larraza-Kintana, 2010). In general, qualitative research is especially effective for theory-building in FF research, as 'it can provide important insights into otherwise hidden interactions between family and business' (Reay, 2014, p. 7). Also, FF-internationalisation literature considering SEW has used it mainly as a background theory, rather than as a measured variable incorporated into the analysis (e.g. Cesinger et al., 2016). Thus, it was natural to choose the case-study method and utilise its opportunities for an in-depth and relational understanding of SEW and international networking. Reay (2014) calls for qualitative researchers to show and tell empirical and theoretical stories, the reason that this paper aims to bring SEW from general-level theoretical assumptions to more concrete, empirically grounded pieces of evidence—namely, by constructing interview-based 'SEW profiles' and connecting them to the FFs' behaviour in building FPRs, thereby maintaining economic and noneconomic goals in internationalisation.

As the theoretical goal of this study was to create a more in-depth understanding of SEW theory in the situations of internationalisation and international networking, the method of reasoning was *elaboration of theory* (Ketokivi & Choi, 2014). Hence, existing theories and the literature (e.g. SEW, the

298   J. Metsola

network model) provide a sufficient basis for formulating the research question, but not explicit a priori hypotheses. So, including an empirical context (i.e. small FFs, FPRs) would help to elaborate more general theoretical insights (Ketokivi & Choi, 2014). The data analysis followed the guidelines of abductive case research, with an emphasis on a back-and-forth movement between existing general theories and data with contextual idiosyncrasies (Dubois & Gadde, 2002; Järvensivu & Törnroos, 2010; Ketokivi & Choi, 2014). Using the typology of Welch, Piekkari, Plakoyiannaki, and Paavilainen-Mäntymäki (2011) for case-study theorising, the analysis aimed at contextualised explanation, with identification and explanation of causal mechanisms under contingent and limited contextual conditions. Theory—in this paper, SEW, the network model—often deductively inspires, and data—small FFs, FPRs—inductively inspire contextualised explanation (Welch et al., 2011).

Contextual conditions and the interplay of theory and data are present in abductive and contextualised explanations of case research. As a result, multiple cases provide broad, yet rigorous information on the similarities and differences between cases (Eisenhardt, 1989), thus enabling 'multiple conjunctural' intertwinement of contexts, theories and data (Rihoux & Ragin, 2008; Welch et al., 2011). Theoretical sampling served to select eight case firms from among firms with apparent experience in the phenomena under study (Patton, 2002). Theoretical sampling enabled the use of cases that increase our understanding of relational constructs in certain phenomena (Eisenhardt & Graebner, 2007), including SEW (Berrone et al., 2012). Selection of the case firms occurred on the basis of the following criteria: *Finnish nationality* (familiar context and knowledge of the language would help in understanding SEW and international networking), *small-firm classification* (staff headcount below 50 and turnover max EUR 10 million, as the European Commission defined it in 2019), *family control* (Arregle, Naldi, Nordqvist, & Hitt, 2012), *degree of internationalisation* (with foreign sales amounting to at least 50% of total sales, indicating a strategic orientation towards internationalisation) and *belonging to the same industry* (i.e. manufacturing; enabling the avoidance of industry-specific differences in the analysis of FPRs). Furthermore, it was important to have FFs with intermediaries, such as agents, distributors or subsidiaries, with whom FPRs are formed and developed. These relationships would also allow study of the role of SEW, as small FFs in these external relationships are likely to consider both SEW and economic goals under the pressure of limited resources, strategically important internationalisation and 'external exposure' through embeddedness in FPRs.

10 Coexistence of Economic and Noneconomic Goals in Building... 299

The deliberate choice to study specifically *family-controlled* firms—that is, firms having family members owning at least 50% of the shares and present in management and governance—responds to the need to distinguish between these and merely *family-influenced* firms (Arregle et al., 2012; Sirmon, Arregle, Hitt, & Webb, 2008; Westhead & Howorth, 2007). Family-influenced firms limit the decision-making power of family members, due to a lack of unilateral control of the firm. In family-controlled firms, family members have a dominant role in ownership and management, with the power to make strategic decisions (Arregle et al., 2012; Sirmon et al., 2008). Family-controlled firms are well suited to research on the SEW perspective, as high levels of family control over strategic decision-making may encourage family members to preserve SEW dimensions (Berrone et al., 2012; Gomez-Mejia et al., 2007; Zellweger et al., 2012). Furthermore, internationalisation is itself a strategic decision that internal family business characteristics influence (e.g. the desire to maintain control and influence) (Gallo, Tàpies, & Cappuyns, 2004). Thus, in family-controlled firms, SEW dimensions may become important in influencing the execution of internationalisation.

The term 'foreign partner relationship (FPR)' describes FFs' relationship with agents, distributors and subsidiaries, indicating elements of the relationship including the foreignness (Zaheer, 1995) and key relationship-marketing assumptions, such as long-term and profit-oriented relationship-building (e.g. Grönroos, 1990). The case firms also operate in a relative niche of B2B markets, in which exchange relationships are often partnerships, rather than mere 'acquaintanceships' (Johnson & Selnes, 2004).

Despite the theoretical sampling and predetermined descriptive delimitation of data, the set of case-firm data enabled 'multiple conjunctural' analysis of the research question. The preliminary delimitation of data was to ensure that the contexts enable explanations, connected or not, of SEW and FPRs. The data enabled the author to assess both history and process, which are important to understand in contextualised explanation (Welch et al., 2011).

Table 10.1 below gives information on the case firms, the criteria applied and the interviews.

The author of this paper conducted 28 semi-structured, face-to-face interviews with between one and three persons from each case firm. Using snowball sampling to contact family CEOs and chairs of the board led to their suggesting other interviewees, including people knowledgeable about the research topics, who might participate. Eventually, the researcher interviewed at least one family member from the firms with management and board positions, to obtain answers on family-specific, SEW-related questions. All the family-member   interviewees   were   also   familiar   with

Table 10.1 Basic information regarding the case firms and interviews

Firm		Interview years	Roles of interviewees (FM = family member)	Total number of interviews (and interview minutes)	% family ownership	Est.	First foreign market entry	Foreign sales to total sales (%)	Most important foreign markets (sales %)	Foreign operation modes
A	Sliding and folding door systems	2015 and 2018	CEO (FM); Export manager	4 (93)	100	1983	1984	50	Sweden, Norway, UK	Export via distributors
B	Wooden design lamps	2015 and 2018	Founder, former CEO and current creative director (FM); CEO; Chairman of the board (FM)	5 (218)	100	1995	2000	85	Germany, UK, Sweden	Export via agents and distributors
C	Hydraulic generators, power washers, and compressors	2015 and 2018	Founder, CEO and Chairman of the board (FM); Sales manager (FM); Design engineer (FM)	5 (183)	100	1986	1989	90	Sweden, North America, UK	Export via distributors
D	Machines and equipment for paper industry	2015	CEO (FM)	1 (46)	100	2006	2010	80	Sweden, Germany	Export via agents

E	Protective gloves for firefighters	2015	CEO (FM)	1 (85)	100	1956	1994	95	Norway, Switzerland, Germany	Export via distributors
F	Clothing items	2015	CEO (FM); Design manager (FM); Subsidiary manager	3 (94)	100	1976	1993	70	China; South Korea	Subsidiaries
G	Electronic detection and control devices	2015 and 2018	CEO; Chairman of the board and former CEO (FM); Board member (FM)	4 (170)	100	1965	1970s	50	Sweden, US, UK	Export via agents
H	Filling stations, tanks and related systems	2015 and 2018	CEO (FM), Sales director; Project manager; Sales director (FM)	5 (177)	98	1966	1980s	50	Norway, Poland, Sweden	Own exports or export via subsidiaries

Source: Author

internationalisation-related issues and FPRs, enabling collection of data on the family perspective on analysing connections between SEW and these topics. Some family CEOs and board chairs also suggested that nonfamily members with international knowledge and experience (e.g. an export manager) participate, to provide not only internationalisation-related answers but also important 'external perspectives inside FFs' on FF- and SEW-related issues.

The number of interviews aligns with Reay's (2014) suggestion that about 30 interviews should generally provide a sufficient breadth of data in qualitative research. Five firms were interviewed twice, first in 2015 and again in 2018. Three firms were interviewed only in 2015, as the author was not able to arrange meeting again in 2018. The interviews were digitally recorded and transcribed verbatim. Interviews are a data-collection method that provides rich data for unveiling underlying factors related to complex, episodic and infrequent phenomena (Eisenhardt & Graebner, 2007). The interviews followed a semi-structured, topic-based format. The questions posed were tentative rather than fixed, so modification of the course of the interview could occur in order to obtain rich details on complex phenomena (Barriball & While, 1994). The main topics of the interviews were *the general background of the case firms, SEW-related questions and the development of internationalisation and FPRs.* Items that Berrone et al. (2012) proposed provided the basis for the SEW-related questions, measuring five central SEW dimensions: *family control and influence, identification of family members with the firm, binding social ties, the emotional attachment of family members, and renewal of family bonds through dynastic succession.*

Case studies often use more than one source of evidence (Eisenhardt, 1989; Woodside & Wilson, 2003). Thus, in addition to the interview data, the author analysed such secondary data as firm websites, news archives and history books, to improve the validity of the data by triangulating the information (Miles & Huberman, 1994). For instance, to validate the chronological development of FPRs, the author investigated firm presentations relating to the timeline of their internationalisation.

Since abductive analysis lies between theory-driven and data-driven analysis (Dubois & Gadde, 2002; Ketokivi & Choi, 2014), directed content analysis provided a useful path to follow. In directed content analysis, initial coding categories emerge from existing theory, prior research or research questions, but new categories and themes can arise from the data in the course of the data analysis, the purpose being to conceptually validate or extend an existing theory (Hsieh & Shannon, 2005). Borrowing from grounded theory, the formation of categories is strongly grounded in the data; however, borrowing also from deductive logic, a priori theoretical considerations provide general categories, to which empirical observations and contextual idiosyncrasies relate (Ketokivi & Choi, 2014). Three main initial coding categories emerged from the research question and existing theory: (1) *Initiating, developing, and maintaining FPRs*, (2) *Characteristics of FPRs* and (3) *The value of having FF status in the context of internationalisation, and SEW profiles*. Subcategories formed under the main categories. For instance, the main category *Characteristics of FPRs* included the subcategory *Strength of relationships*, to address the differing strengths of the relationships in question. The first main category included different subcategories for the initiation, development and maintenance of FPRs. In the third main category, subcategories formed for the case firms' views on the importance of FF status and the SEW profiles, with different SEW dimensions (Berrone et al., 2012).

Regarding the assessment of SEW at the firm level (having formed a range of SEW profiles), the author recognises that the views of the interviewees (placed along the various SEW dimensions) are subjective and individual. However, the significant involvement of the family interviewees in their respective small-sized firms and internationalisation activities over a long period indicated the relevance of their views at the firm level and to the firm's relationship-building with foreign partners.

Within the main categories and subcategories, the author aimed to identify linkages, similarities and differences between the case firms. As an example, a new, data-driven and theory-elaborated category, *Close FPR-building for maintaining both economic and noneconomic goals*, emerged from the initial coding categories. The author went back and forth between the data and the theories to validate and elaborate the new category, to make interpretations as accurate as possible. The author also sent the findings back to the interviewees to check their validity and correct any inconsistencies or incorrect information. This was especially important for ensuring that the constructed SEW profiles match the views of the family owners and managers. Figure 10.2 below depicts the directed-content-analysis process for forming the aforementioned categories. Firm B's answers provide an example. As indicated in the figure, all the subcategories were analysed for each case firm, so that it was possible to conduct not only firm-specific within-case analyses but also cross-case analyses.

Since case-study theorising following contextualised explanation can generalise findings as far as the contingency of contextual conditions allows (Welch et al., 2011), the data analysis yielded three propositions, formatted so that they identify SEW levels and FPR-building activities and set idiosyncratic conditions under which the validity of the propositions is expected (in a critical-realist way). Thus, the findings and propositions of the study aimed

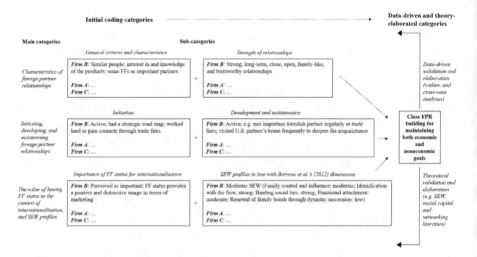

Fig. 10.2 Directed content analysis applied in forming the category 'Close FPR-building for maintaining both economic and noneconomic goals' with Firm B's answers as an example. (Source: Author)

at adopting a 'sceptical' approach to reality (for more critical-realist assumptions, see Easton, 2010; Sayer, 1992), given the relatively abstract and complex natures of FFs, SEW and FPRs.

Overall, it was essential to ensure the quality of the case-study research process. The guidelines of De Massis and Kotlar (2014) guided consideration of the four main criteria (e.g. Campbell, 1975; Yin, 1984) for case-study quality in FF research: construct validity (e.g. SEW measures; theoretical sampling; triangulation of data), internal validity (e.g. contextualised explanation; within-case and cross-case analyses), external validity (e.g. contingent and limited generalisation derived from acknowledged critical realist and 'multiple conjunctural' views) and reliability (e.g. systematic and abductive research process; snowballing sampling in interviews; tables and figures illustrating data collection and analysis).

Findings

SEW Profiles

The analysis of the SEW dimensions that Berrone et al. (2012) present profiled the case firms for SEW level on a scale from high to low, indicating the importance of SEW in their business (see Fig. 10.3 below). A 'high' score

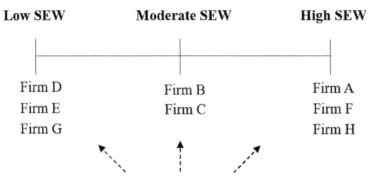

Fig. 10.3 SEW levels of case firms, A–H. (Source: Author)

meant that the case firm showed mostly high levels on the five central SEW dimensions. With a 'low' score, the opposite was true. A 'moderate' score comprised a mix of high, moderate and low scores for individual dimensions or a majority of dimensions earning moderate scores. Three firms scored in both high SEW and low SEW categories, while the moderate SEW category included two firms. Since FFs having 100% family ownership (98% in Firm H) and strong family involvement in management represent different levels of SEW, the findings at this stage of the analysis indicated that (high) family ownership and involvement, as a proxy for SEW, may not be enough to theorise SEW (cf. Kotlar et al., 2018; Zellweger et al., 2012). Due to space limitations here, we discuss each SEW profile (high, moderate, low) that came up for the case firms (presented in the appendix) using *one case firm* representing the profile in question. These descriptions illustrate the manifestations of the five SEW dimensions in the FFs: family control and influence, family members' identification with the firm, binding social ties, emotional attachment and renewal of family bonds to the firm through dynastic succession.

Foreign Partner Relationship (FPR)-Building

The case evidence shows that the case firms differed in the strength of their FPRs. By relating the FPR analysis to the SEW endowments in question, the case firms with higher levels of SEW had at least fairly strong FPRs and active relationship-building. By contrast, the case firms with lower-than-moderate levels of SEW mostly had fairly weak FPRs and relatively more passive relationship-building.

Firm H (high SEW level) discussed its adoption of a 'guerrilla strategy' for internationalisation, meaning that it actively tracked potential opportunities without devoting too many resources. However, setting an example, the family owner-CEO of the firm devoted his time and the firm's limited resources to the establishment of the relationship with the main partner and the customer in the most important market (Norway), which process took about ten years before he made the first big deals. In this process, the CEO had travelled to Norway every year to initiate possible deals, without results. He coincidentally met someone there, and they became good friends. They met regularly at trade fairs and on other occasions but never did any deals. In the tenth year, after regular but unsuccessful promotion, he met the same person at a small trade fair in Italy. There, the person hinted at a very promising deal in Norway. Eventually, after negotiations, the firm signed a major contract with the Norwegian customer, who also became a partner for Firm H. The relationship with the customer/partner has remained strong and close over six years of partnership. Firm H and this customer/partner communicate regularly and have realised not only significant growth in Norwegian sales but also achievements in collaborative product development.

Firm B (moderate SEW level) (see Fig. 10.2 for an example of the data-analysis process) also showed an active approach to both initiating and further developing FPRs. The active search for foreign partners, for example, through trade fairs, resulted in regular contacts and meetings of the partners. Firm B had visited the partner's home in the US many times, not just to talk about business but also (and more importantly) to become familiar with the persons with whom they conducted business. Although the familiarisation process in Japan had been longer, Firm B also had eventually succeeded in building a strong, trustworthy relationship with the partner there.

Similarly, the members of Firm F (high SEW level) had engaged in persistent relationship-building with the foreign partners. They had attended trade fairs regularly to create partnerships. They saw continuous relationship management as important. Thus, on regular occasions, the firm communicated remotely with the managers in China and South Korea. They also met physically several times a year, and the firm invited the partners to the family's summer cottage in Finland. Taking care of the partners was important; Firm F's CEO contended that it was more important to keep a good partner than to constantly tender for new ones.

10 Coexistence of Economic and Noneconomic Goals in Building... 307

The CEO of Firm C (moderate SEW level) recounted how he started marketing and selling products in Middle Europe through active contact at the grassroots level. He drove to different places, knocked on doors and tried to persuade people with his poor language skills. His active approach to making contacts had lasted to the present:

> I had a principle that I had to open at least 15 customer doors in a day when I was abroad [...] Customer contacting is done very much there [abroad], because when one speaks of these international trade fairs, they are just a period of one week in a year—there are 51 other weeks in a year when we should do export work.

Firm C has wanted to actively support partners. Although the firm informants reported that their partners were given the main responsibility for executing operations in their respective markets, Firm C provided constant support for marketing the products and helping the partners, promoting conditions in which they could perform well.

In relation to passive international networking and weaker FPRs, the case firms with low SEW levels (Firms D and E) had been passive throughout their internationalisation and formation of FPRs. The CEO of Firm D stated that he had never gone on any trips to foreign markets to build an agent network. Instead, he had mainly managed the building of relationships remotely, by reacting to incoming inquiries. Managing partner relationships had been passive, as demonstrated by this quote from the CEO concerning the agent partner in Spain:

> [The agent partner in Spain] doesn't load us down with useless inquiries [...] Then there is the extreme end that someone constantly asks about everything [...] it brings about unnecessary work.

Firm E had also been reactive and passive. The CEO indicated that almost all its FPRs had started by coincidence. As with Firm D, Firm E had limited communication with existing partners, and there had been no recent travel abroad to meet them. Usually, the interaction between Firm E and the partners involved nothing more than duties related to orders and delivery processing. Firm E emphasised that it was the partners' responsibility to execute operations in foreign markets, as far as they were able.

Accordingly, the data on FPRs, in association with the data on SEW, provided initial evidence that SEW does not restrain small FFs' developing FPRs for internationalisation but, rather (and somewhat unexpectedly), indicated

308 J. Metsola

its role in facilitating close FPR-building. Thus, further analysing the core part of the research question was important, to find additional evidence of SEW somehow either confining or being utilised in the process of FPR-building. For this purpose, conspicuous and relevant findings were sought relating to whether the case firms mentioned inter-FF or familial partnerships and whether they saw their FF status as important for internationalisation. This would indicate the extent to which SEW might be 'embedded' in FPR-building. Findings on these issues, together with findings on SEW and FPR-building activity levels, appear in Table 10.2 below.

All the case firms with at least a moderate level of SEW and an active approach to FPR-building explicitly mentioned that they had FF partners or familial relationships with the partners. They also mentioned that their FF status plays at least a fairly important role in internationalisation. All the foreign partners of Firm A were FFs, and the partner relationships had been strong, long-term and fruitful, based on mutual trust and similar values over the years and after successions. Firm B's interview demonstrated the familial nature of the partner network. For instance, the relationship with the Swedish agent (also an FF, acting for around 15 years as an agent for Firm B) had initially been somewhat professional and not particularly strong. Over time, it had developed into a very strong and close relationship. The agent and his wife and children were often present at trade fairs. The firm and the partner had spent much time together, discussing family and personal matters. A similar trend had occurred in Germany. There, a Finnish woman acting as an

Table 10.2 SEW, FPR-building activity, and importance of FF status in FPRs and internationalisation

Firm	SEW	FPR-building activity	Existence and importance of FF or familial foreign partners	Perceived importance of FF status for internationalisation
H	High	Active	Yes, and important	Important
A	High	Fairly active	Yes, and important	Important
F	High	Fairly active	Yes, and fairly important	Fairly unimportant
B	Moderate	Active	Yes, and important	Fairly important
C	Moderate	Active	Yes, and fairly important	Fairly unimportant
D	Low	Passive	Not mentioned	Unimportant
E	Low	Passive	Not mentioned	Fairly unimportant
G	Low	Fairly passive	Yes, and important	Fairly important

Source: Author

10 Coexistence of Economic and Noneconomic Goals in Building... 309

agent had become a friend of the founder of Firm B. She represented Firm B until her retirement. Overall, Firm B's mindset was towards developing and maintaining a committed and familial partner network, as the founder of Firm B demonstrated:

> These [foreign partners and customers] are almost part of our firm; they are more like extension. It is very important because then they are committed. For instance, we have these agent meetings, to which all our representatives, well not all, but European representatives have come here and we have spent few days here together, and there many have mentioned that they feel that they are part of Firm B family. [...] I believe that [...] if they remain as business acquaintances, very superficial, it is hard to commit those people to your thing. And if you cannot commit them and make them believe, they pretty easily might switch to other brand and start representing that instead.

Firms A and B also indicated the importance of FF status in creating a positive image for foreign partners. For instance, the Indian FF partner of Firm A mentioned that the firm only conducted business with other FFs. Firm A regarded the FF status as a factor in promoting closer interaction with foreign partners. The relationship-building process with the Indian partner has evolved into a great business relationship, thanks to their similar values, as the nonfamily export manager of Firm A explained:

> It [the partnership] started initially so that we actually had a good situation to choose from a couple [of potential partners] with whom we want to start running this [Indian] business. And then we ended up with this firm. [...] Their set of values were one of the most important criteria, of course in addition to other [business-related] acquirements. [...] And when we have done business, we have taken a sauna bath and else. [...] They have mentioned many times that as we have now started to do this [business together], we are a bit like one family. We openly talk about prices together, and everything is very open.

Firm H, whose fruitful relationship-building process with the major Norwegian customer/partner was mentioned earlier, also pointed to the positive marketing factor of being an FF, as illustrated by the family CEO:

> Yes, we always tell [our FF status] and bring it up [...] It is part of our identity. [...] When we had had partnership with Norwegians, our biggest customer, for six years, [...] they decided to come here two months back with their entire personnel, two busses, 80 persons [...] An essential part was to come see these crazy Finnish. [...] We do not want to be those pinstripe boys.

His son, a family manager, adds:

> In the last trade fairs, when the biggest existing customers were aware of our FF status, they said 'hey, you are the son of the family CEO, where is your dad?' sort of thing. So, in a way, the historical continuum is visible and relations there. It is easier to get to conversations, thanks to this surname.

In the case of Firm F, although there was no explicit mention of the FF status of their foreign partners, indications of warm or even familial relationships came up in the interviews. Firm F had long-term and trustworthy relationships with subsidiary managers in China and South Korea (both key markets). In general, Firm F found it important to identify the 'right kind' of partner—someone who would reflect the identity of Firm F and show its commitment. The family manager summarised the commitment of the Chinese subsidiary manager, emphasising mutual commitment and reciprocity:

> Our current CEO of China [operations], Mary [name changed], worked as a translator for the founder of our firm at the time when we had business with a Chinese textile firm [prior to own subsidiary]. We established our subsidiary in China in 1994 and since then Mary has worked for us. In Chinese context, this shows an exceptionally strong commitment, as it is a prevailing way to tender your value [in terms of a potential job change] regularly in China.

For instance, Firm F helped the Chinese subsidiary manager with housing matters when she got divorced in the 1990s. In his own interview, the South Korean subsidiary manager of Firm F said that he felt like a family member of the firm.

> They [the family members of Firm F] are good persons, so I want to both give back return and also show respect. I want to [...] contribute for the second generation to be inheriting; the first generation was in really good shape.

Case firms D and E, which had low levels of SEW, had been passive in their relationship-building. They did not mention familial FPRs and saw the FF status as unimportant or somewhat unimportant for internationalisation.

Notably, in addition to taking a more active approach to relationship-building with foreign partners, the case firms with at least a moderate level of SEW also indicate better financial results than the case firms with below-moderate levels of SEW. Using the Amadeus database offered by Bureau van

Dijk, the author discovered turnovers and profit margins of the case firms from 2008 to 2017 (with the following exceptions: no data from Firm F 2008–2009, Firm G 2008, or Firm E 2008–2009 and 2016–2017). The numbers indicate that case firms with at least a moderate level of SEW tended to have better results (e.g. a higher turnover and growth rate and higher profit margins) than case firms with lower levels of SEW. The relationship between SEW and performance indicators will undoubtedly require further statistical analyses and a new research setting. Nevertheless, the numbers provide preliminary evidence that among small FFs with higher SEW levels, efforts to collaborate with foreign partners can benefit both SEW preservation and economic goals.

The SEW profiles (see Appendix for examples) indicate how small FFs with moderate or high SEW levels usually value family control, emotional attachment and generational continuity, but imply that family benefit per se and exclusively is not so important. Rather, social relationships are important, and FFs want to include nonfamily employees and other stakeholders (i.e. binding social ties) in the long-term journey of their businesses, which also requires rational economic orientation and cooperative approaches. Simply put, these family owners and managers may want to maintain the pride and heritage of their businesses (firms with high SEW probably a bit more than firms with moderate SEW), which cannot occur at the expense of long-term economic goals. For this purpose, active relationship-building with foreign partners, which can embed the attributes of SEW through trust (e.g. correspondence with identification and binding social ties dimensions) and long-term orientation (e.g. correspondence with family control and renewal of family bonds dimensions), is considered important for internationalisation to gain economic growth and profits. This, in turn, feeds SEW endowments.

Figure 10.4 below depicts the theoretical framework of the study, updated with the findings on SEW and intensity in FPR-building. The findings suggest the association of that SEW with active FPR-building. The case firms with higher SEW levels also regarded the FF status as important for internationalisation and had many foreign partners sharing the FF status. This implies that the preservation of SEW is important for them and is a concern that does not act as an obstacle to their efforts. Rather, it operates as an asset that impels them to promote and succeed in internationalisation. Thus, SEW can act as a bridge for small FFs, assisting them in building strong, trustworthy and long-term relationships with foreign partners. Such efforts lead to reciprocity and more integrated cooperation. Active and close relationship-building may eventually contribute to solid financial results.

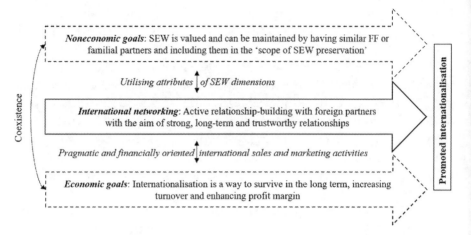

Fig. 10.4 Coexistence of noneconomic and economic goals in driving small FFs' active and close relationship-building with foreign partners for promoted internationalisation (Source: Author)

Overall, when one has other FFs as foreign partners or familial relationships with the partners, it is possible to incorporate the foreign partners within the 'scope of SEW preservation', as a part of the 'extended international family' (see Firm B's quote about creating a 'Firm B family' within the foreign partner network, and Firm A's quote about the familial relationship with the Indian partner, presented earlier). The SEW perspective extends to the international context, with SEW viewed as better preserved through active and close interaction with partners who share one's values and practices. In other words, SEW acts as both a means and an end for the internationalisation of small FFs. However, case-firm evidence shows that implementation of pragmatic and financially oriented international sales and marketing activities that maintain economic goals in FPR-building should accompany utilising attributes of different SEW dimensions and contributing to noneconomic goals (see detail in the discussion section).

In Fig. 10.4, an arrow between noneconomic and economic goals emphasises the possible coexistence of these goals in driving small FFs' active and close relationship-building with foreign partners. Thus, the findings and the figure suggest that the internationalisation of small FFs is not necessarily an 'either/or' mixed gamble of preferring noneconomic or economic goals. Rather, the interactive coexistence of noneconomic and economic goals manifest in active and close FPR-building can promote sustainable internationalisation. Figure 10.1, the theoretical framework for this study, with the separate arrows from noneconomic and economic goal orientations to relationship-building, indicates the more general view in the literature that the effect of one goal orientation or the other is more dominant.

Discussion

The finding that small FFs with higher SEW levels aim at a kind of extended international family with foreign partners, to promote internationalisation and, simultaneously, preserve their SEW, both confirms and contradicts earlier findings. Regarding internationalisation propensity, Gomez-Mejia et al. (2010) argue that FFs are more reluctant to go international than other firms because preservation of SEW acts as an obstacle in decision-making. However, in the context of FPRs, the findings of this study suggest (i) that internationalisation is an economic decision and (ii) that it may help small FFs to preserve noneconomic dimensions and SEW in the longer term. As mentioned earlier, SEW appears to function both as a means and an end regarding the internationalisation of small FFs, given that active establishment of close relationships with foreign partners is their way to succeed in international competition. In this sense, economic and noneconomic goals coexist. More successfully, managing the mixed gamble and associated trade-offs between these two goal orientations (e.g. Alessandri et al., 2018) can occur if they are not mutually exclusive in the long term.

Patel et al. (2012) argue that SEW preservation may make FFs risk-averse in achieving internationalisation, but also that factors derived from SEW preservation (such as stewardship, trust and aligned decision-making) could facilitate internationalisation efforts. In light of this study, small FFs may be able to deploy the beneficial attributes of SEW by extending the scope of SEW preservation to include foreign partners, with whom stewardship, trustworthiness and decision-making flourish. However, the findings on higher SEW levels and higher-level FPR-building activities indicate that those small FFs with higher SEW levels *must* build long-term and close FPRs to preserve SEW in the long run. Close FPRs enable FFs to get to know the partner, increase commitment and, thereby, ensure that the proven partner will contribute to the FFs' economic and noneconomic SEW goals. With weaker FPRs and more passive relationship-building, FFs would not necessarily be aware and knowledgeable enough of the partner's operations and character to convince themselves of the partner's potential for supporting *both* economic and noneconomic SEW goals. Weaker FPRs can contribute to economic goals, and FFs can passively monitor the development of an agent's sales in a host country, but for those FFs with high levels of SEW endowment, purely economic understanding may not be enough. These findings align with Cesinger et al. (2016), who found that collaboration intensity and network trust with network partners play key roles in small FFs' acquiring knowledge crucial to internationalisation. According to them, gaining such knowledge may assist FFs in overcoming threats to SEW. Along similar lines, Kraus et al. (2016) argue that FFs with high levels of SEW may utilise external and international networks for learning and secure both noneconomic SEW and economic goals. The findings of this study elaborate the active FPR-building processes, in which small FFs may need to engage to meet both economic and noneconomic SEW goals.

Proposition 1 *Small FFs with concerns about their SEW do not regard internationalisation as a threat but as a way to secure both economic and SEW-related goals. However, the higher the levels of SEW endowment, the greater the need to engage in active relationship-building with foreign partners and establish strong relationships with them.*

Studies have favoured weak over strong relationships, on grounds that strong ones may narrow readiness for international opportunities outside the immediate network (Oviatt & McDougall, 2005), including in the 'network' of FFs (Kontinen & Ojala, 2012). In contrast, this study's findings suggest that having strong foreign relationships with firms that share the same values and practices may enhance the exchange of information on international opportunities. A network relationship between organisations sharing common interests provides mutual benefits and encourages a long-term relationship (Johanson & Mattsson, 1988; Johanson & Vahlne, 2003). This also seems true for small FFs. Three out of five case-firms, with at least a moderate level of SEW, mentioned explicitly that they had or sought corresponding small FFs as foreign partners, with whom cooperation worked well and who support the establishment of strong, long-term and trustworthy relationships. Notably, the establishment of relationships with foreign FFs is a beneficial strategy for an FF's international networking, due to the advantages of having similar values and characteristics (Fernandez & Nieto, 2005; Gallo & Pont, 1996; Swinth & Vinton, 1993).

Internal family relationships appear to have hampered the international-opportunity-recognition process (Kontinen & Ojala, 2011) and expanding internationalisation to diverse markets (Scholes et al., 2016). This paper's findings suggest that for small FFs, if the persons running the foreign FF partner firms assume a role as foreign family members, a coherent 'international family' may prove effective for internationalisation. Transnational family networks (i.e. family members of a local firm spread over various countries) have been important for gaining new contacts and resources for internationalisation (Hewapathirana, 2014; Mustafa & Chen, 2010). Although the small FFs in this case study did not rely on biological family ties, the findings can extend to familial foreign partners playing a similar role. Indirectly supporting this notion is the finding that FFs tend to create reciprocal social relationships, not just between family members but also with nonfamily members in a FF, increasing a sense of belonging and commitment and leading to better performance and success (Miller & Le Breton-Miller, 2005; Miller, Lee, Chang, & Le Breton-Miller, 2009). The consequent communal embeddedness and fellowship allow FFs to serve those within and around them (Berrone et al., 2010). This may also apply to foreign partners who become incorporated into a small FF's community.

Proposition 2 *The opportunities for achieving both economic and SEW-related goals in parallel in internationalisation increase if small FFs direct active relationship-building and establishment of strong relationships to foreign but similar small FF or familial partners.*

The case firms with above-moderate levels of SEW show how different dimensions of the FIBER-scale (Berrone et al., 2012) manifest themselves in FPR-building. For example, *binding social ties* and related trust, as well as treating nonfamily employees as part of the family and maintaining strong and long-term relationships with other firms, were evident in active FPR-building and extending international family to foreign partners. *Identification* and *emotional attachment* of family members to their firms convey a special meaning to foreign partners, and especially to foreign FF partners, which can then identify with the people in FFs and their willingness to do business for mutual profit in the long run. Affective considerations are not necessarily something family members should belittle. Rather, foreign partners see these as showing pride in the heritage that family owners and managers embody through strong involvement in the daily operations of FFs. For this purpose, the two other dimensions, *family control and influence* and *renewal of family bonds through dynastic succession*, are not necessarily negative, restraining factors but, rather, attributes that convince foreign partners of long-term relationships, effective decision-making and transfer of knowledge among family owners and managers. These dimensions can also convince FFs to invest in active and close FPR-building because stability and capacity to maintain established FPRs will most likely characterise the future and coming generations.

Scholes et al. (2016) and Cesinger et al. (2016) also stress the positive influence of binding social ties on trust between network partners in FF internationalisation. In addition, this study suggests that identification and emotional attachment can beneficially strengthen the bond between FFs and foreign partners towards mutually profitable business in the long run. High levels of family control and a related (assumed) strong SEW-preservation tendency have mainly carried negative connotations for FF internationalisation (e.g. Gomez-Mejia et al., 2010; Sánchez-Bueno & Usero, 2014). However, the findings of this study suggest that family control and generational continuity may prove to be effective for active FPR-building and, thereby, internationalisation in the long run. All the case firms with higher-than-moderate levels of SEW were at least second-generation FFs with a two-decade history of operations and strong family control through ownership and management, indicating that stability does not necessarily stagnate FPR development.

However, the case firms also show that not only noneconomic and SEW-related attributes enable and feed close FPR profitability. For SEW-related attributes to flourish, there must be economic and pragmatic foundations on which to build FPR activity. For example, the case firms broadly expressed criteria for having partners with capabilities and networks in host countries, to do growth-oriented selling and marketing of the case firms' products. The family CEO-owner of Firm C mentioned that the best thing to do in his firm is to give plane tickets to employees so that they can do active grass-roots-level selling and support the customers and partners. Attending trade fairs is important for many case firms, not just for meeting partners and customers but also for seeking new revenues and markets for their products. In general, the case firms with above-moderate levels of SEW were profitable and financially growth-oriented. Accordingly, utilising SEW attributes in FPR-building activities cannot occur in isolation; they also need a strong focus on reaching financial goals, starting from pragmatic operational-level sales and marketing activities. Both noneconomic SEW attributes and economically oriented activities occur from strategic to operational levels, so utilising and pursuing them concurrently are necessary for them to benefit each other in the long run.

Proposition 3 *FFs with higher SEW levels utilise attributes of different SEW dimensions in FPR-building, but their utilisation requires concurrent implementation of pragmatic and financially oriented international sales and marketing activities.*

Conclusions

Drawing upon the notion that SEW lies in social relationships (e.g. Zellweger et al., 2019), this study aimed to investigate whether SEW restrains small FFs' building foreign partner relationships (FPRs) for internationalisation and, in the event that they do not, how the firms might strategically confine or utilise SEW effects. A key differentiating factor from similar studies (e.g. Cesinger et al., 2016; Scholes et al., 2016) was the formation of qualitative 'SEW profiles' for each case firm, through applying Berrone et al.'s (2012) FIBER-scale in the multiple-case study; then, comparing those with how actively and closely FFs initiate, develop and maintain their FPRs. That made possible conclusions about how different SEW profiles or levels might manifest in FPR-building activities, thereby unravelling more generally the extent to which noneconomic (SEW) goals coexist with economic goals in the internationalisation of FFs. The lack of in-depth measurement and analysis of what SEW actually means for the FFs (e.g. Miller & Le Breton-Miller, 2014) has left us uncertain of how SEW manifests itself through different dimensions (Berrone et al., 2012) in the context of FF internationalisation, in which networking behaviour often differs from that of non-FFs (Kampouri, Plakoyiannaki, & Leppäaho, 2017; Kontinen & Ojala, 2010; Pukall & Calabrò, 2014). Essentially, this study elaborates existing theory and findings revolving mainly around the role of SEW as an antecedent or outcome of internationalisation, by providing insights into how SEW manifests itself in the processes of FPR-building activities. Small FFs were chosen as units of analysis as they usually depend on FPRs for internationalisation, and SEW dimensions affect them more heavily than such dimensions affect larger FFs.

The key findings on the close, familial and actively maintained FPRs suggest a strategic orientation among small FFs with higher SEW levels, such that they utilise these partnerships for fruitful cooperation in international operations and ensuring the preservation of SEW. The SEW profiles of the case firms with moderate or high SEW levels usually implied that the SEW dimensions are important (but not exclusively for family benefit, per se), along with engaging nonfamily employees and other stakeholders in the long-term success of the business. This requires that economic goals coexist with noneconomic goals. Indeed, small FFs with higher SEW levels can utilise their internal SEW attributes (e.g. pride, heritage and trustworthiness), stemming from different SEW dimensions, in external relationships and FPRs for economically profitable internationalisation that, in turn, enables noneconomic SEW endowments to endure. Despite the relatively strong emotional attachment to and identifications with FFs, family owners and managers with stronger SEW preservation tendencies also seem to approach their FPRs with strong economic mindsets. Indeed, another key finding was that the utilisation of SEW attributes requires concurrent implementation of pragmatic and financially oriented international sales and marketing activities. Figure 10.4, the theoretical framework updated with the findings of the study, encapsulates the propositions that the analysis prompted.

These findings extend our knowledge of the role of SEW in internationalisation, specifically, how FFs with different SEW profiles act differently in building FPRs for internationalisation and preservation of noneconomic (SEW) and economic goals. This study aligns with studies (e.g. Cesinger et al., 2016; Scholes et al., 2016) that identified international and social-network relationships as key contexts in which SEW manifests itself—for instance, through trust stemming from the SEW dimension of binding social ties. This study also extends that knowledge by pinpointing how FFs engage in those relationships so as to maintain the pursuit of both noneconomic and economic goals. Interrelating SEW and FPRs of small FFs yielded interesting findings of the possible 'bright side' of high SEW levels, contradicting the stream of literature that posits SEW as an unavoidable or difficult-to-alter restraint on internationalisation (e.g. Gomez-Mejia et al., 2010; Sánchez-Bueno & Usero, 2014).

This study has some concrete managerial implications. It indicates how small FFs can harness their SEW-related goals and special features in efforts to promote international networking and internationalisation, especially in terms of having other FF or familial foreign partners. The scope of SEW preservation may not lie merely within the immediate family and nonfamily employees in the small FF. It may also extend to the international context, with the potential for cultivating economic gains without diminishing SEW. For instance, actively attending trade fairs may turn out to be effective for initiating, developing and maintaining FPRs and, hence, for achieving both economic and noneconomic goals. It would benefit small FFs to evaluate and understand themselves through the five dimensions of the FIBER-scale (Berrone et al., 2012), to see whether they can utilise some SEW-related attributes, such as trust and long-term orientation stemming from binding social ties and generational continuity, in FPR-building strategies (e.g. foreign partner selection) and operations (e.g. sales negotiations with foreign partners). The pride, heritage and active involvement of family owners and managers in their businesses could serve as differentiating factors in international sales and marketing to convince potential foreign partners to choose small FFs' products in their resale portfolios over bigger, 'faceless' nonfamily corporations. However, small FFs must be aware of the economic realities of internationalisation. Best outcomes of active FPR-building for internationalisation occur when noneconomic and economic goals coexist. Hence, utilisation of SEW attributes and implementation of pragmatic and financially oriented international sales and marketing activities should occur in unison.

This study has some limitations and implies some avenues for future research. Its particular context (involving small Finnish FFs and their FPRs) was a deliberate choice to exploratively investigate a context familiar to the researcher. The findings of the study, which highlight trustworthy relationship-building and collectivism, are especially applicable not just in a Finnish context but in a Scandinavian context as well, as the Scandinavian countries are a culturally unique group that highly values both individual and collective responsibilities and greatly trusts institutions (e.g. Mullet, Lazreg, Candela, & Neto, 2005). Firm-level attributes reflect these country-level attributes, and since FFs can function as institutions of their own with a special tendency towards SEW preservation, Scandinavian small FFs may have strong confidence in doing international business with foreign FF partners that share the same values. The small Finnish FFs in this study had many FPRs within other Scandinavian countries, including relationships with other small FFs, so the findings and the propositions apply especially in the Scandinavian context. However, considering the evidence of similar SEW preservation tendencies across different countries and cultures (e.g. US-based study by Alessandri et al., 2018; China-based study by Yang, Li, Stanley, Kellermanns, & Li, 2020), the findings of this study are likely to apply more globally. In any case, this study only interviewed small Finnish FFs, so future research could include the views of foreign partners to see whether their views on the nature of FPRs match. In addition to strengthening network-based analysis, this would also bring more cross-cultural generalisability to the findings of this study.

The choices of small FFs were also somewhat narrow in terms of the industry, (manufacturing). However, the small FFs with above-moderate levels of SEW participated in designing and manufacturing niche high-tech and high-quality products (e.g. hydraulic equipment for certain mobile machinery and wooden design lamps). Thus, the paper aligns with the findings by Hennart et al. (2019) on the competitive advantage of small FFs in global niches for these kinds of products, through their ability to create long-term and strong customer and partner relationships. The paper also contributes to these findings with the dynamics of SEW. Future research could look at other industries and whether the dynamics are the same.

Furthermore, although this study presents some financial-performance indicators suggesting a potentially fruitful role for high SEW in international

320   J. Metsola

networking, they receive only limited attention since the study primarily involved qualitative exploration. Thus, future studies might elaborate the findings and propositions via quantitative methods. These could include a range of variables related to SEW dimensions and FPRs. Longitudinal datasets also could shed light on the development of the variables. Furthermore, the use of different kinds of FFs (e.g. family-controlled vs. family-influenced firms) and countries as contexts could provide insights into heterogeneous groups of FFs and different geographical locations.

Appendix: Example Case Firms with High, Moderate or Low SEW Profile

High SEW—Example Firm A. In Firm A, the CEO (second generation) and her father (founder and chairman of the board) had strong identification with and emotional attachment to the firm. For instance, the business had been part of the CEO's everyday life since childhood. They saw continuation of the business from one generation to the next as important. For them, the FF was the embodiment of the people owning it and working for it. There appeared to be good relationships and cooperation between family and nonfamily members. Although the family brought good values to the business, they saw that it is important to keep family matters separate from the business, so that strategic decisions were not biased. However, since family members had full ownership of the firm, their views strongly entered into the firm's decision-making. This resulted in risk-averse decisions, since the family's own money, and thereby the well-being of the family (also all the employees) was in question. However, since the firm was highly growth-oriented and willing to accelerate internationalisation, family benefit per se was not a priority. The export sales representative, a nonfamily employee, indicated that he had been strongly engaged in the business from an early period, and he believed that other employees felt the same. According to him, the feeling was like being part of the family.

Moderate SEW—Example Firm C. Firm C did not strongly represent itself as an FF. Although the CEO (first generation) had strong commitment to the business, and although the firm was fully owned by the family, the firm was, first and foremost, a limited company, set up as a legal entity. Thus, ownership was in principle separated from the family, and the priority was whatever would benefit the firm. The analysis indicated that if there was too much emotional attachment involved, family quarrels could occur. However, there was united power within family members in running the business. Continuing the business from generation to generation was valued, but in the end, it was the interests of the firm that mattered. Despite this, the CEO said that he saw family ownership as best for the firm in the long term. Relationships within the family and with nonfamily members were good: family members were not privileged and were just like any other employees in the firm. The CEO said that he aimed to be the best employee himself. The daughter of the CEO, the Executive Vice President, had fairly strong emotional attachment to and identification with the firm, as she had grown into her position, and had taken on increasing responsibilities over time. There was probably a special passion to work and to contribute, since Firm C was an FF. Nevertheless, the FF status was not excessively emphasised, even if it was a source of pride. More important than being family-centred was the fact that the firm employed so many excellent people, with whom the firm could progress.

Low SEW—Example Firm E. In Firm E, continuing the business from generation to generation was not an end in itself. The business had been transferred from an authoritarian father to his son (the CEO interviewed) as something obligatory; thus, the CEO did not want to pass the business on to the next generation in the same way. There had been emotional attachment previously, but it had diminished, due to challenges in the industry and to the outsourcing of many activities. However, since the FF was felt to be a kind of an embodiment of the persons involved, there was pride and honour to some extent. This had impelled the CEO to manage through severe financial difficulties. The relationships with nonfamily employees had generally been long-term. However, among family members (as distinct from Firms A, B, and C) the relationships were somewhat difficult. The CEO had been the main person to run the business, as the other family members had been somewhat reluctant to participate, and conflicts had occurred.

References

Alessandri, T. M., Cerrato, D., & Eddleston, K. A. (2018). The mixed gamble of internationalization in family and nonfamily firms: The moderating role of organizational slack. *Global Strategy Journal, 8*(1), 46–72.

Arregle, J. L., Naldi, L., Nordqvist, M., & Hitt, M. A. (2012). Internationalization of family–controlled firms: A study of the effects of external involvement in governance. *Entrepreneurship Theory and Practice, 36*(6), 1115–1143.

Barriball, K. L., & While, A. (1994). Collecting data using a semi-structured interview: A discussion paper. *Journal of Advanced Nursing, 19*(2), 328–335.

Bell, J. (1995). The internationalization of small computer software firms: A further challenge to "stage" theories. *European Journal of Marketing, 29*(8), 60–75.

Berrone, P., Cruz, C., & Gomez-Mejia, L. R. (2012). Socioemotional wealth in family firms: Theoretical dimensions, assessment approaches, and agenda for future research. *Family Business Review, 25*(3), 258–279.

Berrone, P., Cruz, C., Gomez-Mejia, L. R., & Larraza-Kintana, M. (2010). Socioemotional wealth and corporate responses to institutional pressures: Do family-controlled firms pollute less? *Administrative Science Quarterly, 55*(1), 82–113.

Bird, M., & Zellweger, T. (2018). Relational embeddedness and firm growth: Comparing spousal and sibling entrepreneurs. *Organization Science, 29*(2), 264–283.

Buciuni, G., & Mola, L. (2014). How do entrepreneurial firms establish cross-border relationships? A global value chain perspective. *Journal of International Entrepreneurship, 12*(1), 67–84.

Campbell, D. T. (1975). "Degrees of freedom" and the case study. *Comparative Political Studies, 8*(1), 178–191.

Cesinger, B., Hughes, M., Mensching, H., Bouncken, R., Fredrich, V., & Kraus, S. (2016). A socioemotional wealth perspective on how collaboration intensity, trust, and international market knowledge affect family firms' multinationality. *Journal of World Business, 51*(4), 586–599.

Chetty, S., & Holm, D. B. (2000). Internationalisation of small to medium-sized manufacturing firms: A network approach. *International Business Review, 9*(1), 77–93.

Chrisman, J. J., & Patel, P. C. (2012). Variations in R&D investments of family and nonfamily firms: Behavioral agency and myopic loss aversion perspectives. *Academy of Management Journal, 55*(4), 976–997.

Cruz, C. C., Gómez-Mejia, L. R., & Becerra, M. (2010). Perceptions of benevolence and the design of agency contracts: CEO-TMT relationships in family firms. *Academy of Management Journal, 53*(1), 69–89.

De Massis, A., & Kotlar, J. (2014). The case study method in family business research: Guidelines for qualitative scholarship. *Journal of Family Business Strategy, 5*(1), 15–29.

Dubois, A., & Gadde, L. E. (2002). Systematic combining: An abductive approach to case research. *Journal of Business Research, 55*(7), 553–560.

Easton, G. (2010). Critical realism in case study research. *Industrial Marketing Management, 39*, 118–128.

Eberhard, M., & Craig, J. (2013). The evolving role of organisational and personal networks in international market venturing. *Journal of World Business, 48*(3), 385–397.

Eisenhardt, K. M. (1989). Building theories from case study research. *Academy of Management Review, 14*(4), 532–550.

10 Coexistence of Economic and Noneconomic Goals in Building... 323

Eisenhardt, K. M., & Graebner, M. E. (2007). Theory building from cases: Opportunities and challenges. *Academy of Management Journal, 50*(1), 25–32.

European Commission (2009). Overview of family-business-relevant issues: Research, networks, policy measures and existing studies. Retrieved from https://www.google.com/url?sa=t&rct=j&q=&esrc=s&source=web&cd=3&ved=2ahUKEwj8 4rzazIXoAhXtkYsKHfk_AooQFjACegQIBRAB&url=https%3A%2F%2Fec. europa.eu%2Fdocsroom%2Fdocuments%2F10388%2Fattachments%2F1%2Ft ranslations%2Fen%2Frenditions%2Fnative&usg=AOvVaw1w_6Mdh6Iech2s9R oZ68ur

European Commission. (2019). What is an SME? Retrieved October 10, 2019, from https://ec.europa.eu/growth/smes/business-friendly-environment/sme-definition_en

Fang, H., Kotlar, J., Memili, E., Chrisman, J. J., & De Massis, A. (2018). The pursuit of international opportunities in family firms: Generational differences and the role of knowledge-based resources. *Global Strategy Journal, 8*(1), 136–157.

Fernandez, Z., & Nieto, M. J. (2005). Internationalization strategy of small and medium-sized family businesses: Some influential factors. *Family Business Review, 18*(1), 77–89.

Gabrielsson, M., Kirpalani, V. M., Dimitratos, P., Solberg, C. A., & Zucchella, A. (2008). Born globals: Propositions to help advance the theory. *International Business Review, 17*(4), 385–401.

Gallo, M. A., & Pont, C. G. (1996). Important factors in family business internationalization. *Family Business Review, 9*(1), 45–59.

Gallo, M. Á., Tàpies, J., & Cappuyns, K. (2004). Comparison of family and nonfamily business: Financial logic and personal preferences. *Family Business Review, 17*(4), 303–318.

Gomez-Mejia, L. R., Cruz, C., Berrone, P., & De Castro, J. (2011). The bind that ties: Socioemotional wealth preservation in family firms. *Academy of Management Annals, 5*(1), 653–707.

Gomez-Mejia, L. R., Haynes, K. T., Núñez-Nickel, M., Jacobson, K. J., & Moyano-Fuentes, J. (2007). Socioemotional wealth and business risks in family-controlled firms: Evidence from Spanish olive oil mills. *Administrative Science Quarterly, 52*(1), 106–137.

Gomez-Mejia, L. R., Makri, M., & Kintana, M. L. (2010). Diversification decisions in family-controlled firms. *Journal of Management Studies, 47*(2), 223–252.

Granovetter, M. S. (1973). The strength of weak ties. *American Journal of Sociology, 78*, 1360–1380.

Granovetter, M. (1985). Economic action and social structure: The problem of embeddedness. *American Journal of Sociology, 91*(3), 481–510.

Grönroos, C. (1990). Relationship approach to marketing in service contexts: The marketing and organizational behavior interface. *Journal of Business Research, 20*(1), 3–11.

Hennart, J. F., Majocchi, A., & Forlani, E. (2019). The myth of the stay-at-home family firm: How family-managed SMEs can overcome their internationalization limitations. *Journal of International Business Studies, 50*(5), 758–782.

Hewapathirana, G. I. (2014). Bridging, bonding and linking global entrepreneurs: The case of Sri Lanka. *Human Resource Development International, 17*(2), 164–182.

Hsieh, H. F., & Shannon, S. E. (2005). Three approaches to qualitative content analysis. *Qualitative Health Research, 15*(9), 1277–1288.

Järvensivu, T., & Törnroos, J. Å. (2010). Case study research with moderate constructionism: Conceptualization and practical illustration. *Industrial Marketing Management, 39*(1), 100–108.

Johanson, J., & Mattsson, L. G. (1988). Internationalisation in industrial systems—A network approach. In N. Hood & J. E. Vahlne (Eds.), *Strategies in global competition* (pp. 287–314). London: Croom Helm.

Johanson, J., & Vahlne, J. E. (2003). Business relationship learning and commitment in the internationalization process. *Journal of International Entrepreneurship, 1*(1), 83–101.

Johanson, J., & Vahlne, J.-E. (2009). The Uppsala internationalization process model revisited: From liability of foreignness to liability of outsidership. *Journal of International Business Studies, 40*, 1411–1431.

Johnson, M. D., & Selnes, F. (2004). Customer portfolio management: Toward a dynamic theory of exchange relationships. *Journal of Marketing, 68*(2), 1–17.

Kampouri, K., Plakoyiannaki, E., & Leppäaho, T. (2017). Family business internationalisation and networks: Emerging pathways. *Journal of Business & Industrial Marketing, 32*(3), 357–370.

Kano, L., & Verbeke, A. (2018). Family firm internationalization: Heritage assets and the impact of bifurcation bias. *Global Strategy Journal, 8*(1), 158–183.

Ketokivi, M., & Choi, T. (2014). Renaissance of case research as a scientific method. *Journal of Operations Management, 32*(5), 232–240.

Kontinen, T., & Ojala, A. (2010). The internationalization of family businesses: A review of extant research. *Journal of Family Business Strategy, 1*, 97–107.

Kontinen, T., & Ojala, A. (2011). International opportunity recognition among small and medium-sized family firms. *Journal of Small Business Management, 49*(3), 490–514.

Kontinen, T., & Ojala, A. (2012). Social capital in the international operations of family SMEs. *Journal of Small Business and Enterprise Development, 19*(1), 39–55.

Kotlar, J., Signori, A., De Massis, A., & Vismara, S. (2018). Financial wealth, socio-emotional wealth, and IPO underpricing in family firms: A two-stage gamble model. *Academy of Management Journal, 61*(3), 1073–1099.

Kraus, S., Mensching, H., Calabro, A., Cheng, C. F., & Filser, M. (2016). Family firm internationalization: A configurational approach. *Journal of Business Research, 69*(11), 5473–5478.

Le Breton-Miller, I., & Miller, D. (2013). Socioemotional wealth across the family firm life cycle: A commentary on "family business survival and the role of boards". *Entrepreneurship Theory and Practice, 37*(6), 1391–1397.

Leppäaho, T., & Metsola, J. (2020). *Family firm internationalisation: A network perspective.* Cham: Palgrave Pivot.

Leppäaho, T., & Pajunen, K. (2018). Institutional distance and international networking. *Entrepreneurship & Regional Development, 30*(5–6), 502–529.

Loane, S., & Bell, J. (2006). Rapid internationalisation among entrepreneurial firms in Australia, Canada, Ireland and New Zealand: An extension to the network approach. *International Marketing Review, 23*(5), 467–485.

Metsola, J., Leppäaho, T., Paavilainen-Mäntymäki, E., & Plakoyiannaki, E. (2020). Process in family business internationalisation: The state of the art and ways forward. *International Business Review, 29*, 101665.

Miles, M. B., & Huberman, A. M. (1994). *Qualitative data analysis: An expanded sourcebook.* Thousand Oaks, CA: Sage.

Miller, D., & Le Breton-Miller, I. (2005). Management insights from great and struggling family businesses. *Long Range Planning, 38*(6), 517–530.

Miller, D., & Le Breton-Miller, I. (2014). Deconstructing socioemotional wealth. *Entrepreneurship Theory and Practice, 38*(4), 713–720.

Miller, D., Lee, J., Chang, S., & Le Breton-Miller, I. (2009). Filling the institutional void: The social behavior and performance of family vs non-family technology firms in emerging markets. *Journal of International Business Studies, 40*(5), 802–817.

Mitter, C., & Emprechtinger, S. (2016). The role of stewardship in the internationalisation of family firms. *International Journal of Entrepreneurial Venturing, 8*(4), 400–421.

Mullet, E., Lazreg, C., Candela, C., & Neto, F. (2005). The Scandinavian way of perceiving societal risks. *Journal of Risk Research, 8*(1), 19–30.

Mustafa, M., & Chen, S. (2010). The strength of family networks in transnational immigrant entrepreneurship. *Thunderbird International Business Review, 52*(2), 97–106.

Oviatt, B. M., & McDougall, P. P. (2005). Defining international entrepreneurship and modeling the speed of internationalization. *Entrepreneurship Theory and Practice, 29*(5), 537–553.

Patel, V. K., Pieper, T. M., & Hair Jr., J. F. (2012). The global family business: Challenges and drivers for cross-border growth. *Business Horizons, 55*(3), 231–239.

Patton, M. Q. (2002). Two decades of developments in qualitative inquiry: A personal, experiential perspective. *Qualitative Social Work, 1*(3), 261–283.

Piekkari, R., Welch, C., & Paavilainen, E. (2009). The case study as disciplinary convention: Evidence from international business journals. *Organizational Research Methods, 12*(3), 567–589.

Pukall, T. J., & Calabrò, A. (2014). The internationalization of family firms: A critical review and integrative model. *Family Business Review, 27*(2), 103–125.

Reay, T. (2014). Publishing qualitative research. *Family Business Review, 27*, 95–102.

Rihoux, B., & Ragin, C. C. (2008). *Configurational comparative methods: Qualitative comparative analysis (QCA) and related techniques* (Vol. 51). Thousand Oaks, CA: Sage.

Sánchez-Bueno, M. J., & Usero, B. (2014). How may the nature of family firms explain the decisions concerning international diversification? *Journal of Business Research, 67*(7), 1311–1320.

Sayer, A. (1992). *Method in social science: A realist approach* (2nd ed.). London, UK: Routledge.

Scholes, L., Mustafa, M., & Chen, S. (2016). Internationalization of small family firms: The influence of family from a socioemotional wealth perspective. *Thunderbird International Business Review, 58*(2), 131–146.

Sirmon, D. G., Arregle, J. L., Hitt, M. A., & Webb, J. W. (2008). The role of family influence in firms' strategic responses to threat of imitation. *Entrepreneurship Theory and Practice, 36*(6), 979–998.

Söderqvist, A., & Chetty, S. (2013). Strength of ties involved in international new ventures. *European Business Review, 25*(6), 536–552.

Stieg, P., Cesinger, B., Apfelthaler, G., Kraus, S., & Cheng, C. F. (2018). Antecedents of successful internationalization in family and non-family firms: How knowledge resources and collaboration intensity shape international performance. *Journal of Small Business Strategy, 28*(1), 14–27.

Swinth, R. L., & Vinton, K. L. (1993). Do family-owned businesses have a strategic advantage in international joint ventures? *Family Business Review, 6*(1), 19–30.

Welch, C., Piekkari, R., Plakoyiannaki, E., & Paavilainen-Mäntymäki, E. (2011). Theorising from case studies: Towards a pluralist future for international business research. *Journal of International Business Studies, 42*(5), 740–762.

Westhead, P., & Howorth, C. (2007). 'Types' of private family firms: An exploratory conceptual and empirical analysis. *Entrepreneurship and Regional Development, 19*(5), 405–431.

Woodside, A. G., & Wilson, E. J. (2003). Case study research methods for theory building. *Journal of Business & Industrial Marketing, 18*(6/7), 493–508.

Yang, X., Li, J., Stanley, L. J., Kellermanns, F. W., & Li, X. (2020). How family firm characteristics affect internationalization of Chinese family SMEs. *Asia Pacific Journal of Management, 37*(2), 417–448.

Yin, R. (1984). *Case study research*. Beverly Hills, CA: Sage.

Yin, R. K. (1994). *Case study research: Design and methods*. Beverly Hills, CA: Sage.

Zaheer, S. (1995). Overcoming the liability of foreignness. *Academy of Management Journal, 38*(2), 341–363.

Zellweger, T. M., Chrisman, J. J., Chua, J. H., & Steier, L. P. (2019). Social structures, social relationships, and family firms. *Entrepreneurship Theory and Practice, 43*(2), 207–223.

Zellweger, T. M., Kellermanns, F. W., Chrisman, J. J., & Chua, J. H. (2012). Family control and family firm valuation by family CEOs: The importance of intentions for transgenerational control. *Organization Science, 23*(3), 851–868.

11

Networking from Home to Abroad: The Internationalization of The Iberostar Group

Elena San Román, Agueda Gil-López, Isabel Díez-Vial, and Sarah Jack

Introduction

Social networks play a particularly important role in the internationalization of family firms (FFs) (Pukall & Calabrò, 2014). Multinational family firms have expanded throughout the world upon the basis of their ability to create and leverage networks of collaboration with other firms in order to gain better access to markets (Colli, García-Canal, & Guillén, 2013). Social capital, created through the set of network relations across firms, constitutes a critical factor that shapes the process and outcomes of family firms' internationalization, including market selection, entry form and the selection of partners (Evers & O'Gorman, 2011; Hohenthal, Johanson, & Johanson, 2014; Montoro-Sánchez, Díez-Vial, & Belso-Martinez, 2018). Interestingly, some studies suggest that family firms find it more difficult to build these critical

---

E. San Román (✉) • I. Díez-Vial
Universidad Complutense de Madrid, Madrid, Spain
e-mail: esanroma@ucm.es

A. Gil-López
Universidad Francisco de Vitoria, Madrid, Spain

S. Jack
House of Innovation, Stockholm School of Economics, Stockholm, Sweden

Lancaster University Management School, Lancaster, UK

© The Author(s), under exclusive license to Springer Nature Switzerland AG 2021
T. Leppäaho, S. Jack (eds.), *The Palgrave Handbook of Family Firm Internationalization*,
https://doi.org/10.1007/978-3-030-66737-5_11

327

328   E. San Román et al.

networks, compared to non-family firms, and that the precise way these networks intertwine with the family issues and how this affects family firm internationalization is still underexplored (Kontinen & Ojala, 2010). In fact, non-family firms have received comparatively more attention in the literature on internationalization and networks, and this has left critical issues concerning family firms unexamined, such as the specific types of networks they use when looking to internationalize, their dynamics and how these networks evolve as internationalization develops over time, and even across countries (Kontinen & Ojala, 2010). From the literature on family firms, there is also a lack of concluding evidence into how these types of firms pursue international opportunities by drawing on their networks. Addressing these issues is particularly important since family firms differ considerably from non-family firms in many issues, including business orientation, risk taking or performance (Arregle, Naldi, Nordqvist, & Hitt, 2012; Naldi, Nordqvist, Sjöberg, & Wiklund, 2007). So, it can be anticipated that internationalization patterns for family firms will differ too.

Notwithstanding the shared characteristics of family firms, national contexts and institutional frameworks can in many ways shape internationalization patterns, creating notable differences among firms and countries (Meyer, Mudambi, & Narula, 2011). Particularly under contexts of resource constraints and institutional imbalances, like Spain during Franco's dictatorship, family firms become an effective channel through which resources are leveraged, connections to foreign players built and operations launched (Puig & Fernández Pérez, 2009). Yet, within the discipline of family firm internationalization, studies have paid limited attention to the issue of context-embeddedness (Leppäaho, Metsola, & Paavilainen-Mäntymäki, 2016). Furthermore, approaches incorporating not only context but also time are even less prevalent.

To address these gaps and move research forward, more empirical work is needed which understands the internationalization of family firms as a longitudinal process of social networking shaped by the context in which the firm is embedded. Therefore, this chapter analyses from a historical perspective the case of a multinational Spanish family firm that relied on its social networks to develop its business at home and launch the firm internationally. Being a Spanish family firm allows us to introduce the context of a country whose institutional imbalances during part of the twentieth century have strongly shaped its business *demography*.[1] Thus, Spanish family-owned companies

---

[1] The internationalization of Spanish family firms has generated a growing body of literature including many case studies. They usually deliver a rich, historical description on the processes, drivers and out-

became a prominent type of organization capable of overcoming domestic market constraints and acted as a virtuous channel for launching connections at home and abroad.[2]

While the context was restrictive, Spanish companies were forced to focus on the domestic market, while trying to access needed resources, located in foreign markets, to supply their operations. Given the existing institutional barriers imposed by the Spanish context, social connections became an alternative channel for accessing those valuable resources including not only financial means but also knowledge and markets abroad, as Puig and Fernández Pérez (2009) pointed out. These personal and social networks, as Spanish scholars have described, conformed the key asset that family firms enjoyed at those times of legal and institutional limitations.

Our chapter is particularly interested in studying how networks between a family firm and foreign companies in a constrained domestic market were deployed and developed through time. It also looks at how these networks supported the internationalization of the family firm. To address our research interest, we consider the case of the Iberostar Group, a 100% family-owned Spanish multinational company based in Palma de Mallorca that has been operating in the tourist sector since 1956 and whose internationalization started in the late 1970s. Nowadays, its business is focused on hospitality, where it has a global portfolio of more than 100 four- and five-star hotels in 16 countries. In 2019, the Iberostar Group ranked fifth in terms of number of hotels in Spain and 46th worldwide in terms of rooms (Hosteltur, 2019). Our case is particularly interesting as it constitutes a multinational family firm operating in an industry that plays a key role in the Spanish economy (Cirer-Costa, 2014): in 2019, tourism accounted for 11.1% of Spanish GDP and 13.3% of total employment.[3]

Our case shows that the Iberostar Group constituted a trustworthy partner through which foreign companies entered the Spanish tourist market and

---

comes of their venture abroad (Fernández-Pérez, 1999; Fernández Moya, 2010; Puig & Fernández Pérez, 2009; San Román, 2009, 2017; Tàpies, San Román, & Gil-López, 2015; San Román & Puig, 2018). If there is something common to this rich, historically detailed body of research it is the particular attention that the Spanish institutional context has received, as well as the prevailing assumption that internationalization has happened through an ongoing process that needs to be examined over the long term (Fernández Moya, 2012; Reuber, 2016).

[2] According to the Spanish *Instituto de Empresa Familiar* (IEF), nowadays family firms account for 89% of Spain's business sector, 57% of the GDP of the private sector and 67% of private employment. They have also played an active, dominant role in the internationalization of Spain and are particularly dominant in industries where the country holds a competitive advantage, like trade, transportation, textiles and clothing and tourism.

[3] Data have been gathered from "España en cifras, 2019", Instituto Nacional de Estadística. https://www.ine.es/prodyser/espa_cifras/2019/3/.

built business alliances with both a domestic and an international scope. Interaction between the Iberostar Group and foreign companies allowed the Spanish family firm to grow and consolidate its domestic business but also provided access to foreign markets, resulting in a learning process that fore-armed the company for venturing abroad. In this process of networking, the family nature of the Iberostar Group was key because it offered the international partners reputation and, therefore, trust, reliability and a long-term vision which helped to counteract the uncertainties and constraints imposed by the domestic context (Pla-Barber, Sanchez-Peinado, & Madhok, 2010; Villar, Pla-Barber, & León-Darder, 2012).

Theoretical Framework: Networks in the Internationalization of Family Firms

Previous studies have confirmed the relevance of relationships with international partners for developing the internationalization process of family firms (Hohenthal et al., 2014; Hutchings & Murray, 2002; Kontinen & Ojala, 2011a). From this perspective, family firms use their network of relationships to search for new international opportunities and knowledge about distant markets, learning about new practices and processes that are useful in their ventures abroad (Chetty & Holm, 2000; Sharma & Blomstermo, 2003). These networks tend to play a particularly important role since family firms usually lack resources (Pukall & Calabrò, 2014) and tend to gradually commit to international markets (Graves & Thomas, 2008).

Within the field of family firms' internationalization, network models play an important role as the social network of the business family can notably influence internationalization activities (Anderson, Jack, & Dodd, 2005; Brydon & Dana, 2011; Byrom & Lehman, 2009; Coviello, 2006; Crick, Bradshaw, & Chaudhry, 2006; Mustafa & Chen, 2010; Wright & Nasierowski, 1994). Many studies indeed suggest that through some family-specific resources, including trust, altruism or social capital, family firms can overcome constraints in their internationalization (Calabrò & Mussolino, 2013; Segaro, 2010; Zahra, 2003). This set of qualitative factors, which emerge from the family nature of a company, can assume a critical role when the company is constrained by the scarcity of financial resources, competences and/or knowledge to pursue international opportunities (Wright, Filatotchev, Hoskisson, & Peng, 2005). This issue is particularly common in family firms due to their predominantly small and medium size and the family unwillingness to lose control due to external funding. Despite the fact that networks matter for a family firm's internationalization, as Pukall and Calabrò (2014) suggest, there is still limited knowledge about the particular role they play and the processes through which they are created and develop over time (Kampouri, Plakoyiannaki, & Leppäaho, 2017; Kontinen & Ojala, 2010, 2011b, 2012; Pukall & Calabrò, 2014).

The network perspective (Ahuja, Soda, & Zaheer, 2012; Phelps, Heidl, & Wadhwa, 2012) has developed abundant research in its attempt to understand how direct and indirect ties between agents—providers, clients, partners, competitors and other agents—evolve over time for business information, advice and problem solving, with some contacts providing multiple resources. In particular, this perspective highlights the importance of social and business ties for international entrepreneurship. Contributions suggest that firms internationalize via domestic business networks and that the type and nature of the network tie might influence many processes and strategies associated to internationalization such as market selection, entry form and even the choice of the exchange partner (Evers & O'Gorman, 2011; Hohenthal et al., 2014; Montoro-Sánchez et al., 2018).

In this sense, the relevant role that brokerage relations play has been observed (Bembom & Schwens, 2018; Coviello, McDougall, & Oviatt, 2011; Kontinen & Ojala, 2011a). International suppliers, clients or competitors are used to identify new opportunities, obtain business advice, assist in foreign negotiations or open doors in their home markets, among others (Agostini & Nosella, 2018; Gao, Ren, Zhang, & Sun, 2016). By brokerage interactions entrepreneurs can obtain valuable knowledge about international markets that is non-redundant within existing ones (McEvily & Zaheer, 1999), decreases the perceived risk (Sharma & Blomstermo, 2003), enhances the establishment of new relationships (Guercini & Runfola, 2010) and helps the firm identify opportunities (Kontinen & Ojala, 2011a).

Previous studies on internationalization have acknowledged this critical role of brokerage positions for firms (Chetty & Eriksson, 2002; Chetty & Holm, 2000; Ellis, 2000; Johanson & Mattsson, 1988; Kontinen & Ojala, 2011a), being concerned with the kind of relationships that firms should have with the broker for success in the international venture (Agndal, Chetty, & Wilson, 2008; Chandra et al., 2009). Some researchers have observed that establishing strong ties with brokers has been pointed out as best for internationalization (Chetty & Eriksson, 2002). Strong ties results from "the combination of the amount of time, the emotional intensity, the intimacy (mutual confiding), and the reciprocal services which characterize the tie" (Granovetter, 1973, p. 1361). Entrepreneurs who identify international opportunities through strong ties will find it easier because of mutual understanding since they have already developed shared routines and procedures and a trustworthy relation (Yli-Renko, Autio, & Tontti, 2002). Studies confirming this point have been mainly based on their being complementary relationships between the entrepreneur and her suppliers or clients (Belso-Martínez, 2006; Chetty & Eriksson, 2002; Hitt, Ireland, & Tuggle, 2006).

Nevertheless, strong ties can behave as real brokers for the entrepreneur, providing new ideas and opportunities for international business, only if no other member of the network has any other strong ties with the same network of the broker (Burt, 1992). The presence of strong ties that are also bridged require the existence of different groups inside the network that are hardly connected, so some parts can have strong relationships that are not shared by all (Granovetter, 1973). As it has been explained, the tendency of the network to increase connectivity and embeddedness across time makes this club network structure increasingly difficult (Baum, McEvily, & Rowley, 2012).

There is also a view in the network literature that weak ties offer the possibility of connections to new markets (Jack, 2005). Weak ties are characterized as infrequent, irregular and loose contacts, such as casual business contacts or association memberships (Hitt et al., 2006), international trade shows (Evers & Knight, 2008), acquaintances of the entrepreneur (Loane & Bell, 2006) or contacts from existing contacts (Coviello & Munro, 1995), among others. Entrepreneurs can get access to information and knowledge through weak ties: "To become established in a new market—that is, a network that is new to the firm—it has to build relationships which are new both to itself and its counterparts" (Johanson & Mattsson, 1988, p. 306).

However, once the firm has been able to enter an international market, the establishment of new brokerage relationships for continuing the internationalization process is fostered by the previous experience of the firm in its domestic market. Firms that have already developed a similar kind of bridging connection in their domestic network would have more chances of establishing useful international bridging ties (Chetty & Eriksson, 2002; Kontinen & Ojala, 2011a). Firms tend to develop specific routines and procedures based on their experience in past network positions that would improve their capacity to develop, store and apply knowledge when they are in a similar position in their current networks, a kind of "network memory" (Soda, Usai, & Zaheer, 2004). As long as the firm can incorporate its previous relational knowledge into specific routines, it will be able to improve its capacity to govern and develop inter-firm sharing routines (Gulati, Nohria, & Zaheer, 2000).

Establishing bridging ties in the domestic network implies a change in the previous relationship (Belso-Martínez, Díez-Vial, López-Sánchez, &

Mateu-Garcia, 2018). Belonging to a network creates dependencies on the resources of others, and new international relationships imply changes to the entire network—that is, deleting some of the existing relationships or incorporating the new one (Johanson & Mattsson, 1988). Firms that can reduce their local commitment to create new international relationships in the domestic market would find it much easier to replicate the structure in relationships once they are in international markets (Ahuja et al., 2012). By having domestic as well as international bridging ties, firms can not only apply similar patterns, routines and norms to the relationships but can also leverage new ideas, experiences and knowledge across them (Soda et al., 2004).

When Context Matters: Spain in the Second Half of the Twentieth Century

Spanish development in the second half of the twentieth century is probably one of the most complex and interesting processes of economic growth and socio-political change in Contemporary European history. The Spanish economy began catching up and consolidated earlier than the socio-political one, the former worked as a virtuous breeding ground for the latter.

After a long period of isolation during the 1940s, and a decade of reforms and substantial economic progress in the 1950s, Spain experienced during the 1960s the so-called "Spanish economic miracle", a period of fast economic growth driven by the increasing openness and deregulation of the internal market: GDP grew at an average annual rate of 8.3% and GDP per capita at 6.9%. This economic expansion had implications on tourism that, although flourishing in the 1950s, turned during the 1960s into the key activity for bringing foreign currencies that compensated the foreign deficit. So, the "mass tourism" of the 1950s gave way in the 1960s to "massive tourism" (Vallejo-Pousada, 2013), which enabled Spain to be ranked among the first in the world in terms of number of visitors and tourism income: in 1969 Spain overtook France and shortly afterwards Italy, and ranked second behind the United States. By the beginning of the 1970s, the Spanish share of world tourism had reached greater heights than ever before in the twentieth century: almost 16% of visitors and over 10% of total income (Sánchez, 2004).

The fast economic growth slowed down abruptly in 1973 due to the oil shock and the resulting international economic downturn that, in Spain, coincided with the instability of the transition to democracy. After Franco's death in 1975, Spain held its first democratic elections in 1977 and approved and signed its Constitution one year later. The arrival of democracy paved

Spain's way towards Europe. Its integration into the EEC, in 1986, allowed the country to initiate another wave of fast growth.

The persisting institutional imbalances and domestic resource constraints in Spain during most of the second half of the twentieth century shaped the way business worked, giving distinctive importance to non-economic resources like social networks. This type of resource was particularly important if we bear in mind that economic and financial means were mostly provided by foreign markets, so turning to foreign markets was a key channel to develop businesses at home.

Our Case Study: Iberostar Group, the History of a Long-Lasting Family Firm

The origins of the Iberostar Group can be traced back to the Fluxá family, initially linked to the footwear industry and the island of Majorca (Spain). In 1877, Antoni Fluxá (1853–1918), first generation of the business family, started work as a shoemaker, opening a small artisanal workshop in the town of Inca (Majorca). In 1956 his son, Lorenzo Fluxá (1908–1993) ventured towards the tourism industry through the purchase of a small travel agency called Viajes Iberia. Two main factors encouraged him towards diversification. On the one hand, during the 1940s the artisanal shoe workshop of Lorenzo Fluxá had suffered the scarcity of foreign currencies needed to import supplies. This imprinted the family with a sense of the importance of being international, so that the limitations of the Spanish context could never hinder the development of the company again. On the other hand, as already pointed out, Spanish tourism entered a flourishing stage in the 1950s which made the sector an interesting activity for business diversification.

Given this flourishing context and the international vision of the family, in 1956 Lorenzo Fluxá acquired Viajes Iberia that, at that time, had eight regional travel agencies. A few years later, his son, Miguel, took the responsibility of the tourism business of the family. Under his leadership, the company expanded its domestic activity towards the three main areas of the tourism industry: outbound, inbound and hotels. While outbound refers to organizing trips as a retailer, through travel agencies or as a wholesaler using tour operators, inbound consists of handling tourist arrivals in a destination, arranging transfers and additional excursions. Meanwhile, hotels are responsible for accommodating travellers. Until the end of the 1970s, all the business activity of the company was mainly focused on the Spanish market.

The internationalization process of the Iberostar Group took place in the same three areas developed at home: inbound, outbound and hotels. The first international venture came in the inbound activity, with the establishment of two affiliates, one in the UK (Iberotravel) and one in the United States (Visit US) in 1979–1980. The second international venture took place in 1991 in the outbound business through the creation of Sunworld, the first Spanish tour operator abroad. Finally, in 1993, the Iberostar Group launched the internationalization of its hotel area through its first resort in the Caribbean. This represented the starting point for a remarkable international expansion of hotels. Between 1993 and 2018, Iberostar added more than 70 hotels to its international portfolio, meaning an average annual accumulated growth of 14%. In 2018, 64% of the total number of Iberostar hotels were located abroad (San Román & Puig, 2018).

Figure 11.1 extends this historical narration by providing a timeline with the milestones in Iberostar's history. Given our interest in researching the role of networks in family firm internationalization, this work focuses on a period of the company's history (1962–1997) that covers the development of the business in Spain, the deployment and enactment of network ties with international companies and the first international venture.

Research Method

Qualitative Case Study Research

Our research relies on a qualitative method which is particularly appropriate given our focus on a "how" rather than "what" or "how many" questions (Yin, 1994). This approach is also in line with previous research that identified qualitative research as being adequate to study linkages between the past and the present of organizations (Bryant, 2014; Garud, Kumaraswamy, & Karnøe, 2010). Given our research interest in understanding how networks between a family firm and foreign companies in a constrained domestic market were deployed and developed through time, and how these networks supported the internationalization of the family firm, descriptive data are required for generating systematic insights, in which the context of the organization is appreciated as a key factor (Reay, 2014). Indeed, an important feature of qualitative inquiry is to demonstrate sensitivity to context and gain a holistic view of social phenomena. Another outstanding characteristic of qualitative research is to approach the fieldwork accounts in their original forms throughout the

336 E. San Román et al.

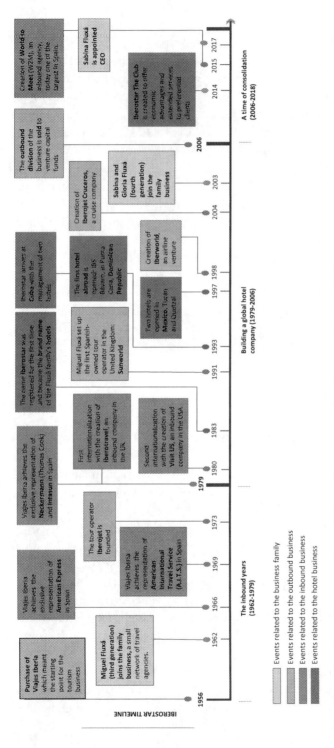

Fig. 11.1 Timeline of Iberostar Group history. (Own elaboration from San Román, 2017)

study, so the reader can capture the context within which the events were observed (Fletcher et al., 2016).

In addition to our qualitative approach, this work is based on a single case study. Although this method prevents the generalizability of our findings, a single case study is useful if the case is particularly representative for the research purpose and when research is focused on a longitudinal case, as ours is (Yin, 2003). Indeed Iberostar is a multinational family firm that relied on social networks for developing the whole possibilities of its tourism businesses—inbound, outbound and hotels—during four consecutive decades. So it seems an appropriate fieldwork to fulfil our interest in the role played by networks in FFs' internationalization.

Moreover, case studies provide unique means of developing theory by utilizing in-depth insights of empirical phenomena and their contexts (Dubois & Gadde, 2002), understood as the "the surroundings associated with phenomena which help to illuminate that phenomena [sic]" (Cappelli & Sherer, 1991, p. 56). Therefore, learning from a particular case, conditioned by its context, should be considered a strength as far as the interaction between a phenomenon and its context is best captured so that contextualizing and explaining can be brought together in a case study (Welch, Piekkari, Plakoyiannaki, & Paavilainen-Mäntymäki, 2011).

Data Collection

Our empirical research is grounded in an extensive and sufficient collection (Reay, 2014) of written and oral sources gathered between 2012 and 2017. Thanks to a business history project commissioned by the Iberostar Group, we were able to set up a fully digitalized historical archive containing over 4000 documents and the transcripts of 71 interviews with owners and managers of the company, external informants, family members and other key players in the tourism industry. Given the purpose of this chapter and following specific suggestions about how to deal with business documentation, from our collection of data sources we selected for closer study those sources that helped shed light on our research interests (Rowlinson, 2004). These include the transcribed interviews with highly knowledgeable informants and selected archived internal company documents. Secondary data including press articles, websites, books and industry reports were also examined to verify and extend data provided by our primary sources. Table 11.1 summarizes our sources of data.

In our interviews, we addressed the issues of bias typically by approaching numerous and highly knowledgeable informants who viewed the phenomena

338   E. San Román et al.

Table 11.1 Summary of data

Data description
Interviews with 38 informants, including:
8 Iberostar's corporate executives (2 family members)
10 (non-family) Iberostar's general managers
15 external informants (owners or managers of other hotel or tourism companies, and independent external advisers)
5 members of the Fluxá family without any role in the company
Interviews procedure:
Interviews were conducted by one of the authors between 2012 and 2017
They lasted between one and three hours
All were recorded and transcribed verbatim
Iberostar Group Archive
Documents about external partners

Partner	Number of document	Type of document	Years
Iberia Líneas Aéreas, American Express, AITS and AARP	3–4	Manuscript on the history of the company written by the Vicepresident	1930–1990
	2	Chronological summary of Viajes Iberia history	1930–1990
	29	Report about the history of the company	1930–2004
	34	Timeline of Viajes Iberia Group	1930–1996
	35	Descriptive memorandum of Viajes Iberia Group	1930–1994
American Express	2565	Assessment of agencies performance	1961
	1458–1460	Summary of subjects covered in the meeting with the board of directors of Viajes Iberia S.A.	1973
	1514–1515	Clearing documents with Viajes Iberia	1975
	1294	Clearing documents with Viajes Iberia	1979

(*continued*)

11 Networking from Home to Abroad: The Internationalization... 339

Table 11.1 (continued)

Intasun	2501	Memorandum about the visit of the accounting department of Intasun to Viajes Iberia	1977
	2514	Documentation related to Intasun clients	1978
	2332–2341 2346–2362 2518–2524	Clearing documents with Intasun	1978–1981
	2504	Accounting protocol agreement	1978
	2506	Intasun Flight arrivals memorandum	1978
	2447–2457 2503, 2505	Documents on several agreements between Viajes Iberia and Intasun	1979–1982
	2448	Statistical study regarding the average stay of Intasun clients	1980
	2449	Correspondence about the comercial agreement with Intasun for the year 1981	1981
Neckermann	1012	Several contracts between agencies	1968–1972
	1006	Agency contract between Neckermann and Viajes Iberia	1974
	2440–2447	Clearing documents with Neckermann	1977–1979
	2512	Agreement appointing Viajes Iberia as the exclusive representative of Neckermann in Spain	1979
	60–61	Several agency contracts between Viajes Iberia and Neckermann	1987
	62–63	Correspondence between Viajes Iberia and Neckermann	1990

(*continued*)

340   E. San Román et al.

Table 11.1 (continued)

Documents about companies of Iberostar Group

Company	Number of document	Type of document	Years
Iberotravel	2635–2645	Correspondence between Viajes Iberia and Iberotravel	1995–2000
Sunworld	1963	Press article on the entry of Miguel Fluxà in the British touroperation market	1992
	2517	Selling contract of Sunworld	1996
Iberojet	259	Correspondence including information about Iberojet future operations	1972
	260	Contracts between Aviaco Airlines and Iberojet	1972
	1455	Summary of subjects covered in the meeting with the board of directors of Viajes Iberia S.A., including Iberojet	1972
	271	Information on advertisement brochures	1973
	1005	Contract between Iberojet and Intasun	1977
Viajes Iberia	3–4	Manuscript on the history of the company written by the Vicepresident	1930–1990
	2	Chronological summary of Viajes Iberia history	1930–1990
	29	Report about the history of the company	1930–2004
	34	Timeline of Viajes Iberia Group	1930–1996
	35	Descriptive memorandum of Viajes Iberia Group	1930–1994

Source: Own ellaboration from Iberostar Group Archive

from diverse perspectives (Eisenhardt & Graebner, 2007). The combination of insiders and outsiders' views and the plurality of testimonies from actors in different positions and motives provided different perspectives to guide our interpretations and support the overall credibility of our oral sources and the validity of our findings (Kipping, Wadhwani, & Bucheli, 2014).

Interviews followed a semi-structured schedule and were focused on tracing key events in the company's evolution, understanding the practices in relation to these events, appreciating the personal history, activities and background of the interviewed, and identifying interactions and network linkages related to the development of ventures in both the domestic market and abroad. As recommended by Pettigrew, Woodman, and Cameron (2001), the use of questions containing "what, who, where, why, when and how" were used to guide the research protocol of the interviews. We also used techniques aligned with active interviewing (Holstein & Gubrium, 1995), allowing respondents to articulate their perceptions and experiences freely and spontaneously, thus assuring the free flow of storytelling (Czarniawska, 2004).

We took steps to identify and minimize retrospective bias by triangulating the interviews with the relevant documentation selected from the Historical Archive of the Iberostar Group. As a family-owned company, there are no minutes of the Annual Meetings of the Board of Directors or minutes of shareholders general meetings, but we have been able to access other documents—see Table 11.1—with valuable information to support our research purpose. These documents complemented and corroborated our interviews and avoided the limitations often associated with relying on a single source (Kipping et al., 2014; Miles & Huberman, 1994).

Data Analysis

To analyse the rich body of data collected, an inductive and iterative process was adopted (Miles, Huberman, & Saldaña, 2014), hence building and refining theory from the case study data (Eisenhardt & Graebner, 2007). Data analysis evolved in different stages. First, the historical evolution of Iberostar was reconstructed by delineating the data and events into a chronological order, avoiding excessive data reduction and allowing the authors to identify interactions and relationships among the different types of data examined (Miles et al., 2014). Furthermore, classifying the data into a chronological order was key to identify events and analyse interactions among different actors and link their actions to other data, which allowed the determination of the context (Van de Van de Ven, 2007; Yin, 2009).

Second, data analysis was theoretically oriented by building on the assumptions about FFs internationalization (Pukall & Calabrò, 2014) and the role played by networks in here (Colli et al., 2013; Evers & O'Gorman, 2011; Hohenthal et al., 2014; Montoro-Sánchez et al., 2018). These assumptions framed theoretical expectations. The authors worked recursively between the case and the theory being developed. When a specific theme was ambiguous, the authors referred to the relevant academic literature for a clear distinction and categorization. In this sense, an inductive approach to elaborate and refine existing theory was followed (Halinen & Törnroos, 2005) by contrasting empirical observations emerging from our case with preexisting propositions of our research theme. In so doing, we refined our initial themes and gradually gained more insights on why and how internationalization of the Iberostar Group developed the way it did. Data were then scrutinized for detail relating to these themes and emerging categories in order to arrive at our contributions and theoretical implications which are presented in our conclusions.

From Home to Abroad: A Longitudinal Process of Networking

In each area of Iberostar's internationalization, inbound, outbound and hotels—discussed below—the process was driven by a set of relationships with local and foreign ties. These ties, which were first deployed in the local market, provided the stock of knowledge and resources that supported the upcoming international venture.

The Internationalization of the Inbound Business

During the period 1962–1979, Iberostar business expanded towards the inbound activity through its original travel company called Viajes Iberia. By the beginning of the 1960s, the company was firmly established in the local market, with an extended retail business that focused on handling tourist arrivals in Spain. The tourism boom that Spain experienced meant an opportunity to change the business approach and start taking advantages of the growing number of foreign visitors.

The company understood that expanding the inbound activity in the local market had to rely on pursuing and establishing network relationships with foreign companies. Indeed, contacts abroad were relevant because they were able to provide Iberostar with clients. Iberostar's current President explains: "[inbound business] doesn't need capital; it needs connections".[4] These connections had to be built on a trust relationship between Viajes Iberia, Iberostar's travel agency, and the foreign companies that would bring their customers to Spain: "We understood that inbound business (…) meant being the representative of other companies [...] In this side of the business we were very successful because the customers trusted us and we did everything that was necessary to solve their problems".[5]

Establishing connections with foreign companies meant going abroad to look for tour operators who were willing to entrust their clients to the Spanish company and, then, deploy and develop these connections in the domestic market. First attempts to find tour operators were taken in culturally similar markets: South and Central America. The role of brokers was relevant for Viajes Iberia to establish first contact with potential clients. The public Spanish airline, Iberia Líneas Aéreas, which already had a history of operations in the American market, played that role. Ultimately, South and Central America did not provide relevant clients to Viajes Iberia but the knowledge accumulated during the searching process oriented Viajes Iberia to look to North America. This shows how the process of looking for network ties was itself a source of knowledge to inform further steps in Viajes Iberia expansion.

The entry in North America was in fact facilitated by the airline that became the channel through which connections were established in this market. One informant explains: "They [the airline company] introduced us abroad".[6] Moreover, the closeness of their businesses (air transport and tourism) and the fact that both companies shared "Iberia" in their names, offered a great opportunity to exploit the synergies: the airline would sell more tickets if it additionally offered its clients the services of a local agency in the country of destination with programmes of tourism.[7] "The airline could offer an additional service that included not only the trip to Spain but also, for instance, circuits through Europe by bus; this was the 'candy' they used to provide the airline with more customers travelling to Spain".[8] The two companies ended up working together and "started having a stable, friendly relationship".[9] Shared idiosyncrasies made business collaboration easier for them: "[We] were

---

[4] Interview with Miguel Fluxá (20 March 2013).

[5] Ibid.

[6] Interview with José Linares (25 September 2012).

[7] Many customers tended to think that Iberia Líneas Aéreas and Viajes Iberia were the same company.

[8] Interview with José Linares (23 October 2012).

[9] Interview with José Linares (18 October 2012).

Spanish men so we could easily understand each other".[10] This collaboration, based on business synergies, regular contacts and cultural closeness, also helped Iberostar reach other markets such as Mexico or Canada, and extended the inbound business from the United States.

At the end of the 1960s, the experience gathered in the United States and all networks developed allowed Viajes Iberia to reach, now independently, the exclusive representation in Spain of three American companies: American Express, American International Travel Services Inc. (AITS) and American Association of Retired Persons (AARP). This resulted in a growing number of American tourists arriving in Spain through Viajes Iberia which soared in the 1970s, providing a great leap forward for the domestic inbound business. Viajes Iberia was still a travel agency whose business was mainly concerned with Spain but it managed to be a part of an international network which nurtured the business in Spain and informed new international opportunities.

Indeed, the case of Viajes Iberia shows that a key resource offered by being part of an international network was the stock of knowledge and the reputation it supplied. These factors were reinforced by Fluxá's remarkable ability to establish personal relationships and generate friendship and trust, as one informant explained: "everything was built on the back of his personality".[11] These factors led to the signing in 1979 of two important inbound contracts that turned the Spanish company into the exclusive representative of two large European tour operators, the German Neckermann and the British Intasun.

The agreement between Iberostar and Neckermann took shape as a result of the many trips Miguel Fluxá made to Germany "to see if they would give us a chance because they had various partners in Spain".[12] Before the contract was signed in 1979, Viajes Iberia was already collaborating with Neckermann as one of its agents, among many, in Spain. However, at the end of the 1970s, Neckermann decided to concentrate all its outbound business in the hands of one sole agent. The German tour operator understood that Viajes Iberia would be the trustworthy partner they needed and the family nature of the company was at the core of the decision for choosing it; the Spanish company also offered a wider vision of the tourism business that was attractive to the tour operator: "Fluxá had, at that time, a wider vision than others (…) The Fluxás were a very solid and honorable family. For us it was critical to choose

---

[10] Ibid.

[11] Interview with Harry Goodman (6 May 2013).

[12] Interview with Miguel Fluxá (20 March 2013).

11 Networking from Home to Abroad: The Internationalization... 345

honest partners, who would be capable of defending our interests. Because our agent is the *long arm* of the company on his home turf".[13]

The contract with Intasun was the result of the personal friendship between Fluxá and Harry Goodman, the founder of the ILG group owner of Intasun. Fluxá and Goodman met in Majorca at the beginning of the 1960s. As Goodman acknowledged, his constant presence in Majorca resulted in a close-tie relationship between them that facilitated the agreement signed in 1979. This agreement between the British tour operator and Viajes Iberia meant an exchange of business: the Spanish company had created its own tour operator in 1973, Iberojet, which entrusted its clients when travelling to the UK to one of Goodman's inbound companies. In exchange, Intasun assigned its inbound clients exclusively to Viajes Iberia in Spain. The agreement with Intasun also meant the entry of Fluxá as a shareholder in Harry Goodman's company, which in turn extended the international network and gave more visibility and reputation abroad to Viajes Iberia.

The links established with Neckermann and Intasun fostered growth in inbound business in Spain but also gave Viajes Iberia the opportunity to widen and diversify its tourist operations in two ways. First, the alliance with Neckerman played a key role in the expansion of the business towards hotels, as we will explain in Sect. 4.3. Second, the alliance with Intasun guided Viajes Iberia to establish its first inbound company outside Spain, called Iberotravel.

The creation of Iberotravel, based in London, made sense: in the words of one of our informants "We wanted to be the Spanish agent of big European tour operators, but, in the destinations where we were sending large numbers of clients, we preferred to be our own agent rather than to be in the hands of a third partner".[14] For this reason, Iberotravel was set up in the UK in 1979 and, one year later, a similar company, called Visit US, was also established in the United States.

While for the case of Iberotravel, the experience and knowledge that Viajes Iberia accumulated in its previous international alliances acted as key driver, the case of Visit US shows the added importance of the strong-tie relationship that joined Fluxá and Goodman. Indeed, the opportunity to create Visit US was provided by Harry Goodman who was looking for a partner to create an inbound company in the United States that would support his airline company already flying from London to Miami. He offered that opportunity to Fluxá, after failing with another British partner and realizing that he preferred to join his trustworthy Spanish agent who had a long experience in the

---

[13] Interview with Wolfgang Besser (21 November 2013).
[14] Interview with Miguel Fluxá (20 March 2012).

inbound business: "[Goodman] had created the inbound business with a British partner but, what happened? The British partner did not understand how the inbound business worked".[15] Again, the family nature of Iberostar was a key reason why Harry Goodman trusted it. Three generations of a solid business gave the company a good reputation. Fluxá and Goodman established Visit US as a joint venture.

The internationalization of the inbound business fostered the growth of Viajes Iberia and consolidated this segment of the business, inbound activity, as being the most solid and profitable in the years up to 1979. It was not, however, the only area of growth, as we explain in the next section.

The Internationalization of the Outbound Business: From Iberojet to Sunworld

The outbound business of Iberostar experienced progressive growth along with the expansion of the inbound activity, but significantly expanded after 1979. The Spanish company managed the development of the outbound business in the local market through the retail travel agencies. After 1973, the creation of the tour operator Iberojet added further support to this expansion. When studying the internationalization of the outbound business, in 1991, there are two main factors that help explain the success achieved by Iberostar. First, the gathered knowledge and network ties deployed in the local market. Second, the prior development of a network tie with an international partner.

Regarding the local market, the establishment of a domestic tour operator in 1973, Iberojet, was drawn on a previous experience with local partners. Indeed, at the end of the 1960s, the change in the economic climate prompted a number of Spanish travel agencies to negotiate the creation of the tour operator Club de Vacaciones, a joint venture owned by several travel agencies including Viajes Iberia. In 1973, Miguel Fluxá felt he preferred to be "at the head of something small rather than at the tail of something big" and decided to split the others and set up his own tour operator. The company experienced difficulties during the start up because of an empty leg in the flights they had booked.[16] Networks again offered support to survive during the first year: a competitor tour operator shared seats on its flights, thus allowing Iberojet to avoid the risk of hiring full flights. In the words of one informant: "[the tour operator offered us] seats enough to let us be alive in the market".[17]

---

[15] Interview with Jaime Cortés (25 September 2012).

[16] An empty leg is an empty plane on the return flight or outbound of an already-booked trip.

[17] Interview with Martin Amengual (17 January 2013).

11 Networking from Home to Abroad: The Internationalization... 347

Despite the difficulties of the early years, from 1975 onwards, Miguel Fluxá's tour operator became one of the most relevant in Spain. At the end of the 1970s, it transported an annual average of 180,000 passengers.[18] In the 1990s, following a process of vertical integration, Miguel Fluxá added an airline and a cruise line to the tour operator, as a result of which Iberojet increased its annual number of clients to over two million.[19]

Given all the experience gathered with the domestic operator, Iberostar was ready to go international. Yet, it still needed the opportunity. Again, the fact that Iberostar already belonged to an international network developed around the inbound business, as explained in the previous section, was key in opening the opportunity in the outbound. Intasun and Harry Goodman were again the providers, although in a different situation than the one that allowed the establishment of Iberotravel and Visit US. In 1991, Goodman's group went bankrupt due to the failure of its airline, Air Europe, which was mainly caused by the outbreak of the Gulf War and the resulting downturn of the international travel and tourism market. The failure of Air Europe brought down the Goodman's holding company ILG in the spring of that year.

The news of the bankruptcy hit Iberostar deeply as Intasun was a very important client. Miguel Fluxá decided to buy Harry Goodman's tour operator in order to keep all Intasun clients for Viajes Iberia's inbound business. As an informant explained, "when ILG collapsed, everybody tried to grow businesses on the back of that collapse, so we had a short special time to do something very quickly".[20] It was a question of gaining control of the tour operator as soon as possible. Goodman's tour operator had a highly skilled management team, long experience in the business and a valuable reservations system which, if recovered, would allow them to continue operating and avoid losing the millions of clients who had been left stranded.

Armed with the reservations system after buying it and keeping the management team, Miguel Fluxá renamed the tour operator as Sunworld. Recovery came quickly under the direction of the previous team. As Sunworld's CEO recalls: "He [Miguel Fluxá] put his trust in me to build and manage the business. We shared the same vision. We wanted to take the good things from ILG but build a different business, much more centred on creating great experiences for our clients. When you start from scratch, you can take the good things from the past and build something quite unique, which is what we

---

[18] "Report on the Fluxá group", 1986, IBA R. 38.

[19] Interview with Miguel Fluxá (20 March 2013).

[20] Interview with Manny Fontenla (18 January 2017).

348   E. San Román et al.

started to do in 1991".[21] The reasons for this success also relied on the international network that Miguel Fluxá had developed in the UK. As one informant explained: "he hit all his initial contacts, his network to know from opposite side how we were doing, but how the industry saw us as well. It was very peculiar".[22]

Only five years later, in 1996, Fluxá sold Sunworld to Thomas Cook. This operation turned out to be very strategic in order to support and finance the expansion of the hotels business.

The Internationalization of the Hotel Business

The development of the Iberostar Group hotel business is closely connected to the agreement signed with Neckermann in 1979. By then, the German tour operator TUI, Neckermann's main competitor, had a strong position in the hotel industry of the Balearic Islands through an agreement with another Spanish hotel company. Neckermann also wanted to establish an alliance with a Spanish company in order to secure its customers' accommodation in Spain and better deal with the socio-cultural environment. As Neckermann's CEO explained: "you need a local partner who knows everyone and knows where the problems are and how to avoid them".[23] "The total and final responsibility has to be in the hands of someone who lives there and who is knowledgeable and in control".[24]

Again, as with the outbound business, two main factors drove the internationalization process of Iberostar's hotel business: the prior development of a network tie with an international partner and the knowledge gathered and network ties deployed in the local market.

The existence of a previous network relationship with Neckermann facilitated the agreement between this tour operator and Iberostar, which was established in simple terms. Miguel Fluxá would build his own hotels, or buy them, and would manage others which were not of his property. Neckermann would fill them all and would help finance the building of some hotels. A close contact between the two partners and the existence of a previous trustworthy relationship facilitated negotiations. "We were always in permanent contact. There were the numbers and we agreed everything in one sentence or a very short protocol: no papers, no attorneys. We never had the help of an

---

[21] Interview with Peter Long (7 February 2017).

[22] Interview with Manny Fontenla (18 January 2017).

[23] Interview with Wolfgang Beeser (21 November 2013).

[24] Ibid.

attorney at the (negotiating) table (…)".[25] At the heart of this agreement was again the family nature of the company, which gave trust to the German multinational.

The agreement between Neckermann and Iberostar fostered Iberostar's expansion in the Spanish market during the 1980s. Between 1984 and 1990, Iberostar built seven hotels in Majorca and one more in the Canary Islands. Moreover, as explained by informants, the agreement resulted in a win-win relationship: on the one hand, for the German tour operator the alliance increased its market share in Spain; on the other hand, Neckermann reinforced Iberostar's brand name and reputation locally and abroad. "Neckermann became the market leader in Spain, thanks mainly to the support of Iberostar, and Iberostar expanded to become a successful hotel chain with the help and support of Neckermann's client base".[26]

By 1992, Fluxá had completed the cycle of growth and construction in Majorca and understood that an opportunity existed abroad, since other competitors were already exploiting it. Two of them, the Majorcan-based family groups Barceló and Riu, had internationalized their hotel business in the Dominican Republic during the first half of the 1980s. For Iberostar, these two companies, with similar origins and a close contact in the island, acted as gatekeepers. Indeed, their pioneering role in the internationalization of the Majorcan hotel business granted them with relevant international knowledge and experience which was disseminated within the Majorcan clustered network (Giuliani, 2011; Giuliani & Bell, 2005; Graf & Krüger, 2011; Munari, Sobrero, & Malipiero, 2012).

Riu's role was especially relevant for Iberostar in driving the international hotel leap. Indeed, when Miguel Fluxá began to think about investing in the Dominican Republic, he met Luis Riu Bertrán, second generation of the Riu company, who encouraged him to try the American market. "Luis Riu senior, an extraordinary person, told me that the demand for hotels in Latin America was enormous and that sales there were incredible. With that kind of encouragement I had no option but to start there".[27] Luis Riu Bertrán asked his son Luis Riu Güell, heading at that time operations in America, to share all his knowledge with Fluxá: "Be quite open. Tell him about the problems and about the advantages too, everything".[28] Miguel Fluxá spent three nights at

---

[25] Interview with Wolfgang Beeser (21 November 2013).
[26] Written testimony of Peter Fankhauser, ex-Thomas Cook CEO (24 May 2017).
[27] Interview with Miguel Fluxá (20 March 2013).
[28] Interview with Carmen Riu (26 February 2016).

the first Dominican hotel of the Riu family and was there giving first-hand information about the ups and downs of the international expansion.[29]

Interestingly, despite the fact that they were technically competitors, the advise given by Riu resulted in the key push for Iberostar to go ahead in the international hotel venture. What this shows is that the Majorca-based tourism local market acted as a cluster of family firms with dense networks containing competitors that cooperated and shared information widely. Those who had pioneered the internationalization venture of hotels acted as gatekeepers driving the internationalization process of the "followers" and helped create a cluster network in the targetted foreign market, the Caribbean. Iberostar, as a follower, based its learning on observation, comparison and on the social proximity with competitors both in the local and the foreign market.

The Iberostar's international partner, Neckermann, also provided support in the American international venture. Although unwilling to provide funding and thus never shared the property of Iberostar hotels, the German tour operator contributed by marketing them in the Caribbean as had prevously been the case in Spain. This shows how the practices deployed in the local market, supported by a trustworthy relationship and a close contact built in the past, reinforced collaboration between the two parties abroad.

Discussion and Conclusions

Our chapter was interested in studying the role played by networks in the internationalization of FFs. More specifically, our research purpose was focused on how networks between a family firm and foreign companies in a constrained domestic market were deployed and developed through time, and how these networks supported the internationalization of the family firm. To explore these topics, this chapter has taken a historical case study of the Iberostar Group, a long-lasting multinational family firm operating in the tourism industry.

The literature suggests that there are no concluding results about the distinctive role of family in internationalization (Sciascia, Mazzola, Astrachan, & Pieper, 2012). Neither are there concluding results about the specific role that networks play in FFs' internationalization (Kampouri et al., 2017; Kontinen & Ojala, 2010, 2011b, 2012). Although most research suggests that networks matter—particularly for compensating the shortage of resources that commonly affect FFs' operations—there is a need to further investigate how

---

[29] Ibid.

networks intertwine with the internationalization process of FFs over time and how business families specifically leverage their social contacts, either domestic or international, to support the development of their business abroad (Pukall & Calabrò, 2014). The role played by the organization's context in this complex process has also been underexplored in the literature (Colli et al. 2014; Puig & Fernández Pérez, 2009). Some studies suggest that in order to advance this stream of research, works need to address and understand FFs' internationalization as a process that develops through time and is rooted in a context whose economic and institutional features constitute powerful dimensions (Kontinen & Ojala, 2010; Leppäaho et al., 2016). Therefore, historical studies seem a strategic tool to further investigate these topics.

Our findings, focused on the case of the Iberostar Group, confirm previous results regarding the importance of networks for launching and supporting FFs' internationalization (Basly, 2007; Fernández & Nieto, 2005; Graves & Thomas, 2008; Kontinen & Ojala, 2011a; Pukall & Calabrò, 2014). Yet, our study extends our knowledge about the process of networking for leveraging internationalization opportunities, the role played by family in it as well as the distinctive way the organization context can shape how relationships with international partners are deployed and evolve and their implications. Our study also depicts the crucial importance of establishing bridging ties in the domestic market. In addition, throughout this work, we have been able to identify the two crucial dimensions of context as suggested by Meyer et al. (2011)—resource endowments and institutional framework—and their implications for FFs' internationalization, as discussed below.

Our case study shows a process of co-evolution, that is, a gradual internationalization that was nurtured by the existence and evolution of previous ties with local and foreign partners. The Iberostar Group constituted, as we have shown, the trustworthy partner through which foreign companies entered the Spanish tourist market and built business alliances with a domestic but also international scope. Networks were originally deployed in the domestic market and provided Iberostar with critical resources, including financial support, brand consolidation, reputation or knowledge, which fuelled Iberostar's domestic growth. Importantly, what these resources also brought was the opportunity to broaden, internationally, the scope of a still domestic business. Therefore, Iberostar was able to internationalize through cross-territorial networking (Andreosso-O'Callaghan & Lenihan, 2008; De Propris & Sugden, 2008) by linking itself to extensive international networks from the domestic market.

Through cooperating with relevant international operators in the domestic market, Iberostar initiated a learning journey that forearmed the company to venture abroad. For instance, the creation of Iberotravel and Visit US—the

352   E. San Román et al.

two inbound agencies of the Iberostar Group in the UK and the United States, respectively—resulted from the domestic network established with Intasun and the growth of tourist flows between Spain and the UK. Albeit indirectly, after the collapse of Instasun, it was also this network which provided the opportunity to internationalize the outbound business of Iberostar through the creation of Sunworld. In the hotel area, the domestic network with Neckermann did not provide the international opportunity, but for many years, Neckermann had offered the Iberostar Group the market knowledge and the reputation that facilitated its internationalization.

Our findings also include many examples that illustrate how the family character of Iberostar facilitated the establishment of networks, from the domestic market, with international partners, and gave these networks a long-term vision (Pla-Barber et al., 2010; Villar et al., 2012). The family nature of the firm helped consolidate relationships and therefore turned an exclusively social network, joining domestic and foreign entrepreneurs, into a business network sustained by strong, sometimes still informal, and trusted relationships nurtured by the joint experience accumulated (Kellermanns, Eddleston, Barnett, & Pearson, 2008). This family nature was key because it helped the international partners trust and rely in long-lasting firms (Andreu, Claver, Quer, & Rienda, 2018). Interestingly, while the networks and partnerships developed and consolidated, and more experience was generated, the family turned into a sort of repository of this accumulated experience which continuously backed the development of the company and then supported, even further, its internationalization (Colli et al., 2013).

Regarding the type and nature of the networks driving the internationalization process, our study shows that ties bridging foreign companies and Iberostar were mostly informal, based on trust, and some emerged from the personal or the social environment of the family members. This is also coherent with previous studies on family firms, in which family and business aspects are mutually influenced and largely affect the relationships that the firm develop in their internationalization process (Arregle, Duran, Hitt, & Van Essen, 2017). Our case study also shows that brokerage and bridging ties constituted a crucial channel to help launch their internationalization (Ciravegna, Majano, & Zhan, 2014), therefore illustrating the importance of the initial relationship but also the later networking processes. The case of the Spanish public airline, Iberia Líneas Aéreas, is a good example of how a supplier was used to identify new opportunities. Another example is Riu, a competitor that advised Iberostar when assessing venturing to America, who also constitutes another example of the brokerage relationship with competitors.

Yet, and more importantly, what our study shows is that the importance of the family nature of the company as well as the crucial role of accessing bridging ties would have had no sense if the context that surrounded the family firm had been different. And this allows us to recall an idea commonly recognized by business and economic historians but usually forgotten in organizational studies: context matters. Family firms perform well in contexts and situations which are characterized by high degrees of uncertainty and variability (Colli et al., 2013). The Iberostar case confirms this. Indeed, all assets associated with the family character of the company, as mentioned above, including trust, reliability, commitment and a long-term vision, were valued by the international partners only because they allowed the uncertainties and constraints imposed by the domestic context to be counteracted (Pla-Barber et al., 2010; Villar et al., 2012). So, following other works (Colli, Fernández Pérez, & Rose, 2003; Puig & Fernández Pérez, 2009), this study has identified that the historical framework of the country needs to be taken into account when exploring the drivers, process and outcomes of family firms internationalization. The case of Iberostar shows that, during the last years of Franco's Regime and the transition to democracy, the institutional barriers and legal restrictions determined the form of the partnership with the foreign firms and granted a preeminent position to Spanish local family firms. Hence, family firms turned out to be the type of organization capable of overcoming the threats that might have prevented the foreign partner from venturing with Spanish companies. In absence of the security provided by a democratic country with stable rules of the game, the foreign tour operators, Neckerman and Intasun, looked for a consolidated family firm, with three generations of experience in business and a proven reputation in Spain. In addition, what our analysis of the Iberostar case suggests is that, for Spanish FFs' internationalization, the crucial dimension of the context is the institutional framework—whose imbalances, in the case of Spain, coexisted with an economic boom between 1953 and 1973. Despite this boom, the strong-tie relationships that linked Iberostar with foreign partners responded to the need to cope with the uncertainties imposed by a non-democratic institutional context.

Hence, appreciating the context that surrounds the organization, including its resource endowments but especially its institutional features (Meyer et al., 2011), seems to be a key lens for a comprehensive understanding of the internationalization of FFs. Moreover, a restrictive context has its implications over the nature of the ties and its outcomes. When constrained by the scarcity of resources and the political imbalances, bridging ties are also critical for allowing the organization to access the resources, knowledge and information provided by foreign markets and companies. To build these kind of bridging ties, the nature of the business as a family firm was also critical, as some other studies have also suggested (Chetty & Eriksson, 2002; Kontinen & Ojala, 2011a). The family nature of the Iberostar Group helped create business alliances with foreign partners and imprinted them with a sense of trust, commitment and long-term vision. This set of distinctive resources allowed the members of the network to overcome the uncertainty and institutional constraints imposed by the Spanish context, and in turn provided the Spanish family firm with critical resources that fuelled its own internationalization. Recalling Douglas North (1990), when explaining economic and business growth, there are explicative variables that matter even more than the economic variables: these are institutions understood as the norms and conventions of a society including law, property rights or the type of government. These institutions are so powerful when it comes to creating order and security, that is the framework that underpins socio-economic progress. Our study of Iberostar follows these ideas and demonstrates that even though the economic context matters, sometimes institutions matter even more.

Acknowledgments We thank Iberostar Group for allowing access and use of the information contained in this paper. We especially thank Sabina Fluxá (CEO of Iberostar Group) for all her support. We also thank funding from Spanish Ministerio de Ciencia, Innovacion y Universidades (MCIU), Agencia Estatal de Investigacion (AEI), and Fondo Europeo de Desarrollo Regional (FEDER), through project PGC2018-093971-B-I00..

References

Agndal, H., Chetty, S., & Wilson, H. (2008). Social capital dynamics and foreign market entry. *International Business Review, 17*(6), 663–675.

Agostini, L., & Nosella, A. (2018). Inter-organizational relationships involving SMEs: A bibliographic investigation into the state of the art. *Long Range Planning, 52*(1), 1–31. Elsevier Ltd.

Ahuja, G., Soda, G., & Zaheer, A. (2012). The genesis and dynamics of organizational networks. *Organization Science, 23*(2), 434–448.

Anderson, A. R., Jack, S. L., & Dodd, S. D. (2005). The role of family members in entrepreneurial networks: Beyond the boundaries of the family firm. *Family Business Review, 18*(2), 135–154.

Andreosso-O'Callaghan, B., & Lenihan, H. (2008). Networking: A question of firm characteristics? The case of the Shannon region in Ireland. *Entrepreneurship and Regional Development, 20*(6), 561–580.

11 Networking from Home to Abroad: The Internationalization... 355

Andreu, R., Claver, E., Quer, D., & Rienda, L. (2018). Family ownership and Spanish hotel chains: An analysis of their expansion through internationalization. *UCJC Business and Society Review, 59,* 40–75.

Arregle, J. L., Duran, P., Hitt, M. A., & Van Essen, M. (2017). Why is family firms' internationalization unique? A meta–analysis. *Entrepreneurship Theory and Practice, 41*(5), 801–931.

Arregle, J.-L., Naldi, L., Nordqvist, M., & Hitt, M. A. (2012). Internationalization of family-controlled firms: A study of the effects of external involvement in governance. *Entrepreneurship Theory and Practice, 36*(6), 1115–1143.

Basly, S. (2007). The internationalization of family SME: An organizational learning and knowledge development perspective. *Baltic Journal of Management, 2,* 154–180.

Baum, J. A., McEvily, B., & Rowley, T. J. (2012). Better with age? Tie longevity and the performance implications of bridging and closure. *Organization Science, 23*(2), 529–546.

Belso-Martínez, A. J. (2006). Do industrial districts influence export performance and export intensity? Evidence for Spanish SMEs' internationalization process. *European Planning Studies, 14*(6), 791–810.

Belso-Martínez, J. A., Díez-Vial, I., López-Sánchez, M. J., & Mateu-Garcia, R. (2018). The brokerage role of supporting organizations inside clusters: how does it work? *European Planning Studies, 26*(4), 706–725.

Bembom, M., & Schwens, C. (2018). The role of networks in early internationalizing firms: A systematic review and future research agenda. *European Management Journal, 36*(6), 679–694. Elsevier Ltd.

Bryant, P. T. (2014). Imprinting by design: The microfoundations of entrepreneurial adaptation. *Entrepreneurship Theory and Practice, 38,* 1081–1102.

Brydon, K., & Dana, L. O. P. (2011). Globalisation and firm structure: Comparing a family-business and a corporate block holder in the New Zealand seafood industry. *International Journal of Globalisation and Small Business, 4*(2), 206–220.

Burt, R. S. (1992). *Structural holes.* Cambridge: Cambridge University Press.

Byrom, J., & Lehman, K. (2009). Coopers Brewery: Heritage and innovation within a family firm. *Marketing Intelligence & Planning, 27*(4), 516–523.

Calabrò, A., & Mussolino, D. (2013). How do boards of directors contribute to family SME export intensity? The role of formal and informal governance mechanisms. *Journal of Management & Governance, 17*(2), 363–403.

Capelli, P., & Sherer, P. (1991). The missing role of context in OB: The need for a meso level approach. *Research in Organizational Behavior, 13,* 55–110.

Chandra, Y., Styles, C., & Wilkinson, I. (2009). The recognition of first time international entrepreneurial opportunities: Evidence from firms in knowledge-based industries. *International Marketing Review, 26*(1), 30–61.

Chetty, C., & Holm, D. B. (2000). Internationalization of small to medium sized manufacturing firms: A network approach. *International Business Review, 9,* 77–93.

Chetty, S., & Eriksson, K. (2002). Mutual commitment and experiential knowledge in mature international business relationship. *International Business Review, 11*(3), 305–324.

Ciravegna, L., Majano, S. B., & Zhan, G. (2014). The inception of internationalization of small and medium enterprises: The role of activeness and networks. *Journal of Business Research, 67*(6), 1081–1089.

Cirer-Costa, J. C. (2014). The explosive expansion and consolidation of the Balearic hotel sector, 1964–2010. *Revista de Historia Industrial, 56,* 189–216.

Colli, A., Fernández Pérez, P., & Rose, M. B. (2003). National determinants of family firm development? Family firms in Britain, Spain, and Italy in the nineteenth and twentieth centuries. *Enterprise & Society, 4*(1), 28–64.

Colli, A., García-Canal, E., & Guillén, M. F. (2013). Family character and international entrepreneurship: A historical comparison of Italian and Spanish 'new multinationals'. *Business History, 55*(1), 119–138.

Colli, A., Mariotti, S., & Piscitello, L. (2014). Governments as strategists in designing global players: the case of European utilities. *Journal of European Public Policy, 21(4),* 487–508.

Coviello, N. E. (2006). The network dynamics of international new ventures. *Journal of International Business Studies, 37,* 713–731.

Coviello, N. E., McDougall, P. P., & Oviatt, B. M. (2011). The emergence, advance and future of international entrepreneurship research? An introduction to the special forum. *Journal of Business Venturing, 26*(6), 625–631. Elsevier Inc.

Coviello, N. E., & Munro, H. J. (1995). Growing the entrepreneurial firm. *European Journal of Marketing, 29,* 49–61.

Crick, D., Bradshaw, R., & Chaudhry, S. (2006). "Successful" internationalising UK family and non-family-owned firms: A comparative study. *Journal of Small Business and Enterprise Development, 13*(4), 498–512.

Czarniawska, B. (2004). *Narratives in social science research.* London: Sage Publications.

De Propris, L., & Sugden, R. (2008). The governance of cross-locality networks as a determinant of local economic development. *Entrepreneurship and Regional Development, 20*(6), 493–515.

Dubois, A., & Gadde, L. E. (2002). Systematic combining: An abductive approach to case research. *Journal of Business Research, 55*(7), 553–560.

Eisenhardt, K. M., & Graebner, M. (2007). Theory building from cases: Opportunities and challenges. *The Academy of Management Journal, 50*(1), 25–32.

Ellis, P. (2000). Social ties and foreign market entry. *Journal of International Business Studies, 31*(3), 443–469.

Evers, N., & Knight, J. (2008). Role of international trade shows in small firm internationalization: A network perspective. *International Marketing Review, 25*(5), 544–562.

Evers, N., & O'Gorman, C. (2011). Improvised internationalization in new ventures: The role of prior knowledge and networks. *Entrepreneurship & Regional Development, 23*(7–8), 549–574.

Fernández, Z., & Nieto, M. J. (2005). Internationalization strategy of small and medium-sized family businesses: Some influential factors. *Family Business Review, 18*(1), 77–89.

Fernández Moya, M. (2010). A family-owned publishing multinational: The Salvat company (1869–1988). *Business History, 52*, 453–470.

Fernández Moya, M. (2012). Creating knowledge networks: Spanish multinational publishers in Mexico. *Business History Review, 86*(1), 69–98.

Fernández-Pérez, P. (1999). Challenging the loss of an empire: González & Byass of Jerez. *Business History, 41*(4), 72–87.

Fletcher, D., De Massis, A., & Nordqvist, M. (2016). Qualitative research practices and family business scholarship: A review and future research agenda. *Journal of Family Business Strategy, 7*(1), 8–25.

Gao, H., Ren, M., Zhang, J., & Sun, R. (2016). Network gatekeeping in SME exporters' market entry in China. *International Marketing Review, 33*(2), 276–297.

Garud, R., Kumaraswamy, A., & Karnøe, P. (2010). Path dependence or path creation? *Journal of Management Studies, 47*, 760–774.

Giuliani, E. (2011). Role of technological gatekeepers in the growth of industrial clusters: Evidence from Chile. *Regional Studies, 45*(10), 1329–1348.

Giuliani, E., & Bell, M. (2005). The micro-determinants of meso-level learning and innovation: Evidence from a Chilean wine cluster. *Research Policy, 34*(1), 47–68.

Graf, H., & Krüger, J. J. (2011). The performance of gatekeepers in innovator networks. *Industry and Innovation, 18*(1), 69–88.

Granovetter, M. S. (1973). The strength of weak ties. *American Journal of Sociology, 78*(6), 1360–1380.

Graves, C., & Thomas, J. (2008). Determinants of the internationalization pathways of family firms: An examination of family influence. *Family Business Review, 21*(2), 151–167.

Guercini, S., & Runfola, A. (2010). Business networks and retail internationalization: A case analysis in the fashion industry. *Industrial Marketing Management, 39*(6), 908–916.

Gulati, R., Nohria, N., & Zaheer, A. (2000). Strategic networks. *Strategic Management Journal, 21*(3), 203–215.

Halinen, A., & Törnroos, J.-Å. (2005). Using case methods in the study of contemporary business networks. *Journal of Business Research, 58*(9), 1285–1212.

Hitt, M. A., Ireland, R. D., & Tuggle, C. (2006). The make or buy growth decision: Strategic entrepreneurship versus acquisitions. In E. Hess & R. Kazanjian (Eds.), *The search for organic growth* (pp. 124–146). Cambridge: Cambridge University Press.

Hohenthal, J., Johanson, J., & Johanson, M. (2014). Network knowledge and business-relationship value in the foreign market. *International Business Review, 23*(1), 4–19. Elsevier Ltd.

Holstein, J. A., & Gubrium, J. F. (1995). *The active interview*. Thousand Oaks, CA: Sage Publications.

Hosteltur. (2019). Ranking Hosteltur de grandes cadenas hoteleras 2019. Retrieved from https://www.hosteltur.com/131601_senales-de-cambio-de-ciclo-en-la-industria-hotelera.html

Hutchings, K., & Murray, G. (2002). Australian expatriates' experiences in working behind the Bamboo curtain: An examination of Guanxi in post-communist China. *Asian Business & Management, 1*(3), 373–393.

Jack, S. L. (2005). The role, use and activation of strong and weak network ties: A qualitative analysis. *Journal of Management Studies, 42*(6), 1233–1259.

Johanson, J., & Mattsson, L.-G. (1988). Internationalization in industrial systems—A network approach. In D. Hood & J.-E. Vahlne (Eds.), *Strategies in global competition* (pp. 303–321). Croom Helm.

Kampouri, K., Plakoyiannaki, E., & Leppäaho, T. (2017). Family business internationalisation and networks: Emerging pathways. *Journal of Business & Industrial Marketing, 32*(3), 357–370.

Kellermanns, F. W., Eddleston, K. A., Barnett, T., & Pearson, A. (2008). An exploratory study of family member characteristics and involvement: Effects on entrepreneurial behavior in the family firm. *Family Business Review, 21*(1), 1–14.

Kipping, M., Wadhwani, R., & Bucheli, M. (2014). Analyzing and interpreting historical sources. In *Organizations in time: History, theory, methods* (pp. 305–329). Oxford, UK: Oxford University Press.

Kontinen, T., & Ojala, A. (2010). The internationalization of family businesses: A review of extant research. *Journal of Family Business Strategy, 1*(2), 97–107.

Kontinen, T., & Ojala, A. (2011a). Network ties in the international opportunity recognition of family SMEs. *International Business Review, 20*(4), 440–453.

Kontinen, T., & Ojala, A. (2011b). Social capital in relation to the foreign market entry and post-entry operations of family SMEs. *Journal of International Entrepreneurship, 9*(2), 133–151.

Kontinen, T., & Ojala, A. (2012). Internationalization pathways among family-owned SMEs. *International Marketing Review, 29*, 496–518.

Leppäaho, T., Metsola, J., & Paavilainen-Mäntymäki, E. (2016). Process view and the internationalization of family businesses. *Academy of Management Conference*, Anaheim, California, USA, 5–9 August 2016.

Loane, S., & Bell, J. (2006). Rapid internationalisation among entrepreneurial firms in Australia, Canada, Ireland and New Zealand: An extension to the network approach. *International Marketing Review, 23*(5), 467–485.

McEvily, B., & Zaheer, A. (1999). Bridging ties: A source of firm heterogeneity in competitive capabilities. *Strategic Management Journal, 20*(12), 1133–1156.

Meyer, K. E., Mudambi, R., & Narula, R. (2011). Multinational enterprises and local contexts: The opportunities and challenges of multiple embeddedness. *Journal of Management Studies, 48*(2), 235–252.

Miles, M. B., & Huberman, A. M. (1994). *Qualitative data analysis: An expanded sourcebook*. Thousand Oaks, CA: Sage Publications.

Miles, M. B., Huberman, A. M., & Saldaña, J. (2014). *Qualitative data analysis: A methods sourcebook* (3rd ed.). Thousand Oaks, CA: Sage.

Montoro-Sánchez, Á., Díez-Vial, I., & Belso-Martinez, J. A. (2018). The evolution of the domestic network configuration as a driver of international relationships in SMEs. *International Business Review, 27*(4), 727–736.

Munari, F., Sobrero, M., & Malipiero, A. (2012). Focal firms as technological gatekeepers within industrial districts: Knowledge creation and dissemination in the Italian packaging machinery industry. *Industrial and Corporate Change, 21*, 429–469.

Mustafa, M., & Chen, S. (2010). The strength of family networks in transnational immigrant entrepreneurship. *Thunderbird International Business Review, 52*(2), 97–106.

Naldi, L., Nordqvist, M., Sjöberg, K., & Wiklund, J. (2007). Entrepreneurial orientation, risk taking, and performance in family firms. *Family Business Review, 20*(1), 33–47.

North, D. C. (1990). *Institutions, institutional change and economic performance.* Cambridge University Press.

Pettigrew, A. M., Woodman, R. W., & Cameron, K. S. (2001). Studying organizational change and development: Challenges for future research. *Academy of Management Journal, 44*(4), 697–713.

Phelps, C., Heidl, R., & Wadhwa, A. (2012). Knowledge, networks, and knowledge networks: A review and research agenda. *Journal of Management, 38*(4), 1115–1166.

Pla-Barber, J., Sanchez-Peinado, E., & Madhok, A. (2010). Investment and control decisions in foreign markets: Evidence from service industries. *British Journal of Management, 21*(3), 736–753.

Puig, N., & Fernández Pérez, P. (2009). A silent revolution: The internationalisation of large Spanish family firms. *Business History, 51*(3), 462–483.

Pukall, T. J., & Calabrò, A. (2014). The internationalization of family firms: A critical review and integrative model. *Family Business Review, 27*(2), 103–125.

Reay, T. (2014). Publishing qualitative research. *Family Business Review, 27*(2), 95–102.

Reuber, A. R. (2016). An assemblage–theoretic perspective on the internationalization processes of family firms. *Entrepreneurship Theory and Practice, 40*(6), 1269–1286.

Rowlinson, M. (2004). Historical analysis of company documents. In C. Cassell & G. Symon (Eds.), *Essential guide to qualitative methods in organizational research* (pp. 301–310). London: Sage.

San Román, E. (2009). *Ildefonso Fierro. La aventura de un emprendedor.* Madrid: LID.

San Román, E. (2017). *Building stars. Miguel Fluxá, an entrepreneurial story.* Madrid: El Viso.

San Román, E., & Puig, N. (2018). German capital and the development of the Spanish hotel industry (1950s–1990s): A tale of two strategic alliances. *EBHA Conference 2018.*

Sánchez, E. M. (2004). Turismo, desarrollo e integración internacional de la España franquista. *EBHA Annual Conference*, Barcelona, 16–18 September 2004.

Sciascia, S., Mazzola, P., Astrachan, J. H., & Pieper, T. M. (2012). The role of family ownership in international entrepreneurship: Exploring nonlinear effects. *Small Business Economics, 38*(1), 15–31.

Segaro, E. (2010). Internationalization of family SMEs: The impact of ownership, governance, and top management team. *Journal of Management & Governance, 16*(1), 147–169.

Sharma, D. D., & Blomstermo, A. (2003). The internationalization process of Born Globals: A network view. *International Business Review, 12*(6), 739–753.

Soda, G., Usai, A., & Zaheer, A. (2004). Network memory: The influence of past and current networks on performance. *Acadademy of Management Journal, 47*(6), 893–906.

Tàpies, J., San Román, E., & Gil-López, A. (2015). *100 families that changed the world. Family businesses and industrialization.* Barcelona: Fundación Jesús Serra.

Vallejo-Pousada, R. (2013). Turismo y Desarrollo Económico En España Durante El Franquismo, 1939–1975. *Revista de Historia de La Economía y de La Empresa, 7*, 423–452.

Van de Ven, A. H. (2007). *Engaged scholarship: A guide for organizational and social research.* Oxford University Press on Demand.

Villar, C., Pla-Barber, J., & León-Darder, F. (2012). Service characteristics as moderators of the entry mode choice: Empirical evidence in the hotel industry. *The Service Industries Journal, 32*(7), 1137–1148.

Welch, C., Piekkari, R., Plakoyiannaki, E., & Paavilainen-Mäntymäki, E. (2011). Theorising from case studies: Towards a pluralist future for international business research. *Journal of International Business Studies, 42*(5), 740–762.

Wright, M., Filatotchev, I., Hoskisson, R. E., & Peng, M. W. (2005). Strategy research in emerging economies: Challenging the conventional wisdom. *Journal of Management Studies, 42*(1), 1–33.

Wright, P. C., & Nasierowski, W. (1994). The expatriate family firm and cross-cultural management training: A conceptual framework. *Human Resource Development Quarterly, 5*(2), 153–167.

Yin, R. K. (1994). *Case study research design and methods: Applied social research and methods series* (2nd ed.). Thousand Oaks, CA: Sage Publications Inc.

Yin, R. K. (2003). *Case study research design and methods* (3rd ed.). Thousand Oaks, CA: Sage Publications.

Yin, R. K. (2009). How to do better case studies. In *The SAGE handbook of applied social research methods* (Vol. 2, pp. 254–282). Los Angeles, CA: SAGE.

Yli-Renko, H., Autio, E., & Tontti, V. (2002). Social capital, knowledge, and the international growth of technology-based new firms. *International Business Review, 11*(3), 279–304.

Zahra, S. A. (2003). International expansion of US manufacturing family businesses: The effect of ownership and involvement. *Journal of Business Venturing, 18*(4), 495–512.

12

Social Capital and Values in the Internationalization of Family Firms: A Multi-Country Study

Spiros Batas, Karine Guiderdoni-Jourdain, and Tanja Leppäaho

Introduction

Social capital (SC) plays an important role in the competitive success of firms (Burt, 2019). The role of SC is especially important for smaller and family firms (FFs; see e.g. Johanson & Vahlne, 2009). FF SC is characterized by high levels of trust, closeness, and duration (Arregle, Hitt, Sirmon, & Very, 2007; Roessl, 2005; Salvato & Melin, 2008; Zellweger, Chrisman, Chua, & Steier, 2019). However, little is known about how FFs build and develop SC overall, especially in the context of internationalization, although SC overall has been proven to be an especially important research for FF internationalization (Arregle, Naldi, Nordqvist, & Hitt, 2012; De Massis, Frattini, Majocchi, & Piscitello, 2018; Graves & Thomas, 2008; Hennart, Majocchi, & Forlani, 2019; Kampouri, Plakoyiannaki, & Leppäaho, 2017; Kontinen & Ojala,

---

S. Batas (✉)
Department of Economics and International Business, University of Greenwich, London, UK
e-mail: S.Batas@greenwich.ac.uk

K. Guiderdoni-Jourdain
CNRS, LEST, Aix-Marseille University, Marseille, France

T. Leppäaho
LUT University, Lappeenranta, Finland

© The Author(s), under exclusive license to Springer Nature Switzerland AG 2021
T. Leppäaho, S. Jack (eds.), *The Palgrave Handbook of Family Firm Internationalization*,
https://doi.org/10.1007/978-3-030-66737-5_12

361

2010, 2012; Leppäaho & Metsola, 2020; Metsola, Leppäaho, Paavilainen-Mäntymäki, & Plakoyiannaki, 2020; Pukall & Calabrò, 2014; Zellweger et al., 2019). SC ties can be categorized as either strong or weak (Granovetter, 1973). Both strong and weak ties are needed in internationalization, but strong ties typically take pride of place in the case of FFs (see e.g. Kontinen & Ojala, 2012).

Recently, among the scholars of FF internationalization, there have been two novel approaches in relation to FF internationalization: (1) discussion on the role of *family structures* (Arregle, Duran, Hitt & Van Essen, 2017; Todd, 1985); and (2) discussion on the role of family and non-family assets and basic human and cultural values related to *bifurcation bias* (BB; Schwartz, 1992; Verbeke & Kano, 2012; Verbeke, Yuan, & Kano, 2020). Both of these discussions are still on a rather conceptual level and empirical studies have been called for (Arregle et al., 2017; Arregle, Hitt, & Mari, 2019; De Massis et al., 2018; Hennart et al., 2019; Metsola et al., 2020; Verbeke et al., 2020).

Indeed, in a recent article, Arregle et al. (2019) noted that there are different family structures (involving e.g. an *egalitarian, authoritarian*, or *absolute nuclear* family) in different cultures and parts of the world. They argue that these are of critical importance for understanding differing FFs' internationalization strategies, calling for studies combining a range of cultural contexts and family heritages to shed new light on FF internationalization (Arregle et al., 2019). On the side of internationalization studies, Terjesen, Hessels, and Li (2016, p. 300) have asked for studies from different countries and cultures of origin, arguing "an appreciation of similarities as well as fundamental differences enables scholars to develop better theories to explain conditions that help or hinder entrepreneurial activity in different countries as well as the implications of entrepreneurship."

The BB approach, as per the definition by Verbeke and Kano (2012) and by Kano and Verbeke (2018), is related to the family-oriented behavior of FFs toward human and non-human resources, including relational assets. Family values play an important role in the shaping of strategies. However, there is a gap in the literature regarding how such values may influence the internationalization of FFs (Yuan & Wu, 2018). Verbeke et al. (2020), adapting Schwartz's theory, explained how FF values are linked to BB. FF values can be categorized as (1) openness to change, (2) self-enhancement, (3) self-transcendence, and (4) conservation (Verbeke et al., 2020). Here we set to investigate the aspect of values in relation to BB.

The aim of this study is to shed light on FF internationalization and their networking in special by studying FFs with different countries of origin (Terjesen et al., 2016) and family structures (Arregle et al., 2019) through the human and cultural values (Schwartz, 1992; Verbeke et al., 2020; Verbeke & Kano, 2012) in the context of building SC in the international markets.

In addressing our research questions ***How do FFs develop social capital in their internationalization? How is their internationalization behavior related to family structures and human and cultural values?***, we conducted an in-depth study of three FF cases, one from Taiwan (TAI), France (FRA), and Finland (FIN). As per the definitions given by Arregle et al. (2019) (please see section "Family Structures"), they represented different family structures, categorizable as an *absolute* nuclear family (the Finnish case), an *exogamous* family (the French case), and an *authoritarian* family structure (the Taiwanese case).

When studying FFs with different family structures we found that the differences in the international networking behavior of FFs were related to *values* bound up with BB and their historically and culturally bound family structures. Weak SC ties played an important role in the first phases of internationalization for all the case firms, despite differing family structures and traditions. In the case of the Finnish and French cases, the post-entry networking behavior was linked to conformity (related to abidance by rules, obligations, and respectfulness for parents) and sometimes to security (related to the protection of family members). By contrast, in the case of the Taiwanese case, there was an emphasis on tradition related to religion and culture, and security was visible more strongly than it was for the Finnish and French cases. Here, we can see that the family structures influenced the building of SC abroad through different values they cherished in this family structure.

We contribute to the discussions on FF international networking (Arregle et al., 2019; Kampouri et al., 2017; Kano & Verbeke, 2018; Kontinen & Ojala, 2010, 2012; Pukall & Calabrò, 2014; Yuan & Wu, 2018) by showing that what seemed to make a difference in the international networking behavior of FFs from different countries and family structures derived from values. The value that drove the international networking behavior was conservation, which encompasses conformity, security, and tradition. The Finnish and French cases were linked more to conformity, whereas the Taiwanese case demonstrated more security and tradition values as Taiwanese societal values are more conservative compared to the European ones. We demonstrate the importance of values and we stress that it will be useful also in the future to further delve into values of FFs to enhance our understanding of their heterogeneity in networking.

This chapter begins with an analysis of literature on FFs' SC, values, and BB and FF structures and how those influence internationalization. This is followed by the methodological choices of this study. We continue to present

364   S. Batas et al.

the empirical evidence of this study by illustrating the mechanism between SC, BB, and family values. This chapter concludes by presenting the key contributions of our study.

Theoretical Background

Nahapiet and Ghoshal (1998, p. 243) define SC as "the sum of the actual and potential resources embedded within, available through, and derived from the network of relationships possessed by an individual or social unit." Members of a network can develop ties that assist in the exchange of resources and knowledge. The strength of ties (i.e. strong or weak) has been a topic of interest to scholars in sociology, especially in terms of how to comprehend the flow of information (Granovetter, 1973; Lin, Ensel, & Vaughn, 1981). There has been debate on whether strong and weak ties can be perceived as similar or as different entities (Dubini & Aldrich, 1991; Hite, 2003; Uzzi, 1997), and on how relationships differ between strong and weak ties (Aldrich & Zimmer, 1986).

Previous studies have linked the strength of ties to various perspectives such as *closeness* (Marsden & Campbell, 1984), *trust* (Elg, 2008; Jack, 2005; Morgan & Hunt, 1994; Singh, 2000), *mutual respect* (Jack, 2005), and *commitment* (Hite, 2003; Morgan & Hunt, 1994). It has been noted that overconcentration on the frequency and duration of strength of a tie can lead to inaccurate results (Marsden & Campbell, 1984); hence, those measures were not applied in the present study. We followed a modified definition drawn from Söderqvist and Chetty (2009), viewing the characteristics of a strong tie as linked to *closeness*, high levels of *trust*, *mutual respect*, and *commitment* between the actors. Conversely, a weak tie can be characterized as "a superficial tie not yet based on strong trust [in which] the parties do not know each other well and are not emotionally close to each other" (Söderqvist & Chetty, 2009, p. 9). One of the main advantages of weak ties is that they offer access to information and new ideas, whereas strong ties may offer more obsolete and less necessary information (Granovetter, 1973). Weak ties can link networks that are disconnected, in contrast to strong ties, which primarily link well-connected networks (Granovetter, 1973). Moreover, weak ties can be more effective, insofar as they allow actors to search more broadly and distantly for other networks, resulting in more alternatives within the business environment (Hansen, 1999).

Individuals tend to have a limited number of strong ties due to the high maintenance costs and the time required to develop close ties (Singh, 2000).

By contrast, weak ties require less time and cost to be maintained, allowing individuals to keep up a large number of such ties. Weak ties are beneficial as they can offer valuable and unique information to an entrepreneur (Granovetter, 1973; Singh, 2000). Weak ties can be described as bridges to information, something that is not available within an entrepreneur's strong ties (Granovetter, 1973).

On the other hand, strong ties are linked to emotional bonds and to high levels of trust. In strong ties, trust is based on mutual experience and cooperation; hence, it should be perceived as a continuous investment in learning among actors. The formation of trust is associated with a general reputation for trustworthiness among the partners; this allows a given firm to deal with partners on the basis of previous experience, having awareness as well that it will be a strategic disadvantage to behave opportunistically (Elg, 2008). Thus, trust enhances the willingness of actors to offer advice and to provide valuable information (Singh, 2000). Information flow can be faster and more reliable when there are strong ties (Granovetter, 1985). Nevertheless, entrepreneurs who rely primarily on strong ties may miss opportunities when they scan the environment as the information they receive will be more local and possibly biased.

FFs tend to form networks—bridging SC ties—with other FFs and, less frequently, with non-FFs (Graves & Thomas, 2004; Roessl, 2005). This could be explained by their inner bonding capital, which exists in a particularly strong form—a point related to the building and developing of bonding SC (Salvato & Melin, 2008). Unification of ownership and management leads to strong bonding capital (Salvato & Melin, 2008). In such cases, the aspirations and capabilities of family members are reflected in the FF; furthermore, the strategy, operations, and administrative structure are influenced by the social elements of the FF. Overall, one needs to be aware of the extent to which FFs emphasize personal relationships and focus on interpersonal trust (Roessl, 2005).

Values and Bifurcation Bias

Bifurcation bias (BB) can be described as a behavioral orientation of FFs toward human and non-human resources, including relational assets (Kano & Verbeke, 2018; Verbeke & Kano, 2012). According to Verbeke et al. (2020, p. 451), "family-based resources are linked to family firm owners' identity." They see these resources as encompassing a range of assets, classifiable as human, physical, or non-physical in nature. As the researchers see it, resources that are not part of the identity and the history of the family should not be perceived as family resources.

When family-based resources are perceived as unique and valuable, and when non-family-based resources are perceived as (merely) a commodity, BB occurs (Verbeke et al., 2020). It is important to note that—viewed through the lens of the BB—human resources (chiefly family members) are seen as loyal and committed to safeguarding and promoting the goals of the firm. Non-family members are seen as having no such loyalty, and as being self-centered in their interests (Verbeke et al., 2020). Other studies (e.g. Chua, Chrisman, & Bergiel, 2009) have shown the negative influence of BB—for example, non-family members felt that the family members treated them unfairly in performance evaluation and in terms of compensation.

In a more recent work of Kano and Verbeke (2018), assets were linked to physical assets, network relations, etc. BB can be observed when two instances occur: (1) family-related assets are perceived as heritage assets, in other words, those are unique and add value, whereas (2) non-family assets are perceived as commodity-type assets, in other words, those can be found easily in markets and they do not offer any advanced add value (Kano & Verbeke, 2018). Another challenge that emerges in FFs when the BB occurs is their prevention from "seeking and engaging complementary resources of external actors" during internationalization decisions (Kano & Verbeke, 2018, p. 168). In our study, we extend those views by examining how BB influences the internationalization of FFs with the use of the SC spectrum (i.e. network relations and ties).

Schwartz (1992) developed a theory related to the basic human values, such as self-direction, achievement, power, security, etc., which can be linked to the personality of an individual and show how individual idiosyncrasies are described with societies. Verbeke et al. (2020) adapted Schwartz's theory and explained how FF values are linked to BB. FF values can be categorized as including (1) openness to change, (2) self-enhancement, (3) self-transcendence, and (4) conservation (Verbeke et al., 2020). Family values play an important role in the shaping of strategies. However, there is a gap in the literature regarding how such values may influence the internationalization of FFs (Yuan & Wu, 2018). There seems little doubt that FF values are associated with BB (Kano & Verbeke, 2018; Verbeke et al., 2020); also that the personality of the owner of the FF may increase the possibilities for BB to occur (Kano & Verbeke, 2018), with consequences for internationalization behavior.

For the purpose of our study we focused on the *conservation* FF values. These include *security*, *conformity*, and *tradition*. *Security* encompasses both personal and societal security, with personal security being related in particular to the protection of family members. *Conformity* highlights the respect of a new generation of family managers toward their parents and the adherence of family members to rules. *Tradition* is a value related to the preservation of the family, and the importance placed by family members on traditions related to religion and culture (Verbeke et al., 2020). We decided to focus on the *conservation* FF values as those may affect the most the internationalization of FF and can offer interesting insights how FFs' internationalization decisions can be hindered or facilitated. *Conservation* values can be perceived as an explanatory factor of the BB occurrence.

Current literature has not examined how the strength of ties could be linked to (or in conflict with) BB. We do not know how the strength of ties can influence the values of FFs when they decide to internationalize, or in their post-entry operations, although this has been mentioned by other scholars as a promising topic (e.g. Verbeke et al., 2020). This study sought to offer insights into this emerging theme.

Family Structures

The *family structure* can shed light on how FFs internationalize (Arregle et al., 2019). In our study we took note of the four family structures of the *authoritarian family*, the *exogamous community family*, the *absolute nuclear family*, and the *egalitarian nuclear family*. Arregle et al. (2019, p. 9) write of the *authoritarian family* thus:

> [This family structure facilitates] the successful inter-generational transfer and preservation of the wealth within the family, creating salient inter-generational perspective. It strongly facilitates the family leader's ability to inherit SC and strategic knowledge from the previous generation.

The *exogamous community family*, for its part, has values that are linked to the egalitarian and symmetric values of the family relationships. In addition, there is strong density and closure of the family network, along with a strong sense of authority and co-dependency of parents with their children; the FF has an important and central role in the family (Arregle et al., 2019).

The *absolute nuclear family* is characterized as being more liberal, and as having low levels of egalitarianism. The family members frequently decide not to work in the FF, with the likelihood that they will be more independent and follow career paths outside the FF. In general, there is weak attachment to the FF (Arregle et al., 2019).

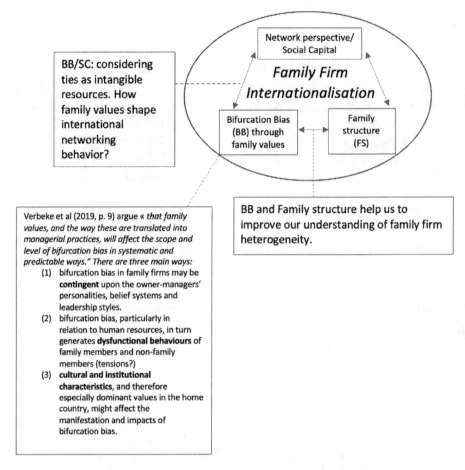

Fig. 12.1 Social capital, bifurcation bias, family values, and family structures in the internationalization of FFs. (Source: Elaborated by the authors)

Finally, an *egalitarian nuclear family* is characterized by the stability of the relationship: the family members have strong SC, with the older generation desiring to pass the FF on to the new generation (Arregle et al., 2019).

Family structures, in conjunction with BB and strength of ties, can offer interesting insights into how FFs internationalize, and how their decisions may be influenced. Figure 12.1 encompasses the objectives of our study and highlights the mechanism between the different aspects mentioned earlier.

Methodology

The objectives of our research were related to understanding the behavior of a firm rather than to quantitative measurement (Jack, 2005); hence, a qualitative research method was regarded as most appropriate for this study. This approach provides "understanding of what really goes on in networks; provides more knowledge about the content of network relations; the processes involved; how networks evolve, change and develop over time" (Jack, 2010, p. 120). We used a multiple case study method, similar to the approaches introduced by Eisenhardt (1989) and by Eisenhardt and Graebner (2007). In following this approach we conducted in-depth interviews with the founders of the FFs, or with a family member who ran the business, and with international business managers.

In this study, an FF was defined as a firm in which the family (1) controlled the largest block of shares or votes, (2) had one or more of its members in key management positions, and (3) had members of more than one generation actively involved with the business. This definition is based on the two criteria of ownership and management presented by Graves and Thomas (2008) and is consonant with the notion of continuity presented by, for example, Zahra (2003).

We selected the *main market entries* as the context of the foreign market entry (FME) (see Table 12.1). This allowed investigation of the FME in a context that would be similar for all the firms, in terms of the most important FMEs, as described by the interviewees. These markets consisted of those that had the largest foreign sales and the largest number of ties. We followed Yin (1994) in selecting cases in which the phenomenon studied was transparently observable. We used a purposeful sampling in order to help us to narrow down the population of the sample (Poulis, Poulis, & Plakoyiannaki, 2013). It allowed us to stress "the need for a theory-driven selection of cases along with a consideration of contextual idiosyncrasies" (Poulis et al., 2013, p. 310). Here, it should be borne in mind that the geographical location of internationalizing entrepreneurs largely dictates their foreign sales ratios, and the number of countries in which they internationalize (Zander, McDougall-Covin, & Rose, 2015).

The research context was interesting as all the case firms were occupied with painting (paints and decorative coatings, or paint brushes and paint rollers); also, because the countries differed in terms of culture, size, geographical location, and family structure. We focused on a single industry (i.e. paint industry) to control the industry effects on internationalization (Reuber & Fischer, 1997).

Table 12.1 Background on FFs

Case Firm	% family ownership	Year of establishment	Generation(s)	Product	Start of internationalization	Three most important foreign markets (on the basis of sales %)	Operation modes in main markets
FIN	100	1978	Second and third	Environmentally friendly paints	1987	Sweden, Netherlands, France,	Exporting via distributors
FRA	100	1864	Fourth	Paints and decorative coating	1984	Japan, Russia, USA	Exporting via distributors (creation of a subsidiary in Japan in 2008) (creation of a subsidiary in Russia in 2009)
TAI	100	1986	Second	Paint brushes and paint rollers	1999	Thailand, Malaysia, Germany	Exporting via distributors

Source: Authors

Data Collection and Analysis

The choice of informants (i.e. the choice of actors) was driven by conceptual questions and not by their "representativeness" (Miles & Huberman, 1994, p. 29). The best approach in seeking to limit interview data bias is to choose informants who view the observed phenomena from different angles (Eisenhardt & Graebner, 2007). We took the view that the objectives of the research would be best served by interviews with the founders of the FF, or with family members who worked in the firms, or with persons in managerial positions.

Gaining access to, and selecting the appropriate number of informants, is challenging and complex. It becomes even more challenging if the researcher does not have personal business contacts, and more specifically, access to business executives (Harvey, 2010; Welch, Marschan-Piekkari, Penttinen, & Tahvanainen, 2002). In the present case, the selection of business executives was based on their involvement with the internationalization decisions of the FF. We used two approaches to make contact with the business executives in the selected FFs: sending cold emails to possible case firms and using our personal networks to gain access.

In total, nine interviews were conducted with founders, family members, and managers of Finnish, French, and Taiwanese FFs. There were either one or two informants from each firm. The interviews lasted from 11 minutes to 2 hours (see Table 12.2) conducted in Finnish, French, and English. These were transcribed by professional translators in English in order to ensure consistency during data analysis process.

Table 12.2 Interviews and informants

Firm	Number of interviews and duration	Informant(s)
FIN	3 interviews; 165 minutes First interview: 63 minutes Second interview: 57 minutes Third interview: 45 minutes	CEO (second generation); Sales Manager (second generation); Sales Assistant (third generation)
FRA	3 interviews: 107 minutes First interview: 11 minutes Second interview: 60 minutes Third interview: 36 minutes	CEO (fourth generation)
TAI	3 interviews: 160 minutes First interview: 45 minutes Second interview: 70 minutes Third interview: 45 minutes	Sales Manager (second generation)

Source: Authors

372 S. Batas et al.

We analyzed SC, through strong and weak ties, within the three case firms by first conducting a within-case analysis, followed by a cross-case analysis. We based our cross-case analysis on (1) the strength of ties in the initial FMEs and (2) the strength of ties in the post-entry operations, plus their relatedness to BB and to family values and structures.

We used NVivo 12 to analyze the data, seeking to increase the trustworthiness of the qualitative research (Sinkovics, Penz, & Ghauri, 2008). In addition, direct quotes were used to support the findings and to illustrate the "underlying phenomena" which our study was attempting to illuminate (Sinkovics et al., 2008, p. 695). We followed Miles and Huberman's (1994) axial coding system in applying categories and concepts to the empirical data (seeking to increase the depth of the categories). The categories included themes related to: *strong ties*, *weak ties*, and *family values*. These categories appeared to be crucial for analyzing the FMEs of the examined FFs. The coding used to classify ties and family conservation values was as follows:

* *Strong ties*: trust, loyalty, friendship, trusted family member
* *Weak ties*: lack of trust, met via trade exhibition for the first time, new partner
* *Security*: family member wanted to protect the new generation, protection from potential buyout
* *Conformity*: family members respecting their parents, agreeing with the decisions of their parents out of respect
* *Tradition*: retention of the FF for family members, decisions taken on the basis of cultural traditions

Case Profiles at the Time of the Interviews

FIN

FIN was a 100% family-owned manufacturer of paints, established in 1978. At the time of the study it was managed by second-generation siblings, one being the CEO and Chairman of the Board and the other the Business Director. Internationalization had started with sales to Sweden in 1987 and expanded to the Netherlands in the mid-1990s. To some extent the international sales were started unintentionally when the founder father and his Finnish partner along with an expert on paints visited France, Spain, and Belgium to obtain suitable raw materials. At the same time, they attended trade fairs and met potential partners and customers. Recently, FIN had invested in an online store to boost foreign sales.

In relation to family values and characteristics, the siblings had a fairly strong emotional attachment to and identification with the FF. There were warm relationships between the family and non-family employees. However, strong emotional attachment had sometimes led to considerable stress. Sometimes the stress had made the siblings consider selling the business. However, ultimately they had decided to continue, and would actually have appreciated successors from the family. Their children had worked for the firm, but in minor roles, and some of them had left for other jobs. FIN represented an *absolute nuclear family* (which is fairly typical of Finnish culture in general), and this comes in contradiction to Arregle et al. (2019), who categorized Finnish families primarily as *exogamous community*.

FRA

FRA was established in 1864. Four generations had succeeded each other in running the firm, which specialized in the manufacture of paints and decorative coatings. This FF was located in the south of France, not far from Marseille, where its headquarters and manufacturing plant were located. The firm had 18 employees at its headquarters and eight abroad. The FF offered organic products made with lime, and utilized the identifier "Made in Provence." In 2017, it achieved a turnover of 1.2 million euros, 60% of which was exported. The company was owned by the current CEO and his wife. His wife and his brother-in-law had managerial positions. The current CEO marketed the firm's products either through local distributors (in the USA, South Korea, Ukraine, Saudi Arabia) or by creating subsidiaries in Japan, Russia, and Brazil. Their most important markets were Japan, Russia, and the USA. For Japan and Russia, the first contacts with customers had come through trade exhibitions. The opportunity to export to the USA came via a friend, who had his own company and encountered a direct opportunity.

The FRA case was interesting because it highlighted the importance of networks, and the role of ties in the context of the possible selling of an old FF. The CEO was very stressed by the question of heritage transmission because he was unable to pass the ownership on to his own children. It was an important issue for him because he was feeling his age and was afraid that when he died, all that he and his family had built would be destroyed. This attachment shaped the strategic decisions of the family members, in that the family members would have liked to transfer their company to someone who shared the same family values. FRA located in South-East France follows the classification of Arregle et al. (2019) and can be categorized as an *exogenous community* family.

TAI

TAI was established in 1986 and produced paint brushes and paint rollers. The FF had kept the firm's headquarters in Taiwan and had set up two manufacturing plants in China and Vietnam. The firm sold its products in approximately 15 countries. The majority of its revenue came from Southeast Asia. The newest manufacturing plant (in Vietnam) was founded in 2014. The founder of the company was the CEO, and his daughters were acting members in the business. The elderly daughter of the founder ran the operations in Vietnam; she acted as the sales manager and dealt with all foreign customers. The younger daughter had recently joined the FF.

The firm had found most of its partners via trade fairs, and the manufacturing plant in Vietnam had been decided on by all the family members. The founder of the FF was very emotionally attached to it, and this had led to some decisions that might not be rational from a purely business perspective. He wanted his daughters to control and run the business in the future. He was afraid that possible dilution would lead to loss of control of the firm. The family is *authoritarian* and followed the traditions of most Asian families.

Findings

As shown in Table 12.3, weak SC ties were the most common way of entering the main foreign markets, but these ties were quickly developed into strong ties. Each case (see Table 12.3) can be linked to the SC ties related to its three most important markets. The preliminary findings indicated that the FFs relied on SC to facilitate their internationalization. In addition, the FFs developed links and built their SC with other FFs. At the initial stages of internationalization, the FFs attended exhibitions to find new customers/clients. Moreover, there were cases where the firms used strong networks to further expand their operations in both geographically close and distant countries. The *evolution of strong ties* is an interesting finding as those ties continued among the next generations of FFs.

Table 12.3 Cross-case analysis: Family values, structure, and networks

Firm	Strength of the initial tie enabling the FME	Strength of ties during post-entry	Family values influencing international networking behavior	Family structure influencing the internationalization
FIN	Sweden: Weak tie. Potential partners met at international trade fairs. The first-generation CEO went to live in Sweden. He approached potential partners and selected one as most suitable. Netherlands: Weak tie. Potential partners met at international trade fairs. The first-generation CEO went to live in the Netherlands, visiting potential partners. France: Weak tie. Potential partners met at international trade fairs, then were contacted (becoming the first and second reseller).	Sweden: The original weak tie was quickly developed into a strong tie. This was possible because the founder CEO lived in Sweden for over a year, and was able to spend a lot of time with the partner (who remains their only Swedish partner). The partner was a leading specialist in renovating old houses in Sweden; this led to very good sales for the first 5–10 years. Netherlands: The weak tie was quickly developed into a strong tie. This was possible because the founder CEO lived in the Netherlands and was able to spend a lot of time with the partner they still have as their only Swedish partner. France: "The first two resellers did not work out. Both of them sold log houses and then our paints, suitable for log houses, on the side. Both of them went bankrupt. And we had spent a lot of resources on them. Inviting them to Finland, training them … With the first one, we traveled to France to investigate whether he was any good, and he has proved to be. He has great contacts with the Louvre and Versailles, where our paints are used. France is not the most important market in relation to sales, but it is the most important market in relation to our image."	*Conformity* The current generation protected the network tie created by the father, although the sales are low and decreasing. *Conformity* The current generation protected the network tie created by the father, although the sales were low. *Security* FIN wanted to have the kind of ties in France that would enable them to pass on the firm to the next generation, after all the difficulties they had faced with the two first agents in the market.	*Absolute nuclear* The previous generation of the FF was responsible for the initial internationalization. The second-generation representatives, currently in charge of the FF, have protected the initial network ties and recreated the lost French market ties. The third-generation representatives are not currently attached to the FF, although they worked for it in an earlier stage, and they follow a different career.

(*continued*)

Table 12.3 (continued)

Firm	Strength of the initial tie enabling the FME	Strength of ties during post-entry	Family values influencing international networking behavior	Family structure influencing the internationalization
FRA	Japan: Weak tie. A Japanese architect sent by his Japanese construction company (to figure out what a "Provencal Villa" might be) met the CEO at an exhibition in Paris, 1984 (weak tie). They talked for a short time (15 min) with the help of an interpreter. Russia: Weak tie. A member of a Russian delegation approached the CEO at an exhibition in Brussels. They talked for a short time (15 min) with the help of an interpreter. USA: Strong ties. A friend was met at an exhibition some years ago. The friend had his own construction company in the USA. He persuaded the CEO to quickly send him its products to seize a business opportunity.	Japan: Weak ties at the initial stage and strong after some years (with creation of a subsidiary in 2008). In 2018, they sold the subsidiary to a French friend. "On the back of that penetration into the [Japanese] market, I created a subsidiary in Tokyo in 2008, where I had Tamaya and Nagoya working for me. You cannot imagine [how close we were with the Japanese]! So, I gave the company to that very same Tamaya who was my technician, so it still exists but I don't own it anymore." Russia: Weak ties at the initial stage, but strong after some years (with creation of a subsidiary in 2009). "Trust with the Russians: it's beautiful, but ephemeral. But at the same time, it is very tense because you are not always sure that the guy won't disappear with the cash. Russia is a complicated country." USA: Strong ties at the initial stage and termination of collaboration after the financial crisis in 2008 (2008: bankruptcy of the US company, the friend lost everything and completely disappeared). "I delivered to Jean-Paul containers of goods that we had in stock. I was his product supplier. He was a close friend. We had loads of fun together in the USA. It lasted about ten years with Jean-Paul. And in 2008, when the crisis in the USA came, his company exploded. He unfortunately disappeared off the map."	*Security* FF CEO decided to protect his wife's job by establishing a contract with his Japanese partner to whom he gave his Japanese subsidiary. *Conformity* *Tradition* The FF CEO refused to search for potential Japanese investors to whom he could sell his Japanese subsidiary. He preferred to give it to a Japanese technician whom he had known for years and considered a member of his family (because the technician had "the right heart"). *Security* The CEO decided to create a subsidiary in Russia with people whom he knew and trusted. *Security* The CEO decided to protect his company from exposure in the US market after the issues faced there.	*Exogamous* The CEO of the FF decides for most of the internationalization plans but he has a strong link with the family members. The new generation follows a different career.

12 Social Capital and Values in the Internationalization of Family... 377

TAI			
Thailand: Weak ties. A customer approached them via the Taiwanese trading department, 2007. Vietnam: Strong ties. Uncle of the founder of the FF introduced them to the Vietnamese business landscape, 2014. Germany: Weak ties. Met manager at an exhibition, 2014.	Thailand: Weak ties at the early stage of the partnership, but developed to strong ties over time (family friends): "They all have become our family friends … because all these customers they are actually family business too … I also know their daughter, their daughter is also my friend … so we kind of, like, visit Bangkok like once a year and they will visit once a year, like, their whole family visits us and our whole family visits them to see friends and to talk about future collaboration." Vietnam: Strong ties throughout the process of setting up a manufacturing plant: "My father's uncle is just a trigger, he gives access to the information, like, we know the land price, we know the […] state of the industry in Vietnam and the supply chain etc., and he just give us the access. The key reason for my father to invest in Vietnam is he thinks Vietnam has […] one of the reasons why my father thinks China is not good for manufacturing is because we are traditional, we are from a traditional industry and we need a lot of labor." Germany: Weak ties at the early stages, but strong over the years: "He comes to our Vietnam factory just like it's a holiday resort, he came, like, twice a year, and … sometimes with his wife, we became very close after that, and he's a general manager of that company, the German company, and, as I mentioned before, he tried to do a merger, but we refused, we rejected it because this is a family business, but he still showed a lot of interest … he's actually coming again to us next week with his wife like, he is the general manager of one of the companies, and he's going to bring his group near here."	*Conformity* *Tradition* TAI (the Taiwan FF) shared the same values and traditions with its partner—an FF in Thailand. *Security* The FF founder decided to set up a manufacturing plant in Vietnam to protect his daughters. *Conformity* *Tradition* The whole extended family was involved in the decision to set up a manufacturing plant in Vietnam. *Security* The FF founder rejected the offer of the German customer to buy shares in TAI.	*Authoritarian* The family leader used his social capital to internationalize the operations and he was in charge of most decisions related to the expansion of the FF. The new generation is emotionally attached to the FF and follows the decisions of the founder of the firm.

Source: Authors

Case FIN

FIN had found all the initial leads to their three foreign markets at international trade fairs. They thus started from weak ties. However, in each case, they had made considerable efforts to develop these originally weak ties into strong ties as quickly as possible. In the case of Sweden and the Netherlands, the founder CEO went to live in these countries to develop the initially weak ties into strong ones:

> My father kind of wanted to leave Finland for a while and went to live in Sweden, hoping to develop good partners for us. The one we still have, they got along with each other very quickly. (second-generation Sales Manager)

This approach seemed to work out well as these agents were still representing them. However, sales in Sweden had declined due to the emergence of a competitive traditional paint company in Sweden, which had taken most of FIN's market share there. Furthermore, the firm had not made any further efforts to renew network ties in Sweden, although times had changed.

Entry to France (their most important market in terms of public image as their paints were used in Versailles and the Louvre) did not start so well. They had started with their first French reseller, who represented Finnish log houses. This ended up in bankruptcy after a couple of years, although FIN had trained them, invited them to Finland, and so on:

> Well, the original partner, we had him from the trade fairs. He was a reseller for a Finnish log house company, someone our paints matched well with. (second-generation Sales Manager)

Exactly the same thing happened with their second French reseller, who had a similar profile to the first. With their third and current reseller (initiated 6 years previously), they wanted to be more systematic in order not to waste their resources again. The second-generation representative traveled to France to get to know the person better. This had worked out as the relationship was good and sales had emerged. They were still fairly moderate, but with potential for major growth, given that France possesses around 60,000 castles where their paints could be used:

> The first two resellers did not work out. Both of them sold log houses and then our paints, suitable for log houses, on the side. Both of them went bankrupt. And we had spent a lot of resources on them. Inviting them to Finland, training them ... With the first one, we traveled to France to investigate whether he was any good, and he has proved to be. He has great contacts with the Louvre and Versailles, where our paints are used. France is not the most important market in relation to sales, but it is the most important market in relation to our image. (second-generation CEO)

12 Social Capital and Values in the Internationalization of Family...

The values related to BB of the firm were especially strongly visible in the approach of FIN in Sweden and the Netherlands. The firm had made efforts to quickly develop network ties into trustworthy ties in order to guarantee security; however, BB was reflected in their inability to renew these ties, even if they had not brought good sales or growth. For FIN, the conformity related to the network ties created by their father was important. In their dealings with France, too, the network ties were renewed out of necessity—due to bankruptcies. This was related to the security value—they wanted to pass the firm on to the next generation, and to ensure that the firm would have decent chances of running as a FF in the future.

Case FRA

FRA was a very old FF (154 years old). The current CEO was the great-grandson of the founder, and he was the only son who decided from his childhood to work in the family business with his father. He was the first of the family who decided to go abroad. The most important markets for FRA were Japan, Russia, and the USA. The Japanese and Russian customers were found via trade fairs. For the US market, the opportunity came from a friend of the CEO. Over time, the CEO had established a closer relationship and trust. Thus, the strength of the ties became strong.

Concerning the Japanese market, FRA started exporting to Japan in 1984. The CEO relied on weak ties to establish an initial contact with Japanese customers in 1984:

> A Japanese architect was sent by his Japanese construction company to figure out what a "Provencal Villa" is like, and he met the CEO at an exhibition. It came from a weak tie: they just exchanged a few words with the help of an interpreter.

It was a similar process for Russian market: a member of the Russian delegation came to the FRA stand during trade fairs in Brussels and asked some questions. A few days later, FRA received an initial order. FRA exported products to Russian distributors from 1992 to 2008 (16 years). In 2009, FRA set up a subsidiary in Moscow.

There was an exception for the US market. The opportunity to export to the USA had come from strong ties: a French friend, who had had his own construction company in the USA, persuaded the CEO of FRA to send him his products:

> The United States is a stroke of luck ... [Name of French friend] called me: "have a gigantic opportunity ... I have a first order, I need two containers of products."

The FRA company exported products to the USA from 1998 to 2008 (10 years). However, in 2008, the financial crisis led FRA to terminate operations there. The FRA CEO gave up staying in this market in order to protect his own company. His decision is based on *security* value. FRA exported products to the Japanese market from 1984 to 2008 (24 years). The CEO explained that in 2008 his Japanese distributor went bankrupt. The Japanese distributor CEO gave him all his stock and let him choose the people to hire, as proof of their level of trust and mutual affection. The CEO created a sales subsidiary in Tokyo from 2008 to 2018 (10 years). It was the same for the Russian market. The CEO explained that every time one of his Russian partners went bankrupt, he continued the business with one of the persons from the previous company who had decided to create his own business. However, in 2009, the situation in Russia was so difficult (following the financial crisis) that the CEO of FRA decided to create a Russian subsidiary with people he knew based on the *security* value.

A long partnership with the FF had caused weak ties to evolve to strong ones, even if there were deep cultural differences. With their Japanese partner this evolution took 34 years. Over time, all the members of FRA were invited to Japan, starting with the father of the current CEO, a few years before his death in 1988:

> He [my father] was a guest in Japan: it was a big moment for him. You cannot imagine [how close we were with the Japanese]! We would meet and spend evenings together. My Japanese colleague took me out. I'm a bit like their father sometimes.

The CEO of FRA was very emotionally attached to his firm. He was afraid that when he died all that he and his family had built up would be destroyed. In this particular context, it might be expected that BB would be absent. The FRA CEO might have been expected to sell his business, being aware there was no direct succession to the next generation. However, this was not the case, and the behavior of the CEO was based on the values of *security* and *conformity/tradition*.

The emotional attachment to the firm shaped the strategic decisions of the family members as the CEO and his wife would have liked to transfer their company to someone they appreciated, someone who would share the same family values. Concerning his Japanese subsidiary, his attitude could be described as paternalistic. He said that in the previous year (2018) they had "given" their sales subsidiary to a Japanese technician. This was someone he had known for years and had hired after the failure of his first Japanese supplier.

In the background, one can identify two main values. Thus, there was the *tradition* value, insofar as he used the verb "give" as if [Tayama] was his son. There was the *security* value, in that he would have liked to choose his substitute in order to protect his wife (who was younger, and who would need to continue working for several years). It was because of the *security* value that he had signed an exclusive contract with the Japanese in exchange for his company. The FRA case is interesting as it highlights the importance of international networks and the role of strong ties in the context of selling an old FF.

Case TAI

The company started exporting to Thailand in 2007 when a customer approached them via the trading department of Taiwan. The majority of the customers were found via trade fairs. The German market was entered in 2014. In that year, the Sales Manager of the FF attended an exhibition, where she met the key person in a German firm, which was one of the main players in the industry. At the initial stages of the FME in Thailand and Germany, the FF relied on weak ties to establish collaboration as the level of trust was low. Over time, the sales manager established a closer relationship, and the parties built trust. Hence, the tie had changed from weak to strong.

The TAI customers/partners also ran their FFs. It was notable that the ties had evolved over time, with partnership continuing from the first to the second generation of FF owners. The long partnership with the FFs had brought about the evolution of weak ties to strong ones. This was bound up with the high levels of trust between the FF members. Such a level of trust had evolved between the second generation of FF owners, emphasizing the role of strong ties in terms of continuing a successful partnership. Other customers also emerged in new markets (e.g. in the Cambodian market via the Thai partner), illustrating the importance of networks for TAI.

The founder of TAI was emotionally attached to his firm, and he was seeking to pass the ownership on to his children. His overall attachment was highlighted by his rejection of an offer by a German customer to buy shares in the company.

BB was observed at different stages of the FF. One of the most interesting events was the refusal of the founder of the FF to accept transfer of shares to the manager of the firm's manufacturing plant in China as he believed that he could lose control:

> We have a Chinese manager ... she helped my father to set up the factory in China. She managed the whole factory and has done he trading in the Chinese

factory for more than ten years … The Chinese factory is 100% owned by my family, but after ten years, or so many years, when her daughter grew up, she also wanted her daughter to be part of this company. So she requested my father to give her some shares in the Chinese factory, but my father decided not to do so, so she retired, she quit the company because of this. (second-generation Sales Manager)

Even though the ties were strong between the founder of the FF and his manager, the *security* value impelled the founder to protect the firm for the future generation (i.e. his daughters).

A result of this decision was that the TAI founder set up a new manufacturing plant in Vietnam in 2014. This demonstrates that BB can actually trigger a firm to expand its operations (based on the *security* value overall, and on personal security):

There's another reason why my father wants to move and change the investment resources from China to Vietnam, because he feels like China is sometimes a bit dangerous to me and my sister, compared with Vietnam … He is slowly moving resources from China to Vietnam. He made the decision, because he wants us to stay in a better environment … so the reason why he decided to do it in Vietnam instead of Western China is to make sure that our family has 100% control of it. (second-generation Sales Manager)

The family of the focal firm shared the values of Confucian philosophy, two pillars of which are loyalty and family obligations. The daughter of the founder respected her father's choice to move to Vietnam:

When my father was going to set up a business in Vietnam he called me and said 'I'm going to set up a factory, a new factory in Vietnam because of blah blah blah, for all these rational reasons, what do you feel?' and … and it's also about our own judgment, either emotional or rational, it doesn't matter, it's a family business, so how we feel would affect his decision, and actually, I felt it's okay, Vietnam for me is pretty nice … and also my father's uncle has helped a lot.

The major German customer, who was a manager in one of the biggest MNEs in the paint brush sector, offered to acquire shares in the FF. The founder of the FF declined the offer as he wanted his daughters to continue the business. This is another interesting example that highlights the *security* value—the wish to preserve the firm for future generations and the lack of trust in non-family members as regards becoming part of the management of the firm. This was linked to the emotional attachment, not just of the father, but of other members of the family, toward the firm:

As I said, also in the German merger case, it is good for our company, but because it's my father's "son" he cannot sell his "son" to a stranger, so this is strongly attached to him, because this is something that is owned by our family, so we are willing to invest more, which is not going to happen if we work in another company. But in return, we also expect more from this company because this is our family, so yeah, it's definitely like the whole company operation and strategic decision-making, all aspects, because of this emotional attachment. (second-generation Sales Manager)

The value related to BB of TAI was clear when the founder of the firm rejected an offer to merge with the German partner and to offer shares to the Chinese manager. This highlights the *conservation* value—the desire of the founder of the company to maintain control of the firm and to secure it for the next generation. It is interesting that even though the ties were strong with the German partner and the Chinese managers, the *conservation* value prevailed.

Cross-Case Analysis

All FF structures: (1) absolute nuclear family, (2) exogamous, (3) authoritarian were associated with strong and long-term SC developed by the previous generations. The internationalization decisions were more influenced by the whole family in the absolute nuclear and exogamous family structures; whereas the authoritarian family structure was linked to the decision of the founder of the firm where the other members had to follow their will and decisions. Another interesting finding is that values played a strong role despite the structure of the FF, for example, more liberal and egalitarian family structures were influenced by conformity and security when decisions to the preservation of the FF had to be taken. The same applied to the authoritarian family in the case of TAI where tradition, conformity, and security affected the decision of the founder of the firm to retain the control of the FF for the future generation.

As regards the strength of the ties in the initial foreign market entries (see Table 12.3), all the case firms (FIN, FRA, and TAI) used weak ties for their initial market entries. They had no ready-made contacts abroad, and it was due to this that they were approached or found a partner via trade fairs/exhibitions. The only exception concerned case FRA; for them, the opportunity to export to the USA came from a French friend located in the USA. It can be concluded that in this case, even though the firms operated in different countries and cultures, weak ties played an important role in the first phases of internationalization.

The family values linked to initial ties and to the important markets were *conservation* and *tradition* as the case forms wanted to preserve the firm for the family members. At the initial FME, all the case firms relied on weak ties. All the FFs had attended trade fairs to find new customers and partners; hence, the initial level of trust was low, lacking emotional attachment between the FFs and their partners. As the FFs were at their initial stages of internationalization, they focused on strategies to retain the control of their firms and to protect the future generations against dilution of the firm ownership structure. *Conservation* and *tradition* were the dominant family values. The only exception was case TAI, which relied on strong ties when they first entered the Vietnamese market.

Regarding TAI, the family value of *tradition* and *conformity*, is very interesting, underlining the difference in family structure between Asian and European FFs. Case FIN had an *absolute nuclear* family structure (as is the norm in Finnish culture). FRA followed the *exogamous community* family structure, whereas TAI followed an *authoritarian* family structure. This might lead one to expect different internationalization behavior on the basis of the family structure, but in fact, the three FFs seemed to be more influenced by their family values, and certain common patterns were observed. This may be explained by the dominant role of the *conservation* value in all three case firms, FIN, FRA, and TAI.

In the post-entry phase, the FFs developed their strength of ties from weak to strong over time. All the case firms developed higher levels of trust with their partners. It is notable that all the FFs developed partnerships with other FFs. In addition, next-generation family members developed close links with the family members of their partners (the daughter of the founder of TAI was a close friend of the daughter of their Thai partner). In the case of FIN, a transition was taking place, in that the daughter of the CEO was visiting the French agent and learning to know his potential successor children.

There were cases in which the strong ties had started to decay; this was occurring between TAI and the firm in China, and between FRA and the firm in the USA. In the case of TAI, the founder of the company had decided to set up a new manufacturing plant in Vietnam because he feared a loss of control in China. He made this decision to protect the next generation from long-term issues in China. The same thing happened with the CEO of FRA, who decided to terminate collaboration with the USA due to a lack of engagement on the part of the American partner. Both developments were linked to the *security* value.

It is striking that TAI received offers to merge with other firms or to sell part of its shares. TAI had an offer to merge with its German partner, but the founder rejected it. Even though the level of trust was high, the family members were biased by the conservation family value. The founder preferred to pass the firm on to the next generation. An exception occurred with FRA because the new generation had no desire to control the firm. The current CEO of FRA had decided to progressively sell his subsidiaries. What was interesting in his behavior is that he wanted to transmit his subsidiary and his brand to people who shared the same values in the manner of an extended family. This was the case with his Japanese technician, to whom he sold the Japanese subsidiary.

It is clear that even though the family structure was different among the three FFs, there were some common patterns. In all three cases, family values tended to play a dominant role when the FFs had to take internationalization decisions. It is important to note that the CEO in FRA followed the *conformity* value in his efforts to sell one of his companies to the right person, while the CEO in TAI followed the *security value* in seeking to save his company from foreign investors.

Discussion and Conclusions

With our study on how FFs with different family structures and countries of origin build SC for internationalization, we contribute to the discussions on FF international networking (Arregle et al., 2019; Kampouri et al., 2017; Kano & Verbeke, 2018; Kontinen & Ojala, 2010, 2012; Pukall & Calabrò, 2014; Yuan & Wu, 2018). First, our findings suggest that to some extent, different values are at the forefront of the decision-making related to international networking among FFs from different countries of origin. The Taiwanese FF based its decisions more strongly on tradition (related to religion and culture) and security; by contrast, among the Finnish and French FFs, conformity (related to the protection of family members) was the strongest family value influencing international networking. We reveal that what seemed to make a difference in the international networking behavior of FFs from different countries and family structures derived from *values* related to *conservation*. The Taiwanese case demonstrated more security and tradition values as Taiwanese values are more conservative compared to the European ones. Altogether, our evidence appears to point in a certain direction, that is, that on a global level, in comparison with other types of firms, FFs may be more similar on the basis of the values they cherish networking (Arregle et al., 2019; Kano & Verbeke, 2018; Verbeke & Kano, 2012).

Second, our findings extend the work of Kontinen and Ojala (2012) to the effect that FFs from cultures beyond Europe use weak ties for foreign market entry. However, in relation to the pace of developing trust in the post-entry phase, we can see some variation: the Finnish high level of trust was visible in the willingness of FIN to quickly develop trust with their new international partners; by contrast, TAI and FRA (representing cultures where trust is not self-evident) developed trust at a slower pace.

Third, our findings also shed light on the trans-generational aspect of international networks (Arregle et al., 2019; De Massis et al., 2018; Kampouri et al., 2017). Our findings show how the FFs made a generational change in parallel with their international collaborators. The father and daughter in TAI developed strong ties with the founder and daughter of their partner FF in Thailand. The same process was under way with FIN, where the daughter of the CEO was visiting the French agent and learning to know his potential successor children. The Finnish case represents an *absolute nuclear* family and the FRA the *exogamous community* family structure. However, in relation to values (related to BB), both FIN and FRA followed *conformity*, meaning that they were compliant with the various rules and that the new generations respected their parents. Although FIN represented an absolute nuclear family, the value of conformity (which it cherished) made its international networking following the traditional approach of a FF. The Asian case was linked to an *authoritarian* structure; here, BB led the FF to take decisions that might not be rational economically. The retention of the FF's control indicated that the *security* value was linked to internationalization, and strong ties were associated mainly with the post-entry phase. All the case firms relied on the *security* value, seeking to protect their family members, and to maintain the structure of the FF. This finding is in line with Verbeke et al. (2020) and Arregle et al. (2019), who noted the tendency of older generations to seek to protect oncoming FF generations. *Tradition* was primarily linked to case TAI, where the family structure was more *authoritarian* (Arregle et al., 2019), with a background of Confucianism (Verbeke et al., 2020), which is part of the worldview of many Asian families.

From a managerial point of view, our study can provide new knowledge for family owners to drive the relationship with their foreign partners and for policy makers to a better understanding of the specificities of FF internationalization and maybe act more as "safeguard" against BB. The owners of FFs should minimize the effects of BB by taking decisions more rationally. Emotions should not influence and hinder business opportunities if those can assist firms to grow and further expand their international operations. The new generations of FFs should advise and explain to older generations that *security* and *tradition* may have a negative impact in the long term. Culture does play an important role and FFs share different values. The Asian FFs tend to be more traditional and authoritarian but new generations could offer new skills and a more open mindset to facilitate internationalization decisions without the dysfunction coming from BB. On the other hand, the European FFs have differences in terms of their geographic location (i.e. South or the North), where South European FFs can be more traditional and the BB higher. North European FFs are more open to changes and the BB has less impact. Networking is equally important among the FFs and they should use their strong ties in order to minimize BB and to get valuable advice on a potential collaboration that could increase their profitability and international exposure and expansion. Policy makers could support FFs with training, for example, how a collaboration could benefit them in order to minimize the negative effect of BB. Another approach that could mitigate BB, which may be linked to preconceptions, is the older FF generation to discuss and seek advice from the new generation as they may offer a fresher approach to a potential collaboration.

Our study is not free of limitations. One of the limitations is the number of cases per country; however, this study was not pursuing a statistical but an analytical generalization (Miles & Huberman, 1994). The second limitation is related to values that were not the original focus of our study, but their importance emerged from the data. That is why we did not have direct questions about values in the interview protocol, which we recommend is an excellent further research direction. Future studies could also conduct a survey and test our framework in multiple locations with different cultures and FFs that operate in various industries.

The field of FF studies has so far left a good many aspects unaddressed. These have included, notably, how the internationalization of FFs can be analyzed in terms of values held by the firms (Schwartz, 1992; Verbeke et al., 2020), and how the structures of the firms can affect their internationalization (Arregle et al., 2019). Here we offer new perspectives in the FF field by showing how the strength of ties appears to influence the internationalization of FF, with inputs from values, and by highlighting the limited effect of family structures. We recommend to go beyond values and to examine through empirical inquiry how social capital could moderate the magnitude of a bifurcation bias and extenuate the effects of family structures. We also suggest investigating other family structures not explored yet in the recent articles (Arregle et al., 2019; Hennart et al., 2019; Verbeke et al., 2020) like anomic family, asymmetrical community family, or egalitarian nuclear family which lead us to privilege multi-country study approach. This has the potential to offer a new stream for future studies.

References

Aldrich, H., & Zimmer, C. (1986). *Entrepreneurship through social networks: The art and science of entrepreneurship.* Cambridge, MA: Ballinger Publ. Company.

Arregle, J. L., Duran, P., Hitt, M. A., & Van Essen, M. (2017). Why is family firms' internationalization unique? A meta–analysis. *Entrepreneurship Theory and Practice, 41*(5), 801–831.

Arregle, J. L., Hitt, M. A., & Mari, I. (2019). A missing link in family firms' internationalization research: Family structures. *Journal of International Business Studies, 50*(5), 809–825.

Arregle, J. L., Hitt, M. A., Sirmon, D. G., & Very, P. (2007). The development of organizational social capital: Attributes of family firms. *Journal of Management Studies, 44*(1), 73–95.

Arregle, J. L., Naldi, L., Nordqvist, M., & Hitt, M. A. (2012). Internationalization of family-controlled firms: A study of the effects of external involvement in governance. *Entrepreneurship Theory and Practice, 36*(6), 1115–1143.

Burt, R. S. (2019). Network disadvantaged entrepreneurs: Density, hierarchy, and success in China and the West. *Entrepreneurship Theory and Practice, 43*(1), 19–50.

Chua, J. H., Chrisman, J. J., & Bergiel, E. B. (2009). An agency theoretic analysis of the professionalized family firm. *Entrepreneurship Theory and Practice, 33*(2), 355–372.

De Massis, A., Frattini, F., Majocchi, A., & Piscitello, L. (2018). Family firms in the global economy: Toward a deeper understanding of internationalization determinants, processes, and outcomes. *Global Strategy Journal, 8*(1), 3–21.

Dubini, P., & Aldrich, H. (1991). Personal and extended networks are central to the entrepreneurial process. *Journal of Business Venturing, 6,* 305–313.

Eisenhardt, K. M. (1989). Making fast strategic decisions in high-velocity environments. *Academy of Management Journal, 32*(3), 543–576.

Eisenhardt, K. M., & Graebner, M. E. (2007). Theory building from cases: Opportunities and challenges. *Academy of Management Journal, 50*(1), 25–32.

Elg, U. (2008). Inter-firm market orientation and the influence of network and relational factors. *Scandinavian Journal of Management, 24*(1), 55–68.

Granovetter, M. (1973). The strength of weak ties. *American Journal of Sociology, 78*(6), 1360–1380.

Granovetter, M. (1985). Economic action and social structure: The problem of embeddedness. *American Journal of Sociology, 91*(3), 481–510.

Graves, C., & Thomas, J. (2004). Internationalisation of the family business: A longitudinal perspective. *International Journal of Globalisation and Small Business, 1*(1), 7–27.

Graves, C., & Thomas, J. (2008). Determinants of the internationalization pathways of family firms: An examination of family influence. *Family Business Review, 21*(2), 151–167.

Hansen, M. T. (1999). The search-transfer problem: The role of weak ties in sharing knowledge across organization subunits. *Administrative Science Quarterly, 44*(1), 82–111.

Harvey, W. S. (2010). Methodological approaches for interviewing elites. *Geography Compass, 4*(3), 193–205.

Hennart, J. F., Majocchi, A., & Forlani, E. (2019). The myth of the stay-at-home family firm: How family-managed SMEs can overcome their internationalization limitations. *Journal of International Business Studies, 50*(5), 758–782.

Hite, J. M. (2003). Patterns of multidimensionality among embedded network ties: A typology of relational embeddedness in emerging entrepreneurial firms. *Strategic Organization, 1*(1), 9–49.

Jack, S. L. (2005). The role, use and activation of strong and weak network ties: A qualitative analysis. *Journal of Management Studies, 42*(6), 1233–1259.

Jack, S. L. (2010). Approaches to studying networks: Implications and outcomes. *Journal of Business Venturing, 25*(1), 120–137.

Johanson, J., & Vahlne, J. E. (2009). The Uppsala internationalization process model revisited: From liability of foreignness to liability of outsidership. *Journal of International Business Studies, 40*(9), 1411–1431.

Kampouri, K., Plakoyiannaki, E., & Leppäaho, T. (2017). Family business internationalisation and networks: Emerging pathways. *Journal of Business & Industrial Marketing, 32*(3), 357–370.

Kano, L., & Verbeke, A. (2018). Family firm internationalization: Heritage assets and the impact of bifurcation bias. *Global Strategy Journal, 8*(1), 158–183.

Kontinen, T., & Ojala, A. (2010). The internationalization of family businesses: A review of extant research. *Journal of Family Business Strategy, 1*(2), 97–107.

Kontinen, T., & Ojala, A. (2012). Internationalization pathways among family-owned SMEs. *International Marketing Review, 29*(5), 496–518.

Leppäaho, T., & Metsola, J. (2020). Conclusions: Implications of family firm internationalisation from a network perspective. In *Family Firm Internationalisation* (pp. 121–135). Cham: Palgrave Pivot.

Lin, N., Ensel, W. M., & Vaughn, J. C. (1981). Social resources and strength of ties: Structural factors in occupational status attainment. *American Sociological Review, 46*, 393–405.

Marsden, P. V., & Campbell, K. E. (1984). Measuring tie strength. *Social Forces, 63*(2), 482–501.

Metsola, J., Leppäaho, T., Paavilainen-Mäntymäki, E., & Plakoyiannaki, E. (2020). Process in family business internationalisation: The state of the art and ways forward. *International Business Review*, 101665.

Miles, M. B., & Huberman, A. M. (1994). *Qualitative data analysis: An expanded sourcebook*. Sage.

Morgan, R. M., & Hunt, S. D. (1994). The commitment-trust theory of relationship marketing. *Journal of Marketing, 58*(3), 20–38.

Nahapiet, J., & Ghoshal, S. (1998). Social capital, intellectual capital, and the organizational advantage. *Academy of Management Review, 23*(2), 242–266.

Poulis, K., Poulis, E., & Plakoyiannaki, E. (2013). The role of context in case study selection: An international business perspective. *International Business Review, 22*(1), 304–314.

Pukall, T. J., & Calabrò, A. (2014). The internationalization of family firms: A critical review and integrative model. *Family Business Review, 27*(2), 103–125.

Reuber, A. R., & Fischer, E. (1997). The influence of the management team's international experience on the internationalization behaviors of SMEs. *Journal of International Business Studies, 28*(4), 807–825.

Roessl, D. (2005). Family businesses and interfirm cooperation. *Family Business Review, 18*(3), 203–214.

Salvato, C., & Melin, L. (2008). Creating value across generations in family-controlled businesses: The role of family social capital. *Family Business Review, 21*(3), 259–276.

Schwartz, S. H. (1992). Universals in the content and structure of values: Theoretical advances and empirical tests in 20 countries. *Advances in Experimental Social Psychology, 25*(1), 1–65.

Singh, J. (2000). Performance productivity and quality of frontline employees in service organizations. *Journal of Marketing, 64*(2), 15–34.

Sinkovics, R. R., Penz, E., & Ghauri, P. N. (2008). Enhancing the trustworthiness of qualitative research in international business. *Management International Review, 48*(6), 689–714.

Söderqvist, A., & Chetty, S. (2009). *Strength of ties and their role in pre-founding, start-up and early internationalization.* In 12th McGill International Entrepreneurship Conference, Vaasa, Finland.

Terjesen, S., Hessels, J., & Li, D. (2016). Comparative international entrepreneurship: A review and research agenda. *Journal of Management, 42*(1), 299–344.

Todd, E. (1985). *The explanation of ideology: Family structures and social systems.* Oxford; New York, NY: B. Blackwell.

Uzzi, B. (1997). Social structure and competition in interfirm networks: The paradox of embeddedness. *Administrative Science Quarterly, 42*, 35–67.

Verbeke, A., & Kano, L. (2012). The transaction cost economics theory of the family firm: Family-based human asset specificity and the bifurcation bias. *Entrepreneurship Theory and Practice, 36*(6), 1183–1205.

Verbeke, A., Yuan, W., & Kano, L. (2020). A values-based analysis of bifurcation bias and its impact on family firm internationalization. *Asia Pacific Journal of Management, 37*, 449–477.

Welch, C., Marschan-Piekkari, R., Penttinen, H., & Tahvanainen, M. (2002). Corporate elites as informants in qualitative international business research. *International Business Review, 11*(5), 611–628.

Yin, R. K. (1994). Discovering the future of the case study. Method in evaluation research. *Evaluation Practice, 15*(3), 283–290.

Yuan, W., & Wu, Z. (2018). Commentary: A value perspective of family firms. *Entrepreneurship Theory and Practice, 42*(2), 283–289.

Zahra, S. A. (2003). International expansion of US manufacturing family businesses: The effect of ownership and involvement. *Journal of Business Venturing, 18*(4), 495–512.

Zander, I., McDougall-Covin, P., & Rose, E. L. (2015). Born globals and international business: Evolution of a field of research. *Journal of International Business Studies, 46*(1), 27–35.

Zellweger, T., Chrisman, J., Chua, J. H., & Steier, L. (2019). Social structures, social relationships and family firms. *Entrepreneurship Theory and Practice, 43*(2), 207–223.

Part IV

Family Firm Internationalization from Emerging Markets

13

The Network Dynamics During Internationalization of a Family Firm: The Case of a New Venture from Colombia

Sascha Fuerst

Introduction

Research on family firm internationalization is attracting more interest due to the increasing involvement of this type of firm in international markets (Arregle, Duran, Hitt, & van Essen, 2017; Kontinen & Ojala, 2010; Pukall & Calabrò, 2014). Family firms, however, suffer from a variety of liabilities such as risk aversion, conservative decision-making, conflict of interests, and lack of capabilities and resources (Metsola, Leppäaho, Paavilainen-Mäntymäki, & Plakoyiannaki, 2020). The presence of these liabilities inhibits internationalization. Capabilities are, therefore, needed that enable internationalization of the family firm (Graves & Thomas, 2006). Research shows that these capabilities are often brought into the firm by outside managers (Arregle, Naldi, Nordqvist, & Hitt, 2012; Claver, Rienda, & Quer, 2009; D'Angelo, Majocchi, & Buck, 2016; Kraus, Mensching, Calabrò, Cheng, & Filser, 2016; Mitter, Duller, Feldbauer-Durstmüller, & Kraus, 2014). Moreover, internationalization of family firms is more effectively accomplished if there is less influence of family members in governance (Arregle et al., 2012). An important capability that enables and drives internationalization is networking. The network perspective is increasingly adopted in family firm research for explaining

---

S. Fuerst (✉)
EGADE Business School, Tecnologico de Monterrey, Guadalajara, Mexico

Turku School of Economics, University of Turku, Turku, Finland
e-mail: sascha@tec.mx

© The Author(s), under exclusive license to Springer Nature Switzerland AG 2021 **395**
T. Leppäaho, S. Jack (eds.), *The Palgrave Handbook of Family Firm Internationalization*,
https://doi.org/10.1007/978-3-030-66737-5_13

internationalization (Kampouri, Plakoyiannaki, & Leppäaho, 2017; Pukall & Calabrò, 2014). Networks provide access to resources and evolve with the changing resource needs of the firm (Hite & Hesterly, 2001).

Given the above-mentioned challenges of family firm internationalization, this chapter aims at contributing to the literature on family firm internationalization from a network perspective. More specifically, it tries to explain how a family-controlled new venture both co-founded by a family member and a non-family member was able to internationalize from its home market in Colombia.

The study focuses on a Colombian new venture in the global, mobile video game industry co-founded by a family member entrepreneur and a non-family member entrepreneur. The family holds 90% of the shares and the non-family entrepreneur the remaining 10%. The video game industry is characterized by an accelerated growth combined with fast-changing technological developments and rapid changes in consumer trends. For the new venture to succeed in such a highly competitive global environment, it requires resources and capabilities mainly accessed through networking. An additional challenge is managing the internationalization from its home base in Colombia, that is, from the periphery and not the centre of the development of the global mobile video game industry such as San Francisco in the U.S. These circumstances provided an interesting setting for studying how activities of networking evolved and eventually contributed to the internationalization of this family venture.

This case study reveals the central role of networking for internationalization. It illustrates the different networking behaviour of the two types of entrepreneurs (family member vs non-family member) and how the activities of networking play out and interact from foundation, to first market entry, through to post-entry in order to secure the resources needed for internationalization. This provides a micro-level perspective on the networking of family firm entrepreneurs (De Massis & Foss, 2018). Furthermore, the case shows how the joint development of strategic ties by the two entrepreneurs to external board members and mentors is an important networking activity able to alleviate the tensions caused by the mixed gamble of non-economic and economic goals within the family firm. In addition, the locational disadvantage was overcome through creating a local support network and through the development of strong strategic ties to external board members and mentors abroad.

The findings of the research presented in this chapter respond, on one hand, to the call by Kampouri et al. (2017) to focus on the entire process of family firm internationalization from a network perspective (beyond first market entry) and, on the other hand, to the recent call by Metsola et al. (2020) to consider the influence of the country of origin context for family firm internationalization and to research the dynamic process of family firm internationalization with the methodology and methods appropriate for capturing and analysing longitudinal process data.

Family Firm Internationalization from a Network Perspective

Research on family firm internationalization is increasing (Casillas & Moreno-Menéndez, 2017; Metsola et al., 2020). However, there is no agreement on the outcome of internationalization of family firms versus other firms. While some authors relate to factors that constrain family firm internationalization, others identified characteristics that facilitate their internationalization. In a recent meta-analysis about family firms and internationalization, Arregle et al. (2017) even found that the relationship between a firm's ownership (i.e. family vs non-family firm) and internationalization is null. Nonetheless, the authors identified, among others, that what makes family firm internationalization unique is the role of family control. That means when the family has a substantial ownership and participation in top management (i.e. the firm is family controlled), the relationship between family firm and internationalization is negative. Consequently, if family control hinders internationalization, then the participation of non-family members within the board and/or top management facilitates internationalization.

Internationalization requires managerial capabilities that family managers often lack (Graves & Thomas, 2006). Therefore, it is the knowledge and the networks brought in from outside of the close family boundaries that provide access to the necessary resources in order to make internationalization happen. While the participation of non-family members in family firms is attracting increasing interest (Hiebl & Li, 2018; Tabor, Chrisman, Madison, & Vardaman, 2018), fewer studies have looked at the relationship of the influence of non-family members on the internationalization of the firm (Arregle et al., 2012; Claver et al., 2009; D'Angelo et al., 2016; Kraus et al., 2016; Mitter et al., 2014). Among these studies, most have focused on the impact of external governance (i.e. board of directors and ownership) on internationalization and fewer on the participation of non-family members in management (Kraus et al., 2016; Mensching, Calabrò, Eggers, & Kraus, 2016; Pongelli, Caroli, & Cucculelli, 2016; Yeoh, 2014). Overall, these studies confirm that external managers and external ownership have a positive influence on internationalization.

It is the combined influence of both externally hired managers and external ownership that exert the most favourable influence on internationalization in family firms (D'Angelo et al., 2016). Internationalization of family firms is more effectively accomplished if there is less influence of family members in governance. Therefore, family-influenced firms where the family does not unilaterally control the firm (i.e. with less than 50% of shares) seem to take greater advantage of external resources and managerial capabilities than family-controlled firms (Arregle et al., 2012).

External managers are able to contribute knowledge, experience, and networks in order to enable and facilitate internationalization (Banalieva & Eddleston, 2011; Kraus et al., 2016; Mensching et al., 2016; Pongelli et al., 2016; Yeoh, 2014). Access to networks is particularly important for family firms in order to overcome the financial and managerial resource constraints (Graves & Thomas, 2008). The network perspective is increasingly considered a dominant feature for explaining internationalization, not only in international business literature but also in literature on family firm internationalization (Kampouri et al., 2017; Pukall & Calabrò, 2014).

Research has shown that networks are particularly important for the internationalization of family firms that suffer from liabilities that inhibit their expansion abroad such as risk aversion, conservative decision-making, conflict of interests, and lack of capabilities and resources (Metsola et al., 2020). Networks are, therefore, considered a capability facilitating internationalization. Furthermore, the network perspective is central in order to explain different paths of internationalization ranking from the incremental path of conquering markets abroad, over rapid internationalization through born global models, and born-again globals that experience rapid international growth periods (Kontinen & Ojala, 2012). The different pathways of internationalization are well explained through the internationalization process model (Johanson & Vahlne, 1977; Johanson & Vahlne, 2009; Vahlne & Johanson, 2017). It is no longer the liability of foreignness that inhibits internationalization but the liability of outsidership. Thus, building relevant positions in international or global networks is the prime task of any firm interested in doing business abroad.

Kampouri et al. (2017) in their literature review on family firm internationalization and networks identified three areas that emerged from research on family firm internationalization from a network perspective, specifically, the role of networks and relationships in the internationalization process, the factors that influence network formation, and strategic/managerial issues in the formation and building of network ties. Regarding the role of networks and relationships, family firms build personal and organizational relationships for internationalizing gradually from their home country to geographically close countries (e.g. Chen, 2003). Relationships with governments, personal contacts, and business associates seem to be important during the initial stages of internationalization (e.g. Senik, Scott-Ladd, Entrekin, & Adham, 2011). However, there is a lack of understanding about the role of networks and relationships during the later stages of internationalization.

The governance structure (i.e. family-controlled vs family-influenced) and the decision-making of family versus non-family owners/managers seem to be the main factors influencing the network formation (e.g. Carney, 2005; Child & Hsieh, 2014). Especially during the initial period of internationalization, the family owner/manager seems to inhibit network formation whereas the non-family owner/manager seems to be more active in forming new relationships (e.g. Arregle et al., 2012; Ciravegna, Majano, & Zhan, 2014). Again, there is a lack of understanding about the factors influencing network formation during the later stages of internationalization. The creation of network ties is strategically important for the family firm as it contributes to the formation of managerial capabilities such as learning, knowledge, and international opportunity recognition (e.g. Edwards, Sengupta, & Tsai, 2010; Kontinen & Ojala, 2011; Minguzzi & Passaro, 2001).

Overall, there is increasing interest in the research of family firm internationalization. Networking is considered an important capability for the internationalizing family firm in order to acquire the necessary resources and to overcome its liability of outsidership. Researching family firm internationalization from a network perspective requires particular methodological choices in order to fully capture the longitudinal and processual dynamics of the individual decision-makers within the firm.

Methodology

I applied a longitudinal research design where I followed the business development and internationalization process of a new venture in the video game industry. C2 Game Studio (C2) was founded by two entrepreneurs Luis and Camilo located in the city of Medellin, Colombia. The company was registered as a Simplified Stock Company (S.A.S. by its acronym in Spanish). Camilo as the non-family member holds 10% of the shares, and Luis, the family member, together with his brother and father the remaining 90%. C2 can, therefore, be considered a family-controlled firm (Arregle et al., 2012). A clear definition of a family firm is still lacking. Some authors define a family firm either by its family ownership (Peng & Jiang, 2010), its family management (Anderson & Reeb, 2003), its intergenerational character (Kontinen & Ojala, 2012; Zahra, 2003), or a combination of the aforementioned, particularly family ownership and management (Chua et al., 1999; Graves & Thomas, 2008). Lately, in an effort to explain family firm internationalization through family heterogeneity, Arregle et al. (2019) proposed a typology of family businesses based on their social anthropological family structure.

C2 can be considered a family firm insofar as it is family controlled (i.e. 90% of the share belong to the family) and family managed (i.e. Luis' role in the top management and Luis' father and brother's roles in the managing board of C2). The intergenerational perspective does not apply in this case as the management of C2 was not passed on yet between generations. C2 was co-founded in 2008 by Luis as the family member and Camilo as the non-family member. Consequently, C2 can be considered a family-controlled and family-managed new venture.

Focusing on one case allowed me to study the unfolding of networking in depth in their natural setting and context. Case studies provide rich, empirical descriptions of particular instances and are useful in order to understand the dynamics present within single settings (Eisenhardt & Graebner, 2007; Yin, 2009). A single case study that explores the depth of a phenomenon in their natural setting is a powerful tool for inductive theory generation (Dyer & Wilkins, 1991; Siggelkow, 2007). Single case studies are often criticized for their lack of sample size or non-representativeness. However, as Langley et al. (2013, p. 7, emphasis in the original) note in regard to longitudinal, process studies "[i]t is a common misconception that longitudinal case studies represent 'samples of one.' However, it is important to note that the sample size for a process study is not the number of cases, but the number of temporal observations. Depending on how researchers structure their analysis, the number of temporal observations in a longitudinal study can be substantial."

I reconstructed the case history through interview data with the firm's founders ranging from the pre-founding period, over the startup period, to the beginning of the internationalization period, and then followed the new venture's internationalization process in real time. Altogether, I was able to reconstruct 12 years of retrospective case history and covered 32 months of longitudinal, real-time data. In order to capture the events as they unfolded in real time, I applied weekly solicited logs in combination with periodic follow-up interviews (Balogun, Huff, & Johnson, 2003; Kenten, 2010). Altogether, between June 2011 and January 2014, a total of nine interviews were conducted face-to-face in order to follow-up on the information reported within

13 The Network Dynamics During Internationalization of a Family... **401**

Table 13.1 Observation period and data sources

	Retrospectively	Real time	Total
Observation period	14 years (1998–June 2011)	32 months (June 2011–January 2014)	15.67 years (1998–January 2014)
Primary data			
Weekly solicited logs including follow-up emails	113 pages (27,291 words)		
Interviews	9 Interviews (9.35 hours)		
Secondary data			
Social media updates (Tweets)	11		
Documents	50	37 Press articles 7 Company presentations 2 Internal documents 4 Workshop presentations	

Source: Author

the logs. The diary approach allowed me to capture in detail the unfolding of micro-events related to the networking process at the level of the entrepreneurs. I complemented the data from the logs and interviews with observational data, the use of follow-up emails for clarification purposes, the collection of media information as they emerged in real time (e.g. Tweets, Internet news), and the consultation of additional documents as they were created during the business development process (e.g. company presentations, workshop presentations). Table 13.1 provides an overview of the different sources I used for collecting the data.

For the analysis of the longitudinal retrospective and real-time data, I used different sensitizing devices and heuristics for the identification of patterns. First, I applied a grounded theorizing strategy (Langley, 1999) and coded the data following Pettigrew's (1990) meta-level analytical framework of content, process, context with the support of MaxQDA (software for qualitative data analysis). In a next step, I applied a visual mapping strategy (Langley, 1999) and constructed a network model (Miles et al., 2014) based on the coded data in order to visualize how events connected over time and unfolded chronologically. The construction of the network model was supported by MaxQDA's visual mapping function MaxMaps. After I had more clarification about the recurrent networking activities of the entrepreneurs and their interactions over time, I constructed an event-listing matrix (Miles et al., 2014) and time-bracketed the unfolding of events according to common themes (Langley, 1999). Finally, based on the event-listing matrix, I created a focused narrative

402 S. Fuerst

(Langley, 1999; Miles et al., 2014; Pentland, 1999) which tells the story about how the case firm experienced rapid internationalization based on the networking of the individual entrepreneurs through interaction with others.

Findings: Focused Case Narrative

This section tells the story of how the networking of the two entrepreneurs unfolded over the observed time period within C2. The narrative follows a chronological order and is structured according to the time-bracketed periods. Some periods might overlap with others and some occur in parallel. Figure 13.1 provides an overview of the networking activities of Luis and Camilo along the different periods of firm development and internationalization. Decision-making within C2 was not solely accomplished by the two entrepreneurs but depended on many occasions on the board of directors. This related especially to decisions that strategically impacted further development of C2 such as the decision to cooperate with the Publisher and the development of strategic ties. Luis' decisions were supported by his family (i.e. father and brother), meaning that the family controlled strategic decision-making through their majority stake in the firm.

In this study I followed Kontinen and Ojala (2011) that define a strong tie as one which is close and is based on trust, mutual respect, and commitment, whereas a weak tie is a more superficial tie not yet based on strong trust and where the parties do not know each other well and are not emotionally close to each other. Furthermore, I differentiate between social and arm's length economic ties in order to distinguish relationships with family and friends from business relationships (Coviello, 2006). I also consider strategic ties as personal relations through which the entrepreneurs access resources such as information, advice, and guidance that impact the strategy of the firm in order to gain or sustain competitive advantage vis-à-vis their competitors outside the network (Jarillo, 1988; Upson, Damaraju, Anderson, & Barney, 2017).

Gaining Professional Competencies and International Work Experience

Camilo and Luis met each other in 1998 during the first semesters of their undergraduate studies in systems engineering at Universidad EAFIT in Medellin, Colombia. While Camilo continued with the same studies, Luis left the country after five semesters and completed in 2005 a bachelor of

13 The Network Dynamics During Internationalization of a Family... 403

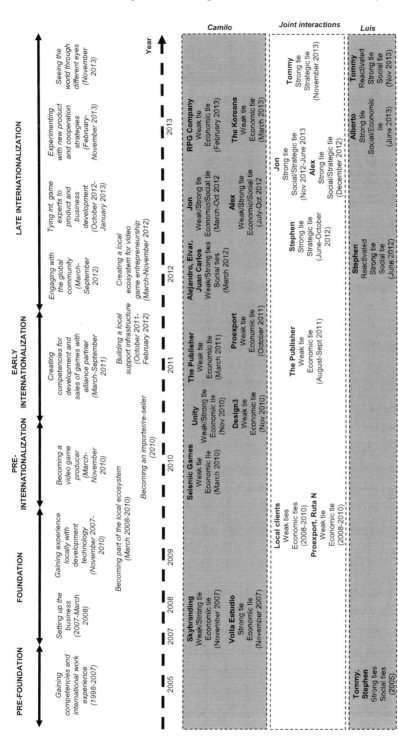

Fig. 13.1 Networking activities along different development periods. (Source: Author)

science degree in real-time interactive simulation in the U.S. Following the completion of his undergraduate studies, Luis extended his stay in the U.S. until 2006 working as a programmer for the video game company Midway Games. Camilo spent two years working as a support engineer in the telecommunication industry in Taiwan. During his bachelor studies in the U.S., Luis developed friendships with his classmates Tommy and Stephen.[1]

Both contacts, Tommy and Stephen, developed into strong, social ties that Luis reactivated after C2 was founded and began operating.

Setting up the Business

While Camilo was still working in Taiwan, Luis returned to Colombia in 2006 with an idea to start up a video game enterprise. Camilo returned in October 2006 to Colombia and Luis told him about his business idea. Together they evaluated the idea and realized the cost and time difficulty for such a small firm of developing a video game for consoles. Without abandoning the idea of video game development, Camilo and Luis decided to explore in parallel alternative products which they found in the production of simulations and visualizations. The exploration of an alternative product did not only mitigate the risk of working on one larger project only (i.e. the video game for console), it also provided an opportunity to familiarize and gain necessary technical expertise with the development software for video games, Unity.

In order to start the activities, Luis took over the role as product developer and Camilo as business developer. The role assignment was based on the entrepreneurs' previous work experience of Luis in video game development and Camilo in customer development. In order to focus on product development, Luis and Camilo decided to outsource the production of artwork to Sky Branding, a local animation studio which Camilo got to know earlier through a friend's recommendation. Similarly, they started to ally with Volta Estudio a local sound producer and friend of Camilo. C2 eventually was registered in March 2008 at the local chamber of commerce.

During the setup period of C2, Camilo actively made use of his relationships with friends in order to establish economic ties to other small, local firms in order to outsource the development of some of the product components.

---

[1] The original names are maintained anonymous.

Gaining Experience Locally with Development Technology

The years 2008–2010 were marked by the production of simulations and visualizations to a variety of renowned clients in the local market in industries such as research, consulting, education, hospitality, utility, retail, food processing, energy, and media. These projects generated vital cash flow in the short term. The projects were attracted through the personal and family networks of both entrepreneurs and their partner firms Sky Branding and Volta Estudio.

During this period, Luis and Camilo established numerous weak ties to clients facilitated by their strong ties (families and friends) for business purpose (economic ties).

Becoming Part of the Local Ecosystem

Felipe, the director of Sky Branding, invited Camilo and Luis to a meeting with the different actors involved in the creative industry in Medellin at the local science park with the aim to evaluate the possibilities of creating a local industry association. The meeting was also attended by representatives of national and local business support organizations. This first meeting and the subsequent gatherings triggered interactions of C2 with business support organizations such as Proexport and Ruta N. Both organizations later became important supporters of C2's international market development.

Felipe from Sky Branding constituted a strong tie for both entrepreneurs and facilitated the creation of weak, economic ties to Proexport and Ruta N for the purpose of securing support for C2.

Becoming an Importer/Re-seller of Technology and Know-How

In 2010 Camilo had the opportunity to sell several Unity licences to a former client, the Colombian agency for vocational training (SENA). After the deal was done, Camilo approached the firm Unity at the industry event Unite in Canada and secured for C2 the sales representation of the software maker for Colombia. At the same event, Camilo negotiated the sales representation for Colombia for Design3 that offers online tutorials for video game development.

Camilo proactively established (weak, economic) ties with both companies in order to access technology at a discounted price and to improve the reputation of C2 nationally and internationally.

Becoming a Video Game Producer

In March 2010 Camilo participated in the Game Developers Conference (GDC) in the U.S. where he got to know C2's first potential international client for a video game. C2 participated in the game bidding procedure which was intermediated by Seismic Games, a U.S.-based video game content creator and consultancy firm for video game producers. Although the bidding was not successful, Seismic Games invited C2 to further bidding procedures with clients based in the U.S. and Australia. None of these business offers were successful, but C2 acquired important knowledge about how to structure and estimate a video game development project based on the design of a potential international client.

At this stage, Camilo deliberately added a new weak, economic tie to C2's network of contacts.

After the participation in several bidding procedures for video games internationally, the successful cooperation with Sky Branding and Volta Estudio for projects in the Colombian market, Camilo and Luis decided that it was time to start developing their first video game. Camilo's visit to Unite in November 2010, however, resulted in a strategic change regarding the development of their first game. The major insight that Camilo took home from the event was the fact that the global video gaming industry shifted towards mobile games. Based on this insight, the decision was taken to split the development of one larger game for PC into four smaller games tailored for the iOS operating system (iPhone, iPad) and for distribution through the App Store. The development of the first game for the mobile gaming market with the title Cowboy Guns began.

It was also during November 2010 that Luis began to work on the vision he had for C2 called C2 Ideal which included a description of the internal operations, the roles of the team members, and the role of innovation within the startup.

Creating Competencies for the Development and Sales of Globally Competitive Mobile Video Games in Cooperation with Alliance Partner

The highly competitive market situation in digital distribution platforms such as the App Store required the cooperation with a specialized publisher for mobile video games. Once the development of Cowboy Guns reached a more mature state in March 2011, Camilo contacted a renowned U.K.-based mobile video game publisher for independent video game development studios (the Publisher[2]).

It was at this stage that Camilo deliberately contacted the Publisher, one of the top publisher's for mobile video games globally that meant adding a new weak, economic tie to C2's network. The subsequent cooperation with the Publisher led to the signing of a new contract with the same publisher during August 2011 for the development and publication of the new game Nitro Chimp. Both Luis and Camilo interacted with the producer of the Publisher and were able to strengthen the relationship with the publisher during Unity's developer's conference Unite in San Francisco (U.S.) in September 2011 in order to promote the game Cowboy Guns.

The experienced lived throughout this period in cooperation with the Publisher and the launch of Cowboy Guns provided an important trigger for Camilo to rethink the firm's strategic plan.

> *And with all the things we learned throughout the development of the game [Cowboy Guns] there is the need for a revision. There we have it [the strategic plan] and it is good to also think about the future.* (Camilo, follow-up interview)

At this time, Camilo did not agree anymore with what was written down by Luis a year ago envisioning the operation and development of the firm in the document C2 Ideal. It was time for a revision based on the experience with the development and the launch of C2 Game Studio's first mobile video game. The free-to-play, freemium business model[3] also became mainstream during this period in 2011 which marked an important trend for mobile video games that especially Camilo felt to be of importance for the future development of the firm.

Building a Local Support Infrastructure

During September 2011, C2 reached the highest sales in history among Colombian firms within the App Store during the launch period of Cowboy Guns. This contributed to C2 becoming the most recognized mobile video game company in Colombia which also caught attention of the

---

[2] The name of the publisher is maintained anonymous.

[3] Free-to-play refers to video games which give players access to a large part of their content without paying. The most common free-to-play game is based on the freemium software model. For freemium games, users are granted access to a fully functional game, but must pay microtransactions to access additional content. Free-to-play can be contrasted with pay-to-play, in which payment is required before using a service for the first time (Wikipedia, 2020a).

government-sponsored business development organizations Proexport and Ruta N. Subsequently, Proexport and Ruta N provided financial support for participation in an export mission to the industry event Game Connection in the U.S. and consultancy services by an expert from Los Angeles, U.S., regarding the design and mechanics for the current game under development, Nitro Chimp, respectively.

The connections to Proexport and the game expert from Los Angeles constituted new weak, economic ties that C2 was able to exploit for international business development (i.e. participation in Game Connection, U.S.) and product development.

Creating a Local Ecosystem for Video Game Entrepreneurship

At Game Connection in San Francisco in the U.S., Camilo strengthened his relationships with the CEOs of other Colombian video game companies (Alejandro from Brainz, Eivar from Efecto Studios, and Juan Carlos from Gara Entertainment). All companies including C2 were invited on behalf of Proexport to participate in an export mission with the aim to showcase and sell Colombian video games in the global market. The interactions with the Colombian video game companies contributed strong, social ties to C2's network.

Camilo returned from San Francisco with the desire of putting together an IGDA[4] Meet & Greet event in order to provide a platform for networking for firms and institutions involved in the video game industry in Medellin.

The event took place in April 2012 with over 80 participants and was repeated in September. For the organization of the second Meet & Greet, Camilo teamed up with Juan Carlos from Gara Entertainment who also participated in the export mission to Game Connection earlier. Due to its success, Camilo and Juan Carlos decided to organize it every second month. For the event they also gained the support of Ruta N. Camilo's increasing involvement in IGDA activities let to his appointment to the board of directors of IGDA Colombia in October. While Meet & Greet provided a unique opportunity for networking among the industry's firms and institutions, it lacked content. Therefore, Camilo took the initiative in October to coordinate a digital content forum together with local universities, Gara Entertainment, and Ruta N. He also led the organization of a workshop for

---

[4] International Game Developers Association (IGDA) (https://igda.org/).

13 The Network Dynamics During Internationalization of a Family...

November 2010 about video game entrepreneurship by IGDA with the support of Ruta N and the participation of Alejandro from Brainz. This workshop was especially helpful to reconfirm the strong relationship Camilo developed with Ruta N and Proexport.

During this period Camilo developed numerous strong, social ties with business support organizations and competitors in C2's home market in Colombia with the intention to create a local ecosystem for video game entrepreneurship in the country.

Engaging with the Global Community of Mobile Video Game Development

Camilo arrived at Game Connection in the U.S. in March 2012 with 27 meetings scheduled in his calendar. Proexport who sponsored the export mission facilitated the location for the buyer-seller meetings. Camilo's priority was the top, well-known publishers in the industry.

Jon, an experienced industry insider and consultant for mobile and game studios, was present during one of Camilo's meetings with a potential client. Although there was no direct contact between Camilo and Jon during this particular meeting (Jon acted as a consultant to the firm that Camilo met with), the event became important for a re-encounter with Jon in October 2012 during Colombia 3.0.

The participation in Game Connection not only provided a platform for networking with potential clients and industry experts, it also provided an opportunity for Camilo to verify the content of C2 Game Studio's strategic plan.

The increasing experience of C2 with the development of mobile video games and the engagement of the firm in the global market for mobile video games led Luis and Camilo to propose to the managing board of C2 to hire an external adviser and additional non-family, board member for the firm. The managing board of C2 included until this moment Camilo as the non-family member and Luis, his father, and his brother as the family members. The role of the adviser included providing support for strategic decision-making in business development, providing access to relevant network contacts, and giving advice regarding a faster and more efficient production process.

Consequently, Luis contacted his former classmate from the university in the U.S., Stephen, who worked as an executive producer for a major

U.S.-based game franchise in order to propose him the participation as shareholder in C2 and a seat on the board of directors.

> *[Stephen] studied with me in the university [in the U.S.] and in that moment he worked in the studio that developed Call of Duty[5] [video game]. So, he had experience with large projects, with ambitious projects, big projects.* (Luis, retrospective interview)

> *[Luis] respects him [Stephen] very much because both studied together.* (Camilo, retrospective interview)

Reactivating this strong tie on behalf of Luis and offering Stephen a seat on the board of directors also meant to turn this previous social tie into a strategic tie.

C2 received financial support from Proexport to participate in an export mission in July 2012 to Casual Connect in San Francisco. Camilo took advantage to engage in conversations with as many people as possible in order to get feedback on the current games Cowboy Guns and Nitro Chimp and on drafts of future games. At Casual Connect, Camilo had the chance to participate in a lunch with Eivar from Efecto Estudios together with game consultant Alex:

> *There is a person who we would like to have very much as a mentor but he is consultant and charges money. [...] He's an eminence! He has designed extremely important games, and he met with the people from Efecto and they invited me. He gave us about half an hour. He talked to us and told us about games and explained us and everything but he charges money per hour, like hundreds of dollars. So, no we don't have the money to hire him as a consultant. But Eivar from Efecto talked to him and to Proexport and they will invite him for a speech to Colombia 3.0 in October.* (Camilo, follow-up interview)

Camilo simply observed the conversation between Efecto Estudios and Alex and kept Alex's business card. The contact with Alex added another weak tie to C2's network of business contacts with the intention to develop it into a strong and strategic tie for the role of a mentor.

The period was marked by establishing important weak ties on behalf of Camilo with the desire to identify advisers and mentors for C2. Luis on his behalf reactivated a dormant, social tie in order to offer him participation in C2's board of directors. All networking activities during this period aimed at

---

[5] Call of Duty is a successful first-person and third-person shooter video game franchise (Wikipedia, 2020b).

Tying International Game Experts to Product and Business Development

Jon and Alex were invited to Colombia 3.0 as guest speakers by Proexport. Jon still remembered Camilo from Game Connection which made it easier to establish the initial contact. As Luis' former classmate Stephen could not take on the role as external adviser for C2, Camilo had the idea to offer this role to Jon:

> *I will try to improve the relationship with Jon because I am interested in that he takes on the role of [Stephen] [...]. We talked about this briefly in Bogota [during Colombia 3.0] but it is a matter of time to get to know each other to see if it is viable.* (Camilo, log)

Camilo also took advantage of Alex's presence and met several times with him during the conference in order to receive feedback on Cowboy Guns and Nitro Chimp, and game design in general. The intense conversations with Alex at Colombia 3.0 helped to establish a closer relationship with him.

The feedback and advice from Jon and Alex motivated Camilo to suggest to the managing board of C2 Game Studio a change of strategy to its business development in order to focus on a particular community of gamers and game design strategy.

Several meetings took place via Skype during November and December between Jon, Camilo, and Luis with the aim to establish a closer relationship and to define Jon's role as an external adviser. Having Jon on board would allow the firm to establish a direct link to the global gaming industry and pull C2 Game Studio out of its isolation from the happenings of the international market.

The continuing conversation with Jon and the feedback and the advice he offered became an important input to rethink C2's development plans for 2013:

> *[U]ntil now what he [Jon] did was scheduling meetings more or less every 20 days where he gives us advice, where we tell him what happened, what we think, let's say. We had a very good meeting where we told him about the plans we have for this year. He gave us feedback and thanks to that we probably think in another way of how to*

approach this year and what we are doing this year is, is thanks to the feedback he gave us. (Camilo, follow-up interview)

Ruta N invited Alex for a workshop about game design in December. Camilo took advantage of his visit and arranged several meetings with Luis and Alex in C2's office. Camilo benefited from his close relationship with Ruta N who paid for Alex's visit and individual firm consultancy services. Receiving Alex's input on game design and feedback on C2's current design strategy was particularly important to Camilo:

Alex we consider him like a mentor for game design. [...] Let's say he analysed how we really work. [...] He questioned many things, he made us think a lot [...] I think his visit really was very, very, very, very constructive for us [...]. I think Alex what he is doing is destroying what you have, destroying the game, and subsequently build on it. He really destroyed us which was very good. (Camilo, follow-up interview)

In January 2013 the design work for the new game began based on the feedback and advice provided by Alex.

This period also saw the launch of Nitro Chimp in December. Compared to the cooperation with the Publisher for Cowboy Guns, the cooperation for Nitro Chimp did not fulfil C2's expectations. It was rather considered disturbing and preventing from other learning opportunities.

In general, we weren't satisfied with anything with [the publisher's] process for the second game. For the first one, yes! For the second one, no! We already were saying, we took the decision with [that publisher] never again. [...] From now on working together with a publisher like that, like we did it, I sincerely think is losing the opportunity to learn more [...]. (Camilo, follow-up interview)

The rather unsuccessful cooperation with the Publisher for Nitro Chimp was largely substituted through the interaction with leading video game experts and consultants. Therefore, the cooperation with the Publisher was finally brought to an end.

The period was marked by tying globally recognized experts to product and business development. Camilo, therefore, pushed for the development of the previously weak ties with Jon and Alex into strong ties, then jointly with his partner Luis.

13 The Network Dynamics During Internationalization of a Family... 413

Experimenting with New Product and Cooperation Strategies

After the production of Nitro Chimp—an endless-runner game for mobile devices digitally distributed through the App Store—Luis started to work on a new type of game, a role-playing video game (RPG). In contrast to Nitro Chimp, the new game was to be distributed through the online platform Steam and the PlayStation Network. Hence, C2 joined Sony's incubation programme with the intention to accelerate the development on the PlayStation platform.

In contrast to the cooperation with the previous publisher which solely focused on the publication process, the new game was already being co-produced with a strategic partner in order to lower the risk associated with game development. Thus, Camilo contacted in February 2013 a renowned game development and publishing company for role-playing games (RPG company[6]) headquartered in the U.S. in order to offer the co-production for the new game. Before Camilo departed for Game Connection in San Francisco, the contract with RPG company was signed. The trip that took place in March 2013 was partly funded by Proexport.

At Game Connection, Camilo established contact with the publishing director for North America of an important mobile game publisher headquartered in South Korea (the Koreans[7]). He was interested in the concept of a sequel of Nitro Chimp, Nitro Chimp 2. The week after Camilo returned from Game Connection, the publishing director for North America presented Camilo to the vice-president for North America of the Koreans in order to close the contract.

Once the contract was signed in May 2013, the intention was to hire additional staff in order to work simultaneously on the two new games. C2 could either follow the usual strategy and hire inexperienced interns or make use of the money to hire an experienced new team member for the Nitro Chimp 2 project. The latter option was adopted and Alberto, a friend of Luis, was hired. Alberto was an experienced IT project manager. His task focused on the optimization of the game development process from a programmer's perspective, especially to make the process faster, more efficient, and agile.

In October 2013 the publishing director of the Koreans told Camilo about his resignation from the company. So did, a few weeks later, the vice-president

---

[6] The name of the company is maintained anonymous.

[7] The name of the company is maintained anonymous.

for North America of the Koreans. Subsequently, the development cooperation for Nitro Chimp 2 was ended on behalf of the Koreans.

During this period, Camilo deliberately looked out for new cooperation partners. This meant the addition of new weak, economic ties to C2's network. However, it also implied the sudden ending of the relationship with the Koreans. A strategic tie could finally be created, Jon signed the contract with C2 and joined the firm as a board member with a 2% participation as a shareholder.

Seeing the World Through Different Eyes

Tommy, the former classmate of Luis from the university in the U.S., visited C2 in November 2013. Tommy had ample work experience in different executive positions in leading video game development and publishing firms on a global level. His industry experience, especially as a producer, motivated Luis to contact him. Tommy visited C2 for three days and offered sessions regarding firm strategy which covered areas such as game design and development, monetization and microtransactions, business models, cooperation strategies, and human resource management.

The communication style with Tommy triggered to rethink the relationship C2 Game Studio developed earlier with other industry experts such as Jon and Alex:

> *Many of the experts that visited us, including Alex who helped us a lot, since they are [professional] consultants who charge a lot of money, they really don't tell you everything, they are ambiguous. [Tommy] really is more the type of, "What do you need?" As if he were a member of our team, he sits down and works with you. So I think that this, this was very, very, very important for us.* (Luis, retrospective interview)

The open and honest communication style with Tommy was attributed to the long-standing friendship between Luis and Tommy dating back to their undergraduate studies in the U.S.:

> *This helped a lot having a friendship, having a previous friendship [before Tommy's visit], because he, he, he, his attitude is, "I want to help my friends. I want my friends to prosper."* (Luis, retrospective interview)

Tommy's visit was important in that Luis changed his attitude towards the free-to-play business model which marked a trend in the global video game industry:

[I] understand or let's say accept that this is the direction where the industry moves. The company [C2 Game Studio] needs to move into that direction, but being faithful and following the firm's objectives. (Luis, retrospective interview)

Although C2 Game Studio was already applying the free-to-play business model to its games, the visit of Tommy was an important event that helped the firm to define its identity within the global game market. During the three-day sessions with Tommy, Luis and Camilo were re-thinking the firm's strategic direction and identified a strategy of how to position the company in the global game industry:

[During Tommy's visit] we gained something that we were searching for a long time which was a, a, a plan, something more specific and, and a direction. [...]. (Luis, retrospective interview)

The period was marked by one major event, the visit of Tommy. Luis was able to reactivate this dormant, social tie and turned it into a strategic tie. The peer-to-peer communication with Tommy was an eye-opener regarding C2's past and current activities. The three-day session provided a unique opportunity to reflect on the firm's current focus and to identify its future course in order to create its identity in the global game market.

This section had the purpose to provide a vivid account of the development of the C2 case from the perspective of the networking activities of the two focal entrepreneurs—Luis as the family member and Camilo as the non-family member of the entrepreneurial team.

In the following section I synthesize the findings of the case for its subsequent discussion with extant literature on family firm internationalization.

Synthesis of Findings

As the case narrative above illustrates, during the foundation period, Luis and Camilo made use of their families' and friends' existing contacts in order to identify business partners, get access to clients, and establish contacts with local business support organizations. It was a mix of weak and strong ties, always with the purpose of engaging in business (economic ties), that characterized the network formation of C2 during this phase.

During the periods of pre-internationalization and early internationalization, Camilo deliberately developed weak ties for the sole purpose of developing the competencies for video game production and sales, and for securing economic support for international business development (economic ties).

After the first international market entry, during the late internationalization period, Camilo continued adding deliberately more weak, economic ties to C2's network. However, many of those weak ties were purposefully turned into strong, social ties with the intention of converting them into strategic ties for strengthening the global business development of C2. During this stage, Luis reactivated strong, social ties from the past with the purpose of developing them into strategic ties.

Generally, over the observed period from pre-foundation, over first market entry, to late internationalization, Camilo's networking behaviour seemed to be proactive, sometimes even aggressive by constantly expanding C2's network through new, weak ties and always driven by the desire for profit-making. Luis, on the other hand, did not actively develop new ties. Only during the period of late internationalization when strategic ties were developed, Luis reactivated his strong, social ties from the past.

Camilo's constant interaction with especially new, weak ties provided him feedback on C2's games in development and insights into industry trends. This information triggered to periodically rethink C2's strategic development and led to disagreements with his partner Luis about the firm's future development. While Camilo showed interest and openness towards adopting industry trends in product and business development, Luis was rather sceptical, preserving the status quo, focusing on core gamers instead of the emerging market of casual gamers.

At the beginning of the late internationalization period, both entrepreneurs observed the need to hire an external board member—an expert in the global video game industry—able to contribute to the business and game development of C2. Therefore, most networking efforts went into the development of strategic ties. The decision of which tie to be developed into a strategic tie did not solely depend on Camilo and Luis. C2's board of directors was equally involved in the decision-making process. Luis found support for his decisions in his father and brother. Consequently, the family controlled the decision-making through their majority stake in the firm.

Whereas Camilo identified strategic ties based on the development of new, weak ties, Luis contributed strategic ties based on already existing strong, social ties. Luis rather showed an adverse attitude towards adding strategic ties that did not originate from long-lasting strong and social ties such as the relationship with Jon, contrary to the relationship with Tommy which was a reactivated strong, social relationship from the past.

13 The Network Dynamics During Internationalization of a Family... 417

Table 13.2 Networking characteristics of both entrepreneurs

	Camilo (non-family member)	Luis (family member)
Networking behaviour	Proactive	Reactive
	Deliberately adding weak, economic ties	Reactivation of strong, social ties
Tie development	Engages in tie development: Turning weak into strong ties and economic in social ties	Does not engage in development of strong or social ties
	Both engage in strategic tie development	
Networking motivation	Profit-oriented: Selling games globally	Product-oriented: Developing high-quality games for the global market of core gamers
Networking result	Rapidly adopting market trends	Conserving status quo

Source: Author

Table 13.2 compares the networking characteristics of both entrepreneurs based on their attitude and behaviour of engaging with contacts over the observed periods. Whereas Camilo seemed to be more proactive, engaged in the development of new strong, social ties, and willing to adopt market trends, Luis was rather reactive towards adding new ties, uninterested in developing new strong, social ties, and rather inclined towards preserving the status quo.

During foundation, early internationalization, and the beginning of the late internationalization period, Camilo actively engaged with local and national business support organizations in order to access, on one hand, financial support for visiting industry events in Canada and the U.S. (i.e. Unite-Montreal, GDC-San Francisco, Game Connection-San Francisco), to gain access to industry experts (i.e. consultants such as Jon, Alex), and, on the other hand, to jointly create and shape with these support organizations and the leading game development studios in Colombia a local ecosystem for video game entrepreneurship.

Not being located at the centre of the global game development industry was perceived as a disadvantage by Camilo.

Therefore, the disadvantage of being located in Colombia and not San Francisco was tried to be overcome, on one hand, by regularly participating in industry events abroad with the financial support of local business support organizations and, on the other hand, by engaging locally with global industry experts such as Jon and Alex, again, with the support of local business support organizations that arranged and financed the visit of these experts to Colombia. Being embedded in a flourishing local video game ecosystem is considered important in order to be competitive globally.

418   S. Fuerst

The lack of a striving, local video game ecosystem in Colombia, and the fact that C2 is located at the periphery (and not the centre) of global video game development, was a characteristic that influenced the networking activities of C2 in order to overcome the locational disadvantage.

In the following section, I discuss the findings of the C2 case with extant literature on family firm internationalization with the intention to map out the insights we are able to gain from the case in form of its contributions to theory and practice.

Discussion

C2 is a family-controlled firm right from inception (Arregle et al., 2012). The firm was co-founded by the two entrepreneurs Camilo and Luis. Camilo as the non-family member holds 10% of the shares and Luis, the family member, together with his brother and father, the remaining 90%. The combination of non-family member and family member as co-founders is an interesting constellation for researching family firm internationalization from the perspective of network development due to the differing roles ascribed by the literature to, on one hand, the manager within the internationalizing family firm (Kraus et al., 2016; Mensching et al., 2016; Pongelli et al., 2016; Yeoh, 2014) and, on the other hand, family firm internationalization in general (Arregle et al., 2012; Claver et al., 2009; D'Angelo et al., 2016; Kraus et al., 2016; Mitter et al., 2014).

The Networking Profile of the Family Member and the Non-family Member

As the case illustrates, the entrepreneurs have opposing networking behaviours that mirror the characteristics found in literature regarding the role of family versus external managers in the internationalization of family firms (see Table 13.2). Family managers have been found to be averse towards internationalization due to their higher perceived psychic distance of international markets (Mensching et al., 2016), lack of international experience (Yeoh, 2014), emotional attachment to their company (Gomez-Mejia, Cruz, Berrone, & De Castro, 2011), and risk aversion in order to maintain control of the firm (Banalieva & Eddleston, 2011). Luis' networking behaviour reflects this rather cautious attitude towards internationalization. Contrary to Camilo, he does not proactively engage in networking and does not develop new ties. He contributes ties he trusts from long-standing relationships from his bachelor studies in the U.S. These strong, dormant ties were awakened or reactivated (Jack, 2005) once C2 entered its post-entry period of internationalization ("late internationalization"), and the development of strategic ties became important.

While Camilo contributed strategic ties (i.e. Jon and Alex) based on the previous development of new, weak ties, Luis did not seem to trust strategic ties that did not originate from long-lasting strong and social ties. Nevertheless, Luis engaged jointly with Camilo in the development of strategic ties, independent of the origin of the tie. The joint development of strategic ties enabled Luis to keep control of the business model, which directly affected the genre or type of games to be developed, the publishing strategy and the revenue model, and, hence, the further internationalization of C2. The preference for engagement in strategic tie development is an interesting aspect that differentiates the networking behaviour of Luis. It, therefore, shows how a family firm liability (i.e. emotional attachment and control attitude) directly shapes the networking behaviour of the managing family member. Therefore, this finding provides a nuanced perspective of networking within the family firm beyond our general understanding that family firms are rather averse to networking.

Camilo's networking behaviour also reflects our general understanding of non-family members more proactively engaging in network development. Moreover, the findings illustrate the deliberate development on behalf of Camilo of completely new ties to strong ties in a short period of time, often turning them into strategic ties if deemed appropriate. This proactive tie development is driven by the purpose of building rapidly an appropriate business model able to generate revenue and profit in the highly competitive, global mobile video game industry. The process of active tie development, therefore, resembles a teleological approach of networking driven by the implementation of an envisioned goal (Slotte-Kock & Coviello, 2010).

The opposing networking behaviour of Camilo and Luis complements each other. While Camilo adds primarily new, weak ties to the firm's network of contacts, Luis contributes his strong, social ties. This mix of weak and strong ties is of particular benefit for C2. While new, weak ties facilitate access to new information (e.g. industry trends) and facilitate new international business opportunities (Kontinen & Ojala, 2011) such as the contact to the Publisher or the Koreans, strong, social ties are useful for joint problem-solving in the form of mentoring as in the case of the relationship with Tommy. Focusing only on a few strong, trustworthy ties with foreign partners, family firms miss out on potential other international opportunities, as

420 S. Fuerst

Kontinen and Ojala (2012) confirm. The complementary networking behaviour confirms research on network benefits, particularly Uzzi (1996) who put forward the idea that the ideal entrepreneurial network includes a particular mix of strong and weak ties. Uzzi (1996) states that "[o]n one hand, networks constituted of embedded ties benefit from trust, joint problem solving, and thick information exchange, which enhance coordination and resource sharing. On the other hand, networks composed of arm's-length ties have wide access to information circulating in the market [...]." Hence, the networking behaviour of both entrepreneurs is able to complement each other in order to deliver a beneficial mix of strong and weak ties over the development period of the new venture.

In broad terms, both entrepreneurs resemble the networking behaviour we assume to expect based on the findings of extant literature that analyses the role of non-family versus family members in internationalizing firms. Yet, the case provides an understanding at the micro-level of how networking is accomplished differently by both types of team members. This responds to a recent call by De Massis and Foss (2018) of advancing family business research from the perspective of its microfoundations. In addition, the case findings add the temporal perspective that extant research is not able to deliver as most studies that look at the non-family versus family member roles are exclusively cross-sectional and lack the longitudinal understanding of network development at the micro-level (Hiebl & Li, 2018; Kampouri et al., 2017). From a practical standpoint, the findings reveal the importance for the entrepreneur as a family member to cooperate with a non-family co-founder in order to create the necessary networking capabilities for the internationalizing new venture.

Shaping the Evolution of the Firm's International Network

From a dynamic, network development perspective, C2 during foundation and pre-internationalization added exclusively new, weak ties to its network for business. Only later, after its first international market entry ("late internationalization"), the entrepreneurs engaged in the development of strong ties originating from either economic or long-standing social ties with the purpose of developing them into strategic ties. These strategic ties were added in the role of advisers, board members, or mentors.

The networking behaviour of C2 resembles the networking strategies of so-called Broad Network Enablers as a particular type of family firm (Leppäaho & Metsola, 2020). Broad Network Enablers are characterized by expanding their network on a global scale, managing a portfolio of strong and weak ties.

The development of weak ties is considered important for new opportunities to emerge. The same as C2 ended its relationship with the Publisher as it did not fulfil its expectations of international growth, Broad Network Enablers commit to "open relationship" that are characterized as close and committed but can be discontinued at any time if the results do not align with the internationalization objectives.

The network development of C2 contradicts the findings of Hite and Hesterly (2001) who found that firms start out during emergence with identity-based networks (i.e. strong, socially embedded ties drawn from a dense, cohesive set of connections) and develop calculative networks (i.e. weak ties for economic benefit obtained from a sparse set of connections that span structural holes) during growth. The network development of C2 rather resembles what Johanson and Vahlne (2009) coined overcoming the liability of outsidership in the context of internationalizing firms.

Establishing and positioning C2 within the global video game industry required the entrepreneurs to continuously develop the necessary relationships as outsiders in order to become insiders within the industry, not only related to the knowledge of developing and selling games but also in relation to their network position vis-à-vis the different stakeholders in the industry. Hite and Hesterly (2001) argue that emerging firms reconfigure their network according to the different resource needs and resource challenges. This is also true for C2. The difference, however, stems from the fact that neither entrepreneur nor any of the board members could be considered an industry insider upon startup, despite Luis' studies and brief work experience in the U.S. Luis and Camilo needed to acquire the necessary knowledge and skills for video game development and sales and to build relationships from scratch. This also differentiates the case from extant research on the participation of external managers in family firms either as board members or part of the management team. This stream of research assumes prior industry and international experience on behalf of the external manager in order to contribute the needed managerial capabilities and the network required for internationalizing the family firm (Tabor et al., 2018). Therefore, the findings provide insights into how the development of a family firm's network is shaped from scratch on behalf of their founders with the purpose of rapidly creating the necessary relationships and knowledge that enable the firm to position itself in a global industry. From a practical perspective, the findings reveal that entrepreneurs do not necessarily need to be insiders upon startup in their respective industry. Consequently, there is the need to overcome their liability of outsidership by deliberately adding new weak ties and to develop select ties into economic, social, and strategic ties depending on the particular resource needs of the moment.

Dealing with the Mixed Gamble During Internationalization

Family firms are said to be influenced by a mixed gamble between economic and non-economic goals (Gomez-Mejia et al., 2014) influencing their internationalization (Alessandri, Cerrato, & Eddleston, 2018). This mixed gamble becomes evident in C2 through the different networking behaviour of the two entrepreneurs. While Camilo's networking motivation is mainly business-oriented with the purpose of generating revenue and profit for the firm (economic goal), Luis is rather (emotionally) attached to the development of high-quality video games targeted at core gamers (non-economic goal). In that sense, Camilo is rather willing to adapt to new market trends with the purpose of profit-making (rational decision-making), whereas Luis is opposed to these trends driven by his passion for the development of games for core gamers (emotional decision-making).

The pursuit of non-economic goals and the tendency of Luis to retain control of the shape of the business model are considered family firm liabilities, whereas Camilo's pursuit of economic goals and rapid adaptation of market trends are considered family firm capabilities (Metsola et al., 2020). Metsola et al. (2020, p. 8) argue that "[a]fter the initial international entry, the liabilities become less significant, and opportunities can be utilised for seeking resources and capabilities enabling more effective internationalisation." This contrasts the experience of C2 where the liabilities appeared after initial entry during post-entry ("late internationalization"). While the early internationalization period of C2 was marked by creating competencies for the development and sales of mobile video games with the Publisher as alliance partner, the succeeding post-entry periods focused mainly on the engagement with the global community of mobile video game development followed by committing international game experts to product and business development. The necessity for strategic tie development occurred at this stage which triggered the liabilities to emerge in order to influence the strategic development of C2 on behalf of Luis. Interesting to observe is how the meeting with Luis's long-time friend Tommy seemed to compromise the emerging mixed gamble and to alleviate the tension between Camilo and Luis regarding the strategic development of C2.

This finding has two important implications for our understanding of the mixed gamble in internationalizing family firms. First, family firm liabilities are not necessarily confined to a particular period of firm development (e.g. initial or later stages)—they might be latent and become visible when

13 The Network Dynamics During Internationalization of a Family... 423

triggered by specific circumstances (e.g. situations that threaten the control of the future course of the firm). Second, strong, trusted, social ties are important mediators able to alleviate the tensions caused by the mixed gamble. This implies that entrepreneurs in family firms should be attentive to their liabilities and how they influence their decision-making. Furthermore, the findings underline the importance of the role of a mentor with a close, trusted relationship to the family member and expert in the industry.

Overcoming the Locational Disadvantage

External contextual factors are hardly considered in family firm internationalization with some exceptions by Eddleston, Sarathy, and Banalieva (2019), Miller, Lee, Chang, and Le Breton-Miller (2009), Tsang (2001). An important contextual element is the fact that C2 is located in Colombia, whereas the centre for video game development in the Western world is San Francisco, as expressed by the entrepreneurs. As stated above, the lack of a striving local video game ecosystem in Colombia, and the fact that C2 is located at the periphery (and not the centre) of global video game development, was a characteristic that influenced the networking activities of C2 with the aim to overcome the locational disadvantage. Therefore, the proactive networking behaviour of Camilo made an important contribution to secure the resources necessary to overcome the locational disadvantage.

Research on family firm internationalization often assumes the firm to be embedded in strong, local networks (Graves & Thomas, 2008; Kontinen & Ojala, 2011). Due to this reason, firms start to exploit their existing local networks first before entering nearby countries. However, what happens when the home country does not provide the needed resources for growth? Camilo deliberately engaged in developing a local support infrastructure from foundation through to early internationalization. Thereby, he did not only reach out to government-sponsored business support organizations, he also built ties to technology and educational providers abroad for importing needed software and know-how. This confirms the findings of others that found relationships with government important for the initial stage of family firm internationalization (Kampouri et al., 2017). Besides, the international business literature emphasizes on importing as an integral part of firm internationalization (Grosse & Fonseca, 2012).

The post-entry period is marked by the creation of a local ecosystem for video game entrepreneurship. Again, the beginning of this period provides evidence of heightened networking activities both locally and internationally

("Engaging with the global community of video game development"). On one hand, Camilo is able to create a leading insider position for C2 within the emerging video game industry in Colombia and, on the other hand, to build a bridge between the periphery and the centre of the global video game industry through deliberately developing new strong, strategic ties with leading game experts in the U.S. (i.e. Jon and Alex).

Overall, C2 has been able to overcome its locational disadvantage through proactive networking on behalf of Camilo, the non-family entrepreneur, both inside C2's home country (the periphery) and outside abroad (the centre). Therefore, new weak ties needed to be proactively developed as either economic ties or strategic ties. This finding reveals the importance of purposeful networking on behalf of the non-family entrepreneur both home and abroad for the creation of needed resources for internationalization. From a practical standpoint, the family member entrepreneur should consider teaming up with a non-family co-founder who possesses the necessary motivation and skills to create economic and strategic relationships from scratch, both within the home market and internationally.

The research was concerned with the question of how a family-controlled new venture both co-founded by a family member and a non-family member is able to internationalize successfully from its home market in Colombia. This endeavour poses challenges from three perspectives for the family new venture. First, family-controlled firms face more obstacles for internationalization than family-influenced firms (Arregle et al., 2012). Second, the engagement of family members within the management of the firm constitutes a liability that hinders internationalization (Pukall & Calabrò, 2014). Third, engaging as a family firm in a global industry from the periphery and not its centre brings additional obstacles along for successful internationalization.

Conclusions

The C2 case showed the central role of networking for internationalization. The networking liability of the family member entrepreneur needs to be complemented by the networking capability of the non-family co-founder in order to create the necessary resources for internationalization. The joint development of strategic ties to external board members and mentors is an important networking activity able to alleviate the tensions stemming from the mixed gamble of non-economic and economic goals within the venture. The locational disadvantage of being located at the periphery and not the centre of global video game development has been ameliorated by building a local support infrastructure and through the development of strong strategic ties to external board member and mentors abroad.

As with all research, this study has its limitations. These limitations relate to the boundary conditions of the findings. As I collected the data in a particular type of firm, managed by a particular team of entrepreneurs and board of directors, operating in a particular industry context, the question is how the findings are generalizable to a broader spectrum of firms and industry contexts. Unlike variance explanations, process explanations do not focus on uniformity and consistency but on versatility (Poole et al., 2000). The generality of a process explanation lies in its ability to encompass a broad domain of developmental patterns for a variety of cases and contexts. The versatility stems from the complexity of narratives and their underlying event sequences. Narratives might differ in event sequences and contextual factors but nevertheless may share the same plot or through-line of a story. Thus, narrative explanations of process theory need to encompass the particularities of individual cases that share a common developmental process. Langley et al. (2013) observe an inference from the particular to the general for process generalization. Climbing the ladder of abstraction through analytical generalization by inferring the general theoretical phenomenon of which the observed particular is a part. Regarding analytical generalization, the question then arises of what the findings are a case of? Or what is the general case of where the findings are part of? I suggest the general case to comprise the following situation and context: Family-controlled new ventures managed by a family and a non-family entrepreneur that are entering global markets with knowledge-intensive offerings located at the periphery of such markets.

For future research it would be interesting to observe more directly the decision-making process of the board of directors and its impact on the activities of the firm. For instance, in the case of C2, it would have been helpful to act as a participant observer during the board of director meetings. This would have allowed to depict in more detail the influence of Luis' father and brother on the networking activities of each entrepreneur. During this study, I depended on the accounts of the diaries and the interviews as made by the entrepreneurs in order to derive conclusions about the impact of the decisions made on behalf of the board of directors.

References

Alessandri, T. M., Cerrato, D., & Eddleston, K. A. (2018). The mixed gamble of internationalization in family and nonfamily firms: The moderating role of organizational slack. *Global Strategy Journal, 8*(1), 46–72. https://doi.org/10.1002/gsj.1201

Anderson, R. C., & Reeb, D. M. (2003). Founding-Family Ownership and Firm Performance: Evidence from the S&P 500. *Journal of Finance, 58*(3), 1301–1327. https://doi.org/10.1111/1540-6261.00567

Arregle, J. L., Duran, P., Hitt, M. A., & van Essen, M. (2017). Why is family firms' internationalization unique? A meta-analysis. *Entrepreneurship: Theory and Practice, 41*(5), 801–831. https://doi.org/10.1111/etap.12246

Arregle, J. L., Hitt, M. A., & Mari, I. (2019). A missing link in family firms' internationalization research: Family structures. *Journal of International Business Studies, 50*(5), 809–825. https://doi.org/10.1057/s41267-019-00213-z

Arregle, J. L., Naldi, L., Nordqvist, M., & Hitt, M. A. (2012). Internationalization of family-controlled firms: A study of the effects of external involvement in governance. *Entrepreneurship: Theory and Practice, 36*(6), 1115–1143. https://doi.org/10.1111/j.1540-6520.2012.00541.x

Balogun, J., Huff, A. S., & Johnson, P. (2003). Three responses to the methodological challenges of studying strategizing. *Journal of Management Studies, 40*(1), 197–224. https://doi.org/10.1111/1467-6486.t01-1-00009

Banalieva, E. R., & Eddleston, K. A. (2011). Home-region focus and performance of family firms: The role of family vs non-family leaders. *Journal of International Business Studies, 42*(8), 1060–1072. https://doi.org/10.1057/jibs.2011.28

Carney, M. (2005). Globalization and the renewal of Asian business networks. *Asia Pacific Journal of Management, 22*(4), 337–354. Springer. https://doi.org/10.1007/s10490-005-4114-z

Casillas, J. C., & Moreno-Menéndez, A. M. (2017). International business & family business: Potential dialogue between disciplines. *European Journal of Family Business, 7*(1–2), 25–40. https://doi.org/10.1016/j.ejfb.2017.08.001

Chen, T. J. (2003). Network resources for internationalization: The case of Taiwan's electronics firms. *Journal of Management Studies, 40*(5), 1107–1130. https://doi.org/10.1111/1467-6486.t01-1-00373

Child, J., & Hsieh, L. H. Y. (2014). Decision mode, information and network attachment in the internationalization of SMEs: A configurational and contingency analysis. *Journal of World Business, 49*(4), 598–610. https://doi.org/10.1016/j.jwb.2013.12.012

Chua, J. H., Chrisman, J. J., & Sharma, P. (1999). Defining the Family Business by Behavior. *Entrepreneurship Theory and Practice, 23*(4), 19–39. https://doi.org/10.1177/104225879902300402

Ciravegna, L., Majano, S. B., & Zhan, G. (2014). The inception of internationalization of small and medium enterprises: The role of activeness and networks. *Journal of Business Research, 67*(6), 1081–1089. https://doi.org/10.1016/j.jbusres.2013.06.002

Claver, E., Rienda, L., & Quer, D. (2009). Family firms' international commitment. *Family Business Review, 22*(2), 125–135. https://doi.org/10.1177/0894486508330054

Coviello, N. E. (2006). The network dynamics of international new ventures. *Journal of International Business Studies, 37*(5), 713–731. https://doi.org/10.1057/palgrave.jibs.8400219

D'Angelo, A., Majocchi, A., & Buck, T. (2016). External managers, family ownership and the scope of SME internationalization. *Journal of World Business, 51*(4), 534–547. https://doi.org/10.1016/j.jwb.2016.01.004

De Massis, A., & Foss, N. J. (2018). Advancing family business research: The promise of microfoundations. *Family Business Review, 31*(4), 386–396. https://doi.org/10.1177/0894486518803422

Dyer, W. G., & Wilkins, A. L. (1991). Better stories, not better constructs, to generate better theory: A rejoinder to Eisenhardt. *Academy of Management Review, 16*(3), 613–619. https://doi.org/10.5465/amr.1991.4279492

Eddleston, K. A., Sarathy, R., & Banalieva, E. R. (2019). When a high-quality niche strategy is not enough to spur family-firm internationalization: The role of external and internal contexts. *Journal of International Business Studies, 50*(5), 783–808. https://doi.org/10.1057/s41267-018-0199-8

Edwards, P., Sengupta, S., & Tsai, C. J. (2010). The context-dependent nature of small firms' relations with support agencies: A three-sector study in the UK. *International Small Business Journal, 28*(6), 543–565. https://doi.org/10.1177/0266242610375769

Eisenhardt, K. M., & Graebner, M. E. (2007). Theory building from cases: Opportunities and challenges. *Academy of Management Journal, 50*(1), 25–32. https://doi.org/10.5465/AMJ.2007.24160888

Gomez-Mejia, L. R., Campbell, J. T., Martin, G., Hoskisson, R. E., Makri, M., & Sirmon, D. G. (2014). Socioemotional wealth as a mixed Gamble: Revisiting family firm R&D investments with the behavioral agency model. *Entrepreneurship: Theory and Practice, 38*(6), 1351–1374. https://doi.org/10.1111/etap.12083

Gomez-Mejia, L. R., Cruz, C., Berrone, P., & De Castro, J. (2011). The bind that ties: Socioemotional wealth preservation in family firms. *Academy of Management Annals, 5*(1), 653–707. https://doi.org/10.5465/19416520.2011.593320

Graves, C., & Thomas, J. (2006). Internationalization of Australian family businesses: A managerial capabilities perspective. *Family Business Review, 19*(3), 207–224. https://doi.org/10.1111/j.1741-6248.2006.00066.x

Graves, C., & Thomas, J. (2008). Determinants of the internationalization pathways of family firms: An examination of family influence. *Family Business Review, 21*(2), 151–167. https://doi.org/10.1111/j.1741-6248.2008.00119.x

Grosse, R., & Fonseca, A. (2012). Learning through imports in the internationalization process. *Journal of International Management, 18*(4), 366–378. https://doi.org/10.1016/j.intman.2012.08.003

Hiebl, M. R. W., & Li, Z. (2018). Non-family managers in family firms: Review, integrative framework and future research agenda. *Review of Managerial Science,* 1–45. https://doi.org/10.1007/s11846-018-0308-x

Hite, J. M., & Hesterly, W. S. (2001). The evolution of firm networks: From emergence to early growth of the firm. *Strategic Management Journal, 22*(3), 275–286. https://doi.org/10.1002/smj.156

Jack, S. L. (2005). The role, use and activation of strong and weak network ties: A qualitative analysis. *Journal of Management Studies, 42*(6), 1233–1250. https://doi.org/10.1111/j.1467-6486.2005.00540.x

Jarillo, J. C. (1988). On strategic networks. *Strategic Management Journal, 9*(1), 31–41.

Johanson, J., & Vahlne, J. E. (2009). The Uppsala internationalization process model revisited: From liability of foreignness to liability of outsidership. *Journal of International Business Studies, 40*(9), 1411–1431. https://doi.org/10.1057/jibs.2009.24

Johanson, J., & Vahlne, J.-E. (1977). The internationalization process of the firm – A model of knowledge development and increasing foreign market commitments. *Journal of International Business Studies, 8*(1), 23–32. https://doi.org/10.1057/palgrave.jibs.8490676

Kampouri, K., Plakoyiannaki, E., & Leppäaho, T. (2017). Family business internationalisation and networks: Emerging pathways. *Journal of Business and Industrial Marketing, 32*(3), 357–370. https://doi.org/10.1108/JBIM-04-2015-0066

Kenten, C. (2010). Narrating oneself: Reflections on the use of solicited diaries with diary interviews. *Forum: Qualitative Social Research, 11*(2) https://doi.org/10.17169/fqs-11.2.1314

Kontinen, T., & Ojala, A. (2010). The internationalization of family businesses: A review of extant research. *Journal of Family Business Strategy, 1*(2), 97–107. https://doi.org/10.1016/j.jfbs.2010.04.001

Kontinen, T., & Ojala, A. (2011). Network ties in the international opportunity recognition of family SMEs. *International Business Review, 20*(4), 440–453. https://doi.org/10.1016/j.ibusrev.2010.08.002

Kontinen, T., & Ojala, A. (2012). Internationalization pathways among family-owned SMEs. *International Marketing Review, 29*(5), 496–518. https://doi.org/10.1108/02651331211260359

Kraus, S., Mensching, H., Calabrò, A., Cheng, C. F., & Filser, M. (2016). Family firm internationalization: A configurational approach. *Journal of Business Research, 69*(11), 5473–5478. https://doi.org/10.1016/j.jbusres.2016.04.158

Langley, A. (1999). Strategies for theorizing from process data. *Academy of Management Review, 24*(4), 691–710. https://doi.org/10.5465/AMR.1999.2553248

13 The Network Dynamics During Internationalization of a Family... **429**

Langley, A., Smallman, C., Tsoukas, H., & Van De Ven, A. H. (2013). Process studies of change in organization and management: Unveiling temporality, activity, and flow. *Academy of Management Journal, 56*(1), 1–13. https://doi.org/10.5465/amj.2013.4001

Leppäaho, T., & Metsola, J. (2020). *Family firm internationalisation: A network perspective.* Springer International Publishing. https://doi.org/10.1007/978-3-030-28520-3

Mensching, H., Calabrò, A., Eggers, F., & Kraus, S. (2016). Internationalisation of family and non-family firms: A conjoint experiment among CEOs. *European Journal of International Management, 10*(5), 581–604. https://doi.org/10.1504/EJIM.2016.078795

Metsola, J., Leppäaho, T., Paavilainen-Mäntymäki, E., & Plakoyiannaki, E. (2020). Process in family business internationalisation: The state of the art and ways forward. *International Business Review, 2018*, 101665. https://doi.org/10.1016/j.ibusrev.2020.101665

Miles, M. B., Huberman, A. M., & Saldaña, J. (2014). Qualitative data analysis: a methods sourcebook. SAGE Publications.

Miller, D., Lee, J., Chang, S., & Le Breton-Miller, I. (2009). Filling the institutional void: The social behavior and performance of family vs non-family technology firms in emerging markets. *Journal of International Business Studies, 40*(5), 802–817. https://doi.org/10.1057/jibs.2009.11

Minguzzi, A., & Passaro, R. (2001). The network of relationships between the economic environment and the entrepreneurial culture in small firms. *Journal of Business Venturing, 16*(2), 181–207. https://doi.org/10.1016/S0883-9026(99)00045-2

Mitter, C., Duller, C., Feldbauer-Durstmüller, B., & Kraus, S. (2014). Internationalization of family firms: The effect of ownership and governance. *Review of Managerial Science, 8*(1), 1–28. https://doi.org/10.1007/s11846-012-0093-x

Peng, M. W., & Jiang, Y. (2010). Institutions behind family ownership and control in large firms. *Journal of Management Studies, 47*(2), 253–273. https://doi.org/10.1111/j.1467-6486.2009.00890.x

Pentland, B. T. (1999). Building process theory with narrative: From description to explanation. *Academy of Management Review, 24*(4), 711–724. https://doi.org/10.5465/AMR.1999.2553249

Pettigrew, A. M. (1990). Longitudinal field research on change: Theory and practice. *Organization Science, 1*(3), 267–292. https://doi.org/10.1287/orsc.1.3.267

Poole, M. S., Van de Ven, A. H., Dooley, K., & Holmes, M. E. (2000) Organizational change and innovation processes. Oxford University Press.

Pongelli, C., Caroli, M. G., & Cucculelli, M. (2016). Family business going abroad: The effect of family ownership on foreign market entry mode decisions. *Small Business Economics, 47*(3), 787–801. https://doi.org/10.1007/s11187-016-9763-4

Pukall, T. J., & Calabrò, A. (2014). The internationalization of family firms: A critical review and integrative model. *Family Business Review, 27*(2), 103–125. https://doi.org/10.1177/0894486513491423

Senik, Z. C., Scott-Ladd, B., Entrekin, L., & Adham, K. A. (2011). Networking and internationalization of SMEs in emerging economies. *Journal of International Entrepreneurship, 9*(4), 259–281. https://doi.org/10.1007/s10843-011-0078-x

Siggelkow, N. (2007). Persuasion with case studies. *Academy of Management Journal, 50*(1), 20–24. https://doi.org/10.5465/AMJ.2007.24160882

Slotte-Kock, S., & Coviello, N. (2010). Entrepreneurship research on network processes: A review and ways forward. *Entrepreneurship: Theory and Practice, 34*(1), 31–57. https://doi.org/10.1111/j.1540-6520.2009.00311.x

Tabor, W., Chrisman, J. J., Madison, K., & Vardaman, J. M. (2018). Nonfamily members in family firms: A review and future research agenda. *Family Business Review, 31*(1), 54–79. https://doi.org/10.1177/0894486517734683

Tsang, E. W. K. (2001). Internationalizing the family firm: A case study of a Chinese family business. *Journal of Small Business Management, 39*(1), 88–93. https://doi.org/10.1111/0447-2778.00008

Upson, J. W., Damaraju, N. L., Anderson, J. R., & Barney, J. B. (2017). Strategic networks of discovery and creation entrepreneurs. *European Management Journal, 35*(2), 198–210. https://doi.org/10.1016/j.emj.2017.01.001

Uzzi, B. (1996). The sources and consequences of embeddedness for the economic performance of organizations: The network effect. *American Sociological Review, 61*(4), 674–698. https://doi.org/10.2307/2096399

Vahlne, J. E., & Johanson, J. (2017). From internationalization to evolution: The Uppsala model at 40 years. *Journal of International Business Studies, 48*(9), 1087–1102. https://doi.org/10.1057/s41267-017-0107-7

Wikipedia (2020a, February 2). Free-to-play. https://en.wikipedia.org/wiki/Free-to-play

Wikipedia (2020b, February 2). Call of Duty. https://en.wikipedia.org/wiki/Call_of_Duty

Yeoh, P.-L. (2014). Internationalization and performance outcomes of entrepreneurial family SMEs: The role of outside CEOs, technology sourcing, and innovation. *Thunderbird International Business Review, 56*(1), 77–96. https://doi.org/10.1002/tie.21597

Yin, R. K. (2009). Case study research: design and methods (4th ed.). SAGE Publications.

Zahra, S. A. (2003). International expansion of U.S. manufacturing family businesses: The effect of ownership and involvement. *Journal of Business Venturing, 18*(4), 495–512. https://doi.org/10.1016/S0883-9026(03)00057-0

14

Internationalisation of a Migrant Family Firm and Contextual Uncertainty: The Role of Ethnic Social Networks

Leonardo Centeno-Caffarena and Allan Discua Cruz

Introduction

This study is motivated by the need to understand the approach and rationale of migrant families in businesses to internationalisation. In this study, a migrant family in business relates to members of a family of migrants, or descendants of migrants, who engage in the foundation, management and continuity of one or several family business ventures over time (Elo et al., 2018; Hamilton, Discua Cruz, & Jack, 2017). Studying migrant families in business is important as recent studies on internationalisation suggest shifting our attention from the firm to the family level of analysis (Kontinen & Ojala, 2011a, 2011b). Such shift can help our understanding about how migrant family firms achieve long-term competitiveness in increasingly challenging environments (Discua Cruz, Basco, Parada, Malfense Fierro, & Alvarado Alvarez, 2019). A migrant family firm can be conceptualised as a venture where members of a migrant family in business participate in the

L. Centeno-Caffarena
Centro de Promoción para el Desarrollo de la Empresa Familiar (CEPRODEF),
Managua, Nicaragua

A. Discua Cruz (✉)
Centre for Family Business, Department of Entrepreneurship and Strategy,
Lancaster University Management School, Lancaster, UK
e-mail: a.discuacruz@lancaster.ac.uk

© The Author(s), under exclusive license to Springer Nature Switzerland AG 2021
T. Leppäaho, S. Jack (eds.), *The Palgrave Handbook of Family Firm Internationalization*,
https://doi.org/10.1007/978-3-030-66737-5_14

431

management of the firm and own enough equity to be able to exert control over strategy (Howorth, Rose, Hamilton, & Westhead, 2010). As strategies to internationalise in migrant family firms may be only understandable within the specific context and place in which they occur (Discua Cruz, Centeno Caffarena, & Vega Solano, 2020; Roscoe, Discua Cruz, & Howorth, 2013), further attention to migrant families in business (Elo & Dana, 2019) and their approach to internationalisation in different contexts is needed (Elo & Minto-Coy, 2019).

The migrant family in business concept links to theoretical discussions around transnationalism, ethnicity, networks and context. Transnationalism refers broadly to the processes by which migrants create and preserve multiple economic, cultural and social relationships that link them to their origin and host societies (Vertovec, 2001). Accordingly, transnational networks relate to multiple social relationships (familial, economic, social, organisational, religious and political) that span borders and link immigrant entrepreneurs to others across borders to provide information or resources to trade or identify international markets (Mustafa & Chen, 2010). Such relationships are extensively regarded in the study of diasporas, transnationalism, ethnic communities and migration (Rodgers et al., 2019; Vershinina, Barrett, & Meyer, 2011). The importance of ethnicity is attributed to the way it allows people from similar backgrounds to share information (Larson & Lewis, 2017). Ethnic networks, that is, networks of social relationships connected by ethnicity may be more relevant than previously believed to explain internationalisation (Brzozowski, Cucculelli, & Surdej, 2017). Such importance may be paramount in uncertain contexts, characterised by weak institutions, social unrest, economic volatility and political turmoil (Lynch, Mason, Beresford, & Found, 2012). Such contexts represent an interesting milieu to understand the role of ethnic networks in the approach of migrant families in business to internationalisation. Thus, this study aims to answer the following question: *What is the role of ethnic networks in the internationalisation of migrant family firms in uncertain contexts?*

To answer our question, we depart from the argument that migrant families in developing economies internationalise their businesses through social relationships in family, ethnic and business networks (Jack, Moult, Anderson, & Dodd, 2010). The relevance of relationships in local and familiar networks as well as transnational networks highlights the nature of strong and weak ties (Anderson, Jack, & Drakopoulou Dodd, 2005; Elo et al., 2018, 2019). The study of relationships between individuals in networks, which facilitates business activities, is studied under a social capital perspective (Anderson et al.,

2007). Social capital is a theoretical perspective that has gained acceptance in studies of family businesses and internationalisation (Nahapiet & Ghoshal, 1998; Oviatt & McDougall, 2005; Uzzi, 1997). While some studies suggest that social capital in ethnic networks in relevant in the emergence and development of a firm created by migrants (Elo and Dana, 2019), other studies suggest that the value of relationships in such networks may become less significant for subsequent generations as descendants become more embedded in their host countries (Deakins, Ishaq, Smallbone, Whittam, & Wyper, 2007).

In this study, we focus on Central America, a context where migrant families in business from developed economies have thrived, often amidst adverse contextual conditions (Discua Cruz, Ramos Rodas, Raudales, & Fortin, 2016; Müller, Botero, Discua Cruz, & Subramanian, 2019). This study relies on a single case study (Leppäaho, Plakoyiannaki, & Dimitratos, 2016) in Nicaragua, where family firms previously dominated the economic landscape (Strachan, 1976) and where migration waves, mainly from European countries, helped Nicaragua's initial economic development (Leogrande, 1996). Yet, contextual crisis (e.g. wars and governmental policies) affected migrant families in business in Nicaragua (Duarte, 2009). Exploring the approach and rationale of a migrant family in business in such a context is relevant as some families when facing diverse contextual pressures may either exhibit resilient behaviour (Discua Cruz et al., 2019) or opt to exit such an environment (Fernández Pérez & Lluch, 2016).

Based on the narratives of a migrant family in business (Hamilton et al., 2017) in Nicaragua, we extend understanding of the role of ethnic networks behind the internationalisation of a family firm. Findings reveal why migrant families in business may rely on ethnic networks to internationalise and how after setbacks occur, such networks allow business continuity and internationalisation. In this study, a deliberate approach to rely on ethnic networks drives and supports the internationalisation of a migrant family firm. Moreover, in uncertain contexts, migrant families may consider relationships outside familiar and ethnic networks to advance business purposes. Taken together, the findings extend understanding in the literature of internationalisation of migrant family firms in uncertain contexts.

The chapter continues as follows: First, it describes the theoretical background, then it explains the contextual scope and the research method. It continues by focusing on case findings and discussion. Finally, it suggests limitations and opportunities for further research.

Theoretical Framework

Migrant Families in Businesses

Migrant families that have established their firms in host countries around the world are more widespread than originally believed (Elo & Minto-Coy, 2019). Many migrant families introduce novel perspectives and ideas into a host country business landscape because their cultural and institutional background and mind-set are different from local counterparts (Elo et al., 2018). To understand how they operate, studies suggest to shift our attention away from the business per se and focus on the family in business, which relates to *"members of a family that engage in the foundation, management and continuity of one or several family business ventures over time"* (Hamilton et al., 2017, p. 3). In this study we suggest that further understanding of migrant families in business, that is, members of a family of migrants, or descendants of migrants, who voice their migrant narrative and leverage ethnic relationships to operate their venture(s), is important to advance our understanding about internationalisation of migrant family firms.

Migrant families in business do not emerge in a vacuum. Migration policy or business opportunity (Elo & Minto-Coy, 2019) may encourage the arrival of migrants, and their families, to developing economies and prompt the establishment of family ventures (Discua Cruz et al., 2016). Many migrant families often settle in peripheral areas of a host country, which do not only refer to distance from urban locations (e.g. large cities) but also to limited business and resource frameworks (Elo et al., 2018). Such periphery may translate into limited resource availability, small market share, investment and information access, straining the pace and breadth of entrepreneurial activities. For migrant families, such starting point may influence the motivation to pursue opportunities outside local boundaries (Discua Cruz & Basco, 2018).

Networks and Social Capital

The internationalisation of migrant family firms has been implicitly associated with the literature on networks and social relationships, which highlight the role of family, ethnic networks and social capital. First, social relationships have been widely regarded in the study of internationalisation (Kontinen & Ojala, 2011a, 2011b), transnationalism, ethnic communities and migration (Vershinina et al., 2011). Prior research posits that family is a source, user and builder of social capital (Bubolz, 2001), which relates to *"the goodwill available to individuals and groups*" (Adler & Kwon, 2002, p. 18; Kwon & Adler, 2014, p. 412), and is considered a social phenomenon embedded in networks of relationships (Stam & Elfring, 2008; Estrin, Mickiewicz, & Stephan, 2013). One feature of family stands out universally: the family helps place individuals into a patterned network of interweaving social relationships (Bubolz, 2001). Migrant families can perform such social function by acting as an agent of social placement for their members in origin and host societies (Stark, 2000). Members of migrant families may have access to local and transnational relationships that may support future business activities (Anderson & Miller, 2003). As a result, diverse ties help to position members of a migrant family in a complex web of social ties that can span beyond local borders.

Second, the relevance of social ties for migrant families in business underscores the strength of relationships between individuals and the formation of network structures by individual and groups (Soetanto, 2017), studied through a strong and weak tie perspective (Granovetter, 1973). "Strong ties" are represented through strong relationships and closely knit networks of family, friends, class and ethnicity circles. The term "ethnic" is linked to a "group" of common origin and culture (Yinger, 1985). For migrant families, close friends and family in the origin and host country are considered strong ties, which would help out the most, and thus facilitate collaboration as migrants know them, trust them and interact frequently. Core members of a migrant community may be naturally inclined to discuss ideas or projects within familiar or close circles. In entrepreneurship literature the terms "ethnic" and "immigrant" are often used interchangeably (Collins & Low, 2010). "Weak ties" cut across diverse social network structures outside closely knit circles and are represented through relationships in business, community and professional associations (e.g. local chambers of commerce, Church, Rotary or Lions Club) (Davidsson & Honig, 2003). Weak ties are important because they represent bridges to access networks or groups of people outside familiar circles providing relevant information and resources (Soetanto, 2017). Nevertheless, in comparison with strong ties, the amount of information, support or empathy to be procured through weak ties is uncertain.

Benefits and Disadvantages of Ethnic Networks

The benefits and disadvantages of ethnic ties can be observed in the role of ethnic networks for migrant entrepreneurs engaged in international business

(Brzozowski et al., 2017). Strong and weak ties are found in the degree of relationships in diverse networks spheres and may include customers, suppliers, financial advisors and often a transnational family network that provide a heterogeneous knowledge base (Rauch, 2001; Bagwell, 2008). If migrants settle in (and remain within) ethnic enclaves, they may benefit from low social distance between members of similar ethnic origin, stimulate social networks between ethnic peers and benefit from knowledge transfer, information access, similar attitudes and ideas, with an increased "quality" of social capital that the interaction within such enclave can provide (Andersson, Larsson, & Öner, 2017). In developed economies ethnic minority businesses have been found to rely heavily on strong ties in the early stages of entrepreneurial development (Deakins et al., 2007).

Thus, migrant families in business may have a unique position to internationalise based on social capital from ethnic strong and weak ties because an extended network of contacts may be activated at any point in time. This occurs as business founders may have gained legitimacy and trust to sustain business activity in the host country (Ensign & Robinson, 2011). Moreover, founders can leverage family ties on transnational networks which are an inherent part of a web of their social relationships (Bagwell, 2008). Most importantly, ties within transnational networks may be leveraged to identify and evaluate opportunities in relation to countries of origin (Katila & Wahlbeck, 2012).

Yet, scholars also warn of the disadvantages of ethnic networks in host countries. Settling in an enclave can cause migrants to experience a social and institutional "distance" to natives and local institutions (Andersson et al., 2017). Deakins et al. (2007) hint that reliance on ethnic networks can also act as a constraint for entrepreneurship or business expansion for future generations of a migrant family. Subsequent generations of migrant families in business may decide to become more embedded within the local cultural landscape over time and minimise their involvement with ethnic networks (Katila & Wahlbeck, 2012). This is particularly evident when second- and third-generation members' adherence to cultural practices in ethnic networks may not be aligned with previous generations (Light & Dana, 2013). Yet, while social capital in ethnic networks may be important to internationalise, literature suggests a gradual disinterest from involvement in such networks by subsequent generations. Little is known whether such a premise prevails in diverse contexts.

Uncertain Contexts, Risk and Instability

Some migrant families in businesses face uncertain, high-risk and unstable environments over time, characterised by weak institutions, social unrest, economic volatility and political turmoil (Lynch et al., 2012). To address the difficulties in launching and developing new ventures in such contexts (Acs & Amorós, 2008) migrants may rely on information and resources from diverse networks (Lajqi & Krasniqi, 2017; Luk et al., 2008). Recent studies suggest that ethnic networks may be relevant for migrant families in business aiming to internationalise their products (Discua Cruz et al., 2020). Yet, further understanding about how (whether) ethnic social networks play any role in firms as a response to contextual uncertainty remains scarce. The next section focuses in such a context.

Context

Nicaragua and German Families in Business

Nicaragua is a developing country located in Central America. It has a population of about 6.2 million and a GDP of about US$13.8 billion (World Bank, 2017). The Nicaraguan economy is strongly associated to agricultural production, which plays a vital role in employment generation, entrepreneurship, food security, poverty alleviation, biodiversity conservation, culture tradition and financial investments (Salcedo, Campos, & Guzman, 2014).

Nicaragua is particularly interesting for this study for several reasons: First, the Nicaraguan government, following similar policies of nearby countries (Discua Cruz et al., 2016), enticed migration from Europe by facilitating land to promote agricultural production and improve the local economy; soon after arrival, exports were dominated by English, Italians, and Germans migrants (Khül, 2014, p. 239). This study concentrates on German families as, of all migrant groups, the presence and relevance of the German community since the 1800s has been well documented (Khül, 2014). Second, early migrants settled primarily near the Atlantic coast and in the northern areas of Nicaragua. From 1852 to 1858, the German government appointed consuls in the most important Nicaraguan cities linked to German trade. To address the limitations of peripheral areas, German families created diverse associations in locations where fellow countrymen gradually settled, such as Managua, Matagalpa and Jinotega, and besides, they created a German club (1932), a

German school (1934) and a German cultural centre (1963) (von Houwald, 1975) which nurtured and strengthened ethnics ties.

Third, the perceived cultural distance between German migrants and Nicaraguan natives was significant (Khül, 2004). Some of the principles that characterised the first Germans arriving in Nicaragua related to punctuality, solidarity among countrymen, hard work, honesty, businesses diversification, frugality and zeal towards excessive expenses, which contrasted with more relaxed attitude of locals (Kühl, 2004; Hofstede, 2001). The need to develop strong ethnic ties to conduct business activities, both in Nicaragua with the German community, was encouraged. Yet, as many German male migrants were single, marriage with local women occurred. Subsequent generations had a mixed background, which enriched a mixed ethnic network that was leveraged often to establish business ventures (Tijerino, 1964).

Finally, several contextual crises have affected German migrant families in Nicaragua in the last century. During the First World War (1914–1918) the German colony endured severe business penalties. In the Second World War (1939) the Nicaraguan government, like most Central American countries honouring pacts with the US, declared war on Nazi Germany and its allies. Government officials confiscated all property and assets (coffee farms, machinery, vehicles, etc.) from any person of German origin, including those born in Nicaragua; all men, including the elderly, were detained and taken to detention centres (Von Houwald, 1975, pp. 150–151; Duarte, 2009). In 1939, the German community accounted for 330 residents, not including descendants, but in the 1970s, the colony only accounted for 300 Germans living in the country (von Houwald, 1975, pp. 44–45). In the 1980s, German families in business suffered the confiscation of assets due to communist policies enforced during the Sandinista government (Leogrande, 1996; Roche, 2006; Tyroler, 1991). Several large companies of German and English origin did not survive the Sandinista era. Such contextual crisis resulted in the development of a generalised distrust of locals by German families and an increased reliance on ethnic networks. Next, we explore the challenges of a German family in business in the export of the most important agricultural product in Nicaragua.

The Coffee Industry

In Central America, production of coffee for export has involved the effort of farming families for centuries (Discua Cruz et al., 2020; Hearst, 1932). Coffee has been an important resource for Nicaragua for the last 200 years; however, the earliest indications of coffee plantations date from the 1750s in the

14 Internationalisation of a Migrant Family Firm and Contextual... 439

Mosquito region (Roberts, 1827). The first coffee plantation began in 1825 by a Spanish migrant (Levy, 1873; Radell, 1969), with the first coffee export made to Mexico in 1848 (La Gaceta, 1848). The first commercial coffee plantation in northern Nicaragua was started by Germans in the 1850s (Khül, 2014, p. 249). Immigration laws granted European migrants large land extensions and subsidies of US$0.05 per tree planted (Merrill, 1994, p.101). By 1870, coffee became the principal export product and has remained in this position to date (Merrill, 1994, p. 1001). From 2010 to 2014 coffee accounted for 19–20% of total exports, followed by beef, gold and sugar (Colburn, 2012, p. 95 and ICO, 2013, p. 3), and in 2017 Nicaragua exported around 3 million coffee sacks, generating US$446 million for the economy (CETREX, 2018).

Several contextual influences affect Nicaraguan farming families, which can be understood through Wright, Chrisman, Chua, and Steier's (2014) levels of contextual importance (organisational, institutional, and temporal (Table 14.1)).

Table 14.1 shows that in terms of a temporal dimension, the coffee sector can be influenced by international market shocks, trends and demands. Fluctuation in coffee prices can have a profound impact across coffee-producing regions as they influence land use decisions and consumer demand over time (Wilson, 1994). The emergence of geographic indications, appellations of origin and international certifications have emerged as mechanisms to guarantee the quality and attributes that global markets demand from coffee

Table 14.1 Contextual framework in the Nicaraguan coffee industry context

Contextual dimensions		
Organis	Institutional	Temporal
Interest in farm preservation	Governmental policy and regulatory agencies	Changing practices in coffee farming (e.g. certifications)
Tacit and formal knowledge	Technology processes (e.g. GPS)	Regulations in land property (e.g. confiscation)
Strong intra- and inter-generational bonds	Strong community social capital	Family lifecycles
Specialised human capital	Tradition of farming sector	Expectations of family succession
Family financial support	Inheritance laws	Changes in society/ environmental concerns
Family emotional support	Cultural expectations (local and ethnic)	Industry trends and market demands
Resilience during difficult times	Business networks	International policy changes

Source: Adapted from Wright et al. (2014) and Discua Cruz et al. (2020)

(Paz Cafferata & Pomareda, 2009). Consumer demand for differentiation in coffee has been growing significantly, relying on intrinsic characteristics or perceived product attributes that relate to place, process and circumstances by which coffee is cultivated, produced, processed and marketed (Lara Estrada, Rasche, & Schneider, 2017). In terms of an institutional dimension, coffee producers are influenced by local legal frameworks, international certifications and competitions, government systems and worldwide trade policies (Wilson, 2010). For example, political instability may prompt families in business to reconsider their local strategies and sell their products overseas. Moreover, trends fuelled by gourmet, eco-concerned consumers are modifying the coffee value chain (Rueda & Lambin, 2013). In terms of an organisational dimension, Table 14.1 shows that while coffee farming families may benefit from idiosyncratic resources (Sirmon & Hitt, 2003), they also deal with diverse family skills and knowledge, unpredictable working conditions and limited financial resources (Wilson, 2007).

The previous description is important as at the beginning of the twentieth century German migrants accounted for the largest value of Nicaraguan exports, mainly to Germany, with several corporations, managers and workers migrating and settling in the country (von Houwald, 1975, pp. 41–42). Initial German migrants who engaged in coffee production were physically "isolated" in the central and northern mountain regions known as the Matagalpa region (Bro, Clay, Ortega, & Lopez, 2019), developing a strong ethnic enclave (Khül, 2014). In 1934, 260,000 coffee sacks were exported, with 51,796 units sold to Germany (Von Houwald, 1975, p. 295). Mejía-Lacayo (2018) argues that descendants of German migrants have remained in such location producing coffee for export as well as have developed diversified businesses, contributing more than any other ethnic group to the development of Matagalpa and nearby regions.

Recently, the sophistication of the coffee industry has pushed exporters to transform their product into an added value offering for the international market (Kilian, Jones, Pratt, & Villalobos, 2006). The demand for specialty coffee prompts exporters to consider their unique approach to sourcing, processing, brewing and serving coffee to differentiate existing products (Bacon, 2008). Recent studies suggest that coffee farming families in developing countries may leverage diverse networks to internationalise specialty coffee (Discua Cruz et al., 2020). Yet, there is limited insight about migrant families involved in the production of specialty coffee and the networks they rely on. Thus, the coffee industry represents an ideal context to understand how (whether) a migrant family firm in Nicaragua engages in internationalisation and the extent to which the process is influenced by ethnic networks.

Methodology

To answer our research question, detailed and in-depth insights from those involved directly in internationalisation, which could illustrate what it means, the tensions involved, rooted in actual context, are needed (Miles, Huberman, & Saldana, 2013). Qualitative research allows answering "how" questions, understanding the world from the perspective of those studied, examining and articulating processes (Pratt, 2009). As the interest is in exploring and interpreting internationalisation of migrant family firms, a single case study research is ideal (Stake, 2008). Single case studies offer rich insights when focusing on understanding the complex processes of unique family businesses (Leppäaho et al., 2016) and can be used to explore internationalisation (Poulis, Poulis, & Plakoyiannaki, 2013). Our interest was to find a migrant family in business in Nicaragua that engaged in the production and internationalisation of specialty coffee. In 2018, a family who fulfilled the definition of a migrant family in business was approached by the first author. As detailed information is difficult to obtain in Latin American family firms (Jones, 2004), access was procured through family and professional relationships. The actual name for the participant migrant family in business and their venture(s) are utilised in this study.

The Khül Family and the Selva Negra Estate

The Khül family, descendants of German migrants in the Matagalpa region, acquired the La Hammonia farm in 1975, a farm with 528.75 hectares. The farm now hosts several business ventures currently owned by Eddy and Mausi Khül and is now known as Selva Negra Estate (Black Forest). To date 300 people work at Selva Negra Estate. Among the employees, three families of workers have accompanied the Khül family for three generations, 27 families for two generations, with intermarriages occurring between worker's children. The new families formed have remained in the farm and work with the Khül family. Selva Negra Estate provides a school and a library for its employees.

During the 1980s, the Khül family had to flee the country due to the Sandinista revolution. Eddy and Mausi have four daughters, Victoria, Karen, Gretel and Ursula who were educated in both Germany and the US during their exile. The family returned to Nicaragua after democratic governments were re-established in the 1990s and reclaimed the Hammonia farm. Soon after the family restarted farm operations, their coffee began to be exported as a specialty estate-grown origin product in 1992, with the name "Selva Negra

442   L. Centeno-Caffarena and A. Discua Cruz

Estate Coffee." In 2000, Selva Negra Estate exported 250 tonnes of coffee: 80% to the US and the rest to Europe, and by 2017, they exported around 5000 sacks to the same geographical areas.

For the Khül family, and most German families in business, Nicaragua represented a small market, unable to provide them with the resources they needed to develop their businesses and thus diversification was sought (Grant, 2002). Over 45 years, the Khül family developed different businesses in the agro-industrial and tourism sectors. Diversification was pursued to ensure the sustainability of their farm (Alsos, Ljunggren, & Pettersen, 2003). Eddy and Mausi created a small network of family businesses housed at the Selva Negra Estate. According to Eddy and Mausi, Selva Negra Estate (http://www.sel-vanegra.com/) is the most diversified agribusiness in Nicaragua with some 12 different ventures, including horticulture, coffee (from plantation to roasting), coffee export, hotel and restaurant services, livestock, poultry, pig, vegetable production, dairy products, processed meat and tourism in virgin mountains. One-third of the farm (141 hectares of virgin jungle) remains unexploited as the family wanted to create a tropical microclimate, procure water supply and as a tourist attraction. Residual products are used to create compost and material to be reused throughout the farm complex. Table 14.2 shows important milestones in Selva Negra Estate and the Khül family.

Table 14.2 Important dates for the Kühl family and the Selva Negra Farm. Source: Kühl family

Date	Event
1888	Mausi's great-grandfather marries a woman from Matagalpa
1890	Hans Bosche, a German immigrant, buys La Hammonia farm and establishes a shade-grown coffee farm
1956	Fred Bosche, Hans Bosche's son, sells the farm to Renaldo Rivera. Hans retires and settles in the US
1967	Eddy and Mausi marry; they represent the fourth and fifth generation of German coffee producers in Nicaragua
1968	Eddy and Mausi create their first company (metal and steel structures)
1975	Mausi and Eddy purchase La Hammonia coffee farm from the Rivera family
1978/1979	Family exile due to the Sandinista revolution. Extended family members remain to run La Hammonia day-to-day operations
1989	Mausi and Eddy return to Nicaragua, and resumed the management of La Hammonia farm
1992	First coffee export under the name Selva Negra Coffee Estate

Source: Kühl Family

Data Analysis

The initial data analysis was in Spanish; translation into English was done later. Interpretive methods were used to analyse how and why migrant families in business internationalise. The early stages of the analysis included categorising responses to uncertainty which highlighted the relevance of ethnic networks. Data analysis was inductive as the study sought to understand individual perceptions and experiences (Grbich, 2007). The search for meaning led us to gain an in-depth understanding of meanings and diverse perspectives about internationalisation. Based on Neergaard and Leitch (2015), the authors started by independently examining the data in interviews, observation notes and documents. Then, a coding process was carried out by reading and re-reading transcripts, notes and documents in order to organise data. Once coding was completed, data were organised to identify emerging themes. Analysis of the data was reiterative in moving between data and emerging findings (Alvesson & Skoldberg, 2000). The interpretation of emergent findings was discussed with case study participants to inform ongoing analysis. In analysing the data, experience of the Nicaraguan culture was important, as was the experience in being part of family businesses (Discua Cruz et al., 2020). Finally, findings were "re-contextualised" by comparing them to arguments in existing literature (Neergaard & Leitch, 2015).

Table 14.3 summarises the data coding, themes and concepts that emerged in the process. In the findings section, compelling excerpts from the data are used to illustrate arguments made. Manual analysis methods support the key themes emerging from the analysis (Pratt, 2009). The aim was to increase transparency and address the validity of the study (Gibbert & Ruigrok, 2010).

Findings

Ethnic Identity and Networks as Starting Points

Evidence from the interviews (Table 14.3) highlighted that family members shared the view that German ethnic networks were crucial for internationalisation. The main feature from ethnic networks that fuelled such shared vision was the appreciation of ethnic identity and solidarity over time. Eddy explained ethnic solidarity when describing that the first German families that arrived in Nicaragua settled in the Matagalpa region around the 1800s. These families were encouraged to produce coffee given the good quality of

Table 14.3 Data coding

Excerpts from data	First-order concepts	Second-order themes
"Our farm is frequently visited by professors and students from prestigious national and international business schools who try to understand the success of Selva Negra Estate from a financial perspective, but fail to do so; our success is because of our German heritage, which always accompanies us and we cannot 'renounce' to it; besides, we are descendants of the first coffee producers in Nicaragua." (Eddy)	Strong ethnic heritage	Ethnic identity and networks as starting points
"Selva Negra's café [a venture within the estate] is like a German museum where we keep old books, documents, photos, objects, machines and tools that highlight the German heritage in Matagalpa. It is visited daily by local and international visitors, both for socializing and to do business." (Eddy)	Safeguarding ethnic heritage	
"We feel more Germans than Nicaraguans." (Eddy)	Shared ethnic identity	
"My wife, contrary to the Latin American culture, made a deal with our daughters: 'do not ask for parties, on the contrary you can travel'; and in fact, they began to travel, which has given them a cultural, linguistic, professional, discipline, contact with others, etc. that otherwise they would not have had access to." (Eddy)	Family objectives in building alliances	

"The products offered by Selva Negra Estate have been improved with technical assistance, i.e., two German technicians were brought in … given that they [Selva Negra's products] are aimed at highly competitive markets, such as the market of Europeans living here and people abroad. … There is always a technician present to guarantee the quality of the product in its different phases…" (Eddy)	Specialised knowledge in ethnic network	Relevance of ethnic relational resources for succeeding generations
"Well, we export 80% of its coffee to the US, partly to German-owned companies, and the rest to Europe." (Eddy)	Relevance of ethnic networks for future businesses	
"One of the problems is that in Matagalpa (where Selva Negra Estate is located) there wasn't a university for years, so it was often the case that the next generation that came to the country as a settler, did not study, yet brought with them a tradition in farming or working ethics that was useful in blending family and business goals … The descendants of Europeans usually study in good schools in Nicaragua, and then do their undergraduate and postgraduate studies abroad." (Eddy)	Traditional knowledge to complement lack of specialised knowledge	
"However, all the daughters, together with their relatives, have shown interest in the future to settle in the property of Selva Negra. The son of the oldest daughter (grandson of the founders) is studying two careers (agriculture and journalism) … everyone, in one way or another, will be involved in the various activities that comprise the company because there is space for everyone." (Mausi)	Complementing family objectives with future business growth	

(continued)

Table 14.3 (continued)

Excerpts from data	First-order concepts	Second-order themes
"Many of the new products were emerging because of the exclusivity of the market that visits Selva Negra Estate, since the majority of visitors are foreigners who have settled in the country or who are visiting from overseas; then we can talk to them in our nearby restaurant to talk and get a lot of feedback on the quality of the services, new (coffee) products, etc." (Mausi)	Non-family networks' support for differentiation	The relevance of a mixed network for future international purposes
"Selva Negra Coffee Estate is very well positioned among foreigners, mainly European; whenever Eddy is in the farm or the restaurant or the hotel there are different personalities such as diplomats, journalists, doctors, Protestant pastors which forces us to maintain many international relations, which makes our interest to be proficient in English increase." (Mausi)	Ethnic network outside enclave	
"Selva Negra Estate has managed to position itself properly in the international market for our marketing we patented our name in the United States. When the consumer sees the symbol of the registered trademark, he has more confidence in the product, and also because he knows that the farm exists, and can check it whenever he wants." (Mausi)	Shared understanding of international requirements	
"Our coffee is now exported and consumed by the Club of the Boston Revolution Daughters in the US, who always ask for coffee with the same consistency as the previous year, which for us is easier to comply with as our coffee has a computerised code specifying the specific lot by GPS, height, soil properties, bean variety—it is just similar to how the wine is produced. This club pays more because it knows the quality of the product and the family behind it." (Eddy)	Development of relationships based on external consumers	
"Mausi speaks Spanish, English and German and gives international talks about community improvement topics around coffee. She has already delivered talks in Barcelona, Austria and Seattle, which is the capital of gourmet coffee, about 'women building community,' and also in New York…." (Eddy)	Dissemination of information where family coffee is produced outside local border	

Source: Author

the soil. Over the years the demand for coffee grew and these contacted others in Germany to come and settle in Nicaragua to increase supply and create an ethnic community dedicated to coffee production. Eddy and Mausi belong to the fourth and fifth generations of German families in business who started and developed coffee plantations, which they are proud of. Such initial preference for ethnic families in the development of the Nicaraguan coffee industry grounded a strong reliance on ethnic networks. Ethnic networks provided a trusted group to work with, not only to produce coffee but also to secure transnational links for export to their preferred market: Germany.

Eddy suggested that early German settlers fuelled a shared vision, among migrant families producing coffee, that their main market was not Nicaragua but Germany. Germany was considered the place where future generations of migrant families have to return to continue higher education, to look for partners, resources and new markets. The gradual growth of coffee farms, and the close psychological distance (Hofstede, 2001) between the German enclave in Matagalpa with Germany, facilitated that unplanned requests to export coffee were addressed through trust on ethnic ties. Doing business with families that had the same cultural background became an early and essential aspect for internationalisation based on trust in the transnational network involved. Eddy argued that ethnic networks facilitated international trade between Nicaragua and Germany for several decades.

Moreover, the relevance of ethnic networks related to fostering strong links locally to preserve an ethnic identity, which was considered critical for the continuity of international trade. This was noted when Eddy expressed:

> *If you ask me what has been the secret of our success I can say that it is the Lutheran ethics, good family habits and being of German origin: the values that we all share here is not to waste money, avoid loans with local banks, avoid unnecessary luxuries, being an example to the workers by not being drunk, carrying weapons, avoid foul language and other German values … The descendants of Europeans (in Nicaragua) normally study in good schools, and then do their undergraduate and postgraduate studies abroad; Germans descendants have studied in Germany and the USA for example … my wife has maintained contact with family in Germany, and we have sent our 4 daughters to study German and train there in different subjects; Our grandson, who grew up with us in this farm, has followed the same path, we want to preserve our identity.*

Eddy and Mausi expressed that the German ethnic network in Nicaragua has preserved over time-specific values, skills and cultural features. Such cultural items have endured since the first migrants arrived and endured through diverse crisis. Such values were supported by ethnic institutions (e.g. schools, cultural centres). Eddy argued that distinctive benefits over local entrepreneurs were achieved due to culturally determined attitudes such as dedication and hard work, suggesting that cultural and social factors differences influenced internationalisation. Table 14.3 shows that ethnic solidarity and loyalty, personal motivation to help fellow countryman, hardworking ethics, good relationships with people from the same ethnic group and flexible financing arrangements between fellow countrymen supported the importance to maintain ties to ethnic networks. Ethnic networks then allowed continued access to co-ethnic producers and suppliers to engage in internationalisation.

Relevance of Ethnic Relational Resources for Succeeding Generations

Findings suggest that migrant families in business may strengthen links with the community of migrants from their country, contacts with the country of origin and family structures in business over time based on family narratives. Table 14.3 shows that in Selva Negra Estate, an intentional strengthening of ties with ethnic networks was evidenced by the accounts passed on by family members about critical events. Eddy and Mausi recalled the stories told by their ancestors about the expropriation of their family assets in the past around WWI, WWII and the Sandinista era in Nicaragua. The narratives around such adverse circumstances became part of a collective family memory for generations of the Khül family in business. Such shared understandings supported a distrustful attitude towards non-German descendants and government officials and reinforced the relevance of strengthening relationships within ethnic networks.

In the 1980s, the Khül family experienced a critical event due to the Sandinista government. As properties in the Matagalpa area were being confiscated, the Khül family fled to the US, where they remained for about 10 years until democratic order was restored. Eddy's mother refused to leave the country and stayed behind looking after the family assets. Due to the good employee-owner relationships that persisted since the farm was founded, workers vouched for the family when government officials considered seizing the family estates. Moreover, ethnic networks in Nicaragua spread the rumour that the farm was part of a larger German foreign investment. Such actions prevented Sandinista officials to confiscate family assets. Given the neutral policy of Germany towards Nicaragua during the Sandinista era, the Khül family ventures were largely unaffected.

14 Internationalisation of a Migrant Family Firm and Contextual... 449

Upon the restoration of democratic governments in Nicaragua in the 1990s, Eddy, Mausi and their oldest daughter, Victoria, returned to Nicaragua. Victoria brought her husband and children to continue with the family business. The remaining daughters decided to stay overseas completing postgraduate education before returning to Nicaragua. Today the entire family is integrated in the management of sensitive areas of the corporation; Mausi and the eldest daughter Victoria are in charge of the La Hammonia coffee farm, attending the day-to-day activities along with 300 workers; Karen, the second daughter manages the Selva Negra Hotel; Gretel, the third daughter handles international coffee sales in the US through Javavino (http://www.javavino.com/). Selva Negra Estate currently exports 10% of their coffee production to Gretel's venture. Ursula, the youngest daughter, is the artistic director, helping with logos, decorations, promotions, etc.

Mausi suggested that the exile experience allowed them to appreciate the significance of their ethnic networks and prioritised the relevance of export markets for their coffee. After their exile, the Khül family reinforced a shared view of Nicaragua as a place where their businesses would be located but where ethnic identity and reliance on ethnic networks should be reinforced. Family relationships, technical training and business relationships were to be linked to external markets. For the Khül family, what happened in Germany or the US became more important to whatever happened in Managua, especially in terms of price and market dynamics of their main export item—coffee. Upon their return from exile, Mausi and Eddy prompted the reactivation of ties in transnational ethnic networks to procure trustworthy information, knowledge and skills that would benefit their firm's internationalisation process. Eddy expressed:

> The products offered by Selva Negra Estate have been improved with technical assistance, i.e., two German technicians were brought in ... given that they [Selva Negra's products] are aimed at highly competitive markets, such as the market of Europeans living here and people abroad. ... There is always a technician present to guarantee the quality of the product in its different phases....

By relating the improvement of existing products based on relationships to ethnic circles, the intention of the Khül family was to increase the perception of quality, both locally and internationally, linked to a German identity in business. An ethnic relational resource, related to supporting a narrative of ethnic influence in products made in a host country, highlighted the importance of strengthening the importance of ethnic networks for future generations.

The Relevance of a Mixed Network for Future International Purposes

While ethnic networks could be reactivated for internationalisation by the Khül family upon return from exile, evidence shows that development of stronger relationships outside of ethnic circles was not underestimated. Table 14.3 shows that while Eddy and Mausi relied on relationships within ethnic networks upon return, the development of instrumental relationships outside ethnic networks and with diverse actors in Nicaraguan society was relevant for further exports efforts. Eddy commented that exile was relevant in several ways. First, it allowed them to be exposed to what demanding international markets expected, in terms of quality of coffee, which prompted the interest to develop new relationships and create an export venture. Eddy recalled:

> Upon our return [from exile]... Mausi told me that we were spending a lot [of money] on exporting coffee the way we were traditionally doing it—by paying an export office. We needed to set up our own export office; my first reaction was that it was only for large companies. Yet Mausi asked around for someone with such experience, and found, through our networks a retired lady who had worked in an export company before. Mausi asked her "what do I need to set up an export office?," and the lady said: "only an office in Managua, I am going to move there soon." And that was it, they started the export office.

Second, Eddy and Mausi seized the opportunity to become better informed about the coffee market while in exile. They investigated how to patent the name of their farm in the US as well as the relevance of export certifications for export markets. Upon return from exile, they realised that relationships with officials in local and national institutions would allow them to comply with export requirements. Moreover, their discussions in networks overseas prompted them to introduce new technologies, such as GPS, to address the increased interest for traceability of coffee batches by international consumers (Niederhauser, Oberthür, Kattnig, & Cock, 2008). The introduction of environmental practices, such as the production of compost from residual products (Ronga, Pane, Zaccardelli, & Pecchioni, 2016) and the creation of coffee trails, where visitors can experience coffee culture, plantation and production (Jolliffe, 2010) emerged from interaction with diverse circles in the farm (Table 14.3).

Finally, during exile, Eddy and Mausi became aware of groups and associations that would appreciate the rich production heritage and quality in coffee by German families in Nicaragua (e.g. in the US, Table 14.3). Upon return from exile, the Khül family shared the view that diversification into other export products would depend on ethnic networks and identity but also on a deliberate effort to cultivate local relationships in parallel. Moreover, as they improved their firm over the years following their return Eddy suggested that ethnic solidarity became more evident as fellow countrymen promoted the value of their products not only locally but also internationally. Eddy expressed: *"Café Selva Negra is strongly positioned with the country's tourism agencies, foreigners living in Nicaragua, and inhabitants of the city of Matagalpa, many of whom are of German origin, and they are proud that a company founded by countrymen has achieved so much success and fame."*

Contextual uncertainty encouraged the Khül family to consider diversification and further internationalisation. While coffee exports would remain their core business, the family shared the view to export new products such as wood, cocoa and others to Germany as well as other markets. At the time of the interview they considered further diversification into hospitality (mountain lodges) with an international consumer base in mind. Moving forward, the interest to internationalise further their different products would be supported by networks that combine the advantages of ethnic, local and transnational ties.

Discussion

This study concerned the role of ethnic networks in the internationalisation of migrant family firms in uncertain contexts. There are three main items for discussion based on the findings and their relationship with literature. First, findings support prior literature suggesting that ethnic enclaves provide advantages and disadvantages for migrant families in business. Yet, some of the mechanisms that provided advantages for internationalisation were elusive. In this study, several generations of migrant family members endured adverse contextual conditions yet relied constantly on strong ties in ethnic networks to overcome challenges (Soetanto, 2017). A deliberate interest over generations to adhere to cultural identity and ethnic networks appears to create relevant ethnic relational resources. Institutional crisis (e.g. WWI, WWII) appears to nurture a shared narrative (Hamilton et al., 2017) around ethnicity that supports migrant families' vision to be in business together and consider internationalisation as a relevant strategy (Discua Cruz, Howorth, & Hamilton, 2013). Adherence to Lutheran ethics highlighted the relevance of a common religion of migrant families in business to support business operations locally (Discua Cruz, 2015). This suggests that continued crisis in an uncertain context may nurture a collective narrative by migrant families. Such shared narratives become an ethnic relational resource which would support the value of ethnicity to procure information and resources for internationalisation.

Second, prior literature suggested that the role of ethnic networks may relate mainly to how information and resources could support the founding generations of a family firm. Yet, this study suggests that as context remains uncertain over time, the role of ethnic networks may depend on how ethnicity provides resources to respond to diverse (and adverse) circumstances (Danes et al., 2009; Danes, Rueter, Kwon, & Doherty, 2002). Findings suggest that adverse conditions in Nicaragua such as government regimes or policies created an interruption of commercial activities yet did not severe the strength of relationships within German ethnic networks. As a result of strengthening ties in ethnic networks, German migrant families in Nicaragua appear to possess over time a level of institutional gravitas and internal solidarity that provides descendants with an advantage in mobilising ethnic resources compared to natives (Aldrich & Waldinger, 1990).

Finally, findings suggest that when critical events occur (Cope & Watts, 2000), the role of ethnic networks for migrant family firms can be supported by social capital in local networks. As families face setbacks, including forced migration, ethnic and extended networks may be relevant for the mitigation of risks and setbacks in firms left behind temporarily. This was first evidenced when a family affected by exile was benefited by strong ties in close circles (family, German community) but also by seemingly "weak" ties (native employee workers) to safeguard existing assets. Such finding suggests that while a greater preference for ethnic ties may be encouraged, the actions of migrant families for the benefit of peripheral communities may grant them goodwill within the local community. Critical events then provided the opportunity to appreciate that diverse risks can be addressed by nurturing relationships outside their close circles (Danes et al., 2002). Institutional uncertainty may then prompt migrant families in business to act upon the patterns of change in diverse networks (Jack et al., 2010) that become relevant for internationalisation over time.

Taken together, the findings in this study suggest that ethnic networks in uncertain context have a crucial role in the internationalisation of migrant family firms. A migrant narrative and identity may influence internationalisation over generations, thus challenging the notion that subsequent generations of migrants may diminish the reliance on ethnic networks over time. Subsequent generations in a migrant family firm may be motivated to nurture social capital within ethnic circles, particularly where shared common challenges have been faced (e.g. persecution, unfair treatment). Thus, the role of ethnic networks may not only pertain to the initial internationalisation of a migrant family firm but also to its continuity in an uncertain context. Institutional uncertainty may prompt migrant families to deliberately nurture relationships in diverse networks to safeguard their internationalisation efforts. Such an approach enhances our understanding of the role of ethnic networks for migrant family firms.

Limitations and Further Research

This study has a few caveats, and so its findings must be interpreted with caution. First, this is a single case study; the sampling logic would have been stronger if a broader sample of cases from developing countries with significant levels of coffee production and migrant families had been included, such as Honduras, Brazil, Mexico and Colombia. Second, research on migrant family firms in other industries or across industries in different countries (e.g. see Fernández Pérez & Lluch, 2016), where unique narratives by descendants of migrant families can be examined in relation to a place, should be conducted (see Spielmann, Discua Cruz, Tyler, & Beukel, 2019). Further research on migrant families in business can be extended to different levels and units of analysis (Discua Cruz & Basco, 2018) and contexts that are affected by changing conditions (e.g. see Estrada-Robles, Williams, & Vorley, 2018). Contexts where migrant or mixed nationality families cater for international markets (e.g. see Arias & Discua Cruz, 2018) offer an interesting milieu to investigate. Future studies that follow up on the findings in this chapter will enhance understanding about the relational resources that migrant families leverage to internationalise their firms.

References

Acs, Z., & Amorós, J. (2008). Entrepreneurship and competitiveness dynamics in Latin America. *Small Business Economics, 31*(3), 305–322. https://doi.org/10.1007/s11187-008-9133-y

Adler, P. S., & Kwon, S.-W. (2002). Social Capital: Prospects for a new concept. *Academy of Management Review, 27*(1), 17–40.

Aldrich, H. E., & Waldinger, R. (1990). Ethnicity and Entrepreneurship. *Annual Review of Sociology, 16*(1), 111–135. https://doi.org/10.1146/annurev.so.16.080190.000551.

Alsos, G. A., Ljunggren, E., & Pettersen, L. T. (2003). Farm-based entrepreneurs: What triggers the start-up of new business activities? *Journal of Small Business and Enterprise Development, 10*(4), 435–443.

Alvesson, M., & Skoldberg, K. (2000). *Reflexive methodology: New vistas for qualitative research*. London: Sage.

Anderson, A. R., Jack, S. L., & Drakopoulou Dodd, S. (2005). The role of family members in entrepreneurial networks: Beyond the boundaries of the family firm. *Family Business Review, 18*(2), 135–154. https://doi.org/10.1111/j.1741-6248.2005.00037.x

Anderson, A. R., & Miller, C. J. (2003). "Class matters": Human and social capital in the entrepreneurial process. *The Journal of Socio-Economics, 32*(1), 17–36. https://doi.org/10.1016/S1053-5357(03)00009-X

Andersson, M., Larsson, J. P., & Öner, Ö. (2017). *Ethnic enclaves and immigrant self-employment: A neighborhood analysis of enclave size and quality* (Working Paper No. 1195). Retrieved from IFN Working Paper website https://www.econstor.eu/handle/10419/183424

Anderson, A., Park, J., & Jack, S. L. (2007). Entrepreneurial Social Capital: Conceptualizing Social Capital in New High-tech Firms. *International Small Business Journal, 25*(3), 245–272. https://doi.org/10.1177/0266242607076526.

Arias, R. A. C., & Discua Cruz, A. (2018). Rethinking artisan entrepreneurship in a small island: A tale of two chocolatiers in Roatan, Honduras. *International Journal of Entrepreneurial Behavior & Research, 25*(4), 633–651. https://doi.org/10.1108/IJEBR-02-2018-0111

Bacon, C. M. (2008). *Confronting the coffee crisis: Fair trade, sustainable livelihoods and ecosystems in Mexico and Central America*. MIT Press.

Bagwell, S. (2008). Transnational family networks and ethnic minority business development: The case of Vietnamese nail-shops in the UK. International Journal of Entrepreneurial Behaviour & Research, 14(6), 377–394. https://doi.org/10.1108/13552550810910960.

Bro, A. S., Clay, D. C., Ortega, D. L., & Lopez, M. C. (2019). Determinants of adoption of sustainable production practices among smallholder coffee producers in Nicaragua. *Environment, Development and Sustainability, 21*(2), 895–915. https://doi.org/10.1007/s10668-017-0066-y

Brzozowski, J., Cucculelli, M., & Surdej, A. (2017). The determinants of transnational entrepreneurship and transnational ties' dynamics among immigrant entrepreneurs in ICT sector in Italy. *International Migration, 55*(3), 105–125. https://doi.org/10.1111/imig.12335

Bubolz, M. M. (2001). Family as source, user, and builder of social capital. *The Journal of Socio-Economics, 30*(2), 129–131. https://doi.org/10.1016/S1053-5357(00)00091-3

14 Internationalisation of a Migrant Family Firm and Contextual...   455

Colburn, F. D. (2012). Nicaragua, Forlorn. *World Policy Journal, 29*(1), 91–100.

Collins, J., & Low, A. (2010). Asian female immigrant entrepreneurs in small and medium-sized businesses in Australia. *Entrepreneurship and Regional Development, 22*(1), 97–111. https://doi.org/10.1080/08985620903220553

Cope, J., & Watts, G. (2000). Learning by doing—An exploration of experience, critical incidents and reflection in entrepreneurial learning. *International Journal of Entrepreneurial Behaviour & Research, 6*(3), 104–124.

Danes, S. M., Lee, J., Amarapurkar, S., Stafford, K., Haynes, G., & Brewton, K. E. (2009). Determinants of family business resilience after a natural disaster by gender of business owner. *Journal of Developmental Entrepreneurship, 14*(4), 333.

Danes, S. M., Rueter, M. A., Kwon, H.-K., & Doherty, W. (2002). Family FIRO model: An application to family business. *Family Business Review, 15*(1), 31–44.

Davidsson, P., & Honig, B. (2003). The role of social and human capital among nascent entrepreneurs. *Journal of Business Venturing, 18*(3), 301–331.

Deakins, D., Ishaq, M., Smallbone, D., Whittam, G., & Wyper, J. (2007). Ethnic minority businesses in Scotland and the role of social capital. *International Small Business Journal, 25*(3), 307–326. https://doi.org/10.1177/0266242607076530

Discua Cruz, A. (2015). Rethinking family businesses through a Christian perspective. *Faith in Business Quarterly, 17*(1), 23–30.

Discua Cruz, A., & Basco, R. (2018). Family perspective on entrepreneurship. In R. V. Turcan & N. M. Fraser (Eds.), *The Palgrave handbook of multidisciplinary perspectives on entrepreneurship* (pp. 147–175). Palgrave Macmillan. https://doi.org/10.1007/978-3-319-91611-8_8

Discua Cruz, A., Basco, R., Parada, M. J., Malfense Fierro, A. C., & Alvarado Alvarez, C. (2019). Resilience and family business groups in unstable economies. In M. Rautianinen, P. Rosa, T. Pihkala, M. J. Parada, & A. Discua Cruz (Eds.), *The family business group phenomenon—Emergence and complexities* (pp. 315–352). Cham: Palgrave Macmillan.

Discua Cruz, A., Centeno Caffarena, L., & Vega Solano, M. (2020). Being different matters! A closer look into product differentiation in specialty coffee family farms in Central America. *Cross Cultural & Strategic Management*, ahead-of-print. https://doi.org/10.1108/CCSM-01-2019-0004

Discua Cruz, A., Howorth, C., & Hamilton, E. (2013). Intrafamily entrepreneurship: The formation and membership of family entrepreneurial teams. *Entrepreneurship Theory and Practice, 37*(1), 17–46. https://doi.org/10.1111/j.1540-6520.2012.00534.x

Discua Cruz, A., Ramos Rodas, C., Raudales, C., & Fortin, L. (2016). Large family businesses in Honduras: The influence of state intervention and immigration in the twentieth century. In *Evolution of family businesses: Continuity and change in Latin America and Spain*. Edward Elgar Publishing.

Duarte, L. E. (2009). Los Nazis y Nicaragua. *La Prensa*. Retrieved November 13, 2019, from www.laprensa.com.ni/magazine/reportaje/los-nazis-y-nicaragua

Elo, M., & Dana, L.-P. (2019). Embeddedness and entrepreneurial traditions: Entrepreneurship of Bukharian Jews in diaspora. *Journal of Family Business Management,* ahead-of-print(ahead-of-print). https://doi.org/10.1108/JFBM-03-2019-0016.

Elo, M., & Minto-Coy, I. (Eds.). (2019). *Diaspora networks in international business: Perspectives for understanding and managing diaspora business and resources.* Retrieved from www.springer.com/us/book/9783319910949

Elo, M., Sandberg, S., Servais, P., Basco, R., Discua Cruz, A., Riddle, L., et al. (2018). Advancing the views on migrant and diaspora entrepreneurs in international entrepreneurship. *Journal of International Entrepreneurship, 16*(2), 119–133. https://doi.org/10.1007/s10843-018-0231-x

Elo, M., Servais, P., Sandberg, S., Discua Cruz, A., & Basco, R. (2019). Entrepreneurship, Migration, and Family in Peripheral Contexts – Avenues for Growth and Internationalisation. *International Journal of Entrepreneurship and Small Business, 36*(1/2), 1–15. https://doi.org/10.1504/IJESB.2019.096973.

Ensign, P. C., & Robinson, N. P. (2011). Entrepreneurs because they are immigrants or immigrants because they are entrepreneurs? A critical examination of the relationship between the newcomers and the establishment. *Journal of Entrepreneurship, 20*(1), 33–53. https://doi.org/10.1177/097135571002000102

Estrada-Robles, M., Williams, N., & Vorley, T. (2018). Navigating institutional challenges in Mexico. *International Journal of Entrepreneurial Behavior & Research.* https://doi.org/10.1108/IJEBR-05-2017-0180

Estrin, S., Mickiewicz, T., & Stephan, U. (2013). Entrepreneurship, Social Capital, and Institutions: Social and Commercial Entrepreneurship Across Nations. *Entrepreneurship Theory and Practice, 37*(3), 479–504. https://doi.org/10.1111/etap.12019.

Fernández Pérez, P., & Lluch, A. (2016). *Evolution of family business: Continuity and change in Latin America and Spain.* Cheltenham: Edward Elgar Publishing.

Gibbert, M., & Ruigrok, W. (2010). The "what" and "how" of case study rigor: Three strategies based on published work. *Organizational Research Methods, 13*(4), 710–737. https://doi.org/10.1177/1094428109351319

Granovetter, M. (1973). The strength of weak ties. *American Journal of Sociology, 78*(6), 1360–1380.

Grbich, C. (2007). *Qualitative data analysis: An introduction.* London: Sage.

Hamilton, E., Discua Cruz, A., & Jack, S. (2017). Re-framing the status of narrative in family business research: Towards an understanding of families in business. *Journal of Family Business Strategy, 8*(1), 3–12. https://doi.org/10.1016/j.jfbs.2016.11.001

Hearst, L. (1932). Coffee industry of Central America. *Economic Geography, 8*(1), 53–66. https://doi.org/10.2307/140470

Hofstede, G. (2001). *Culture's consequences, comparing values, behaviors, institutions, and organizations across nations.* Thousand Oaks, CA: Sage Publications.

14 Internationalisation of a Migrant Family Firm and Contextual... 457

Howorth, C., Rose, M., Hamilton, E., & Westhead, P. (2010). Family firm diversity and development: An introduction. *International Small Business Journal, 28*(5), 437–451. https://doi.org/10.1177/0266242610373685

ICO. (2013). ICO Annual review 2012/13. Retrieved from http://www.ico.org/news/annual-review-2012-13-e.pdf

Jack, S., Moult, S., Anderson, A. R., & Dodd, S. (2010). An entrepreneurial network evolving: Patterns of change. *International Small Business Journal, 28*(4), 315–337. https://doi.org/10.1177/0266242610363525

Jolliffe, L. (2010). *Coffee culture, destinations and tourism*. Channel View Publications.

Jones, V. (2004). The rhythms of Latin America: A context and guide for qualitative research. In R. Marschan-Piekkari & C. Welch (Eds.), *Handbook of qualitative research methods for international business* (pp. 439–457). Cheltenham: Edward Elgar.

Katila, S., & Wahlbeck, Ö. (2012). The role of (transnational) social capital in the start-up processes of immigrant businesses: The case of Chinese and Turkish restaurant businesses in Finland. *International Small Business Journal, 30*(3), 294–309. https://doi.org/10.1177/0266242610383789

Khül, E. (2014). *Primeros Inmigrantes a Nicaragua por Origen*. Revista de Temas Nicaraguenses, No. 77, ISSN: 2164-4268, September, pp. 228–258.

Kilian, B., Jones, C., Pratt, L., & Villalobos, A. (2006). Is sustainable agriculture a viable strategy to improve farm income in Central America? A case study on coffee. *Journal of Business Research, 59*(3), 322–330. https://doi.org/10.1016/j.jbusres.2005.09.015

Kontinen, T., & Ojala, A. (2011a). Social capital in relation to the foreign market entry and post-entry operations of family SMEs. *Journal of International Entrepreneurship, 9*(2), 133–151. https://doi.org/10.1007/s10843-010-0072-8

Kontinen, T., & Ojala, A. (2011b). International opportunity recognition among small and medium-sized family firms. *Journal of Small Business Management, 49*(3), 490–514. https://doi.org/10.1111/j.1540-627X.2011.00326.x

Kwon, S.-W., & Adler, P. S. (2014). Social Capital: Maturation of a Field of Research. *Academy of Management Review, 39*(4), 412–422. https://doi.org/10.5465/amr.2014.0210.

La Gaceta. (1848). Leon, Nicaragua. September 23.

Lajqi, S., & Krasniqi, B. A. (2017). Entrepreneurial growth aspirations in challenging environment: The role of institutional quality, human and social capital. *Strategic Change, 26*(4), 385–401.

Lara Estrada, L., Rasche, L., & Schneider, U. A. (2017). Modeling land suitability for Coffea arabica L. in Central America. *Environmental Modelling & Software, 95*, 196–209. https://doi.org/10.1016/j.envsoft.2017.06.028

Larson, J. M., & Lewis, J. I. (2017). Ethnic networks. *American Journal of Political Science, 61*(2), 350–364. https://doi.org/10.1111/ajps.12282

Leogrande, W. M. (1996). Making the economy scream: US economic sanctions against Sandinista Nicaragua. *Third World Quarterly, 17*(2), 329–348. https://doi.org/10.1080/01436599650035716

Leppäaho, T., Plakoyiannaki, E., & Dimitratos, P. (2016). The case study in family business: An analysis of current research practices and recommendations. *Family Business Review, 29*(2), 159–173. https://doi.org/10.1177/0894486515614157

Levy, P. (1873). *Notas geográficas y económicas sobre la República de Nicaragua.* Paris: Librería E. Denne Schmitz.

Light, I., & Dana, L.-P. (2013). Boundaries of social capital in entrepreneurship. *Entrepreneurship Theory and Practice, 37*(3), 603–624. https://doi.org/10.1111/etap.12016

Luk, C. L., Yau, O. H., Sin, L. Y., Alan, C. B., Chow, R. P., & Lee, J. S. (2008). The effects of social capital and organizational innovativeness in different institutional contexts. *Journal of International Business Studies, 39*(4), 589–612.

Lynch, J., Mason, R. J., Beresford, A. K. C., & Found, P. A. (2012). An examination of the role for business orientation in an uncertain business environment. *International Journal of Production Economics, 137*(1), 145–156. https://doi.org/10.1016/j.ijpe.2011.11.004

Merrill, T. (1994). *Nicaragua: A country study* (3rd ed.). Federal Research Division, Library of Congress.

Miles, M. B., Huberman, A. M., & Saldana, J. (2013). *Qualitative data analysis: A methods sourcebook* (3rd ed.). Thousand Oaks, CA: SAGE Publications, Inc.

Müller, C., Botero, I. C., Discua Cruz, A., & Subramanian, R. (2019). *Family firms in Latin America.* New York: Routledge.

Mustafa, M., & Chen, S. (2010). The strength of family networks in transnational immigrant entrepreneurship. *Thunderbird International Business Review, 52*(2), 97–106. https://doi.org/10.1002/tie.20317

Nahapiet, J., & Ghoshal, S. (1998). Social capital, intellectual capital, and the organizational advantage. *The Academy of Management Review, 23*(2), 242–266.

Neergaard, H., & Leitch, C. M. (2015). *Handbook of qualitative research techniques and analysis in entrepreneurship.* Edward Elgar Publishing.

Niederhauser, N., Oberthür, T., Kattnig, S., & Cock, J. (2008). Information and its management for differentiation of agricultural products: The example of specialty coffee. *Computers and Electronics in Agriculture, 61*(2), 241–253. https://doi.org/10.1016/j.compag.2007.12.001

Oviatt, B. M., & McDougall, P. P. (2005). Defining international entrepreneurship and modeling the speed of internationalization. *Entrepreneurship Theory and Practice, 29*(5), 537–553.

Paz Cafferata, J., & Pomareda, C. (2009). *Indicaciones geográficas y denominaciones de origen en centroamérica: Situación y perspectivas.* Retrieved from International Centre for Trade and Sustainable Development (ICTSD) website https://www.ictsd.org/sites/default/files/research/2012/02/indicaciones-geograficas-y-denominaciones-de-origen-en-centroamerica.pdf

Poulis, K., Poulis, E., & Plakoyiannaki, E. (2013). The role of context in case study selection: An international business perspective. *International Business Review, 22*(1), 304–314. https://doi.org/10.1016/j.ibusrev.2012.04.003

14 Internationalisation of a Migrant Family Firm and Contextual... 459

Pratt, M. G. (2009). For the lack of a boilerplate: Tips on writing up (and reviewing) qualitative research. *Academy of Management Journal, 52*(5), 856–862.

Rauch, J. E. (2001). Business and social networks in international trade. *Journal of Economic Literature, 39*(4), 1177–1203.

Roberts, O. W. (1827). Narrative of voyages and excursions on the East Coast and the interior of Central America, Edinburgh, London.

Roche, M. (2006). Competing claims: The struggle for title in Nicaragua note. *Vanderbilt Journal of Transnational Law, 39*(2), 577–606.

Rodgers, P., Vershinina, N., Williams, C. C., & Theodorakopoulos, N. (2019). Leveraging symbolic capital: The use of blat networks across transnational spaces. *Global Networks, 19*(1), 119–136. https://doi.org/10.1111/glob.12188.

Ronga, D., Pane, C., Zaccardelli, M., & Pecchioni, N. (2016). Use of spent coffee ground compost in peat-based growing media for the production of basil and tomato potting plants. *Communications in Soil Science and Plant Analysis, 47*(3), 356–368. https://doi.org/10.1080/00103624.2015.1122803

Roscoe, P., Discua Cruz, A., & Howorth, C. (2013). How does an old firm learn new tricks? A material account of entrepreneurial opportunity. *Business History, 55*(1), 53–72. https://doi.org/10.1080/00076791.2012.687540

Rueda, X., & Lambin, E. F. (2013). Linking globalization to local land uses: How eco-consumers and gourmands are changing the Colombian coffee landscapes. *World Development, 41*, 286–301. https://doi.org/10.1016/j.worlddev.2012.05.018

Salcedo, S., Campos, A., & Guzman, L. (2014). El concepto de agricultura familiar en América Latina y el Caribe. In S. Salcedo & L. Guzman (Eds.), *Agricultura Familiar en América Latina y el Caribe: Recomendaciones de Política*. Chile: FAO.

Sirmon, D. G., & Hitt, M. A. (2003). Managing resources: Linking unique resources, management, and wealth creation in family firms. *Entrepreneurship Theory and Practice, 27*(4), 339–358. https://doi.org/10.1111/1540-8520.t01-1-00013

Soetanto, D. (2017). Networks and entrepreneurial learning: Coping with difficulties. *International Journal of Entrepreneurial Behavior & Research, 23*(3), 547–565. https://doi.org/10.1108/IJEBR-11-2015-0230

Spielmann, N., Discua Cruz, A., Tyler, B. B., & Beukel, K. (2019). Place as a nexus for corporate heritage identity: An international study of family-owned wineries. *Journal of Business Research*. https://doi.org/10.1016/j.jbusres.2019.05.024

Stam, W., & Elfring, T. (2008). Entrepreneurial Orientation and New Venture Performance: The Moderating Role of Intra- And Extraindustry Social Capital. *Academy of Management Journal, 51*(1), 97–111. https://doi.org/10.5465/amj.2008.30744031.

Stark, C. (2000). *Families today: Informing the family debate*. London: Family Policy Studies Centre.

Strachan, H. (1976). *Family and other business groups in economic development: The case of Nicaragua*. Praeger.

Tijerino, T. (1964). *Reminiscencias Históricas*. Nicaragua, Revista Conservadora, No. 40. Enero.

Tyroler, D. (1991). Nicaragua: Recent debate surrounding property confiscated by Sandinista Government, pp. 1–2. Retrieved from https://Digitalrepository.Unm.Edu/Noticen/5557

Uzzi, B. (1997). Social structure and competition in inter-firm networks: The paradox of embeddedness. *Administrative Science Quarterly, 42*, 35–67.

Vershinina, N., Barrett, R., & Meyer, M. (2011). Forms of capital, intra-ethnic variation and Polish entrepreneurs in Leicester. *Work, Employment and Society, 25*(1), 101–117. https://doi.org/10.1177/0950017010389241

Vertovec, S. (2001). Transnationalism and identity. *Journal of Ethnic and Migration Studies, 27*(4), 573–582. https://doi.org/10.1080/13691830120090386.

Von Houwald, G. (1975). *Los Alemanes en Nicaragua.* Serie Histórica No. 2, Colección Cultural, Banco de América, Nicaragua.

Wilson, B. R. (2010). Indebted to fair trade? Coffee and crisis in Nicaragua. *Geoforum, 41*(1), 84–92. https://doi.org/10.1016/j.geoforum.2009.06.008

Wilson, L.-A. (2007). The family farm business? Insights into family, business and ownership dimensions of open-farms. *Leisure Studies, 26*(3), 357–374. https://doi.org/10.1080/02614360600661120

Wilson, O. (1994). "They changed the rules": Farm family responses to agricultural deregulation in Southland, New Zealand. *New Zealand Geographer, 50*(1), 3–13. https://doi.org/10.1111/j.1745-7939.1994.tb00395.x

World Bank. (2017). Nicaragua data can be accessed through https://data.worldbank.org/ (Last accessed December 2018).

Wright, M., Chrisman, J. J., Chua, J. H., & Steier, L. P. (2014). Family enterprise and context. *Entrepreneurship Theory and Practice, 38*(6), 1247–1260. https://doi.org/10.1111/etap.12122

Yinger, J. M. (1985). Ethnicity. *Annual Review of Sociology, 11*, 151–180.

15

Internationalization of Small Indian Family-Firms: An Emergent Theory

Tulsi Jayakumar

Introduction

Small family-firm[1] (FF) internationalization in large, fast-growing emerging economies (EES) presents interesting paradoxes, especially in the face of growing global protectionism and adverse geopolitical factors. With its attractive fastest growing economy status (IMF, 2019), third largest number of family run businesses in the world (Credit Suisse, 2018) and the significant contribution of such family businesses—most of which are small firms—to India's Gross Domestic Product, manufacturing output, exports and employment (https://evoma.com/business-centre/sme-sector-in-india-statistics-trends-reports/; Reserve Bank of India, 2019a), India emerges as a front-runner as a potential source for gaining insights into such paradoxical internationalization of small FFs in the emerging world.

Extant research on internationalization of small FFs is still nascent and scanty, restricted mainly to firms from developed economies. Small FFs from large, fast-growing emerging economies (FGEEs) such as China and India are under-represented in such studies. We found no studies addressing small

---

[1] We use the term 'small' in a generic sense to mean the small and medium enterprises (SMEs) throughout the chapter, although some of the case firms considered were 'micro enterprises' at the time of internationalization.

T. Jayakumar (✉)
S.P. Jain Institute of Management and Research, Mumbai, India
e-mail: tulsi.jayakumar@spjimr.org

© The Author(s), under exclusive license to Springer Nature Switzerland AG 2021
T. Leppäaho, S. Jack (eds.), *The Palgrave Handbook of Family Firm Internationalization*,
https://doi.org/10.1007/978-3-030-66737-5_15

461

family-firm internationalization in the Indian context. This is an important gap area, given that such firms contribute close to 50 per cent of India's exports and to India's status both as an exporting nation and as an important host as well as home nation to global foreign direct investment (UNCTAD, 2019). Studies on Indian family-firm internationalization dwell mostly on large, listed, Indian family businesses (Chitoor, Aulakh, & Ray, 2019; Ray, Mondal, & Ramachandran, 2018; Shanmugasundaram, 2019; Shukla & Akbar, 2018; Singh & Kota, 2017). This gap in the literature, together with the paradox of context, inspired us to explore the internationalization decisions of small FFs in India, a fast-growing emerging economy. Following Metsola, Leppäaho, Paavilainen-Mäntymäki and Plakoyiannaki (2020), our approach was to focus not just on the antecedents and outcomes of the phenomenon of internationalization—what is referred to as a *variance theorizing approach*—but also on the *process* of internationalization.

Our research questions were as follows:

(a) What are the internationalization pathways followed by small Indian family-firms?
(b) What prompts small Indian FFs, faced with lucrative domestic opportunities of high consumption-driven gross domestic product (GDP) growth rates amidst global challenges posed by protectionist policies and adverse geopolitical factors, to internationalize?

Our study suggests that a mix of environmental factors (both state and change variables) within the home and host countries, together with family factors, impacts the ability and willingness of small FFs to internationalize. These, in turn, affect the three key dimensions of the internationalization process corresponding to the pre-entry, entry and post-entry stages. The contribution of this study is an integrated model of small FF internationalization in fast-growing EEs incorporating two additional classifications of internationalization pathways to those available in extant theoretical models (Bell, McNaughton, Young, & Crick, 2003). We term these new pathways 'cohesive' pathways and 'de-internationalization' pathways. Further, the processual approach adopted in this study, in line with Metsola et al. (2020), helps us in better envisioning the future of internationalization of small FFs in emerging economies (EEs), even as environmental contexts in home and host countries change.

This chapter is organized as follows. A review of extant literature points to a gap in the research, and we present and discuss an integrative model of small FF internationalization in emerging economy contexts. The research methodology section is followed by a section on the findings of the study. The study then discusses the findings in light of the integrative model of small FF internationalization in fast-growing emerging economies. The limitations of the study and ideas for future research constitute the final section.

Review and Synthesis of Literature

Internationalization Literature in Perspective: Three-Circle Framework

Extant literature of internationalizing firms reveals a taxonomy based on three criteria and the combinations thereof: (a) origin of the firm—developed versus emerging economy firms; (b) size of the firm—large corporates/multinational enterprises (MNEs) versus small and medium enterprises (SMEs); and (c) form of business organization—family-firms versus non-family-firms. Such a three-circle framework helps us to place extant internationalization literature in perspective and uncover potential research gaps. Using this framework, we find that most extant studies either cover aspects of developed economy, small FF internationalization or emerging economy MNE internationalization, leaving a large gap at the cusp of the three-circle classification. This cusp—encompassing aspects of origin, size and organizational structure—comprises small FFs from emerging economies like India (Fig. 15.1).

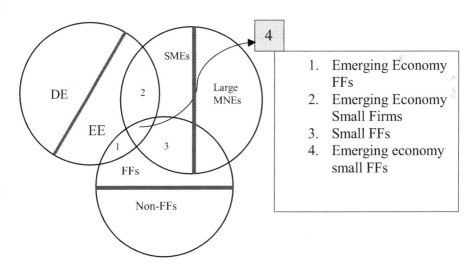

Fig. 15.1 Three-circle framework of internationalization literature: finding a research gap. (Source: Author)

Internationalization of Small Family-Firms (FFs)

Extant studies spanning about three decades integrate aspects of family-firm literature with existing theoretical frameworks to explain internationalization of small FFs as illustrated in Table 15.1. The individual/family features considered by these studies include entrepreneurial orientation (EO) (Alayo, Maseda, Iturralde, & Arzubiaga, 2019; Calabrò, Brogi, & Torchia, 2016), psychic distance (Baronchelli, Bettinelli, Del Bosco, & Loane, 2016; Kontinen & Ojala, 2010), socio-emotional wealth (SEW) (Hernández-Perlines, Ariza-Montes, & Araya-Castillo, 2019; Scholes, Mustafa, & Chen, 2016; Yang, Li, Stanley, Kellermanns, & Li, 2018), family ownership and involvement/familiness (Cerrato & Piva, 2012; Crick, Bradshaw, & Chaudhry, 2006; Fernández & Nieto, 2005; Graves & Thomas, 2008; Merino, Monreal-Pérez, & Sánchez-Marin, 2015), bifurcation bias (Majocchi, D'Angelo, Forlani, & Buck, 2018), network ties (Leppäaho & Metsola, 2020) and social capital (D'Angelo, Majocchi, & Buck, 2016; Kontinen & Ojala, 2011; Tasavori, Zaefarian, & Eng, 2018). Based on the internationalization experience of developed economies' small FFs, these studies focus largely on the mode of entry and country selection during the internationalization process using variants of the Uppsala model (Johanson & Vahlne, 1977; Johanson & Wiedersheim-Paul, 1975). FFs are seen as following traditional internationalization pathways comprising exports, into markets with low geographic and psychic distance, followed by incremental expansion into more remote markets as knowledge and resources expand (Pukall & Calabrò, 2014). Bell et al.'s (2003) 'integrative' model of small firm internationalization, with its two additional internationalization pathways, has provided a useful reference point to several studies, such as Leppäaho & Metsola, 2020; Metsola et al., 2020, who have bridged an important gap in this model by further integrating family features into small firm internationalization. Most studies seek to explain intra- and inter-firm heterogeneity of internationalization experience among family and non-FFs on the basis of 'family influence'.

Welch and Paavilainen-Mäntymäki (2014) and recently Metsola et al. (2020) have called for a processual approach to the study of family-firm internationalization. In their review of the studies on family-firm internationalization, Metsola et al. (2020, p. 2) point to the variance-theorizing approach of most of these studies and the need for conceptualizing internationalization as a process, '*occurring within different time periods, typically encompassing international evolution, episodes and epochs*'. Their *internationalization process model* integrates process-based internationalization pathways with variance-based

15 Internationalization of Small Indian Family-Firms: An Emergent... 465

Table 15.1 Studies on internationalization of small family-firms

S.No	Author (year)	Focus	Nature of the study	Theoretical framework	Relevant findings
1	Alayo, Maseda, Iturralde, and Arzubiaga (2019)	Spanish small FFs	Quantitative:191 firms	Entrepreneurial Orientation	Entrepreneurial orientation (EO) explains the degree of internationalization in FFs. Diversity in the top management team (TMT) with presence of non-family managers promotes internationalization, while involvement of multiple generations hampers it.
2	Baronchelli, Bettinelli, Del Bosco, and Loane (2016)	Small and medium FFs—Italy	Quantitative-122 manufacturing companies	Psychic distance & family involvement	Higher family involvement is associated with lower number of foreign direct investments in psychically distant countries
4	Calabrò, Brogi, and Torchia (2016)	SME FFs—Italy	Case study approach: 4 firms	International entrepreneurship literature and stewardship theory Resource-based view	Involvement of new generations with altruism and competence-based trust positively affects internationalization decisions
5	Calabrò, Mussolino, and Huse (2009)	SME FFs—Norway	Quantitative-146 Norwegian family businesses		Higher levels of non-family board members in FFs improve internationalization.
6	Cerrato and Piva (2012)	SME FFs—Italy	Quantitative-1324 Italian manufacturing firms	Family involvement, foreign shareholders and human capital	Family involvement in management negatively influences export propensity, but once the choice to go international has been made, family-managed firms are no different from non-family-managed firms.
7	Chen, Hsu, and Chang (2014)	SME FFs—Taiwan	Quantitative	Agency theory & resource-based view	Family ownership encourages internationalization, especially when combined with institutional ownership.

(continued)

Table 15.1 (continued)

S.No	Author (year)	Focus	Nature of the study	Theoretical framework	Relevant findings
8	Crick, Bradshaw, and Chaudhry (2006)	SME FFs—UK	Postal survey followed by interviews	Family ownership	High-performing family and non-family-owned SMEs are similar in respect of measures and sources of performance.
9	D'Angelo, Majocchi, and Buck (2016)	SME FFs—Italy	Quantitative: 417 Italian manufacturing firms	Theories of corporate governance and social capital	Externally hired professional managers can only fully exert their potential if coupled with external ownership, allowing bridging and bonding social capital to emerge with the alignment of the positive effects of agency, stewardship and SEW processes.
11	Fernández and Nieto (2005).	Family SMEs—Spain	Quantitative	Family ownership	Negative relationship between family ownership and internationalization, measured by export activities
12	Graves and Thomas (2008)	Family SMEs—Australia	Case study-eight firms	Stage theory; family influence	Three key determinants of the internationalization pathways of FFs are the level of commitment towards internationalization, the financial resources available and the ability to commit and use those financial resources to develop the required capabilities. Also explore how the family unit influences these determinants.
13	Hernández-Perlines, Ariza-Montes, and Araya-Castillo, L. (2019)	Family enterprises—Spain	Quantitative-106 FFs listed in the Spanish Family-firm Institute	Socio-emotional wealth	The inclusion of SEW improves the capacity of EO to explain variations in international performance

14	Kontinen and Ojala (2010)	Finnish family SMEs operating in France	Case study approach: 4 firms	Uppsala model and distance-creating and distance-bridging factors	Family SMEs followed a sequential process and favoured indirect entry modes before entering the psychically distant French market.
15	Kontinen and Ojala (2011)	Eight family SME firms operating in the French market	Case study-eight firms	Social capital theory	Internationalization requires FFs to find the networks to gain bridging social capital that will enable foreign operations, in addition to their strong bonding social capital and strong national social capital.
16	Leppäaho and Metsola (2020)	Family SMEs—Finland	Case study—24 firms	Network relationships	Identify two major international networking strategies—narrow network maximizers (NNMs) and broad network enablers (BNEs).
17	Majocchi, D'Angelo, Forlani, and Buck (2018)	Family SMEs-Europe	Quantitative-6893 firms	Bifurcation bias	Exporting is positively associated with the presence of outside owners and managers and from the interaction between them. International work experience of family managers has a positive impact on exporting.
18	Merino, Monreal-Pérez, and Sánchez-Marin (2015)	Family SMEs—Spain	Quantitative-500 firms	Familiness	Family experience and its culture orientation positively affect the firm's export activity, whereas family governance/management does not have any significant influence.

(continued)

Table 15.1 (continued)

S.No	Author (year)	Focus	Nature of the study	Theoretical framework	Relevant findings
19	Scholes, Mustafa, and Chen (2016)	Family SME—Singapore	Qualitative: six small FFs	Socio-emotional wealth	Family harmony, trust in external relationships, social and business networks and organizational resources and capabilities are important in the internationalization process
20	Tasavori, Zaefarian, and Eng (2018)	SME FFs—Turkey	Quantitative-192 firms	Internal social capital	FFs can improve their international firm performance by utilizing the internal social capital of family relationship, which is further mediated by participative governance capability
21	Yang, Li, Stanley, Kellermanns, and Li (2018)	Family SMEs—China	Quantitative-1542 firms	Socio-emotional wealth	Family ownership negatively affects international expansion. Family-firm characteristics (i.e. presence of founder CEOs and family succession intention) strengthen this negative relationship.

capabilities or liabilities that drive/restrain internationalization over time. It, however, concedes the need for further research to incorporate contextual aspects for a better understanding of FF internationalization as also '*a need for more studies linking the different internationalisation pathways, capabilities, and liabilities to an integrative reference point covering both the economic and non-economic goals of FB internationalisation*' to understand heterogeneity among family-firms. Our research seeks to address this call for studies on small family-firms from diverse contexts integrating multiple family goals.

Emerging Economy Firms and Internationalization

Emerging economies provide different contextual scenarios as compared to developed economies. As such, another strand of literature compares EE firms to their developed economy peers and finds distinct motivations, paths, processes and performances between them, justifying the attempt to build new theories for EE firm internationalization.[2] Extant literature in the field traces the motivations of EE firms for internationalization to their economic goals, including the need to gain scale, to acquire legitimacy by supplying in developed markets and overcoming negative country-of-origin labels, to overcome a mismatch between firm capabilities and home institutional environments, risk-diversification, to get first-mover advantage by investing in institutionally unattractive locations and reaping higher rewards in these high-risk locations and presence of ethnically similar customers and competitors (Gaur & Kumar, 2010). Such motivations are linked to home-country 'push' and host-country 'pull' factors.

The internationalization paths followed by such EE firms were historically treated as uni-directional—limited to geographically close and similarly developed emerging markets (Wells, 1977). However, increasing global integration has resulted in EE internationalization paths changing—directed towards developed markets which are geographically and psychically different. This is true for Indian internationalizing firms as well, especially since India's economic liberalization in 1991 (Gaur & Kumar, 2010; Narula & Dunning, 2000).

In fact, some studies attest to EE firms becoming important sources of foreign direct investment (FDI) through a process of 'accelerated internationalization' (Mathews, 2006; Shrader, Oviatt, & McDougall, 2000) driven by *linkage, leverage and learning* (LLL) strategies (Mathews, 2006).

---

[2] See Gaur and Kumar (2010, pp. 607–609), for a summary of such studies on emerging economy firm internationalization.

However, extant literature on internationalization of emerging economy firms largely examines multinational enterprises (or at best SMEs) rather than small, internationalizing family-firms. The latter's motivations, driven by the need to balance between economic and non-economic goals involving a 'mixed gamble' (Gomez-Mejia et al., 2014), differ—not just from the developed economy firms, but also compared to their non-family peers from their own economy contexts. The justification for the pathways chosen, based on such 'mixed gamble', may be different, and so might be the processes. As such, research areas in EE internationalization are far from exhausted, with size and organizational structure of internationalizing firms providing rich fodder for further research.

Internationalization of Small Indian FFs: The Paradox of Environmental Context

Contextually, within emerging economies, India holds a special significance as a potential research subject for studying small family-firm internationalization. First, India was the fastest growing economy in the world in 2019, along with China, to record the highest global growth rates at 6.1 per cent in 2019 (IMF, 2019). Such high growth rates were fuelled by very high domestic consumption of almost 57 per cent of nominal GDP (RBI, 2019b). Having opened up its economy to the rest of the world in 1991, it was also one of the top ten host recipients of foreign direct investment in the world in H1 2019, with a 20 per cent surge in FDI inflows (UNCTAD, 2019). It also had the third largest number of family-run businesses in the world (Credit Suisse, 2018). What would be the motivations for small family businesses to leave promising domestic markets in search of distant markets? Second, there has been a rise in protectionism globally. A Credit Suisse report of 2019 documents a significant rise in trade-distorting protectionist measures since the global financial crisis in 2009, with more than 1000 trade barriers introduced worldwide since 2009. The proportion of global exports affected by these measures has risen from 40 per cent to 70 per cent since 2009 (Hunziker & Gachet, 2019). Third, the contribution of the micro, small and medium enterprises (MSMEs) to the Indian economy is significant. These 63.38 million MSMEs, comprising mostly family-firms, constitute about 95 per cent of the industrial units in the country (https://evoma.com/business-centre/sme-sector-in-india-statistics-trends-reports/). They contribute one-third of the Indian manufacturing output (Sahoo & Bishnoi, 2019), 29 per cent of India's GDP and close to 50 per cent of India's overall exports (GOI, 2019). There would be policy implications associated with the success or failure of such internationalization for the country's economic growth. Fourth, such small family-firms are also the second largest employment providers in India, creating employment for about 111 million people (GOI, 2019). Decisions to internationalize and forms of internationalization would have ramifications for the country's employment as well.

Even as global protectionism grows (Canals, 2019; Hunziker & Gachet, 2019), adverse geopolitical conditions exacerbate the natural hazards associated with internationalization for small family-firms, which already face the burden of 'liability of foreignness' (Johanson & Vahlne, 2009), lack of legitimacy (Kostova & Zaheer, 1999) and lack of technology, marketing, capital and managerial resources (Wells, 1983). Internationalization of small family-firms from a fast-growing economy like India then presents a paradox worthy of research.

Gap in Research

The extant internationalization literature pertaining to small EE family-firms suffers from a serious gap in that these studies do not integrate the three dimensions, namely, emerging economy, small and family, and consider at best two of these dimensions. Thus, most studies fall either in Zone 2 (Fig. 15.1), studying EE small firms, or in Zone 3, studying small family-firms. Studies in the Indian context fall further short by looking at either small firms (SMEs) (without considering either the impact of their 'emerging' status or their 'familiness') or large business groups which have undertaken international expansion (Table 15.2). Clearly missing are studies to understand the motivations, paths, processes and performance of small Indian FFs undertaking internationalization in the face of global challenges amidst domestic opportunities. Further, in keeping with Metsola et al.'s (2020) classification, most of the extant Indian studies are cross-sectional, variance-theorizing approaches.

Given the context of fast-growing emerging economies like India, we need fresh theoretical frameworks following a processual approach to explain internationalization of small FFs originating in these countries. Such frameworks should adopt multidimensional perspectives in recognition of the fact that small FFs are nested within families, which themselves are nested within a specific institutional environment (Fig. 15.2). As such, we propose an integrated model of FGEE small family-firm internationalization incorporating family-level, organizational-level and environmental-level drivers and their

Table 15.2 Studies on internationalization of Indian family-firms

S. No.	Author (year)	Focus	Nature of the study	Relevant findings
1	Todd and Javalgi (2007)	SME—India	Conceptual	Technology is the primary method of growth of entrepreneurship for Indian SMEs to develop a competitive position in the international marketplace.
2	Javalgi and Todd (2011)	SME—India	Quantitative, 150 case firms	Entrepreneurial orientation, a commitment to internationalization and the ability to leverage human capital influence the international success of Indian SMEs.
3	Narasimhan, Ravi Kumar, and Sridhar (2015)	SMEs India	Qualitative, 3 case firms	Studies the dynamics of internal transformation during the internationalization process of technology-based SMEs. The domestication and initiation stages act as the antecedents of an effective internationalization process.
4	Ray, Mondal, and Ramachandran (2018)	Large Indian FFs	Quantitative (303 leading Indian FFs registered on the BSE 500 Index from 2007 to 2013)	FFs tend to be more averse to internationalization when family control over the firm's actions is greater due to higher family ownership or participation in management. However, greater foreign institutional partnership and presence of professional managers reduce the fear and aversion to internationalization.

(continued)

15 Internationalization of Small Indian Family-Firms: An Emergent... 473

Table 15.2 (continued)

S. No.	Author (year)	Focus	Nature of the study	Relevant findings
5	Chitoor, Aulakh, and Ray (2019)	Large Indian FFs	Quantitative (226 large owner-led (i.e. owner CEO) manufacturing firms registered on the BSE 500 Index from 2002 to 2011)	Owner CEOs, aided by their strategic leadership, long-term orientation and less-restricted decision-making powers, are more risky and exhibit higher internationalization.
6	Shukla and Akbar (2018)	Large business groups	Quantitative study involving 55 business groups	Business group networks arising from three different types of ties—director interlock, direct equity and indirect equity—act as conduits for diffusion of information and resources pertaining to internationalization.
7	Shanmugasundaram (2019)	Large business groups	Case study of 4 large business groups	Ownership concentration negatively influences internationalization, while transparency and professionalization have a positive association. Overall, good corporate governance practices have a positive influence on group internationalization.
8	Singh and Kota (2017)	Large Indian FFs	Quantitative (large firms registered on the BSE 500 Index between 2005 and 2015)	Family businesses, especially younger firms, are more innovative and internationalized compared to non-family businesses and older FFs.

(continued)

Table 15.2 (continued)

S. No.	Author (year)	Focus	Nature of the study	Relevant findings
9	Singh and Gaur (2013)	Indian listed firms	Quantitative (firms listed over the years 2001–2009)	Governance is a response to the prevailing institutional environment and affects the innovation and internationalization strategies of firms
10	Lodh, Nandy, and Chen (2014)	Large Indian FFs	Quantitative (395 Bombay Stock Exchange (BSE) listed Indian firms during the years 2001 and 2008)	Family ownership impacts innovation productivity positively. Affiliation with top business groups affects innovation activities of the FFs positively.

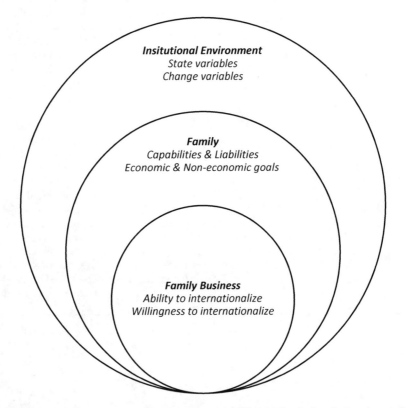

Fig. 15.2 Family-firm internationalization: Institutional-level, family-level and firm-level drivers. (Source: Author)

dynamic inter-relationships. In doing so, we draw on extant influential models (Bell et al., 2003; Johanson & Vahlne, 1977; Metsola et al., 2020) as reference points.

Integrated Model of Emerging Economy Small Family-Firm Internationalization

Our integrated model comprises of *state* and *change* variables (Johanson & Vahlne, 1977, 2009) in the environment, which interact dynamically with family factors comprising both *family characteristics/features* (*capabilities* and *liabilities*) and *family goals* (*economic* and *non-economic goals*) (Metsola et al., 2020). Family features and goals are interdependent, with each shaping the other. The environmental and family factors, in turn, impact the family-firm's *ability* and *willingness* to internationalize. Such ability and willingness impacts and influences the three key dimensions of internationalization: (a) the decision to internationalize and the resultant internationalization pathways, (b) internationalization strategies and (c) sustainability of internationalization (seen as the propensity to continued and intensified internationalization), corresponding to the pre-entry, entry and post-entry stages of internationalization. The model thus uses an *ability-willingness framework* to analyse internationalization decisions of these small FFs. Figure 15.3 presents this integrated model, with the key drivers, their dynamic inter-relationships and their impact on the three key dimensions of internationalization.

The Ability to Internationalize

We define ability to internationalize as the *power* to act/ execute the internationalization decision. The 'ability to internationalize' of small family firms, shaped by family features, depends on their *dynamic* capabilities and *liabilities*. Dynamic capabilities refer to the family-firm's ability to build and adapt internal and external competencies to rapidly changing environments, while liabilities arise due to high family involvement in ownership and management (Metsola et al., 2020, p. 6). These, in turn, are connected to (a) knowledge (Pukall & Calabrò, 2014), (b) the extent and nature of network relations and ties (Chen & Chen, 1998; Elango & Pattnaik, 2007; Kampouri, Plakoyiannaki, & Leppäaho, 2017), (c) the firm's internal human and financial resources and management competencies (Bell et al., 2003) and (d) presence and involvement of new generations and external non-family managers, with the latter affected by a bifurcation bias (D'Angelo et al., 2016; Kano & Verbeke, 2018).

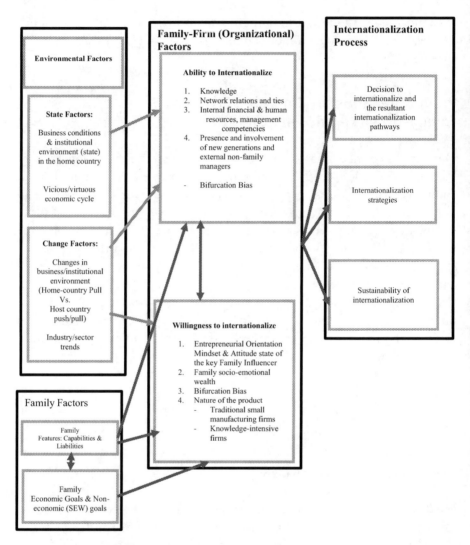

Fig. 15.3 An integrated model of fast-growing emerging economy small family-firm internationalization. (Source: Author)

Small FFs, especially at the onset of internationalization, need knowledge about foreign markets and the respective networks (Pukall & Calabrò, 2014), which may be provided by family managers with international work experience (Majocchi et al., 2018). Besides this, the family's network relations and ties provide the trust, comfort, valuable connections and access to scarce resources and, in a dynamic sense, may also help fill knowledge voids which FFs require for opportunity identification (Kampouri et al., 2017). Such network ties are typically characterized by high level of trust, closeness and long-term commitment (Arregle, Hitt, Sirmon, & Very, 2007; Zellweger, Chrisman, Chua, & Steier, 2019).

The family's internal resources and capabilities, including financial, human and managerial resources and competencies (Bell et al., 2003), affect the FF's ability to internationalize and thus its internationalization decisions. Such resources and capabilities can be impacted by the presence of a *bifurcation bias*—a family liability—which makes FFs treat family members and other 'heritage assets' preferentially as compared to professional, non-family managers and other non-heritage resources (Kano & Verbeke, 2018, p. 158). The bifurcation bias may limit the family-firm's ability to utilize 'non-heritage' domestic as well as new host market resources, especially given its own limited family resources, to create firm-specific advantages (FSAs) and thus affect internationalization, especially its sustainability negatively.

Applying Johanson and Vahlne's (1977, p. 26) terminology of 'state' and change 'variables' to environmental factors, we distinguish between state (stock) variables, such as macroeconomic aggregates (GDP, interest rates, inflation, etc.) and institutional environment factors (regulations, legal frameworks, etc.) as opposed to 'change' (flow) variables, such as recessions and imposition of high tariff and non-tariff barriers. While stock variables affect the onset of internationalization and internationalization strategies, change variables would affect primarily the sustainability of internationalization.

It appears that so long as the positive state variables and FF dynamic capabilities exceed the negative FF liabilities, the FF possesses the ability to go international. Any negative environmental change variables which come into play to upset this balance would impact the ability of the FF towards sustained internationalization.

However, the ability to internationalize is only a necessary condition. Internationalization and its sustainability require 'Willingness'—itself a dynamic concept—which would be affected by family, as also environmental antecedents.

Willingness to Internationalize

We define 'willingness to internationalize' as the *inclination* to act upon/execute the internationalization decision. Willingness is a mental construct, and as such related to individual experiences, biases and heuristics. As such, the FF's 'willingness to internationalize' is affected by the family and individual family members' characteristics and the family's overall economic and non-economic (socio-emotional) goals. Such willingness is concerned primarily with (a) the entrepreneurial orientation (EO) mindset (Lumpkin & Dess, 1996) and the psychic distance (Sousa & Bradley, 2006) of the *'Family (member) Influencer'*—a family member (not necessarily the founder/promoter) who proactively influences the family processes, practices and decision-making activities in favour of/against internationalization and all its attendant decisions; (b) the family socio-emotional wealth (SEW) (Berrone, Cruz, & Gomez-Mejia, 2012; Hernández-Perlines et al., 2019); (c) the bifurcation bias (Kano & Verbeke, 2018); and (d) the nature of the product (Bell et al., 2003; Bell, Crick, & Young, 2004).

The *EO mindset* is identified through five constructs: pro-activeness, innovativeness, autonomy, riskiness and competitive aggressiveness (Lumpkin & Dess, 1996, p. 136). While the push/pull factors (such as the opening up of the Indian economy in 1991 and its integration into a global economy) may be common to an industry or even several industries, the mindset of the family influencers accounts for heterogeneity among small FFs in their internationalization decisions. Family dynamics, such as induction of the next-gen and succession, may create new influencers, possessing (not possessing) the requisite EO, giving a push (reverse push) to internationalization. However, even the existing family members may become 'influencers', as dynamics of the business environment alter family goals. The 'Psychic Distance' of the influencer, operationalized as the individual's *perceived* differences between the home and the host country (Sousa & Bradley, 2006, p. 57), impacts internationalization negatively.

The *family socio-emotional wealth (SEW)*, defined as 'the non-economic wealth or the "affective endowments" of family owners' (Berrone et al., 2012, p. 259) and measured by the five dimensions of the FIBER scale[3] (Berrone et al., 2012, pp. 262–264), is an important influence on the willingness to internationalize, including the willingness to commit the family-firm's internal resources. Extant literature attests to the need for preservation of SEW taking precedence over even financial goals (Berrone et al., 2012, p. 260). Thus, internationalization decisions posing a risk to family SEW may actually get rejected, even if they reduce the family-firm's financial risks. SEW also impacts the EO of the family influencer and thus determines the success or otherwise of internationalization (Hernández-Perlines et al., 2019). A *bifurcation bias*, through the family's unwillingness to utilize non-family human and

---

[3] These dimensions include family control and influence, identification of the family members with the company, binding social ties, emotional attachment of family members and renewal of family bonds with the company through dynastic succession

other resources, affects the willingness to internationalize, at least in the short run (Metsola et al., 2020).

Finally, the nature of the product also impacts the willingness to internationalize, with 'traditional' small manufacturing firms seen as less aggressive and, in fact, reluctant to pursue internationalization unless they went through a 'near death experience', compared to 'knowledge-intensive' firms (Bell et al., 2003, 2004).

The FF's 'willingness to internationalize' is also shaped by changes in the macroeconomic and institutional environment, which act as push-pull factors in the home-host countries (Fabian, Molina, & Labianca, 2009; Patterson, de Ruyter, & Wetzels, 1999), as also industry/sectoral trends (Bell et al., 2003). Such change variables can, in fact, cause sudden 'stops'/'surges' in the capital and entrepreneurial commitments by small family-firms. Such environmental factors affect the family-firm's willingness to internationalize, both directly and through their impact on the family characteristics and goals. Extant theories have held a home-country push and a corresponding host-country pull as factors responsible for internationalization. In contrast, the present-day contextual factors in FGEEs, as discussed earlier, suggest a home-country 'pull' and a host-country 'push', with internationalization notwithstanding these paradoxical features of emerging economies.

With environmental factors favouring a domestic-pull and host-push, the family-firm's willingness to internationalize would have to be shaped by the family's economic and non-economic goals, which would have to be sufficiently strong to outweigh the negative environmental factors.

Ability-willingness mix: Based on their ability and willingness to internationalize, small family-firms in fast-growing emerging economies may pursue different internationalization pathways. The integrated model helps us in distinguishing between such potential pathways based on the ability-willingness framework, which we will discuss in a following section.

Research Methods

We undertook a qualitative case study research to understand the 'why' and 'how' of the internationalization process of small Indian FFs and the role of family-firm features in such internationalization (Eisenhardt, 1989; Yin, 1989). A multiple case research design with four to ten case studies (Eisenhardt, 1989, p. 545) is considered to be the ideal number to help understand patterns. The research design, thus, involved an in-depth investigation of eight selected Indian small FFs which have chosen the path of internationalization.

480 T. Jayakumar

Table 15.3 Definitions of micro, small and medium-sized enterprises

A) IFC Definition			
Indicator/size of the enterprise	Micro enterprise	Small enterprise	Medium enterprise
Number of employees	<10	10–50	50–300
Asset size	<$100,000	$100,000–<$3 million	$3 million–<$15 million
Annual sales	<$100,000	$100,000–<$3 million	$3 million–<$15 million
B) Indian definition			
	Micro	Small	Medium
Manufacturing enterprise (investment in plant and machinery)	Up to ₹2.5 million[a]	> ₹2.5 million–₹50 million	> ₹50 million–₹100 million

Notes: [a]In 2019, the average rupee-dollar exchange rate was ₹70 to 1 USD
Source: International Finance Corporation (2012). *Assessing private sector contributions to job creation: IFC Open Source Study.* Retrieved on November 28, 2019, from http://documents.worldbank.org/curated/en/602291468183841622/pdf/819960BRI0Meas00Box379851B00PUBLIC0; Reserve Bank of India (2019a, June 25). *Report of the Expert Committee on Micro, Small and Medium Enterprises.* Retrieved December 12, 2019, from https://www.rbi.org.in/Scripts/PublicationReportDetails.aspx?UrlPage=&ID=924

The overall objective of the research was to gain a deeper understanding of Indian small FFs' internationalization processes.

We used a criterion sampling method (Patton, 2001, p. 238), which involved selecting cases which met certain predetermined criteria. We considered Indian manufacturing firms, which classified as MSMEs *at the time of* internationalization, based on the official definition of investment in plant and machinery/equipment (RBI, 2019a) as also the World Bank classification based on employee size, asset size or annual sales (IFC, 2012) (see Table 15.3). The firms considered have used such internationalization to transition out of their initial status, with some outgrowing even the MSME tag. We did not exclude the micro sector from our choice set, despite being aware that this would increase the category size, since we found most small firms have actually started off as 'Micro' enterprises even at the time of internationalization. We considered only *family-controlled enterprises*, that is, those having majority family ownership, as also majority family members, as part of the management team. All the small FFs considered were drawn from the manufacturing industry to control the effect of industry type on the process of internationalization.

We measured the intensity and scope of internationalization using the proportion of foreign sales to total sales (FSTS) (minimum 30 per cent criteria) and the number of foreign countries operating in (minimum 3) at the time of study. One of the firms selected, Sidharth Campisa, had a lower proportion of foreign sales due to its embarking on internationalization only recently. It was included since it provided an insight into the dynamics at the onset of internationalization, especially the impact of networks and networking activity. We look at various modes of operating internationally, ranging from exports to having their own foreign intermediaries (agents)/foreign partners to even having their offices and companies abroad or a combination of these.

Based on these criteria, an opportunistic sample was drawn from small family-firms through the author's professional contacts, consistent with the recommendation of researchers that random selection of cases is neither necessary nor preferable (Eisenhardt, 1989, p. 537). We contacted 62 case firms, of which we received a positive response from 15. After a preliminary round of discussions with family managers from these 15 firms, we selected eight firms—which seemed to fit our criteria more closely than the others—as our final case firms. A case protocol was maintained meticulously.

Data were collected mainly through one-to-one semi-structured interviews of the senior family managers/owners of the case firms or non-family owner managers in certain cases, conducted face-to-face or over phone. We conducted 17 interviews over a four-month period, with an average duration of 74 minutes per interview. At least two interviews of people who had been the key influencers or had a detailed knowledge of the phenomenon under study were conducted per case firm, in order to reduce biases.

A preliminary set of questions to understand the context of the interviewees' businesses as well as the internationalization was followed by more detailed questions to address the research questions. Table 15.4 summarizes the characteristics of the case firms. We followed the guidelines for developing questions for a qualitative research exercise (Agee, 2009). Interviews conducted were non-threatening, with no leading questions and with a goal to draw out stories which could provide rich material for the cases. All interviews were digitally recorded and transcribed verbatim, rechecked and a follow-up carried out for clarificatory comments. Finally, the completed case record was shared with the respondents to ensure that there were no inconsistencies/inaccuracies and corrections made accordingly.

The interview material was supplemented with observations, field notes and firm documents to understand the internationalization pathways of these small FFs. Additionally, we used secondary data to understand certain events such as the institutional environments—both in India and in some of the destination countries—to make better sense of the internationalization process. A thematic analysis was carried out manually, and NVivo qualitative

Table 15.4 Characteristics of case firms included in the study

Case firm (location)	Product	Year of establishment (year of establishment of the parent/original family business)	Classification category at the time of internationalization (Size of investment in plant and machinery in Rs. million)	Size of the company (in 2019)		Start of internationalization
				Number of employees	Sales turnover (in million dollars)	
1. Jawand Sons (Ludhiana)	Soft home furnishing products (own factory)	2003 (1975)	Small (20)	2500	35.76 (INR 25000 m)	2003
2. Swati Exports (Mumbai)	Scarves for women	1987	Micro (job-work commissioned)	30 +3 (US) +3 (Spain)	5	1987
3. KLA India Public Ltd. (Uttarakhand)	Rice and frozen fruits and vegetables	2001 (1973)	Micro (2.5 million)	100 FT, 100 contractual	32.89 (INR 2300 m)	1997–1998
4. ABC Kitchenware Private Ltd. (Mumbai)	Stainless steel utensils	1994 (1989)	Small (6 million)	18 workers + 3 Managers	6.86 + 20 (China trade)	1999
5. Z.A Sea Foods Pvt. Ltd. (Kolkata)	Processed shrimp	2008 (1975)	Small (35 million)	150 (100 workers on roll and 50 administrative staff)	25.03	2010
6. Sidharth Campisa (Jaipur)	Dock-levellers and loading bay equipment	2018 (1996)	Micro	9	1.01	2018
7. Dev Publishers & Distributors (Delhi)	Publishing and distribution of books	2011(1952), 1870	Micro	25	1.15	2015 (de-industrialization)
8. R R Global (Mumbai)	Manufacturing and export of wires and cable	1985 (1965)	Small (6)	4000	800	1991
Total						

Source: Author
[a]Extent of internationalization is presented as intensity—the proportion of foreign sales to total sales and scope—the number of foreign countries where the case firm operates (displayed in brackets)

Extent of internationa-lization*	% family owned	Ownership and management		Duration of interviews (in minutes)	Important foreign markets	Operating mode in foreign markets
		Generation in ownership (no. of family owners)	Generation in management as employees/ managers (no. of family managers)			
100 (15)	100	Gen (G) 1 & 2 (6)	Gen 1 and 2 (4)	170	US, Germany, Sweden, UK, Australia, Japan	Exports to foreign clients, major European retailer of household goods and home accessories and other clients
100 (5)	100	Gen 1 & 2 (4)	Gen 1 and 2 (3)	167	Spain, the Netherlands, Germany, Italy, US	Direct exports; office in the US and Spain
90 (40 spread over 4 continents)	100	G1, G2, G3 (7)	G1, G2, G3 (7)	190	South Africa, Switzerland, Saudi Arabia, West Africa	Direct exports, office in South Africa, subsidiary in Mozambique jointly owned
100 (3)	100	G1 (4)	G1, G2(5)	143	Western Africa: 3 countries	3 offices in Western Africa to which direct exports from India and China
100(more than 5)	60	G1 (2)	G1, G2 (3)	135	US, Vietnam, Japan, Malaysia, European Union, Far East and Middle East	Through agents
4 (3)	50 (JV subsidiary of the 100% family-owned parent firm)	G1 (8)	G1 & G2 (7)	144	Sri Lanka, Dubai, Qatar	Direct exports to clients (through joint venture)
50(3 countries/ regions)	100	G1 (2)	G1 & G2 (3)	130	US, UK, ROW	Distributors and sourcing agents, retailers
30 (80)	100	G1, G2, G3 (8)	G2, G3 (8)	180	Europe and Middle East	Direct exports, offices (Dubai, Burma, Bangladesh)
				1259 minutes		

analysis software was used to store and manage the data and to carry out within-case and cross-case analyses.

The validity and reliability of research were ensured through various methods including using theory to structure interview topics (Eisenhardt, 1989), meticulous record-keeping in order to demonstrate a clear decision trail and ensuring consistency and transparency of data interpretation (Long & Johnson, 2000), including verbatim descriptions of respondents' accounts (Slevin, 2002), sending back the interview transcripts to the respondents and inviting them to comment on the same (Long & Johnson, 2000) and data triangulation (Noble & Smith, 2015).

Findings and Empirical Analysis

We analysed the eight Indian small FFs in light of extant theory and with earlier models of internationalization attributable to Bell et al. (2003), Johanson and Vahlne (1977) and Metsola et al. (2020) as the reference points. The original idea was to carry out theory-testing research. However, as attested by Eisenhardt (1989, p. 536), we found serendipitous findings, which led us to convert our study into a possible theory-building research.

Internationalization Process

Following a processual approach involves looking at not just the onset of internationalization but also at the internationalization strategies and the sustainability of such internationalization. Table 15.5 summarizes the case findings on the various dimensions of the internationalization process.

Decision to Internationalize and Internationalization Pathways

We found that while some of the case firms traversed well-recognized internationalization pathways, this was not true of all case firms. Of the eight FFs studied, three—Jawand Sons Pvt. Ltd., KLA India Public Ltd. and ABC Kitchenware Pvt. Ltd.—were well-established firms that had focused on the domestic market place for an extended period of time. Certain critical incidents, stoked by both environmental and family factors, triggered the need/desire for internationalization. In Jawand Sons, it was the participation in a trade fair in Germany in response to a growing family and the need for expansion and diversification; in KLA, it was the entry of a family member who, frustrated with corruption in the domestic environment, acted as the influencer; in ABC it was a botched export consignment to Western Africa, requiring the travel of a family member. These FFs responded to these critical incidents, following which they embraced rapid internationalization in a manner such that they gave up their domestic markets to become highly global, illustrating 'Born-Again Global' (BAG) pathways. Two firms—Swati Exports Pvt. Ltd. and Z.A. Seafoods—exhibit characteristics of 'Born Global' (BG) firms, having followed proactive internationalization right from their inception.

One firm—Dev Publishers and Distributors—has responded to adverse geopolitical factors as also the induction of a relatively risk-averse next-generation, by reducing FSTS from 100 to 50 per cent in just four years, since 2015. It exhibits a *de-internationalization* (DI) pathway.

Two FFs—RR Global and Sidharth Campisa—display characteristics which are not captured by extant models, and we classify these as following *'cohesive'* pathways (Co)—pathways of concurrent expansion in domestic and foreign markets, with a clear intent to treat the domestic market as the primary one.

RR Global—a manufacturer and exporter of wires—commenced internationalization in 1991, after being in the business for more than 26 years. The motivation was to take advantage of new regulations which allowed export income to be tax-exempt at home and also to tap the potentially lucrative textile markets of the Middle East through trading in chemicals and colourants. The group quickly went about its internationalization journey in a structured, planned manner.

The initial few years were spent on exporting traded chemicals and colourants. The company entered a phase of exporting its own manufactured goods from 1999, acquiring certifications from Germany, England, the US, Canada and so forth, so that they could become credible exporters to these countries. Currently, it operates in more than 80 countries, with more than 40 per cent of the wires and cables exported to Western countries.

> We were a zero exporter when we started. ….Once we decided to go global, we branched out very quickly. We went after European approvals, since we knew these would be important for our Asia business as well. (Sanjay Taparia, non-family owner manager, RR Global)

Between 1999 and 2004–2005, the company increased its exports as a percentage of its total sales and attained a 25 per cent exports volume as a

486   T. Jayakumar

Table 15.5 Details of the internationalization behaviour of the case firms

Internationalization behaviour	Jawand Sons	Swati Exports	KLA India Public Ltd.	ABC Kitchenware Private Ltd.
Trigger	Critical incident— knowledge of Heimtextil and participation in trade fair; approach by the major European retailer of household goods and home accessories	Proactive search on the part of the founder	Critical incident— Induction of next-gen who could not accept the current status quo (unsystematic working pattern and corruption)	Critical incident—FF faced a demurrage liability when an African client introduced through networks reneged on making payments for the consignment exported to him; this led to a family member travelling to the Western African country to recover the consignment held up at the port. Found attractive opportunities, leading to a family member relocating and setting up a base within the next year.
Motivation for onset / reduction of internationalization (reduction for Dev Publishers)	Diversify risks and exploit the new networks from the critical incident	First-mover advantage into Nordic markets Rapid penetration of global niches or segments Competitive advantage in producing scarves	⁂ To explore new markets which would pose lesser wastage of time. ⁂ To carry out clean business	⁂ Exploit the new networks from the critical incident ⁂ Growth in new markets which offered potential

Z.A. Sea Foods	Sidharth Campisa	Dev Publishers & Distributors (de-internationalization)	RR Global
Proactive search on the part of the founder, together with using networks of associates	● Proactive response to opportunities posed in the business environment ● Opportunity to manufacture the erstwhile products for which they were the India distributors through a JV with the Italian partner. ● Strong domestic presence and reputation	Geopolitical factors leading to loss of markets Induction of next-gen with lower risk appetite Next-gen sees India as a promising emerging market, given the large-sized population.	● Proactive ● Favourable domestic and host market conditions ● Strong base in home country ● Sufficient funds to expand scale into new geographies ● Active management
Rapid penetration into global niches or segments, since Indian shrimps enjoy good global demand	● To reap economies of scale ● To leverage the core competencies ● To diversify risks	● To gradually have a greater proportion of domestic sales to ensure no losses ● Nationalistic sentiments	● To exploit economies of scale after tapping the domestic market ● To diversify risks ● To leverage core competencies abroad

(continued)

488 T. Jayakumar

Table 15.5 (continued)

Internationalization behaviour	Jawand Sons	Swati Exports	KLA India Public Ltd.	ABC Kitchenware Private Ltd.
International expansion patterns	Long epoch of domestic expansion (28 years) followed by rapid internationalization into 15 countries	International from inception; Strong evidence of networks, which have helped it establish major presence in 7 countries, besides catering to other smaller markets.	Epoch of domestic market orientation followed by rapid industrialization into 40 countries Evidence of networks Expression of nationalistic sentiments and intent to increase proportion of domestic operations	Office set up in the first foreign market and in 2 other Western African countries in subsequent waves of internationalization
Pace of internationalization	Late, but rapid (within 2 years); Currently 100% FSTS	Rapid; Many markets at once.	Rapid after a late start. From 100% domestic, they had transformed to almost 100% export sales within 10 years. Currently 90% FSTS	Late, but rapid. Had become 100% FSTS within 2 years. Currently, 100% FSTS. Restricted to 3 Western African countries
Method of entry into foreign markets	Direct exports to a lead client-major European retailer through participating in a trade fair. Other partners sourced as part of a strategic move later, also through fairs.	Direct exports followed by offices in two foreign markets	Direct exports and offices in South Africa and a jointly owned subsidiary in Mozambique	Direct exports from India and China; offices in three West African countries

Z.A. Sea Foods	Sidharth Campisa	Dev Publishers & Distributors (de-internationalization)	RR Global
International from inception Strong evidence of working with networks of agents	● Concurrent expansion in domestic and international markets, after long period of domestic expansion ● Foreign markets are those which have been 'released' by the Italian partner ● Geographically close markets for economic viability reasons ● Is looking to tap the distant Australian markets which have been released as well through setting up manufacturing facilities there	Epoch of international markets followed by rapid domestic expansion	● Domestic expansion first ● International expansion commences within 10 years of establishment of manufacturing arm, after opening up of the Indian economy ● start with trading of chemicals ● Switch to export of manufactured electricals within few years as a domestic manufacturing base is created. ● Concurrent growth of domestic and foreign markets thereafter, with equal or greater emphasis on domestic ● Not influenced by cultural proximity of markets/psychic distance, but rather by assured economic returns ● Networks important, though not critical in the initial stages ● Further expansion is based on networks.
Rapid; Many markets at once	Rapid after a late start in terms of scope. Extent of internationalization is small as of now (4%); however, does not plan to expand at the cost of the domestic market	Rapid move back into domestic markets. From 100% international, they transformed to almost 50% foreign to total sales (FSTS) within 2 years. Currently 50% FSTS	● Initial period of domestic expansion ● -Several markets tapped simultaneously ● Extent of internationalization remains restricted (25–30% FSTS) as a matter of choice
Exports through agents	Direct exports through a joint venture with a global partner	–	● Flexible ● Direct exports through an export arm Setting up of overseas manufacturing units through JVs based on networks

(*continued*)

490   T. Jayakumar

Table 15.5 (continued)

Internationalization behaviour	Jawand Sons	Swati Exports	KLA India Public Ltd.	ABC Kitchenware Private Ltd.
Internationalization strategies	• Reactive in response to a critical incident but more planned thereafter • Expansion of newly acquired networks • New product development to fulfil Western compliances	Structured, with concentration on Nordic markets Based on few but strong network ties	• Rapid expansion and transformation into almost fully export-oriented, based on learning and network ties	• Reactive in response to critical incident • Mix of manufactured (30%) and traded products (70%) exported to increase profits; larger proportion of exports comprise of traded goods. • Lesser assumption of manufacturing risk relative to turnover
Factors in the business environment affecting internationalization	Host-country pull	Host-country pull	Home-push, host-pull (at the onset) Home-pull in recent years	Host-country pull
Typology of internationalization pathway	Born-again global	Born global	Born-again global	Born-again global

Source: Author

Z.A. Sea Foods	Sidharth Campisa	Dev Publishers & Distributors (de-internationalization)	RR Global
⊛ Structured Based on the strong network ties with agents	Structured Based on few but strong network ties	⊛ Rapid reversal and transformation into domestic-oriented	⊛ Planned approach to international expansion involving acquisition of required global quality certifications, which could help sell in Western markets as well as Asia ⊛ Structured ⊛ Use of global business networks over time ⊛ Decision on the extent of FSTS to be 25–30%; as such, expansion not ad hoc and opportunistic. ⊛ The company continues to expand in domestic markets
Host-country pull	Home-country pull > host-country pull	Host market adverse conditions (reverse push) Home-pull	Home-country pull> Host-country pull
Born global	Cohesive	De-industrialization	Cohesive

proportion of its total production. It has since then retained this proportion. The group has a policy of exporting 25–30 per cent of its overall sales. With the group turnover increasing by more than thrice between 2005 and 2019, this has meant higher volumes of exports. In addition to carrying out direct exports, the group has three foreign offices in Bangladesh, Dubai and Burma. The company has also formed two joint ventures in Bangladesh and Dubai for manufacturing overseas. Despite strong internationalization, the company does not see itself relinquishing its domestic markets at any stage.

> We don't want to starve the domestic market in order to go for the export market. (Sanjay Taparia, RR Global)

This is true of Sidharth Campisa—a manufacturer and trader of dock levellers and loading bay equipment—as well. The new joint venture between Sidharth (the parent manufacturing firm) and Campisa, an Italian firm, used the latter's networks to expand its global reach in just about a year, entering three markets through exports and eyeing other global markets as well. However, it does not view entering foreign markets as being mutually exclusive to operating in domestic markets. In fact, it is using its foreign partner network to expand domestically as well.

> Amazon is building its largest warehouse in Bhiwandi for which it needs 48 dock levellers. The biggest contenders for this contract are my company—Sidharth Campisa and my competitor. Campisa is doing everything to help us bag this order. They have already flown us the raw material required for manufacturing these dock-levellers. Using air transport rather than shipping is very expensive. Yet, Campisa understands the potential of India and this important project.
>
> I have huge export demand in South Asian and other markets. Campisa also wants me to take over other markets. But my domestic demand itself is so high that I can't export too much. As of now, in 10 months, I am doing 4 per cent exports. I may go up to 20 per cent. (Bhavya Jain, Family Manager, Sidharth Campisa)

Both RR Global and Sidharth Campisa, given the high domestic demand, wish to use their international sales to supplement their domestic sales. We call these pathways of concurrent expansion 'cohesive' pathways. More importantly, we found that contrary to extant internationalization theories positing a home-country domestic push, it is attractive domestic opportunities influencing family economic goals together with non-economic SEW (to be discussed in a following section) which constitute a domestic-pull. These shape

Internationalization Strategies

While the case firms following BG pathways exhibit rapid *pace* of internationalization, entering several markets simultaneously, those following BAG pathways exhibit late, but rapid, industrialization. Foreign sales in the three BAG firms currently account for 90–100 per cent of total sales. The two firms following *'cohesive pathways'* exhibit rapid internationalization, but with the extent of internationalization, measured through the proportion of FSTS, restricted as a matter of choice. In the case of Dev Publishers, there has been rapid de-internationalization in just about four years.

The *mode of entry* in almost all cases has been exports. BG as well as BAG firms exported either directly to key clients or through agents. This was followed by setting up of foreign offices in three of these cases, itself shaped by family capabilities, especially network relations, and by the family's economic and non-economic goals. Both firms following cohesive pathways have formed joint ventures with foreign supplier networks for exports or even manufacturing in domestic/overseas units.

Internationalization strategies in the case of BAG firms studied comprised a 'reactive' response to critical incidents, followed by a more planned approach towards internationalization. Case firms following BG pathways exhibit strategies based on strong network ties.

Dev Publishers, an erstwhile BG firm—with the seventh generation in the family business of publishing—illustrates the de-internationalization pathway. The de-internationalization, which commenced in 2015 and which has become intense especially since 2017, has been due to a mix of domestic government policies, global economic conditions and disruptions posed by technology. The family scion attributes it to the shrinking of their main business based in the UK by 70 per cent due to the uncertainties associated with Brexit. The family managers—scions belonging to the next-gen—have decided to concentrate on the domestic market and have reduced foreign operations rapidly.

The two *Co* pathway firms exhibit a planned and structured approach to international expansion, using global business networks. Decisions on the extent of internationalization (FSTS), driven by economic and non-economic goals, are not ad hoc and opportunistic, but deliberated upon within the family and well planned.

Based on the nature of the product, six manufacturing firms classified as 'Traditional', and two firms (RR Global and Sidharth Campisa) were 'Knowledge-intensive' manufacturing firms. The internationalization decisions for the traditional firms were based on the presence of global markets and the relative lack of home demand. This was true for both scarves and shrimps as in the case of Swati Exports and Z.A. Sea Foods, respectively. In the case of the knowledge-intensive firms following cohesive pathways, the decision to export or manufacture overseas is also based on the transportation and logistics costs.

> India is a low consumer of shrimps, and more than 80 per cent of its production is anyway exported. We have more lucrative markets abroad, (Devansh Goenka, Z.A. Sea Foods)
>
> In commodity markets like electrical wires and cables, packaging and transportation costs have a crucial role in determining the reach and extent of internationalization. Even if the intent is there, because of these costs, you may not have competitive advantage. Hence extent of internationalization becomes limited. (Sumeet Kabra, RR Global)

Sustainability of Internationalization

The extent and sustainability of internationalization is more a function of willingness to internationalize, given the ability of the family-firm to internationalize. We found that of the case firms studied, two BG case firms and two of the three BAG firms had no intent of changing the status quo in terms of FSTS, despite a strong home-country pull. This behaviour can be explained through non-economic family variables, especially the psychic distance of the key family influencer (to be discussed later). The two cohesive pathway firms, driven by family and environmental factors, similarly, envisaged status quo, with domestic sales being the primary drivers and the consequent extent of internationalization being restricted.

However, interestingly, we found that a BAG firm like KLA International Public Ltd.—with 90 per cent of FSTS currently—is keen on increasing the proportion of its domestic sales. While this is partly on account of *change* factors in the institutional environment, given the attractive home-country environment and the adverse geopolitical factors and expectations regarding trade and foreign operations, we also found an expression of nationalistic sentiments as a reason for increasing the proportion of domestic sales.

With the change in the business environment in India in 2017, post the implementation of the Goods and Services Tax (GST), we now wish to extend our domestic sales to an extent so as to match our exports over a period of time. We see 50 per cent of our overall sales coming from domestic markets over the next few years.

…As exporters, we have been brand ambassadors for India outside our country for long. We have kept learning silently and have developed manufacturing to global standards. We are happy to bring these technologies to India now, so other smaller players can learn…. we know rice is a necessity, and the country does take precedence…. (Ashok Agarwal, Owner Manager, KLA India Public Ltd.)

The positive changes in India's business and institutional environment, and the increasing difficulties in operating internationally, especially in the wake of the US-China Trade Wars, were commented on by most case firm family managers. Three of these managers spoke about a strategy of greater domestic sales over time, expressing sentiments such as 'India needs us'. Besides environmental factors, individual/family factors which stem from the evoking of nationalistic sentiments may have an important role to play in the sustainability of the internationalization process, going beyond merely the pre-entry/entry stage.

Family-Specific Factors Affecting Internationalization

The ability and willingness to internationalize is contingent upon certain family-specific factors, which affect the three dimensions of the internationalization process. Table 15.6 summarizes our findings with respect to the family-specific factors for the case firms.

Entrepreneurial Orientation of the Key Influencer

An important feature for internationalization is the presence of a key family influencer with the requisite entrepreneurial orientation (EO) who acts as the catalyst prompting and effectuating the decision. In KLA India Public Ltd., it was the induction of the second-generation family member, Ashok Agarwal, which acted as the trigger. The personal values of this influencer clashed with the rampant corruption in the business environment, which prompted him to explore internationalization and eventually enter global markets. He saw internationalization as a means of providing assured and clean profits to the

Table 15.6 Analysis of family factors affecting internationalization in the case firms

Family factors	Jawand Sons	Swati Exports	KLA India Public Ltd.	ABC Kitchenware Private Ltd.	Z.A. Sea Foods	Sidharth Campisa	Dev Publishers & Distributors (de-interna-tionalization)	RR Global
Financing options	Initially financed by the parent company; later equity of the founder	Own equity	Family equity	Family equity	Equity of the founder	Joint venture with funding done by the parent company (FF)	Equity of the founder, after split with the family	• Self-financed via rapid growth • Gone in for private equity in Sept 2018
Psychic distance of the family influencer from the host markets	Low	Low	Low	Low	Low	Low	–	• Not influenced by the psychic proximity of the markets • Proactive approach to target multiple markets and reduce the psychic distance through networks/active knowledge seeking, etc.
Family SEW	High	High	Very high	High	Medium-high	High	High	Very high
Presence of bifurcation Bias	Medium; professional involvement, although family holds key management positions	Very high	Very high	Very high	Medium	High	Very high	Medium (key positions held by family friends/family members). However, non-family owners present; move towards professionalization

Nature of the product	Traditional mass item (home furnishings)	Traditional mass item (scarves)	Traditional (rice, frozen fruits and vegetables)	Traditional, low-end mass items (stainless steel utensils)	Traditional (processed shrimps)	Knowledge-based (dock-levellers)	Traditional (book publication)	Knowledge-intensive
Firm's internal resources and capabilities	Medium to high	Medium	Medium to high	Medium	Low to medium	Medium	Low to medium	High
Networks	Networks of the major European retailer of the household goods and home accessories	Strong network ties with few people	Weak network ties at onset; over time this has transformed to strong networks enabling the firm to move up the value chain from exporting to overseas farming in Mozambique	Strong networks in the host country	Networks of agents	Strong network ties with Italian partner	—	• Networks not critical in the early stages of internationalization • Critical as internationalization has progressed • Such networks responsible for overseas manufacturing arms

Source: Author

498   T. Jayakumar

family business and preferred to convert the family business into almost completely international. Similar EO is seen in Virendra Jain, founder of Swati Exports, who simply landed up in Finland with his samples of scarves without knowing a single person in the country.

> When I go cold-calling in a foreign country, I go to the Indian Consulate, go to their trade section, and ask them: Can you help me with some addresses of the people here? I was pleasantly surprised in Finland—the first country I went to—where one of the officials in the Indian consulate said: 'You don't have to waste your money making phone calls from the hotel. Come to the consulate, sit down, I will give you a room, a phone and also the contacts and you can make calls from here'. Such a beautiful thing it was. (Virendra Jain, Founder, Swati Exports Private Ltd.)

Dynamic changes in family, with the induction of new influencers, could equally influence successive waves of internationalization/de-internationalization.

> As of now, the family business is what I am into. But one never knows what will happen in the future. (Devansh Goenka, scion and family manager, Z.A. Sea Foods)
> I think the population is here, the markets are here. We also ought to be here (in India). (Parichay Jain, scion and family manager, Dev Publishers & Distributors)

We found that 'psychic distance' of the key influencer has a key role in determining the internationalization destinations, especially in BG and BAG firms. Thus, we found that some influencers chose to operate in the 'culturally distant' markets of the US and Europe which, however, were 'psychically closer', since they assured 'clean' profits and the influencers felt no need to compromise on their personal values relating to adherence to compliances and ethical norms.

> Exports require greater compliance—both quality norms and social compliance. As such, our products are costlier relative to manufacturers for Indian markets. We do business only with those who respect compliances. (Balwant Singh, Family Owner Manager, Jawand Sons Private Ltd.)
> The product that we sell is mostly for the Western market … Yes, we could sell these things in India as well, since all top brands sell in India today as well … In India, we find that dealing with local clients, they are bad in payments, margins are extremely low, and they are not worried about compliances. Unless you are able to find a good fit, it doesn't work. In our case, we don't need to work

here, so we don't do it. (Arpit Jain, Family Owner Manager, Swati Exports Pvt. Ltd.)

In the case of the cohesive pathway firms, we found that having taken the decision to limit the proportion of foreign sales to total sales, psychic distance has little relevance. The destination countries may be based on a systematic and pragmatic assessment of opportunities, combined with the presence of networks, as is seen in the case of RR Global which currently operates in 80 countries.

Family Socio-Emotional Wealth (SEW)

We found that internationalizing firms conform with extant theory in that they exhibit high SEW in terms of family control and influence, binding social ties and emotional attachment of family members.

The concept of SEW is well-captured by the statement of the third-generation family owner manager of RR Global:

> When taking decisions, we have agreed that there may be 'Matbhed' (Hindi, for differences in opinion), but there can be no 'Manbhed' (Differences in our mind). (Sumeet Kabra, Family Owner Manager, RR Global)

In the absence of a bifurcation bias, such socio-emotional wealth does not just restrict itself to family members but also to a 'wide set of constituencies', including vendors, suppliers and other non-family employees (Berrone et al., 2012, p. 263), as we found, albeit in a limited sense in certain case firms.

Key family influencers' entrepreneurial initiatives towards internationalization constituting 'critical incidents' were supported by the presence of high SEW in the case of BAG firms. Thus, the family supported Gurbakshish Singh, the founder of Jawand Sons, to establish the company at the age of 44, after being part of the family business, *Oster*, for more than 20 years. Production was undertaken in the same factory as the domestic brands marketed by the family, and financial resources were made available from the common pool. The family split in 2011 with the intent of efficient financial control, providing roles to the next-gen and maintaining family harmony and thus preserving SEW. When ABC Kitchenware, following a critical incident (see Table 15.6), found lucrative opportunities in Western Africa, one of the brothers relocated out to Africa based on mutual consensus, even while his immediate family continued to be part of the joint family staying in India. We witness high SEW in this case. Similarly, in the case of KLA Public Ltd., the key family influencer quit his well-paid, secure government job and joined the family business when the need arose. However, his dissonance, as he found his personal values clashing with that of the business requirements, was respected by his family who supported him in his decision to enter export markets.

High SEW, however, manifests itself even in decisions relating to limited internationalization of the firms following cohesive pathways or even de-internationalization, as we found, with family members taking such decisions based on mutual consensus through the operation of a Family Council. In this sense, we found high SEW to be associated with high levels of family governance, which relates to multiple decisions taken by the business family, including the decision to internationalize.

We found that family SEW holds high significance during times when the family may decide to initiate/change the internal resources committed to such internationalization initiatives. In such scenarios, the family consensus on the extent of internal resources to be committed shapes the internationalization pathways. However, the family may arrive at a consensus to commit high, limited or little/no resources, resulting in BG/BAG, cohesive or de-internationalization pathways, respectively.

Bifurcation Bias

We found the presence of a bifurcation bias in most of the case firms studied, which affected the firms' available internal resources and capabilities and limited the reach and intensity of internationalization.

On why the family has not thought of increasing its presence beyond three countries in Western Africa, the founder of ABC Kitchenware states:

> How can we trust people (other than family)? It is a matter of money. (Founder, ABC, Kitchenware Pvt. Ltd.)

The same is echoed by Lakshya Agarwal, generation-3 member of KLA India Public Ltd.

> We would not want to give the task of handling the clients to (non-family) managers, since such information may be leaked out to competitors were they to leave us and join others. Moreover, they may start a competing firm on their own. Why should I create my own competitors?

15 Internationalization of Small Indian Family-Firms: An Emergent... 501

In Swati Exports similarly, it is the founder, his son and daughter-in-law—the three family owners—who travel four times a year meeting up with clients and being in direct touch with them. Decision-making rests with the family owners in Z.A. Sea Foods as well.

Some FFs did try to overcome this skill gap through hiring consultants and experts to assist them, especially in the initial days as in the case of RR Global and Z.A. Sea Foods. Firms like Jawand Sons and RR Global have mitigated some of these biases by going in for professional recruitment as they have grown in size towards large corporates. However, decision-making still rests with the family principals to a very large extent.

Such bifurcation bias impacts the firm's internal resources and capabilities, and thus the sustainability of internationalization.

> As of now, the four brothers are already in charge of individual functions/territories. When the next generation comes in after proper education, we can think of expanding our presence beyond Western Africa, into Europe and US. (Founder, ABC Kitchenware Pvt. Ltd.)
>
> There were only me and two peons. ... We were doing the maximum we could do. I have never had the time to think of doing anything else. (Virendra Jain, Swati Exports Private Ltd. on being asked why he did not think of diversifying from scarves)

Network Relations and Ties

Networks are particularly important in determining the extent and direction of internationalization, especially for small internationalizing firms which suffer from a knowledge-deficit required for internationalization.

The significance of such network effects for internationalization was captured in multiple statements. Such networks determined the destination countries and helped in risk mitigation. Such networks were based on the family's social capital and, in turn, affected the same.

Arpit Jain, family owner and manager in Swati Exports, a BG firm, attests to the importance of such network ties. Their first hire in the US office—an Indian—was through their family friend who had an office in the vicinity in the US. Similarly, their Spanish office was set up only because of their Spanish connect, who they regard as a family member.

> Networks matter. Either you know people in the foreign country, or someone here who knows someone there. It matters. ... What I am doing in the US (set-

ting up an office), I could do in any state. it doesn't matter. We chose to be there, since our family friend of 40 years was there. (Arpit Jain, Swati Exports)

Only networks are important. We took one and a half years to convince our Bangladeshi partner. It is always easy to set up a manufacturing unit with people you know. (Sanjay Taparia, RR Global)

The Bangladesh Joint Venture happened because of Sanjay's (Taparia)chemical background. He (the JV partner) used to be our distributor of chemicals, who was known to Sanjay, who helped us in setting up a factory for manufacturing super-enamelled wires and Low Voltage (LV) cables. (Sumeet Kabra, RR Global)

Sidharth Campisa, a joint venture, owes its origin to the trusted network ties established by the parent company Sidharth, with the Italian firm, Campisa. When the Italian company was left in the lurch by an Indian distributor of their dock-levellers, Campisa approached Sidharth who had been working with other Italian companies. The latter started importing and selling dock-levellers in India. Soon, Campisa offered Sidharth the opportunity to manufacture these products in India and also gave up some of its export markets, so that it could concentrate on other markets. Sidharth Campisa has already started exporting to three countries. When asked which markets he would like to expand next, Bhavya Jain, family manager, Sidharth Campisa, stated:

I would go to countries which are closer to where I already am, and also to countries like New Zealand and Australia regarding which I can get knowledge from my partners. My partners have a big set of data, they know the people who are going to buy. I do not need to waste my energy in finding new clients.

On the risk-mitigating role of networks, Manish Phushkania, non-family owner and manager, Z.A. Sea Foods, states:

The networks of agents help in mitigating risks, both for the buyers as also suppliers like us. They also provide guidance and match the assortments to the buyers' requirements.

Networks of buyers in the client firms also play a critical role.

Sometimes you work with clients, when the buyer leaves and joins another company-she still wants to come back to her old vendors and you get a new client that way. If the buyer is the decision maker, you get a chance to get a new client thereby. (Arpit Jain, Swati Exports)

Internal Resources and Capabilities

A firm's internal resources and capabilities impinge on the internationalization strategies, as also the sustainability of internationalization. Among the most critical are financial resources, determining the ability to internationalize, as also the family's risk-appetite and commitment to fund internationalization, influencing its willingness.

On being asked what was the chief constraint to further internationalization, Bhavya Jain stated:

> …Solely finance. When I expand, I cannot be dependent on manpower. I need robotic arms which can weld with precision, I need robotic paint-booths. So I need investment. I have clients, I have a market, but I am able to do only this (limited) number because of these constraints. (Bhavya Jain, Sidharth Campisa)

Swati Exports' chief constraint in further internationalization is its willingness to commit internal resources, and a bifurcation bias. When asked why Swati Exports Private Ltd. had given up H&M, a key client, the founder said:

> H&M stayed with us for 12 years. Then they grew too big and we found it difficult to handle and we stopped. …Earlier we were supplying 1000 pieces per colour. Then they went up to 120,000 pieces per colour. That was difficult for us. Then they came with several conditionalities attached to it. You are almost working on a cost plus basis which we don't like. We want our margins. It depends on whether you want to scale up or not. We didn't want to. There is too much risk. One season you may get a huge order, next season nothing. (Virendra Jain, Swati Exports Pvt. Ltd.)

Small family businesses seem to be reluctant to borrow from banks or even go for private equity or venture capital. Most firms studied, except RR Global, were categorical in their desire not to allow any outside control through funding; in fact, there was pride in being 'zero debt" companies. Using their own funds acquired through growth seemed to be the most preferred means of financing.

> ***Luckily***, my father very quickly just started using his own funds. He was always averse to taking any kind of credit. He wanted to use his own funds. So we continued like that. Today we have no debt for business purposes. (Arpit Jain, Swati Exports Pvt. Ltd.)

> Since 1952, we have been zero-debt. (Parichay Jain, Dev Publishers)

504 T. Jayakumar

Indian small manufacturing firms have managed to overcome production constraints for internationalization through contracting to third party vendors domestically or even by dealing in traded goods. Close to 50 per cent of production for Swati Exports is through known vendors. RR Global has entered into joint ventures overseas to expand production capacity. ABC Kitchenware, while exporting 100 per cent of its manufactured products, derives a greater proportion of its turnover through trading goods procured from China.

Discussion

Alternative Typology for Small FF Internationalization

The opening up of the Indian economy in 1991 and the government's attempt to boost exports through declaring export incomes tax-exempt have constituted significant 'state' variables within the environment. They presented uniform opportunities for internationalization to all firms. Yet, the internationalization decisions in a dynamic sense, namely, the decision to internationalize, the pathways followed, the internationalization strategies (such as pace, mode of entry, country selection and products exported) and the sustainability of internationalization, have not been uniform. They are shaped by the small family-firm's ability and willingness to internationalize. Such ability and willingness in turn are influenced and shaped by family factors—the family's dynamic capabilities and liabilities, as also its economic and non-economic goals.

Small family-firms in fast-growing emerging economies like India do not all conform to the four types of internationalization pathways suggested in extant literature (Bell et al., 2003, p. 350; Metsola et al., 2020, p. 6). Driven by 'change' variables within the environment and certain family factors, some family-firms exhibit 'Cohesive Pathways', while some others 'De-internationalization pathways'. The family factors responsible for such pathways include the family influencers' entrepreneurial orientation mindset, family socio-emotional wealth, presence of network ties, bifurcation bias and a potential new factor, that is, ethnic nationalism/nationalistic sentiments.

We define *a 'cohesive' pathway* as a hybrid pathway involving domestic as well as foreign sales. However, such hybrid pathways are not to be confused with any of the extant pathways. These FFs are in no way the reactive, ad hoc opportunists of the 'traditional' pathways; nor do they resemble firms following the born-global or born-again global pathways in terms of their being international from inception, or even changing their focus from domestic to global suddenly in response to a 'critical incident', respectively. These are FFs which are comfortable operating domestically, especially given the large size of the domestic market; yet, they believe in proactively tapping several global markets simultaneously, using and also creating networks along the way.

The reasons for the greater preference for domestic markets are part pragmatic—borne of economic goals shaped by environmental state and change variables in the home-host countries. However, we found non-economic family goals, especially family SEW and an associated nationalistic sentiment—an area which can be taken up for further research—also crucial to these decisions. Thus, cohesive pathway firms exhibit *limited internationalization* as a matter of *choice*, planning the proportion of FSTS. Foreign sales do not replace domestic sales over time; in fact, domestic sales continue to be primary and dominant. These pathways, then, are cohesive in the sense they allow for amalgamation of new export markets, even while the firms continue to expand their presence in the primary domestic markets. This classification then points to a set of small family-firms which may continue with their internationalization in a planned, structured manner, while managing to expand their domestic markets in a cohesive manner.

We also found evidence of a possible 'De-internationalization pathway, with firms which were following BG/BAG pathways earlier, now seeking to expand the proportion of domestic sales to total sales (DSTS). Extant models do consider de-internationalization, but treat these as one-off, sporadic events, followed most likely by firms which had chosen traditional incremental pathways (Bell et al., 2003, p. 350). Contrary to this, we found that even erstwhile BG firms, driven by adverse geopolitical factors, may exhibit de-internationalization. Such geopolitical factors are exacerbated by the dynamics of a family-firm, especially succession and the EO of the next-generation, and by the inability of the family-firm to find the appropriate networks to tide through such adverse conditions.

Table 15.7 extends Bell et al.'s (2003) classification and presents the augmented typology of internationalization pathways and the internationalization motivation and behaviour of firms following 'traditional', 'born global', 'born-again global', 'cohesive' and 'de-internationalization' pathways.

We use the ability-willingness (A-W) matrix to classify the internationalization pathways followed by fast-growing EE small family-firms (Fig. 15.4). Thus, firms lying in Quadrant 1 (low A-low W) are those following *sporadic* internationalization pathways. Quadrant 2 (low A-high W) corresponds to *traditional incremental* pathway firms, and Quadrant 3 (high A–high W) to

Table 15.7 Internationalization pathways of small Indian family-firms: An Augmented framework (based on Bell et al., 2003)

Key characteristics	Internationalization pathways				
	Traditional	Cohesive	Born global	Born-again global	De-industrialization
Trigger	Reactive (pushed) Adverse domestic market Unsolicited orders Insufficient funds to finance product or process improvements • Reluctant management	• Proactive • Favourable domestic and host market conditions • Strong base in home country • Sufficient funds to expand scale into new geographies • Active management	Proactive (active search) Pursue global niche markets Committed management International from inception	Reactive to critical event (management buyout (MBO), takeover, acquisition, etc.) Sudden change in focus from domestic to global orientation	Adverse host market conditions (geopolitical factors) Critical incident (management buy-out, succession, etc.)
Motivation	Firm survival/growth Increasing sales volume Gaining market share Extending product life cycle	To exploit economies of scale after understanding the domestic market to diversify risks To leverage core competencies abroad	Competitive advantage first-mover advantage locking-in customers Rapid penetration of global niches or segments protecting and exploiting proprietary knowledge	Exploit new networks and resources gained from critical incident	To avoid losses Firm survival/growth

International expansion patterns	• Incremental • Domestic expansion first • Focus on psychically close markets • Target low-tech/less sophisticated markets • Limited evidence of networks	• Not international from inception • Domestic expansion first • International expansion commences within 5–10 years of establishment, given non-restrictive trading regime and openness to trade and capital flows • Concurrent growth in domestic and foreign markets thereafter • May start with dealing in traded goods, followed by exporting own manufactures • Networks important, though not critical in the initial stages • Further expansion is based on networks.	• Concurrent • Commences within 2–6 years of establishment[a] • Near-simultaneous domestic and export expansion • Not influenced by psychic proximity of markets • Focus on lead markets • Some evidence of client followership • Strong evidence of networks	• Epoch of domestic market orientation, followed by dedicated and rapid internationalization • Strong evidence of networks (parent company's networks, client followership, suppliers and other-channel partners)	• Reversal of internationalization • not sporadic, but in response to adverse geopolitical factors and family factors. • Could be erstwhile traditional pathway firms or BG/BAG firms • Move from largely foreign markets to largely domestic markets

(continued)

Table 15.7 (continued)

Key characteristics	Internationalization pathways				
	Traditional	Cohesive	Born global	Born-again global	De-industrialization
Pace	● Gradual ● Slow internationali-zation (focus on small number of key markets) ● Single market at a time	● Initial period of domestic expansion ● Followed by rapid internationalization in terms of number of markets (scope) ● Several markets are tapped simultaneously ● intensity of internationalization may still remain restricted (<30% FSTS) as a matter of choice	● Rapid ● Speedy internationalization (large number of markets) ● Many markets at once	● Late/rapid ● No internationalization focus then rapid and dedicated internationalization ● Several markets at once	Reverse internationalization in a short span of time (2 years or so)
Method of entry into foreign markets	● Conventional ● Use of agents/distributors or wholesalers ● Direct to customers	● Flexible and networks ● Use of agents, distributors, licensing, joint ventures, overseas production ● Also evidence of integration with client's channels	● Flexible and networks ● Use of agents, distributors, licensing, joint ventures, overseas production ● Also evidence of integration with client's channels	● Networks ● Use of agents, distributors, licensing and joint ventures ● Existing channel(s) of new parent company, partner(s) or client(s)	Reverse entry Tapping domestic markets

| Internationalization strategies | • Ad hoc and opportunistic
• Evidence of continued reactive behaviour to new opportunities
• Atomistic expansion, unrelated new customers/markets
• Adaptation of existing offerings | • Planned approach to international expansion (e.g. acquisition of required global quality certifications)
• Structured
• Decision on the extent of FSTS (not to exceed a certain percentage); as such, not ad hoc and opportunistic internationali-zation.
• continues to expand in domestic markets which remain dominant | • Structured
• Evidence of planned approach to international expansion
• Expansion of global networks
• Global product development | • Reactive in response to critical incident but more planned thereafter
• Expansion of newly acquired networks
• Adaptation/new product development | Increase in domestic sales to total sales adaptation of product to suit domestic needs |
| Factors in the business environment affecting internationalization | Home-country push | Home-country pull> host-country pull | Host-country pull | Home-country push | Host-country push |

Source: Author

[a]Definition suggested by McDougall, Shane, and Oviatt (1994)

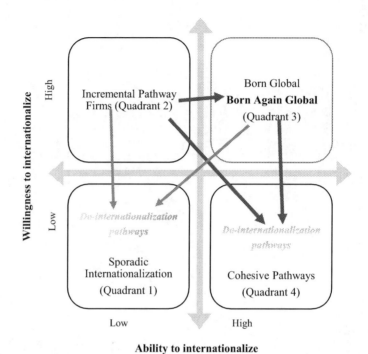

Fig. 15.4 Ability-willingness (A-W) matrix of small family-firm internationalization in fast-growing emerging economies. (Source: Author)

Born Global or *Born-Again Global* firms, with BAG firms entering Quadrant 3 from Quadrant 2. Quadrant 4 (high A–low W) would comprise of firms following cohesive pathways. Firms following de-internationalization pathways may lie either in Quadrant 1 or 4, based on the ability-willingness mix. In both cases, they could move to these quadrants from Quadrants 2 or 3. If, as a result of environmental and/or family factors the firms have lost both the ability and willingness to internationalize, they may move into Quadrant 1; a loss in willingness alone, with relatively high ability, would lead them to occupy Quadrant 4 (Fig. 15.4).

Figure 15.5 depicts these internationalization pathways graphically, with domestic operations along the x-axis and international involvement (measured by foreign sales to total sales, FSTS) along the y-axis. Cohesive pathways firms continue to expand domestically after the internationalization, even as the proportion of foreign sales is maintained. The dotted lines from the BG or BAG pathways indicate de-internationalization. Such firms, based on their ability-willingness, could either reduce the extent of international involvement to converge into cohesive pathways or move towards completely domestic operations.

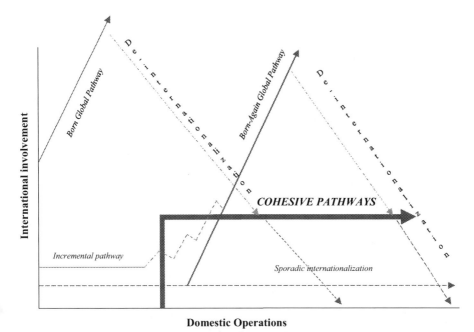

Fig. 15.5 Internationalization pathways followed by fast-growing emerging economy small family-firms. (Source: Author)

The study then offers three key contributions to the general SME internationalization literature and to the nascent literature on internationalization of small family-firms from emerging economies:

First, in keeping with the call for internationalization studies involving a temporal and contextual perspective (Metsola et al., 2020), the study looks at the *internationalization process* of small family-firms through an ability-willingness lens. The study integrates the environmental and family-level factors which determine and influence the ability and willingness of the family-firm to internationalize.

Second, the focus on context helps us in contributing to extant literature on internationalization by suggesting an alternative typology to the internationalization pathways followed by small family-firms from emerging economies. We find that FFs, driven by environmental and family factors, follow additional pathways we term 'cohesive' and 'de-internationalization' pathways.

Third, global geopolitical conditions and non-economic family factors such as entrepreneurial orientation of the (new) key family influencers, family socio-emotional wealth and ethnic nationalism of the individual influencer/family may impact the sustainability of internationalization adversely. Together, they may be responsible for limited internationalization or even sudden 'stops'.

Limitations and Opportunities for Future Research

This study is exploratory and tries to integrate extant views of internationalization, recognizing earlier observations (Coviello & McAuley, 1999) that no single view may be appropriate. Some of the dimensions highlighted in this study, such as that of planned limited internationalization or the non-economic goals of ethnic nationalism, impacting small family-firm decisions regarding the direction and extent of internationalization, may require further investigation for a deeper understanding of the phenomena involved. The results of the eight case firms studied may be idiosyncratic in that they may not be generalizable to all industries and to other emerging market small family-firms. Following earlier researchers in the field, Coviello, Kano, and Liesch (2017), Metsola et al. (2020), Santangelo and Meyer (2017), we would also support the call for diverse methodological approaches—quantitative, mixed methods and longitudinal approaches—to better understand the complex phenomena involved.

As the world becomes more closed, adverse geopolitical factors increase the risks of internationalization, emerging economies' growth rates exceed those of advanced economies and extant theories offering explanations of internationalization based on home-country push factors become redundant. These paradoxical contexts pose opportunities to understand small family-firms from emerging economies which continue with their internationalization orientation, choosing different pathways and strategies. Future research on FF internationalization may explore these contexts further, especially the influence of non-economic variables such as ethnic nationalism amidst growing ethnocentrism on limited internationalization or even de-internationalization. Such studies may adopt different methodologies to understand the impact of different variables over time and may extend to study small family-firms in other fast-growing EEs like China. Overall, the context of fast-growing emerging economies with their preponderance of small family-firms presents exciting opportunities to understand the nuances of small family-firm internationalization even further.

References

Agee, J. (2009). Developing qualitative research questions: A reflective process. *International Journal of Qualitative Studies in Education, 22*(4), 431–447.

Alayo, M., Maseda, A., Iturralde, T., & Arzubiaga, U. (2019). Internationalization and entrepreneurial orientation of family SMEs: The influence of the family character. *International Business Review, 28*(1), 48–59.

Arregle, J. L., Hitt, M. A., Sirmon, D. G., & Very, P. (2007). The development of organizational social capital: Attributes of family firms. *Journal of Management Studies, 44*(1), 73–95.

Baronchelli, G., Bettinelli, C., Del Bosco, B., & Loane, S. (2016). The impact of family involvement on the investments of Italian small-medium enterprises in psychically distant countries. *International Business Review, 25*(4), 960–970.

Bell, J., McNaughton, R., Young, S., & Crick, D. (2003). Towards an integrative model of small firm internationalization. *Journal of International Entrepreneurship, 1*, 339–362.

Bell, J., Crick, D., & Young, S. (2004). Small Firm internationalization and business strategy. An exploratory study of 'Knowledge-Intensive' and 'Traditional' manufacturing firms in UK. *International Small Business Journal, 22*(1), 23–56.

Berrone, P., Cruz, C., & Gomez-Mejia, L. (2012). Socioemotional Wealth in family firms: Theoretical dimensions, assessment approaches, and agenda for future research. *Family Business Review, 25*(3), 258–279.

Calabrò, A., Mussolino, D., & Huse, M. (2009). The role of Board of Directors in the internationalization process of small and medium sized family business. *International Journal of Globalization and Small Business, 3*(4), 393–411.

Calabrò, A., Brogi, M., & Torchia, M. (2016). What does really matter in the internationalization of small and medium-sized family businesses? *Journal of Small Business Management, 54*(2), 679–696.

Canals, C. (2019). *The threat of protectionism in the global economy.* CaixaBank research. Retrieved March 21, 2020, from https://www.caixabankresearch.com/en/threat-protectionism-global-economy

Cerrato, D., & Piva, M. (2012). The internationalization of small and medium-sized enterprises: The effect of family management, human capital and foreign ownership. *Journal of Management and Governance, 16*, 617–644.

Chen, H., & Chen, T. J. (1998). Network linkages and location choice in foreign direct investment. *Journal of International Business Studies, 29*(3), 445–468.

Chen, H. L., Hsu, W. T., & Chang, C. Y. (2014). Family ownership, institutional ownership, and internationalization of SMEs. *Journal of Small Business Management, 52*(4), 771–789.

Chitoor, R., Aulakh, P. S., & Ray, S. (2019). Micro foundations of firm internationalization: The owner CEO effect. *Global Strategy Journal, 9*(1), 42–65.

Chittoor, R., Sarkar, M. B., Ray, S., & Aulakh, P. (2009). Third-world copycats to emerging multinationals: Institutional changes and organizational transformation in the Indian pharmaceutical industry. *Organization Science, 20*, 187–205.

Coviello, N. E., & McAuley, A. (1999). Internationalisation and the smaller firm: A review of contemporary empirical research. *MIR: Management International Review, 39*, 223–256.

Coviello, N., Kano, L., & Liesch, P. W. (2017). Adapting the Uppsala model to a modern world: Macro-context and microfoundations. *Journal of International Business Studies, 48*(9), 1151–1164.

Credit Suisse Report. (2018, September). *The CS Family 1000 in 2018*. Retrieved September 27, 2019, from https://www.credit-suisse.com›docs›about-us›research›publications

Crick, D., Bradshaw, R., & Chaudhry, S. (2006). 'Successful' internationalising UK family and non-family-owned firms: A comparative study. *Journal of Small Business and Enterprise Development, 13*, 498–512.

D'Angelo, A., Majocchi, A., & Buck, T. (2016). External managers, family ownership and the scope of SME internationalization. *Journal of World Business, 51*(4), 534–547.

Eisenhardt, K. M. (1989). Building theories from case study research. *Academy of Management Review, 14*(4), 532–550.

Elango, B., & Pattnaik, C. (2007). Building capabilities for international operations through networks: A study of Indian firms. *Journal of International Business Studies, 38*, 541–555.

Fabian, F., Molina, H., & Labianca, G. (2009). Understanding decisions to internationalise by small and medium-sized firms located in an emerging market. *Management International Review, 49*(5), 537–563.

Fernández, Z., & Nieto, M. (2005). Internationalization strategy of small and medium-sized family businesses: Some influential factors. *Family Business Review, 18*, 77–89.

Gaur, A., & Kumar, V. (2010). Internationalization of emerging market firms: A case for theoretical extension. *Advances in International Management, 23*, 603–627.

Gomez-Mejia, L. R., Campbell, J. T., Martin, G., Hoskisson, R. E., Makri, M., & Sirmon, D. G. (2014). Socioemotional wealth as a mixed gamble: Revisiting family firm R&D investments with the behavioral agency model. *Entrepreneurship Theory and Practice, 38*(6), 1351–1374.

Government of India (2019). Annual report 2018–19. Ministry of micro, small and medium enterprises. Retrieved November 15, 2019, from https://msme.gov.in/sites/default/files/Annualrprt.pdf

Graves, C., & Thomas, J. (2008). Determinants of the internationalization pathways of family firms: An examination of family Influence. *Family Business Review, 21*(2), 151–167.

Hernández-Perlines, F., Ariza-Montes, A., & Araya-Castillo, L. (2019). *Socioemotional wealth, entrepreneurial orientation and international performance of family firms*. Economic Research-Ekonomska Istraživanja. https://evoma.com/business-centre/sme-sector-in-india-statistics-trends-reports/

Hunziker, T., & Gachet, E. (2019, August). *Export hurdles in practice*. Credit Suisse AG, Investment Solutions & Products. Retrieved March 1, 2020, from https://www.s-ge.com/sites/default/files/publication/free/s-ge-20193-c1-credit-suisse-sme-study-en_0.pdf

International Finance Corporation. (2012). *Assessing private sector contributions to job creation: IFC open source study*. Retrieved November 28, 2019, from http://documents.worldbank.org/curated/en/602291468183841622/pdf/819960BRI0Meas00Box379851B00PUBLIC0.pdf

International Monetary Fund. (2019, October). World economic outlook: Global manufacturing downturn, rising trade barriers. Washington, DC.

Javalgi, R. G., & Todd, P. R. (2011). Entrepreneurial orientation, management commitment, and human capital: The internationalization of SMEs in India. *Journal of Business Research, 64*(9), 1004–1010.

Johanson, J., & Vahlne, J.-E. (1977). The internationalization process of the firm—A model of knowledge development and increasing foreign market commitments. *Journal of International Business Studies, 8*(1), 23–32.

Johanson, J., & Vahlne, J.-E. (2009). The Uppsala internationalization process model revisited: From liability of foreignness to liability of outsidership. *Journal of International Business Studies, 40*, 1411–1431.

Johanson, J., & Wiedersheim-Paul, F. (1975). The internationalization of the firm—Four Swedish cases. *Journal of Management Studies, 12*(3), 305–323.

Kampouri, K., Plakoyiannaki, E., & Leppäaho, T. (2017). Family business internationalisation and networks: Emerging pathways. *Journal of Business & Industrial Marketing, 32*(3), 357–370.

Kano, L., & Verbeke, A. (2018). Family firm internationalization: Heritage assets and the impact of bifurcation bias. *Global Strategy Journal, 8*(1), 158–183.

Kontinen, T., & Ojala, A. (2010). Internationalization pathways of family SMEs: Psychic distance as a focal point. *Journal of Small Business and Enterprise Development, 17*(3), 437–454.

Kontinen, T., & Ojala, A. (2011). Social capital in relation to the foreign market entry and post-entry operations of family SMEs. *Journal of International Entrepreneurship, 9*, 133–151.

Kostova, T., & Zaheer, S. (1999). Organizational legitimacy under conditions of complexity: The case of the multinational enterprise. *Academy of Management Review, 24*, 64–81.

Leppäaho, T., & Metsola, J. (2020). *Family firm Internationalization. A network perspective.* Palgrave Macmillan.

Lodh, S., Nandy, M., & Chen, J. J. (2014). Innovation and family ownership: Evidence from emerging markets. *Corporate Governance: An International Review, 22*(1), 4–33.

Long, T., & Johnson, M. (2000). Rigour, reliability and validity in qualitative research. *Clinical Effectiveness in Nursing, 4*(1), 30–37.

Lumpkin, G. T., & Dess, G. G. (1996). Clarifying the entrepreneurial orientation construct and linking it to performance. *Academy of Management Review, 21*(1), 135–172.

Majocchi, A., D'Angelo, A., Forlani, E., & Buck, T. (2018). Bifurcation bias and exporting: Can foreign work experience be an answer? Insight from European family SMEs. *Journal of World Business, 53*(2), 237–247.

Mathews, J. A. (2006). Dragon multinationals: New players in 21st century of globalization. *Asia Pacific Journal of Management, 23*, 5–27.

McDougall, P. P., Shane, S., & Oviatt, B. M. (1994). Explaining the formation of international new ventures: The limits of theories from International Business Research. *Journal of Business Venturing, 9*(6), 469–487.

Merino, F., Monreal-Pérez, J., & Sánchez-Marin, G. (2015). Family SMEs' internationalization: Disentangling the influence of familiness on Spanish firms' export activity. *Journal of Small Business Management, 53*(4), 1164–1184.

Metsola, J., Leppäaho, T., Paavilainen-Mäntymäki, E., & Plakoyiannaki, E. (2020). Process in family business internationalisation: The state of the art and ways forward. *International Business Review, 29* (2), N.PAG. https://doi.org/10.1016/j.ibusrev.2020.101665

Narasimhan, R., Ravi Kumar, M. V., & Sridhar, M. K. (2015). Internationalization of technology-based SMEs in India: Critical factors of transformation. *South Asian Journal of Management, 22*(2), 144–166.

Narula, R., & Dunning, J. (2000). Industrial development, globalisation and multinational enterprises: New realities for developing countries. *Oxford Development Studies, 28*(2), 141–167.

Noble, H., & Smith, J. (2015). Issues of validity and reliability in qualitative research. *Evidence Based Nursing, 18*(2), 34–35.

Patterson, P. G., de Ruyter, K., & Wetzels, M. (1999). Modelling firms propensity to continue service exporting: A cross-country analysis. *International Business Review, 8*, 351–365.

Patton, M. Q. (2001). *Qualitative research and evaluation and methods* (3rd ed.). Beverly Hills, CA: Sage.

Pukall, T. J., & Calabrò, A. (2014). The internationalization of family firms: A critical review and integrative model. *Family Business Review, 27*(2), 103–125.

Ray, S., Mondal, A., & Ramachandran, K. (2018). How does family involvement affect a firm's internationalization? An investigation of Indian family firms. *Global Strategy Journal, 8*, 73–105.

Reserve Bank of India. (2019a, June 25). *Report of the Expert Committee on Micro, Small and Medium Enterprises*. Retrieved December 12, 2019, from https://www.rbi.org.in/Scripts/PublicationReportDetails.aspx?UrlPage=&ID=924

Reserve Bank of India. (2019b, August 29). *Annual Report*. Retrieved December 15, 2019, from https://www.rbi.org.in/Scripts/AnnualReportPublications.aspx?year=2019

Sahoo, P., & Bishnoi, A. (2019). *Budget 2019: Why MSME sector must be priority for Modi government*. Financial Express.

Santangelo, G. D., & Meyer, K. E. (2017). Internationalization as an evolutionary process. *Journal of International Business Studies, 48*(9), 1114–1130.

Scholes, L., Mustafa, M. J., & Chen, S. (2016). Internationalization of small family firms: The influence of family from a socioemotional wealth perspective. *Thunderbird International Business Review, 58*(2), 131–146.

Shanmugasundaram, S. (2019). Internationalization and governance of Indian family-owned business groups. *Journal of Family Business Management*, vol. ahead-of-print no. ahead-of-print, https://doi.org/10.1108/JFBM-06-2019-0040.

Shrader, R. C., Oviatt, B. M., & McDougall, P. P. (2000). How new ventures exploit trade-offs among international risk factors: Lessons for the accelerated internationalization of the 21st century. *Academy of Management Journal, 43*(6), 1227–1247.

Shukla, D., & Akbar, M. (2018). Diffusion of internationalization in business group networks: Evidence from India. *Management Decision, 56*(2), 406–420.

Singh, D. A., & Gaur, A. S. (2013). Governance structure, innovation and internationalization: Evidence from India. *Journal of International Management, 19*(3), 300–309.

Singh, R., & Kota, H. (2017). A resource dependency framework for innovation and internationalization of family businesses: Evidence from India. *Journal of Entrepreneurship in Emerging Economies, 9*(2), 207–231.

Slevin, E. (2002). Enhancing the truthfulness, consistency, and transferability of a qualitative study: Utilising a manifold of approaches. *Nurse Researcher, 7*(2), 79–197.

Sousa, C. M. P., & Bradley, F. (2006). Cultural distance and psychic distance: Two peas in a pod? *Journal of International Marketing, 14*(1), 49–70.

Tasavori, M., Zaefarian, R., & Eng, T. Y. (2018). Internal social capital and international firm performance in emerging market family firms: The mediating role of participative governance. *International Small Business Journal, 36*(8), 887–910.

Todd, P., & Javalgi, R. (2007). Internationalization of SMEs in India: Fostering entrepreneurship by leveraging information technology. *International Journal of Emerging Markets, 2*(2), 166–180.

UNCTAD. (2019, October). *Investment Trends Monitor*, Issue 32, UN, New York.

Welch, C., & Paavilainen-Mäntymäki, E. (2014). Putting process (back) in: Research on the internationalization process of the firm. *International Journal of Management Reviews, 16*(1), 2–23.

Wells, L. T. (1977). The internationalization of firms from developing countries. In T. Agmon & C. Kindleberger (Eds.), *Multinationals from small countries*. Cambridge, MA: MIT Press.

Wells, L. T. (1983). *Third world multinationals: The rise of foreign investment from developing countries*. Cambridge, MA: The MIT Press.

Yang, X., Li, J., Stanley, L. J., Kellermanns, F. W., & Li, X. (2018). How family firm characteristics affect internationalization of Chinese family SMEs. *Asia-Pacific Journal of Management*, 1–32. https://doi.org/10.1007/s10490-018-9579-7

Yin, R. K. (1989). *Case Study research: Design and methods*. Beverley Hills, CA: Sage.

Zellweger, T. M., Chrisman, J., Chua, J., & Steier, L. (2019). Social structures, social relationships, and family firms. *Entrepreneurship Theory and Practice, 43*(2), 207–223.

16

Family Firms' Internationalization: The Importance of Home Country Institutions

Elham Kalhor and Jesper Strandskov

Introduction

The extant conceptualization and empirical research on family firms' internationalization indicate that family ownership and family involvement matter for internationalization. Still, the relationship between family governance and internationalization is contradictory, unclear, and inconclusive (for recent literature reviews, see Pukall & Calabrò, 2014; Alkaabi & Dixon, 2014; Arregle, Duran, Hitt, & Van Essen, 2017). The heterogeneity of results arises from a variety of formal and informal institutional factors in different societies affecting family firms' internationalization. The relationship between family firms and internationalization is highly context-dependent. As a result, the contextual influence may explain the mixed results of prior studies (Arregle et al., 2017). A cross-national institutional differences study seems essential for explaining family firms' distinctive internationalization tendencies and strategies compared to non-family firms.

E. Kalhor (✉) • J. Strandskov
Department of Marketing and Management, University of Southern Denmark,
Odense, Denmark
e-mail: elham@sam.sdu.dk; Jst@sam.sdu.dk

© The Author(s), under exclusive license to Springer Nature Switzerland AG 2021

519

T. Leppäaho, S. Jack (eds.), *The Palgrave Handbook of Family Firm Internationalization*,
https://doi.org/10.1007/978-3-030-66737-5_16

In the following, we use both ownership-based and management-involved criteria in the definition of the family business, as discussed in the literature (De Massis, Sharma, Chua, & Chrisman, 2012). Inspired by Graves and Thomas (2008), we define "a family business as a firm that is majority family-owned (more than 50% of ordinary voting shares) and has at least one family member on the management team." As pointed out in the literature, family firms pursue non-economic objectives more often than non-family firms (Zellweger & Nason, 2008), which can negatively affect internationalization. As a disproportionate share of the family's wealth is invested in the firm and since families are often reluctant to take the risk of losing control (Carney, 2005; Heugens, van Essen, & van Oosterhout, 2009) by attracting equity from stock markets, family owners may be relatively risk-averse (Claver, Rienda, & Quer, 2008). Moreover, family businesses are more likely to be capital rationed than non-family firms (Gomez-Mejia, Makri, & Larraza Kintana, 2010; Graves & Thomas, 2008) as they obtain their financial resources from either current earnings or loans, whereby they typically lack financial support to carry out internationalization (Sirmon & Hitt, 2003).

Furthermore, existing research on family businesses also highlights several factors enhancing the internationalization of family firms. These factors include the general long-term orientation of family owners and their commitment to the firm (Segaro, Larimo, & Jones, 2014) as well as their speed and flexibility in strategic decision-making (Casillas & Moreno-Menéndez, 2014). Lately, in a study of the importance of heritage assets on family firms' internationalization, Kano and Verbeke (2017) point out that there is no generic difference between family and non-family internationalization paths. Instead, they argue that bifurcation bias—a kind of governance dysfunctionality built into the family ownership—negatively influences internationalization motives, patterns, and timing. Bifurcation is brought about by differential treatment of family-based or heritage assets versus non-family assets (Verbeke & Kano, 2012).

Although a large number of factors and conditions have been examined concerning family firms' internationalization, including unique organizational characteristics and features of family ownership per se, there have been only a very few studies that have focused on the interaction between family ownership and the institutional environment in which the family businesses are embedded.

According to the institutional-based view (Friel, 2017; Leaptrott, 2005), firms' internationalization may be facilitated or constrained by a multitude of institutional forces, including formal and informal institutions. Both formal and informal institutions may promote and hinder the upgrading of existing resources and capabilities, direct internationalization strategies, legitimate behavior, practices, and so forth. In general, institutions have been defined as the rules of the game and their enforcement mechanisms (Filatotchev, Jackson, & Nakajima, 2013; North, 1990).

Within the field of international business, scholars have primarily studied how institutions in host countries affect MNEs' entry strategies in emerging economies, for example, foreign entry strategies (Meyer, Estrin, Bhaumik, & Peng, 2009; Trevino, Thomas, & Cullen, 2008), marketing strategies (Dawar & Chattopadhyay, 2002), and management practices (Ferner, Quintanilla, & Varul, 2001), while the role of home country institutions has received little attention in the literature (Estrin, Meyer, Nielsen, & Nielsen, 2015).

This chapter aims to answer the following question: How do home country institutions influence family firms' internationalization strategies and behavior? The answer to this question partly consists of an analysis of the overall society and institutional processes and mechanisms, that is, rules, norms, and values that shape the behavior of family businesses. It also partly consists of an analysis of the context-specific home market institutions, formal (i.e., government instruments) as well as informal (i.e., customs and cultural norms), that directly influence the internationalization strategies of family businesses vis-à-vis non-family firms. Since organizations are driven by pressure from the institutional environment, it is crucial to examine the specific institutional mechanisms and processes influencing the firms' behavior and ownership, mainly to analyze how the institutional mechanisms affect and potentially delimit the internationalization strategies of family firms.

We contribute to the literature in several ways. First, we extend the institutional perspective by exploring how home country institutions affect a highly widespread and significant form of ownership, namely, family-owned firms. Although the existing literature has sporadically investigated the importance of home and host country institutions on firm internationalization (Gaur, Ma, & Ding, 2018; Li & Ding, 2017), only a very few studies have looked at the influence of home country institutional factors on the internationalization of different ownership forms. For instance, Hernández-Linares, Sarkar, and Cobo (2018) studied the effects of institutional distance on decision-making in family and non-family firms concerning international location choice. However, they mostly capture the impact of host country's institutional factors and the gap between home and host country institutions. Most of the research on family firms' internationalization focuses on the ownership structure as a home country institutional factor and its effects on internationalization. Geppert, Dörrenbächer, Gammelgaard, and Taplin (2013) studied the impacts of ownership, concentrated (family- or bank-based) and dispersed (stock market-based), on risk-taking and managerial decision-making in the international acquisition. Similarly, Luo, Chung, and Sobczak (2009) have examined the influence of corporate governance on shaping foreign firms' choice of local partners. Panicker, Mitra, and Upadhyayula (2019) concluded that family ownership positively moderates pressure-resistant investors toward internationalization. However, there is not an investigation of how various factors related to home contexts moderate the effects of family governance concerning internationalization. Since family firms tend to internationalize less than non-family businesses in general, identifying factors that enhance or hamper this process in family firms can be a breakthrough in family firms studies. Second, we apply both a sociological and an economic perspective on institutions by focusing on (1) institutional mechanisms and pressure pertaining to the internationalization of family firms (as non-irrational and path-dependent constraints of firms' decision alternatives), and (2) three pillars of institutions that specifically support or restrain family firms' internationalization. We do so on the basis that there is a need to open and expand the research domain to include not only the importance of institutions per se but also the institutional and legitimacy processes. This process directly and indirectly shapes organizational behavior and practices in which this chapter highlights the institutional implications for family firms' internationalization. Third, we derive hypotheses regarding the importance and influence of seven specific home country institutions that are expected to have moderating effects on family firms' internationalization. A few of these institutional factors have already been studied; however, we identify and discuss some further highly relevant and essential home country institutions that have not yet been investigated.

The chapter consists of four parts. In the first, we present two theoretical perspectives on institutions, that is, the institutional economics and neo-institutional theory that can be applied to explain the internationalization of family businesses. Then, we present and discuss three institutional mechanisms or pillars and isomorphic pressures (coercive, mimetic, and normative) arising from institutional context that drive and shape family firms' adoption of internationalization strategies—vis-à-vis non-family counterparts—in certain common directions. In the third part, we propose a conceptual model that delineates the essential home country institutions moderating family firms' internationalization. In the fourth part, we provide a discussion and reflection on home country institutions' influence on family firms' internationalization. The article concludes with a brief unfolding of future research avenues in relation to the importance of home country institutions on family firms' internationalization.

Institutional Theory and Internationalization of Family Businesses

In general, previous studies of institutions have been carried out using two different orientations: "institutional economics" (Coase, 1998; North, 1990) and "neo-institutional organization theory" (DiMaggio & Powell, 1983; Scott, 2001). Institutional economics emphasizes the influence of macro-environment on firms' strategies and outputs. The main concern of this approach is related to the adoption of effective policies and regulations by governments (Li & Ding, 2013). Formal and informal institutions are, respectively, devised rules and codes of behavior in society (North, 1990). The formal institution is the codified rules that, for example, define property rights and ownership arrangements, and which are stable and effectively enforced. North (1990) terms informal institutions as customs, cultural traditions, and religious norms that underpin society. These are seen as the deepest rooted and slowest changing institutions. Institutions drive actors' behavior in a specific direction through a set of incentives and disincentives, thereby constructing stable arrangement and upgrading human efficiency by reducing uncertainty and transaction costs (Friel, 2017). According to North (1990), humans invent institutions to help them meet their goals, and stable institutions may reduce uncertainty and transaction costs and facilitate interaction between social actors. Therefore, institutional economics emphasizes economic efficiency and effectiveness at the organizational (firm) level, but neglects the social embeddedness of organizations in the institutional environment (Meyer & Gelbuda, 2006).

Neo-institutional organization theory (DiMaggio & Powell, 1983; Scott, 2001) is based on sociological orientation and is related to social legitimacy focusing on firms' behavior driven by social norms and values in the external organization field (Li & Ding, 2013). In contrast to North, Powell and DiMaggio (1991) claim that institutions are not human designs but arise from historical and cultural contexts. Scott (2007) provided a less deterministic explanation of institutions by focusing on individual interpretations rather than a social process (Friel, 2017). He elaborated that cognitive institutions represent peoples' perception of their environment. Meanings arise in interactions, and they are perceived and modified by human behavior (Scott,

1995). He also explained the term normative and regulative institutions. Normative institutions include norms and values. Norms explain how things should be done and define legitimate means to achieve valued objectives (Scott, 1995). Values are desirable and preferred proffered concepts that construct standards by which existing behavior and structure can be compared and evaluated (Scott, 1995). Regulative institutions constrain and regularize behavior. Both institutional economics and neo-institutional theory are essential for survival in a challenging environment. While the former promotes macro-level institutional framework such as government policies and regulation, the latter emphasizes organizations' behavior formed by isomorphic pressure from shared norms and values in society (Li & Ding, 2013).

Both perspectives of institutional theory can be applied to explain firms' internationalization. Some scholars studying firms' internationalization have focused on economic institutions (e.g., Deng, 2009; Hessels & Terjesen, 2010), while others have adopted the sociological perspective (e.g., Li & Ding, 2013; Luo, Xue, & Han, 2010). Since social norms and values strongly affect families in society, a sociological perspective thus seems more efficient in explaining social legitimacy for the family firm to survive in a challenging environment. Neo-institutional theory can clarify the interaction between family and business with shared values and norms in a particular context relating to internationalization drivers and motives. Furthermore, neo-institutional theory based on Scott's definition (2001) of pillars of institutions can analyze the effects of the country-level institutions, including formal and informal institutions that are implicitly favorable for family businesses and to explicit instruments supporting family firms' internationalization process.

The regulative, cognitive, and normative pillars of institutional settings in home and host countries influence internationalization decisions (Lim, Morse, Mitchell, & Seawright, 2010), entry modes (Brouthers & Hennart, 2007), and target markets. These choices can be affected by psychic distance, cultural distance, and institutional distance (Torkkeli et al., 2019). Advanced formal institutions provide opportunities through competition for organizations. Such a market-supporting institutional environment decreases transaction costs, encourages organizations to participate in complex transactions, and promotes impersonal exchange via market efficiency instead of using personal networks or political power (Sun, Peng, Lee, & Tan, 2015). Informal institutions at the country level may affect internationalization expansion as well. For instance, a high level of self-expression and performance orientation and a low level of social desirability may increase internationalization in some new firms (Muralidharan & Pathak, 2017). According to Chen, Saarenketo, and Puumalainen (2018), ventures' social value orientation negatively moderates the effects of home country's formal institutions shaping internationalization relationships (Torkkeli et al., 2019). Social networks also appear as a mediator or substitute, compensating for the resource deficiency of entrepreneurs in the context of internationalization. The extent to which owners rely on social networks varies across countries and institutional contexts. In less developed countries, entrepreneurs rely more on social networks compared to developed economies. Networking activities in less developed contexts are more intense in countries with weak and unstable formal institutions and inefficient legal supports (Kiss & Danis, 2008).

Neo-institutional theory includes "institutional isomorphism" (DiMaggio & Powell, 1983) and the "three pillars of institutions" (Scott, 2001). We first explain institutional isomorphism as concerns family internationalization and then describe the institutional process through the three pillars of institutions. Institutional isomorphism expresses irrational and environment-bounded choices of firms based on isomorphic pressure. The three pillars of institutions explain the reasonable consequences of distinct institutions in specific contexts influencing the strategy choice of firms (Shen, Puig, & Paul, 2017).

Institutional Isomorphism and Family Firms' Internationalization

According to neo-institutional organization theory, internationalization is not just based on profit maximization and economic considerations of the individual firm. It is also driven by isomorphic pressures arising from institutional context (Li & Ding, 2013). Organizations adopt strategies that are legitimate within a specific environment and acceptable in an organizational field (Li & Ding, 2013). Isomorphic forces push organizations to common structures and processes through three mechanisms in which isomorphic institutional change occurs. These mechanisms are coercive isomorphism, mimetic isomorphism, and normative isomorphism (DiMaggio & Powell, 1983). Coercive isomorphism stems from government policies and legitimacy requirements, mimetic isomorphism results from rational reactions to uncertainty, and normative isomorphism is concerned with professionalization.

Coercive Pressure and Family Firms

Coercive isomorphism reflects the enforcement of government policies and regulations in society on firms (Granlund & Lukka, 1998). Organizational behavior is controlled by rules and monitoring activities exerted by force, persuasion, and invitations to join in collusion (Neilson, 2002). Coercive isomorphism is a result of pressure exerted on firms by key organizations or government mandates (DiMaggio & Powell, 1983). Consequently, organizational change occurs in response to government policies and rules. Government intervention has a significant influence on initiating the structural transformation of organizations (Deng, 2009). Regulative structures in society impose boundaries on the strategies and behaviors of organizations (Leaptrott, 2005).

Governments' policies and regulations may have distinct coercive pressure on family firms vis-à-vis non-family counterparts. Although public policies are common among family and non-family businesses in society, formal institutions impact family firms differently due to family businesses' particularism (Carney, 2005; Soleimanof, Rutherford, & Webb, 2018). Family organizations are likely to be more flexible with some institutional forces, and they adopt particular responses to formal institutions (Soleimanof et al., 2018). For instance, family businesses are less influenced by corporate social responsibility (CSR) standards and rules because family owners and managers have significant discretion to establish a customized relationship with different shareholders (Cruz, Larraza-Kintana, Garcés-Galdeano, & Berrone, 2014). In contrast, some other public regulations and policies may influence family organizations more than other types of businesses. For example, the implementation of a one-child policy for controlling the population in China caused many family firms to potentially face human resource constraints (Cao, Cumming, & Wang, 2015; Man, Mustafa, & Fang, 2016).

In emerging economies, government regulatory authorities exert a significant influence on resource allocation (Li & Ding, 2013). Firms in these countries depend on governments to acquire scarce resources such as access to finances, land, and human resources (Meyer & Lu, 2005). Therefore, to access government-controlled resources, firms need to adopt practices and structures recognized as legitimate by government authorities (Li & Ding, 2013). Concerning internationalization, governments in emerging economies, for example, promote internationalization by supporting firms' internationalization through rules and policies (Luo et al., 2010) and firms move toward internationalization to meet the expectations of the governments (Li & Ding, 2013). The government's policies in these countries include easing capital controls, reducing risks associated with politics and investment, streamlining administrative procedures such as decentralization of authority to local levels of government, and providing information and guidance for exporting and investment opportunities (Luo et al., 2010).

16 Family Firms' Internationalization: The Importance of Home... 527

Nevertheless, family firms in emerging markets may respond to government policies quite differently from other types of businesses. Mostly, family businesses are the prevailing type of businesses in emerging countries because they can benefit from informal institutions to compensate for weak formal supports (Liu, Yang, & Zhang, 2012). Family involvement in business decreases the risk of agency costs that stem from lack of interpersonal trust, inefficient monitoring mechanisms, and inadequate labor markets (Soleimanof et al., 2018). Furthermore, weak property rights systems, underdeveloped capital markets, and insufficient contract enforcement push entrepreneurs to rely on family ties for acquiring resources (Soleimanof et al., 2018). Hence, family-owned companies can overcome the scarcity of their resources through enduring relationships, strong social capital, a higher level of trust, and other informal institutions. In terms of internationalization, since family businesses are not very dependent on the governments in emerging markets, they may be less pressured by government mandates.

In developed countries, efficient formal institutions such as monitoring and contracting mechanisms, protection of minority shareholders, and transparent financial regulations decrease the risk of agency cost in family firms and push family businesses to international expansion. Developed formal institutions act as an external governance mechanism, reducing agency costs and increasing external investments in family firms (Fernando, Schneible Jr, & Suh, 2014). Family involvement in business in a developed context has a less distinguishing effect on firms' performance in general (Liu et al., 2012; Soleimanof et al., 2018).

Mimetic Isomorphism and Family Firms

Uncertainty is an intense pressure to encourage imitation in organizations. When the environment creates symbolic uncertainty or goals are vague, organizations tend to model themselves on other organizations. Modeling is a response to uncertainty. Models can be disseminated indirectly by transferring employees or directly by consulting firms or industry trade associations. Mimetic isomorphism leads firms to change and adopt similar practices to other organizations (DiMaggio & Powell, 1983). Imitation is not just based on competitive necessity; more importantly, it is a function for obtaining legitimacy or social fitness in a large social structure (Li & Ding, 2013). The higher the uncertainty in an environment, the more likely companies are to mimic the actions of peer firms. Therefore, in emerging economies, which are characterized by rapid evolution and a higher level of fear of failure due to higher uncertainty of the environment, firms are more influenced by mimetic pressure compared to developed contexts (Li & Ding, 2013).

Internationalization is a high-risk strategy. Hence, firms usually imitate the procedures of competitors to overcome the uncertainty and risk associated with the internationalization process. When companies enter international markets, their competitors are urged to internationalize not through direct imitation but through application of strategies employed by competitors (Yang, Jiang, Kang, & Ke, 2009). Firms are likely to imitate rivals' expansion strategies, that is, location strategy (Delios, Gaur, & Makino, 2008), entry mode (Li, Yang, & Yue, 2007), and operational strategy (Salomon & Wu, 2012). Prevalent and successful internationalization practices are considered reliable and legitimate internationalization methods (Li & Ding, 2013). Imitation is an efficient approach to reducing uncertainty in foreign direct investment (FDI) decisions. Imitation decreases search costs for making strategic decisions (Fourné & Zschoche, 2018).

Family governance may affect imitation strategies in internationalization. Family-owned companies adopt different strategies in internationalization that may not be in line with conventional approaches in non-family counterparts (Arregle et al., 2017). They usually enter fewer markets, narrow their geographic scope, maintain long-lasting foreign partnerships, and invest less (Fourné & Zschoche, 2018). Hence, they follow the internationalization strategy through exclusive approaches. Family companies tend to conform to the behavior of other organizations to avoid social losses. However, the higher motivation for them is to participate in legitimate practice as considered in a specific context (Mazzelli, Kotlar, & De Massis, 2018). Therefore, even if we find that imitation stems from different factors that influence all firms, such as political conditions in society, family firms do not just follow general industry trends and the biggest non-family companies (Fourné & Zschoche, 2018). Instead, they rely on trait-based imitation behavior, that is, copying practices of other companies with certain features, and they may follow leading family firms' peers (Fourné & Zschoche, 2018). There are essential traits for the identification of peers when family owners intend to model themselves on other family firms. For example, the reputation of family companies, particularly among other family firms and partner organizations, seems essential. A superior choice for a family firm in a foreign location may be a firm from the same home country and the same industry. Similarity also arises from being family-owned and having similar economic and non-economic concerns (Fourné & Zschoche, 2018).

Normative Pressure and Family Firms

The third source of isomorphic change is normative pressure derived from professionalization (DiMaggio & Powell, 1983). Normative pressure is concerned with collective cognitive-based shared understanding and definition of norms and legitimated activities within the professional sphere (Larson, 1991). While universities and professional training are essential centers for expanding and distributing organizational norms among managers and staff, professionals and trade associations are also channels for defining and promoting normative rules about professional and organizational behavior. These mechanisms create interchangeable individuals who work in a similar position in different organizations and promote the same orientation and arrangement for shaping corporate behavior toward homogeneity (DiMaggio & Powell, 1983). Normative pressures manifest through internal organizational networks, for instance, among firms and suppliers or firms and customer networks. Norms are disseminated through relational channels, and the dissemination of norms leads to reinforcing them. Thus, individual firms change their behaviors to conform to shared norms (Li & Ding, 2013).

In a globally interconnected world where global ambitions are valued practices in the business environment, pursuing an internationalization strategy can provide excellent credit for firms and cause firms to have significant potential and profitability (Li & Ding, 2013). Therefore, internationalization can be considered a shared norm among organizations that puts pressure on organizations to conform to this strategy.

In addition to pervasive organizational and business norms, family owner-managers may have particular norms and non-economic objectives within their organizations. The family business is not just a link between family and business institutions but mediates the interactions and confluences of these institutions (Soleimanof et al., 2018). The dual nature of family firms and the discrepancy between normative orders of family and business (e.g., generalized long-term objectives related to family and short-term balanced reciprocity linked to business) cause family firms to face a contradictory situation (Soleimanof et al., 2018).

In the context of internationalization, family firms' particular norms create some advantages and disadvantages. For instance, trust is a principle norm in family firms, which is a core component of other attributes such as stewardship and altruism (Arregle et al., 2017). Trust increases the speed of decision-making and ensures that family members will have their interests met without monitoring each other (Carney, 2005). Trust has a unique effect on strategic decisions and plays a positive role in family business internationalization (Arregle et al., 2017). In contrast, the protection of socioemotional wealth may negatively influence family firms' internationalization strategy. Since family owners try to protect socioemotional wealth and are not willing to alleviate financial and managerial resources through non-family partners, they will be more reluctant to internationalize compared to other businesses (Arregle, Naldi, Nordqvist, & Hitt, 2012).

Home Country Institutions on Family Firms' Internationalization

Recently, there has been a growing interest in how home country institutions influence firms' internationalization (Gaur et al., 2018; Lee, Yin, Lee, Wang, & Peng, 2015; Li & Ding, 2017). Since there are specific restrictions in terms of technological deficiency, lack of ownership advantages, and managerial capabilities in emerging economies, the institutional-based view has especially been applied to explain firms' internationalization in emerging markets (Peng, Wang, & Jiang, 2008). Scholars argue that home country institutions may create incentives as well as constraints on strategic choices, which in turn influence firms' motivations and ability to internationalize rather than only conduct domestic operations (Estrin et al., 2015). In examining the effects of home country institutions, most studies have investigated the decisive role of the institutional environment in promoting internationalization, while the negative role has received relatively little attention (Li & Ding, 2017).

Furthermore, government policy may offer several incentives and measures that help firms to face the liability of foreignness and thus mobilize resources aimed at international expansion. Home country institutions shape firms' ability to access resources in their home environment and may enhance the legitimacy of foreign operations and activities. A number of countries have created formal institutions that support the international business activities of firms from their country, especially exports or export-enhancing foreign direct investments (Luo et al., 2010; Nguyen, Le, & Bryant, 2013). Government policies also include policies such as streamlined administrative procedures, low interest financing, favorable exchange rates, and reduced taxation. Research has shown that market-supporting institutions such as export assistance programs (Lages, Jap, & Griffith, 2008) and government programs promoting outward FDIs (Luo et al., 2010) have a positive influence on firm internationalization.

16 Family Firms' Internationalization: The Importance of Home... 531

On the other hand, firms can focus on internationalization to avoid the hostility of their home market institutions (Witt & Lewin, 2007) due to institutional constraints and costs (high taxes, corruption, strong regulations, government inefficiencies, etc.). Informal or poor home country institutional factors such as government corruption, regulatory uncertainty, weak law enforcement practices, and insufficient protection of intellectual property rights may also push the firm to internationalize in pursuit of more efficient institutions (Luo et al., 2010). Prior study shows that new business ventures export more as government corruption increases (Lee et al., 2015). In several cases, home country institutions also aim to constrain firm internationalization, particularly outward FDI, due to the potential of losing domestic jobs and so forth (Hartman, Shaw, & Stevenson, 2003).

Nevertheless, investigations of the effects of host country institutions on internationalization strategies have not elaborated on how the two environmental forces of "support" and "escapism" coexist (Witt & Lewin, 2007) or how they interact with different ownership structures: state-ownership, private-investor ownership, family ownership, and so forth. For example, state-owned enterprises (SOEs) are expected to be driven to internationalize by government promotion and support, while investor-owned firms are more likely to internationalize to escape institutional home environment constraints. However, it is rather unclear how home country institutions influence family firms' internationalization strategies, a highly neglected topic in the IB literature.

According to the new institutional perspective, institutional factors can be grouped into three categories: regulative, normative, and cognitive pillars of institution structure (Scott, 2007). In contrast with this typological view, Trevino et al. (2008) suggested that the institutional pillars should not be considered a classification of the type of institution; rather, these pillars determine the process by which institutions affect managerial and organizational actions (Trevino et al., 2008). Based on this suggestion, a classification of the institutionalization process (instead of a grouping of institutional types) can develop a theoretical framework that explains how national institutions influence family business' intention and capability for internationalization. Hence, family firms' internationalization behavior can be shaped by the process associated with all the pillars of institutions, perhaps simultaneously but not necessarily equally.

To clarify the role of institutional contexts in family firms' internationalization, we propose a conceptual model that delineates essential determinates enhancing family firms' internationalization. The model elaborates on the relations between family firms' institutions with the three pillars of institutions structure based on Scott's definition (see Fig. 16.1).

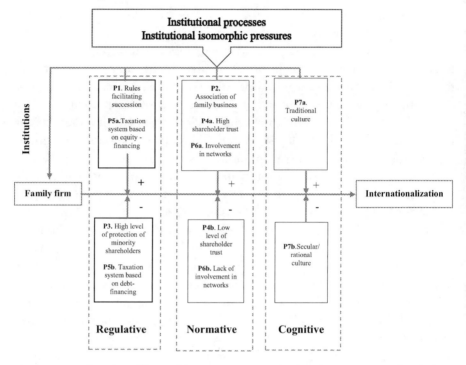

Fig. 16.1 Moderating effects of home country institutional processes on family firm internationalization. A conceptual model. (Source: Author)

In the following, we review essential regulatory, cognitive, and normative institutional factors related to family firms in particular, and processes that may positively or negatively impact family firms' internationalization depending on the specific managerial and organizational context. These institutional factors have been extracted from prior research and official (i.e., government) reports in the field of family firms, mostly from European countries (e.g., see Austria, 2008; Pittino et al., 2017).

We will focus on the following institutions: (1) laws and regulations facilitating business transfer, (2) associations of family businesses, (3) protection of minority shareholders, (4) generalized trust toward family business, (5) taxation of reinvested profits, (6) networks, and (7) culture.

Laws and Regulations Facilitating Business Transfer

Succession is a unique factor related to family businesses, which empirically influences internationalization (Graves & Thomas, 2008). Evidence shows that subsequent generations have a higher tendency to internationalize compared to first-generation family members. The higher tendency may arise from the higher capability of the subsequent generation in terms of acquired knowledge and other resources. A successful succession can drive family firms toward adopting new strategies such as international expansion. Commitment to internationalization is related to the vision and abilities of the successor (Graves & Thomas, 2008). For instance, Starmould and Pioneer Wines companies demonstrated internationalization behavior in family firms that is similar to "born-again global" firms. They were well-established firms that had focused on the domestic marketplace and then instantly embraced rapid and dedicated internationalization due to a "critical incident." The incident was succession and transferring the business to the next generation that led to a global orientation and long-term commitment to internationalization. The development of organizational capabilities such as the requisite managerial expertise acquired by the new generation is the logical reason (Graves & Thomas, 2008). Hence, in line with born-again triggers such as management buyout (MBO), takeover, and acquisition (Bell, McNaughton, Young, & Crick, 2003), succession to the next generation of family firms can also be a trigger for family firms to pursue a born-again pathway to internationalization (Graves & Thomas, 2008).

Studies on the impact of succession on family firms' internationalization reveal that a successful succession provides essential opportunities that may increase firms' international commitment (e.g., Meneses, Coutinho, & Carlos Pinho, 2014). As a result, regulations that facilitate business transfer are favorable for family business internationalization. Generational change is an important incident in family businesses since family owners tend to maintain the sustainability of the firm beyond the professional life of the founder. At the same time, generational change exerts substantial challenges on family enterprises influencing their survival (Austria, 2008).

A relevant law that affects business transfer is inheritance and gift tax, which causes a significant challenge for family organizations. If the tax burden is insupportable for family owners' budgets, it can prevent successful business transfer (Austria, 2008). Concerning this issue, some European countries enacted rules to eliminate inherence and gift tax for business transfer or significantly reduced the financial burden arising from taxation. Another major problem for failure in a business transfer is lack of planning and information in terms of the importance of timely preparation and procedures facilitating the succession process (Austria, 2008). These supportive instruments were offered in European countries about three years ago by governmental authorities or employers' organizations.

534 E. Kalhor and J. Strandskov

From the perspective of institution construction, particular regulations supporting the succession process such as tax reforms and legal assistance from government authorities primarily take place through the regulative pillars of institutions because of the tangibility of the rules and probable sanctions for non-compliant actions. Thus, we establish the following proposition:

P1 *Laws and regulations that facilitate and promote business transfer to the next generation (succession process) positively moderate internationalization in family businesses.*

Associations of Family Businesses

Associations of family businesses are usually non-profit organizations that serve as executive business platform and key intermediary between family businesses and public administration. It aims to defend the interests of family businesses, identify corporate governance and management best practices, and secure the education and networking of future generations. For instance, Instituto de la Impresa Familiar (IEF) in Spain has 16 regional associations of family businesses consisting of 1100 companies from all sectors that are leading companies in their respective regions (Pittino et al., 2017).

Associations of family businesses support family firms' development and growth by exchanging knowledge and experience across different industries. These institutions help family owners overcome the lack of managerial capabilities and risk aversion as key deterrent factors in family-owned companies influencing essential strategies such as internationalization. Associations of family businesses also secure networks for future generations and help family owners protect socioemotional wealth and positively affect the adoption of new strategies (Pittino et al., 2017).

From the institutional perspective, associations of family businesses primarily legitimize through normative pillars of institutions because they do not set punitive measures and only act to facilitate and guide internationalization behavior. Hence, a regional association of family businesses may increase the tendency toward internationalization in family firms. Based on this discussion, we establish the following proposition:

P2 *The existence of an association of family businesses positively moderates family business internationalization.*

Protection of Minority Shareholders

Family involvement in firms and the consequence of the integration of family goals and business objectives lead to specific attributes in organizations (Carney, 2005). A common concern about family involvement in governance is the assumption that family owners formulate strategies without significant interference from minority non-family shareholders (Arregle et al., 2017). However, research has shown that non-family shareholders bring specific resources that positively affect firms' strategies, such as internationalization (Arregle et al., 2012). Minority shareholder protection increases the ability of non-family members to monitor family activities and intervene if necessary. This formal institution is essential to restrain family manipulation and increase the power of non-family members in family firms. According to previous research, family involvement negatively affects internationalization (e.g., Verbeke & Kano, 2012), and minority ownership protection can increase the opportunity for internationalization in family organizations (Singla, Veliyath, & George, 2014).

In contrast, the economic perspective and some other theories suggest that minority shareholders may not be beneficial in all situations. Opposing views argue that a high level of minority shareholders can impede internationalization in several ways. For instance, this institution neglects the potential conflict between family and minority shareholders because it influences the interaction between family and non-family shareholders. Furthermore, a high level of minority shareholder protection may block crucial strategic decisions and lead to defensive strategies when there is a possibility of expropriation. Finally, the protection of minority shareholders alters the nature of strategic decision-making in family firms from long-run strategies to short-term investments. Therefore, it may hamper the internationalization process (Arregle et al., 2017).

From an institutional perspective, protection of minority shareholders legitimizes through regulative pillars of institutions since it places restrictions on family business organizations. Consequently, we propose the following proposition:

P3 High level of protection of minority shareholders negatively moderates family business internationalization.

Generalized Trust Toward Family Businesses

Prior research has examined the effects of the "trust of other nations" on the internationalization process in family firms (Arregle et al., 2017). However, trust is a multidimensional factor, and one crucial dimension can be generalized trust in society toward family firms. Trust, or the ability to generate trust, is one of the essential elements distinguishing family businesses from other types of companies. Anecdotal evidence indicates that family businesses have an advantage over non-family firms in generating trustworthiness in stakeholders' perceptions and, as a result, stakeholders' trust. This evidence stems from a stereotypical belief about family-owned companies. Furthermore, long-term corporate philosophies are a crucial component in family firms that increase the trustworthiness of family companies (Krappe, Goutas, & von Schlippe, 2011). Some scholars investigated family business behavior (e.g., Dyer & Whetten, 2006) and found that family companies are less likely to engage in irresponsible practices. According to Cooper, Upton, and Seaman (2005), family companies pay more attention to customer concerns and satisfaction compared to non-family companies. Family businesses exhibit more responsibility for work relationships and secure employment and ethical contracts for eternal recruits (Stavrou, Kassinis, & Filotheou, 2007).

One of the main concerns of family owners about the internalization process is the risk of losing the socioemotional wealth endowment (SEW). Threats to SEW can derive from the need for funding, which is seen as a potential dilution of family shareholding, or may arise from inexperienced owners/ managers and consequently the need for external managers to deal with the complexity of the internationalization process, which also reduces the power of family owners. Moreover, it is necessary to adhere to foreign shareholders, which may lead to a loss of SEW (Pukall & Calabrò, 2014).

According to organizational identity theory, family influence promotes a trustworthy manner toward stakeholders because the effects of these manners and attitudes lead to the preservation of family socioemotional wealth (Hauswald, 2013). Based on categorization research, people hold predefined categorizations about family business' trustworthiness in general. Based on the integration model of trust, increased perception of trustworthiness establishes the trust that, in turn, stimulates risk-taking behavior (Hauswald, 2013). Stakeholders' trust generates a competitive advantage for family businesses over non-family firms (Hauswald, 2013). Trust affects firms' performance by promoting network relationships, reducing conflicts, and decreasing transaction costs (Kramer, 1999).

16 Family Firms' Internationalization: The Importance of Home... 537

Regarding the effects of trust on firms' performance, stakeholders' trust toward family-owned companies can influence family businesses' internationalization by decreasing transaction costs and risk aversion in family firms. From the institutional construction point of view, social acceptance of "trust toward family companies" primarily legitimates through the normative pillar of institutions because of the less tangible essence of this construct. Against this background, we propose the following proposition:

P4a *High level of "shareholder trust" toward family firms positively moderates family business internationalization.*

P4b *Low level of "shareholder trust" toward family businesses negatively affects internationalization in family firms.*

Taxation of Reinvested Profits

Tax is an essential issue for private owners. In many countries, taxation systems support debt financing. A benefit of debt financing is that the interest on the debt is a tax-deductible income expense. As a result, the corporate tax system authorizes the deduction of interest from debt; however, it does not take into account the cost of capital in the form of equity financing (Flören, 2010). This policy discriminates in favor of debt financing (against retained earnings) and decreases the relative debt cost, which hinders growth and access to cheaper debt financing.

Reinvestment is crucial to family business capitalization. In general, family firms' debt-equity ratio is lower than non-family businesses. A lower debt-equity leads to more sustainability during recessions and structural changes. The taxation system, which promotes debt-equity, is not advantageous for family firms (Flören, 2010). In contrast, an equity financing-based tax system facilitates family business capitalization. Hence, the choice of financing methods, that is, debt versus equity financing and reinvesting of profits, affects family business capitalization. Reinvestment of profits and capitalization systems in family businesses influences firms' investment decisions (Austria, 2008), such as foreign market investment and internationalization strategies.

From the perspective of institution building, government policy of favorable tax treatment of retained profit and supporting family business capitalization can positively influence family firms' internationalization. Since this construct is tangible and restrictive, the taxation system of reinvestment primarily operates through the regulative pillar of institutions due to the tangibility of tax rules and the presence of sanctions for non-compliant behavior. Thus, we formulate the following proposition:

P5a *Taxation systems that support equity financing positively moderate family business internationalization.*

P5b *Taxation systems supporting debt financing negatively moderate family business internationalization.*

Social Networks

Classical internationalization theory assumes that firms internationalize when the benefits of internationalization exceed the costs. However, studies based on this theory do not consider governance mechanisms based on the interaction among actors, for instance, business networking among individuals and cooperation among firms (Enderwick & Buckley, 2017). Rondi, Debellis, De Massis, and Garzoni (2020) express three complexities related to internationalization: (1) information costs referring to the cost of acquiring knowledge and transferring them to a strategic partner, (2) coordination costs relating to the costs of communication about joint actions with partners, and (3) motivation costs including the cost of supervision and aligning interests with partners. Formal contracts are insufficient to manage these complexities; therefore, the presence of networks can facilitate mutual trust and interaction between parties.

Strong social capital is a distinctive characteristic of family firms and is a deeply embedded resource that is immensely difficult to imitate (Rondi et al., 2020). The structural component of social capital is social networks that are materialized into measurable phenomena such as social participation and relational goods consumption. Social network plays a double-sided role in economic development and growth (Sabatini, 2009). Networks may nurture or hamper social cohesion and economic activities. The conventional distinguishing among bonding, bridging, and linking social capital reflects the different roles of networks in economic development (Sabatini, 2009).

Family firms have two forms of social capital: family social capital and organizational social capital (Arregle et al., 2007). Family social capital develops among family members and is the most potent and durable (Rondi et al., 2020). Organizational social capital refers to the need to access the resources beyond the family firm, specifically those resources that cannot be purchased, such as knowledge, information, trust, and connection to other organizations that may affect the family firm's performance. Although family social capital can reduce agency and transaction costs significantly, the conceptual examination should not be limited to a single-family firm (Feranita, Kotlar, & De Massis, 2017).

Hence, it is vital to study social networking beyond the boundaries of a single organization to explore the potential of social networking in cross-organizational cooperation.

Recently, scholars have started to explore the importance of organizational social capital in family business' internationalization (e.g., Zahra, 2020; Rondi et al., 2020). The results show that family firms with high organizational social capital internationalize more than non-family firms (Zahra, 2020).

In contrast, Donckels and Frohlich (1991) express that family businesses are reluctant to expand their social networks and tend toward less cooperation with other firms and less participation in socioeconomic networks such as government programs. The reluctance may arise from family firms' privacy (Graves & Thomas, 2004). They explain that family owners may not even be aware of networks, such as government programs and non-profit agencies, that are intermediary between public and private sectors. The lack of involvement in social networks leads to family companies facing more challenges for internationalization compared to non-family firms because networks play an essential role in the internationalization process. Nevertheless, in terms of internationalization, the role of networks can be more significant for family firms compared to non-family businesses. Family companies are restricted by conservative behavior and a higher level of risk aversion (Minetti, Murro, & Zhu, 2015), and they tend to internationalize less than their non-family counterparts in general. Social networks may counteract the negative influence of family governance on firms' internationalization by providing knowledge about markets, access to international partners and resources, and capabilities required for internationalization.

The role of the network can be different in internationalization from country to country. For example, in emerging markets where formal institutions are not efficient in supporting firms, the role of the network is crucial in firms' internationalization. According to previous research, the higher level of uncertainty of the institutional environment leads to managers and owners relying on networks for entering international markets (Shirokova & McDougall-Covin, 2012).

From the institutional perspective, involvement in socioeconomic networks enables family firms to manage international operations in foreign markets more efficiently. In contrast, when family owners try to rely only on internal networks and family ties, they will miss out on acquiring capabilities for entering international markets.

Social networks legitimize through normative-cognitive pillars of institutions as they act as guiding behavior and symbolic representation. Networks provide a dynamic platform for exchanging opinions, knowledge, and experiences, thereby driving family firms from ethnocentrism toward globalization. Based on this discussion, the following proposition is proposed:

P6a *Involvement in socioeconomic networks positively moderates family businesses' internationalization.*

P6b *Lack of involvement in socioeconomic networks negatively affects family firms' internationalization.*

Culture

Culture has been defined in several different ways based on dominant theoretical and methodological approaches. We adopt the definition of culture as "a set of values that are shared in a given social group and distinguish this group from others" (Beugelsdijk, Kostova, & Roth, 2017). Several studies have shown the effects of culture on international businesses and explained that internationalization is embedded in the culture of societies (e.g., Beugelsdijk et al., 2017; Verbeke, Yuan, & Kano, 2020).

Culture can affect family and business systems and the linkage between them. Societal values embedded in societies affect family firms' practices and determine family firms' desirable behavior (Verbeke et al., 2020). Societal values justify people's actions in society. Family business owners legislate their own firm culture over time, and they address both external and internal challenges.

At the macro-level (external environment), they need to meet a variety of demands, such as producing required goods and gaining legitimacy. At the firm level (internal environment), they need to interact with organization members and coordinate different units and functions. Family business owners need to gain some level of approval from the societies in which they operate. The values of family owners and their firms should be aligned with prevalent societal norms; otherwise, family firms may be subjected to pressures or sanctions (Verbeke et al., 2020). Scholars have studied different dimensions of culture relating to firms' performance and internationalization in family firms. For instance, Verbeke et al. (2020) have examined the role of relational contracting culture, formal contracting culture, embeddedness culture, hierarchal cultures, and egalitarian culture. They investigated the role of individual values and social values in the context of bifurcation bias in family firms and the effects on internationalization.

In addition to these dimensions, two dimensions of culture seem especially crucial in the investigation of country culture relating to family firms' output and internationalization: traditional culture and rationalistic or secular culture. Traditional culture is a culture in which tradition is the authority guiding social life. Authorities promote traditions and transfer them to new generations. The authorities of tradition are localized in family and religious leaders. Traditions are exercised when people seek advice and listen to the authorities (Schott & Cheraghi, 2012). The traditional culture is in contrast with rationalistic culture (secular or rational culture). In rationalistic culture, the social system is more guided by cost and benefit, mainly based on science. It is localized in professions that guide people in the pursuit of well-being and advantage (Schott & Cheraghi, 2012). In a traditional culture, social relationships are based on solidarities; however, in a rationalistic culture, social exchanges are based on perceptions of benefit (Schott & Cheraghi, 2012).

Family businesses have strong values and norms and are known as traditional organizations. Tradition is understood as "consciously transmitted beliefs and practices expressing identification with a shared past" (Dacin, Dacin, & Kent, 2019). Traditions shape family firms' identity and support continuity and induce the next generation to accept it. Shared beliefs, practices, and legacy support family firms' survival, albeit they pose a substantial constraint to change (Erdogan et al., 2019). Family business systems are built on solidarities and family ties, and they benefit from enduring relationships and steward behaviors and altruism. Family business owners pursue some non-economic objectives which are not pursued by non-family firms (Erdogan et al., 2019). The non-economic objectives are more in line with traditional culture rather than a rationalistic culture, which is driven by cost and benefit and by professionalism. The traditional culture is likely to provide a more efficient social system for supporting family endeavors in business. Recently a cross-national study conducted by Liu (in press) in 54 countries around the world has shown that institutional factors in societies with traditional culture are more favorable and supportive for family firms compared to societies based on rationalistic or secular culture. Since internationalization is embedded in the culture of societies, traditional culture may support family firms' internationalization, particularly compared to rationalistic culture, and traditional culture-based countries may increase family firms' internationalization.

In contrast, rationalistic culture may not support the non-economic goals of family owners, which are priorities in family businesses; moreover, it is incompatible with the traditional structure of family firms. Therefore, Western countries that are constructed on rationalistic culture may not particularly lend themselves to a beneficial environment for family firms' internationalization. From the institutional point of view, culture is less tangible and effectively legitimizes through the cognitive pillars of institutions. Based on the earlier discussion, we state the following propositions:

P7a *Traditional culture positively moderates the internationalization of family businesses.*

P7b *Rationalistic culture* (secular or rational culture) negatively moderates the *internationalization of family businesses.*

Discussion and Conclusions

Drawing insight from institutional theory, we have conceptually examined how home country institutions and processes play an essential role in family firms' internationalization. Several studies have researched the importance of home and host country institutions on firms' internationalization. This chapter has focused explicitly on home country institutions' impact on family firms' internationalization. These institutions regulate family ownership with laws on business transfer (generation succession), taxes, and so forth and promote and propagate family ownership informally and implicitly through family business networks and associations as well as sociocultural influences (norms and values).

To address the research question, we have adopted both perspectives of institutional economics and neo-institutional theory by focusing on institutional isomorphism and the three pillars of institutions, including regulative, normative, and cognitive pillars. The institutional process through the three pillars of institutions has also been elucidated for family business internationalization. We have derived propositions regarding the moderating effects of seven home country institutions on family firms' internationalization process. Most of these factors have not been applied in empirical studies yet. The next step—in a cross-country setting—is to empirically test how the seven identified institutional factors influence family firms' internationalization.

The article raises several crucial issues regarding the relationship between family business characteristics and the importance of the institutional setting on firms' internationalization. As family-owned firms are the dominant form of ownership in highly industrialized countries, as well as in emerging market economies and less developed countries, a key issue—in a globalized world—is whether the family business is particularly suitable for using internationalization as a growth strategy. The IB research literature cannot provide a clear answer to this since family ownership as an organizational form has both weaknesses and strengths concerning foreign market expansion, that is, internationalization. So far, research has shown various economically ineffective factors embedded in family ownership that negatively influence internationalization. In particular, factors pertain to non-economic objectives of family businesses such as firm survival, family succession, risk aversion, protection of socioemotional wealth, and preservation of local jobs. Furthermore, the research in this area also has found some positive elements of family ownership that promote firms' internationalization. These elements include speed of strategic decision-making, long-term orientation, and trustworthiness in business affairs, which, in turn, foster network relationships, reduce conflicts, decrease transaction costs, and so forth.

Institutional processes and factors creating isomorphic pressures may increasingly promote the spread of family ownership, for example, by facilitating generational shift, providing exclusive tax benefits to family businesses, and low level of minority shareholders' protection. As a result, it can make family ownership more competitive vis-à-vis other forms of ownership (e.g., private investor firms). However, it may have the paradoxical effect that family-owned firms will be better suited for exportation and internationalization due to government regulation and embedded sociocultural factors in favor of family ownership. But alternative ownership and organizational forms (e.g., private investor-owned firms) will have a competitive disadvantage even though they have greater capabilities and opportunities to internationalize (e.g., greater risk willingness, higher investment capacity). The macroeconomic implications for the home country can thus be detrimental in terms of foreign exchange earnings and long-term competitiveness.

The present study has some limitations. First, we have primarily analyzed the importance of home institutions for the internationalization of family businesses on a general level. However, institutional processes and factors influencing various strategy dimensions of internationalization have not been addressed in this chapter, such as family firms' aspirations and motivations, their location strategies (i.e., choice of markets and supply locations), their entry mode strategies (e.g., exports, contracts, or direct foreign investment), the pace or speed of their internationalization, and other essential dimensions of internationalization. However, internationalization is not just related to outward activities. It is also concerned with inward activities that are related to how family firms supply themselves by importing raw materials, foreign technology, human resources, and so forth (i.e., inward internationalization), which ultimately affect the competitiveness of family businesses. For family businesses, internationalization involves significant capital budget allocation decisions, exposing them to multiple dimensions of distance and causing them to face dilemmas and circumstances radically different from those experienced domestically. For example, entry mode decisions that involve significant investments (i.e., equity FDIs, JVs, cross-border M&As) are essential, as well as overall international market expansion strategies. The research concerning these relevant strategic dimensions of internationalization is only in its infancy, and there is still little knowledge about how external institutional factors affect family ownership per se and key internationalization choices.

Second, the study on home country institutional factors only provides a partial explanation for the understanding of family firm internationalization. While home country institutions may be assumed to act as push factors that motivate/force the family business to internationalize, the analysis must be further supplemented by the pull factors represented by host country institutions. These are primarily assumed to influence the family firms' choice of foreign location and type of entry mode. Further explanatory factors, such as industry-related factors and firm-specific advantages, must be included in the analysis to gain a more comprehensive understanding of the primary drivers of family firms' internationalization.

Future Research

For further advancing our understanding of host country institutions on family firms' internationalization, we suggest that future research should be directed toward analyzing (1) how different configurations of majority family ownership in correspondence with strong protection of minority shareholders influence firms' internationalization, and in particular how non-family board members may exert their influence on internationalization decisions vis-à-vis family owners, (2) how home country institutions may have an impact on specific internationalization decisions related to localization of foreign operations (i.e., market selection) or mode of foreign entry, and (3) how regulatory, normative, and cognitive institutional processes influence one another and, through their interplay, affect both organizational and governance characteristics of family businesses on the one hand, and family business' internationalization choices on the other.

References

Alkaabi, S. K., & Dixon, C. (2014). Factors affecting internationalization decision making in family businesses: An integrated literature review. *Journal of Applied Management and Entrepreneurship, 19*(2), 53.

Arregle, J. L., Duran, P., Hitt, M. A., & Van Essen, M. (2017). Why is family firms' internationalization unique? A meta-analysis. *Entrepreneurship Theory and Practice, 41*(5), 801–831.

Arregle, J. L., Hitt, M. A., Sirmon, D. G., & Very, P. (2007). The development of organizational social capital: Attributes of family firms. *Journal of management studies, 44*(1), 73–95.

Arregle, J. L., Naldi, L., Nordqvist, M., & Hitt, M. A. (2012). Internationalization of family-controlled firms: A study of the effects of external involvement in governance. *Entrepreneurship Theory and Practice, 36*(6), 1115–1143.

Austria, K. F. (2008). *Overview of family business relevant issues.* Contract No. 30-CE-0164021/00-51 Final Report.

Bell, J., McNaughton, R., Young, S., & Crick, D. (2003). Towards an integrative model of small firm internationalization. *Journal of International Entrepreneurship, 1*(4), 339–362.

Beugelsdijk, S., Kostova, T., & Roth, K. (2017). An overview of Hofstede-inspired country-level culture research in international business since 2006. *Journal of International Business Studies, 48*(1), 30–47.

Brouthers, K. D., & Hennart, J.-F. (2007). Boundaries of the firm: Insights from international entry mode research. *Journal of Management, 33*(3), 395–425.

Cao, J., Cumming, D., & Wang, X. (2015). One-child policy and family firms in China. *Journal of Corporate Finance, 33*, 317–329.

Carney, M. (2005). Corporate governance and competitive advantage in family-controlled firms. *Entrepreneurship Theory and Practice, 29*(3), 249–265.

Casillas, J. C., & Moreno-Menéndez, A. M. (2014). Speed of the internationalization process: The role of diversity and depth in experiential learning. *Journal of International Business Studies, 45*(1), 85–101.

Chen, J., Saarenketo, S., & Puumalainen, K. (2018). Home country institutions, social value orientation, and the internationalization of ventures. *International Business Review, 27*(2), 443–454.

Claver, E., Rienda, L., & Quer, D. (2008). Family firms' risk perception: Empirical evidence on the internationalization process. *Journal of Small Business and Enterprise Development, 15*(3), 457–471.

Coase, R. H. (1998). The new institutional economics. *American Economic Review, 88*(2), 72–74.

Cooper, M. J., Upton, N., & Seaman, S. (2005). Customer relationship management: A comparative analysis of family and nonfamily business practices. *Journal of Small Business Management, 43*(3), 242–256.

Cruz, C., Larraza-Kintana, M., Garcés-Galdeano, L., & Berrone, P. (2014). Are family firms really more socially responsible? *Entrepreneurship Theory and Practice, 38*(6), 1295–1316.

Dacin, M. T., Dacin, P. A., & Kent, D. (2019). Tradition in organizations: A custodianship framework. *Academy of Management Annals, 13*(1), 342–373.

Dawar, N. D. N., & Chattopadhyay, A. (2002). Rethinking marketing programs for emerging markets. *Long Range Planning, 35*(5), 457–474.

Delios, A., Gaur, A. S., & Makino, S. (2008). The timing of international expansion: Information, rivalry and imitation among Japanese firms, 1980–2002. *Journal of Management Studies, 45*(1), 169–195.

De Massis, A., Sharma, P., Chua, J. H., & Chrisman, J. J. (2012). *Family business studies: An annotated bibliography.* Edward Elgar Publishing.

Deng, P. (2009). Why do Chinese firms tend to acquire strategic assets in international expansion? *Journal of World Business, 44*(1), 74–84.

DiMaggio, P. J., & Powell, W. W. (1983). The iron cage revisited: Institutional isomorphism and collective rationality in organizational fields. *American Sociological Review, 48*(2), 147–160.

Donckels, R., & Frohlich, E. (1991). Are family businesses really different? European experiences from STRATOS. *Family Business Review, 4*(2), 149–160.

Dyer, W., & Whetten, D. (2006). Family firms and social responsibility: Preliminary evidence from the S&P 500. *Entrepreneurship: Theory & Practice, 30*(6), 785–802.

Enderwick, P., & Buckley, P. J. (2017). Beyond supply and assembly relations: Collaborative innovation in global factory systems. *Journal of Business Research, 103*, 547–556.

Erdogan, I., Rondi, E., & De Massis, A. (2019). Managing the tradition and innovation paradox in family firms: A family imprinting perspective. *Entrepreneurship Theory and Practice, 44*(1), 20–54.

Estrin, S., Meyer, K. E., Nielsen, B. B., & Nielsen, S. (2015). Home country institutions and the internationalization of state-owned enterprises: A cross-country analysis. *Journal of World Business, 51*(2), 294–307.

Feranita, F., Kotlar, J., & De Massis, A. (2017). Collaborative innovation in family firms: Past research, current debates and agenda for future research. *Journal of Family Business Strategy, 8*(3), 137–156.

Fernando, G. D., Schneible Jr., R. A., & Suh, S. (2014). Family firms and institutional investors. *Family Business Review, 27*(4), 328–345.

Ferner, A., Quintanilla, J., & Varul, M. Z. (2001). Country-of-origin effects, host-country effects, and the management of HR in multinationals: German companies in Britain and Spain. *Journal of World Business, 36*(2), 107–127.

Filatotchev, I., Jackson, G., & Nakajima, C. (2013). Corporate governance and national institutions: A review and emerging research agenda. *Asia Pacific Journal of Management, 30*(4), 965–986.

Flören, R. H. (2010). Overview of family-business-relevant issues: Research, networks, policy measures and existing studies.

Fourné, S. P. L., & Zschoche, M. (2018, forthcoming). Reducing uncertainty in follow-up FDI: Imitation by family firms. *Global Strategy Journal.* https://doi.org/10.1002/gsj.1331.

Friel, D. (2017). Understanding institutions: Different paradigms, different conclusions. *Revista de Administração (São Paulo), 52*(2), 212–214.

Gaur, A. S., Ma, X., & Ding, Z. (2018). Home country supportiveness/un favorableness and outward foreign direct investment from China. *Journal of International Business Studies, 49*(3), 324–345.

Geppert, M., Dörrenbächer, C., Gammelgaard, J., & Taplin, I. (2013). Managerial risk-taking in international acquisitions in the brewery industry: Institutional and ownership influences compared. *British Journal of Management, 24*(3), 316–332.

Gomez-Mejia, L. R., Makri, M., & Larraza Kintana, M. (2010). Diversification decisions in family-controlled firms. *Journal of Management Studies, 47*(2), 223–252.

Granlund, M., & Lukka, K. (1998). It's a small world of management accounting practices. *Journal of Management Accounting Research, 10*, 153–179.

Graves, C., & Thomas, J. (2004). Internationalization of the family business: A longitudinal perspective. *International Journal of Globalization and Small Business, 1*(1), 7–27.

Graves, C., & Thomas, J. (2008). Determinants of the internationalization pathways of family firms: An examination of family influence. *Family Business Review, 21*(2), 151–167.

Hartman, L. P., Shaw, B., & Stevenson, R. (2003). Exploring the ethics and economics of global labor standards: A challenge to integrated social contract theory. *Business Ethics Quarterly, 13*(2), 193–220.

Hauswald, H. (2013). *Stakeholder trust in family businesses.* Springer Science & Business Media.

Hernández-Linares, R., Sarkar, S., & Cobo, M. J. (2018). Inspecting the Achilles heel: A quantitative analysis of 50 years of family business definitions. *Scientometrics, 115*(2), 929–951.

Hessels, J., & Terjesen, S. (2010). Resource dependency and institutional theory perspectives on direct and indirect export choices. *Small Business Economics, 34*(2), 203–220.

Heugens, P., van Essen, M., & van Oosterhout, J. (2009). Meta-analyzing ownership concentration and firm performance in Asia: Towards a more fine-grained understanding. *Asia Pacific Journal of Management, 26*(3), 481–512.

Kano, L., & Verbeke, A. (2017). Family firm internationalization: Heritage assets and the impact of bifurcation bias. *Global Strategy Journal, 8*(1), 158–183.

Kiss, A. N., & Danis, W. M. (2008). Country institutional context, social networks, and new venture internationalization speed. *European Management Journal, 26*(6), 388–399.

Kramer, R. M. (1999). Trust and distrust in organizations: Emerging perspectives, enduring questions. *Annual Review of Psychology, 50*(1), 569–598.

Krappe, A., Goutas, L., & von Schlippe, A. (2011). The "family business brand": An enquiry into the construction of the image of family businesses. *Journal of Family Business Management, 1*(1), 37–46.

Lages, L. F., Jap, S. D., & Griffith, D. A. (2008). The role of past performance in export ventures: A short-term reactive approach. *Journal of International Business Studies, 39*(2), 304–325.

Larson, A. (1991). Partner networks: Leveraging external ties to improve entrepreneurial performance. *Journal of Business Venturing, 6*(3), 173–118.

Leaptrott, J. (2005). An institutional theory view of the family business. *Family Business Review, 18*(3), 215–228.

Lee, M., Yin, X., Lee, S., Wang, D. H., & Peng, M. (2015). The impact of home country institutions on new venture export: Examining new ventures in transition economies. *International Entrepreneurship and Management Journal, 11*(4), 823–848.

Li, F., & Ding, D. Z. (2013). The effect of institutional isomorphic pressure on the internationalization of firms in an emerging economy: Evidence from China. *Asia Pacific Business Review, 19*(4), 506–525.

Li, F., & Ding, D. Z. (2017). The dual effects of home country institutions on the internationalization of private firms in emerging markets: Evidence from China. *Multinational Business Review, 25*(2), 128–149.

Li, J., Yang, J., & Yue, D. (2007). Identity, community, and audience: How wholly owned foreign subsidiaries gain legitimacy in China. *Academy of Management Journal, 50*(1), 175–190.

Lim, D. S. K., Morse, E. A., Mitchell, R. K., & Seawright, K. K. (2010). Institutional environment and entrepreneurial cognitions: A comparative business systems perspective. *Entrepreneurship Theory and Practice, 34*(3), 491–516.

Liu, W., Yang, H., & Zhang, G. (2012). Does family business excel in firm performance? An institution-based view. *Asia Pacific Journal of Management, 29*(4), 965–987.

Liu, Y. (in press). Institutionalization of family business and its regulative, normative and cognitive pillars: Embedded in traditional culture. *European Journal of International Management.*

Luo, X., Chung, C. N., & Sobczak, M. (2009). How do corporate governance model differences affect foreign direct investment in emerging economies? *Journal of International Business Studies, 40*(3), 444–467.

Luo, Y., Xue, Q., & Han, B. (2010). How emerging market governments promote outward FDI: Experience from China. *Journal of World Business, 45*(1), 68–79.

Man, T. W. Y., Mustafa, M., & Fang, Y. (2016). Succession in Chinese family enterprises: The influence of cognitive, regulatory and normative factors. *International Journal of Management Practice, 9*(4), 412–432.

Mazzelli, A., Kotlar, J., & De Massis, A. (2018). Blending in while standing out: Selective conformity and new product introduction in family firms. *Entrepreneurship Theory and Practice, 42*(2), 206–230.

Meneses, R., Coutinho, R., & Carlos Pinho, J. (2014). The impact of succession on family business internationalization: The successors' perspective. *Journal of Family Business Management, 4*(1), 24–45.

Meyer, K. E., Estrin, S., Bhaumik, S. K., & Peng, M. W. (2009). Institutions, resources, and entry strategies in emerging economies. *Strategic Management Journal, 30*(1), 61–80.

Meyer, K. E., & Gelbuda, M. (2006). Process perspectives in international business research in CEE. *Management International Review, 46*(2), 143–164.

Meyer, M. W., & Lu, X. (2005). Managing indefinite boundaries: The strategy and structure of a Chinese business firm. *Management and Organization Review, 1*(1), 57–86.

Minetti, R., Murro, P., & Zhu, S. C. (2015). Family firms, corporate governance and export. *Economica, 82*, 1177–1216.

Muralidharan, E., & Pathak, S. (2017). Informal institutions and international entrepreneurship. *International Business Review, 26*(2), 288–302.

Neilson, J. E. (2002). *The accountability reporting and focus of local government entities in Western Australia from agency and institutional theory perspectives.* PhD thesis, School of Accounting, Curtin University of Technology, Perth.

Nguyen, T. V., Le, N. T. B., & Bryant, S. E. (2013). Sub-national institutions, firm strategies, and firm performance: A multilevel study of private manufacturing firms in Vietnam. *Journal of World Business, 48*(1), 68–76.

North, D. C. (1990). *Institutions, institutional change, and economic performance.* Cambridge, MA: Harvard University Press.

Panicker, V. S., Mitra, S., & Upadhyayula, R. S. (2019). Institutional investors and international investments in emerging economy firms: A behavioral risk perspective. *Journal of World Business, 54*(4), 322–334.

Peng, M. W., Wang, D., & Jiang, Y. (2008). An institution-based view of international business strategy: A focus on emerging markets. *Journal of International Business Studies, 39*(5), 920–936.

Pittino, D., Martínez, A. B., Chirico, F., & Galván, R. S. (2017). Psychological ownership, knowledge sharing and entrepreneurial orientation in family firms: The moderating role of governance heterogeneity. *Journal of Business Research, 84*, 312–326.

Powell, W., & DiMaggio, P. (1991). Introduction. In W. Powell & P. DiMaggio (Eds.), *The new institutionalism in organizational analysis* (pp. 1–40). Chicago: University of Chicago Press.

Pukall, T. J., & Calabrò, A. (2014). The internationalization of family firms: A critical review and integrative model. *Family Business Review, 27*(2), 103–125.

Rondi, E., Debellis, F., De Massis, A., & Garzoni, A. (2020). Bonding and bridging social capital in family firm internationalization. *Sinergie.*

Sabatini, F. (2009). Social capital as social networks: A new framework for measurement and an empirical analysis of its determinants and consequences. *The Journal of Socio-Economics, 38*(3), 429–442.

Salomon, R., & Wu, Z. (2012). Institutional distance and local isomorphism strategy. *Journal Of International Business Studies, 43*(4), 343–367.

Schott, T., & Cheraghi, M. (2012). Entrepreneurs' networks: Size, diversity and composition shaped by cultures of rationality and trust. *2012 IEEE/ACM International Conference on Advances in Social Networks Analysis and Mining,* IEEE, pp. 220–226.

Scott, W. R. (1995). *Institutions and organizations. Foundations for organizational science.* London: A Sage Publication Series.

Scott, R. (2001). *Institutions and organizations* (2nd ed.). Thousand Oaks, CA: Sage.

Scott, W. R. (2007). *Institutions and organizations: Ideas and interests* (3rd ed.). Thousand Oaks, CA: Sage.

Segaro, E. L., Larimo, J., & Jones, M. V. (2014). Internationalization of family small and medium sized enterprises. The role of stewardship orientation, family commitment culture and top management team. *International Business Review, 23*(2), 381–395.

Shen, Z., Puig, F., & Paul, J. (2017). Foreign market entry mode research: A review and research agenda. *The International Trade Journal, 31*(5), 429–456.

Shirokova, G., & McDougall-Covin, P. (2012). The role of social networks and institutions in the internationalization of Russian entrepreneurial firms: Do they matter? *Journal of International Entrepreneurship, 10*(3), 177–199.

Singla, C., Veliyath, R., & George, R. (2014). Family firms and internationalization-governance relationships: Evidence of secondary agency issues. *Strategic Management Journal, 35*(4), 606–616.

Sirmon, D. G., & Hitt, M. A. (2003). Managing resources: Linking unique resources, management, and wealth creation in family firms. *Entrepreneurship Theory and Practice, 27*(4), 339–358.

Soleimanof, S., Rutherford, M. W., & Webb, J. W. (2018). The intersection of family firms and institutional contexts: A review and agenda for future research. *Family Business Review, 31*(1), 32–53.

Stavrou, E., Kassinis, G., & Filotheou, A. (2007). Downsizing and stakeholder orientation among the Fortune 500: Does family ownership matter? *Journal of Business Ethics, 72*(2), 149–162.

Sun, S. L., Peng, M. W., Lee, R. P., & Tan, W. (2015). Institutional open access at home and outward internationalization. *Journal of World Business, 50*(1), 234–246.

Trevino, L. J., Thomas, D. E., & Cullen, J. (2008). The three pillars of institutional theory and FDI in Latin America: An institutionalization process. *International Business Review, 17*(1), 118–133.

Torkkeli, L., Kuivalainen, O., Saarenketo, S., & Puumalainen, K. (2019). Institutional environment and network competence in successful SME internationalisation. International Marketing Review.

Verbeke, A., & Kano, L. (2012). The transaction cost economics theory of the family firm: Family-based human asset specificity and the bifurcation bias. *Entrepreneurship Theory and Practice, 36*(6), 1183–1205.

16 Family Firms' Internationalization: The Importance of Home... 551

Verbeke, A., Yuan, W., & Kano, L. (2020). A values-based analysis of bifurcation bias and its impact on family firm internationalization. *Asia Pacific Journal of Management, 37*, 449–477. https://doi.org/10.1007/s10490-018-9598-4.

Witt, M. A., & Lewin, A. Y. (2007). Outward foreign direct investment as escape response to home country institutional constraints. *Journal of International Business Studies, 38*(4), 579–594.

Yang, X., Jiang, Y., Kang, R., & Ke, Y. (2009). A comparative analysis of the internationalization of Chinese and Japanese firms. *Asia Pacific Journal of Management, 26*(1), 141–162.

Zahra, S. A. (2020). Technological capabilities and international expansion: The moderating role of family and non-family firms' social capital. *Asia Pacific Journal of Management, 37*(2), 391–415. https://doi.org/10.1007/s10490-018-9607-7.

Zellweger, T. M., & Nason, R. S. (2008). A stakeholder perspective on family firm performance. *Family Business Review, 21*(3), 203–216.

17

Internationalization Process of Developing-Country Family SMEs: The Case of Solanos Hermanos S.A. of Guatemala

Jose Godinez and José Solís Sierra

> *Our internationalization approach can be described assustainable, conservative, and strategic.*
> *CFO Solanos Hermanos S.A.*

Introduction

Small and medium-sized enterprises (SMEs), usually controlled by family members, account for a large share of firms and employment in the private sector of most economies (Ayyagari, Beck, & Demirguc-Kunt, 2007; Siakas, Naaranoja, Vlachakis, & Siakas, 2014), especially in developing ones. In fact, family SMEs from emerging countries provide seven out of every ten jobs in those locations. Hence, family SMEs in developing countries are considered the base for their private sector growth (McKinsey, 2012). Family SMEs from developing countries are characterized by their long-term orientation and their risk aversion. Also, these firms are more constrained in their operations

---

J. Godinez (✉)
University of Massachusetts Lowell, Lowell, MA, USA
e-mail: jose_godinez@uml.edu

J. S. Sierra
Universidad del Valle de Guatemala, Guatemala City, Guatemala
e-mail: jsolis@uvg.edu.gt

© The Author(s), under exclusive license to Springer Nature Switzerland AG 2021
T. Leppäaho, S. Jack (eds.), *The Palgrave Handbook of Family Firm Internationalization*,
https://doi.org/10.1007/978-3-030-66737-5_17

553

due to insufficient resources (Dikova & Brouthers, 2016) and the challenging environment characteristic of the countries on which they are headquartered. Nevertheless, despite their apparent unfavorable position, a large number of family SMEs from developing countries are expanding their operations internationally (Ciravegna, Lopez, & Kundu, 2014), usually via exporting (Majocchi, D'Angelo, Forlani, & Buck, 2018). Thus, this chapter seeks to understand how family SMEs from developing countries utilize their limited resources to start an export strategy while accounting for the challenging institutional environment of their country of origin.

Indeed, expanding our knowledge of how family SMEs from developing countries internationalize could prove to be valuable as they can face serious difficulties to start operations abroad. Such difficulties can derive from their lack of necessary resources, knowledge, and information regarding foreign markets. In addition, such deficiencies can be intensified if these firms are headquartered in a developing market, due to the many socioeconomic difficulties and structural deficiencies inherent to those locations. However, for some of these organizations, internationalizing can be crucial for their survival, since their local market might not be large enough or might not present the necessary conditions to support their operations .

To carry out our research, we studied Solanos Hermanos S.A., a Guatemalan family SME that produces and commercializes coffee. This firm is considered a family SME because it is under total control of a family, the CEO is a fourth-generation member of the firm, while his two sons operate as the CFO and CMO. Solanos Hermanos S.A. is currently producing 1.5 million pounds of coffee annually. However, despite its large-scale operation, Solanos Hermanos S.A. took a conservative approach to start its exporting strategy. In fact, their exporting strategy began 150 years after its inception. Nowadays, the company exports 80% of its production, their most important markets being the United States, Australia, Germany, The Netherlands, and Japan. Nevertheless, despite their current success, Solanos Hermanos S.A. faced serious challenges to their export strategy. These challenges are derived from their lack of resources, when compared to family SMEs from developed countries, and the challenging and unstable environment of the country on which it is headquartered.

Relying on the resource-based view (RBV) of the firm, we acknowledge that to begin an export strategy, family SMEs from developing markets need to prioritize their limited resources due to their size and because of the challenging institutional environment on which they operate. To do so, we rely on previous studies of family SMEs (i.e. Kontinen & Ojala, 2012) to use as a framework to analyze the internationalization process of family SMEs from developing markets. In doing so, we acknowledge that to start an exporting strategy, a family SME from a developing country has to have a combination of structural and experiential resources. However, we expand our knowledge of the RBV by providing a fine-grained description of how a family SME from a developing country leveraged its family nature and its limited resources to start a successful exporting strategy.

This research makes three contributions to the study of the determinants of exporting of family SMEs from developing markets under the lens of RBV theory. First, it provides a definition of family SMEs from developing countries. In our study, we define family SMEs from developing countries as those firms with 250 employees or fewer that comprise a combination of the reciprocal economic and non-economic values that have been forged through a family and guide the firm's business systems in place and operate in a location characterized by an underdeveloped institutional environment. Second, recent scholarship has placed a special emphasis on the needs of firms, especially smaller ones, to acquire financial resources to begin an exporting strategy (Santangelo & Meyer, 2017), while downplaying other important determinants of starting an export strategy. Thus, this chapter presents how family SMEs from developing markets can start an exporting strategy by leveraging their nature as family businesses without needing to mortgage their valuable assets. Specifically, we propose that to begin an exporting strategy, family SMEs from developing markets are able to leverage their family nature to establish long-lasting relations with intermediaries to overcome uncertainties in their country of origin. Additionally, family SMEs can leverage experiential knowledge gained in other companies to be deployed on their own when needed. Third, given the scarceness of studies analyzing the internationalization process of family SMEs from developing markets, this study is novel in terms of the data collected and the results presented. Specifically, this study relied on a unique interview with the CFO of a family SME headquartered in Guatemala that currently exports 80% of their coffee production.

The rest of the chapter is organized as follows. First, we provide a review on the literature of the internationalization of family businesses from developing markets through the lens of the RBV. Second, we present our methodology consisting of an in-depth interview with Solanos Hermanos S.A.'s CFO. Third, we present the results of our analysis. Finally, we discuss the implications of our study and our conclusions.

Theoretical Underpinning

We utilize the RBV to understand the determinants of exporting of a family SME from a developing country. We focus on this theoretical framework because it allows us to analyze how these firms utilize the limited resources they have at their disposal to achieve their goal while operating in a challenging environment characteristic of developing markets (Godinez & Liu, 2018). Also, in this study, we acknowledge that what makes a family business unique is that members of a family are involved in its ownership and management. Thus, for this chapter, we define a family SME from a developing market as a small or medium-sized enterprise with 250 employees or fewer that is controlled by a family and that has one or more members of such family in managerial positions and is headquartered in a developing market. Therefore, what makes a family SME from a developing market different from a non-family SME is the involvement of family members in the management and ownership of the firm, and the lack of development of its country of origin. This means that a family SME comprises a combination of the reciprocal economic and non-economic values that have been forged by the family and business systems in place and operates in a location characterized by an underdeveloped institutional environment.

The RBV assumes that organizations are collections of distinctive bundles of resources that help improve organizational performance. This assumption is based on the heterogeneity of resources, and the heterogeneity of organizations in specific industries that are the result of the lack of perfect mobility across organizations. Moreover, Dhanaraj and Beamish argue that the RBV should be the foundation of a rigorous theory building in the export strategy discipline. Previous work analyzing SMEs export strategies have implicitly relied on such firms' resources. However, less attention has been paid to understanding how SMEs utilize those resources to achieve their exporting goals, especially if such SMEs are headquartered in developing markets. Thus, since the RBV has served as an adequate vehicle to analyze the determinants of exporting of SMEs from developed markets, it can also be utilized as an appropriate framework to study the determinants of exporting of SME family business from developing markets.

The RBV regards resources as the basis of business results (Barney, 1991). However, not all resources have the potential to create a competitive advantage for a firm. To create a competitive advantage, a resource must have the following characteristics: it must be valuable, rare, difficult to imitate, and should not have substitutes. Generally, there are two types of resources necessary to create a competitive advantage: assets and capabilities. Assets are the means that a firm has accumulated. On the other hand, capabilities are the bundles of skills and accumulated knowledge deployed through organizational procedures that allow the firm to coordinate activities to effectively and efficiently utilize their assets. The relation between assets and capabilities, and the propensity of SME family firms from developing markets to utilize them to internationalize through an exporting strategy, has not received enough attention in current scholarship. To bridge this gap, this analysis considers two kinds of resources (both, assets and capabilities), concurrent with RBV: structural and experiential .

Structural resources are those that are embedded in the organizational configuration of a firm (Navarro-Garcia, Arenas-Gaitan, Rondan-Cataluna, & Rey-Moreno, 2016). In this regard, studies have argued that some of the most important structural resources that SMEs need to start an exporting strategy are financial, an export department (Navarro-Garcia et al., 2016), product mix, and organizational configuration. Experiential resources refer to the general experiences that the members of an organization have. These include knowledge related to the reduction of improvisation and the decrease of the likelihood of making erroneous decisions when conducting operations (Navarro-Garcia et al., 2016). Nevertheless, because of their nature and the location on which they are headquartered, family SMEs might have a different arrangement of structural and experiential resources to initiate an exporting strategy.

Exporting is the most popular method for many family SMEs as well as for SMEs from developing markets to internationalize. This internationalization mode is preferred by smaller firms because it requires less resources than establishing foreign operations via foreign direct investment (FDI), for instance (Wilkinson & Brouthers, 2006). Additionally, because of the nature of the product (coffee beans), exporting is the only option that the firm can have to sell their product in most developed markets since this bean does not grow in those locations. Also, exporting allows firms to achieve economies of scale in a speedy manner and enables them to become more competitive. There is a vast amount of research analyzing factors that enhance the internationalization of family SMEs. Such research proposes that family SMEs internationalize when they have a long-term orientation, are willing to use information technology, and have capabilities for innovation. Also, there is evidence that when the new generations take control of the family SME, they have a positive influence on internationalization. However, less attention has been paid to how family SMEs internationalize through exports, especially those from developing markets.

However, prior research on the determinants of exporting of family SMEs has been done mainly in the context of developed countries. These countries are characterized mainly by a stable institutional environment and high standards of living of their citizens. Additionally, SMEs from developed countries also have greater access to resources available in their home locations such as exporting offices and access to capital, which might also be the case for family SMEs. However, a better understanding of how family SMEs internationalize when they originate in locations that are characterized by a weaker institutional environment and a lack of support from their local government is overdue in the business discipline.

Developing markets are characterized by weak, incoherent, and continually changing formal institutional environment and by a weak or inexistent infrastructure that fosters the internationalization of firms. Thus, SMEs in these settings are unable to calculate their operation costs due to changing laws and regulations (Zhu, Wittmann, & Peng, 2012). They also have difficulties accessing credit in these locations since financial institutions might favor larger enterprises instead of smaller organizations (Quartey, Turkson, Abor, & Iddrisu, 2017). Additionally, they face increased hardship to transport their products to service distant markets. In these cases, when the formal institutional environment is weak or non-existent, informal institutions take precedence. Thus, smaller firms in developing markets, such as Guatemala, need to resort to personal informal relations with relevant actors in order to operate. These actors include stakeholders along the value chain, which includes business partners, intermediaries, and costumers to name a few.

To carry out our analysis, we will study how an SME family business from a developing market, Guatemala, enacted its internationalization strategy through exports. Research on internationalization of family SMEs proposes that these firms tend to be less prone to start an exporting strategy when compared to public companies. The obstacles to SME family firms beginning an export strategy include limited capital, unwillingness to hire experts from outside the family, inflexibility and resistance from their top-management teams, differences in family goals, and conflicts among successors (Tsang, 2018). However, as previously mentioned, these studies have mainly focused on family SMEs from developed countries, and thus less is known about the process of developing markets SME family firms to start an exporting strategy.

Family SMEs from developing markets might be at a disadvantage to start their exporting process. The disadvantages stem from their perceived lack of ownership advantages, their status as late entrants into international markets, their poorly developed proprietary technology, and their liabilities of foreignness. Thus, it is expected that these organizations have less developed resources

17 Internationalization Process of Developing-Country Family SMEs...

than well-established family SMEs from developed markets (Jamali, Lund-Thomsen, & Jeppesen, 2017). Additionally, developing market family SMEs face obstacles stemming from the weak institutional environment characteristic of developing markets. However, these companies are increasingly entering new markets, especially by exporting (Paul, Parthasarathy, & Gupta, 2017), and for that reason, their motives to initiate an exporting strategy should be analyzed.

Methodological Approach

This is an exploratory, qualitative study that helps an in-depth analysis of how a family SME from a developing country utilizes its structural and experiential resources to start an export strategy. Thus, a case study method was appropriate to carry out this research due to its usefulness to understand international business phenomena and allows to answer "how" questions. Additionally, this research follows Welch and Welch who argue that empirical analyses on internationalization should be carried out with the help of a detailed case analysis instead of a broad survey study. This is because of the former's complexity and because of the need of developing a clear understanding of the exporting process over time. This study is based on a single case study, following Vissak and Francioni. Although this approach decreases the generalizability of the results, it allows to investigate the determinants of exporting of a family SME from a developing market in an in-depth manner that would not be possible otherwise. Also, it allows to present the results in a rich manner that allows a better understanding of the complexity of this issue and the factors that influence it.

Purposeful sampling was utilized to uncover a case that was rich in information. At first, four potential firms were considered to analyze in this study, but Solanos Hermanos S.A. was selected. The decision was reached after a conversation with its CFO in September 2019, since this company is considered an SME, is headquartered in a developing country, is controlled by family members, and had successfully started an exporting strategy. Additionally, the suitability of this firm to be used in our analysis stemmed from the fact that the firm has entered several international markets while simultaneously maximizing its limited resources while encountering impediments inherent to the developing market on which this firm is based. The information was then gathered with the help of a semi-structured in-depth interview guide that was conducted in late September 2019. The interview protocol included questions regarding the organizational structure of the firm, a description of the chronology of the internationalization of the firm from its inception until its first international sale, the utilization of networks to achieve its internationalization goals, and a description of success and failures in its internationalization process. The interview lasted 50 minutes and was conducted and analyzed in Spanish, since that was the language the respondent deemed most suitable to present all the nuances of the exporting process of the SME. The interview was recorded and later transcribed verbatim before it was analyzed.

To analyze the data, a content analysis was performed using NVivo 12.0. This software was appropriate for qualitative research since it allowed to manipulate data without affecting or deteriorating it while facilitating the analysis of the rich account provided by the respondent. This research utilized a conventional content analysis because it allowed the categories and names for categories to emerge from the data to uncover new insights. Additionally, this approach is relevant for this study since it helped "describe a phenomenon for which existing theory or research literature is limited." A chronological account of the exporting activities of Solanos Hermanos S.A. was also created to identify all critical events that impacted this process. Following the explanation of the methodology, the main characteristics of the setting and of the firm are presented below to then analyze why and how it started its exporting strategy.

Setting

We chose Guatemala because it is a developing market characterized by a large number of SME family businesses and a challenging institutional environment inherent to developing markets. In the past five years, Guatemala's GDP per capita has oscillated between $4200 and $4500. Also, Guatemala is the second largest economy in Central America, after Panama, and is the source of many successful firms with international operations. Nevertheless, Guatemala also presents a weak institutional environment and is characterized by poverty and inequality, weak law and contract enforcement, as well as few support systems for SMEs to begin an exporting strategy (Godinez & Liu, 2015; Godinez & Garita, 2015). As with many developing countries, Guatemala presents high levels of income inequality (15th most unequal country in the world) (World Bank, 2019) and presents a low literacy rate of 75%. Additionally, Guatemala is home to 16 million people of which 59.3% live below the poverty line .

We also chose the coffee industry to conduct our study. This industry is suitable for this research since it is a long-standing, international agricultural commodity that is based mainly in developing countries since coffee grows only in the tropics. Also, the coffee industry is one of the most important products of the Guatemalan economy and can be traced back to the 1850s. Guatemala is the main coffee producer in the Central American industry and is the tenth largest producer in the world. In 2018, the coffee accounted for 4% of Guatemala's GDP, or $3.14 billion. However, most Guatemalan firms do not directly engage in the internationalization of their products (Godinez & Garita, 2016). Instead, because of their limited resources, limited knowledge of international markets, and lack of help from public and private organizations, coffee producers rely on larger, international intermediary companies to carry the sales of their product internationally (Palacios, 2019). By doing this, coffee producers allow third parties to take all the risk of selling their product internationally but at the same time gaining all the benefits of this activity. Thus, it is important to understand how a few firms are now challenging the status quo in this industry by taking on the exporting of their coffee themselves. Such understanding can allow us to create a roadmap for not only the owners of these firms to enjoy the benefits of their exporting activities, but also could be generalized to other similar firms in developing markets.

Firm

Solanos Hermanos S.A. is a four-generation family business that was established in 1859. Currently, the firm's upper management is comprised of a CEO, a CFO, and a CMO. The CEO is the father of the other two members of the upper management team. The firm has been in the hands of the same family since its inception. The current CEO acquired the shares from all other family members and now shares control only with his two sons. At the beginning, this firm focused on growing beans, corn, and coffee. After the third generation took control of its operations, it became an exclusive coffee production. This shift was the result of the grandson of the founder returning from a short tenure at a coffee plantation and bringing the newly acquired knowledge with him. The farm is ideal for growing coffee since it has an elevation of 5912 feet over sea level and it is over volcanic soil, which is ideal for harvesting specialty coffee. Currently the farm is producing 1.5 million pounds of coffee annually. Its main markets are the United States, where the firm exports 80% of its production. Then, the firm exports 15% of its production to Australia, Germany, The Netherlands, and Japan, while 5% of its products remain for the local market.

Fig. 17.1 Solanos Hermanos S.A. value chain. (Source: Author)

To better understand how Solanos Hermanos S.A. operates, Fig. 17.1 presents a detailed account of their activities. As presented below, it can be seen that Solanos Hermanos S.A. is in charge of growing and harvesting coffee. The company then outsources the roasting of some of their coffee while the rest remains green (unroasted). Following the roasting of coffee, the company packages it and exports it on their own or with the help of local and international agents. The company also sells their coffee locally through their own coffee shop or through third wholesalers to distribute the product in Guatemala.

Results

This section presents the findings of our study. Here, we describe when Solanos Hermanos S.A. firm decided to start their internationalization process by exporting. We also present how the company had considerable structural resources, but they were not enough to begin their exporting strategy. Instead, they needed to acquire and utilize experiential resources by establishing informal linkages with intermediaries to achieve their goals.

Descriptive Information

Solanos Hermanos S.A. firm began its exporting activities in 2009, 150 years after its inception. The internationalization efforts began, according to the respondent, "*when local prices became so low that they could not cover the firm's operations. That was when the firm began trying to find new markets.*" Additionally, during the same period of time, the world was in "*the middle of the third wave of coffee*" (Light, 2019). The third wave of coffee meant that "*both consumers and manufacturers were focused on high-quality coffee that was a high-end differentiated product as opposed of just being a commodity. This meant that high quality coffee was sought after and had higher market value in international markets.*"

17 Internationalization Process of Developing-Country Family SMEs... 563

When the firm began testing its product in international markets in 2009, they did so by *"exporting 20% of their products while commercializing 80% locally to not affect the company's finances."* Four years after their initial exporting venture, the company reached their current exporting arrangement, on which 95% of their product is sold abroad. In order to begin their exporting strategy, Solanos Hermanos S.A. had to utilize both structural and experiential resources while operating in an underdeveloped home market that made their internationalization process more difficult than the journey faced by firms headquartered in developing countries.

Structural Resources

The main structural resource the firm had to begin its international operations was a large plot of land with coffee plants already producing high-quality beans. Nevertheless, while the conditions were right for Solanos Hermanos S.A. to begin exporting, they decided to undertake this activity at a slow pace in part because they did not have the structure in place to undertake this strategy on their own. Specifically, the company lacked enough financial resources and an export department. Also, the slow approach was taken because they *"needed to find the optimal point between local and international sales in order to make their international strategy sustainable."* The respondent elaborates on this approach by arguing that they *"could have expedited their internationalization by being more aggressive to take advantage of international prices, but this idea was discarded because this would jeopardize their liquidity."* In fact, while both the CEO and the CMO wanted to begin an exporting strategy when realizing how attractive the market was for their product at the time, the CFO was able to convince them otherwise to *"protect the family patrimony."* In fact, the CFO argued that if they had not been part of the same family, probably the cautious approach to initiating exporting would not have been possible and would have *jeopardize their operations*. However, the respondent argued that the CEO and CMO listened to his concerns because they *"were family and that preserving the family's patrimony was paramount"* for the three family members.

As is the case with many agricultural enterprises, most of Solanos Hermanos S.A. assets were invested in their land, which made access to liquid assets to cover their exporting strategy difficult. While in many developed countries there are a plethora of resources for SMEs to access financial products and services when their assets are all tied in productive activities, the same is not the case for many developing-country SMEs. Additionally, Solanos Hermanos

S.A. chose not to resort to a financial institution for the liquidity they needed to internationalize, since, as is the case with many family firms, they would prefer not to mortgage their main assets in exchange for cash. Additionally, *"because of their legal characterization in Guatemala, their financial liabilities would have to be covered not only by the firm's assets but also for those of the family."* This statement is corroborated by the law offices of Salazar and Munoz, who describe that, in many cases, banks in Guatemala can go after the personal patrimony of business owners if such businesses fail to repay their debts (Salazar Munoz, 2018).

As is the case with many SMEs, Solanos Hermanos S.A. could not afford a traditional marketing strategy that would allow the firm to identify, qualify, and manage overseas agents and distributors. Moreover, since this family SME is located in a developing market, they face increased obstacles for exporting because distribution channels in the country where they are headquartered are scarcer and underdeveloped. For instance, while SMEs from developed markets had export departments and/or access to offices that helped them position their products abroad, Solanos Hermanos S.A. *"did not have these resources at their disposal."* This means this family SME had to prioritize which aspects of a marketing strategy better satisfied their needs. For that reason, firm Solanos Hermanos S.A. had to resort to establishing relations with an intermediary with resources to store, roast, and ship coffee overseas. Additionally, as the respondent says, *"these organizations [beneficios] have the connections and can position our products in international markets. Nevertheless, this approach was risky and required a great deal of trust because [the producer] gives all the product to the intermediary and does not receive payment until the coffee is sold abroad."* This kind of transaction is common in Guatemala since there the law is weak, and enforcement of contracts in the country is a lengthy and costly endeavor (Macours, 2014). According to the respondent, *"generating the trust needed to establish a relation with the intermediary took time. However, [Solanos Hermanos S.A.] leveraged the fact that they were a family business and their traditional principles … This was done because the intermediary already knew our family name and we knew theirs. A relationship began because we trusted each other."*

To be able to promote their products, Nisar et al. argue that SMEs need to focus mainly in three specific marketing areas, namely, participation in trade shows, television and radio campaigns, and printed press. Nevertheless, those activities might be too costly and may yield underwhelming results. For that reason, Solanos Hermanos S.A. needed to prioritize their limited resources. To do so, they began *"competing in world barista competitions. By competing in these competitions, such as the one in Boston this year, allows our firm to showcase our coffee and find new overseas clients.*" In this case, while the barista competitions are happening, the CMO of the company "*approaches specialty coffee enthusiasts from around the world and offers to supply them with coffee.*" This approach has proved successful because the CMO not only "*sells coffee but the history of the company that includes family values.*" In turn, the potential clients "*prefer our products because they understand our uniqueness and they recognize that coffee for us is not just a product, is our lives, it's our name.* Additionally, the company *opted for focusing on promoting [their] product in social media because of their wide reach and relatively low cost.*"

In sum, to start an exporting strategy, Solanos Hermanos S.A. needed to overcome structural resources inherent to their size and the underdeveloped nature of the country on which they are located. While the opportunity to begin exporting their products was attractive, they realized they did not have enough financial resources and access to marketing channels to successfully sell their products abroad. Instead, they leveraged their knowledge of the industry and their family name and history to forge relations with intermediaries to begin exporting their product and to access clients abroad.

Experiential Resources

To begin their own exporting strategy, Solanos Hermanos S.A. had to acquire and exploit experiential resources. In this study, we also analyze the importance of experiential resources as determinants of exporting family SMEs from developing countries. Specifically, we focus on the role that being a family business played in acquiring and utilizing experiential resources. Our analysis shows that the most important experiential resources that Solanos Hermanos S.A. acquired and exploited were the education level of the managers, as well as the experience they acquired working in other organizations. We acknowledge that knowledge on how to run an SME can be acquired through prior experience or formal education of management. However, family SMEs from developing markets differ from their counterparts from developed markets because access to education and experiential learning is scarcer in the former locations. In fact, it is common for family SMEs to start international operations in a more "ad-hoc" approach. Hence, the education level of the top managers of family SMEs from developing markets should be taking into account as to why and how these firms begin an export strategy.

According to the respondent, all three members of the upper-level management have college degrees that serve a specific purpose in the firm. Additionally, while they were "*not forced to choose these degrees,*" the CEO made a case for his two sons to specialize in "*something that could help the business.*" In fact, according to the respondent, the CEO "*had the expectation that us [the CFO and CMO] majored in something that would be of use to the business and not on something that 'had no value.*'" The respondent, the current CFO, declared to have earned "*an engineering degree with a business administration minor.*" His brother, the CMO, earned a "*degree in marketing,*" and the CEO has a *degree in business administration.*" As presented by the respondent, "*each member of the upper-level management has strengths and weaknesses when it comes to running the company.*" As for the strengths, the respondent argues that he "*is in charge of making sure the company has a proper financial management to be able to operate profitable, while* his *brother is in charge of promoting their product.*" Due to their different profiles, there can also be disagreements. In fact, the respondent argued that "*sometimes [he] wished his brother had more knowledge about the production side of the business, however, [their] father helps them bridge the two perspectives to make sure they continue their operations,*" which, as was presented before, relies mainly in international sales.

Additionally, as presented before, Solanos Hermanos S.A. began growing coffee at a larger scale when the grandson of the founder applied the knowledge acquired at another coffee plantation to his own farm. This tradition of acquiring knowledge elsewhere to then translate it to their firm has continued by the current administration. According to the respondent, his father (the CEO) "*values education and experience because that is what he learned from his own father.* Thus, even though the respondent and his brother *had been going to the farm since children,*" and "*that the farm has been part of their lives, they knew that there was the expectation of going to gain experience of how to run a business in other companies.*"

This approach is a unique distinction that might be more easily found in family businesses since the two sons had to "*comply with [their] father's wishes and directions.*" Hence, because of this mandate, the respondent and his brother "*[were] employed in other organizations before joining their family SME full time.*" In the case of the respondent, he worked at the financial department of a multinational enterprise that did not focus on agricultural products, while his brother, the CMO, did the same, but in the marketing department of another organization. Actually, the respondent said that "*his brother and him*" spent time working in other firms to master their skills. When the CEO of Solanos Hermanos S.A. deemed that his two sons were ready, they were called to join the company full time. The experience acquired allowed the CFO and CMO to gain the necessary knowledge "*in the logistics of exporting to start selling their product in international markets without the help from intermediaries.*" Additionally, according to the respondent, the CEO also expected his sons to "*understand how businesses were conducted in Guatemala because*," since the laws and regulations are weak and enforcing contracts is too burdensome, "*it was necessary for us [the CFO and CMO] to learn how to deal with people here.*"

In sum, to acquire and exploit experiential resources, the CEO, and father of the CMO and CFO, of Solanos Hermanos S.A. encouraged his children to receive formal education that could be used to run the business. Additionally, the CEO continued the family tradition of having his sons go to different companies in different industries to gain work experience. These results show how the family tradition was applied to acquiring experiential resources that would help the business overcome their limited experiential resources in a challenging institutional environment characteristic of a developing country.

Discussion and Conclusions

This study attempts to examine and identify how a family SME from a developing market started exporting activities. To do so, we analyzed the determinants of exporting of a Guatemalan family SME with the aid of the RBV. Family SMEs from developing markets are firms with 250 employees or fewer that comprise a combination of the reciprocal economic and non-economic values and that have been forged by family that has control over the firm's operations and operates in a location characterized by an underdeveloped institutional environment.

With the aid of classic RBV (Barney, 1991), we acknowledged that family SMEs from developing countries have limited resources, and thus they should carefully utilize such resources to start an export strategy. Current scholarship has agreed that firms, especially smaller ones, are more resource-constrained than their larger counterparts, especially if such firms are headquartered in a developing country (Bianchi, 2019). Additionally, if an SME is controlled by a family, it is likely to be more conservative when deciding to start an exporting strategy. Nevertheless, we uncovered that despite these adverse conditions, Solanos Hermanos S.A. was able to start an export strategy by utilizing a third party before they could do it on their own. In this manner, they reduced their risk and were able to test how their product would be received in international markets. However, because of its condition as a developing market, the laws and regulations of the country are uncertain. For that reason, Solanos Hermanos S.A. had to develop enough trust in the intermediary before they utilized their services. In this case, trust was necessary because the intermediary received all the product and would pay Solanos Hermanos S.A. once all the coffee of a specific harvest had been sold overseas. Nevertheless, establishing trust was not a difficult task because both companies are family businesses and, as such, they had a special bond that helped them operate in this informal setting. Concurrently, the firm realized that they could start their exporting strategy without the help of intermediaries. To do so, Solanos Hermanos S.A. started utilizing social media and leveraged their participation in trade shows where they would advertise not only their high-quality coffee but also the family history to gain maximum exposure while minimizing the use of valuable resources to promote their product abroad.

Once Solanos Hermanos S.A. was certain that their product was well received abroad, they moved to maximize their experiential resources to sell the majority of their products abroad and without the help of intermediaries. To do this, the founder of Solanos Hermanos S.A. encouraged his two sons to receive higher education degrees that would be useful in running the business. Additionally, the CEO continued with the family tradition to gain work experience in other companies. Once the CEO deemed that his two sons had gained the necessary skills of how to operate in the business world, which included how to operate in the Guatemalan uncertain institutional environment, he recalled them into the family firm. By doing this, the CEO leveraged the knowledge their top-management team had acquired in their formal education and the knowledge acquired while they worked in other organizations. This approach allows the firm to minimize the uncertainty regarding starting international operations, which is necessary for family SMEs from developing countries since they are less well-known in international markets and they might have only one chance to make their internationalization strategy succeed.

Our study offers important managerial implications. First, we show that although family SMEs from developing markets lack resources that larger firms from developed countries may enjoy, they can still be successful at implementing an export strategy. Thus, our findings reaffirm that although having resources is important for family SMEs from developing markets, how they use such resources is more important. Thus, managers should understand how their structural and experiential resources are configured, and how the family nature of the business is leveraged to successfully utilize them to begin an export strategy.

Our results are also of relevance for policymakers. Family SMEs from developing markets have been known to benefit from public resources. This research can serve as guidance for policymakers to offer help in the internationalization of these organizations by placing special emphasis on how to

17 Internationalization Process of Developing-Country Family SMEs...

access liquid financial resources and marketing channels that are proven to help these firms to start an exporting strategy.

Finally, due to the nature of the study, to analyze in depth the determinants of exporting of a family SME from a developing market, we were confined to one home country and one firm. Also, due to their size and resources, Solanos Hermanos S.A. does not produce public reports, and private financial records were off limits. Hence, although their claims are fair, it was not possible to corroborate them independently. However, our results show an initial insight on why and how a family SME from a developing market initiates an export strategy even though we relied only on one observation. Thus, future scholarship should analyze the determinants of exporting a family SME from a developing market from different developing countries to validate and generalize the results presented in this document.

References

Ayyagari, M., Beck, T., & Demirguc-Kunt, A. (2007). Small and medium enterprises across the globe. *Small Business Economics, 29*(4), 415–434.

Barney, J. (1991). Special theory forum the resource-based model of the firm: Origins, implications, and prospects. *Journal of Management, 17*(1), 97–98.

Bianchi, C. (2019). Investigating the export behavior of family SMEs from Chile. In W. Newburry, L. Liberman, & M. Oliveira Jr. (Eds.), *Contemporary influences on international business in Latin America* (pp. 155–178). London: Palgrave Macmillan.

Ciravegna, L., Lopez, L., & Kundu, S. (2014). Country of origin and network effects on internationalization: A comparative study of SMEs from an emerging and developed economy. *Journal of Business Research, 67*(5), 916–923.

Dikova, D., & Brouthers, K. (2016). International establishment mode choice: Past, present and future. *Management Interntional Review, 56*(4), 489–530.

Godinez, J., & Garita, M. (2015). Corruption and foreign direct investment: A study of Guatemala. In L. Tihanyi, E. Banalieva, T. Devinney, & T. Pedersen (Eds.), *Advances in International Management* (Vol. 28, pp. 297–326). Bingley, UK: Emerald.

Godinez, J., & Garita, G. (2016). The dimensions of corruption and its impact on FDI decision-making: The case of Guatemala. *Business and Politics, 18*(2), 123–141.

Godinez, J., & Liu, L. (2015). Corruption distance and FDI flows into Latin America. *International Business Review, 24*(1), 33–42.

Godinez, J., & Liu, L. (2018). Corruption and its effects on FDI: Analysing the interaction between the corruption levels of the home and host countries and its effects at the decision-making level. *Journal of Business Ethics, 147*(4), 705–719.

Jamali, D., Lund-Thomsen, P., & Jeppesen, S. (2017). SMEs and CSR in developing countries. *Business & Society, 56*(1), 11–22.

Kontinen, T., & Ojala, A. (2012). Internationalization pathways among family-owned SMEs. *International Marketing Review, 29*(5), 496–518.

Light, M. P. (2019, October 4). Trish Rothgeb coined 'third wave'—And is now looking toward coffee's future. *Los Angeles Times.*

Macours, K. (2014). Ethnic divisions, contract choice, and search costs in the Guatemalan land rental market. *Journal of Comparative Economics, 42*(1), 1–18.

Majocchi, A., D'Angelo, A., Forlani, E., & Buck, T. (2018). Bifurcation bias and exporting: Can foreign work experience be an answer? Insight from European family SMEs. *Journal of World Business, 53*(2), 237–247.

McKinsey. (2012). *Micro-, small and medium-sized enterprises in emerging markets: How banks can grasp a $350 billion opportunity.* Retrieved from https://www.mckinsey.com/~/media/mckinsey/industries/financial%20services/our%20insights/tapping%20the%20next%20big%20thing%20in%20emerging%20market%20banking/micro_small_and_med_sized_enterprises_in_emerging_markets_full_report.ashx

Navarro-Garcia, A., Arenas-Gaitan, J., Rondan-Cataluna, J., & Rey-Moreno, M. (2016). Global model of export performance: Moderator role of export department. *Journal of Business Research, 69*(5), 1880–1886.

Palacios, B. (2019, December 19). Guatemala mejora posición en 'Top 10' de países exportadores de café. *La Republica.*

Paul, J., Parthasarathy, S., & Gupta, P. (2017). Exporting challenges of SMEs: A review and future research agenda. *Journal of World Business, 52*(3), 327–342.

Quartey, P., Turkson, E., Abor, J., & Iddrisu, A. (2017). Financing the growth of SMEs in Africa: What are the constraints to SME financing within ECOWAS? *Review of Development Finance, 7*(1), 18–28.

Salazar Munoz. (2018). *Iniciar un negocio: Preguntas frecuentes.* Retrieved from http://consultajuridicagt.blogspot.com/2012/07/iniciar-un-negocio-preguntas-frecuentes.html.

Santangelo, G., & Meyer, K. (2017). Internationalization as an evolutionary process. *Journal of International Business Studies, 48*(9), 1114–1130.

Siakas, K., Naaranoja, M., Vlachakis, S., & Siakas, E. (2014). Family businesses in the new economy: How to survive and develop in times of financial crisis. *Procedia Economics and Finance, 9*, 331–341.

Tsang, E. (2018). Family firms and internationalization; An organizational learning perspective. *Asia Pacific Journal of Management, 37*, 205–225.

Wilkinson, T., & Brouthers, L. (2006). Trade promotion and SME export performance. *International Business Review, 15*(3), 233–252.

World Bank. (2019). *Small and medium enterprises (SMEs) finance: Improving SME's access to finance and finding innovative solutions to unlock sources of capital.* Washington, DC: World Bank.

Zhu, Y., Wittmann, X., & Peng, M. (2012). Institution-based barriers to innovation in SMEs in China. *Asia Pacific Journal of Management, 29*, 1131–1142.

Index[1]

B

Behavioral theory, 135–163
Bifurcation bias (BB), viii, ix, xiii, xxxviii, xliv, 3–28, 65, 70, 71, 90–92, 94, 114, 138, 145, 153, 362–368, 372, 379–383, 386, 387, 475, 477, 478, 499–501, 503, 504, 520, 541

C

Calculative ties, xlv, 210–222, 224, 225
Case study, xii, xlvii, 179, 181, 182, 239, 240, 246–249, 251–253, 257, 258, 279, 297, 298, 302–304, 315, 328n1, 334–337, 341, 350–352, 369, 396, 400, 433, 441, 443, 453, 479, 559
Conceptual, xxxix, xlvii, xlviii, 5, 6, 20, 27, 28, 81, 136, 137, 162, 180, 250, 267, 362, 371, 522, 531, 532, 539

D

Degree of internationalization (DOI), viii–x, xxii, xliv, 38, 43, 44, 47, 50, 53–55, 65, 70, 72, 74, 80, 81, 84–86, 88, 89, 91–94, 104, 138, 298
De-internationalization, xv, 136, 137, 140, 141, 149–162, 462, 485, 493, 498, 500, 504, 505, 510, 512
Developing country, xiv, 208, 437, 440, 453, 553–569
Developing economy, xlviii, 432, 434
Discontinuous, xxxviii, xlv, 135–163
Domestic, xi, xii, xiv, xxiv, xxv, xxvn1, xxviii, xxix, xxxi, xliii, xlv–xlviii, 23, 67, 68, 75, 93, 103, 107, 149, 182, 199–202, 208, 210, 211, 213–225, 238, 239, 242–244, 248, 252, 253, 256, 273, 329–335, 341, 343, 344, 346, 347, 350–353, 461, 462,

[1] Note: Page numbers followed by 'n' refer to notes.

© The Author(s), under exclusive license to Springer Nature Switzerland AG 2021
T. Leppäaho, S. Jack (eds.), *The Palgrave Handbook of Family Firm Internationalization*,
https://doi.org/10.1007/978-3-030-66737-5

572   Index

470, 471, 477, 484, 485, 492–495, 499, 504, 505, 510, 530, 531, 533

E

Economic, vii, ix–xi, xxvi, xxxix, xliii, 8n1, 9, 43, 63, 105, 143, 176, 204, 245, 267, 289–320, 333, 396, 432, 469, 522, 555
Embedded ties, 204, 226, 420, 421
Entry, ix, xxx, xxxviii, xliv, 6, 38, 44–46, 103–126, 140, 237–259, 278, 293, 327, 378, 396, 462, 521
  mode, ix, xxxviii, xliv, 6, 11, 14, 15, 38, 44–50, 52–54, 56, 104–121, 123–126, 140, 237, 238, 240, 242–244, 246, 278, 524, 528, 543, 544
  node, x, 237–259
Ethnic social networks, 431–439
Export, xiv, xxiv, xlii, 16, 87, 111, 139, 182, 212, 242, 278, 302, 373, 408, 437, 461, 530, 554

F

Family business, vii, xxxvii, xli, xliv, 4, 38, 66, 103, 137, 177, 200, 266, 289, 379, 400, 431, 434, 437–438, 461, 520, 523–525, 534, 536–537, 555
Family firm (FF), vii, xxi–xxxiii, xxxvii, xli, xliii, 3–28, 37, 39–46, 63, 66–72, 103–126, 135–163, 173–193, 199–227, 237, 241–242, 265–280, 289–320, 327, 330–335, 361–369, 395–425, 431–439, 461–512, 519–544, 557
Family managed, xxii, xxiii, xxviii, xxx–xxxiii, 48, 68, 237–259, 400

Family member, viii, xxii, xxvii, xxviii, xxx–xxxii, xliii, xlvi, xlvii, 9, 11, 12, 17–19, 24–26, 39, 42, 45, 48, 53, 54, 63, 64, 66–68, 70, 73–75, 81, 86, 87, 89–91, 94, 103, 104, 106, 124, 125, 135, 145, 160, 161, 177, 206, 207, 213, 238, 245, 252, 253, 271, 272, 275, 276, 279, 290, 293, 295, 299, 302, 305, 310, 314, 315, 337, 352, 363, 365–369, 371–374, 380, 384–386, 395, 396, 398–400, 409, 415, 418–420, 423, 424, 443, 448, 451, 477, 478, 478n3, 480, 485, 495, 499–501, 520, 529, 533, 538, 553, 556, 559, 561, 563
Family ownership, viii, xxii, xxiii, xlii, xlvii, 9, 12, 16, 38, 43, 45, 48, 50, 52–56, 73, 81, 86, 88–90, 92, 104, 114, 116, 119, 123–125, 138, 145, 150, 154, 160, 180, 239, 247, 258, 305, 400, 464, 480, 519, 520, 522, 531, 542–544
Family SMEs, ix, x, xiv, xxxix, 63–94, 553–569
Family structure, viii, xii, xxxi, xxxix, xlvi, xlvii, 362, 363, 367–369, 383–387, 400, 448
Family value, xxxviii, xlv, xlviii, 103, 156, 174, 177, 178, 180, 183, 192, 193, 245, 271, 274, 279, 362, 364, 366, 368, 372, 373, 375–377, 380, 384, 385, 565
Foreign market entry (FME), 5, 44, 54, 55, 71, 89, 120, 121, 237–259, 369, 372, 381, 384, 385
Foreign partner relationship (FPR), x, xxxix, xlvi, 289–320
Founder-entrepreneur, xlv, 182, 200, 201, 204, 205, 208, 210, 224, 225

Framework, xiv, xxxix, xliv, 8n1, 17n3, 41, 55, 103–126, 136, 175, 180, 202–207, 239, 240, 247, 250, 268, 292, 296, 311, 312, 318, 328, 330–333, 351, 353, 354, 387, 401, 434–437, 439, 440, 463–471, 475, 477, 479, 506–509, 524, 531, 555, 556

G

Generation, viii, ix, xii, xxx, xliii, xliv, xlvii, xlviii, 14, 23, 28, 38–40, 42–46, 49, 50, 52–56, 67, 69, 70, 73, 89, 94, 110, 111, 115, 116, 123–125, 139, 145, 148, 183, 200, 201, 205–208, 210–219, 221, 222, 224–227, 245, 266, 274, 275, 295, 296, 310, 315, 334, 346, 349, 353, 367–369, 372–374, 379–387, 400, 433, 436–438, 441, 447–449, 451, 452, 475, 493, 501, 532–534, 541, 542, 557, 561
Global value chain (GVC), xiv, xlvi, 265–280

H

Heterogeneity, vii, ix, xxi, xxxi, xlvii, xlviii, 4, 38–40, 48, 53, 55, 67, 69, 126, 138, 139, 150, 177, 258, 280, 363, 400, 464, 469, 478, 519, 556
Historical case, 201, 207, 210, 350
Home country, xiv, xv, xxi, xxiv, xxvn1, 8, 14, 17, 18, 20, 27, 49, 126, 183, 190, 399, 423, 424, 462, 469, 478, 479, 492, 494, 505, 512, 519–544, 569
Host country, xiii, xv, xxi, xxvii, xlvii, 8, 10–13, 15, 20–23, 27, 49, 50, 104, 113, 117, 118, 120, 126, 141, 242, 274, 290, 293, 313, 316, 433–436, 449, 462, 469, 470, 478, 479, 505, 521, 524, 531, 542, 544

I

Identification, x, xxiii, xxx, xxxviii, xlvi, 21, 39, 45, 66–69, 73–75, 81, 123, 204, 206, 207, 238, 240, 245, 249, 250, 253, 254, 258, 270, 273, 275, 295, 298, 302, 305, 311, 315, 316, 318, 373, 401, 476, 478n3, 528, 541
Identity-based ties, 211, 212, 214, 218, 221, 223–225
Institution, vii, xiii–xv, xxi, xxxi, xxxix, xlvii, 11, 13, 16, 22, 117, 139, 158, 242, 253, 279, 319, 354, 408, 432, 436, 437, 448, 450, 519–544, 558, 564
International, viii, xxi, xxxvii, xli, xliii, 5, 10–16, 38, 64, 104, 136, 173, 199–227, 237, 251–257, 266, 289, 292–294, 328, 363, 395, 402–404, 411–412, 420–421, 432, 450–451, 464, 521, 558
Internationalization, vii, xxi–xxxiii, xxxvii, xli, xliii, 3–28, 37–56, 63–94, 104, 135–163, 174, 200, 202–203, 237, 241–242, 267, 289, 327–354, 361–369, 395–425, 431–453, 461–512, 519–544, 553–569
process, xxvii, xxxviii, xxxix, xliv, xlv, xlviii, 5, 37–39, 41, 44, 53, 55, 68–70, 72, 86, 87, 92, 104, 119, 137, 140–143, 150, 154–156, 162, 163, 199, 200, 202, 203, 205, 210, 225, 239, 246, 267, 290, 293, 330, 332, 335, 348, 350–352, 398–400, 449, 462, 464, 479–481, 484–495, 511, 524, 528, 535, 536, 539, 542, 553–569

574 Index

Internationalization (*cont.*)
   strategy, xxxii, xlii, xliii, xlvii, xlviii,
      42, 89, 90, 139, 141, 143, 148,
      154, 155, 160, 362, 475, 477,
      484, 493–494, 503, 504, 521,
      522, 528–531, 537, 558, 568
International networking legacy, xii,
   xxxviii, xlv, 202, 221–224, 226
Interpersonal network ties, 199–227

L

Long-term, xii, xxx, xxxii, xxxix, xliv,
   xlvi, 12, 21, 22, 27, 37, 38,
   40–45, 50, 68, 69, 75, 80,
   88–91, 93, 107, 109, 110, 115,
   119, 123, 125, 126, 139, 145,
   155, 159, 177, 200, 203, 206,
   212, 220, 223, 224, 254, 255,
   267, 271, 273–278, 291,
   293–295, 299, 308, 310, 311,
   313–315, 317–319, 329n1, 330,
   352–354, 383, 384, 386, 431,
   477, 520, 529, 533, 536, 543,
   554, 557

M

Migrant family, xii, xxxix,
   xlvi, 431–439
Model, ix, xiv, xxvi–xxxii, xxxvii–xxxix,
   xlv–xlviii, 4–6, 17n3, 46, 50, 52,
   53, 70, 84–86, 112–114, 119,
   136, 137, 140, 142, 143, 148,
   173–193, 265–270, 277, 278,
   298, 330, 398, 401, 407, 407n3,
   414, 415, 419, 422, 462–464,
   471, 475–479, 484, 485, 505,
   522, 527, 528, 531, 532, 536
Multi-country, xlviii, 361–369, 387

Multinational company (MNC), xiv,
   xxxviii, xlv, 173–193, 329
Multinational enterprise (MNE), xiv, 3,
   8, 10–13, 15, 17, 21–27, 110,
   113, 114, 120, 266, 269, 270,
   277, 382, 463, 521, 566
Multinational family firm, 327, 329,
   337, 350
Multiple case study, 239, 246, 247,
   279, 291, 317, 369

N

Networking, x, xii, xxxviii, xxxix, xliv–
   xlvi, xlviii, 63–94, 199, 201–203,
   205, 210, 211, 215, 217,
   221–227, 239–241, 246, 248,
   252, 257–259, 290–298, 307,
   314, 318, 320, 327–354, 362,
   363, 385–387, 395, 396,
   399–403, 408–410, 415–420,
   422–425, 481, 525, 534,
   538, 539
Networking behaviour, viii, xii, xxxix,
   223, 317, 396, 416, 418–420,
   422, 423
Networks, vii, xxvii, xxxviii, xli, xliv,
   12, 65, 114, 138, 173, 199–227,
   239, 269, 289, 327, 364,
   395–425, 432, 464, 524, 560
New venture, 204, 272, 395–425, 437
Non-economic/noneconomic, vii,
   ix–xi, xxxix, xliv, 5, 11–13, 16,
   24, 66, 67, 69, 86, 87, 93, 94,
   104, 105, 110, 115, 123, 125,
   148, 200, 245, 289–320, 334,
   396, 422, 424, 469, 470, 475,
   477–479, 492–494, 504, 505,
   511, 512, 520, 528, 529,
   541–543, 555, 556, 567

Non-family member, viii, x, xii, 9, 138, 271, 275, 276, 279, 296, 302, 315, 366, 382, 396, 397, 399, 400, 409, 415, 418–420, 424, 535

P

Post-entry, 126, 237–259, 363, 367, 372, 384–386, 396, 419, 422, 423, 462, 475

R

Re-internationalization, 136, 137, 140–142, 149–160
Relationship, vii, xxi, xxxix, xliv, 8, 38, 64, 106, 138, 175, 202, 237, 267, 289–320, 330, 364, 397, 432, 519, 564
Resource-based view (RBV), 6, 105, 106, 108, 112, 115–119, 121, 123, 124, 143, 554–557, 567

S

SEW preservation, ix, x, xiii, xiv, xxxii, 28, 63, 65–69, 71, 73, 87, 89, 90, 238, 240, 245, 246, 253, 258, 289–292, 294, 297, 311–313, 316–319, 478

Single case, xlvii, 180, 337, 400, 433, 441, 453, 559
Social network, xxxix, 201, 204, 206, 318, 327–330, 334, 337, 352, 431–439, 525, 538–540
Socioemotional, ix, 20, 28, 86, 226, 245, 267, 270
Socio-emotional wealth (SEW), ix, xiii, xxii, xliv, 4, 40, 63–94, 137, 206, 207, 289, 464, 478, 499–500, 504, 511, 536
Stewardship, viii, xliv, 19, 37–56, 68, 105, 108, 142, 176, 293, 295, 313, 529
Subsidiary, xiv, xv, xxiv–xxvi, xxvn1, xxxviii, xlv, 13–15, 26, 45, 105, 107, 110, 112, 113, 116, 117, 120, 123–125, 140, 161, 173–178, 180–182, 184, 186–193, 243, 244, 290, 298, 299, 310, 373, 379, 380, 385

T

Tradition, viii, xlvi, 17, 155, 188, 206, 273, 274, 280, 363, 366, 367, 372, 374, 380, 381, 383–386, 437, 523, 541, 566–568

Printed in the United States
by Baker & Taylor Publisher Services